# PHOTOGRAPHY VISIONARIES

MARY WARNER MARIEN

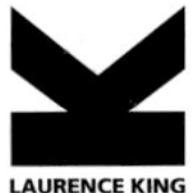


Published in 2015 by
Laurence King Publishing Ltd
361–373 City Road
London EC1V 1LR
e-mail: enquiries@laurenceking.com
www.laurenceking.com



A catalogue record for this book is available from the British Library.

ISBN: 978 1 78067 475 9

Printed in China

Book Design: Jon Allan
Cover Design: Pentagram
Cover Image: Robert Capa, self-portrait, 1938.
Senior Editor: Sophie Wise
Picture Researcher: Peter Kent

# PHOTOGRAPHY VISIONARIES

MARY WARNER MARIEN

Laurence King Publishing

# PHOTOGRAPHY VISIONARIES


Introduction 6

Eugène Atget 1857–1927 8

Alfred Stieglitz 1864–1946 12

Frances Benjamin Johnston 1864–1952 16

Lewis Hine 1874–1940 20

August Sander 1876–1964 24

Edward Steichen 1879–1973 28

Imogen Cunningham 1883–1976 32

Edward Weston 1886–1958 36

Raoul Hausmann 1886–1971 40

Hannah Höch 1889–1978 44

Man Ray 1890–1976 48

Paul Strand 1890–1976 52

John Heartfield 1891–1968 56

Alexander Rodchenko 1891–1956 60

André Kertész 1894–1985 64

Claude Cahun 1894–1954 68

Dorothea Lange 1895–1965 72

Laszlo Móhóly-Nagy 1895–1946 76

Germaine Krull 1897–1985 80

Berenice Abbott 1898–1991 84

Weegee 1899–1968 88

Brassaï 1899–1994 92

George Hoyningen-Huene 1900–1968 96

Lisette Model 1901–1983 100

Ansel Adams 1902–1984 104

Manuel Álvarez Bravo 1902–2002 108

Walker Evans 1903–1975 112

Bill Brandt 1904–1983 116

Margaret Bourke-White 1904–1971 120

Lee Miller 1907–1977 124

Minor White 1908–1976 128

Henri Cartier-Bresson 1908–2004 132

Gordon Parks 1912–2006 136

Helen Levitt 1913–2009 140

Robert Capa 1913–1954 144

Sunil Janah 1918–2012 148

W. Eugene Smith 1918–1978 152

Dickey Chapelle 1919–1965 156

Roy DeCarava 1919–2009 160

Nacho López 1923–1986 164

Richard Avedon 1923–2004 168

Robert Frank b. 1924 172

Mario Giacomelli 1925–2000 176

Garry Winogrand 1928–1984 180

Shōmei Tōmatsu 1930–2012 184

Bernhard and Hilla Becher 1931–2007, b. 1934 188

Peter Magubane b. 1932 192

Eikoh Hosoe b. 1933 196

Lee Friedlander b. 1934 200

Pedro Meyer b. 1935 204

Don McCullin b. 1935 208

Robert Adams b. 1937 212

Ed Ruscha b. 1937 216

Josef Koudelka b. 1938 220

Daidō Moriyama b. 1938 224

William Eggleston b. 1939 228

Ernest Cole 1940–1990 232

Mary Ellen Mark b. 1940 236

Nobuyoshi Araki b. 1940 240

Graciela Iturbide b. 1942 244

Raghubir Singh 1942–1999 248

Martha Rosler b. 1943 252

Sebastião Salgado b. 1944 256

Lewis Baltz b. 1945 260

Jeff Wall b. 1946 264

Stephen Shore b. 1947 268

Deborah Willis b. 1948 272

Annie Leibovitz b. 1949 276

Roger Ballen b. 1950 280

Carrie Mae Weems b. 1953 284

Nan Goldin b. 1953 288

Cindy Sherman b. 1954 292

Andreas Gursky b. 1955 296

Santu Mofokeng b. 1956 300

Liu Zheng b. 1969 304

Further Reading 308

Index 309

Credits and Acknowledgements 312

# Introduction

The lives, thoughts and images of the photographers featured in this book affected others in the medium as well as the general public. Their careers and works illustrate how diverse photographic vision can be. Some created images that became cultural icons; others experimented with style, expanding the medium's expressive capacity. Many led lives attuned to the historical events and cultural values of their time.

Photography is much too varied in its visual qualities and venues for any one person to alter it fundamentally. Instead, the medium's diversity encourages the flow and adaptation of ideas from one genre to another. For example, fashion photographers and photojournalists respond to visual motifs in art photography, which has long investigated and interpreted the objectivity imputed to newspaper images. Photographers whom the world has considered to be visionary, work in the context of multiple sources, fluidity, and change.

Consequently, the image-makers in this book are not only creative, they are savvy borrowers. Their inventions draw from a wide-range of visual experiences in the other arts, like painting and graphic design, as well as from advertising, journalism and social science, and are sometimes reabsorbed into these fields. For example, Lewis Hine's images of child labour were among the early documentary photographs to stem from urban studies and economic reform, and they in turn helped shape the concept of documentary in these fields.

Unlike the cartoonish 'a ha' moments attributed to innovators, most inventive photographers seem to have plugged along, convinced of their own ideas, and not needing an apple to fall on their heads to get started. Also, many photographers were concerned with what the poet Percy Bysshe Shelley called 'startl[ing] the reader from the trance of ordinary life'. New ways to look at things occur across the many photographic genres. For instance, Bill Brandt wanted people to experience 'a sense of wonder' when they engaged his pictures.

For some photographers, enlivening vision has rested on freewheeling experimentation. Man Ray delighted in doing all the wrong things, like resting objects directly on light sensitive photographic paper to create eerie and sensuous images. The sharp contrast of desolate white and deeply saturated black produced by Mario Giacomelli in his works counters the infinite cascade of subtle grey tones that have been a marker of achievement in photographic practice.

Whether or not they employ it extensively, photographers who break new ground are usually well versed in the technology of photography. The shift from analog – that is film and darkroom photography, to digital, with its computer-based image altering software – has not altered that propensity. Photographers were among the first artists to employ computers in image-making, and they continue to do so today, often using digital means to exam the enduring cultural construction of truth and falsehood. In addition, exceptional photographers often seek stimulation and inspiration beyond the visual arts. Ansel Adams, a skilled pianist, credited music for teaching him the discipline required in photographic practice. Literature, especially poetry, has been a frequent interest. Walker Evans may have honed his skill with visual allusion through his devotion of poetry.

The notion of the visionary is a tricky concept, perhaps because it seems to ignore the variety of ways that photgraphers learned from each other. To say that Lewis Hine was influenced by Alfred Stieglitz is not to say that Hine took up the aesthetics of Stieglitz's photographs. Their work is visually dissimilar. Yet Hine greatly admired Stieglitz's intense dedication to photography, and made a similarly powerful commitment to his own work. It is not clear whether Dickey Chapelle was more influenced by Margaret Bourke-White's shiny celebrity or by the distinctive composition and subject matter of her photographs. Feminists in the 1980s focused more on Chapelle's fortitude, enlarging her contribution for another generation. The multitude of photographers who claim to be influenced by Cartier-Bresson's 'decisive moment' did not find it necessary to shoot only black and white photographs, nor to avoid cropping. Instead, they adapted Cartier-Bresson's vision that pictures came and went in the midst of human experience, and that the photographer needed to be in the middle of things, ready to acknowledge the eruption of a picture

The twists and turns of photographers' lives and their images, indeed, the very range of their work, speaks to the notion of a visionary as a 'visioneer': not a prophet, but a dedicated experimenter, whose ideas and pictures enlarge the medium while expanding the scope and range of human understanding.

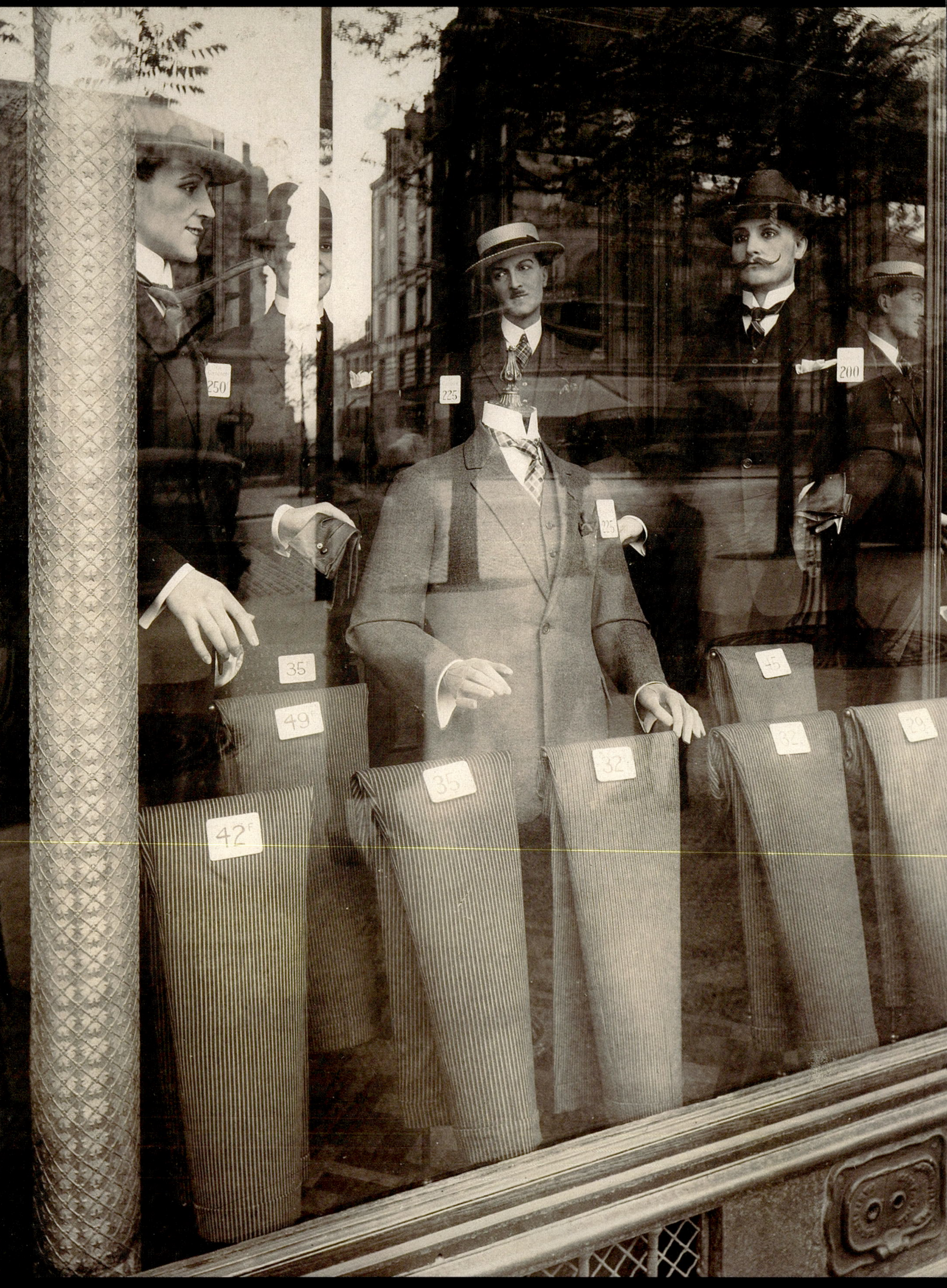


Avenue des Gobelins, 1927.

'A good photograph is like a good hound dog, dumb, but eloquent.'

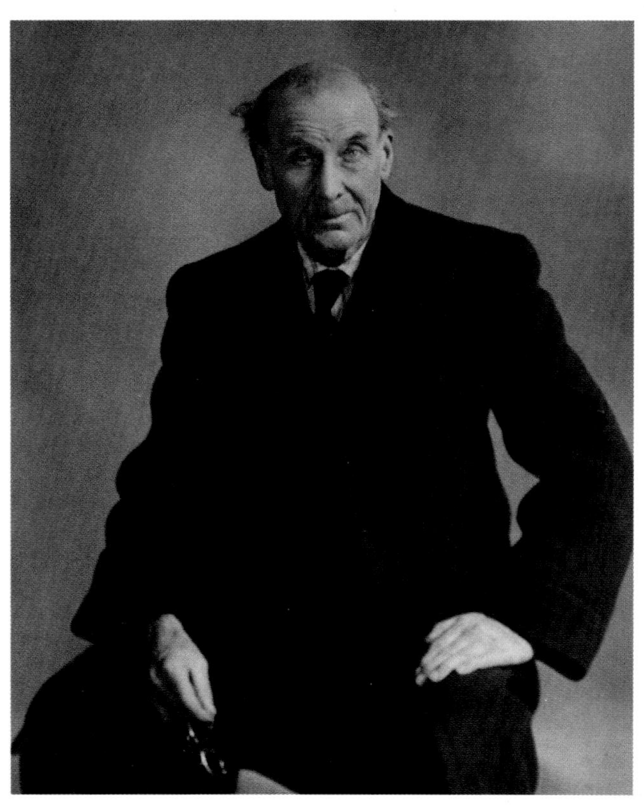

# Eugène Atget

1857–1927

FRANCE

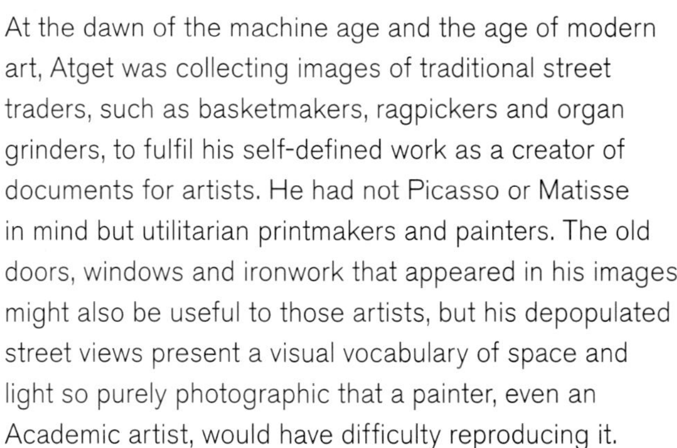

At the dawn of the machine age and the age of modern art, Atget was collecting images of traditional street traders, such as basketmakers, ragpickers and organ grinders, to fulfil his self-defined work as a creator of documents for artists. He had not Picasso or Matisse in mind but utilitarian printmakers and painters. The old doors, windows and ironwork that appeared in his images might also be useful to those artists, but his depopulated street views present a visual vocabulary of space and light so purely photographic that a painter, even an Academic artist, would have difficulty reproducing it.

Detail can be discerned in these photographs, but it is embedded in the flow of life and light by the camera lens. The sometimes luminous, sometimes grainy atmosphere in Atget's work is a co-subject with the ancient buildings that he recorded. Its insistent presence seems like an open-ended visual metaphor for the persistence of the past in the present. Certainly Atget's complicated rendering of reflections is beyond the scope of simple documentary. In some of his images of storefronts, illusory picture-planes infiltrate each other: foregrounds and backgrounds mix; mannequins appear animated and ready to step out for a stroll. Notably, among the 10,000 photographs Atget created, there are no views of the Eiffel Tower, that symbol of progress erected in 1889.

Most of those who knew Atget did not know him very well, and he left few clues to his interests beyond the photographs he made. The institutions that bought or commissioned his work seem to have accepted his proclamation that he was not an artist but a commercial photographer. Yet many artists, photographers and cultural critics in Atget's time and since have insisted that his distinctive use of the camera and idiomatic compositions offered much more than utilitarian views. His images excited the Surrealists, who found in them intimations of the uncanny, which they believed spontaneously erupted into the overly rational present. Man Ray (p. 48) not only bought prints from Atget but also tried to contextualize them as Surrealist by including them in his publications. For critic Walter Benjamin, Atget's views evoked an eerie feeling of being at the scene of a crime. Summing up the cumulative multiplicity of Atget interpretations, Postmodern critic Abigail Solomon Godeau observed that there was 'a surrealist Atget, a primitive Atget, a documentary Atget, a modernist Atget, and a Marxist Atget'.

Towards the end of his life, he offered a large number of his negatives to the French Minister of Art, writing that his work was finished: 'I can say that I possess all of Old Paris.' But it is still too soon to think we possess all of Atget.

Portrait of Eugène Atget by Berenice Abbott, 1927.

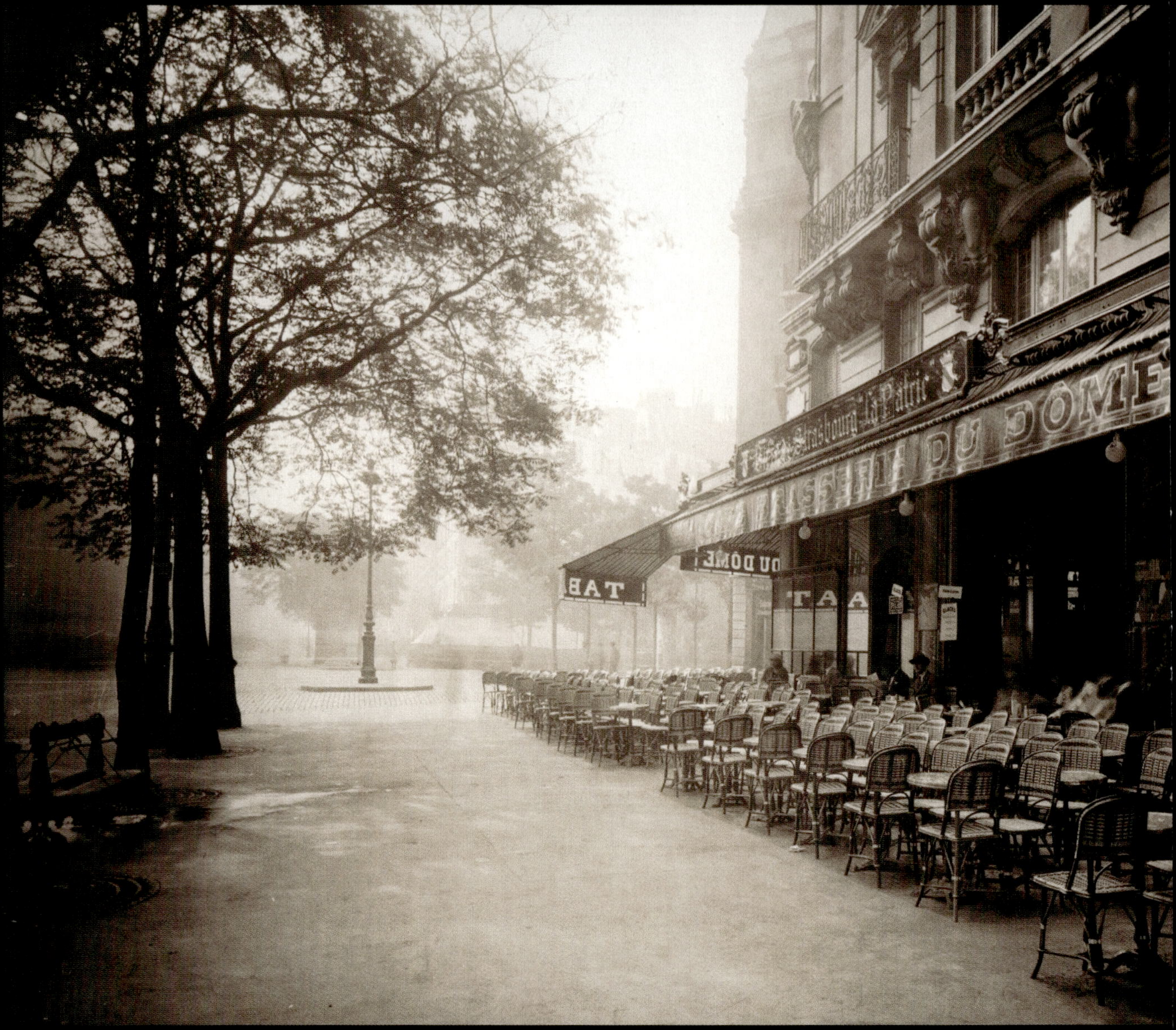

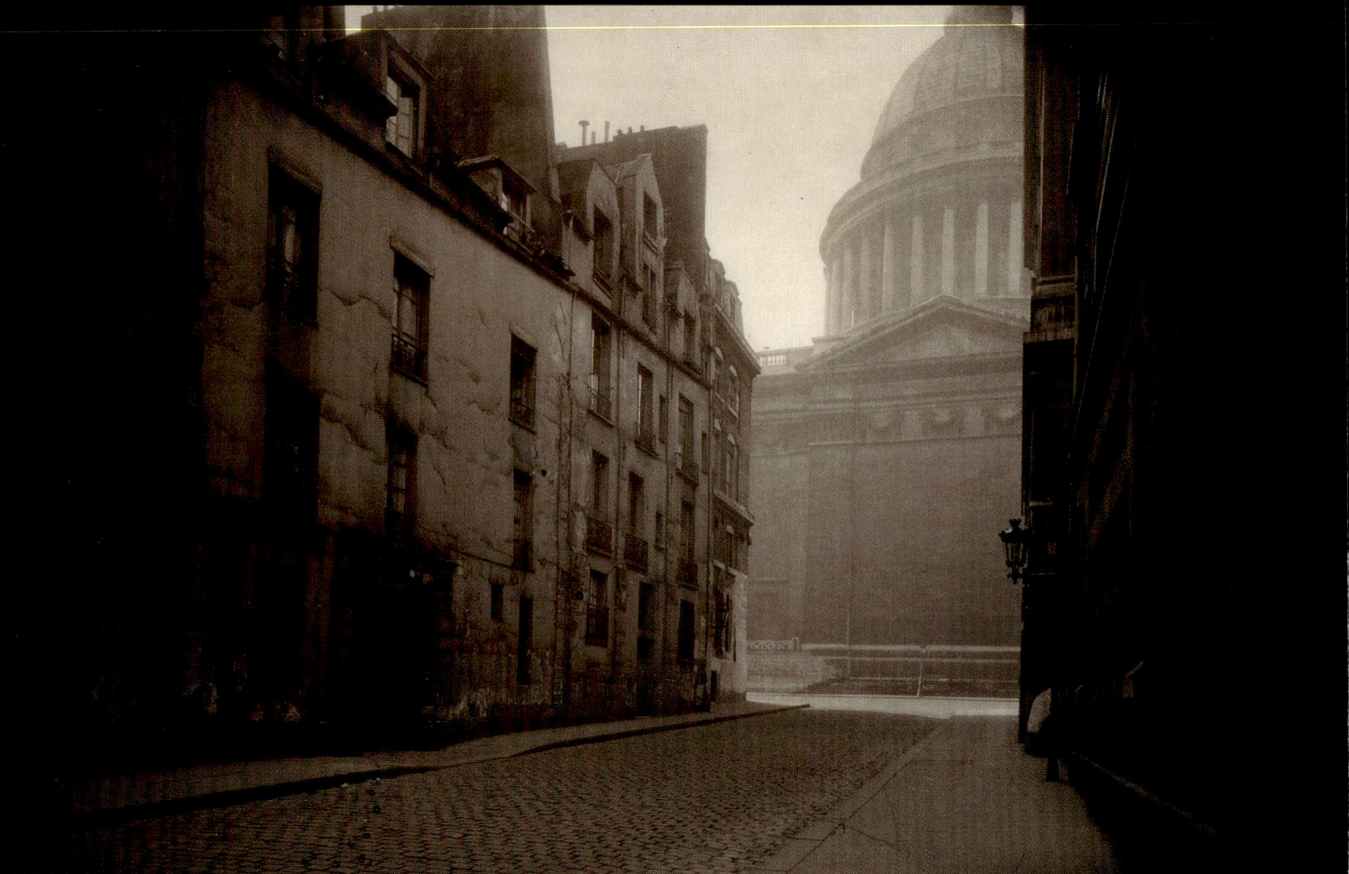

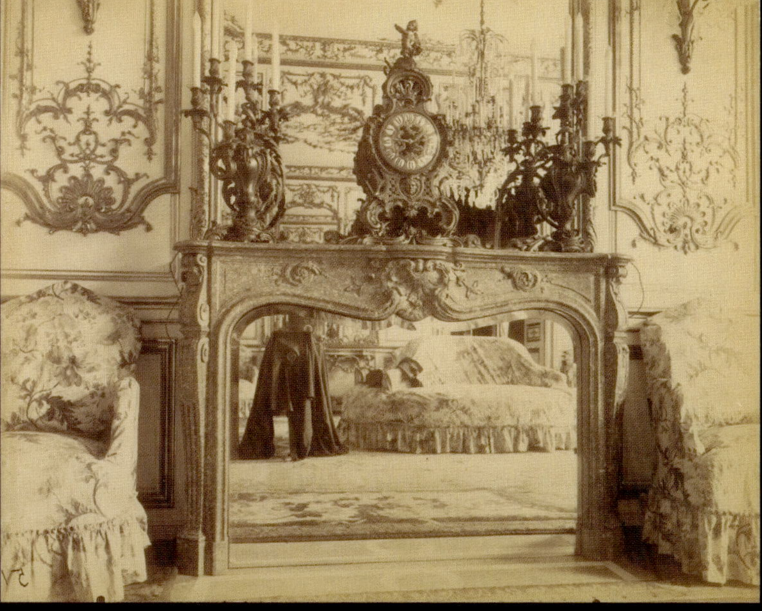

**Opposite top** Le Dôme, Boulevard Montparnasse, 1925.

**Opposite bottom** Valette and Panthéon, 1925.

**Above** Fireplace, Hôtel Matignon, 1905.

## Eugène Atget

1850

**1857** Born in Libourne, France

1860

1870

1880

1890

**1892** First advertises 'documents for artists'

**1898** Begins to photograph 'Old Paris'

1900

**1910** Composes albums of his work for the Bibliothèque Nationale

1920

**1926** Man Ray publishes an Atget image in *La Révolution surréaliste*

**1927** Dies in Paris, France

**1928** Berenice Abbott buys Atget prints that become foundation of MoMA collection

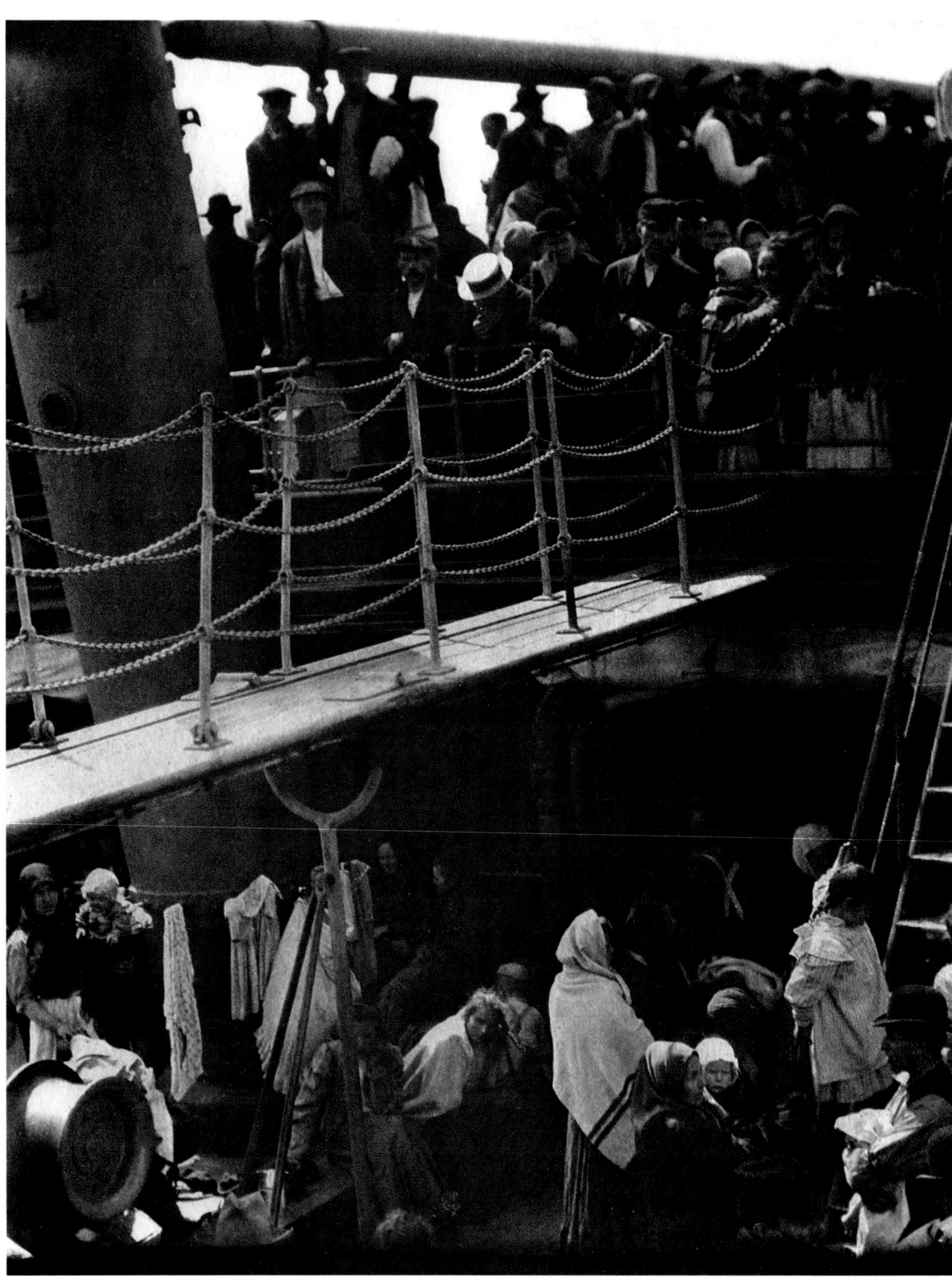

*The Steerage*, from *Camera Work* no. 34, 1907.

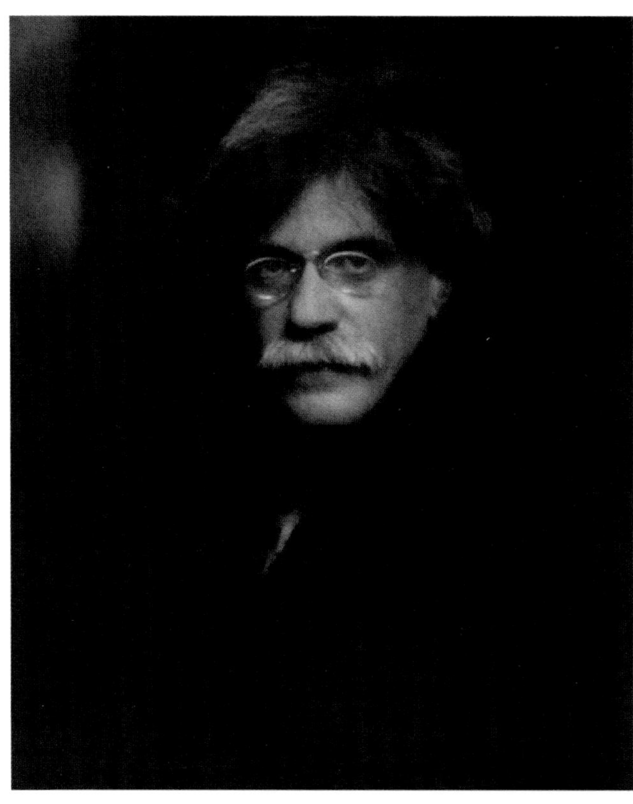

'Photography is my Passion. The Search for Truth is my Obsession.'

# Alfred Stieglitz

1864–1946

United States

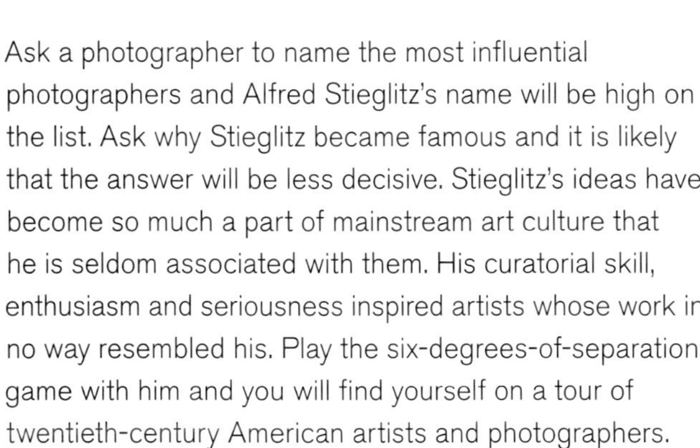

Ask a photographer to name the most influential photographers and Alfred Stieglitz's name will be high on the list. Ask why Stieglitz became famous and it is likely that the answer will be less decisive. Stieglitz's ideas have become so much a part of mainstream art culture that he is seldom associated with them. His curatorial skill, enthusiasm and seriousness inspired artists whose work in no way resembled his. Play the six-degrees-of-separation game with him and you will find yourself on a tour of twentieth-century American artists and photographers.

He created a different take on the connection of art and photography. For Stieglitz, art photography was the expression of aesthetic perception, located not in any medium but in the mind and spirit of the art-maker. He demonstrated this belief in the exhibitions he presented in the various galleries he ran for more than 30 years, and in the short-lived but influential journal *Camera Work*.

Stieglitz's first gallery, named the Little Galleries of the Photo-Secession, presented European avant-garde painting and sculpture as well as American art and photography – including work by the then unknown young painter Georgia O'Keeffe, whom he would eventually marry. Stieglitz was a point man for abstraction expressed through the unique characteristics of the artist's medium. He was not interested in photographers who made images that looked like paintings, or painters who made pictures that looked like photographs. He contended that artists in all media should be modern artists, acutely attuned to new practices and outlooks. It would be another half-century before the sale price of photographs matched that of paintings, but Stieglitz planted the seed of equality.

His own work evolved away from the fashionable haze of Gilded Age photography to clear-eyed, angle-loving Cubist studies. The willing, intuitive mind was alert to moments where abstraction occurred. Recalling how he felt when he saw the scene he photographed for *The Steerage* (1907), he wrote that it was a picture based on shapes, but also on the deepest human feeling.

Like Picasso, Cézanne and Matisse, he rooted his images in everyday experience, including his private life. He took the family snapshot and transformed it from the realm of private memory to public expression. From the early photographs he took in Germany to the images he made towards the end of his career at Lake George, New York, his work is imprinted with his personal experience. Most of his images have recognizable subjects, but the nearly abstract, enigmatic sky studies he called 'Equivalents', produced for a decade from the mid-1920s, seemed to draw inward, withholding access from the viewer. Often dark and small, with no horizon line or other indication of up and down, they teetered on the edge of abstraction. As exponents of Stieglitz's inner life, the 'Equivalents' cannot be fully deciphered. But their effect on subsequent photographers, such as Minor White (p. 128), was both an authorization of abstraction and an endorsement of the place of private meaning in art.

**Above** Self-portrait, 1907.

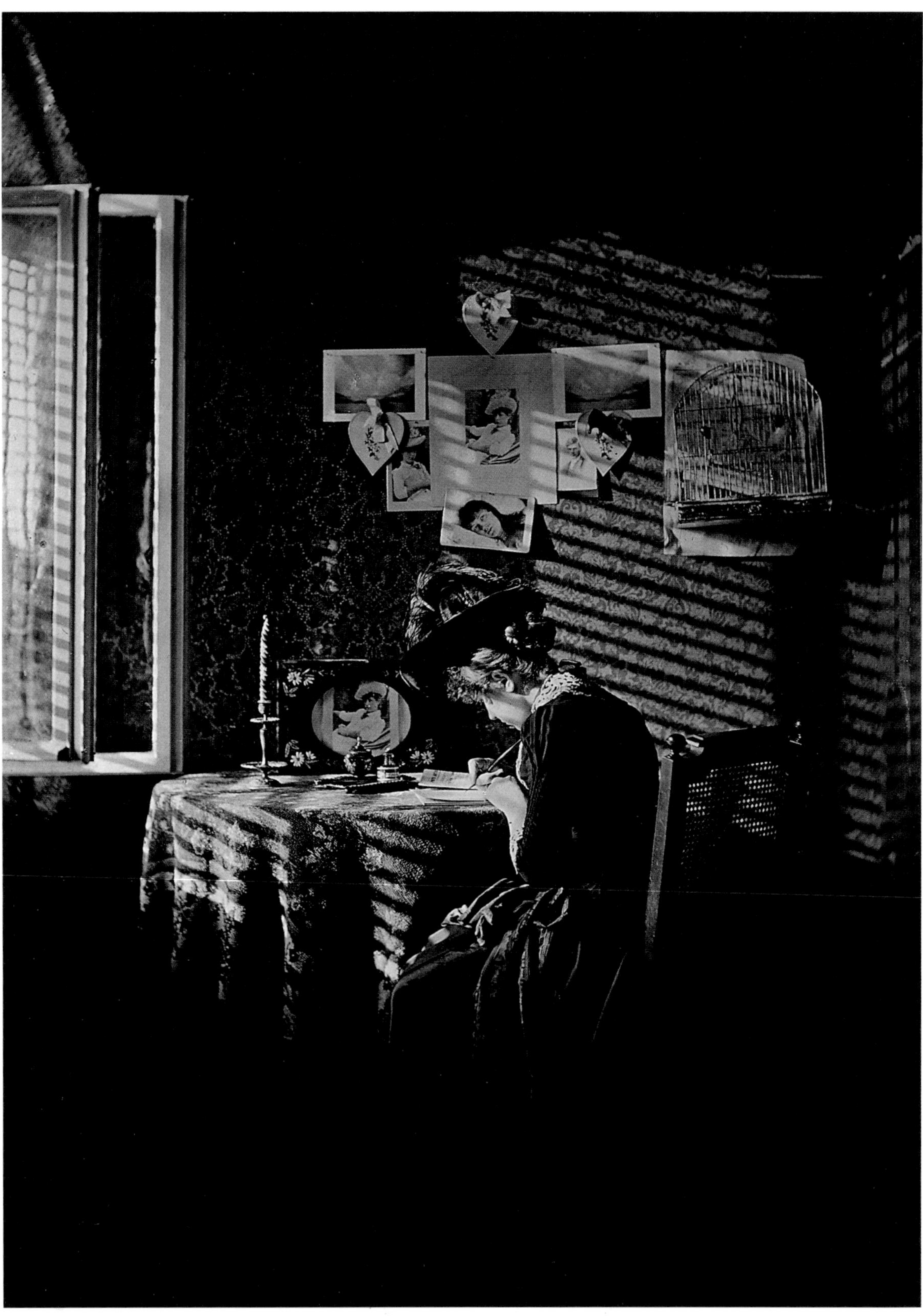

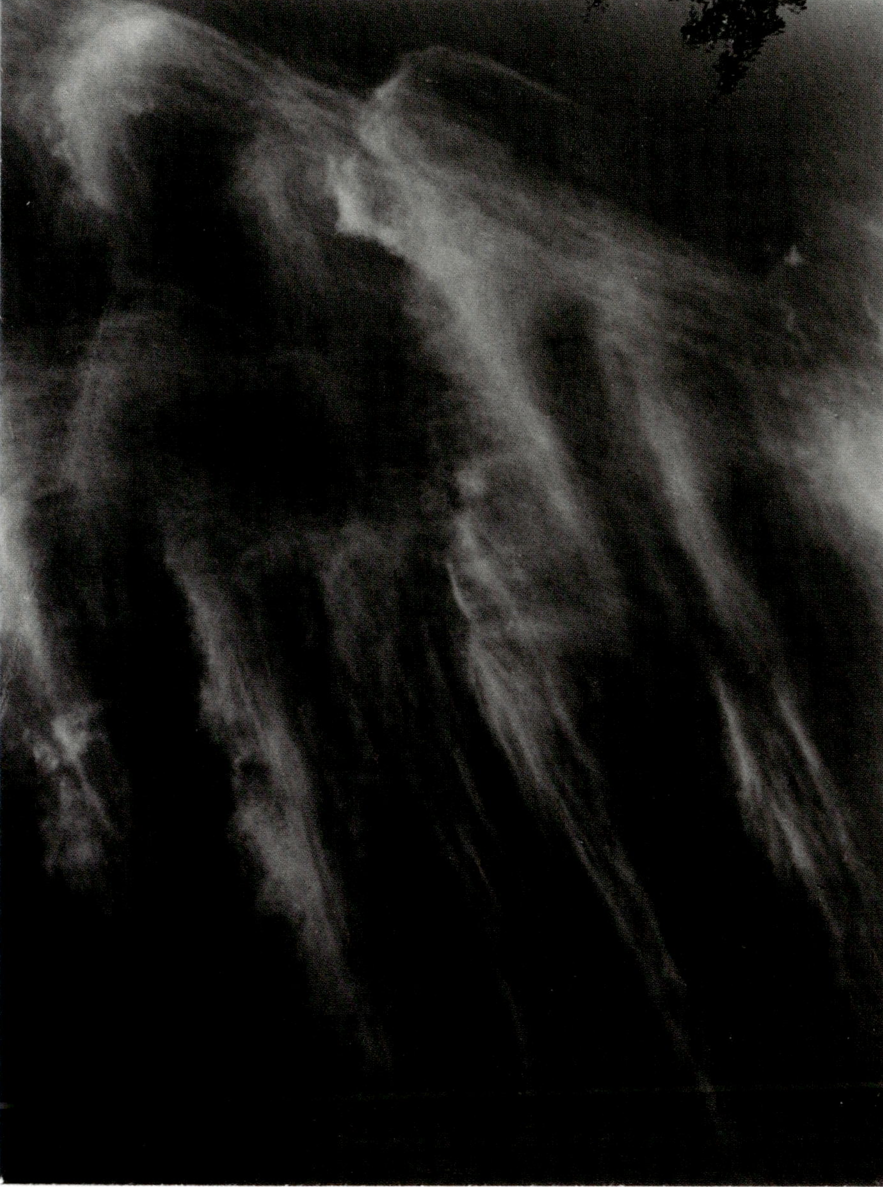

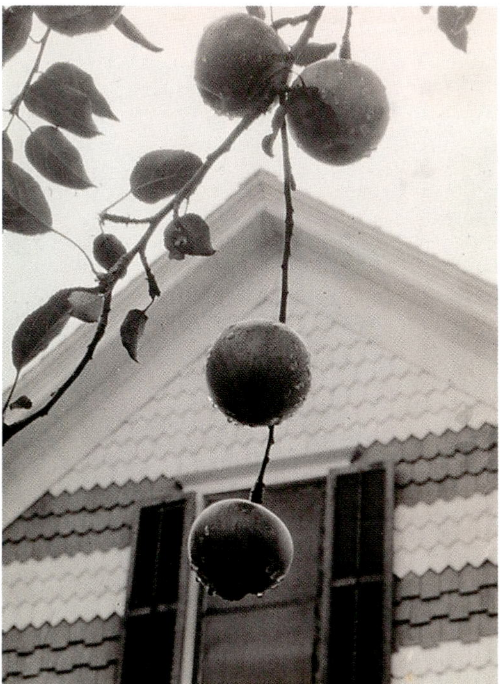

**Above** *Equivalent*, 1930.

**Left** *Apples and Gable*, Lake George, 1922.

**Opposite** *Sun's Rays – Paula*, Berlin, 1889.

## Alfred Stieglitz

1860

1864 Born in Hoboken, New Jersey, USA

1870

1880

1890

1900

1902 Creates the Photo-Secession and publishes *Camera Work*

1905 Opens the Little Galleries of the Photo-Secession, later known as 291, in New York

1910

1913 First one-person show, coinciding with the Armory Exhibition

1920

1922 Makes first sky photographs, known as 'Equivalents'

1924 Marries artist Georgia O'Keeffe

1929 Founds the gallery An American Place, New York

1936 Gives Ansel Adams a solo show at An American Place

1940

1946 Dies in New York, USA

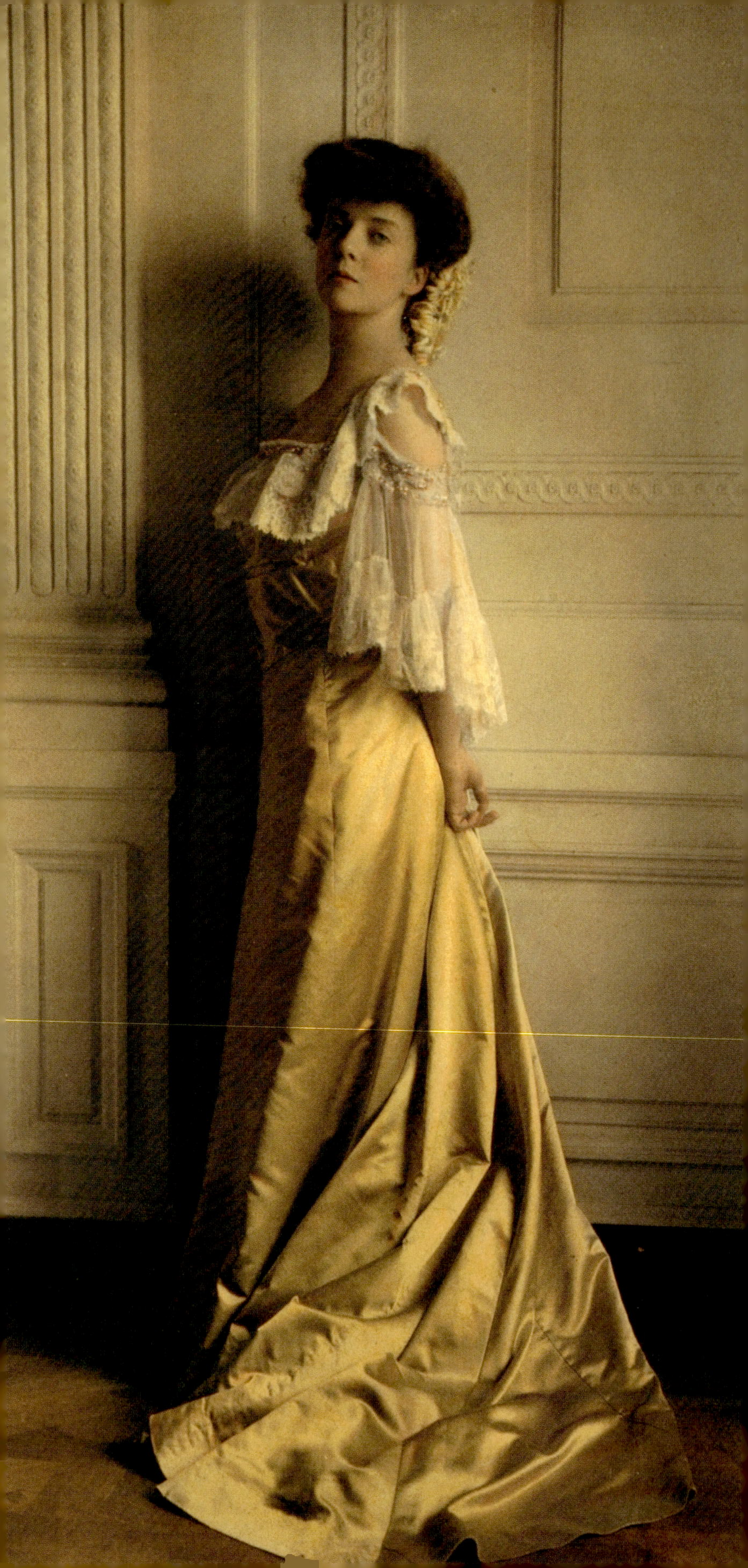

'Photography as a profession should appeal particularly to women.'

# Frances Benjamin Johnston

1864–1952

UNITED STATES

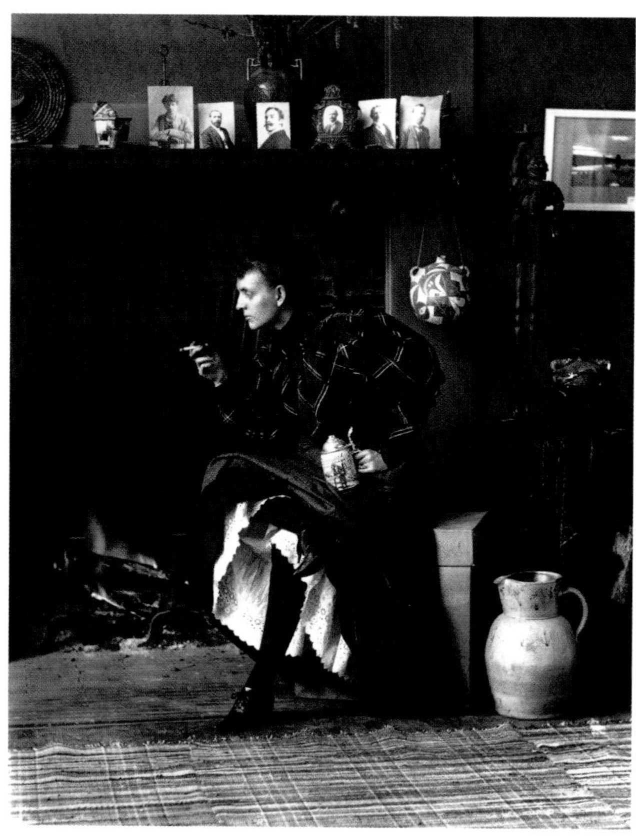

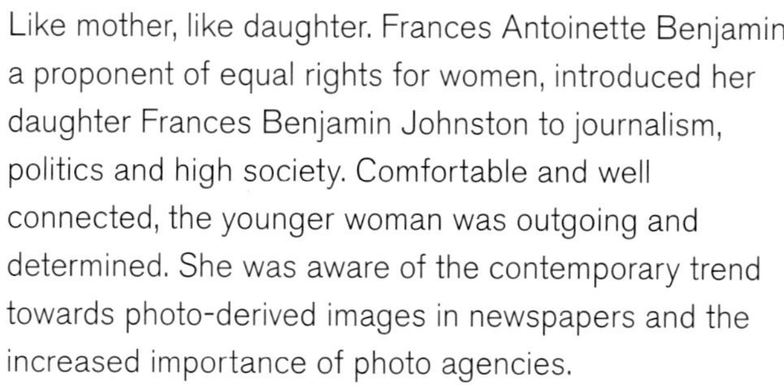

Like mother, like daughter. Frances Antoinette Benjamin, a proponent of equal rights for women, introduced her daughter Frances Benjamin Johnston to journalism, politics and high society. Comfortable and well connected, the younger woman was outgoing and determined. She was aware of the contemporary trend towards photo-derived images in newspapers and the increased importance of photo agencies.

She soon emerged as the informal 'court photographer' for the Washington elite, and for presidents from Benjamin Harrison to William Howard Taft. Her photographs of Theodore Roosevelt's daughter Alice, a media darling and fashionista, contributed to her celebrity. But when Johnston created her own portrait, she depicted herself in a somewhat comic stereotypical male pose, drinking beer, smoking and surrounded by souvenirs of world travel. In articles for popular magazines, she encouraged women to take up photography as a means of employment as well as expression.

Johnston helped organize an exhibition of women photographers in Paris during the Universal Exposition of 1900. During the pre-World War I years, she not only ran her Washington studio and started one in New York, but took and conceived news and documentary assignments. These ranged from life in Minnesota's coal-mining areas to the efforts of the Hampton Institute in Virginia to educate and train African-American youths. For the Bain News Service, she finagled her way on to the ship carrying Admiral Dewey, grabbing the first shot of him after he won the Battle of Manila during the Spanish–American war. She pursued architectural photography and garden photography throughout her life, and experimented with different photographic media as well as colour. Reflecting on the variety of photographic genres she worked in, she coyly announced that she never knew what should not be done in photography.

In an era when art photographers valued consistency and considered commercial photography a betrayal, Johnston's work was more appreciated by the general public than the avant-garde. She did not live to see the start of her current fame, which sprang from the writings of feminists during the 1970s.

Self-portrait (as 'New Woman'), c. 1869.

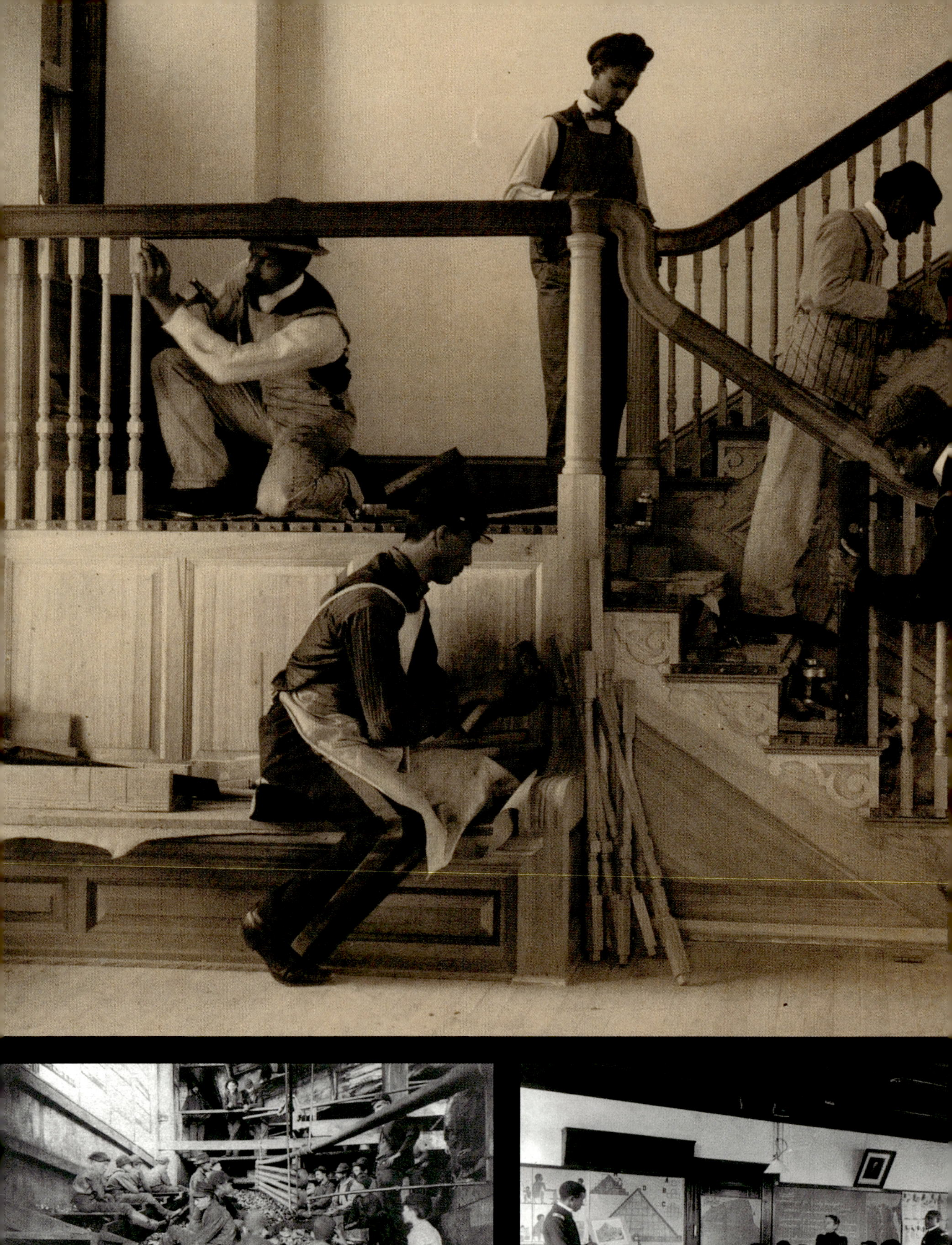

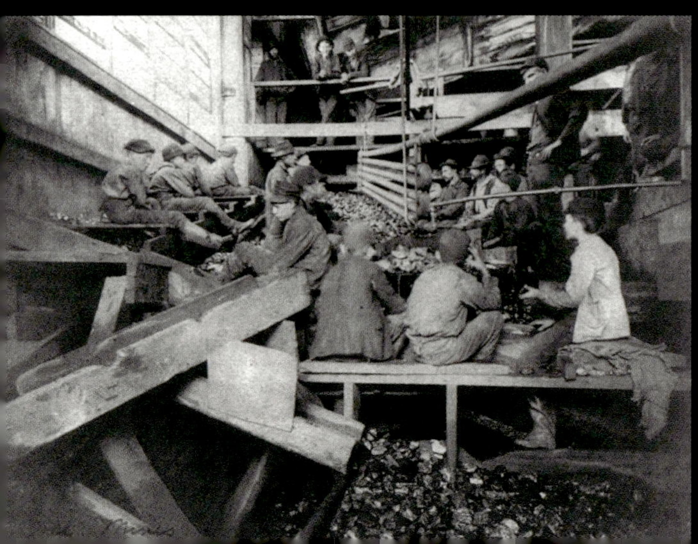

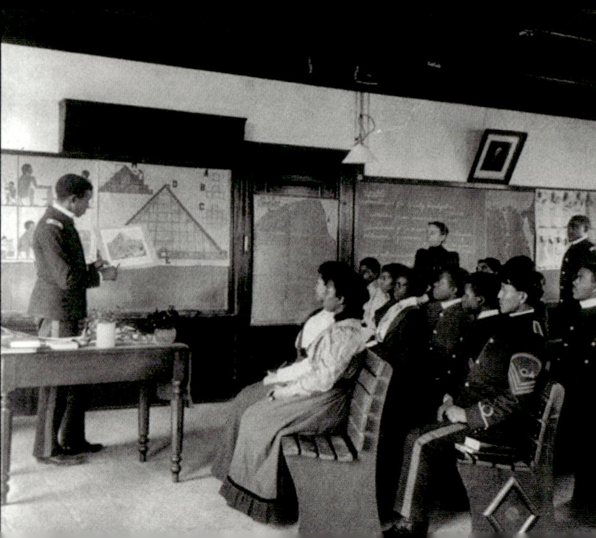

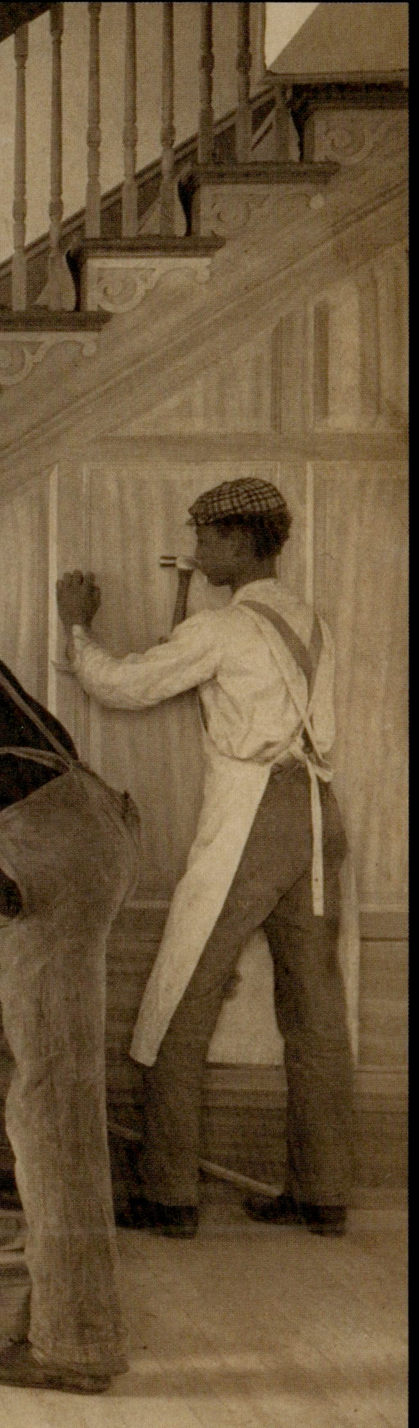

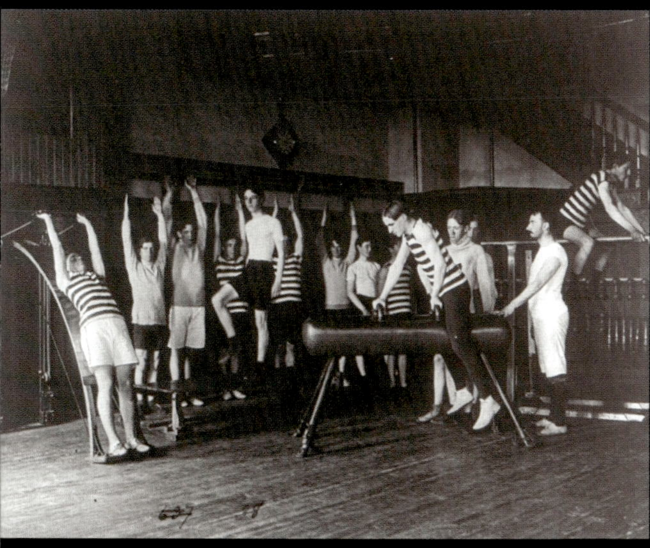

**Left** Students at work on a house largely built by them, c. 1900.

**Opposite left** Breaker boys, Kohinor Mine, 1891.

**Opposite right** Students in Ancient History class, Hampton Institute, Hampton, Virginia, 1899.

**Below** Male students exercising, Western High School, Washington, DC, 1899?

## Frances Benjamin Johnston

1860

1864 Born in Grafton, West Virginia, USA

1870

1880

1888 Studies photography at the Smithsonian Institution

1890

1897 Publishes 'What a Woman Can Do With a Camera'

1898 Begins work for Bain News Service

1899 Documents Hampton Institute

1900 Exhibits American women's photography in Paris during the Universal Exposition

1910

1920

1927 Starts creation of what will become the Carnegie Survey of the Architecture of the South

1930

1940

1950

1952 Dies in New Orleans, Louisiana, USA

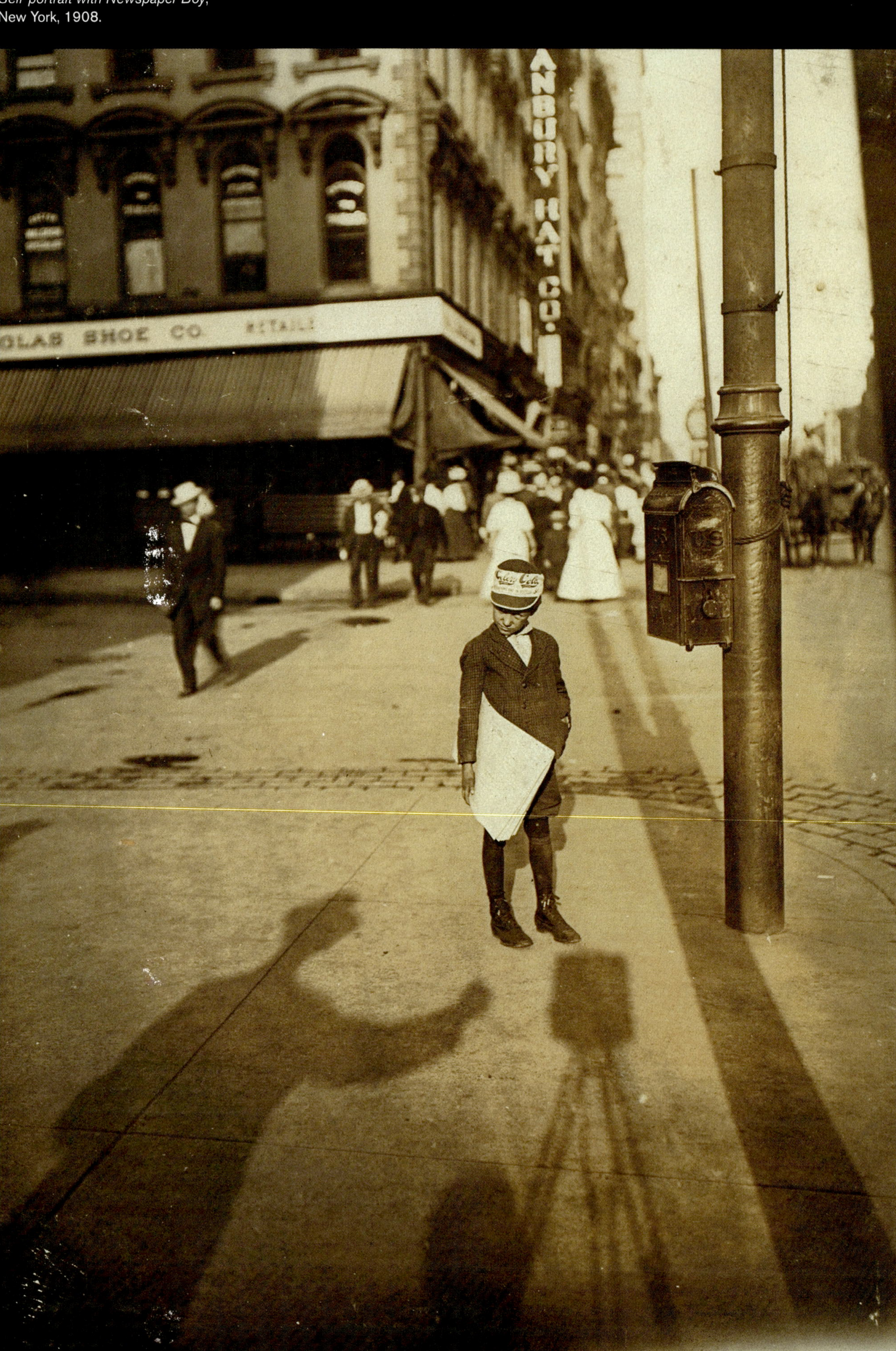


*Self-portrait with Newspaper Boy*,
New York, 1908.

'While photographs may not lie, liars may photograph.'

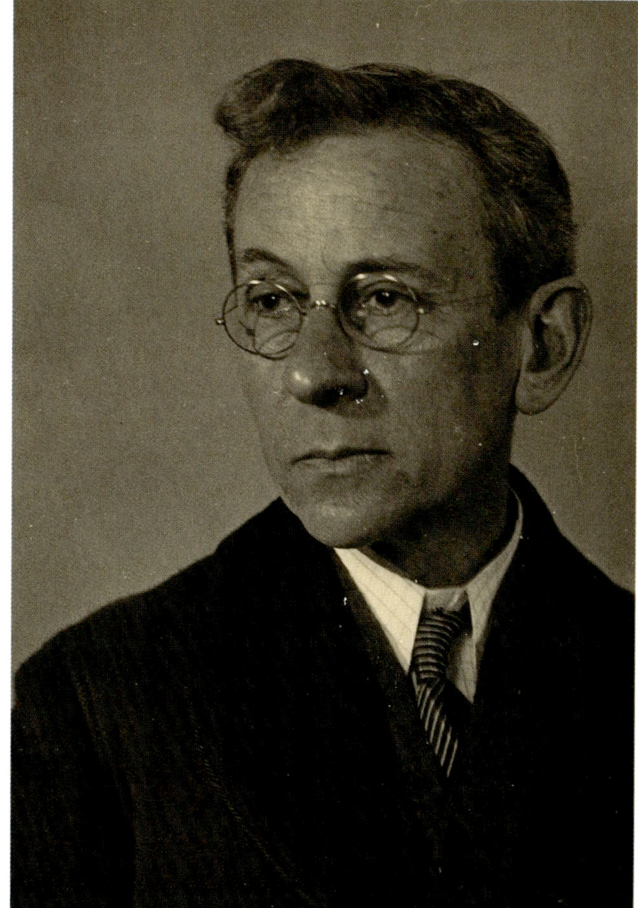

# Lewis Hine

1874–1940

UNITED STATES

Lewis Hine's photographs are part of the communal American memory. His pictures of child workers, immigrants and industrial labourers regularly appear as facts and as symbols of the past. But would Hine himself, who died nearly penniless, endorse the nature of his current success?

Hine was dismayed by the abuse of children in the workplace. Yet his photographs are usually not preachy, but calm, distanced and respectful of children in crisis. On assignment, he collected data like an anthropologist: images of the children in his National Child Labor Committee work came with names, ages, dates, place and occupation. (Nevertheless, he was not above lying to employers to gain access to the mills and factories where children were employed.)

Hine did not want to encourage a short-lived emotional response from viewers. He counted on the public to engage his photographs as 'social facts'. He recognized that photojournalism was the major social medium of the early twentieth century. People talked and wrote about what they saw in newspapers and magazines, quoting and describing ideas like eager proto-tweeters. Commercial advertising and what Hine called 'social photography' mixed information and emotion to effect psychological change in the observer. Like an advertiser, Hine calculated that an active internalized engagement with a picture and text would motivate the viewer more than a simple fact or momentary emotion. Ironically, Hine also emphasized that similar techniques could be used to deceive viewers.

Just as early advertisers quickly learned to increase their effect by using more than one medium to present the same idea, Hine showed his work in slide presentations as well as in exhibitions, posters and articles, and he addressed different segments of society, from philanthropists to labour unions. Through the Hine Photography Company, he offered his pictures to photo agencies and to social service and reform organizations.

Hine produced similar work for the Pittsburgh Survey, a portrayal of the modern industrial city and hint at the future of the United States. He and other photographers were employed, along with 50 or so social scientists, to create a panoply of the city's economic and social life. During the Great Depression, however, Hine changed his focus to a commemoration of collective achievement. His book *Men at Work* was a celebration of labour, not a plea for reform.

Self-portrait, c. 1930.

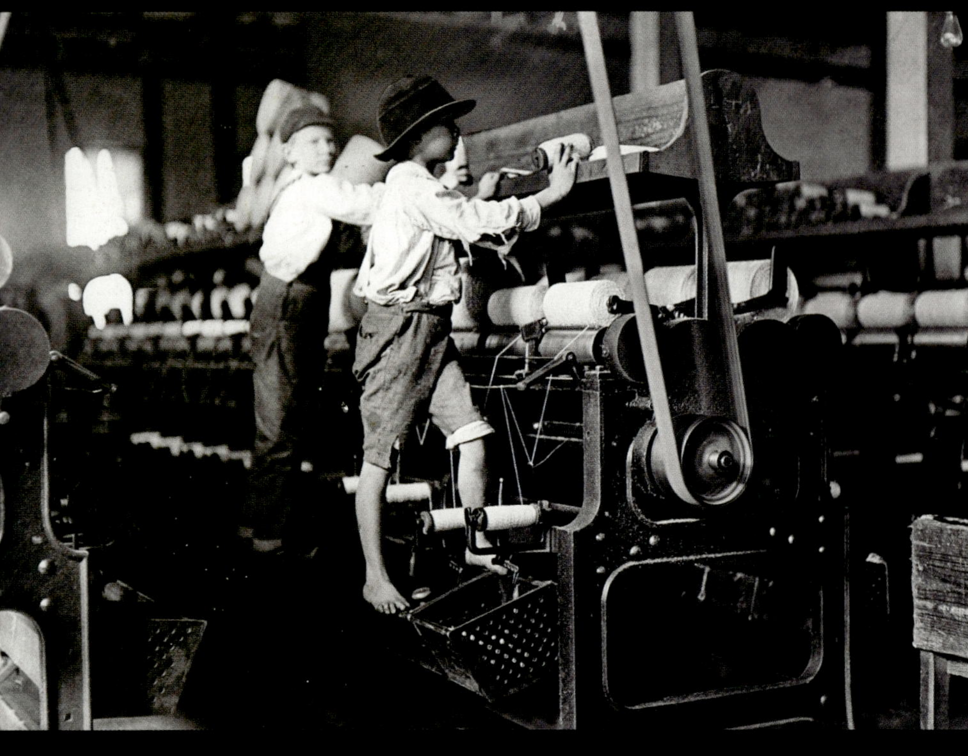

**Above** Children climbing the spinning frame, Georgia, 1909.

**Below** Newspaper advertisement from *The Ogden Standard*, 14 September 1915.

**Opposite** Italian family looking for lost baggage, Ellis Island, New York, 1905.

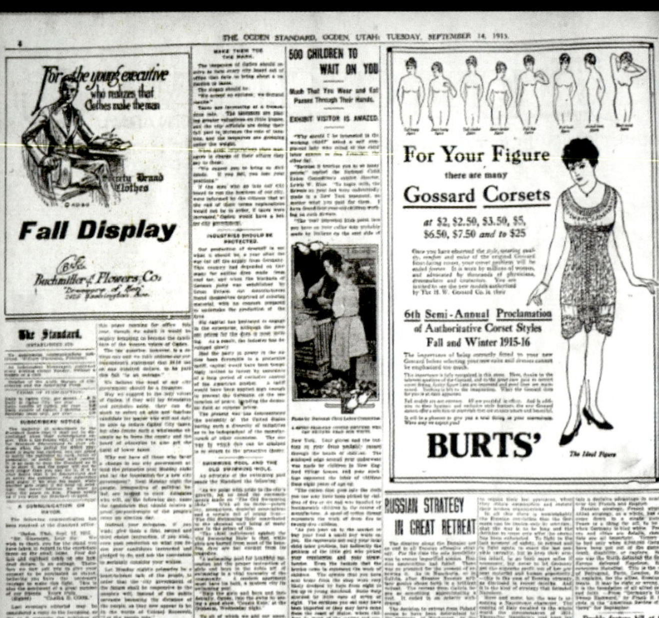

THE OGDEN STANDARD, OGDEN, UTAH, TUESDAY, SEPTEMBER 14, 1915.

For the young executive who realizes that Clothes make the man

Fall Display

Bachmiller & Flowers Co.

500 CHILDREN TO WAIT ON YOU

For Your Figure there are many Gossard Corsets at $2, $2.50, $3.50, $5, $6.50, $7.50 and to $25

6th Semi-Annual Proclamation of Authoritative Corset Styles Fall and Winter 1915-16

BURTS'

RUSSIAN STRATEGY IN GREAT RETREAT

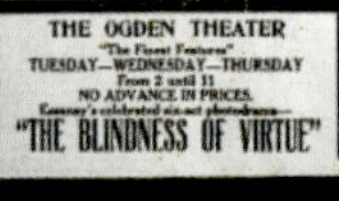

THE OGDEN THEATER

"THE BLINDNESS OF VIRTUE"

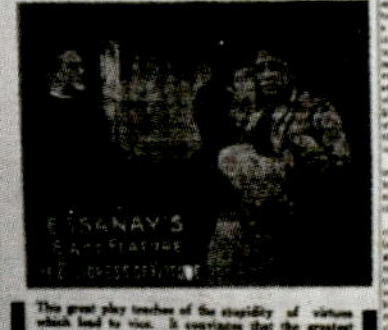

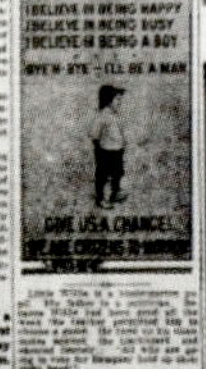

A CHILD'S CREED

Last Time Tonight at the Orpheum

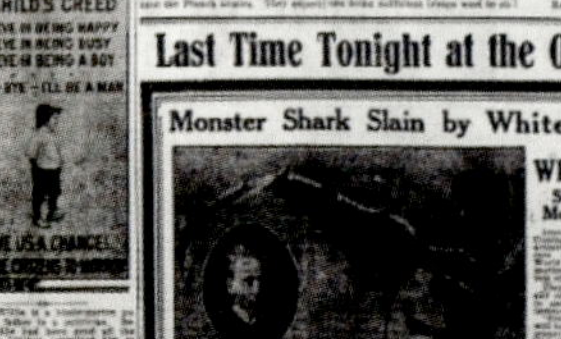

Monster Shark Slain by White Man in The Famous WILLIAMSON SUBMARINE Moving Pictures

## Lewis Hine

1870

1874 Born in Oshkosh, Wisconsin, USA

1880

1890

1901 Hired by the Ethical Culture School in New York City to teach science. Begins photographing immigrants at Ellis Island

1906 Starts photographing for the National Child Labor Committee

1907 Begins graduate study of sociology; hired to work on Pittsburgh Survey

1910

1918 Photographs effects of war in Europe

1920

1932 Publishes *Men at Work*

1940 Dies in Dobbs Ferry, New York, USA

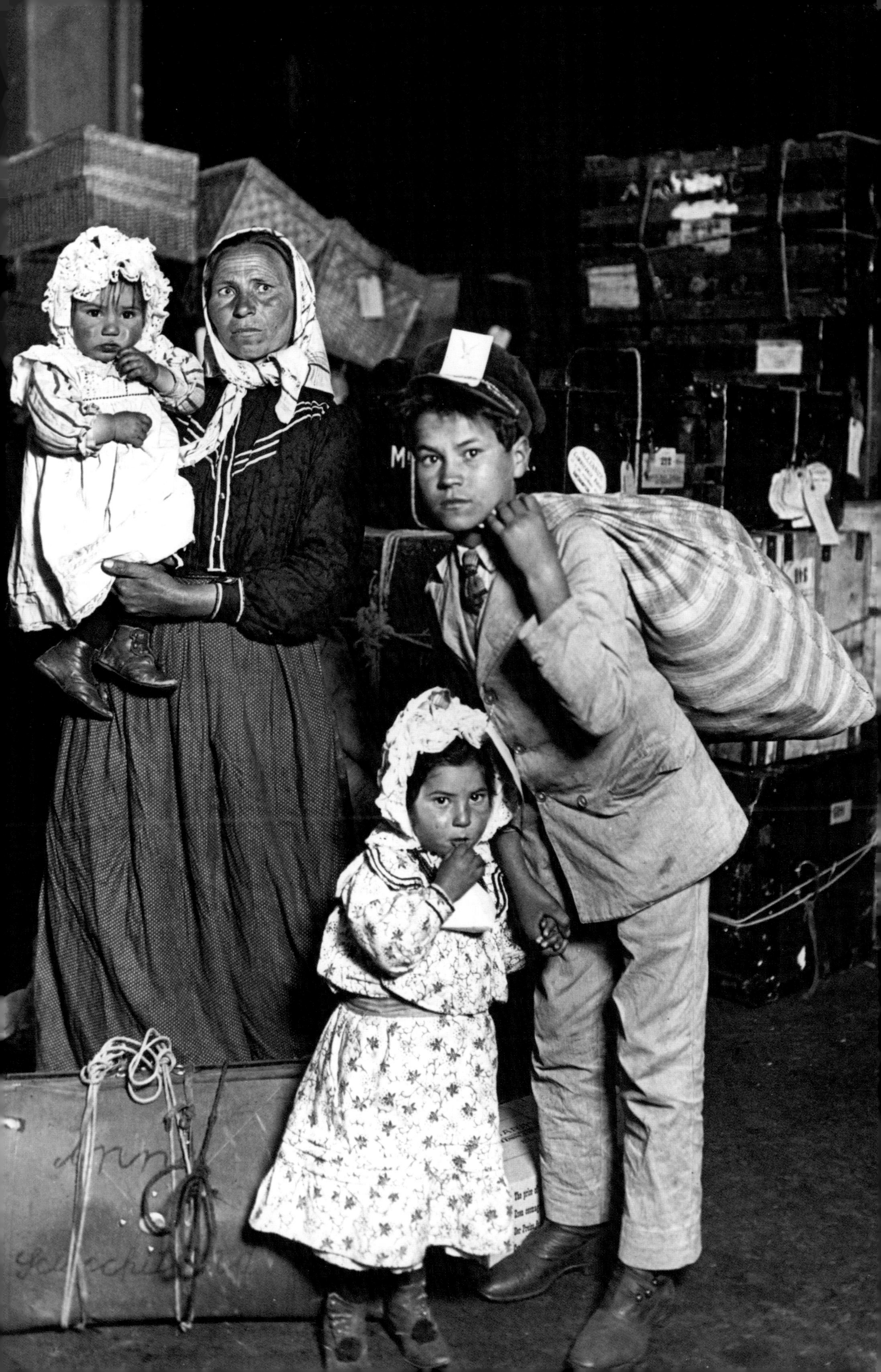

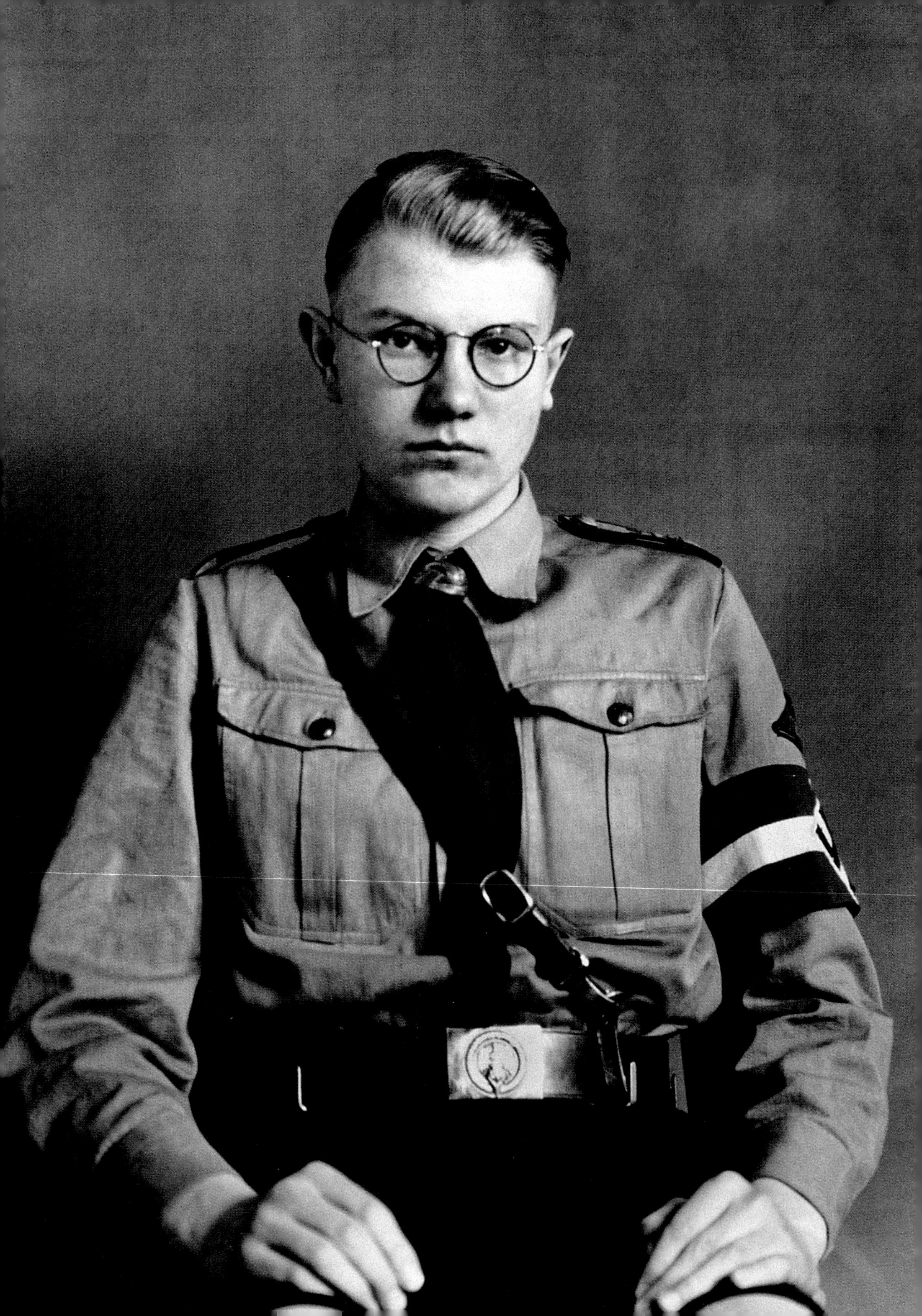

'Documentary photography is less concerned with aesthetic requirements ... than with the significance of what is represented.'

# August Sander

1876–1964

GERMANY

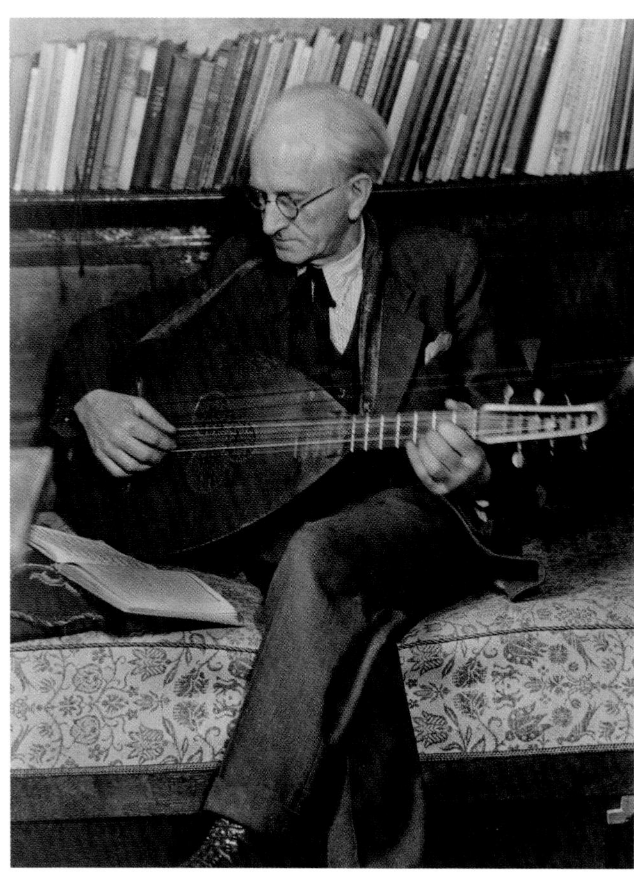

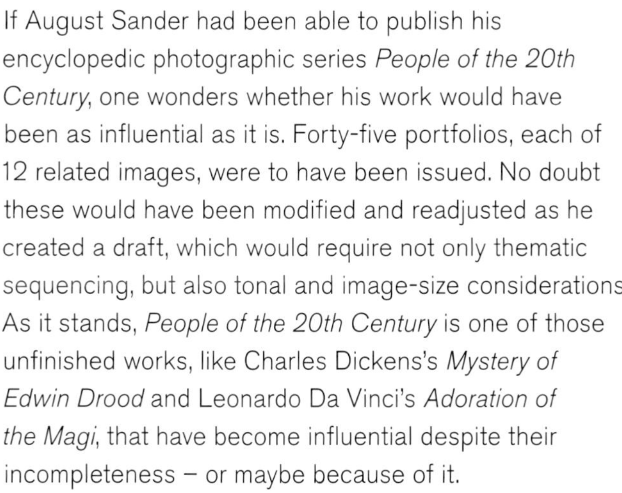

If August Sander had been able to publish his encyclopedic photographic series *People of the 20th Century*, one wonders whether his work would have been as influential as it is. Forty-five portfolios, each of 12 related images, were to have been issued. No doubt these would have been modified and readjusted as he created a draft, which would require not only thematic sequencing, but also tonal and image-size considerations. As it stands, *People of the 20th Century* is one of those unfinished works, like Charles Dickens's *Mystery of Edwin Drood* and Leonardo Da Vinci's *Adoration of the Magi*, that have become influential despite their incompleteness – or maybe because of it.

That very incompleteness has allowed later photographers, ranging from Diane Arbus to Andreas Gursky (p. 296), to find a sympathetic forebear and guide in Sander. For Arbus, Sander seemed to accentuate inherent human idiosyncrasies; for Gursky and the post-World War II Düsseldorf school of photography, Sander's techniques for isolating and distancing individuals underscored the potential of objectivity to be an art language. Taken before the outbreak of World War II, Sander's photographs of Nazi soldiers and functionaries have a historical resonance he could not have imagined. His portraits of women showed them as sophisticated or maternal or unemployed, but not as sex workers. As persecution of minorities increased in the 1930s, Sander added Jews and gypsies to his panoply of modern life and all its contradictions.

There is a rough consistency to Sander's style. His pictures are usually in sharp focus, and show people at full- or half-length. Because he wanted to chronicle the variety of people in Germany generated by rural life, urban values, different occupations and various pastimes, he set out to show regional and metropolitan contrasts. But if this was his goal, it broke down as sitters physically declared their individuality. The humour in his work seems to come from his acceptance of variations that could not be eliminated by standardized distances from the sitters and similar lighting schemes.

Despite having lost the printing plates to an earlier, smaller effort called *Face of Our Time,* as well as about 30,000 negatives in a 1946 fire, Sander attempted to complete his vision, and left detailed notes for those who might succeed him.

**Opposite** Member of the Hitler Youth, 1938.

**Above** Portrait with lute by unknown, 1942.

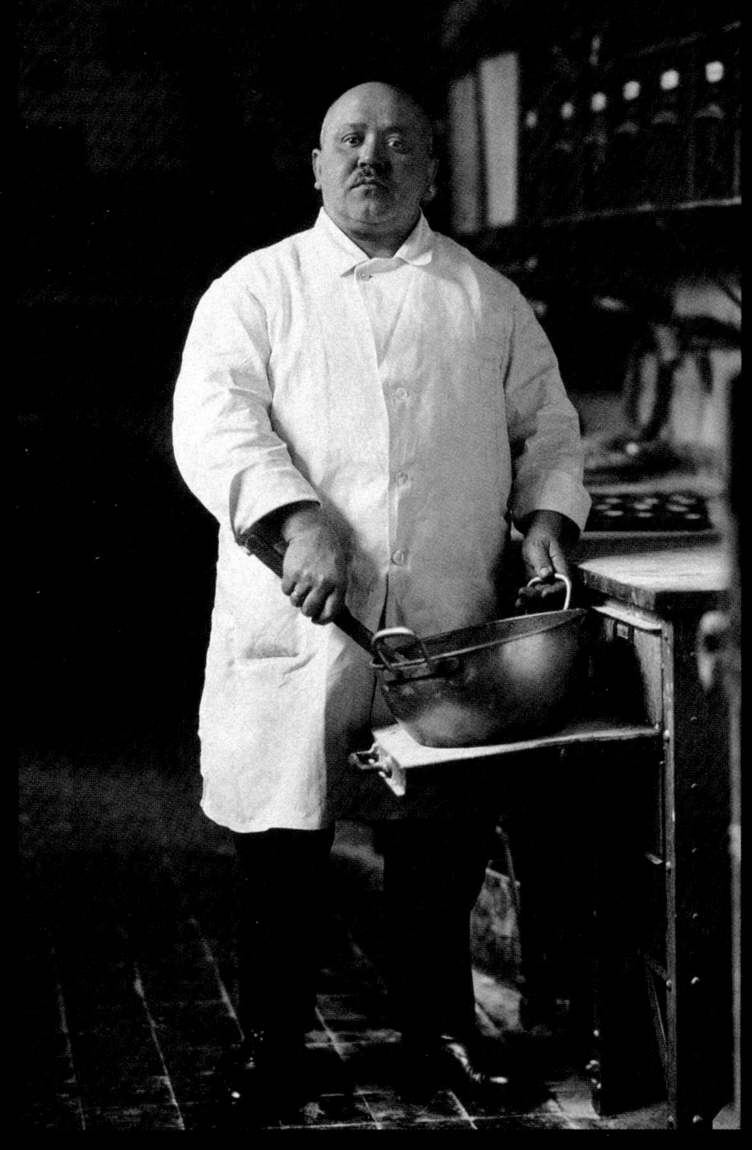

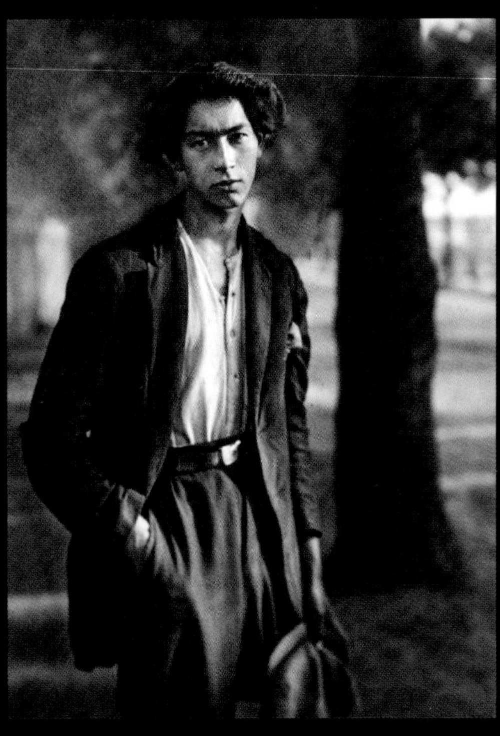

**Above** Pastrycook, 1928.

**Left** Gypsy, 1932.

**Right** Secretary at West German Radio, Cologne, 1931.

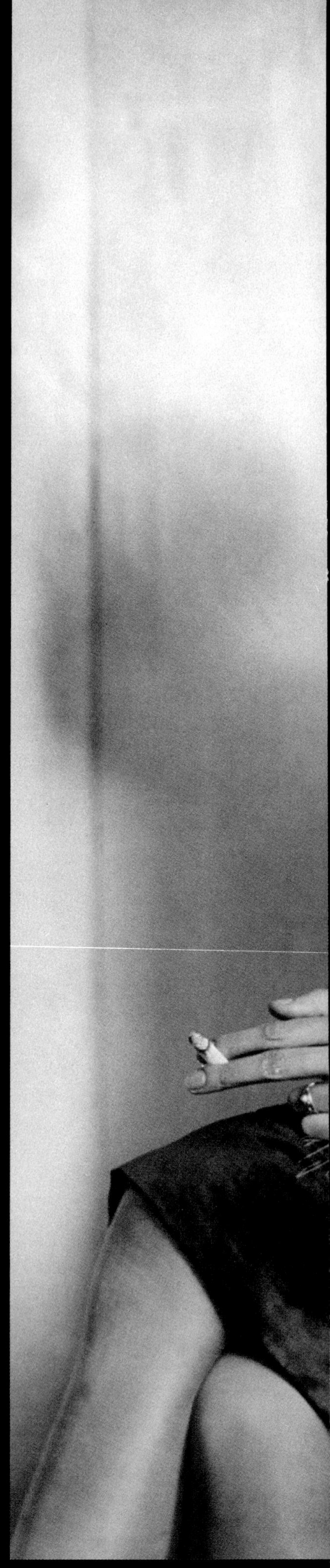

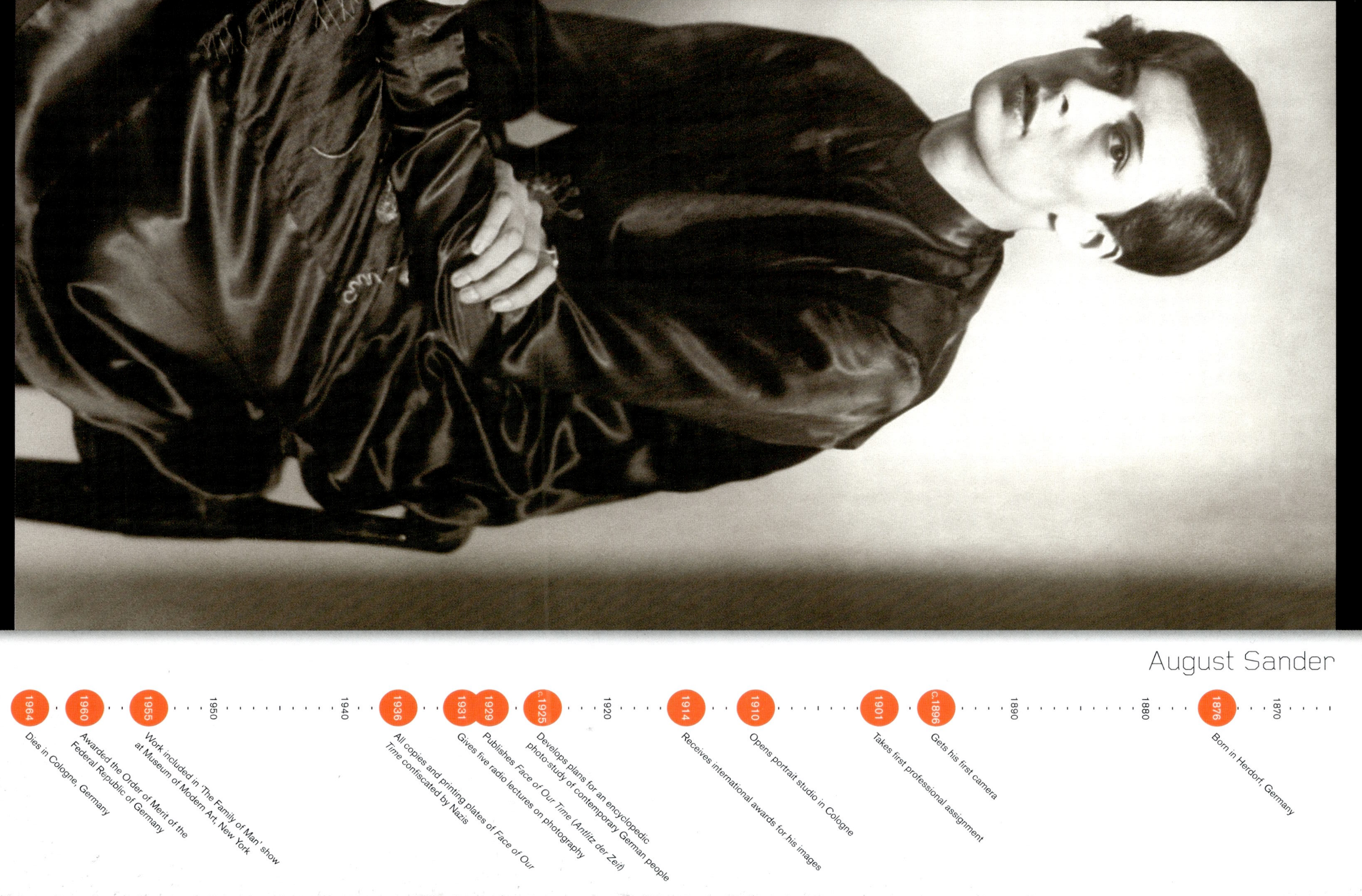
August Sander
1870
1876 Born in Herdorf, Germany
1880
1890
c.1896 Gets his first camera
1901 Takes first professional assignment
1910 Opens portrait studio in Cologne
1914 Receives international awards for his images
1920
c.1925 Develops plans for an encyclopedic photo-study of contemporary German people
1929 Publishes *Face of Our Time* (*Antlitz der Zeit*)
1931 Gives five radio lectures on photography
1936 All copies and printing plates of *Face of Our Time* confiscated by Nazis
1940
1950
1955 Work included in 'The Family of Man' show at Museum of Modern Art, New York
1960 Awarded the Order of Merit of the Federal Republic of Germany
1964 Dies in Cologne, Germany

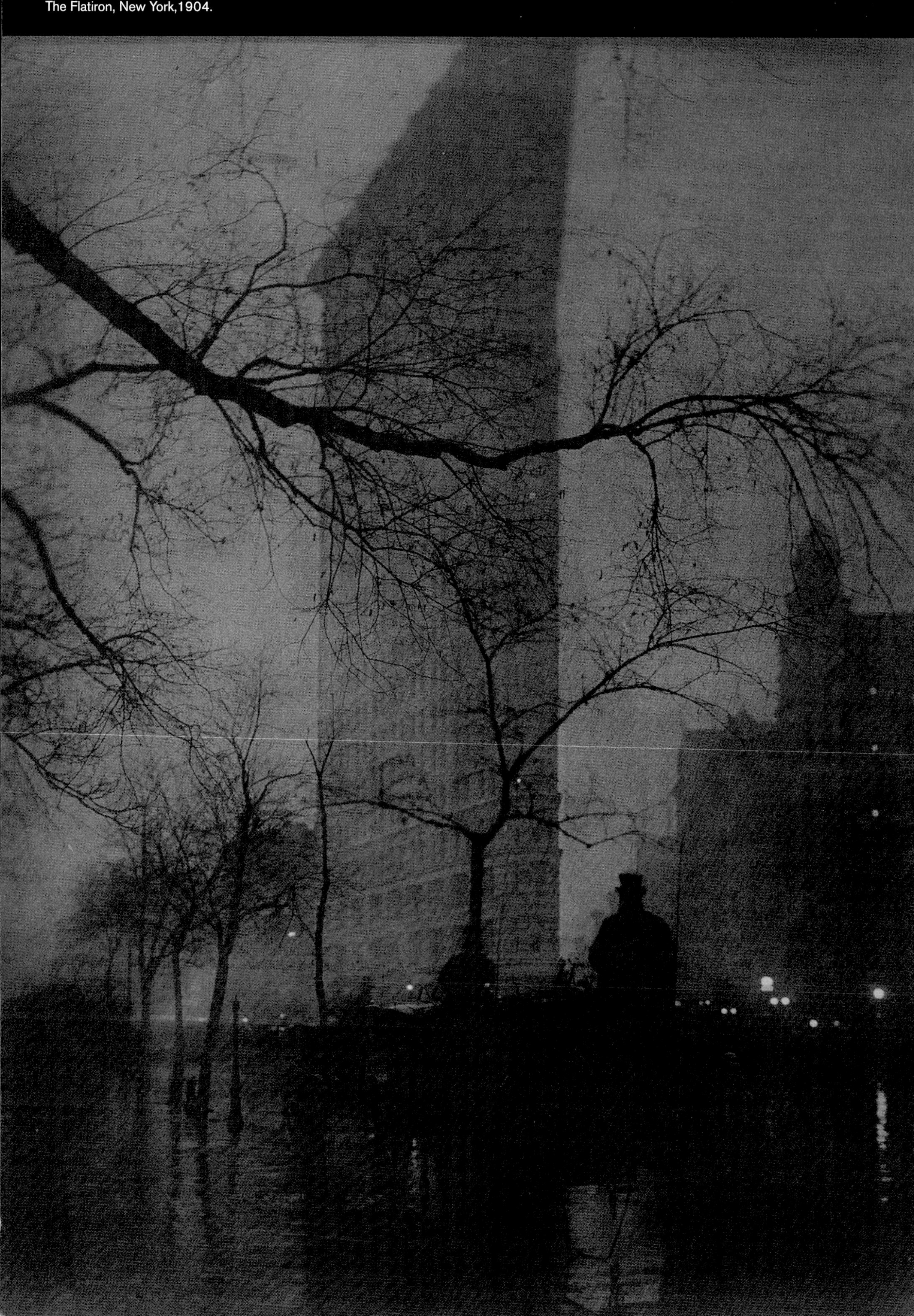

The Flatiron, New York,1904.

'Every ten years a man should give himself a good kick in the pants.'

# Edward Steichen

1879–1973

LUXEMBOURG

From the criticism heaped on Edward Steichen for doing commercial work, you would think that he had sold his soul. It was not so much that he made a living in magazine photojournalism – many art photographers did that – but that he was unapologetic about it. Today, his varied interests and activities, including fashion and advertising photography, make him the Photo-Secessionist most like contemporary photographers, who also hopscotch among media and genres, as well as between commercial and personal work, though without the criticism Steichen faced.

Cosmopolitan despite his working-class roots, young Steichen wanted to be a painter. He met Alfred Stieglitz (p. 12) in New York, just before sailing for France to study art. Eventually he became Stieglitz's eyes and ears on artistic trends in that country, and emerged as the vital steady hand in the Photo-Secession, the art-photography movement created by Stieglitz. While still hoping to succeed in painting, Steichen created a successful photographic portrait studio in New York. About the same time, he took a gamble and tried his hand at high-fashion photography, suggesting through his inventive lighting and composition that both couture and its photography were art forms. Eventually, he was the top photographer for fashion magazines such as *Vogue* and *Vanity Fair,* and took on assignments at J. Walter Thompson, a leading advertising agency. When he finally rejected painting, he ceremonially burned all the canvases he had in his studio.

It was not that Steichen was a restless individual but that so many things interested him, and he was good at them. When World War I broke out, Steichen joined the United States Army Air Service as head of the photographic section; he took a similar but wider role in World War II, which led to his directing the Oscar-winning documentary film *The Fighting Lady,* about life on an aircraft carrier. His military obligations did not seem to interfere with his ability to mount two wartime-themed exhibitions at the Museum of Modern Art. When he became Director of the Department of Photography at MoMA, he attempted to produce a collective, unifying portrait of the world's people, in the still discussed and disputed exhibition 'The Family of Man'.

Self-portrait as a painter, 1901.

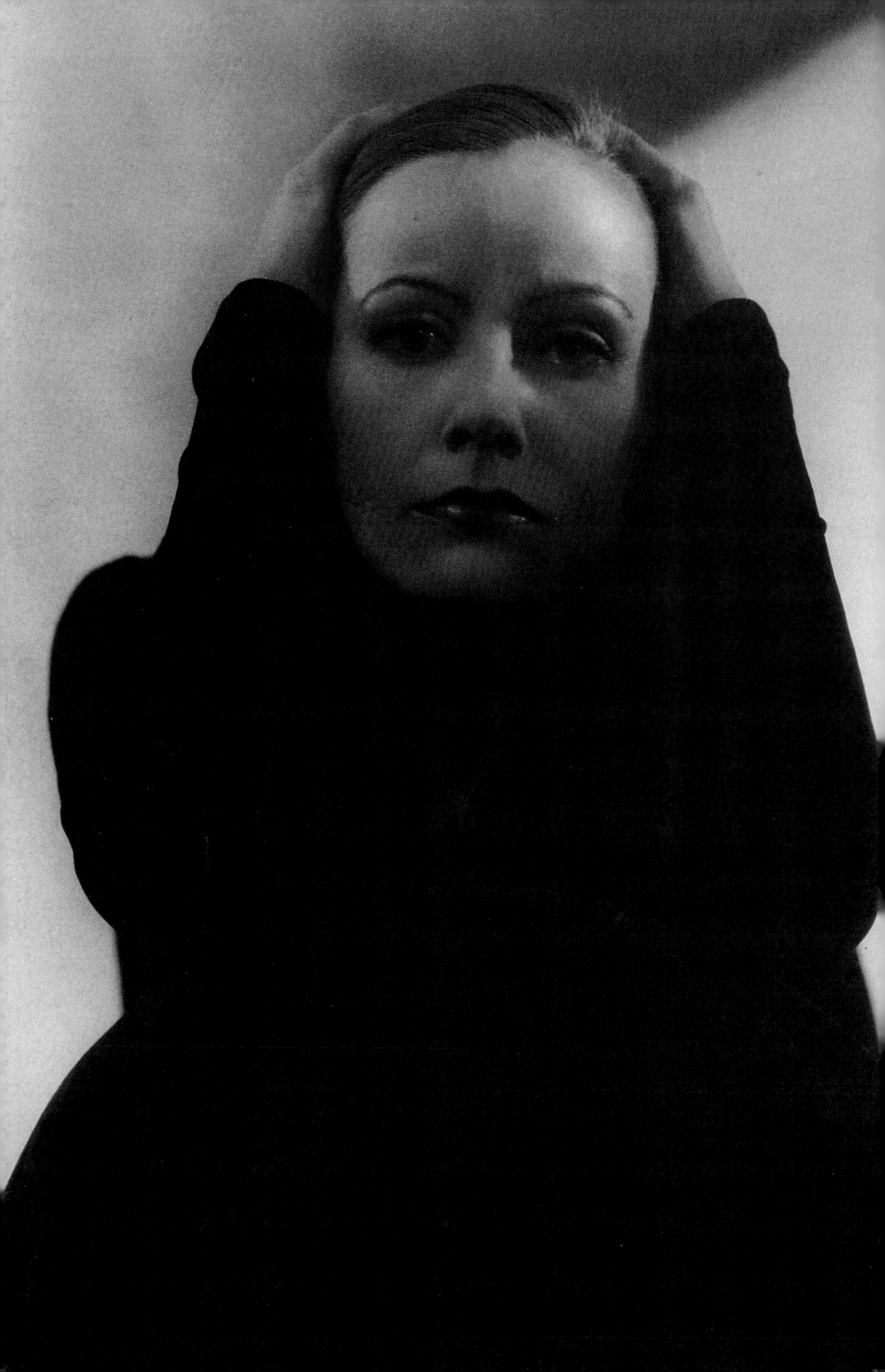

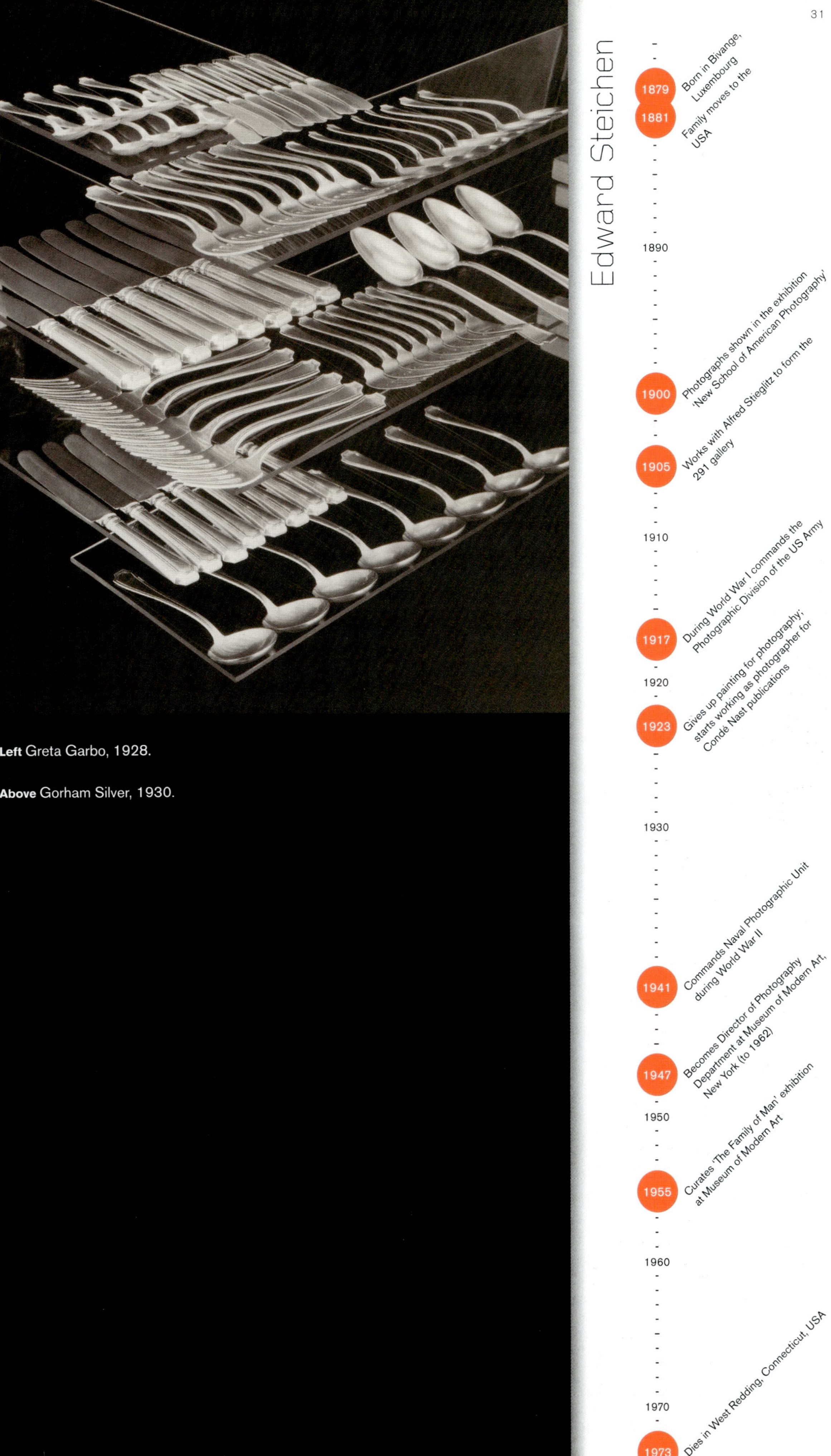

**Left** Greta Garbo, 1928.

**Above** Gorham Silver, 1930.

## Edward Steichen

1879 Born in Bivange, Luxembourg

1881 Family moves to the USA

1890

1900 Photographs shown in the exhibition 'New School of American Photography'

1905 Works with Alfred Stieglitz to form the 291 gallery

1910

1917 During World War I commands the Photographic Division of the US Army

1920

1923 Gives up painting for photography; starts working as photographer for Condé Nast publications

1930

1941 Commands Naval Photographic Unit during World War II

1947 Becomes Director of Photography Department at Museum of Modern Art, New York (to 1962)

1950

1955 Curates 'The Family of Man' exhibition at Museum of Modern Art

1960

1970

1973 Dies in West Redding, Connecticut, USA

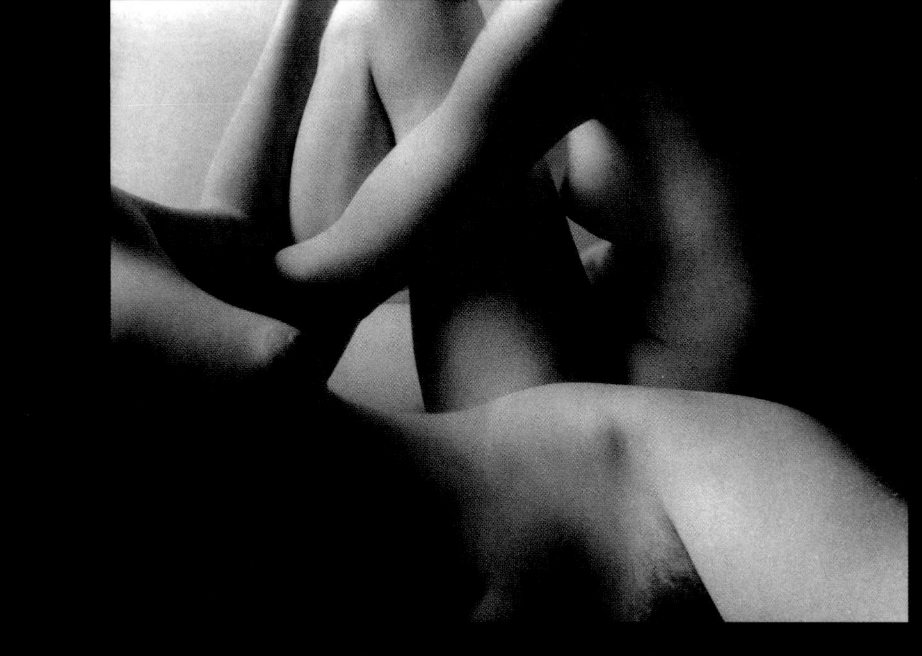

**Right** *Triangles Plus One*, 1928.

**Below right** *John Bovington 2*, 1929

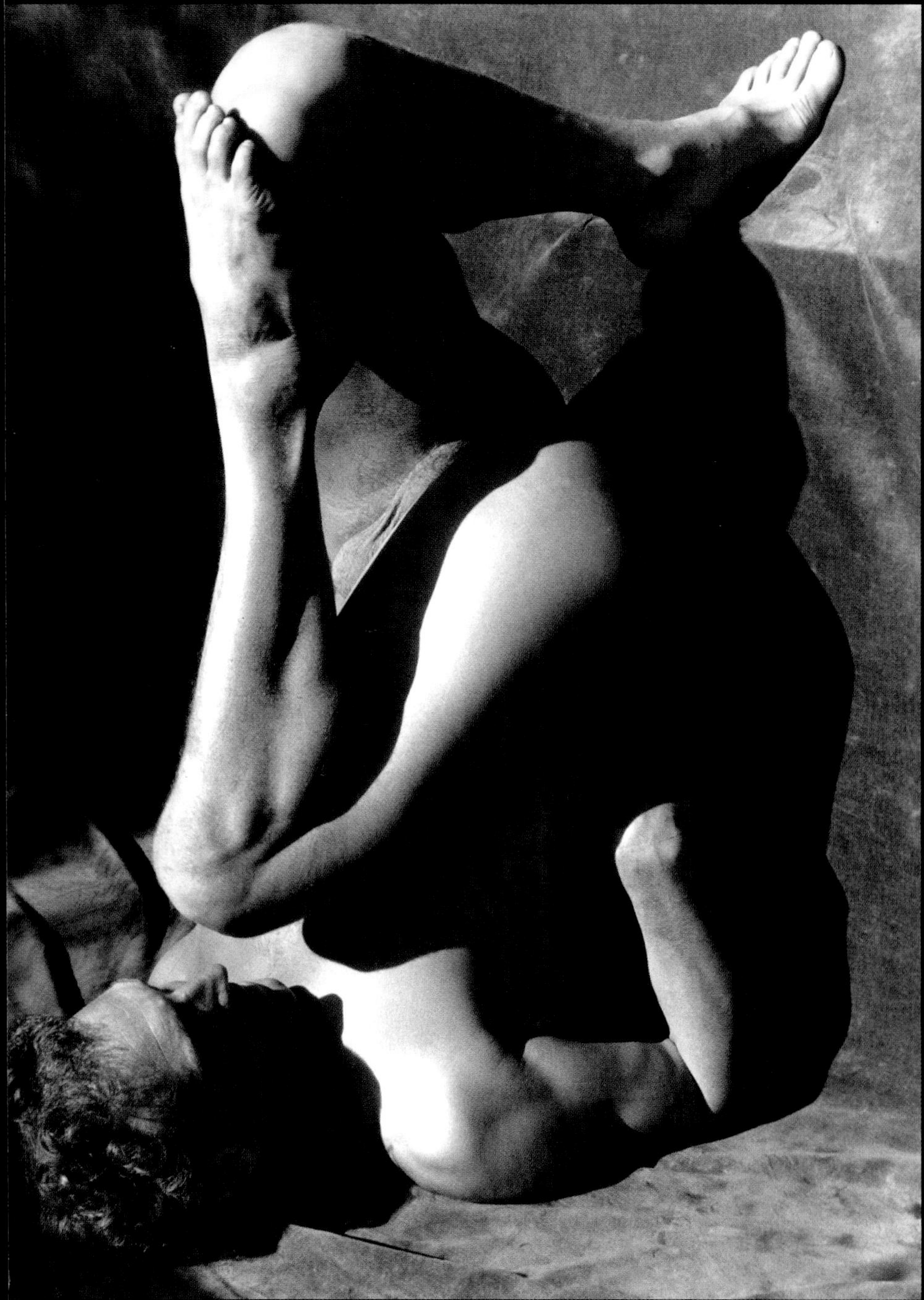

'Photography is ... not a better profession for a woman than for a man, it is simply a profession.'

# Imogen Cunningham

1883–1976

UNITED STATES

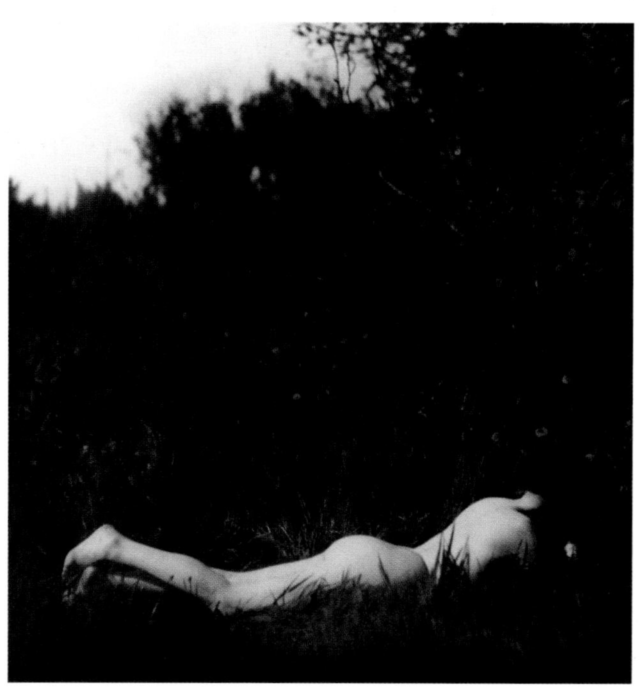

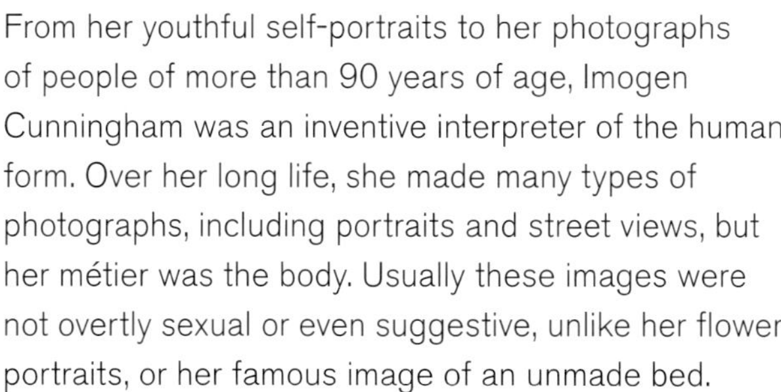

From her youthful self-portraits to her photographs of people of more than 90 years of age, Imogen Cunningham was an inventive interpreter of the human form. Over her long life, she made many types of photographs, including portraits and street views, but her métier was the body. Usually these images were not overtly sexual or even suggestive, unlike her flower portraits, or her famous image of an unmade bed.

In her early work, she visually referenced Christianity and Greek mythology to justify her choice of subject – a ploy that did not succeed when nude photographs of her husband, posed as Narcissus, made her work a scandal in Seattle.

Her subsequent images were so creatively composed and original that they were without a familiar precedent, and even confusing to those hoping to glimpse willing flesh. For example, there is more to *Triangles* than angles: the way that the body forms a frame around the recess space invites the viewer to look into the space, passing by curves emphasized in the intricate lighting scheme. A similarly composed photograph of the dancer John Bovington is surprising in its pose and the way that light chisels triangles on and around his body.

Cunningham's images of pregnancy present women looking like powerful fertility goddesses. Her book *After Ninety* set out to show spry men and women in their tenth decade of life. None of the images is more powerful than that of Irene 'Bobby' Libarry, who displays her bountiful tattoos with such dignity and poise that the viewer is put at ease.

Nude self-portrait, 1906.

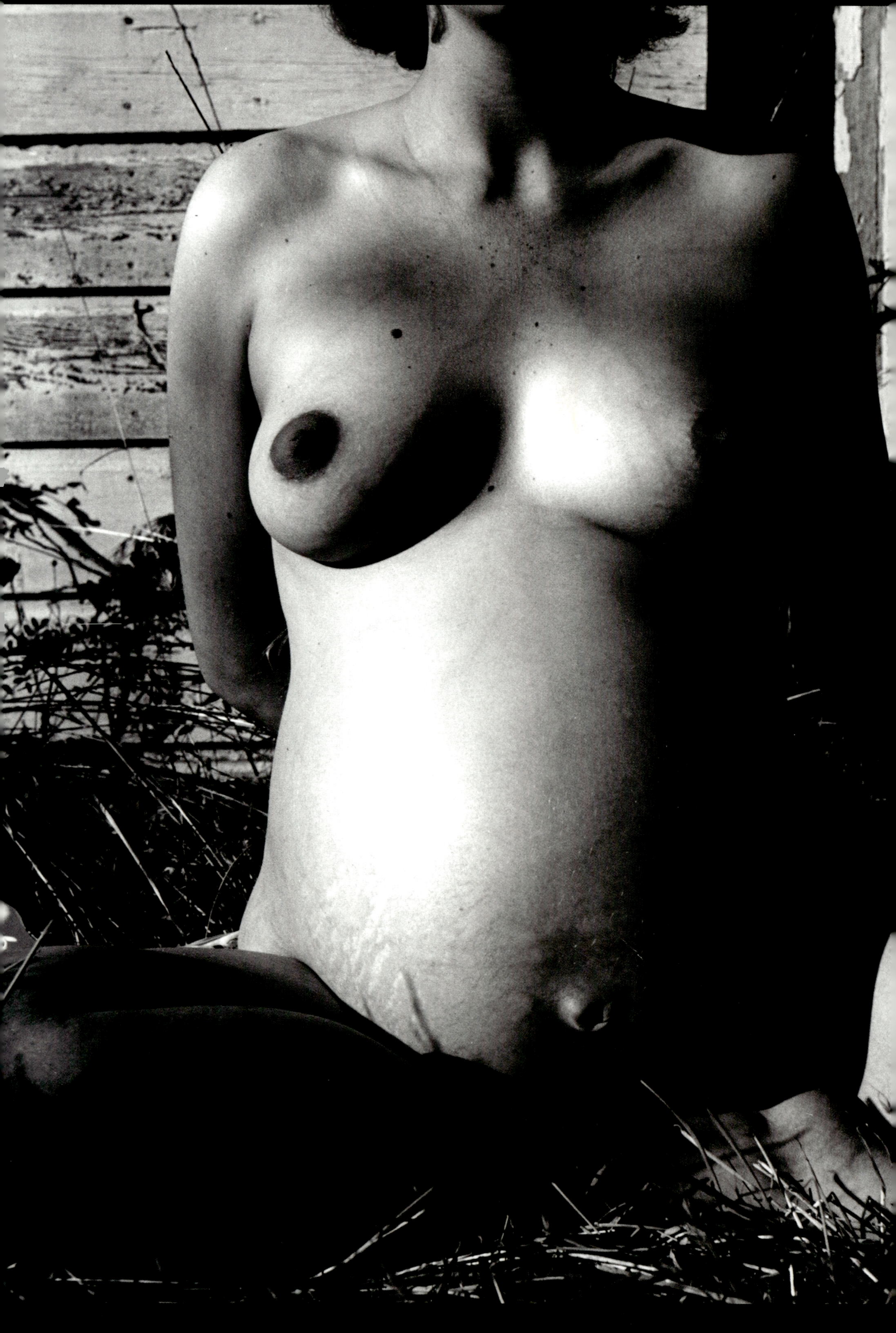

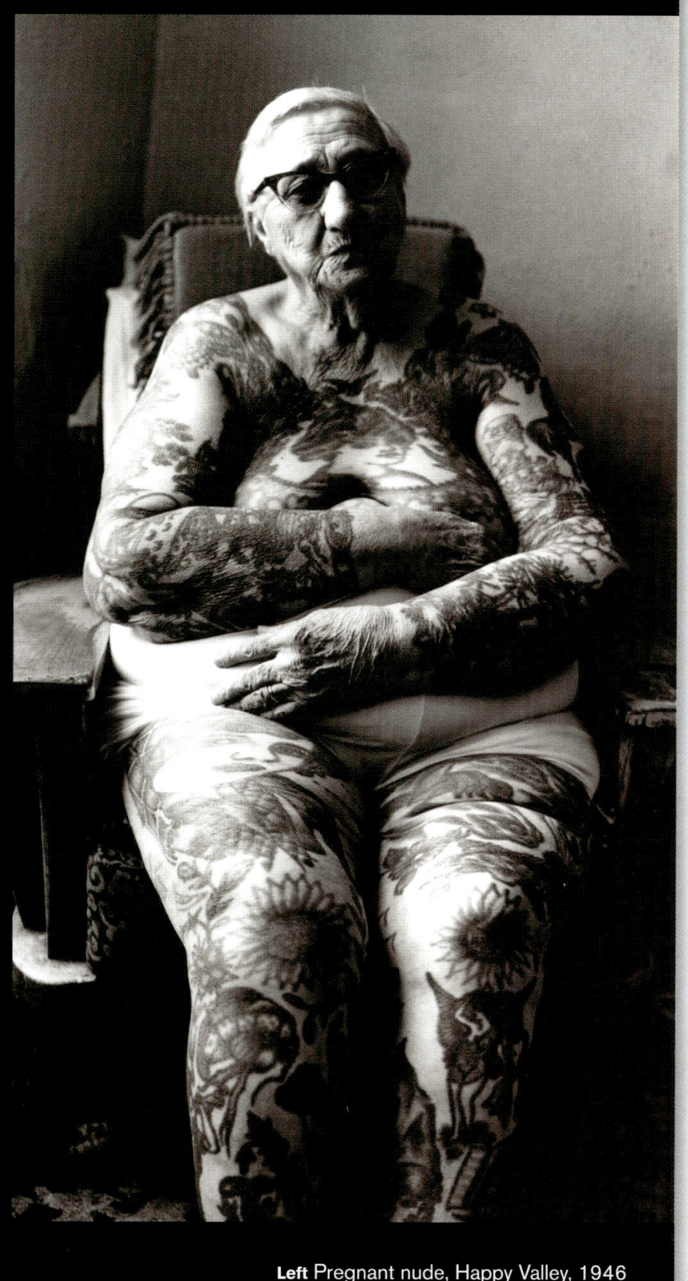

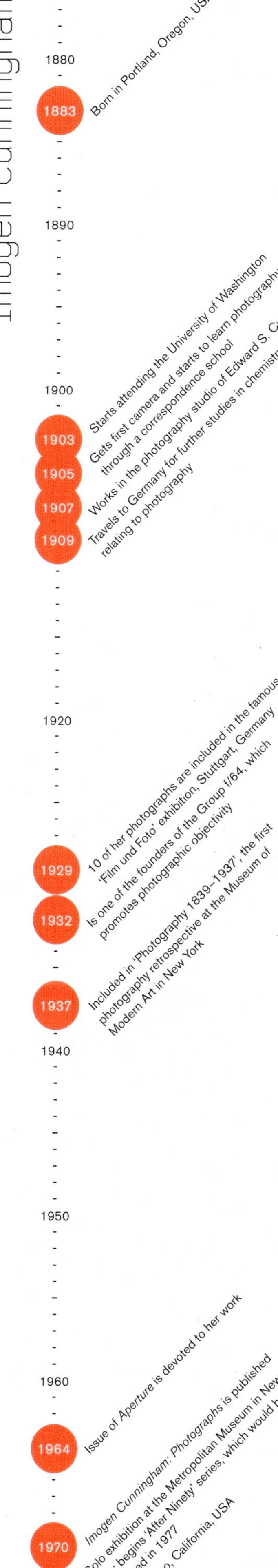


**Left** Pregnant nude, Happy Valley, 1946

**Above** Irene 'Bobby' Libarry from *After Ninety*, 1976.

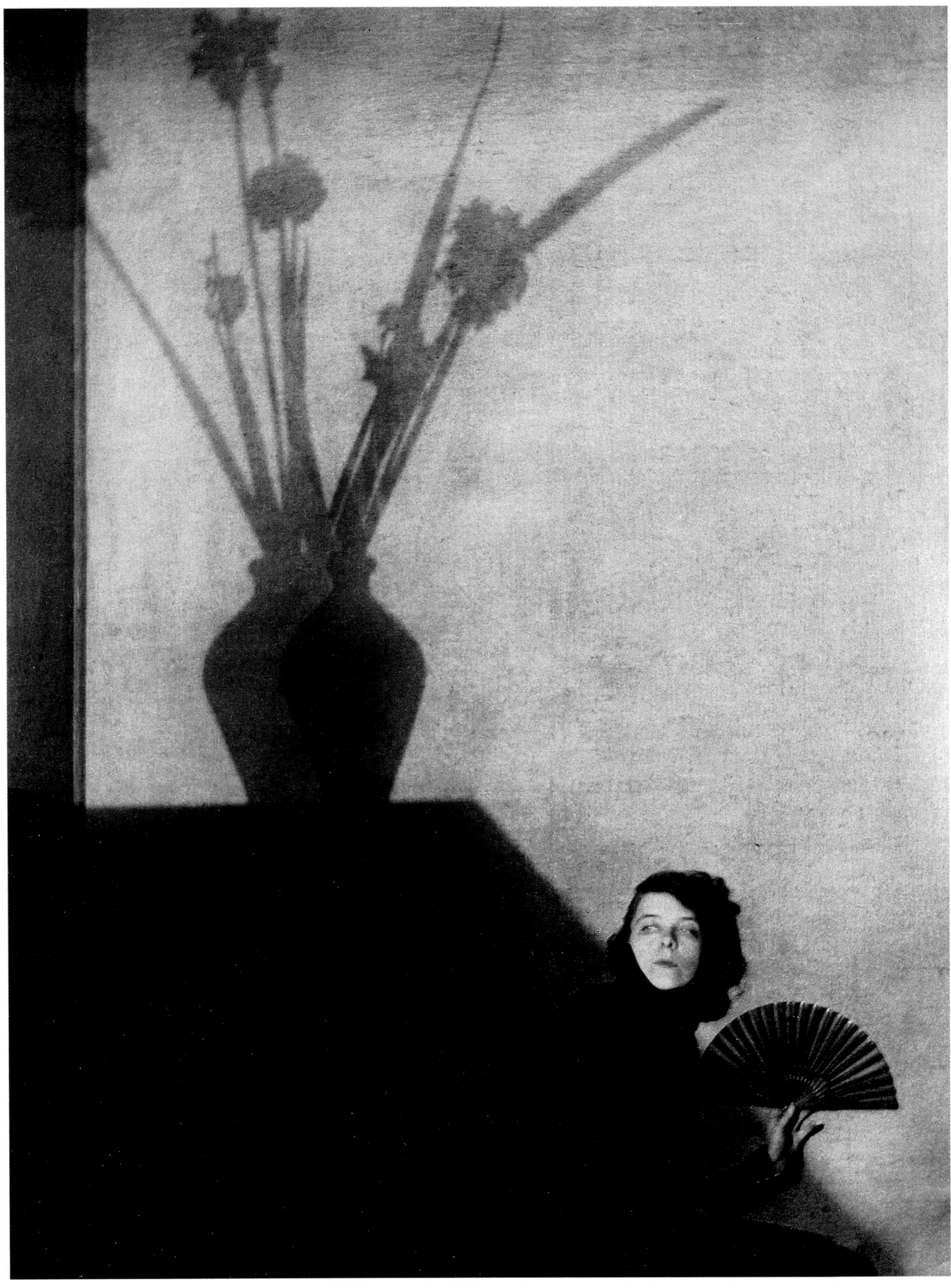

*Epilogue*, 1920.

'To consult the rules of composition before making a picture is a little like consulting the law of gravitation before going for a walk.'

# Edward Weston

1886–1958

UNITED STATES

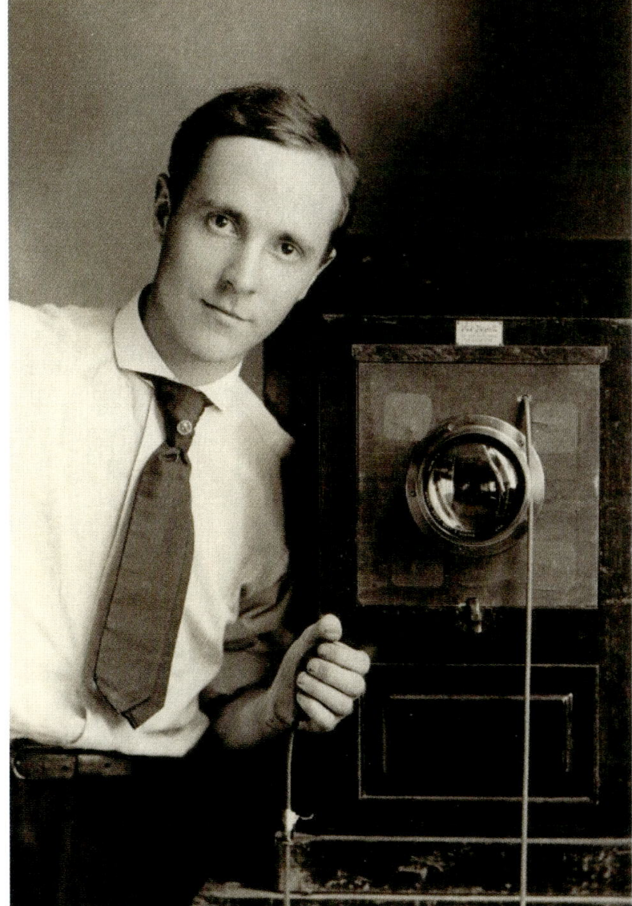

Even when he was young and caught up in soft-focus Pictorialist photography, Edward Weston favoured definitive angles and suggestive tonal contrast in his photography. Those inclinations were underscored by his study of Modernist painting. For him, as for many young photographers, Alfred Stieglitz (p. 12) was a prophet, and he travelled to New York to meet him, gushing in his notebooks that even though Stieglitz tossed many of his prints in a discard pile, he gained strength and a finer understanding of the medium.

Certainly, post-Stieglitz, Weston was more of a chance taker, moving to Mexico and living there on and off for two years. A new minimalism entered his work, and he produced tabletop character studies of ordinary things, such as seashells and vegetables. His famous depiction of a lavatory bowl, or *excusado* in polite Spanish, was taken in Mexico, and painstakingly described in his journal ('Daybook') notations for the period. Similarly, some of his minimalist nudes owe to his perception that he could conjoin the real and the abstract. 'Nature,' he wrote, 'has all the "abstract" (simplified) forms Brancusi or any other artist can imagine.'

What he dubbed 'seeing plus' continued throughout the remainder of his career, especially in landscape work in the desert and along the Pacific coastline near his highland retreat, Wildcat Hill, outside of Carmel, California. His creative life was cut short by serious illness, and by the sombre turn taken in the arts during World War II.

No doubt Weston would be startled to learn that he is now dubbed an old master and that some of his simplified pictures of natural objects have fetched more than a million dollars at twenty-first century auctions.

Self-portrait, 1933.

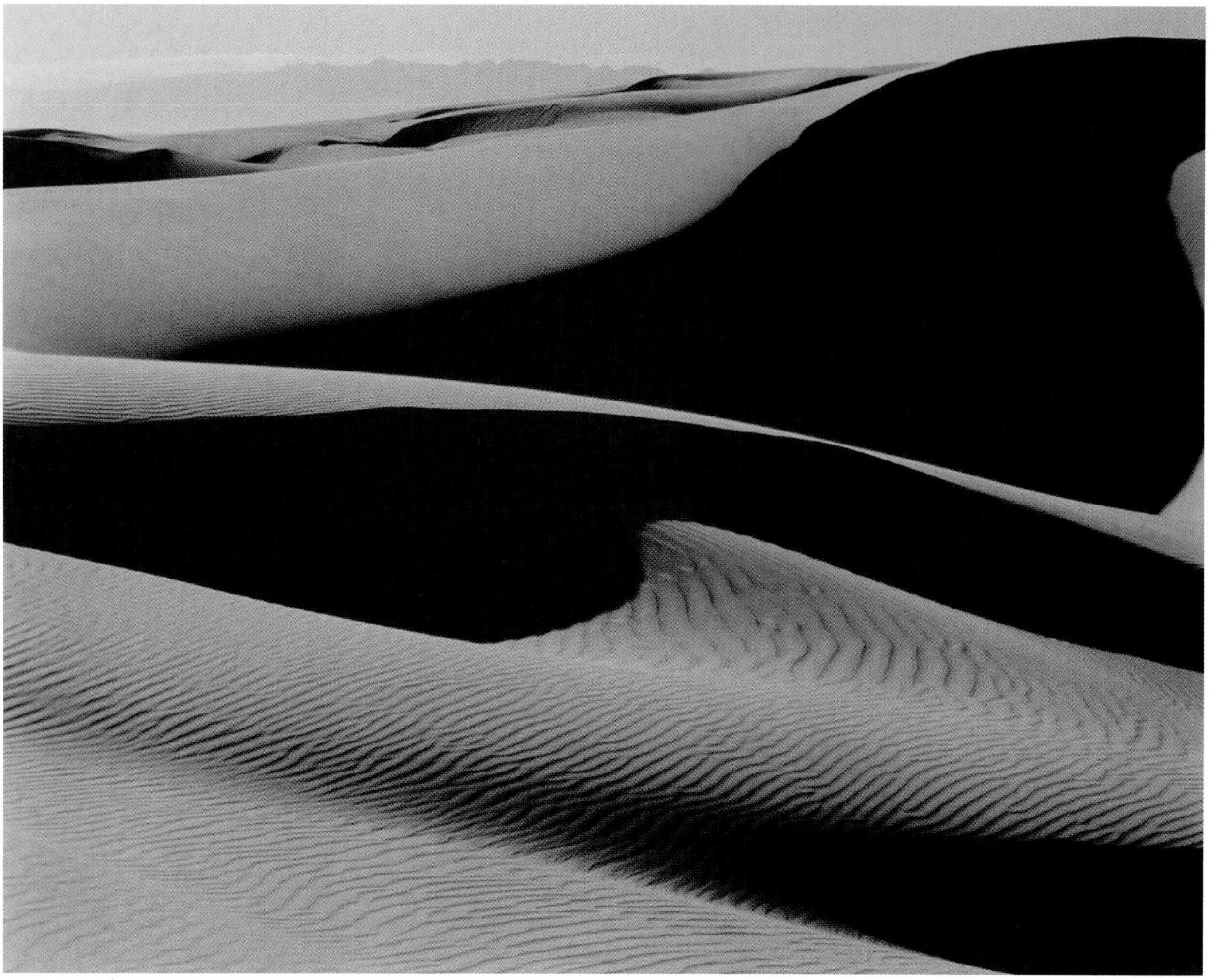

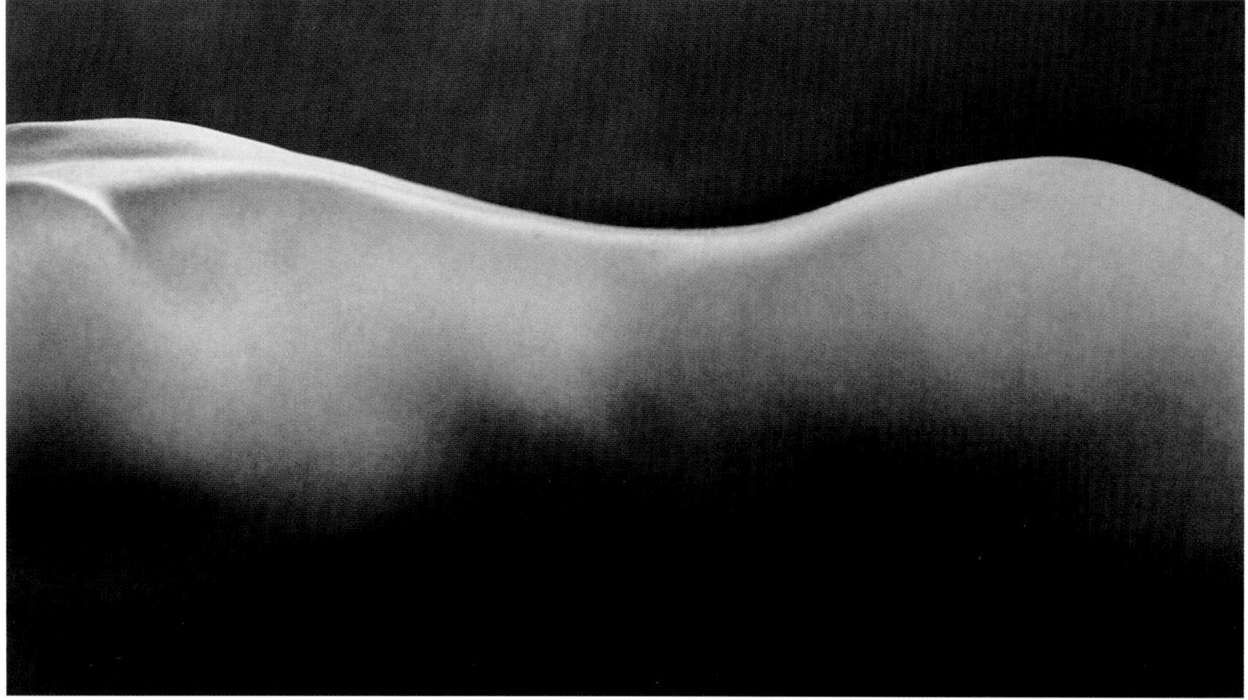

**Top** *Dunes, Oceano*, 1936.

**Above** *Nude*, 1925.

**Opposite top** *Excusado*, 1925.

**Opposite right** *Pepper #30*, 1930.

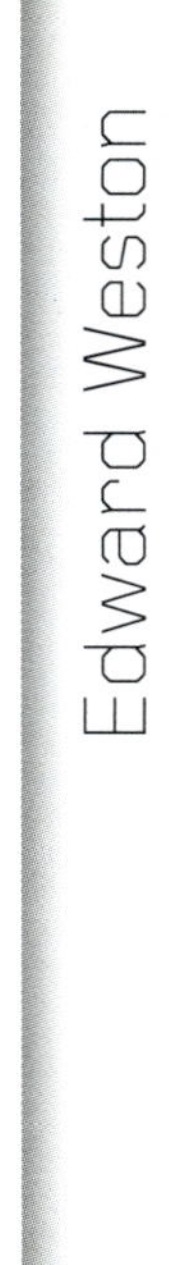
Edward Weston

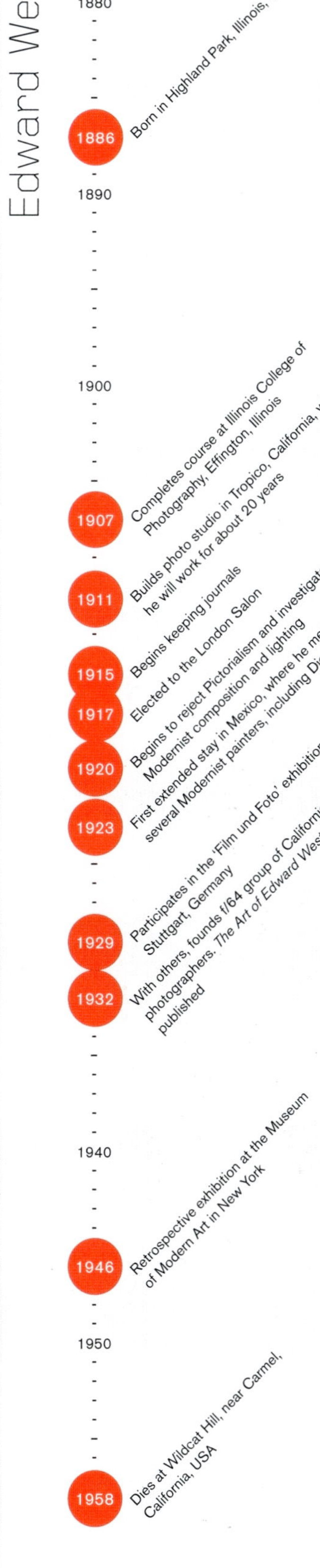
1880
1886 Born in Highland Park, Illinois, USA
1890
1900
1907 Completes course at Illinois College of Photography, Effington, Illinois
1911 Builds photo studio in Tropico, California, where he will work for about 20 years
1915 Begins keeping journals
1917 Elected to the London Salon
1920 Begins to reject Pictorialism and investigate Modernist composition and lighting
1923 First extended stay in Mexico, where he meets several Modernist painters, including Diego Rivera
1929 Participates in the 'Film und Foto' exhibition, Stuttgart, Germany
1932 With others, founds f/64 group of California photographers. The Art of Edward Weston is published
1940
1946 Retrospective exhibition at the Museum of Modern Art in New York
1950
1958 Dies at Wildcat Hill, near Carmel, California, USA

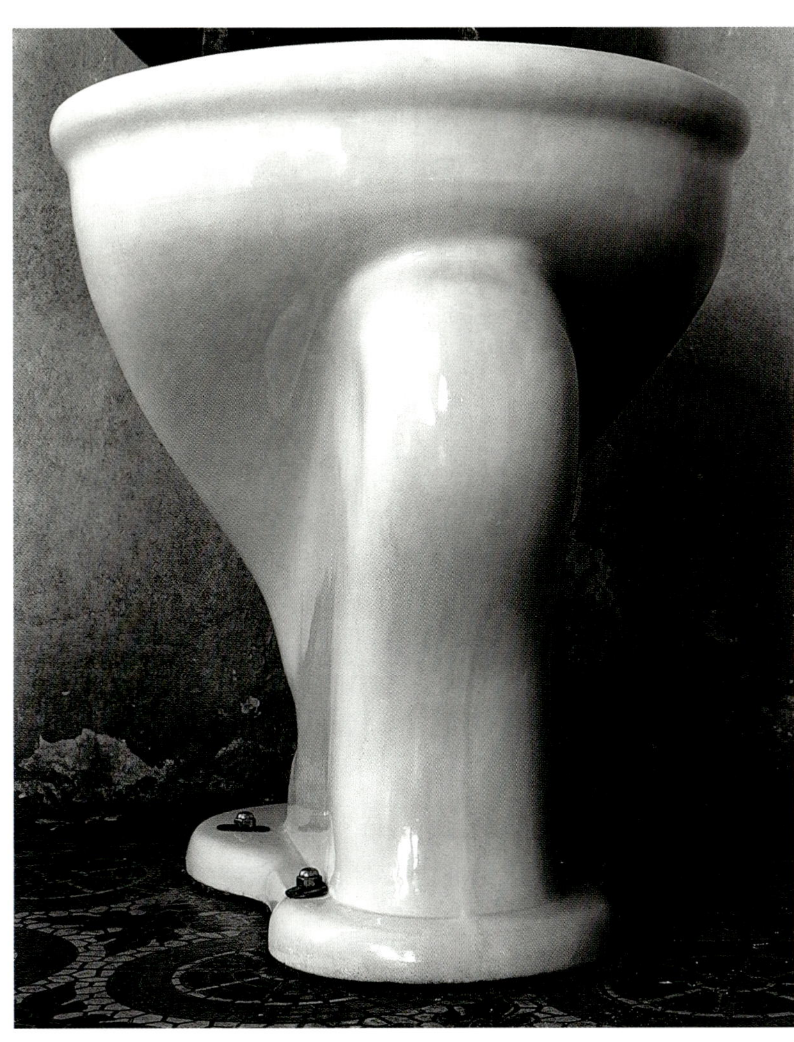

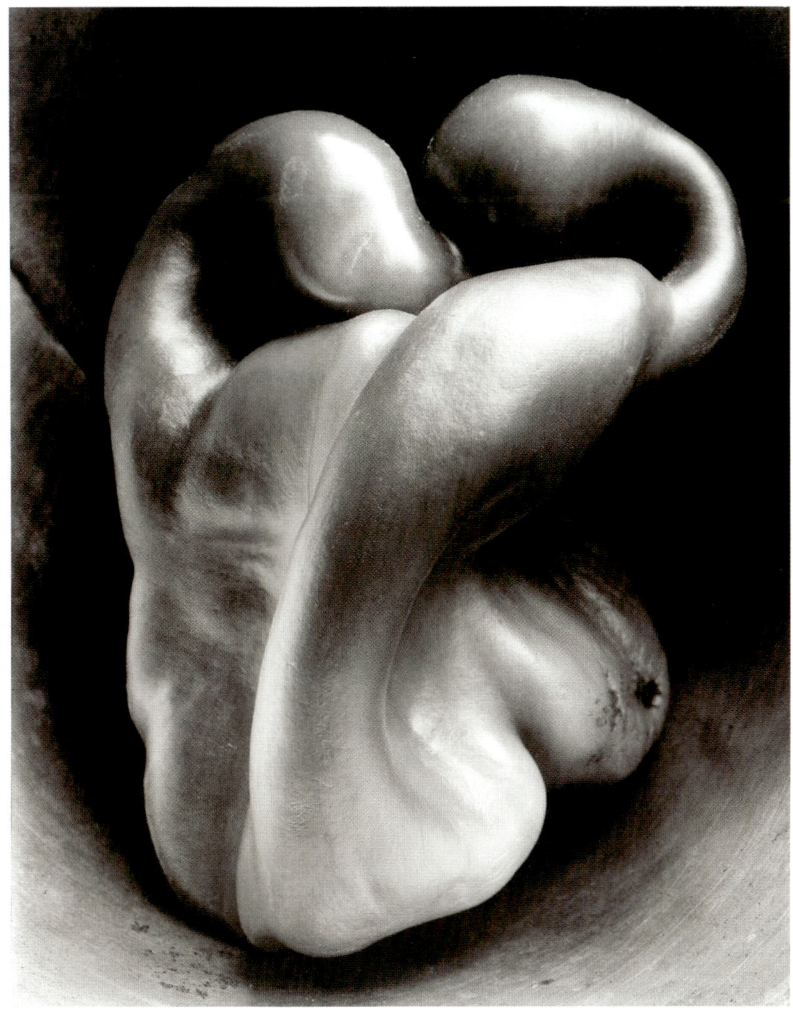

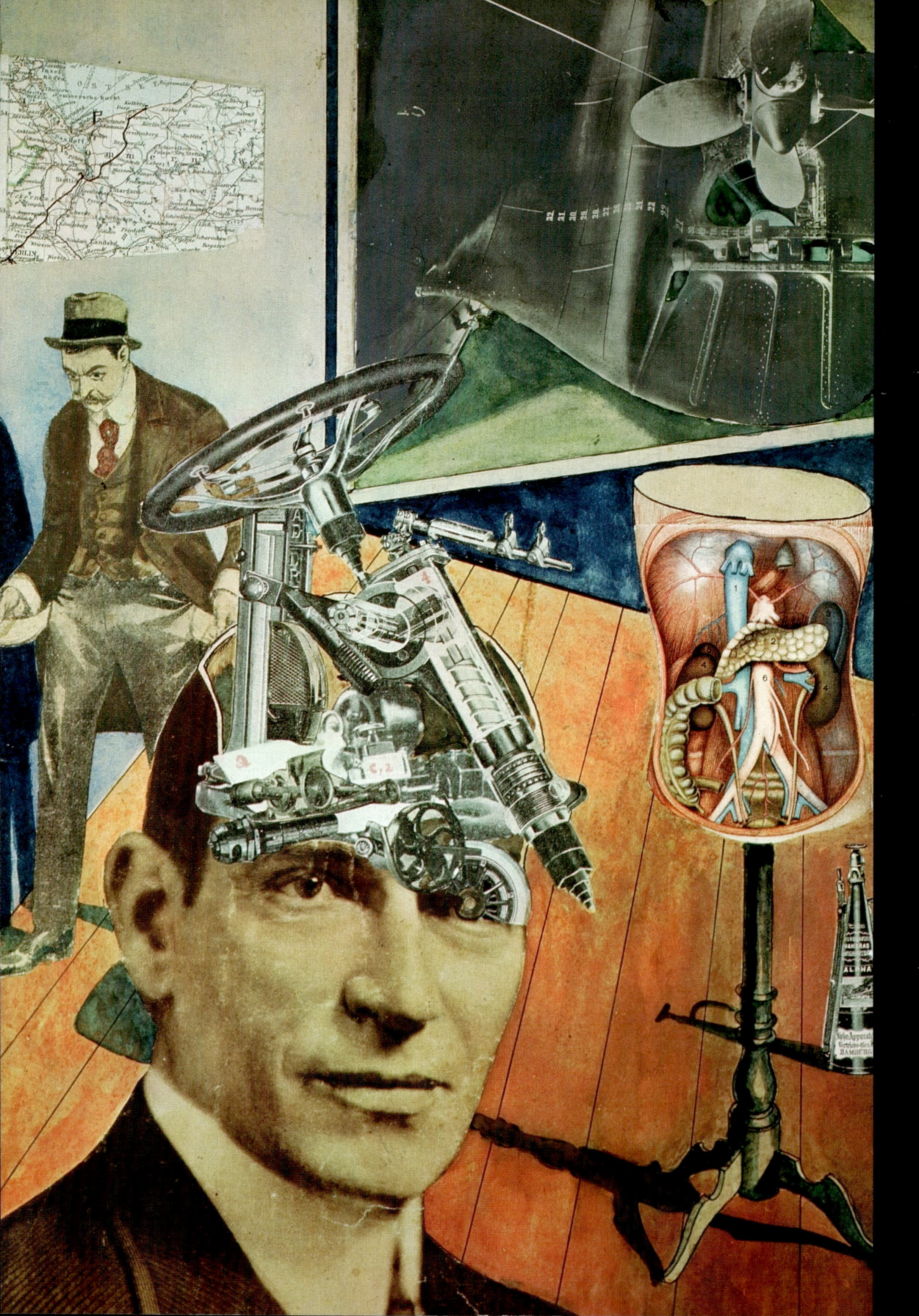
Kolberg
Belgard
Anklam
Bublitz
Stettin
Stargard
ALPHA

'Why don't we paint works today like those of Botticelli, Michelangelo, Leonardo or Titian? Because our spirits have utterly changed.'

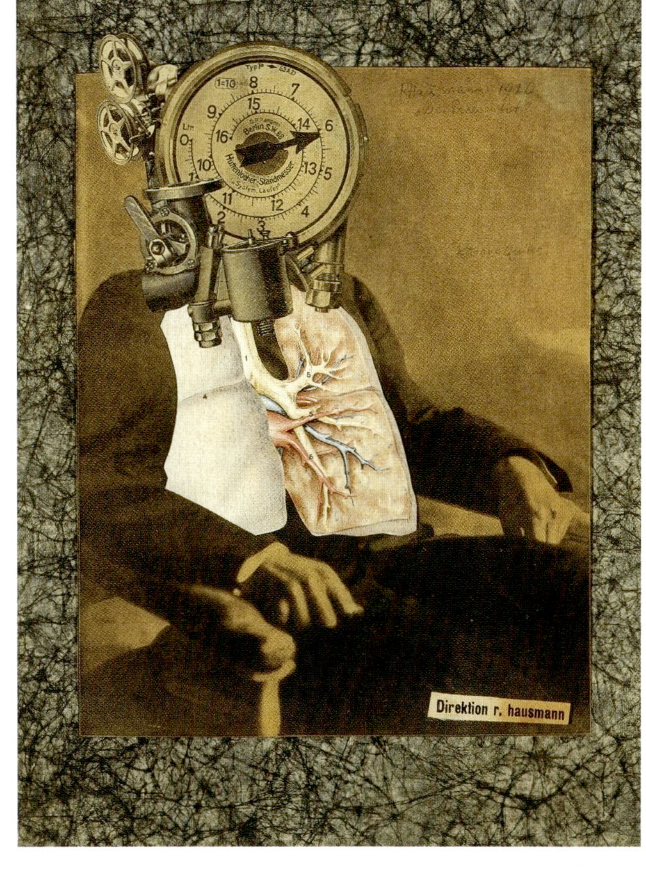


# Raoul Hausmann

1886–1971

AUSTRIA

Who invented photomontage? Two duos claim to have created or discovered the technique: John Heartfield (p. 56) and George Grosz; and Raoul Hausmann and Hannah Höch (p. 44). Grosz, a painter and draughtsman, made few photographs; he is remembered for his inspiring contempt towards life's peccadilloes, as evidenced in his many cynical caricatures. Even if the remaining three contenders did not invent photomontage, they certainly explored its possibilities.

Hausmann was the brainiac and dreamer of Dada, the early twentieth-century avant-garde 'anti-art' movement. His calling card referred to him as 'President of the Sun, the Moon, and the little Earth (inner surface), Dadasoph Dadaraoul, Ringmaster of the Dada Circus'. His Dada colleagues came up with Dadasoph because of his stress on uniting art and social theory in an international framework. For Hausmann, disjunct and perplexing photomontages, along with invented languages, might serve to change human consciousness and weaken the force of nationalism.

*ABCD,* which features a self-portrait, is an anti-alphabet for an unstable present made up of different viewpoints, which Hausmann expressed in images and also in sound poems. In his depiction *Tatlin at Home,* he employed no images by or from the Russian avant-garde architect; instead, his photomontage is an exercise built from freewheeling mental associations. Hausmann explained that he added machinery, including a car's steering wheel, to the main figure's head because he was interested in portraying a man who had machines for brains. The man with his pockets turned inside out was included because Hausmann fancied that Tatlin could not be rich. Despite the jumble of shapes and dimensions, his conventional art training appears in his tendency to paint the backgrounds of his montage works.

Hausmann's flame burned brightly during the Dada era, and many were influenced by his optimism, a rare commodity in Dada circles. As Dadism cooled, so did its Dadasoph, who became a fashionable society photographer until his emigration from Nazi Germany.

Self-portrait as a Dadasoph, 1920.

**Above** *The Art Critic*, 1919–20.

**Opposite** *ABCD*, 1923–24.

## Raoul Hausmann

1880

**1886** Born in Vienna, Austria

1890

1900

**1908** Enrols at art school in Berlin

1910

**1915** Meets Hannah Höch and they develop photomontage techniques

**1918** Helps to form Berlin Dada

1920

1930

**1933** Leaves Germany

1940

1950

1960

**1971** Dies in Limoges, France

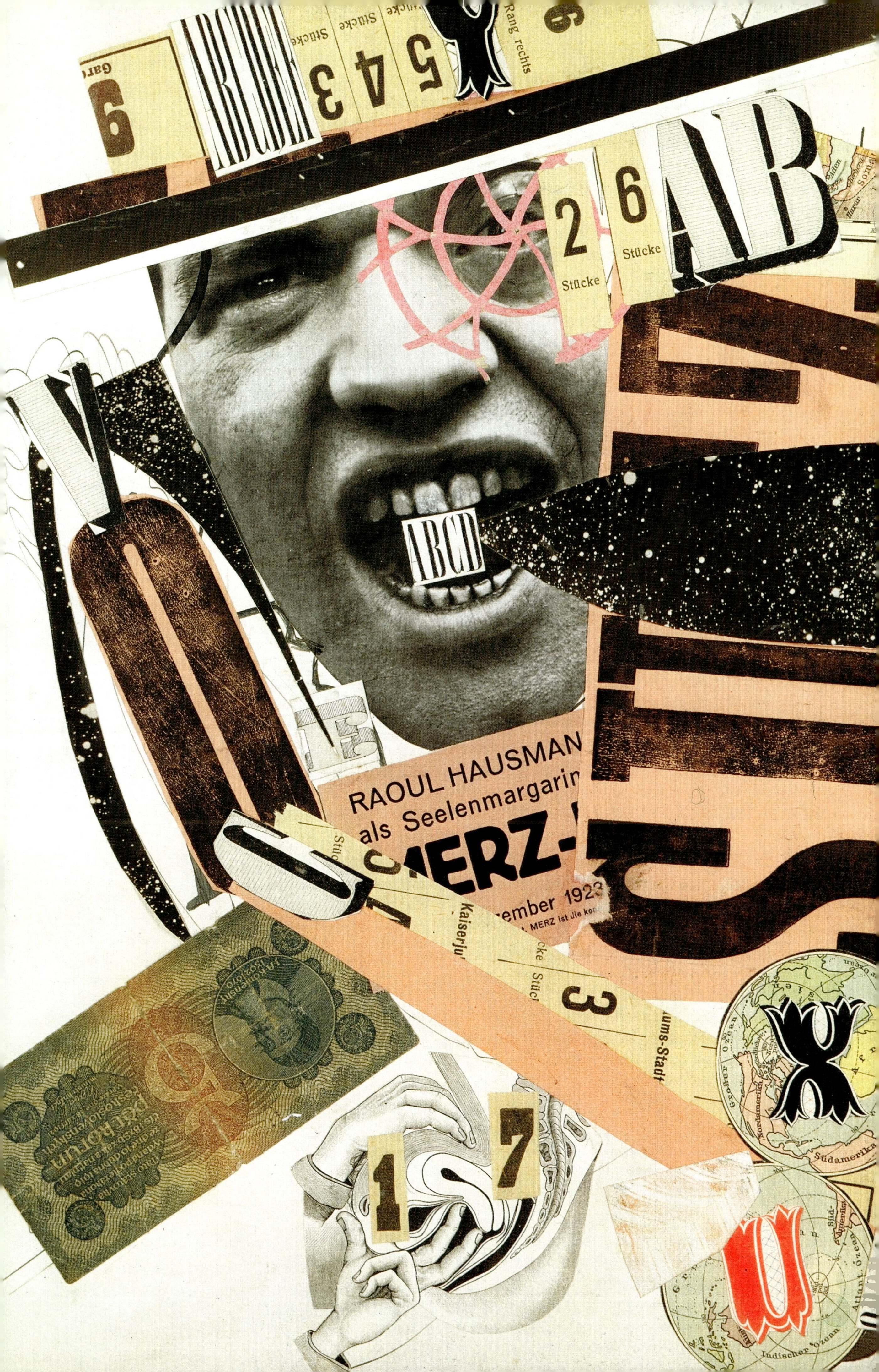
Rang rechts
Stücke
AB
2
Stücke
6
Stücke
ABCD
RAOUL HAUSMAN
als Seelenmargarin
MERZ-
ember 1923
MERZ ist die kon
Kaiserju
3
ums-Stadt
Südamerika
Indischer Ozean
1
7

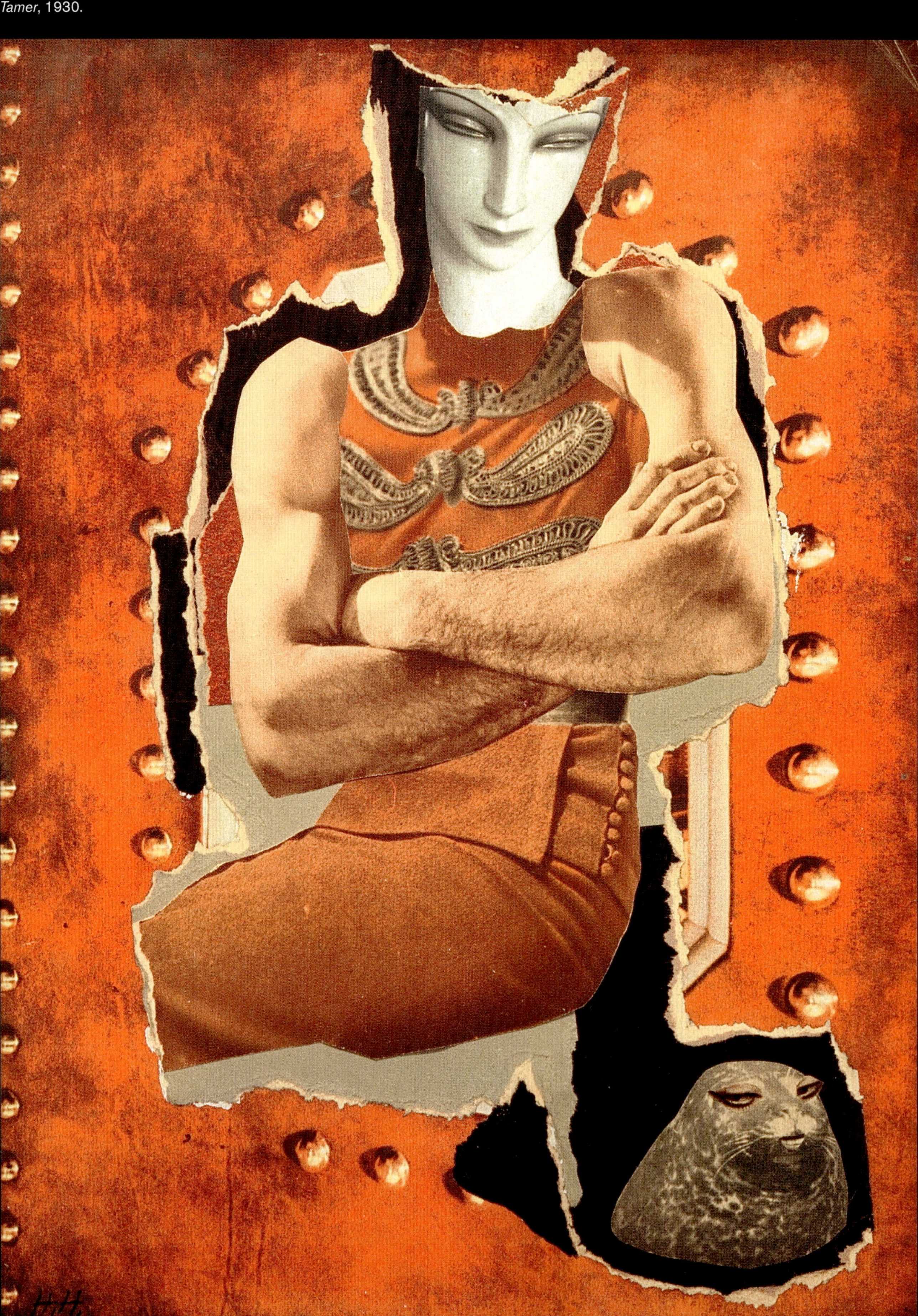

*Tamer*, 1930.

'We called it photomontage because it reflected our aversion to claiming to be artists.'

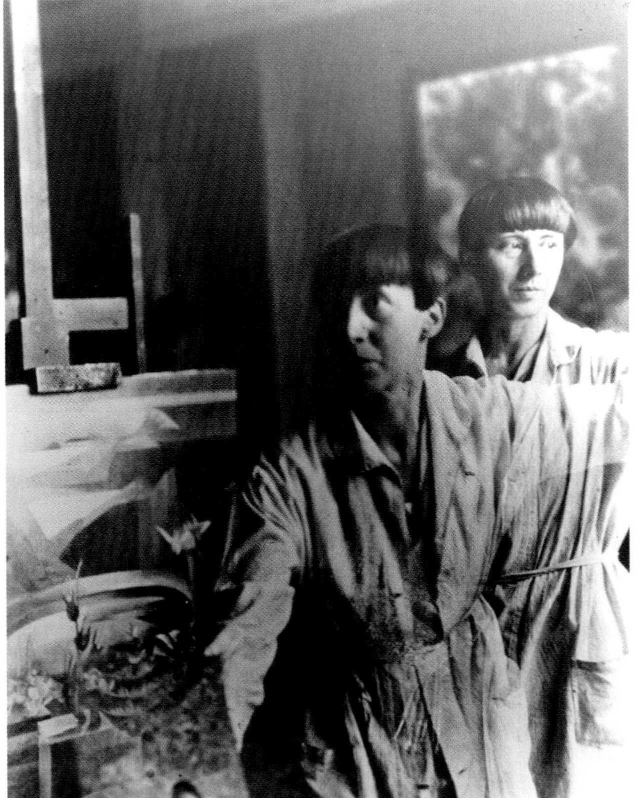

# Hannah Höch

1889–1978

GERMANY

Women artists who fall in love with famous male artists sometimes have a difficult time in achieving recognition for their own work. Which are better known: Pablo Picasso's portraits of the elegant, doe-eyed Dora Maar, or Maar's uncanny Surrealist photographs?

Raoul Hausmann (p. 40) was Hannah Höch's Picasso: until recent decades, Hausmann's work overshadowed Höch's, even though they were equally involved in the invention of photomontage in the early twentieth century. Höch's intriguing and complex images, which often centre on gender, were rediscovered in the 1970s and 1980s, when feminism and art history took a theoretical turn.

Indeed, Höch was a feminist, who found in the fragments and mismatched pieces of a montage's photographic snippets a way to convey society's discontinuities. In her famous effort, *Cut with the Kitchen Knife,* she embedded women's achievements in a network of contradictions. The people whose pictures she clipped, cut and rearranged were known to the newspaper-reading public, which gave the work its intense poignancy. Karl Marx and Vladimir Lenin intermingle with contemporary artists and politicians in a setting that indicates the force of industrialization. There is no easy summing-up of this, or any of Höch's art, as the constituent parts are incommensurate. How does Albert Einstein relate to a headless dancer and ball bearings?

Although fewer individual items appear in pictures that constitute her decade-long series 'From an Ethnographic Museum', the meaning of these works is still elusive. Höch mixed colour with black and white, and combined anthropological and modern photographs. Ceremonial tribal masks cover European faces; the bobbed hair of a German New Woman contrasts with the angular anatomy of the sculptural body she has somehow acquired. The fluidity of identity, which became central to late twentieth-century art theory, was previewed in such works as *Tamer,* where a female mannequin, sporting athletic male arms, stares coldly down at a sea lion with human eyes.

Self-portrait (double exposure), c. 1930.

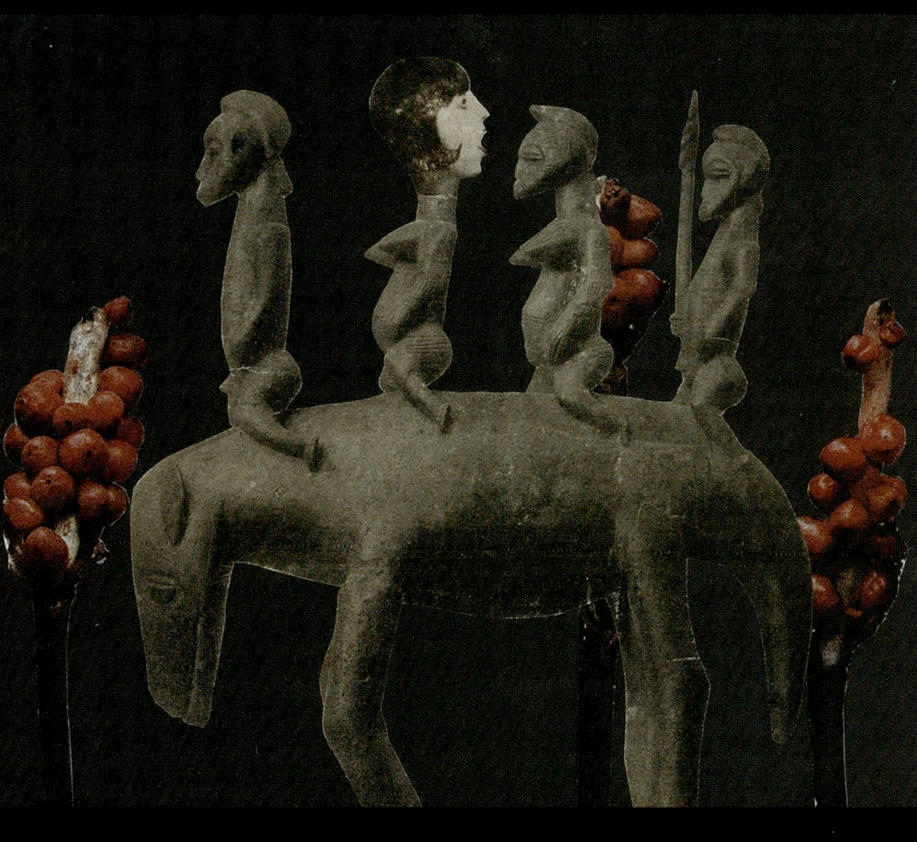

Opposite *Cut with the Kitchen Knife*, c.1919.

**Above** *Abduction* from 'Ethnographic Museum' series, 1925.

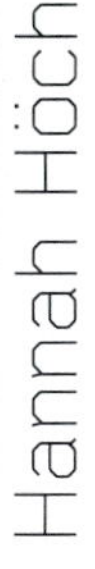


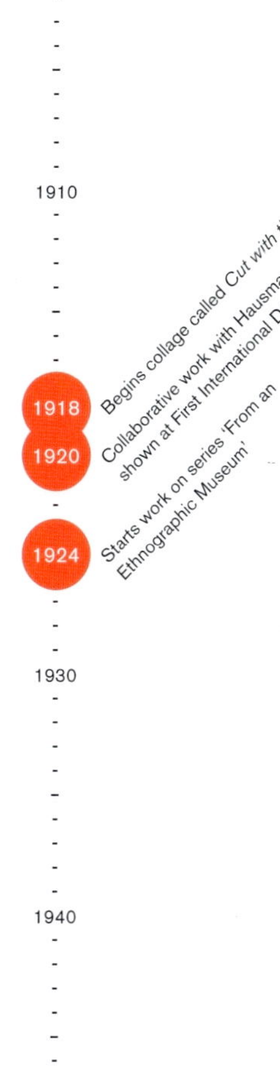


1930

1940

1950

1960

1970

1976 Retrospective at the Modern Art Museum of Paris and the National Gallery in Berlin

1978 Dies in Berlin, Germany

1980

1997 Retrospective at the Museum of Modern Art, New York

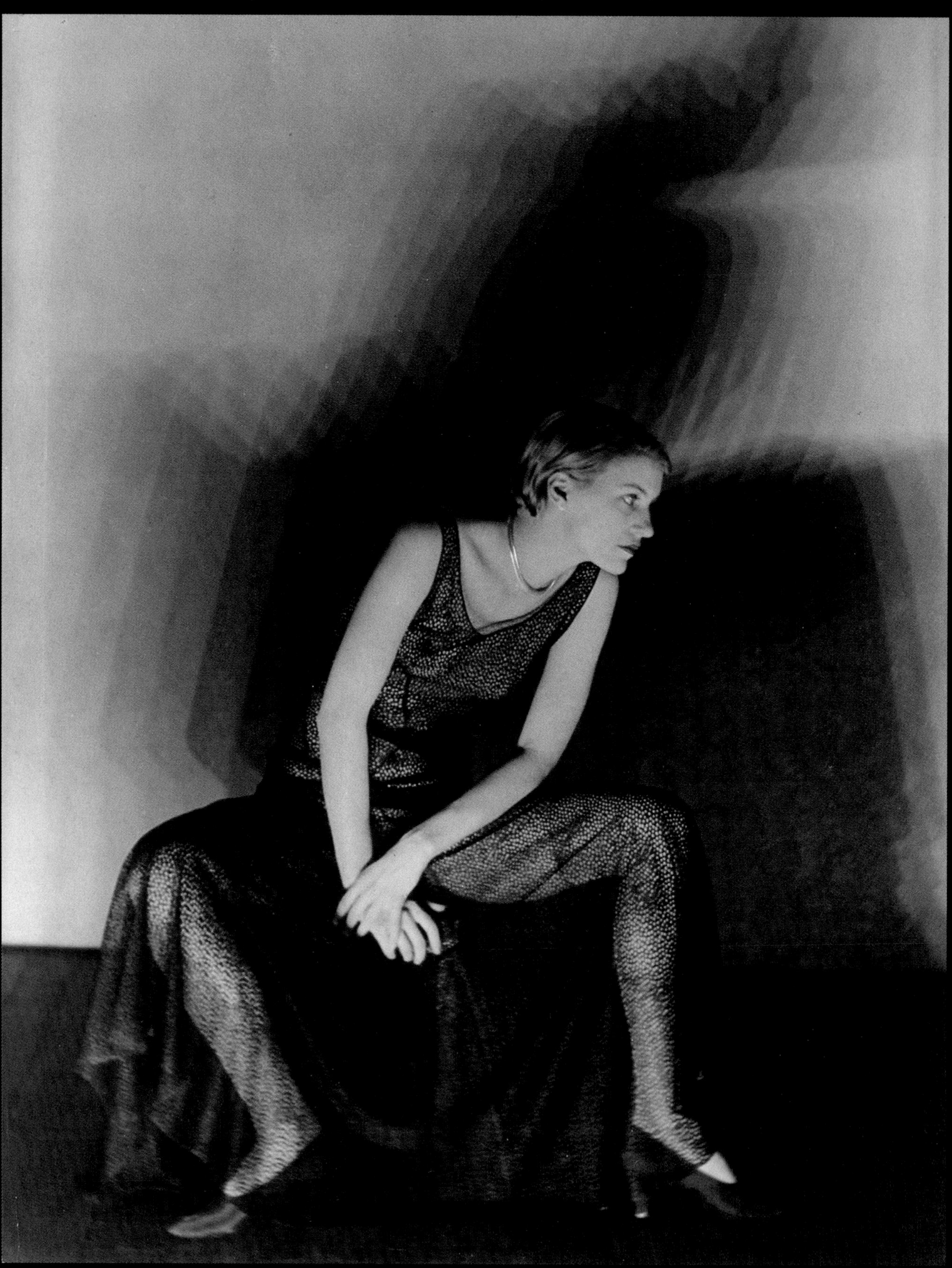

'I maintain that photography is not artistic!'

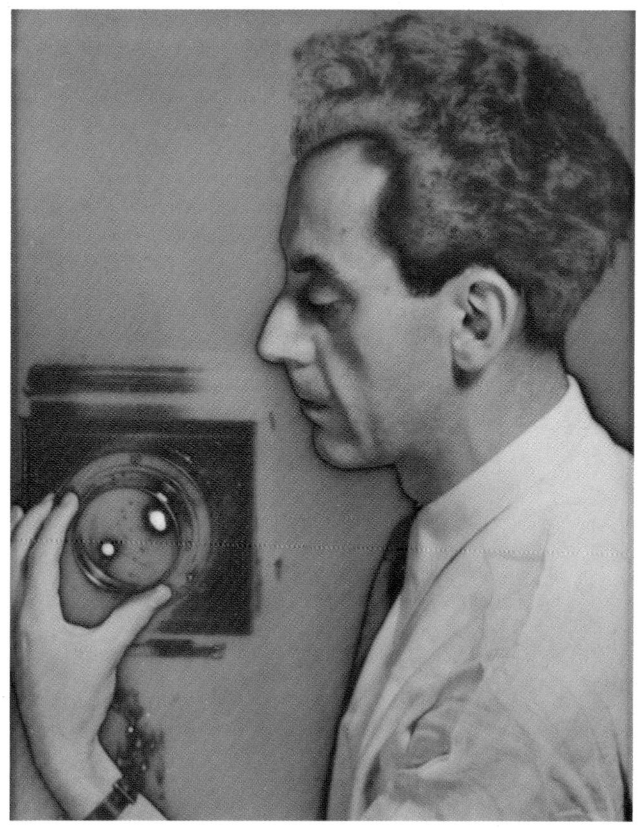

# Man Ray

1890–1976

UNITED STATES

Man Ray's paintings and sculptures were moderately successful in New York, and appreciated in its avant-garde art and literary circles. Yet with characteristic bravura, he turned his back on the city, concluding that 'Dada cannot live in New York. All New York is dada, and will not tolerate a rival.'

He moved to Paris, where he worked until World War II made it impossible for him to stay. Paris was more at ease with his making a living through portraiture and fashion photography, while he experimented with light-imaging. Writing from Paris to a benefactor, he claimed that 'my new role of "photographer" has made it possible to go everywhere and be much talked of'. He created camera-free abstract photograms by placing objects near or on photosensitive paper and exposing the composition to light: these rayographs, as he called them, were valued in art galleries and shown in high-end fashion magazines such as *Vanity Fair.* Man Ray may have claimed that he selected the objects for rayographs with his eyes closed, but the composition and light control evident in the works belie a strict allegiance to Dada's notion of chance.

Similarly, when his photography shifted towards Surrealism, the implausible and uncanny were sometimes diluted by humour. One of his most famous creations, *Le Violon d'Ingres,* placed a model in a pose reminiscent of the 1808 *La Baigneuse Valpinçon* by Jean-Auguste-Dominique Ingres. The louche carnality of the painting is sharply undercut by the dark silhouettes of sound-box openings, which the artist created on the woman's body when he printed the photograph. In other work, Man Ray was the master of sensuality, which he often polished and accentuated with solarization, a reversal of tones created through the manipulation of light that he claimed to have discovered independently of its earlier uses.

There are hardly any out-of-doors photographs by Man Ray. City scenes, landscapes and nature did not interest him as much as the pictures he could concoct in the studio. Ironically, the artist who declared that he had freed himself from 'the sticky medium of paint' to work 'directly with light itself' spent a decade in sunny Hollywood, California. Yet California for him was a 'beautiful prison', perhaps because he was cut off from his major works, which he was forced to leave in France.

**Opposite** Lee Miller, 1929.

**Above** Self-portrait with camera, 1930.

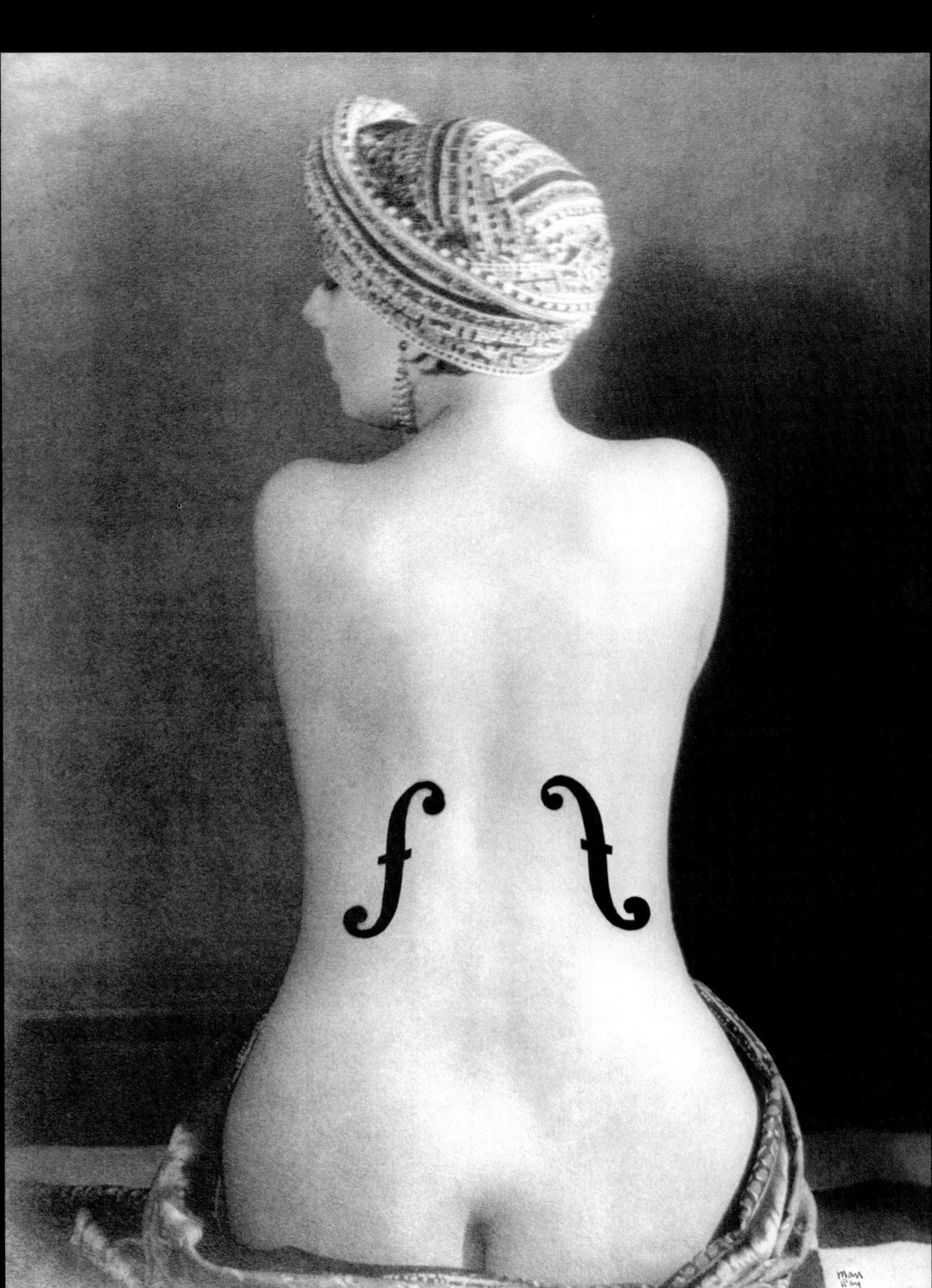
Man
Ray
1924

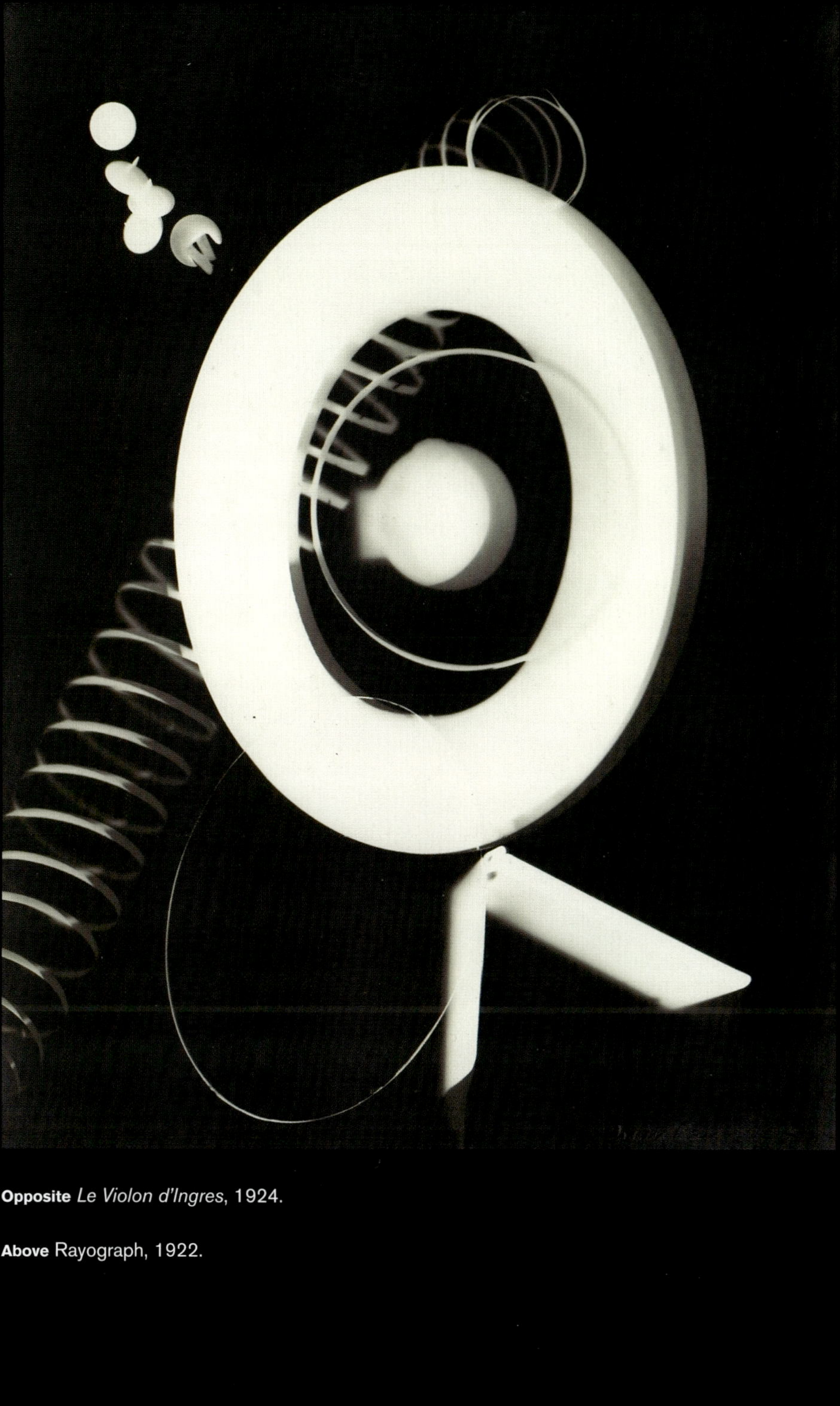

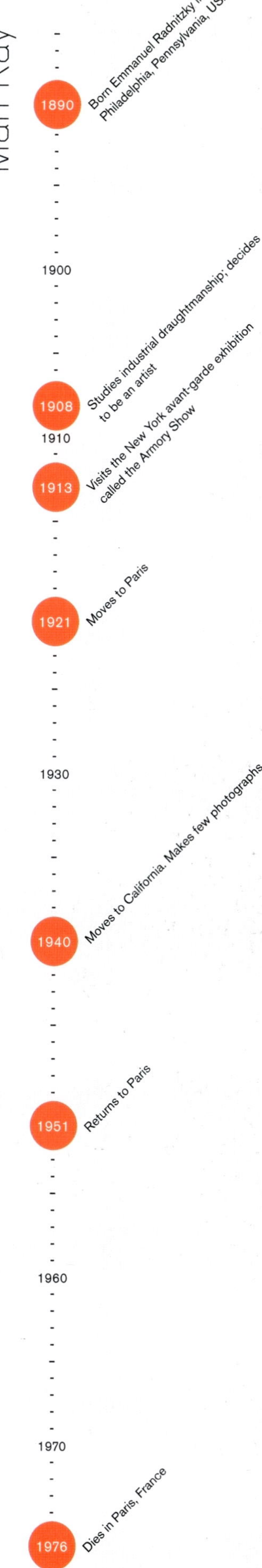


**Opposite** *Le Violon d'Ingres*, 1924.

**Above** Rayograph, 1922.

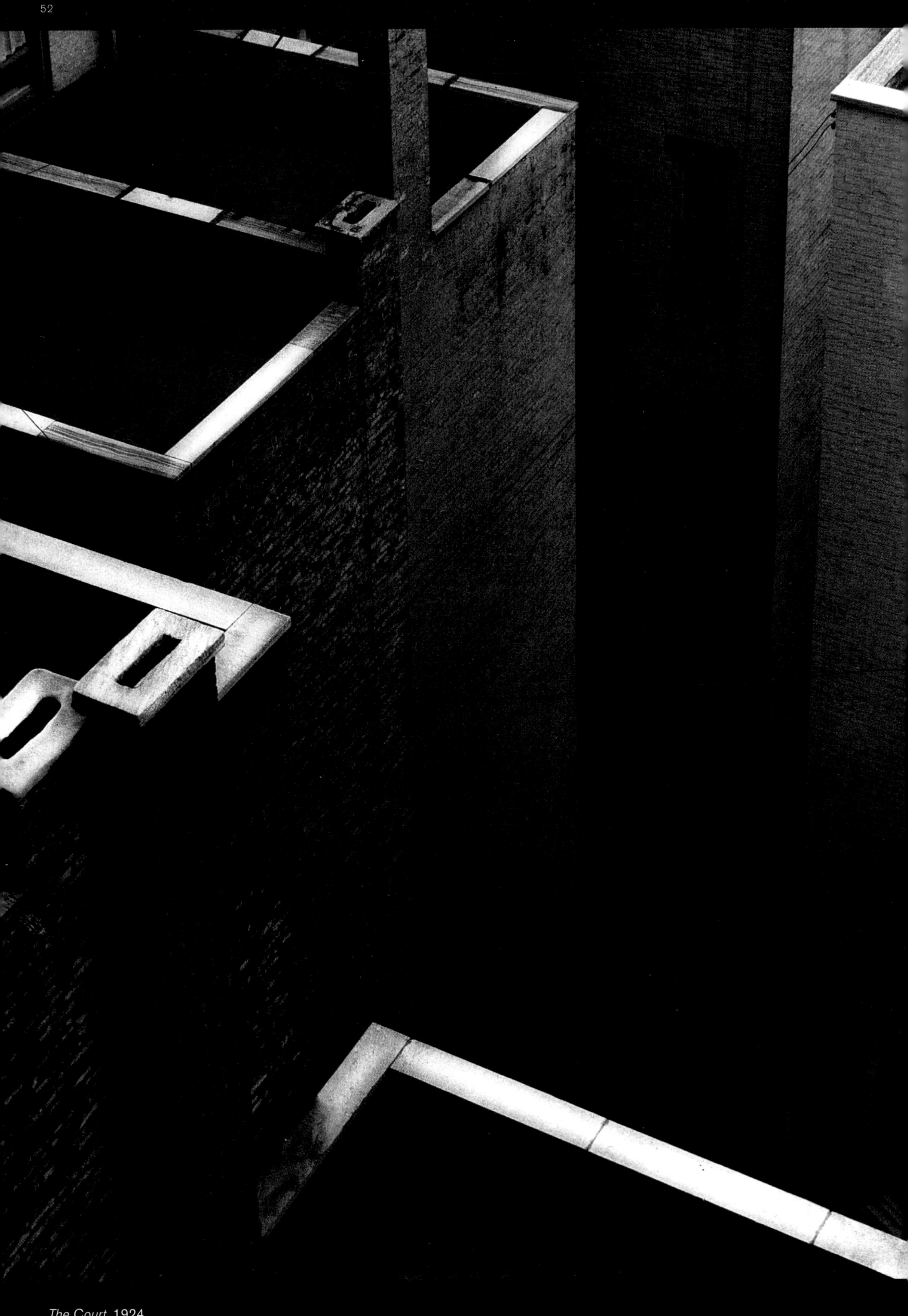

*The Court*, 1924.

'The material of the artist lies not within himself ... but in the world around him.'

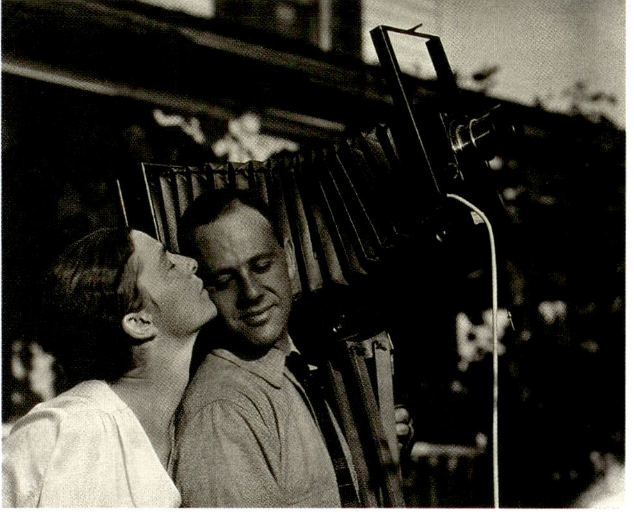

# Paul Strand

1890–1976

UNITED STATES

Stieglitz, Steichen and Strand: in common parlance they have become the Three Musketeers of Modern American Photography. But the phrase dulls the distinctive contributions of each image-maker, especially Paul Strand. While his early work was promoted by Stieglitz (p. 12), Strand grew out of Stieglitz's ambit, and ultimately distanced his work from Stieglitz's self-documentation and spirituality. Edward Steichen (p. 28), who tirelessly aided Stieglitz's needs, seems to have been more of a friend-of-a-friend to Strand, one whom he ultimately chastised for embracing 'corporate age' values in his commercial work.

Strand rejected his early nature studies, shot with a soft-focus lens, concluding that he had 'mushified' the pictures. He replaced phony fog with clear ambient light, and literally moved closer to his topics. The stern indifference to human subjects that Strand affected for the series of New York city street photographs he took with a disguised lens can still make viewers wince. This detachment – an experiment in seeing freed from knowing or caring – also shaped his selection of near-abstract subjects from everyday life, ranging from porch shadows to stacked crockery. In these works light, shadow, volume and line hold the eye long enough to produce self-sufficient visual events, before the mind resolves the image into recognizable bowls, spindles, wheels and backyard laundry lines.

Strand's investigation of abstraction and the thingness of visual phenomena was short-lived. His experience with the fluidity of motion picture film, which began in 1920 and occupied him for decades, likely nudged him away from the discrete semi-abstract image to a looser, aggregated series of images, which trust the viewer to interpret. With a nod to Picasso and Cézanne, he began incorporating scenes from everyday life into his work. During travels in Canada, Mexico, Italy and France, he thought in series, not in isolated images, and he arrayed pictures of people, landscape and architecture that viewers could consider both as art and as a documentary expression of culture and values.

Portrait of Paul and Rebecca Strand by Alfred Stieglitz, early 1920s.

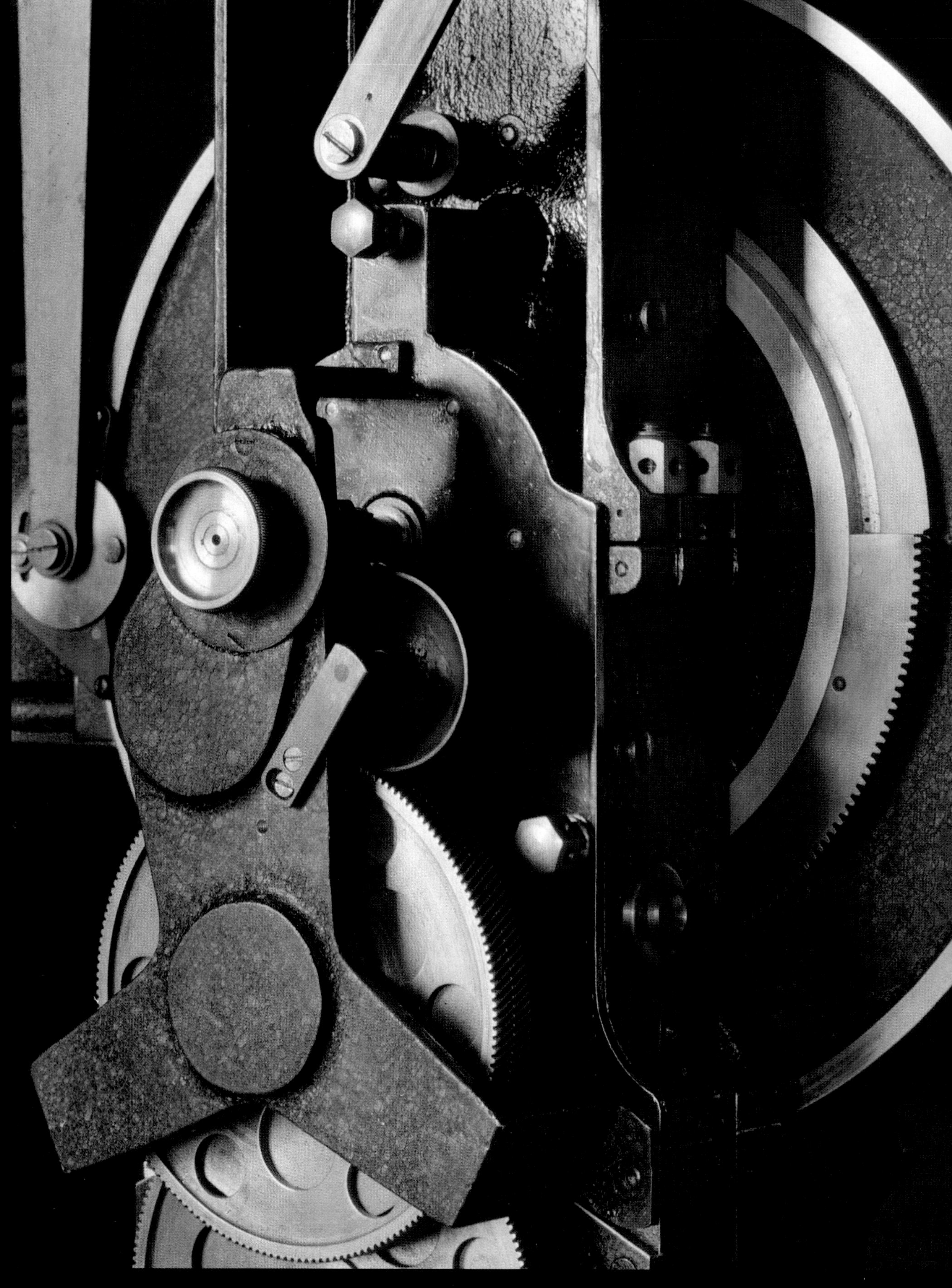

*Double Akeley*, 1922.

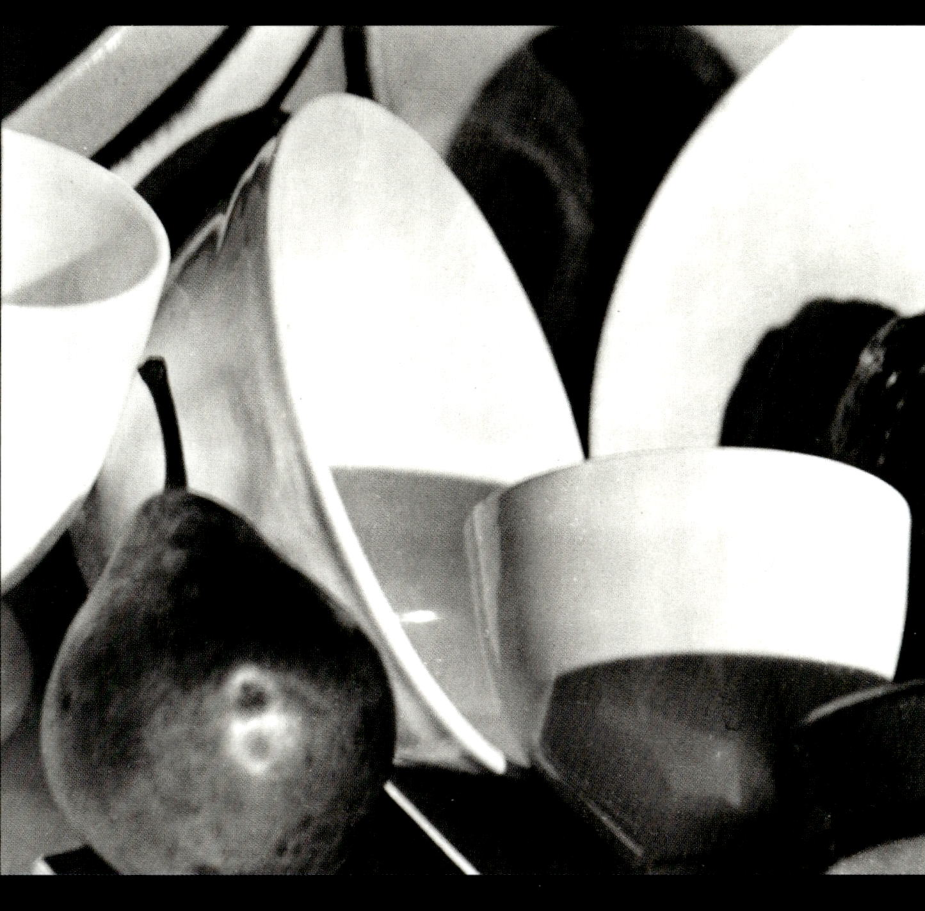

**Above** *Pears and Bowls*, 1916.

**Below** Wire *Wheel*, 1920.

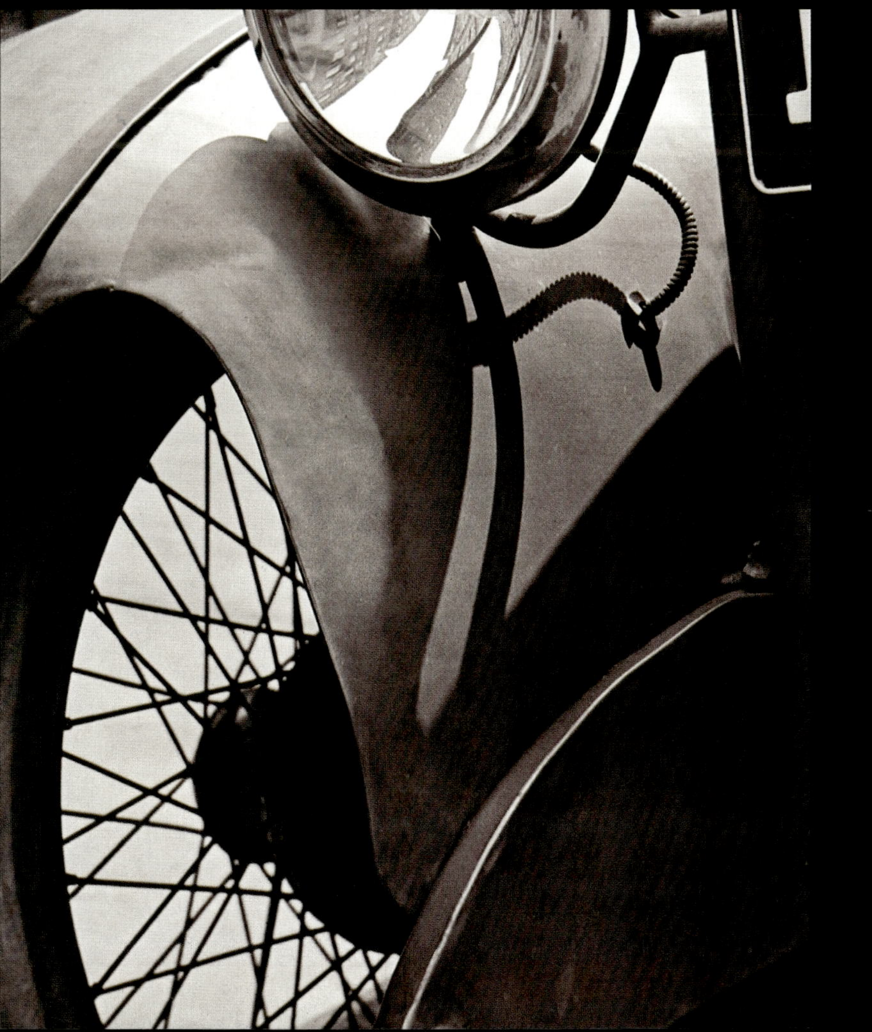

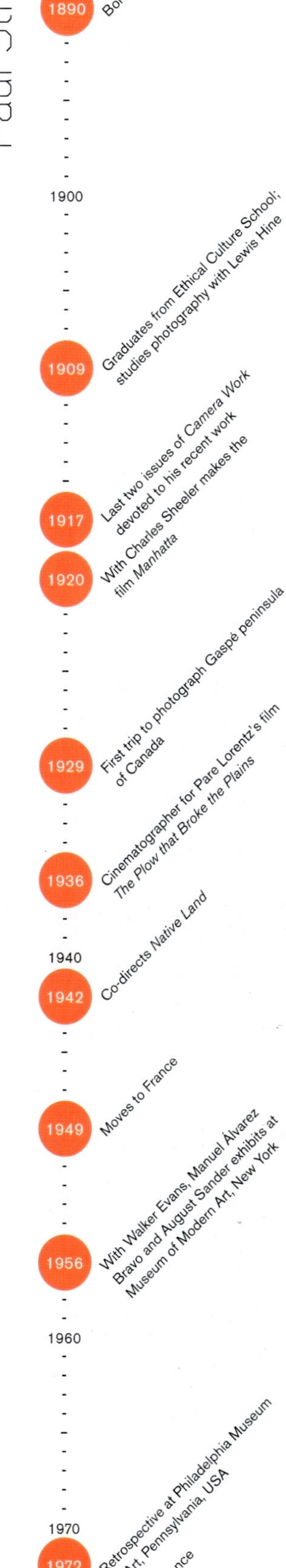

# MILLIONEN

## stehen hinter mir

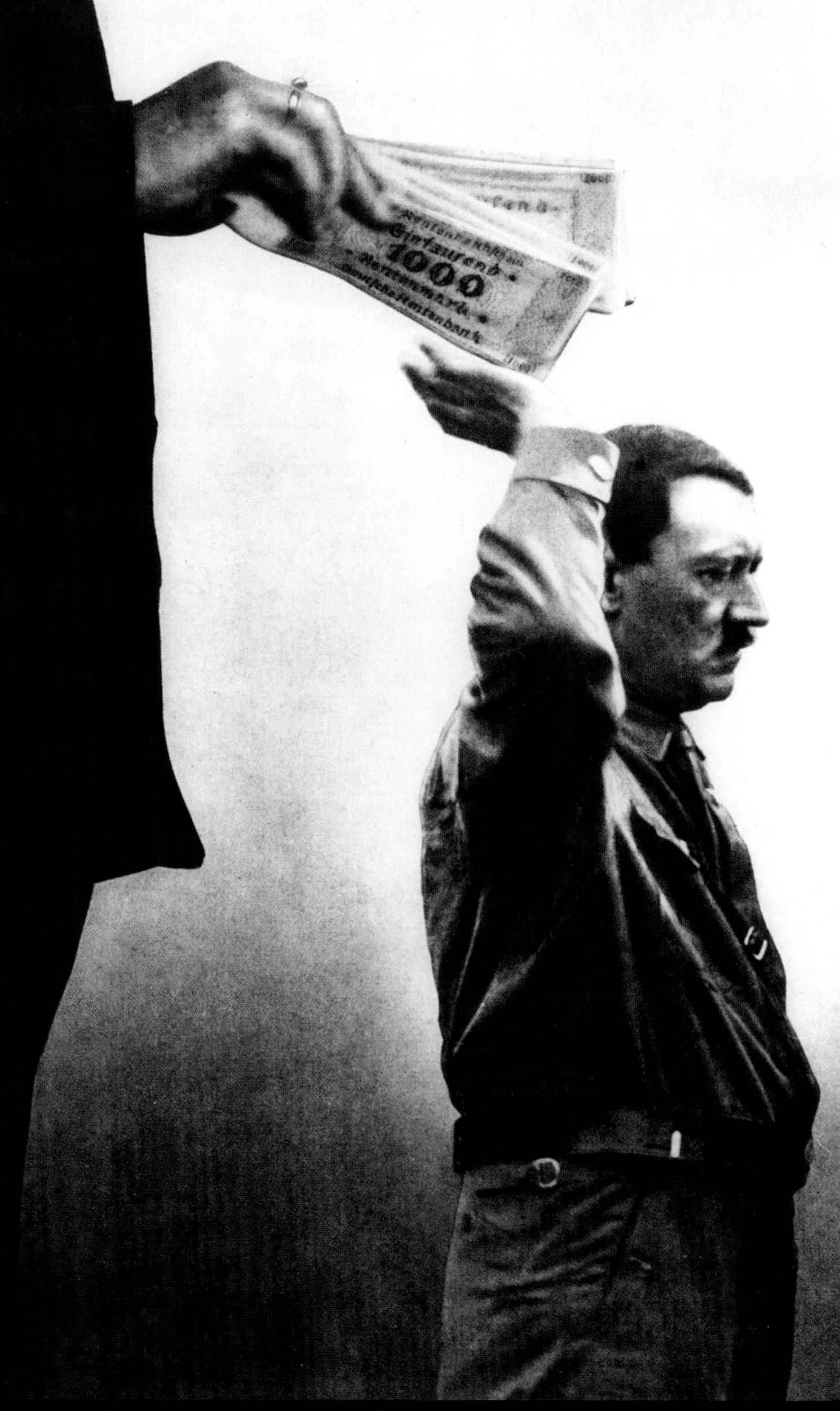

'If I assemble documents and juxtapose them with intelligence and skill, the effect of agitation and propaganda on the masses will be enormous.'

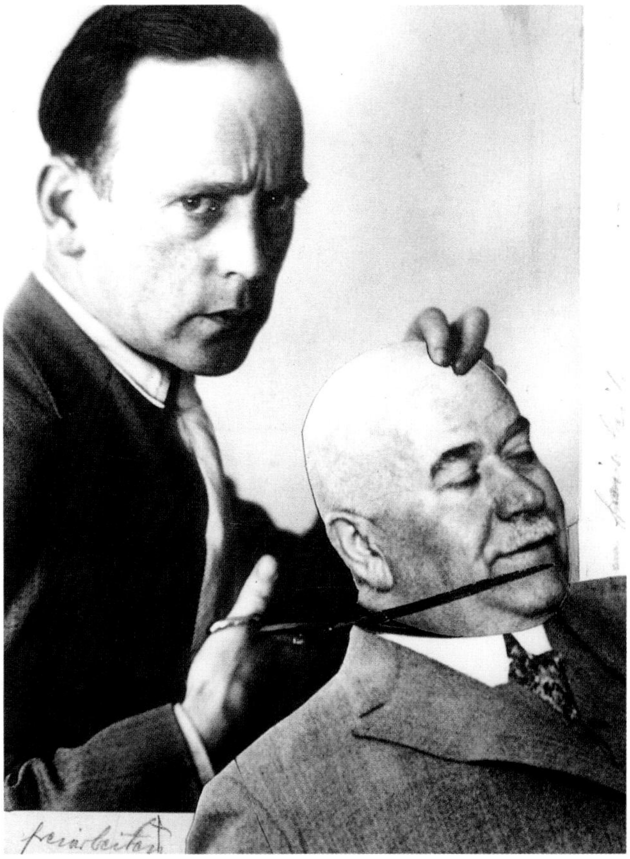

# John Heartfield

1891–1968

GERMANY

The force of John Heartfield's appropriation of advertising techniques is still felt by designers active in social change and anti-war campaigns, though few would want to be as dedicated to detail as he was. He concocted images designed to jolt rather than to reason with the viewer. Through alterations in scale and perspective he manipulated emotion, but he also depended on his own sense of documentary realism. Bertolt Brecht found his work ingenious, calling it a new form of social criticism. In *Der Sinn von Genf* (*The Meaning of Geneva*), which criticized the German unwillingness to make concessions during disarmament talks in the Swiss city, Heartfield insisted that a real dove, symbolizing peace, be run through by a bayonet.

It is too easy to blame the fury that erupts through Heartfield's pictures on his having been abandoned in a forest by his parents at the age of eight, along with his sibling, and being reared in foster homes – a story somewhat inflated to explain the source of his raw political criticism. However they may have shaped his inner life, the childhood traumas cannot account for his calculated photomontages, in which he clipped or created photographs, and rearranged them in unnaturalistic compositions, often adding type to underline his message.

On one level, Heartfield's montages incite fear. At the same time, they often combine horror and humour by destabilizing and mocking revered symbols, such as the Nazi swastika. Hitler is literally belittled in many of Heartfield's images, where the Führer is reduced to a petty bribe-taker, a child playing with toy weapons, a puppet or an ape. Heartfield's mix of typology and montage also extended to the numerous book jackets he produced, the photo shoots for some of which, such as Upton Sinclair's novel *So Macht Man Dollars* (the German version of *Mountain City*), required a shooting script.

Ironically, Heartfield's post-war life in East Berlin was filled with fear and suspicion. He was not trusted by the East German police, and found it difficult to find employment. The few anti-war and anti-nuclear montages he produced lean on dread, and lack the derisive humour of his earlier efforts.

**Opposite** *AIZ* cover: *The Meaning of the Hitler Salute, Millionen stehen hinter mir* ('Millions stand behind me'), 1932.

**Above** Self-portrait with Berlin President of Police, 1929.

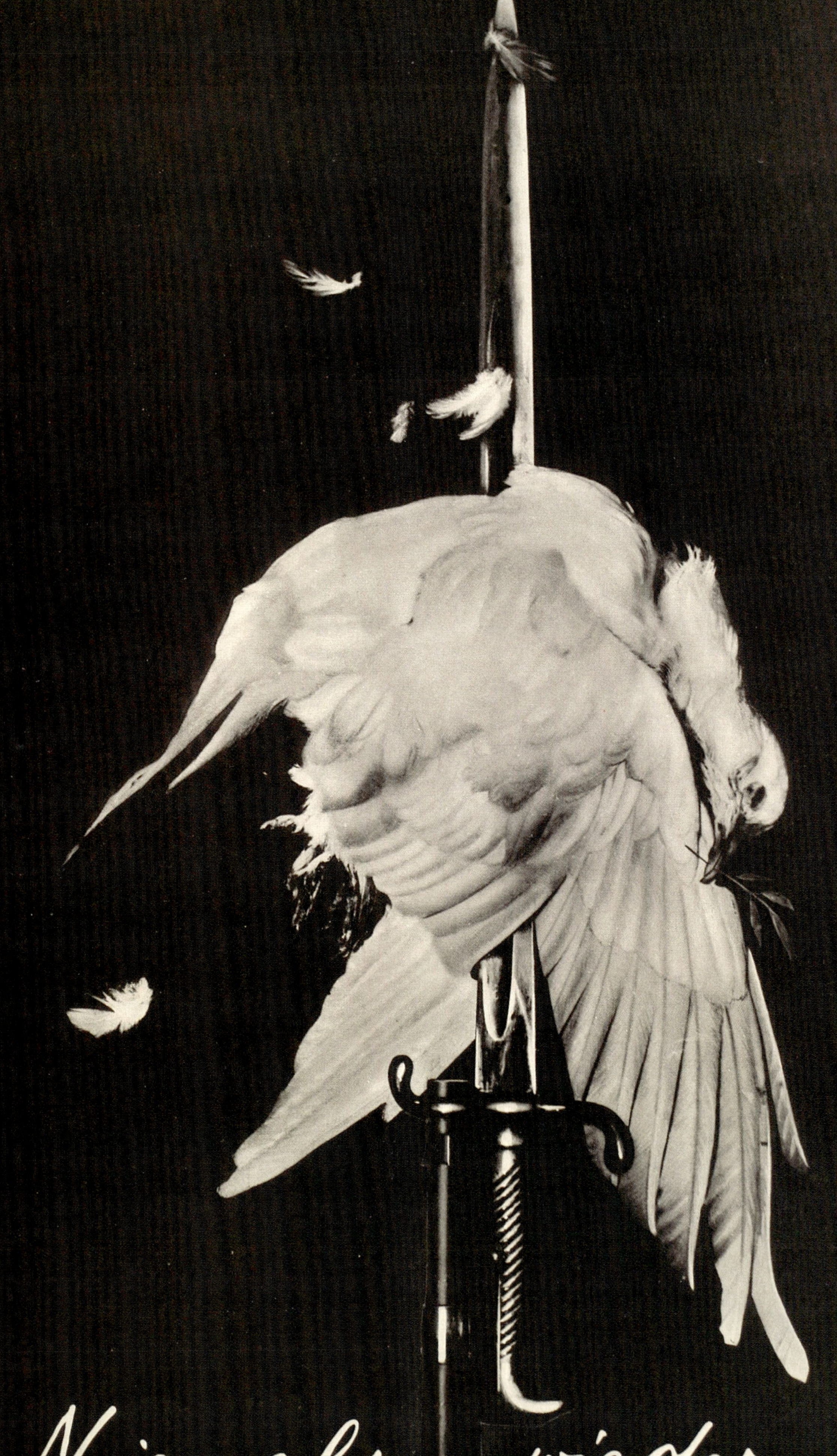
Niemals wieder!

**Opposite** *AIZ* cover: *The Meaning of Geneva, Niemals wieder!* ('Never again!'), 1932.

**Below** Cover of Upton Sinclair, *So Macht Man Dollars* (German translation of *Mountain City*), 1931.

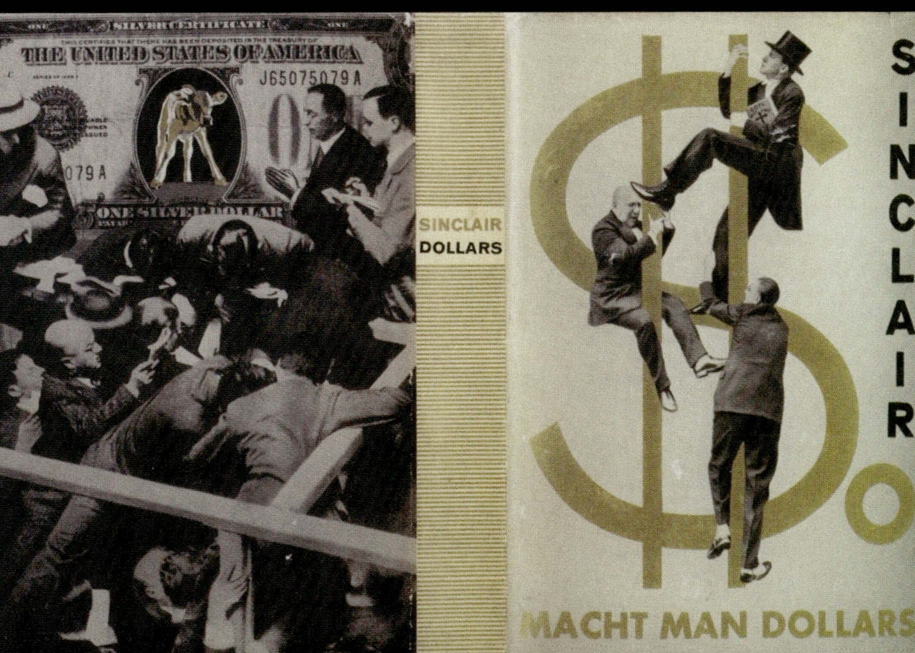


## John Heartfield

- **1891** Born Helmut Herzfelde in Munich, Germany
- 1900
- **1907** Starts studying graphic art and advertising
- 1910
- **1915** Burns his oil paintings
- **1916** Anglicizes name to protest anti-British propaganda
- **1921** Starts to design book jackets and layouts for the publishing firm he founded, Malik-Verlag
- **1931** Starts creating anti-Nazi illustrations
- **1933** Adolf Hitler named Chancellor of Germany; Heartfield flees to Prague
- **1938** Flees to London
- 1940
- **1950** Returns to East Berlin
- 1960
- **1968** Dies in East Berlin, East Germany
- 1970
- 1980
- **1993** Major retrospective, Museum of Modern Art, New York

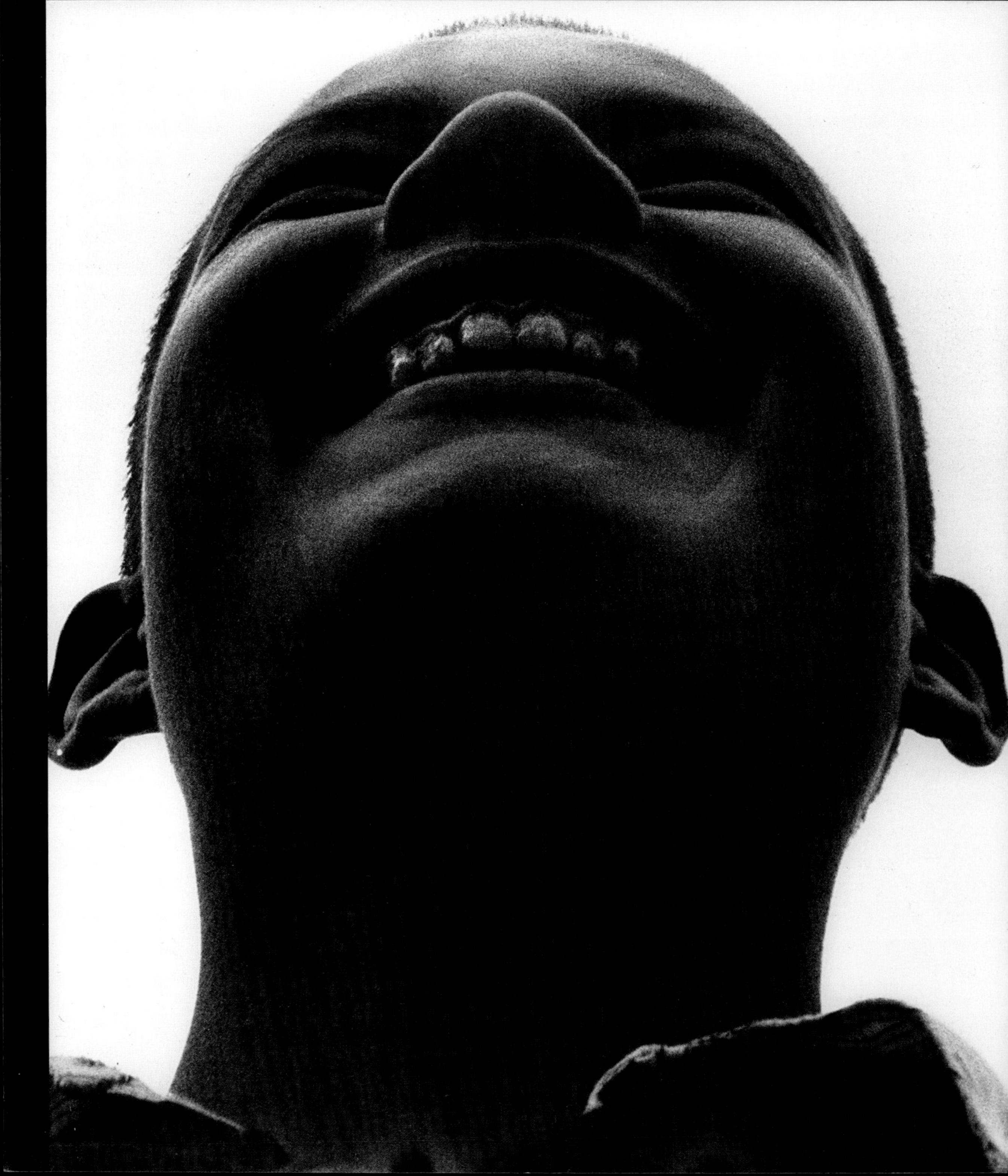

'We were for the new world ...
We were for the new man.'

# Alexander Rodchenko

1891–1956

RUSSIA

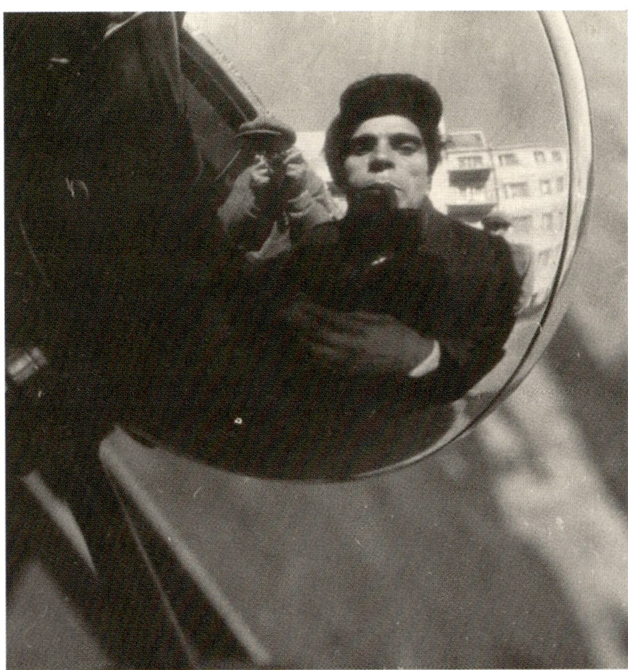

Like many photographers, Alexander Rodchenko initially learned the craft of photography so that he could record his artwork in other media. Nevertheless, he was fascinated with the burgeoning presence of photography in mass media, and made photocollages well before he picked up a camera to create his own lens work.

He used the technique to create idiosyncratic collages to illustrate the poem 'Pro Eto' ('That's What'), by Vladimir Mayakovsky, with whom he collaborated on advertisements for goods and for communist ideas. They hoped to use this capitalist creation against capitalism, in ads for products ranging from cookies made by the Red October factory to stock in the newly established state airline. Perhaps working 'in pieces' helped Rodchenko cast off the traditional notion of the single grand work of art. His photographs indicate a freer, more experimental approach, and a tendency to work in series.

Shooting from unexpected positions and angles, Rodchenko tried not only to refresh vision, but also to open minds to new ideas. His camera seems to glide above, below and around people and objects in the environment, visually claiming a freedom from fixed viewpoints and, sometimes, from gravity. Although the images are unorthodox, they are not subjective or confessional. They operate within a broad definition of documentary practice. This in later years morphed into his commitment to photojournalism aimed at the masses through images in popular publications, which he defended as reaching the people in ways that painting and drawing could not.

Though devoted to events and sites in everyday life, Rodchenko's work was still artfully cropped and framed. Yet his 3,000 photographs of the building of the White Sea Canal (1931–33) demonstrated that eye-catching form is no guarantee of full reporting. The vast project required a conspicuous multitude of workers, many of whom died from hunger and abuse in what was labelled a corrective labour camp – facts that Rodchenko did not picture.

**Opposite** *Young Pioneer*, 1930.

**Above** *Chauffeur*, self-portrait, 1929.

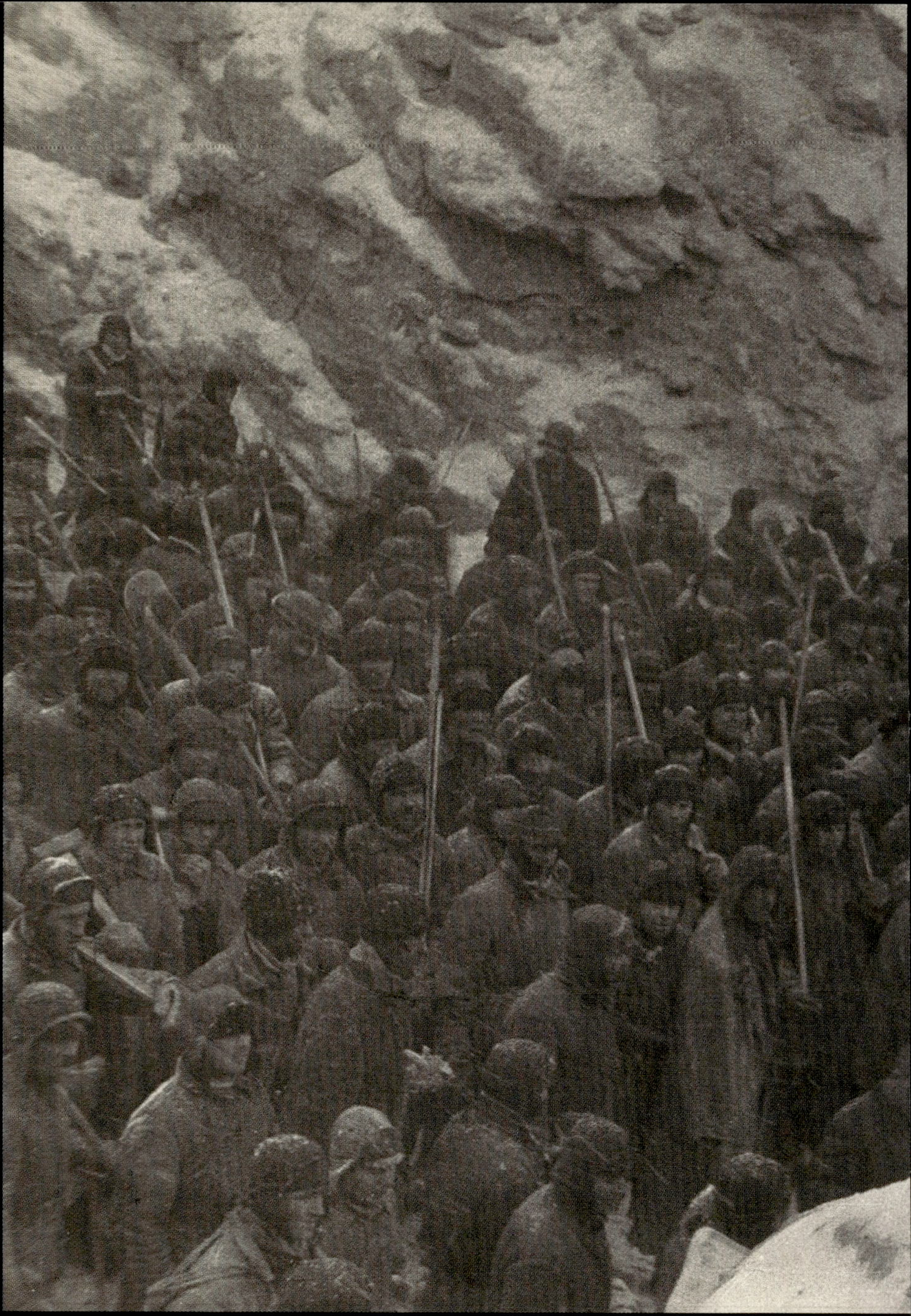

**Right** *White Sea Canal*, 1933.

**Below right** *Pro Eto* ('That's What'), 1923.

**Opposite** Advertising poster for the Leningrad Department of Gosizdat (State Publishing House), 1924.

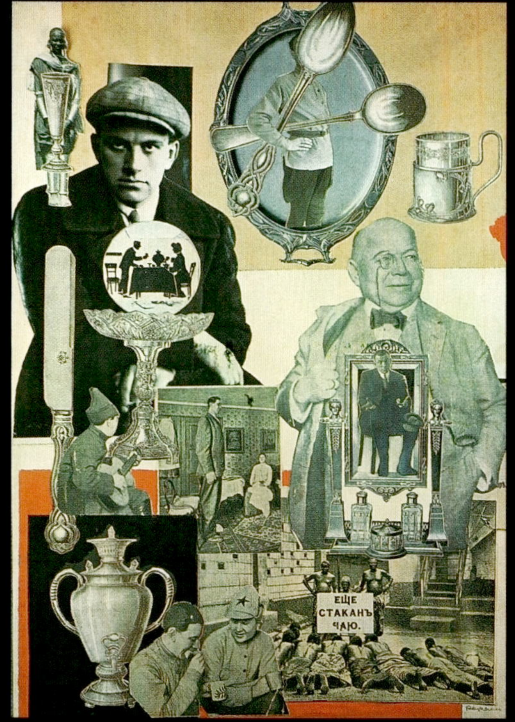

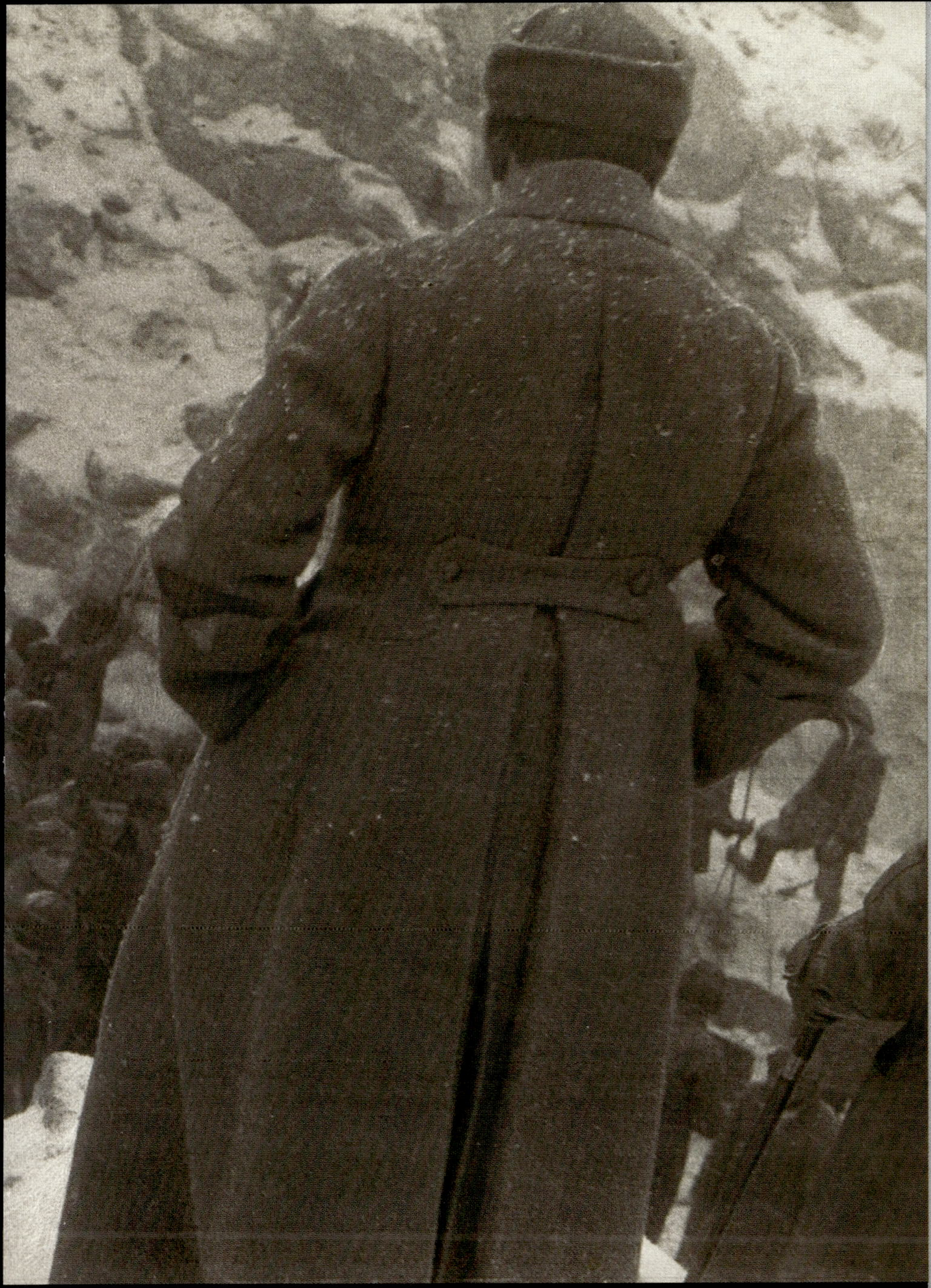

## Alexander Rodchenko

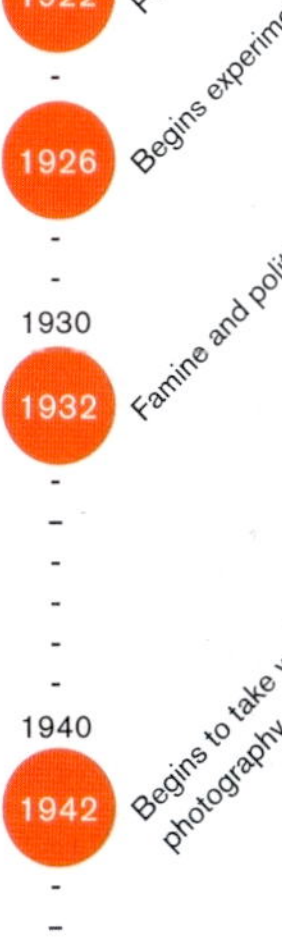

**1891** Born in Saint Petersburg, Russia

1900

**1910** Starts to study painting and drawing

**1915** Moves to Moscow and enrols in a school of applied arts

1920

**1922** Publishes first photocollages

**1926** Begins experimental street photography

1930

**1932** Famine and political unrest in Russia

1940

**1942** Begins to take wartime newspaper photography

1950

**1956** Continues design projects and exhibits work
Dies in Moscow, Russia

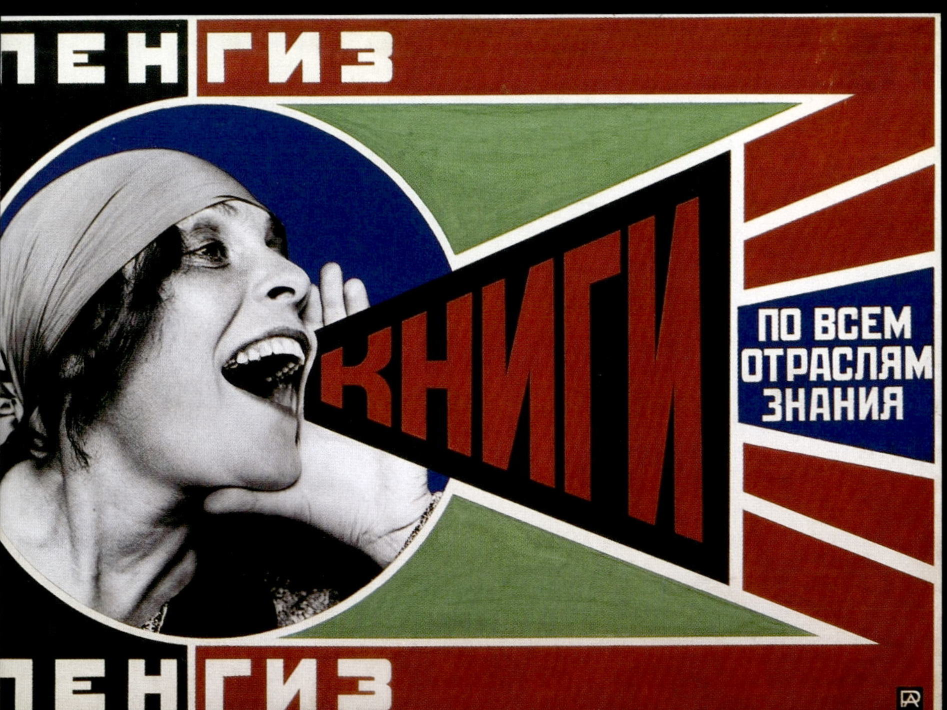

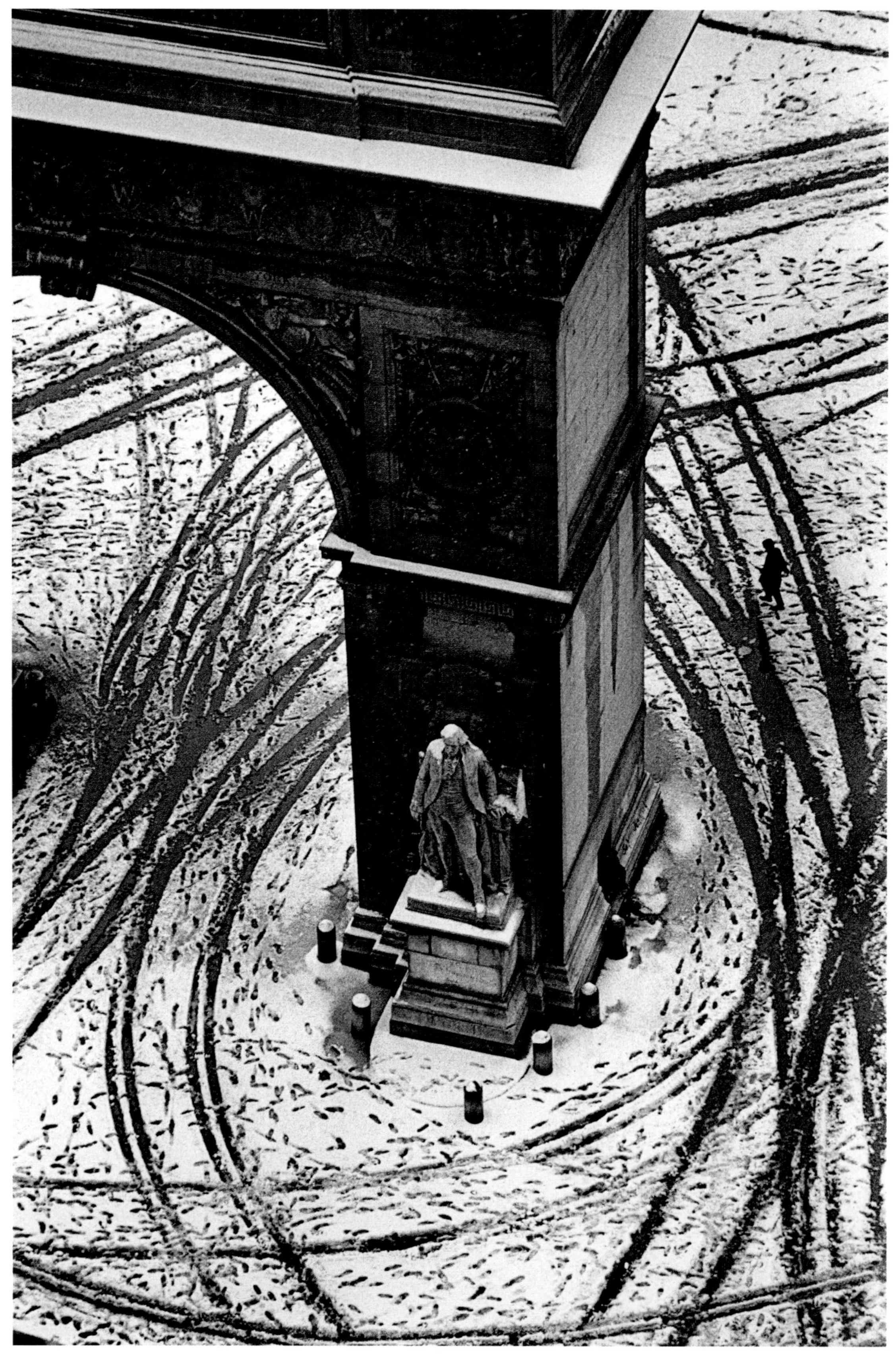

'The camera is my tool. Through it I try to give a reason to everything that happens around me.'

# André Kertész

1894–1985

HUNGARY

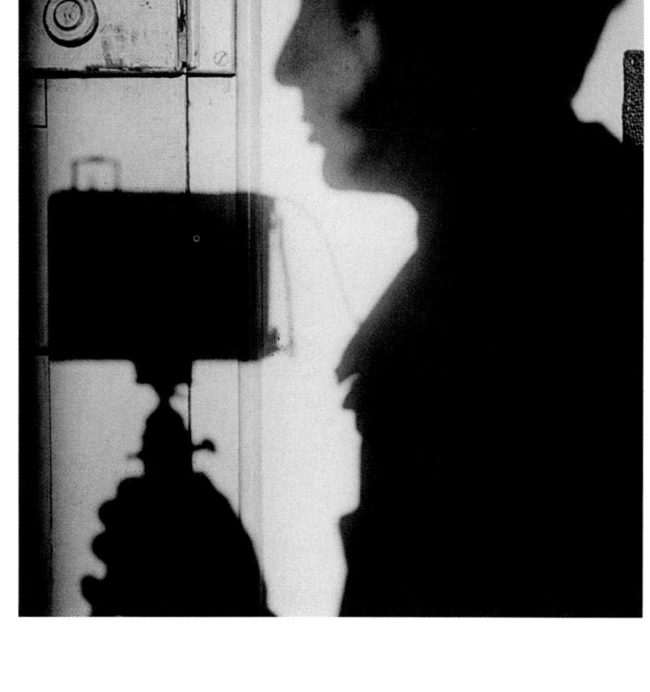

Gertrude Stein pronounced: 'Paris was where the twentieth century was.' Indeed, Cubism, Surrealism and abstraction were at home there. Artists came to Paris hoping to be caught up in what they called modern art. Though André Kertész drifted into Parisian avant-garde circles, his art acquired only a slight French accent; his seemingly Surrealist series of distorted nude figures was created on assignment from a risqué magazine, not as experimental art. The oblique angles, intricate architectural geometries and uncanny points of view that appeared in his work seldom disrupted his humanist inclinations for very long. By the same token, his early work never dawdled in foggy Pictorialism or sentimentality. *Wandering Violinist*, in which a blind musician is helped across a dirt road, remains taut and affecting because it is not mawkish.

In Paris, he succeeded in selling individual photographs and series to popular illustrated magazines, such as *Vu* in France and *Münchner Illustrierte* in Germany. At the same time, his images also appeared in specialized art and photography publications. His photography became more dynamic when he acquired a Leica camera, whose small size let him be both more spontaneous and more anonymous in the street. Disconcerting scenes such as that in *Meudon* resulted as much from his newly acquired speed as from the influence of Surrealism. The stop-action effect that Kertész achieved influenced many twentieth-century photographers, including Henri Cartier-Bresson (p. 132).

Although his work was shown in New York, Kertész's move to the United States was troubled. He was not able to secure permanent employment at *Life* magazine, and through a fluke in the immigration laws he was listed as an enemy alien during World War II, making it difficult to find employment. After the conflict, he toiled at *House and Garden*, a magazine that he felt wasted his talents. Although he never shook off that notion, his energies were renewed by retirement and by increasing recognition of his former achievements. He began photographing his adopted city with new vigour. A major retrospective of his work opened at the Metropolitan Museum of Art in New York several weeks after he died.

**Opposite** *Washington Square with Arch*, 1966.

**Above** Self-portrait with camera, 1927.

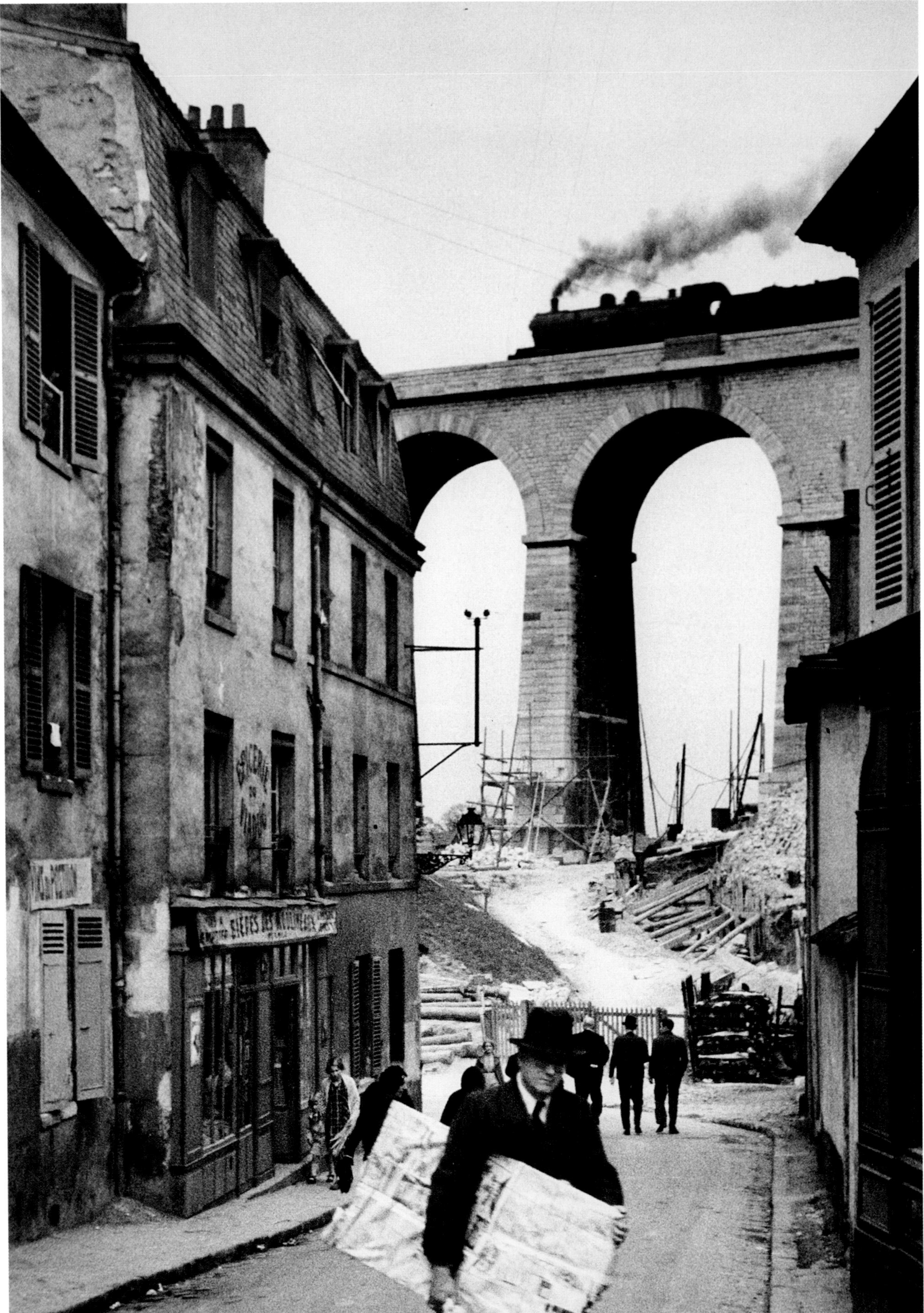

*Meudon*, 1928.

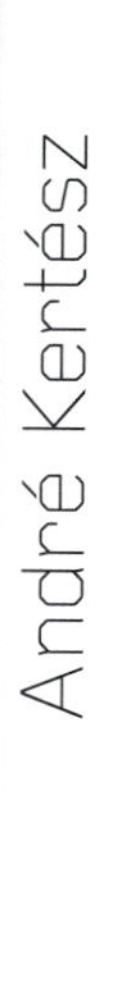

# André Kertész

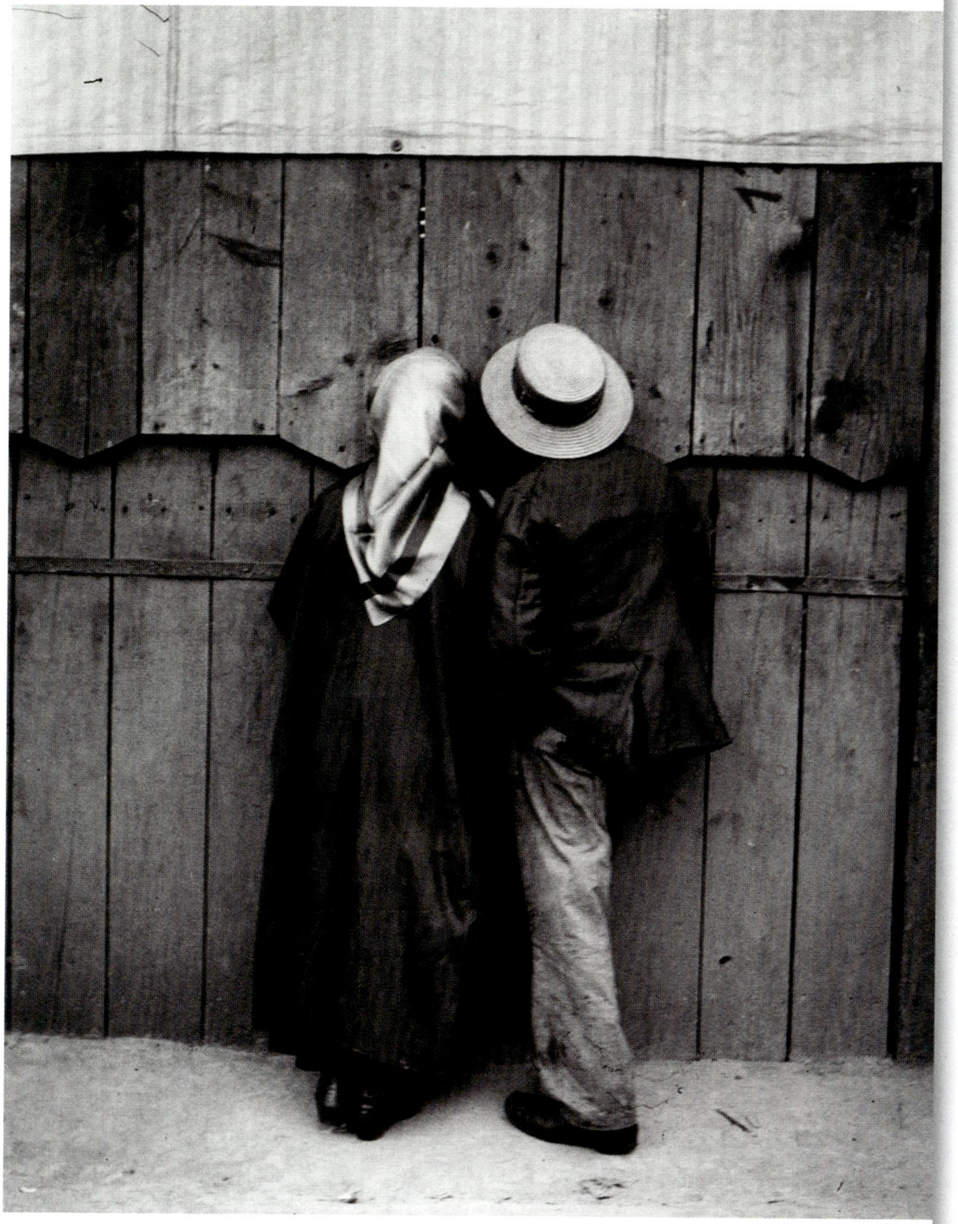

- **1894** Born Andor Kertész in Budapest, Hungary
- **1925** Moves to Paris
- **1928** Buys Leica camera
- **1929** His images appear at the 'Film und Foto' exhibition, Stuttgart, Germany
- **1936** Moves to New York
- **1945** Works for *House and Garden* magazine (to 1962)
- **1985** Dies in New York, USA
  'André Kertész: Of Paris and New York' appears at the Art Institute of Chicago and the Metropolitan Museum of Art, New York

**Above** *Circus*, 1920.

**Below** *Mondrian's Glasses and Pipe*, 1926.

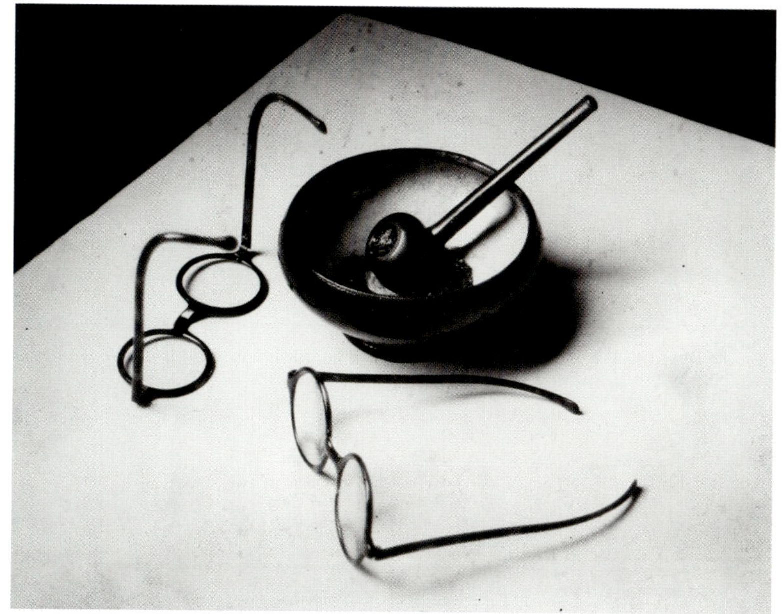

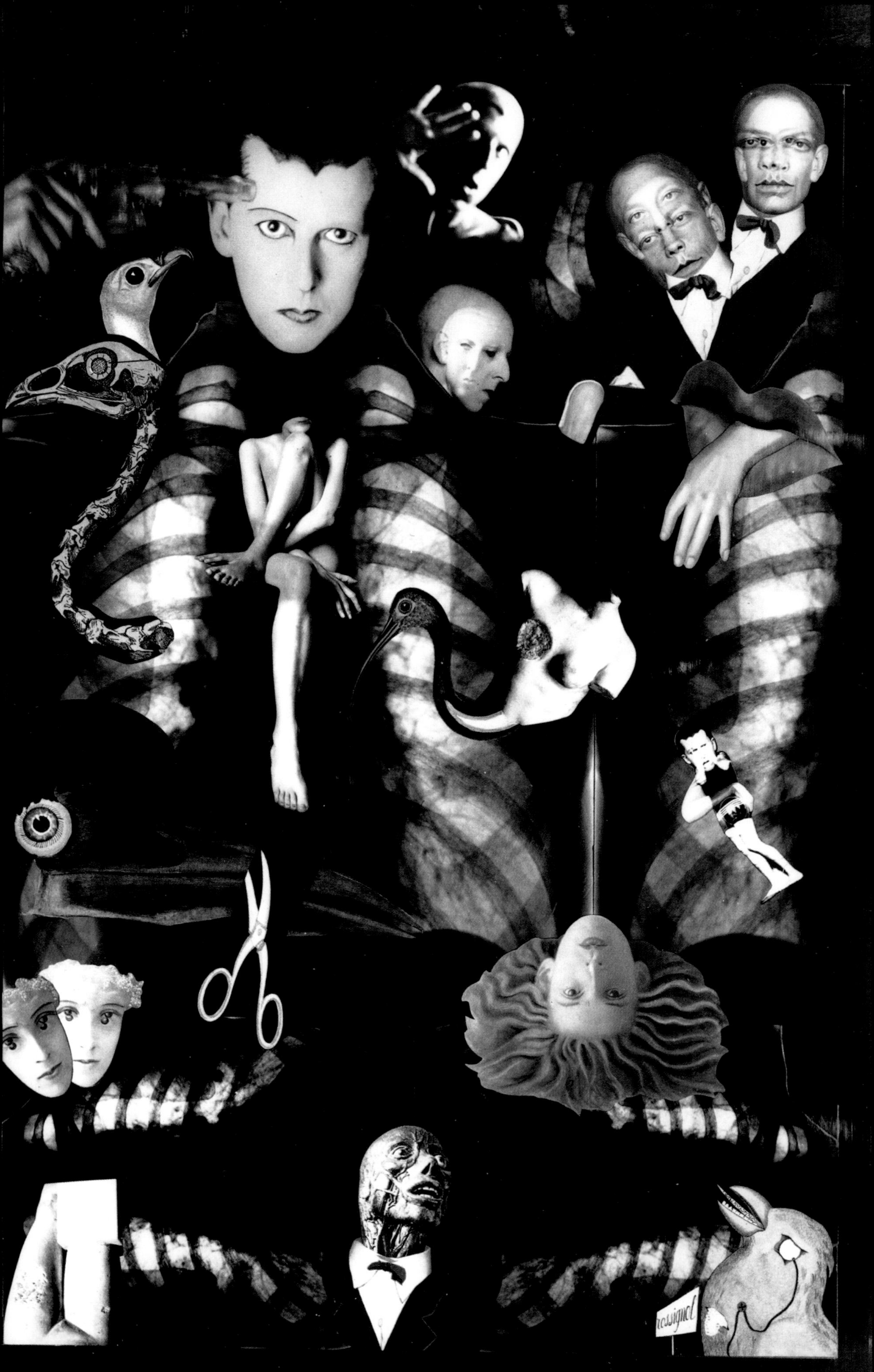

'Realities disguised as symbols are, for me, new realities that are immeasurably preferable.'

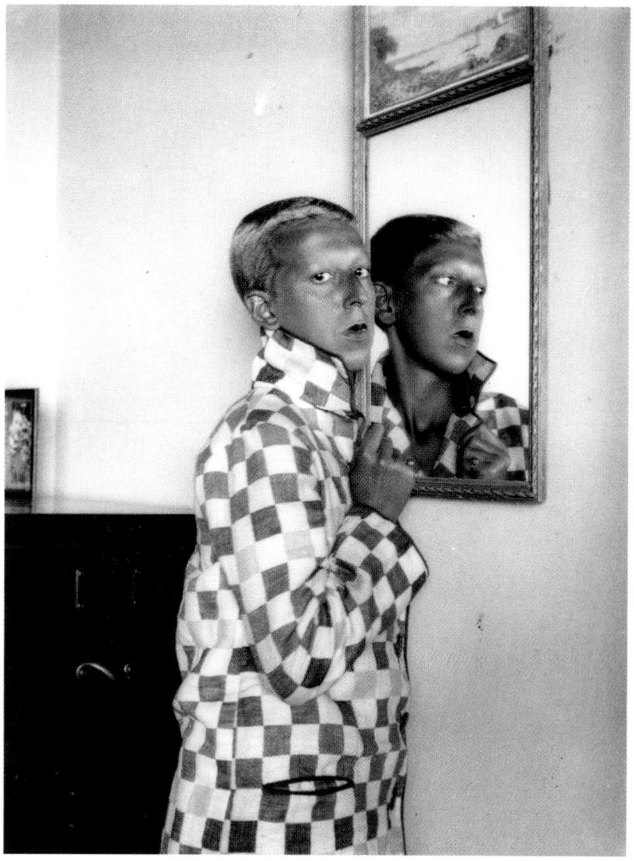

# Claude Cahun

1894–1954

FRANCE

Claude Cahun was two people, and not just because she had two names. Her life partner, stepsister and art collaborator, Suzanne Malherbe, who adopted the name Marcel Moore, lived and worked with Cahun for 40 years. The photocollages credited to Cahun were likely done by both of them, and Moore may have been the person behind the camera when Cahun posed. Trying to reduce them to one artist is as impossible as figuring out exactly which of them initiated what part of each project. The puzzle goes back to photography's earliest days, when the conceptualizer of the image was given all the credit, and the person behind the camera was called the operator. In several cases, it appears that Moore was that operator, but we cannot know how much direction she gave the sitter.

The photocollages published as photolithographs in the book *Aveux non avenus* (published in English as *Disavowals*) were produced mutually. They owe a debt to Surrealism, not only for the uncanny juxtapositions but also for the mixture of religious symbols with sexual allusions. Mirrors play a role in the work of Cahun and Moore, as do masks, and symbols of sight, used to indicate insight. Cahun's experience in experimental theatre during the 1920s allowed her to hone the acting skills apparent in her self-portraits, whereas Moore sometimes seems ill at ease in front of the camera and more comfortable at the drawing table. The seeming ease with which Cahun and Moore explored personal and sexual identity is all the more remarkable because Surrealists, as a group, were mostly men who, despite their philosophy of art, were traditional in their viewing of women as angels or trollops.

Their work was rediscovered by feminist and gay scholars in the 1970s and 1980s. It is understood as part of the history of gender exploration and as an antidote to the devious self-censorship with which many artists struggle.

**Opposite** *H.U.M.* from *Aveux non avenus*, 1930.

**Above** Self-portrait, 1928.

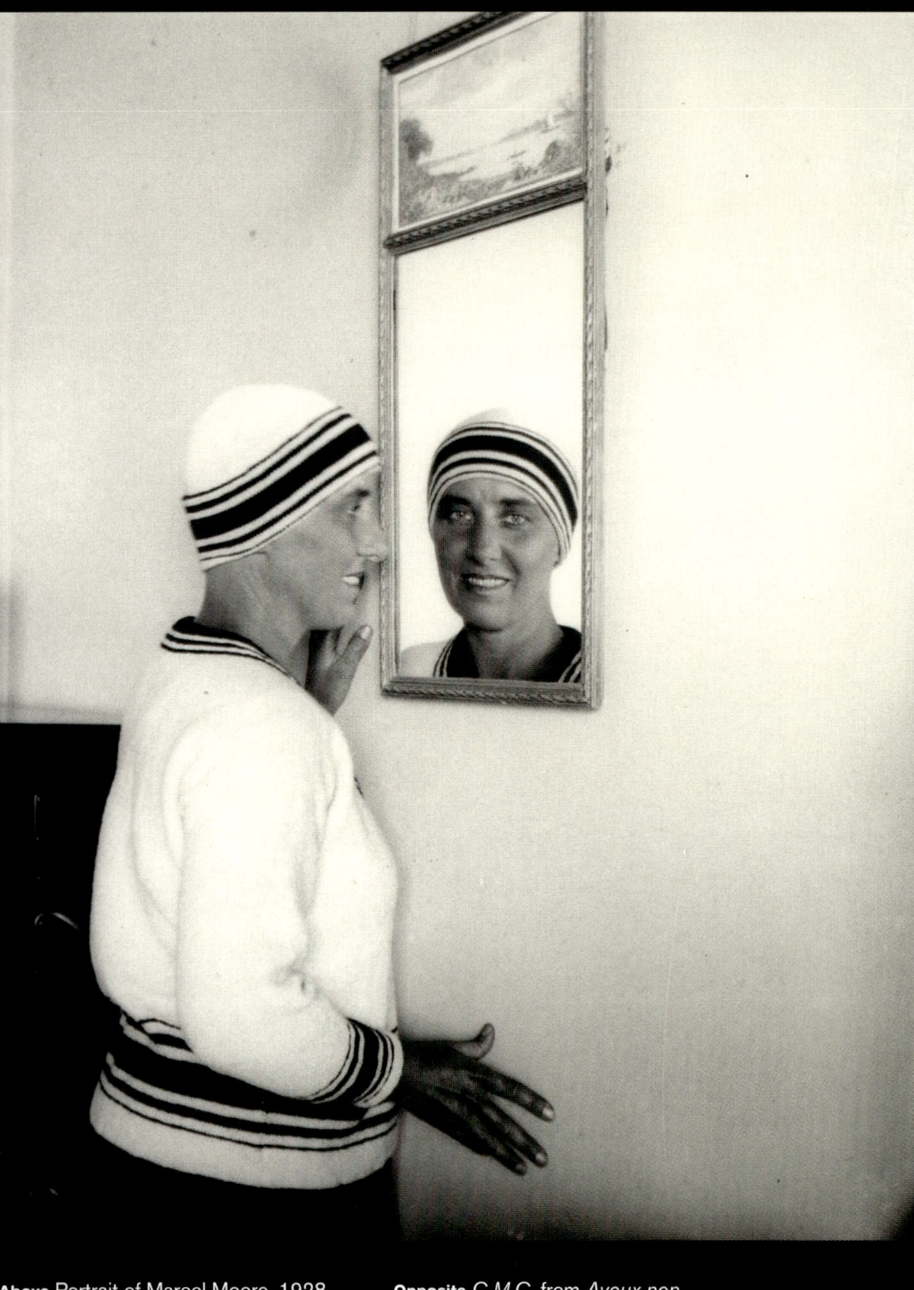

**Above** Portrait of Marcel Moore, 1928.

**Opposite** *C.M.C.* from *Aveux non avenus*, 1930.

## Claude Cahun

1890

1894 Born Lucy Renée Mathilde Schwob in Nantes, France

1900

1910

1913 Collaborates with *Le Phare de la Loire* newspaper, illustrated by Suzanne Malherbe

1914 Writes 'Vues and Visions' for *Mercure de France*

1920 Works with Malherbe to create autobiographical photomontages (to c. 1929)

1930 Publishes *Aveux non avenus*

1937 Moves to the island of Jersey

1938 Jersey invaded by Germany; joins the Resistance

1940

1944 Arrested by Gestapo

1945 Jersey is liberated on 9 May

1946 Begins a series of photographs and self-portraits

1950

1954 Dies in Jersey

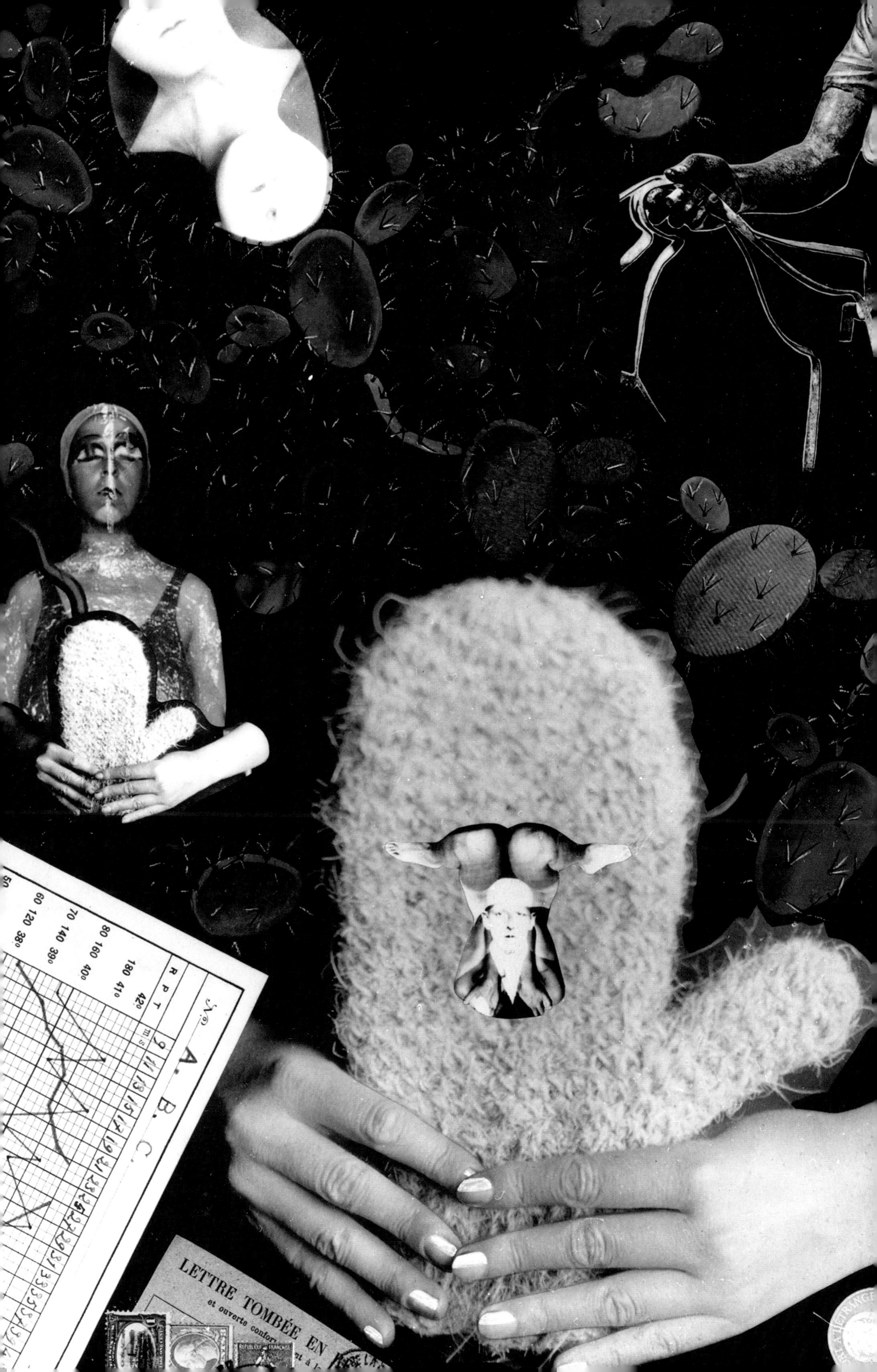
A. B. C.
R P T
42°
180 41°
80 160 40°
70 140 39°
60 120 38°
LETTRE TOMBÉE EN

*Migrant Mother*, 1936.

'A camera is a tool for learning how to see without a camera.'

# Dorothea Lange

1895–1965

UNITED STATES

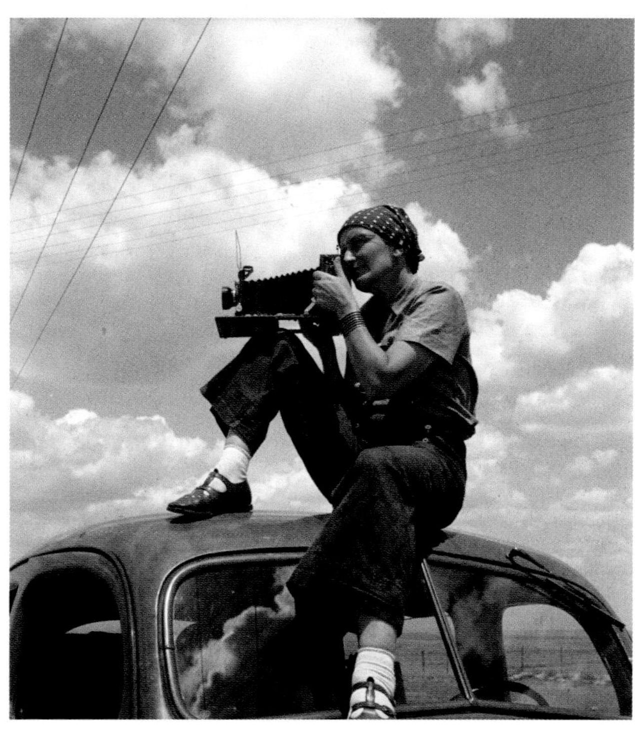

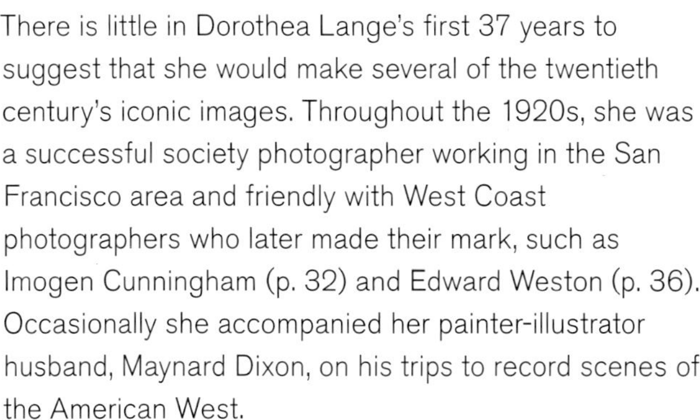

There is little in Dorothea Lange's first 37 years to suggest that she would make several of the twentieth century's iconic images. Throughout the 1920s, she was a successful society photographer working in the San Francisco area and friendly with West Coast photographers who later made their mark, such as Imogen Cunningham (p. 32) and Edward Weston (p. 36). Occasionally she accompanied her painter-illustrator husband, Maynard Dixon, on his trips to record scenes of the American West.

The soft-focus portraits she made of Native Americans during these journeys were free of the then prevalent clichés about indigenous peoples. Nevertheless, they do not hint that she would one day leave her studio, walk to a gathering of the unemployed in a breadline and record the stricken face of a man holding an empty cup. She recalled that 'the discrepancy between what I was working on . . . and what was going on up the street was more than I could assimilate'. Yet it was not an 'a-ha' moment in which she saw her future clearly, but a crisis of personal, social and moral values that prompted her to accept the struggle involved in refocusing her portrait skills towards the world outside the studio and to define her understanding of photography's obligations as a record-keeper.

In 1936, she stopped at a field of frozen pea plants and photographed a desolate woman and her children sheltering there, creating the enduringly popular image *Migrant Mother*. By then, she trusted her aesthetic instincts and was more at ease with people. She was not only working full-time for the Farm Security Administration, a national agency collecting information about the effects of the Depression, but also divorced and remarried to Paul S. Taylor, a progressive economist with whom she published *An American Exodus*. She was mostly on the road until the United States entered World War II.

Her powerful interpretations of the Great Depression, the Dust Bowl and the internment of Japanese Americans treat people as heroes of their own lives. Perhaps this attitude was an outgrowth of her portrait practice, but she referred to her work as evidence. If so, it is evidence minus humiliation and exposé. Because so many of her images have repeatedly appeared in newspapers, it is easy to think of her as a photojournalist. Certainly she embraced the idea of the photo-essay. At the same time she rebelled against the growing practice of taking hundreds of shots and finding the key pictures after the film was developed. For her, photography was like writing, slow and cerebral.

*Dorothea Lange in Texas on the Plains* by Paul S. Taylor, c. 1935.

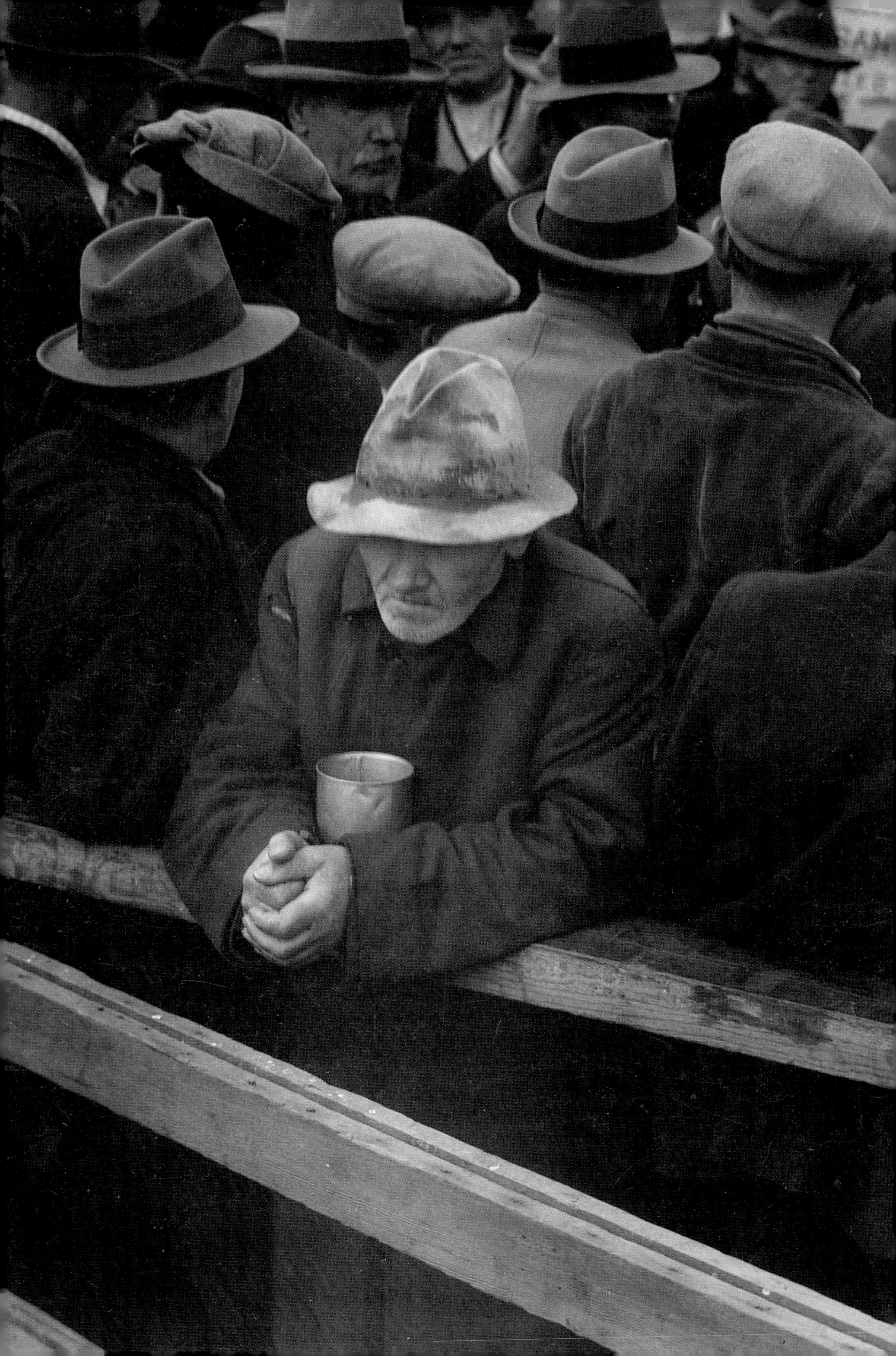

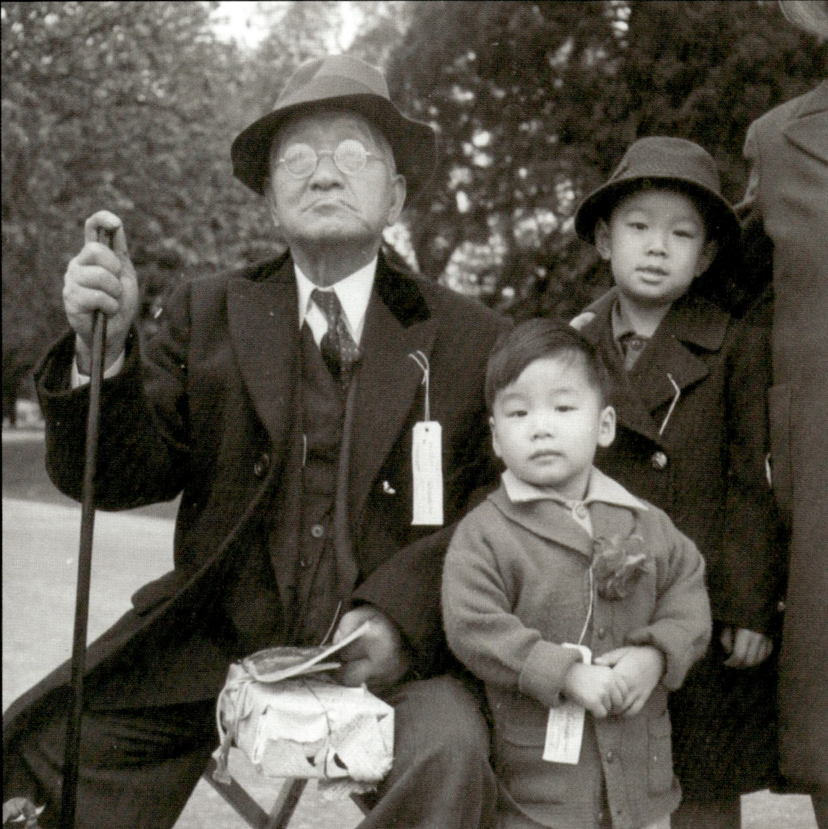

**Opposite** *White Angel Breadline*, 1934.

**Above** Grandfather and grandchildren awaiting evacuation bus, 1942.

## Dorothea Lange

1890

**1895** Born in Hoboken, New Jersey, USA

1900

1910

1920

1930

**1936** *Migrant Mother*; publishes *An American Exodus* with Paul S. Taylor

1940

**1942** Co-founds *Aperture* magazine with Ansel Adams and others

1950

1960

**1965** Dies in San Francisco, California, USA

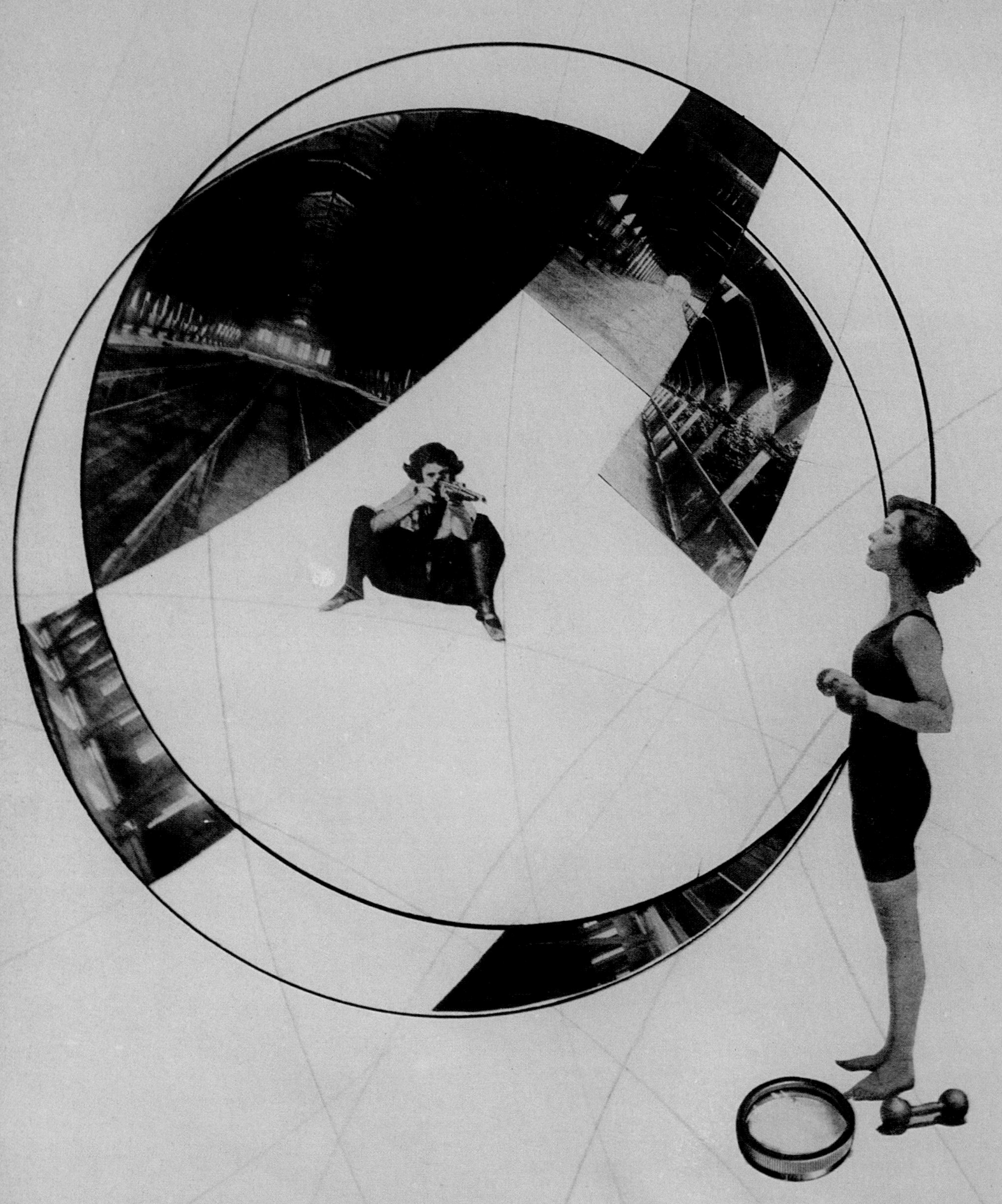

'The enemy of photography is convention, the fixed rules of "how it's done".'

# László Moholy-Nagy

1895–1946

HUNGARY

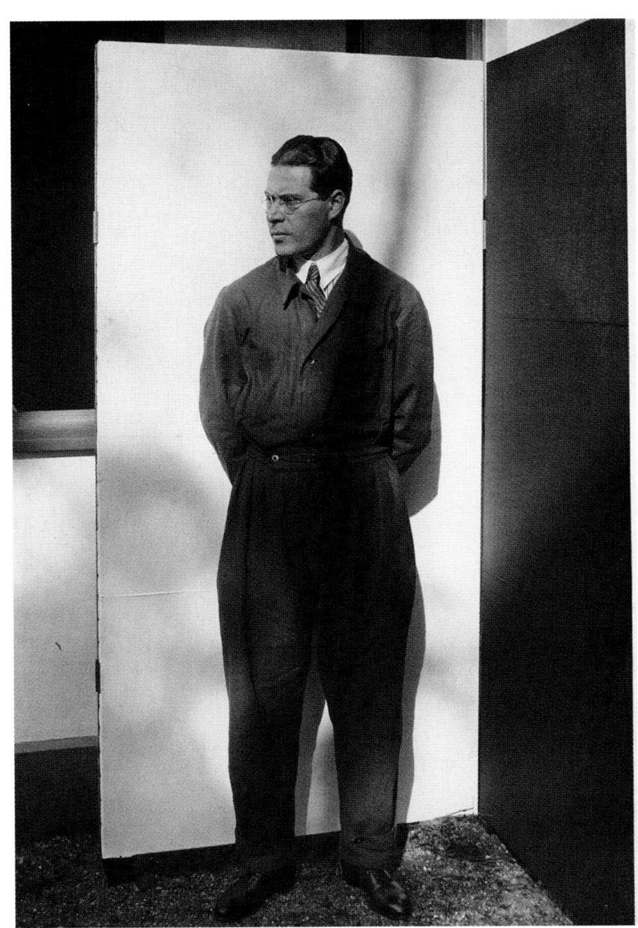

Moholy-Nagy should have an energy drink named after him. His dynamism, inventiveness and polymathic interests suggest indefatigable vitality. Like many artists in the period between the world wars, he believed that the traditional arts were weighty vestiges of the past that should be replaced with the new media of the twentieth century, particularly photography.

For him, photography replaced painting, not for its documentary possibilities but for its inherent qualities of modulating light. To that end, he created abstract images by placing objects on light-sensitive paper and then exposing them, to produce what he called a 'photogram', or camera-less photograph. In addition, he noted and approved the increased use of photography in magazines and newspapers, some of which he appropriated for photomontages. Sometimes he photographed these montages, making them available in multiples. He also used the camera to make images of street life, which he energized by shooting from unexpected angles or by using clever cropping. In all of his photographic work, he employed the diagonal line as both symbol and generator of the new off-kilter view of the world that he proselytized.

Moholy, as he was known, often used everyday items to create his photograms, or to set up lights and shadows that emphasized abstract patterns. His photomontages often alluded to topical social and political figures who are now obscure. His comments on the 'New Woman' of the early twentieth century are more explicable, and the tone of anxiety in such montages as *The Eccentric II* shows how he tempered an uncritical love of abstraction to reference modern anxiety.

**Opposite** *Love Your Neighbour; Murder on the Railway*, 1925.

**Above** Portrait of László Moholy-Nagy by Lucia Moholy, 1926.

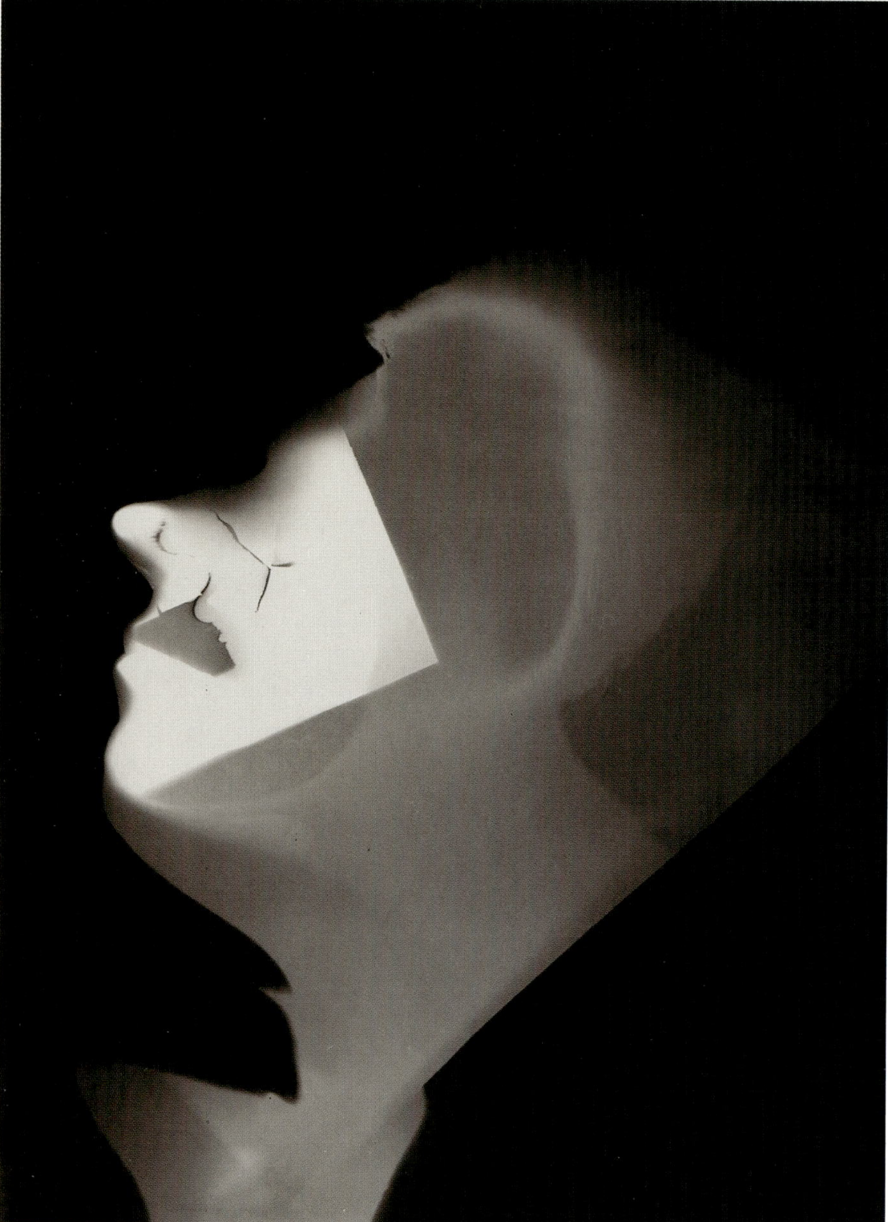

**Above** *Fotogramm*, 1929.

**Opposite** Radio Tower, Berlin, 1928.

## László Moholy-Nagy

1890

1895 Born László Weisz in Borsod (now Bácsborsód), Hungary

1900

1910

1918 Decides to become an artist

1920

1922 Conceives the idea of photograms

1923 Begins teaching foundation course at the Bauhaus and writing about photography

1930

1935 Moves to London; does commercial art, including book covers

1937 Accepts position in Chicago at what will be called the 'New Bauhaus'

1939 Opens his own Chicago institution, the School of Design

1946 Dies in Chicago, USA

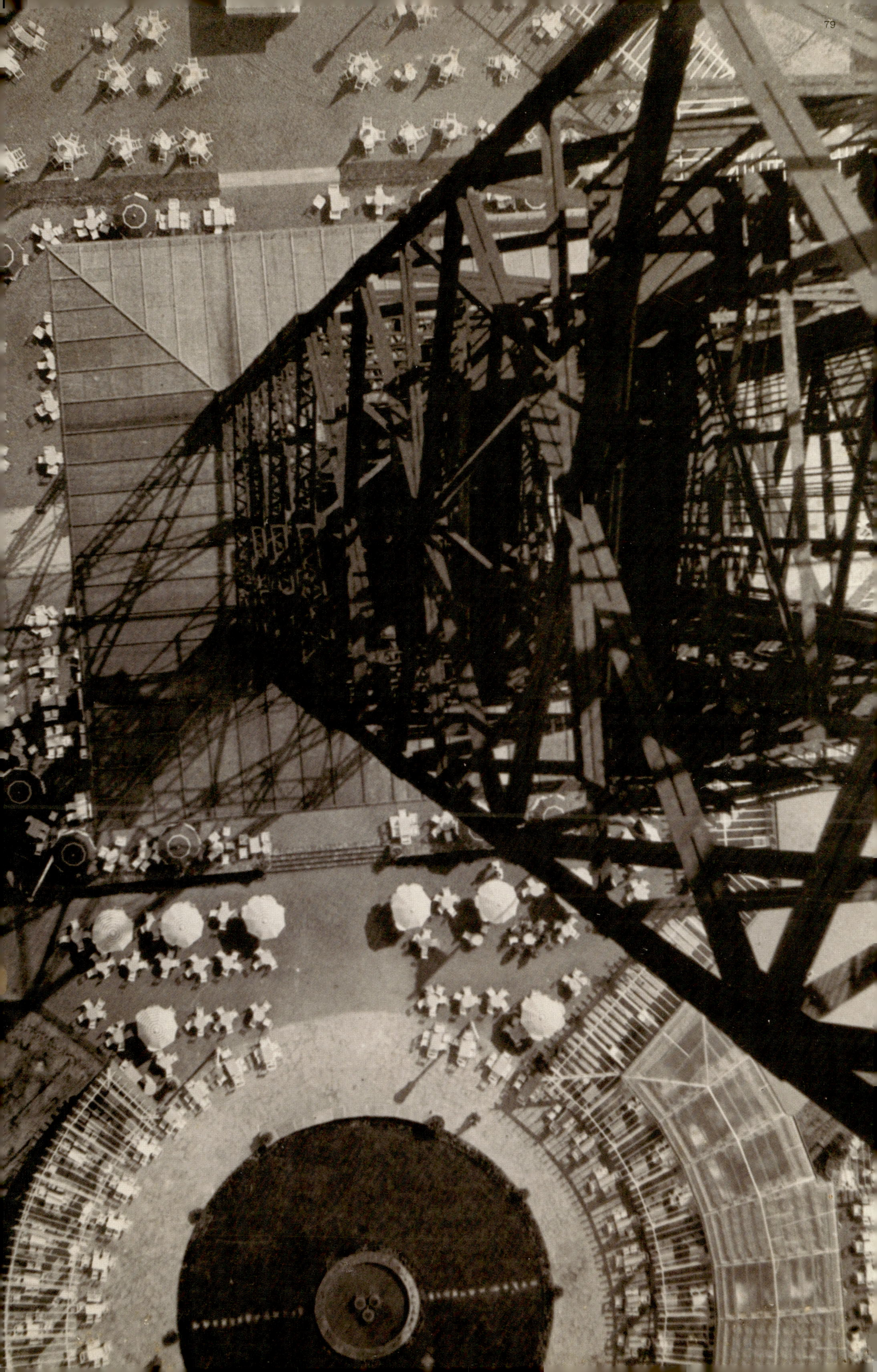

Eiffel Tower from *Métal*, 1928.

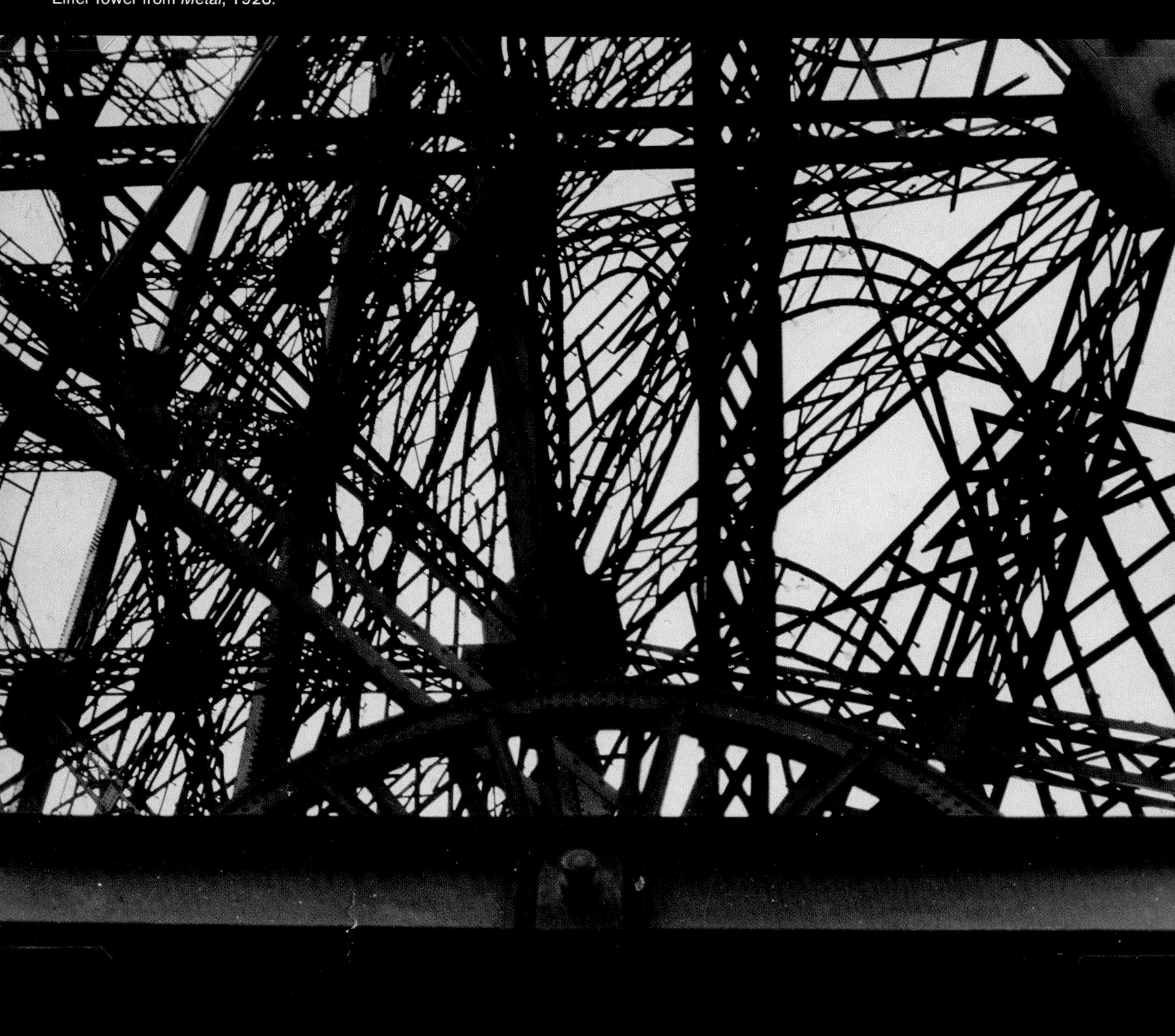

'These steel giants revealed something to me that made me love photography again.'

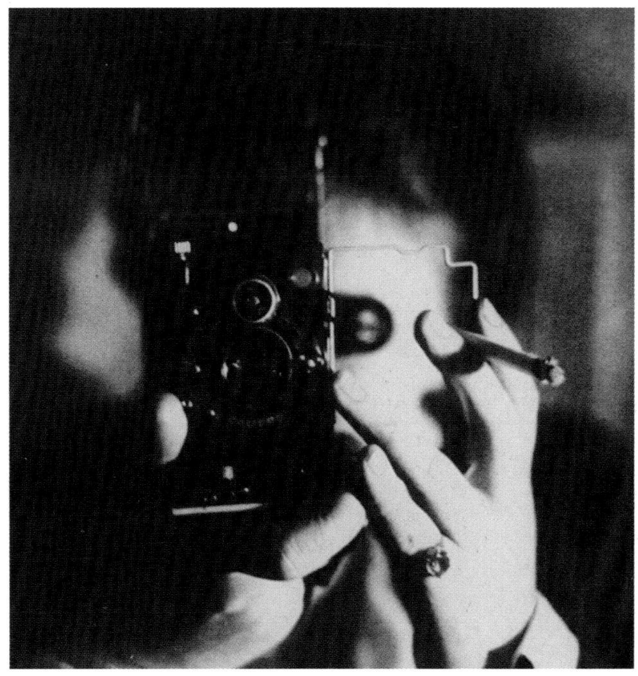

# Germaine Krull

1897–1985

POLAND

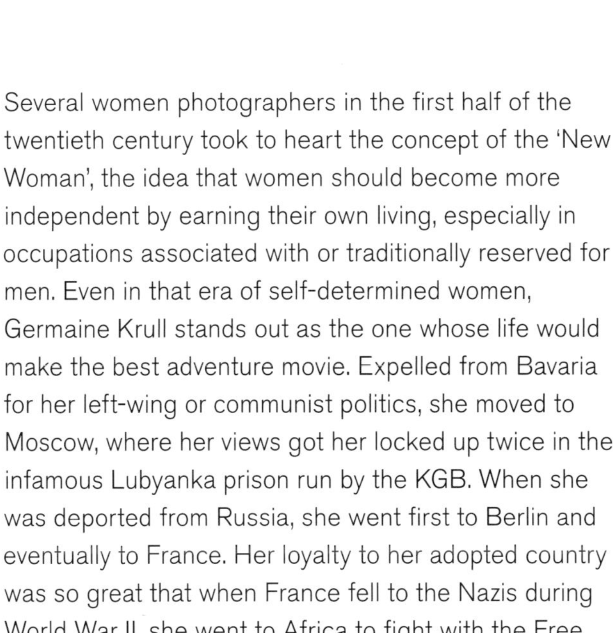

Several women photographers in the first half of the twentieth century took to heart the concept of the 'New Woman', the idea that women should become more independent by earning their own living, especially in occupations associated with or traditionally reserved for men. Even in that era of self-determined women, Germaine Krull stands out as the one whose life would make the best adventure movie. Expelled from Bavaria for her left-wing or communist politics, she moved to Moscow, where her views got her locked up twice in the infamous Lubyanka prison run by the KGB. When she was deported from Russia, she went first to Berlin and eventually to France. Her loyalty to her adopted country was so great that when France fell to the Nazis during World War II, she went to Africa to fight with the Free French legions.

The early photographs she created in her Berlin studio include some thoughtful portraits and jejune nude scenes, none of which hints at the inventiveness of her later portfolio of industrial forms titled *Métal*. Shot in Holland and France, the images are unprecedented in her work. Although they have geometric qualities familiar from abstract art, they are not so much an art expression as an impersonal field guide to manufactured metal objects in the landscape. As Joris Ivens would later do in his 1929 film *Rain*, Krull offers us in *Métal* an impressionistic compendium of form. Soon, other modern photographers would make modern metal architecture fly and swoon. But for Krull, the emerging industrial landscape was beautiful but also aloof. The gleaming conduits, slim extruded cables, bony support girders and ethereal cranes allow only a few small humans in their midst. Her unique approach did not catch on, and resembles in its quietude the late twentieth-century photography of dead tech. Despite her experimentation with *Métal*, Krull was no purist. She happily kept up her portrait practice and her work for corporate clients.

Krull's subsequent voluminous work in fashion and photojournalism made her a success throughout Europe. When she photographed the Eiffel Tower, it became a complex network of lacy beams. At the same time, her photo projects became more varied. Inevitably for a Paris art photographer, she explored Surrealism's ideas. Her last decades were peripatetic – Brazil, Thailand, India – always working on a commission or on entrepreneurial projects.

Self-portrait with Ikarette, 1925.

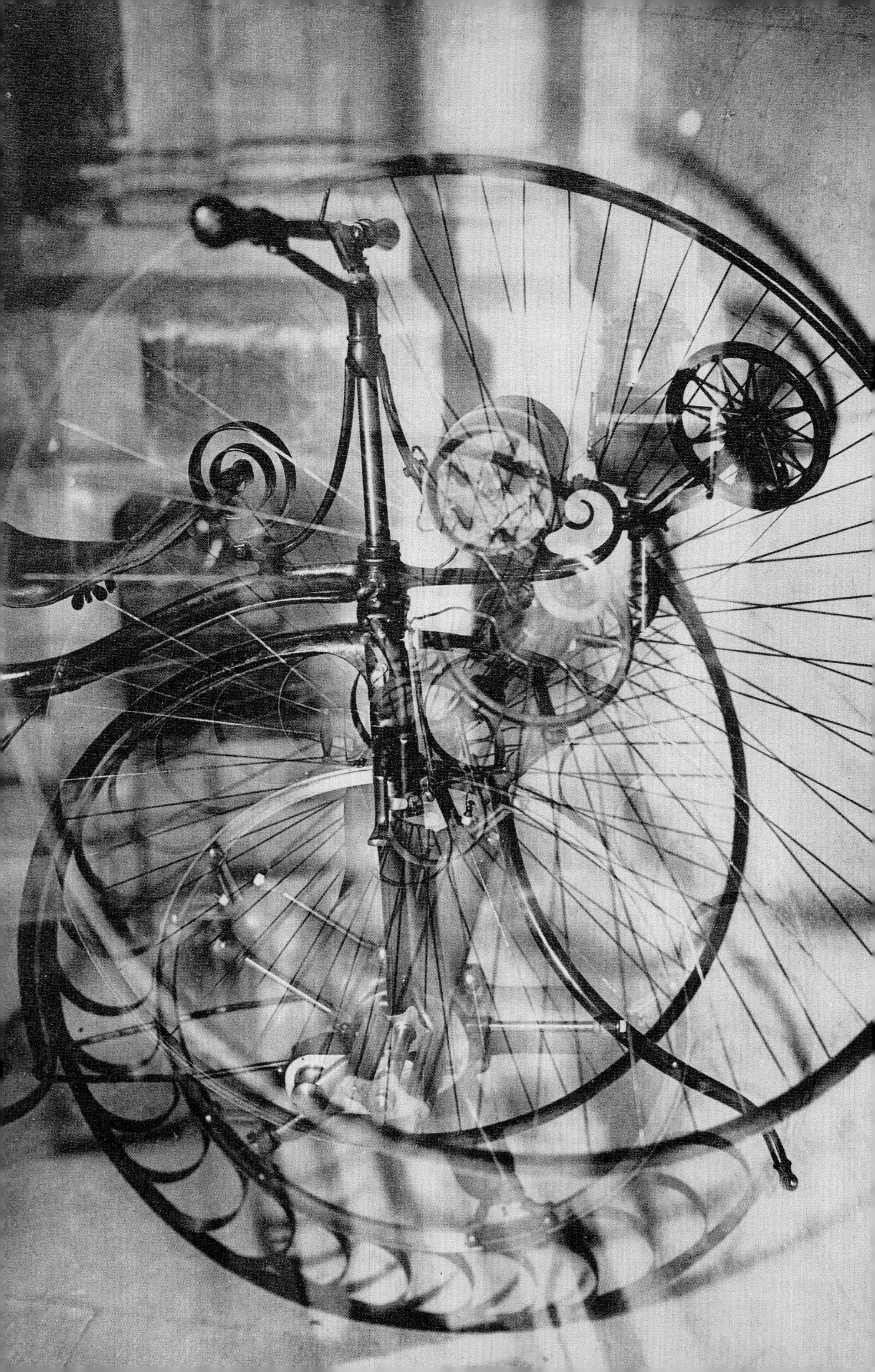

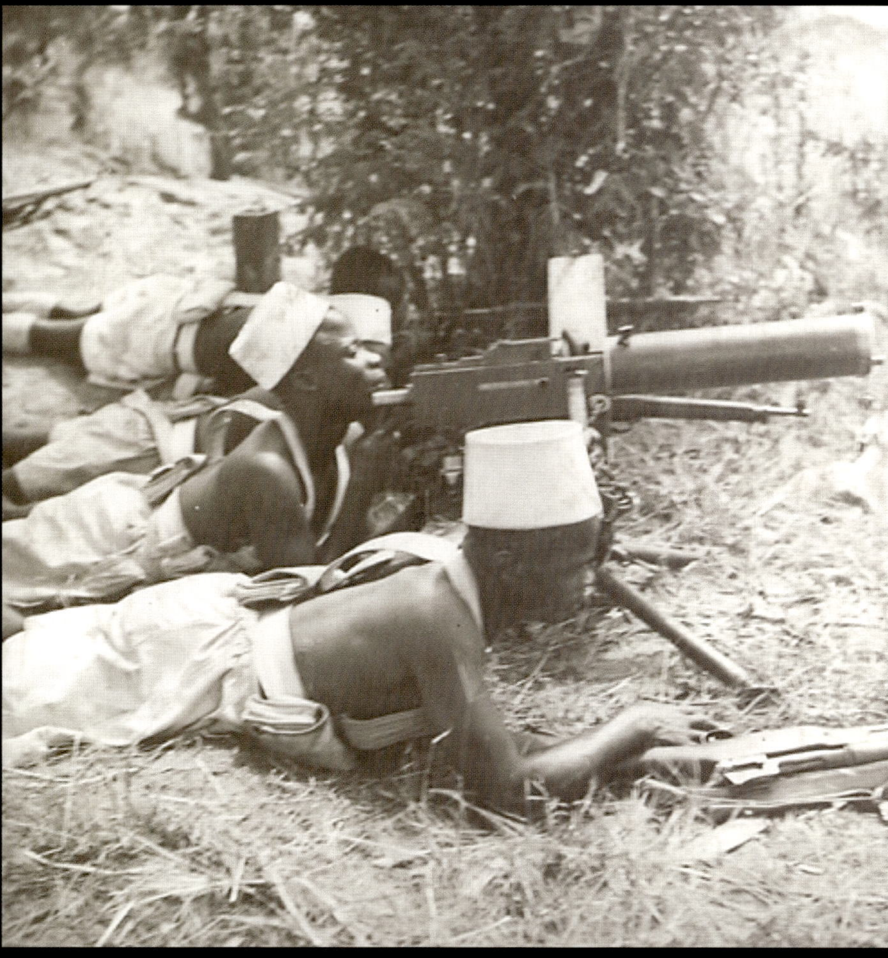

**Opposite** Bicycle wheels from *Métal, 1928.*

**Above** Military exercise in Brazzaville, 1943.

## Germaine Krull

1890

1897 Born in Wilda, Poznan, Poland

1900

1910

1920

1923 Establishes photo studio in Berlin

1925 Travels with avant-garde film-maker Joris Ivens to Holland, where some of *Métal* is photographed

1928 Publishes *Métal*

1930

1940

1950

1960

1970

1977 Retrospective in Bonn, Germany

1980

1985 Dies in Wetzlar, Germany

Janet Flanner, 1927.

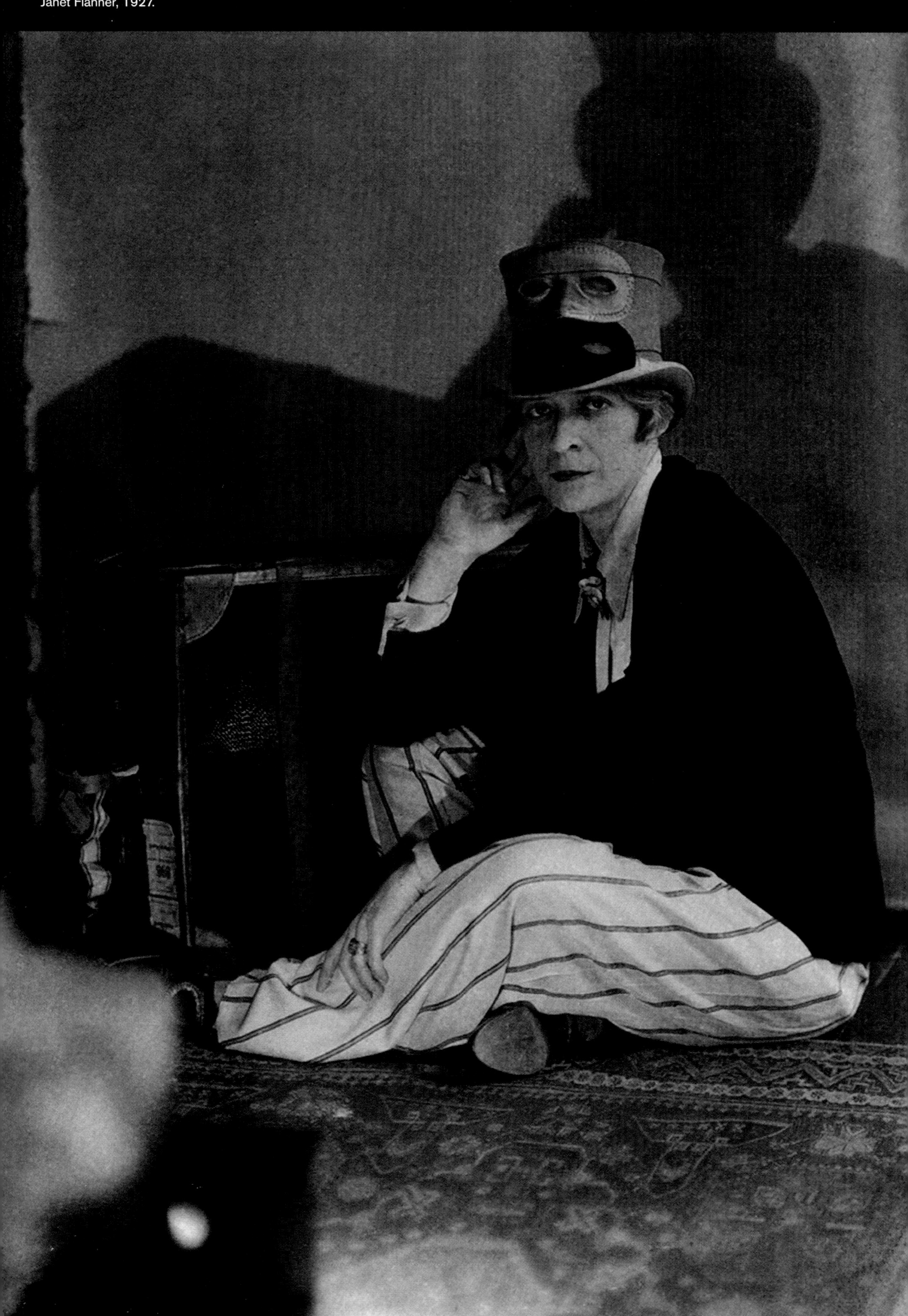

'I wanted to combine science and photography in a sensible, unemotional way.'

# Berenice Abbott

1898–1991

UNITED STATES

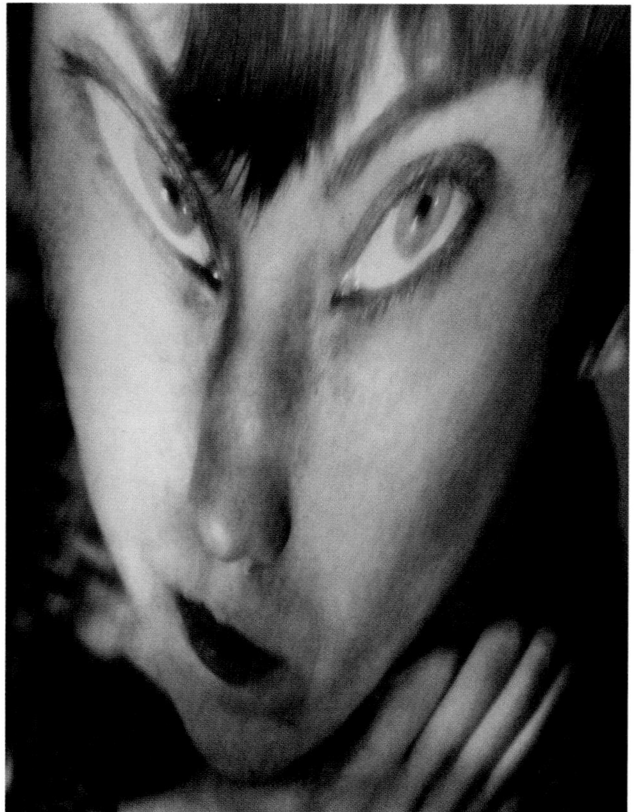

Berenice Abbott was always interested in the arts, but it took her a while to find photography. Or, more correctly, for photography to find her – in the form of the artist Man Ray (p. 48). He was looking for a darkroom assistant to train who knew nothing about the medium, and she fit the bill. He taught her the darkroom techniques that he favoured, but he did not teach her how to use a camera. She taught herself by trial and error, acquiring enough skill to open a portrait studio in Paris, where she photographed figures in the art and fashion world, including Coco Chanel and Jean Cocteau. Her photographs of gay and lesbian local and expat artists preserve a record of the self-determination Abbott and other gay people enjoyed in Paris during the 1920s.

Abbott returned from Paris to New York just before the stock market crashed in 1929, taking with it her customers for upmarket portrait photography. As she would in the future, Abbott reinvented herself, this time as a documentary photographer and editor. She photographed New York with the assistance of the Federal Art Project, a relief agency for artists. *Changing New York* was her invention: a book of photographs incorporating history, maps and plans to orient the viewer, prepared and researched by unemployed artists and writers and distributed to schools and libraries in the metropolitan area.

The success of *Changing New York* spurred Abbott to invent herself again, as a photographer who used the medium to explain scientific concepts such as gravity and phenomena such as electricity. She founded the short-lived House of Photography to promote her work and inventions. Her efforts culminated with her work for the Physical Science Study Project at the Massachusetts Institute of Technology (MIT) in 1958.

Self-portrait, 1945.

Daytona Beach, Florida, 1954.

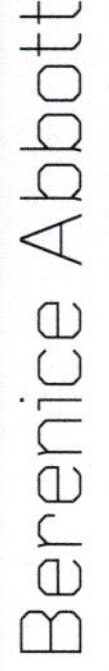


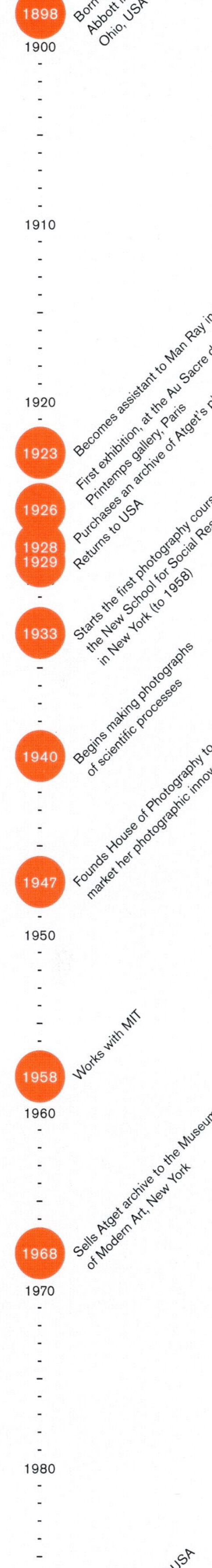


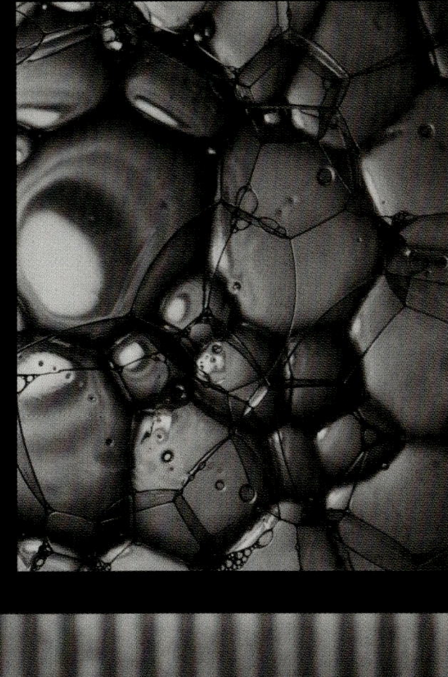

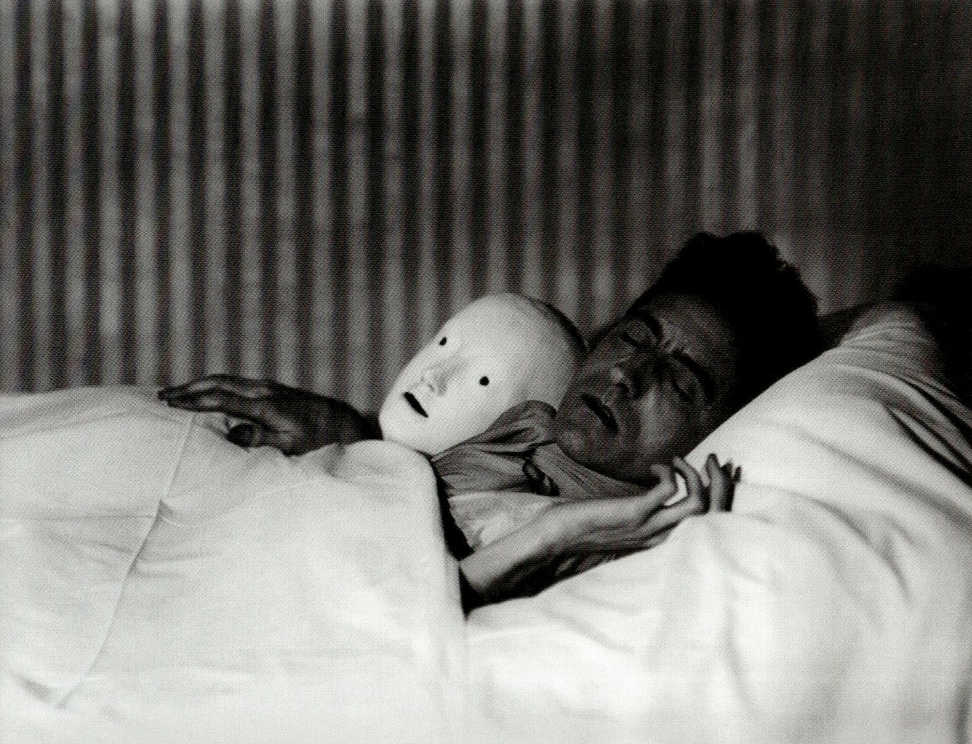

**Above top** Soap bubbles, 1945.

**Above** Jean Cocteau, 1927.

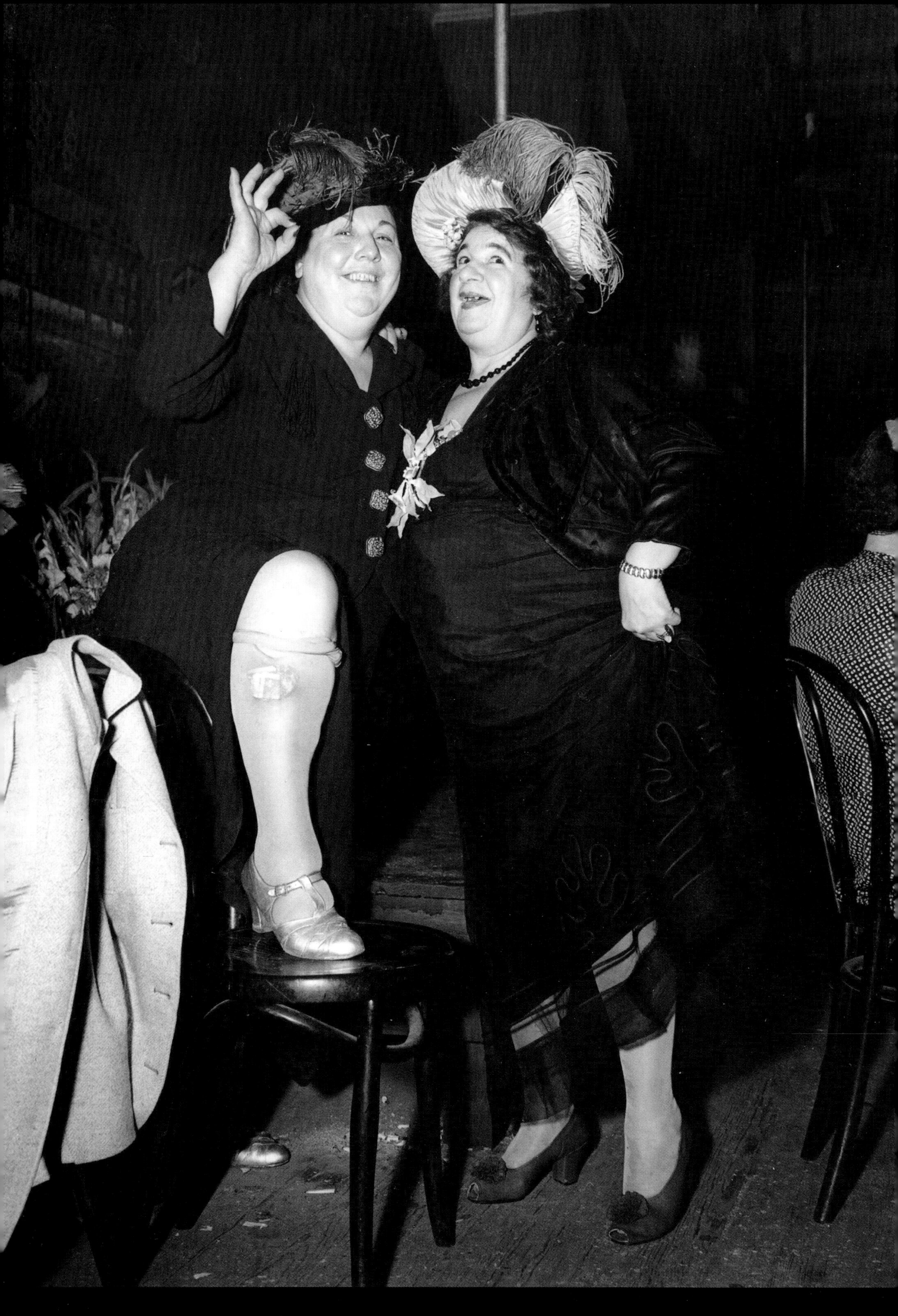

'You can't be a Nice Nelly and take news pictures.'

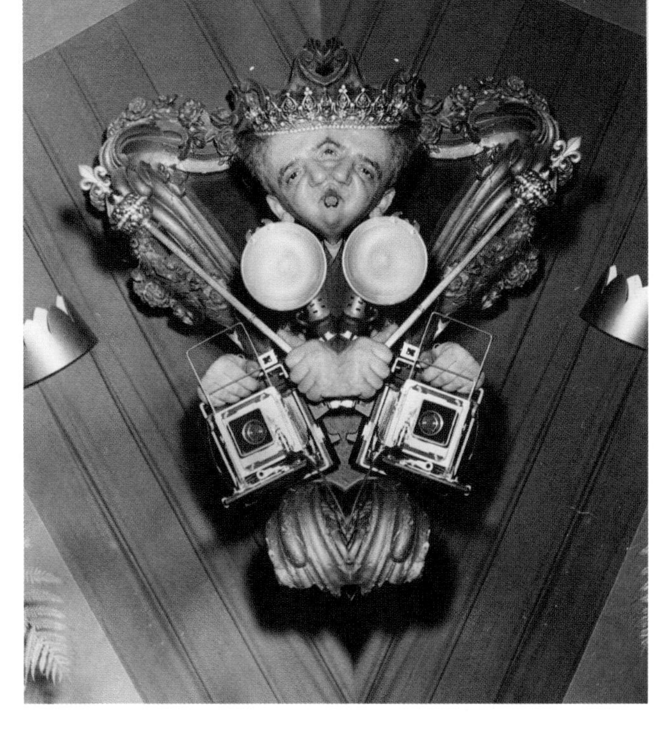

# Weegee

1899–1968

AUSTRIA

Weegee is the photographer people loved to hate. He is known to have introduced himself by saying, 'My name is Weegee. I'm the world's greatest photographer.' His lack of humility was accompanied by an athletic boorishness that sent him energetically elbowing through crowds to get a picture.

His nickname has two sources, one of which is 'squeegee boy', a title referring to the lowly job of running a squeegee over a wet photographic print to get the water off, which Weegee may have done in his early jobs. The second source, and Weegee's favourite, was a reference to the Ouija board, or 'spirit board' – a device popular at the time for trying to receive messages from the spirit world. It was said that Weegee arrived so quickly at the scene of a murder or crime, it was as if he had a Ouija board. In fact, he had a police radio and other equipment in the back of his car.

In his introduction to *Weegee on Weegee*, editor Bruce Downes remarked that Weegee 'accumulated an impressive collection of pictures, the photographic quality of which was uniformly poor. But however bad they were technically, what was in them was true and alive.' Surprisingly, that basic contradiction between talent and technique endeared him to artists, photographers and curators who were looking for a new direction. Diane Arbus, who sometimes tagged along with him as he followed police calls, carried on his indifference to subjects' feeling, as did Robert Frank (p. 172), who, like Weegee, also retreated from technical standards of the medium. Weegee's greatest influence, however, was on Andy Warhol, who loved tabloid photojournalism and reproduced it in his work.

Weegee's notion of 'Rembrandt lighting', derived more from its understanding in popular culture than art history, referred to the sharp white highlights caused by the flash, which accentuated faces while making the backgrounds seem dark. It pervaded photography in the 1950s and 1960s as a sign of rebelliousness.

**Opposite** *At Sammy's on the Bowery*, 1944.

**Above** Self-portrait, 1956.

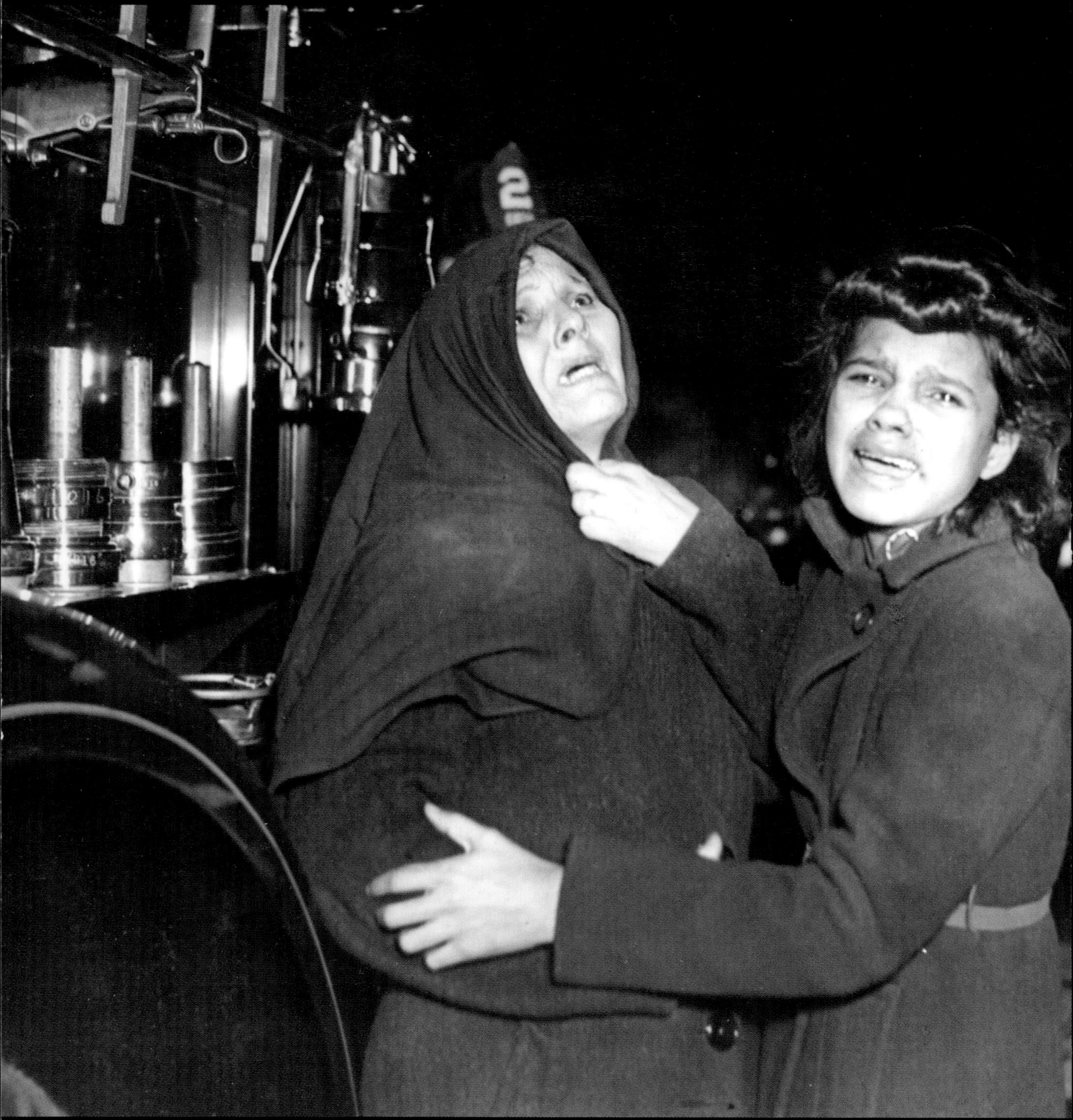

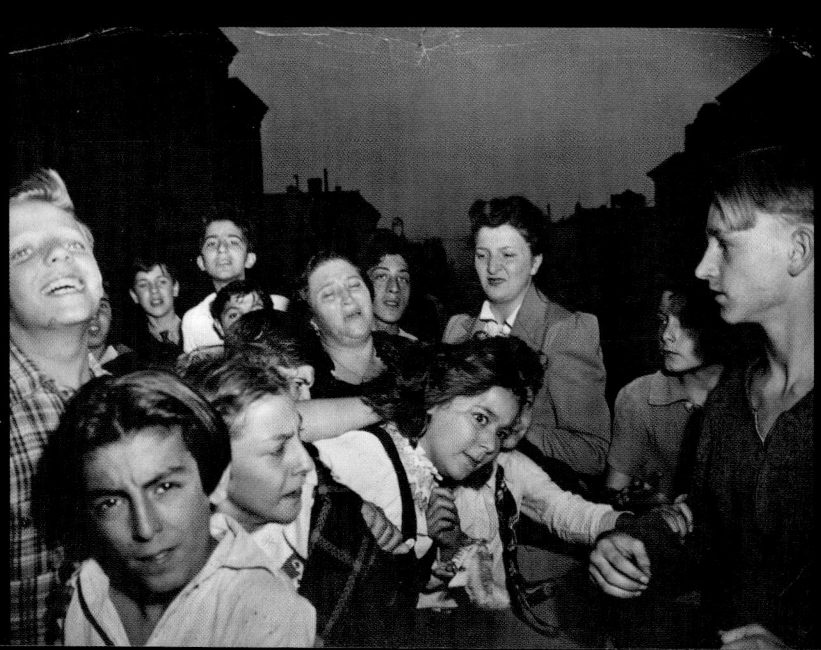

*Their First Murder*, c. 1941.

*Tenement Fire*, Harlem, 1942.

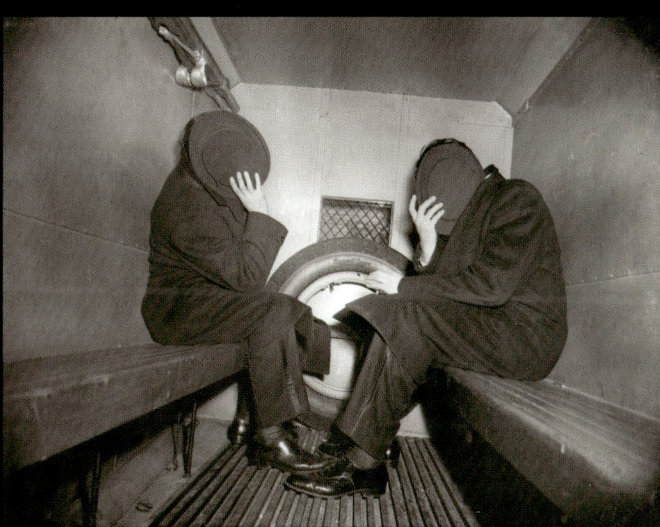

*Charles Sodokoff and Arthur Webber Use Their Top Hats to Hide Their Faces*, 1942.

## Weegee

1890

**1899** Born Usher Fellig, Lemberg (Lvov), Austria (now Ukraine)

**1910** Family moves to the USA; Usher's name is changed to Arthur

**1913** Leaves school

**1918** Takes various jobs in photo studios (to 1924)

1920

**1924** Joins Acme Newspictures (later United Press International)

1930

**1935** Begins freelancing with an emphasis on crime photographs

**1941** Exhibits 'Weegee: Murder is My Business' at the Photo League in New York

**1943** Museum of Modern Art buys five of his prints

**1945** Publishes *Naked City*

**1946** Publishes *Weegee's People*

1950

**1961** Publishes *Weegee by Weegee*

**1968** Dies in New York, USA

*Group in Dance Hall, 1932.*

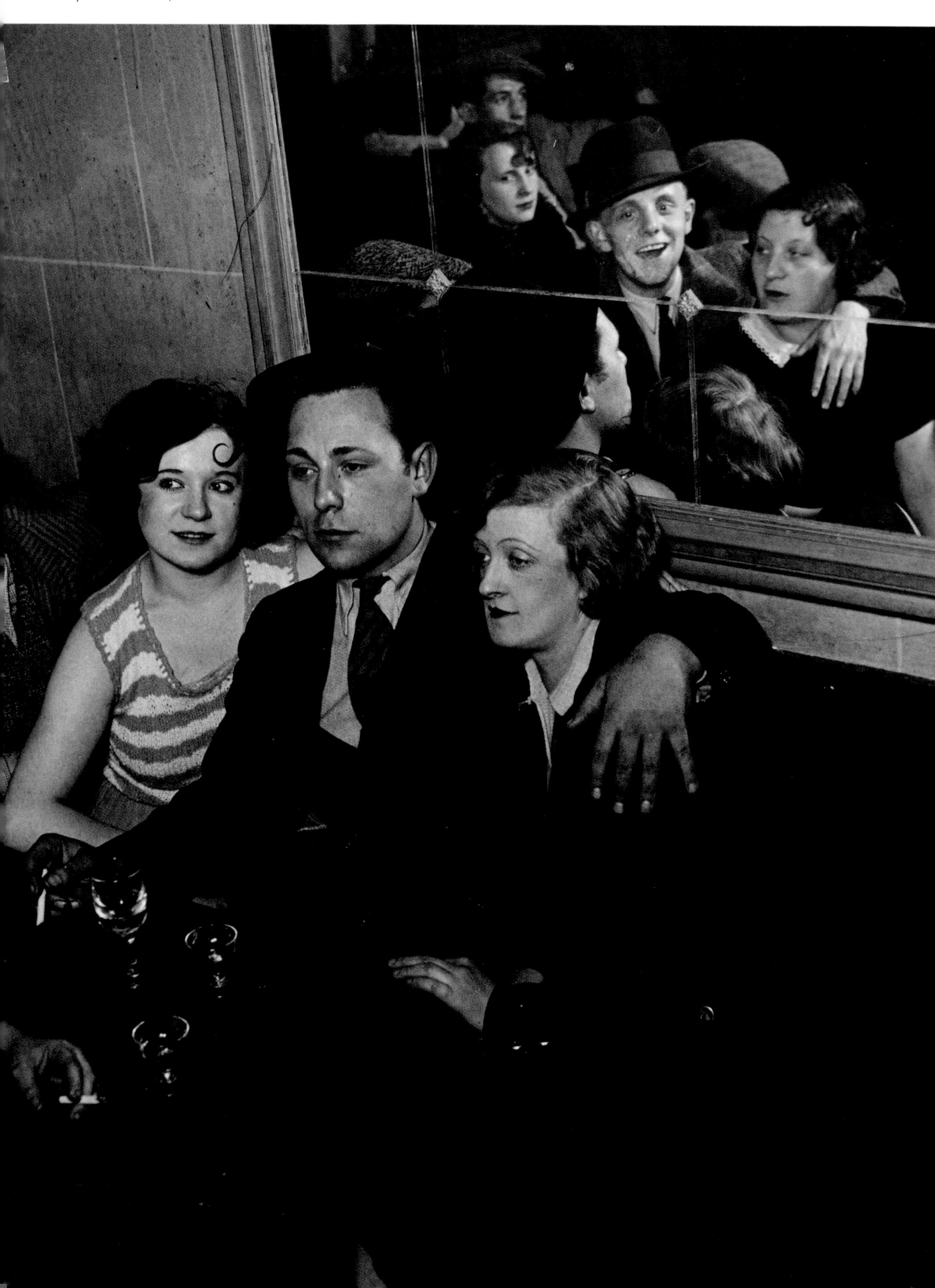

'Yes, I only take one or two or three pictures of a subject ... I find it concentrates one more to shoot less.'

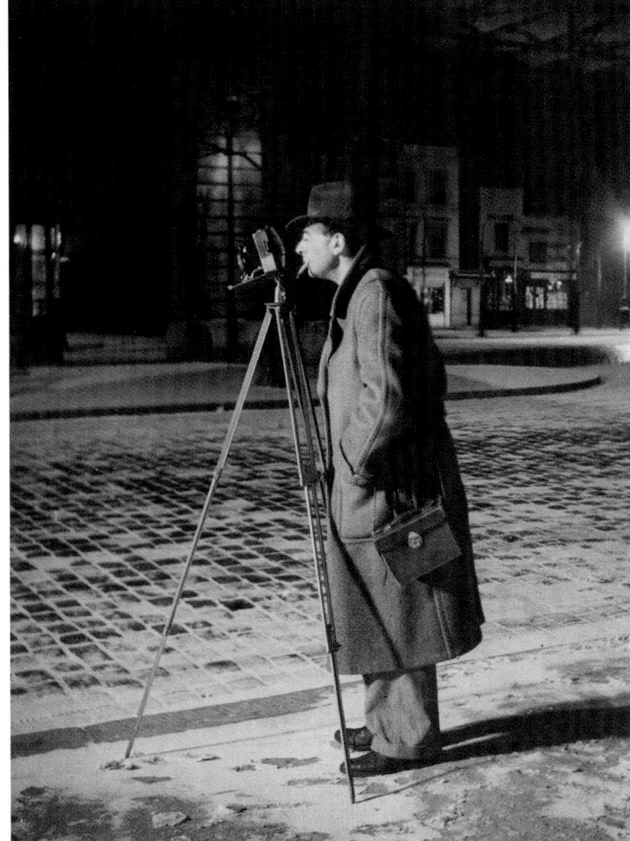

# Brassaï

1899–1984

HUNGARY

Brassaï greatest work was the creation of himself as an anthropologist of the uncanny. An enthusiastic borrower of contemporary ideas, Brassaï was never a fully fledged adherent of any art movement. He engaged most of the great artists living in Paris in the 1930s, vacuuming up their ideas, which energized him, and may have been indirectly aware of Freud's theories.

Throughout his life, Brassaï collected images that suggested, rather than dissected, ulterior aspects of human nature, eruptions of inscrutability in ordinary life, and marks made by anonymous graffiti-makers in public places. Despite dwelling on passion and strangeness, most of his photographs are multivalent and non-judgmental. A series of so-called 'involuntary sculptures' homed in on tiny discarded objects – bits of chewing gum, train tickets, pocket lint – transforming them from incidental detritus to looming sculptural forms. One of his much-discussed female nude studies, first published in the avant-garde magazine *Minotaure,* is so truncated and twisted as to suggest its imminent transformation into the male sex organ.

Like the Surrealists, he was fascinated with mirrors and their ability to double and complicate scenes. The text and photographs in his book *Paris by Night* range across social classes, but the emphasis is on sexual transgression in a lush and evocative Paris after dark. His wide-ranging interests in literature, music and poetry brought Brassaï into contact with such art-world stars as Edgard Varèse, Salvador Dalí and Henry Miller, the latter succinctly describing Brassaï's character as one of 'malicious benevolence'. A 40-year friendship with Picasso led not only to a book but also to Picasso's conclusion that Brassaï was the best photographer to record his entire sculptural output in interpretive, rather than objective, photographs. While Brassaï's work appeared in art publications, he also worked full-time for popular magazines and newspapers, unapologetically supporting himself by writing articles as well as making pictures.

Self-portrait, 1931–32.

Picasso holding one of his sculptures, 1939.

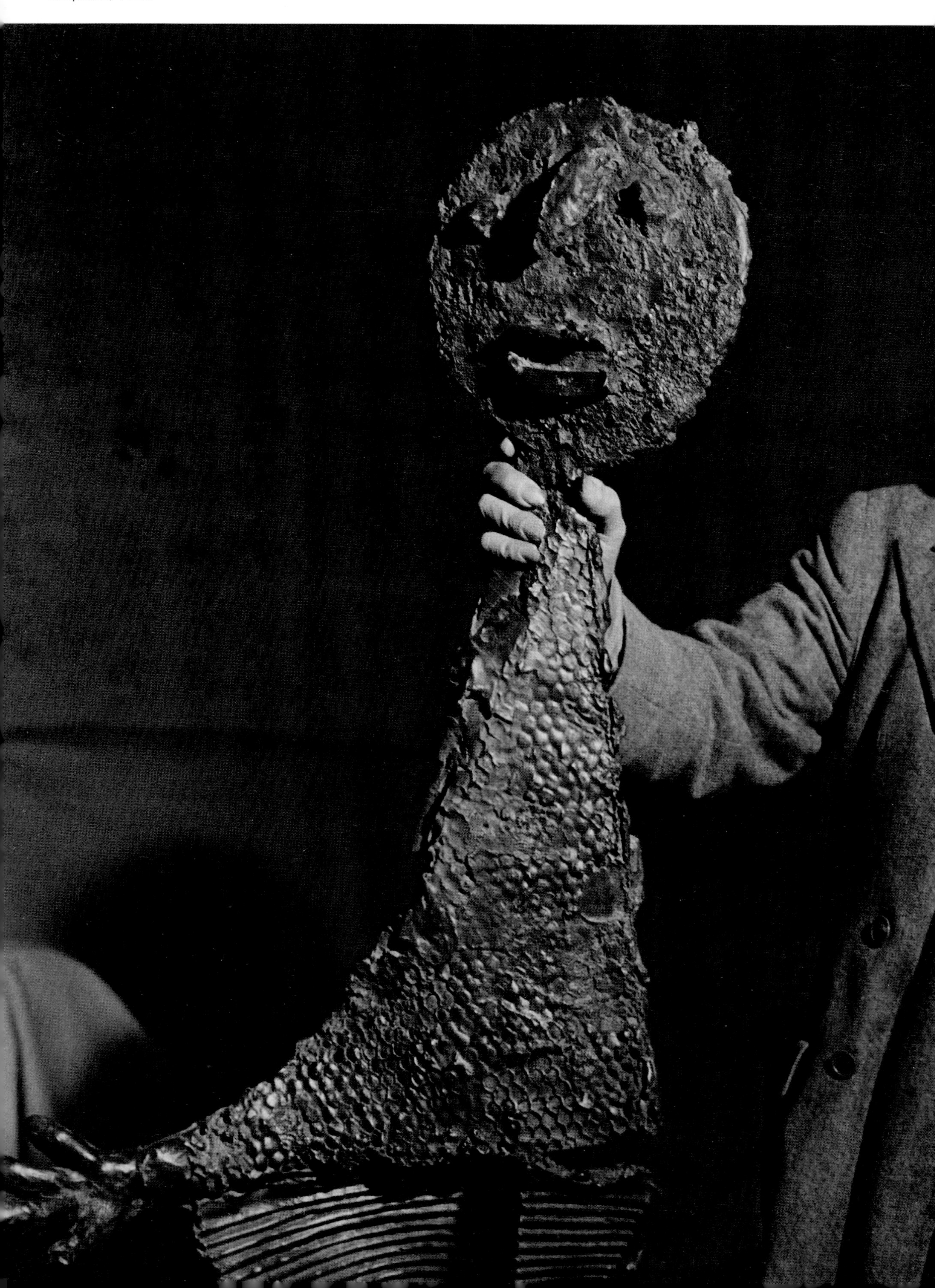

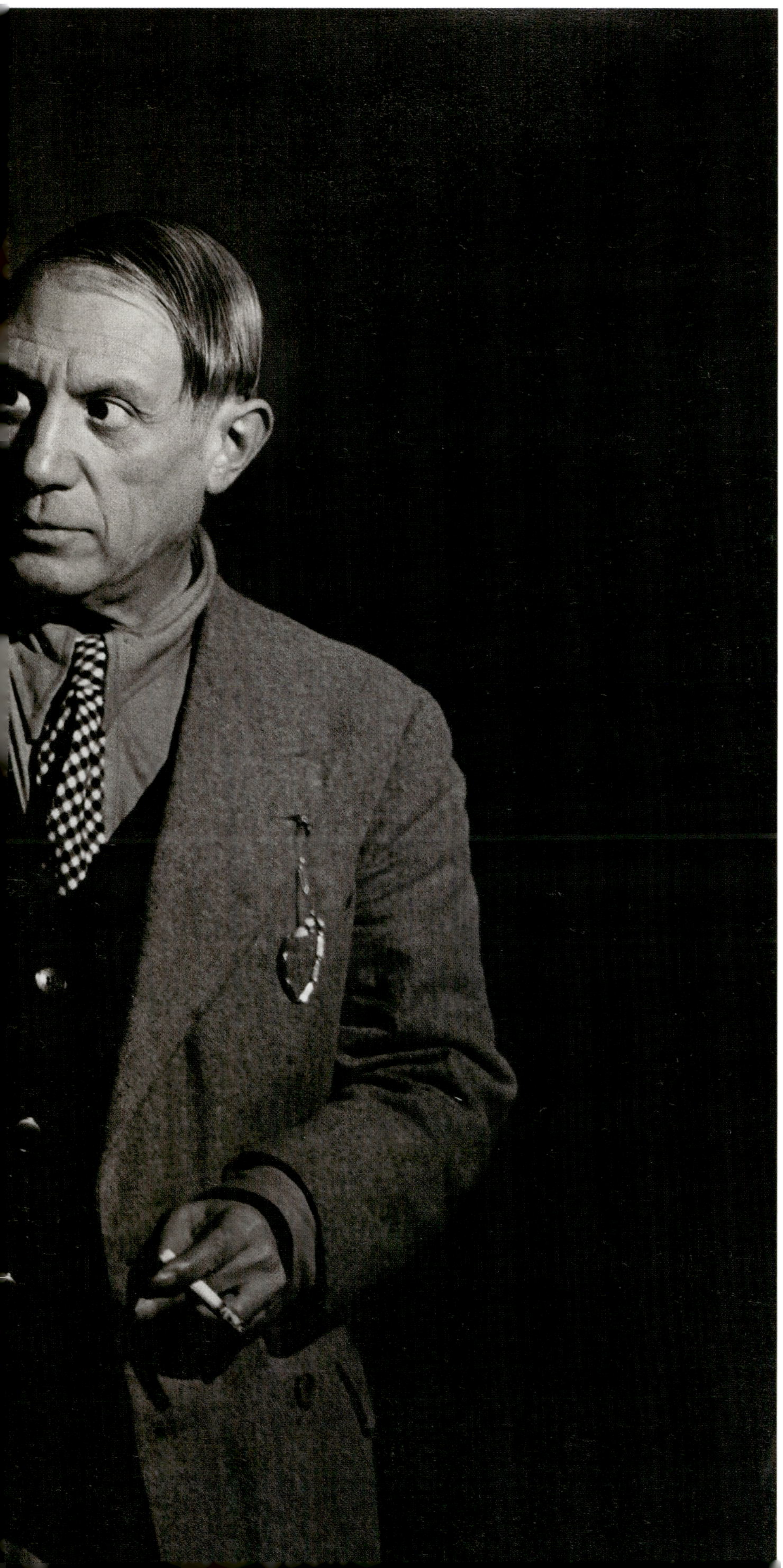

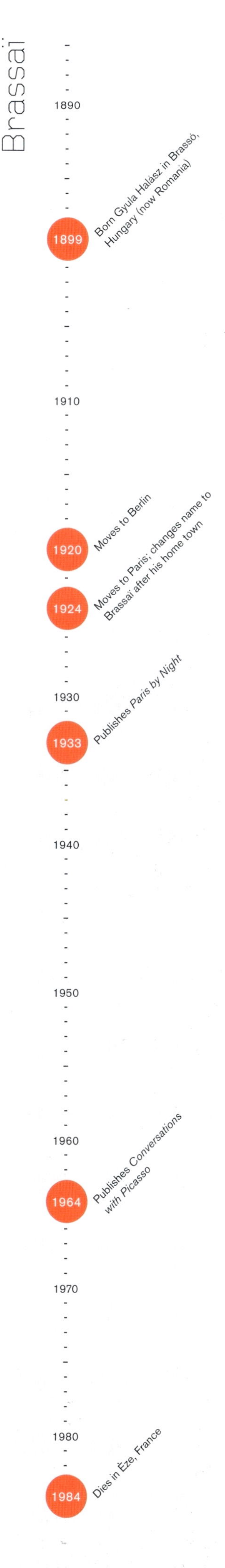

Brassaï
1890
1899
Born Gyula Halász in Brassó, Hungary (now Romania)
1910
1920
Moves to Berlin
1924
Moves to Paris; changes name to Brassaï after his home town
1930
1933
Publishes *Paris by Night*
1940
1950
1960
1964
Publishes *Conversations with Picasso*
1970
1980
1984
Dies in Èze, France

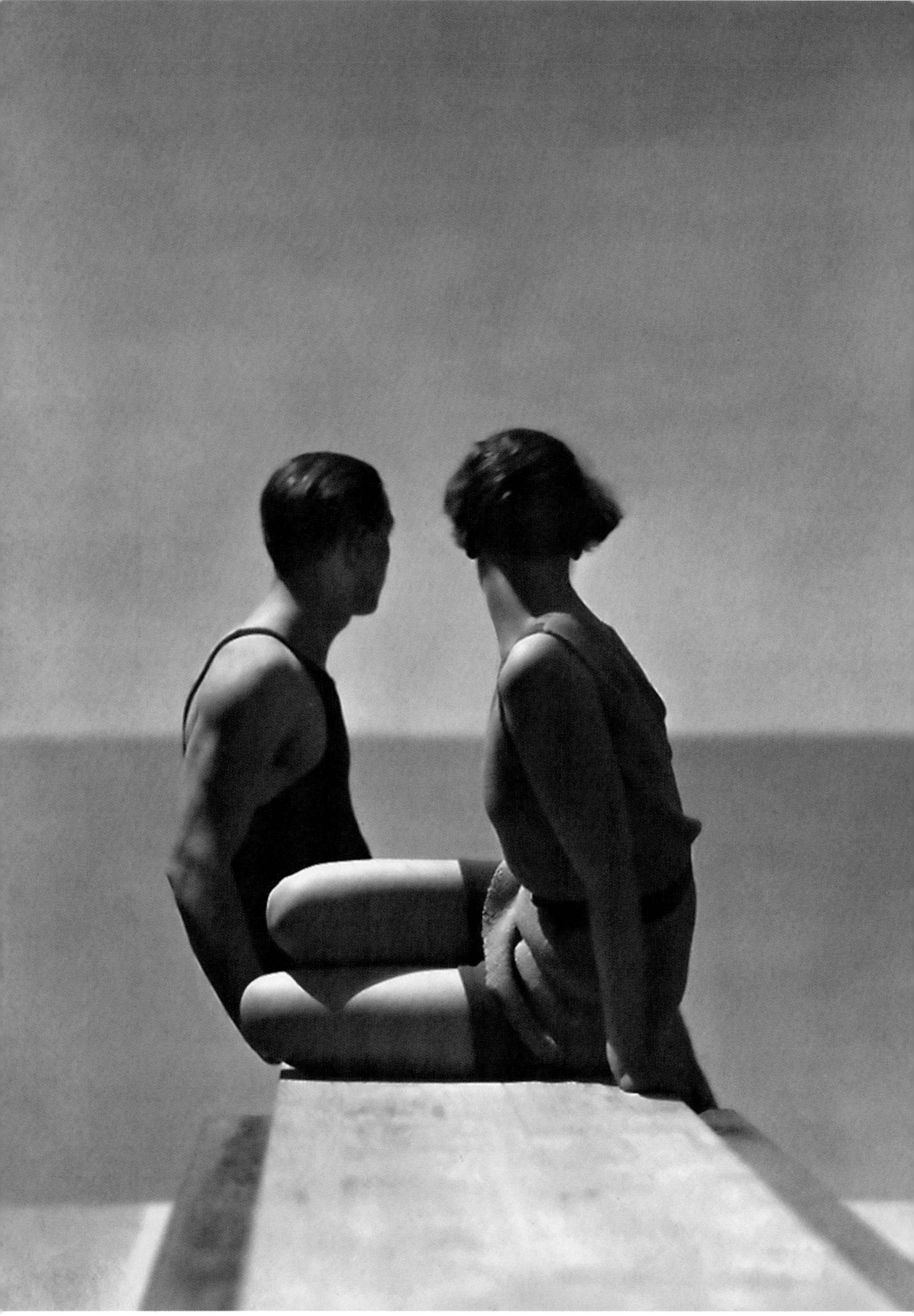

'How would I represent the modern woman in the true light of the period?'

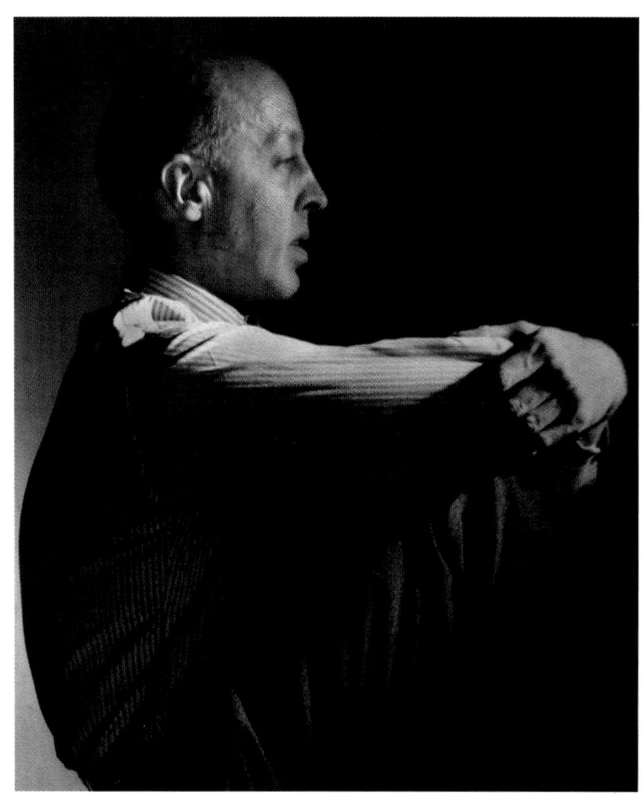

# George Hoyningen-Huene

1900–1968

RUSSIA

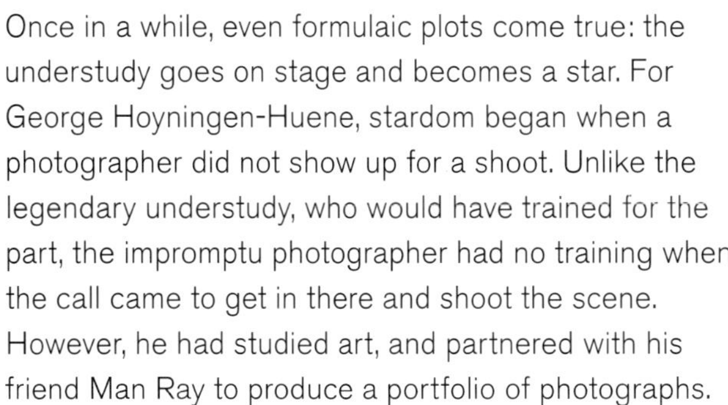

Once in a while, even formulaic plots come true: the understudy goes on stage and becomes a star. For George Hoyningen-Huene, stardom began when a photographer did not show up for a shoot. Unlike the legendary understudy, who would have trained for the part, the impromptu photographer had no training when the call came to get in there and shoot the scene. However, he had studied art, and partnered with his friend Man Ray to produce a portfolio of photographs.

True, false or embellished, the story of Hoyningen-Huene's entry into fashion photography is not surprising. He previously worked as an illustrator, and witnessed at first hand the degree to which photography was eclipsing close rendering in publications. The Paris of the 1920s was not only the capital of Western fashion, but also home to fashion periodicals, such as the French edition of *Vogue*, in which the so-called 'modern woman' was often featured.

Hoyningen-Huene's images blended Classicism with Surrealism. Columns, sculptural heads and busts appear in his work, directly, or by inference in the stances and attitudes of fashion models. In the 1920s, models did not move quickly in front of the camera, as they do today. Instead, they were carefully put into fixed positions by photographers. Hoyningen-Huene, who relished control, sometimes used mannequins in place of humans. Similarly, people who sat for a portrait by him had little choice in how they would be portrayed. Hoyningen-Huene's photography is mainly studio work, where he became skilled at designing spaces and faces with artificial light. Even images that seem to have been taken outdoors, such as the beach- and sportswear pictures he made, were mostly created in the studio, sometimes using lighting equipment of his own invention.

In the post-war era, Hoyningen-Huene's fashion photography quickly lapsed, especially after he moved to Southern California and became an American citizen. He turned his attention to making short movies and consulting on the aesthetics of colour in motion picture films. His tightly controlled studio work was quickly replaced, in the work of such photographers as Richard Avedon, by freer outdoor and location shooting. Despite their differences Avedon called Hoyningen-Huene 'the master of us all', admiring how Hoyningen-Huene's work confirmed that both fashion and fashion photography are art forms.

**Opposite** *Divers,* 1930.

**Above** Portrait of George Hoyningen-Huene by Horst P. Horst, c. 1934.

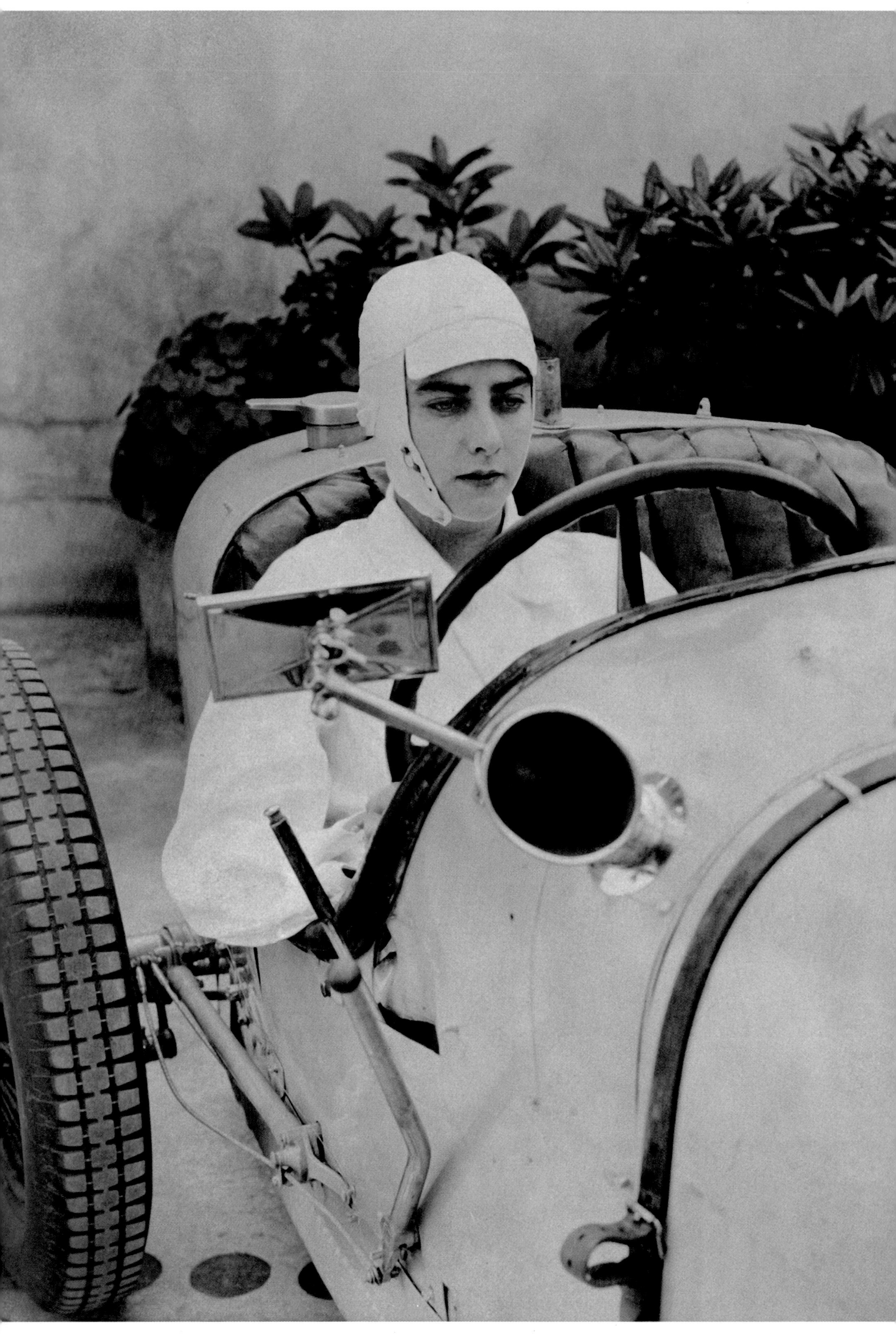

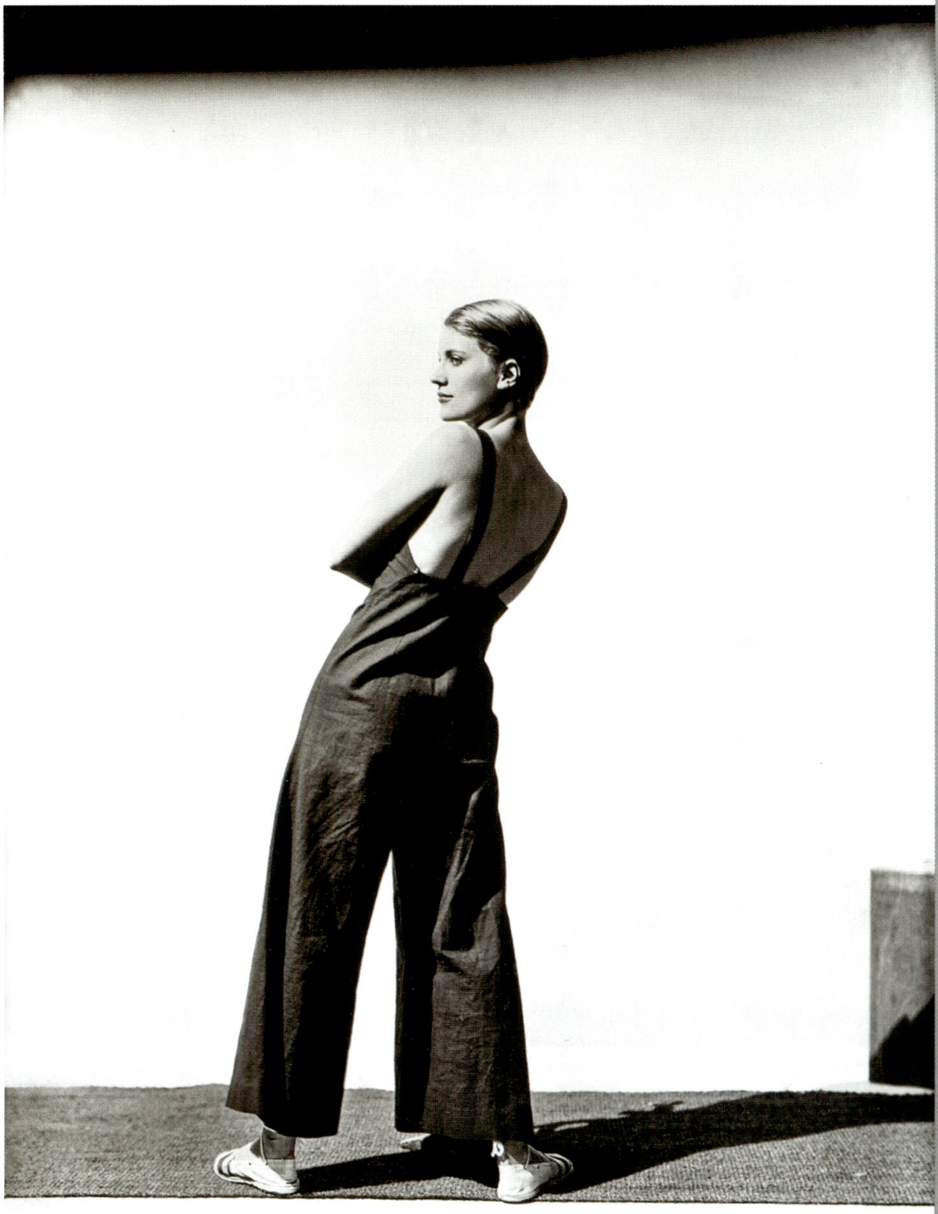

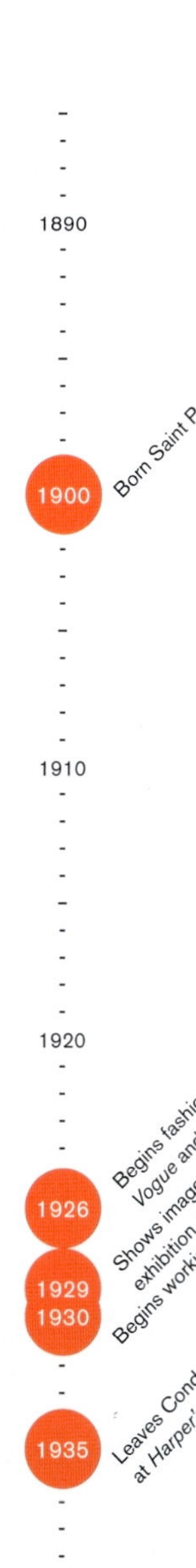

## George Hoyningen-Huene

1890

**1900** Born Saint Petersburg, Russia

1910

1920

**1926** Begins fashion photography at French *Vogue* and *Vanity Fair*

**1929** Shows images in the 'Film und Foto' exhibition, Stuttgart, Germany

**1930** Begins working for Condé Nast

**1935** Leaves Condé Nast and begins working at *Harper's Bazaar* in Paris

1940

**1946** Becomes an American citizen; starts to work on Hollywood motion pictures

1950

1960

**1963** Receives Photokina Photographic Award, Cologne, Germany

**1968** Dies in Los Angeles, USA

**Opposite** *Colette Salomon as 'the modern woman', Vogue,* 1927.

**Above** *Lee Miller Wearing Yraide Sailcloth Overalls*, 1930.

**Right** Mrs Hubbell, 1930.

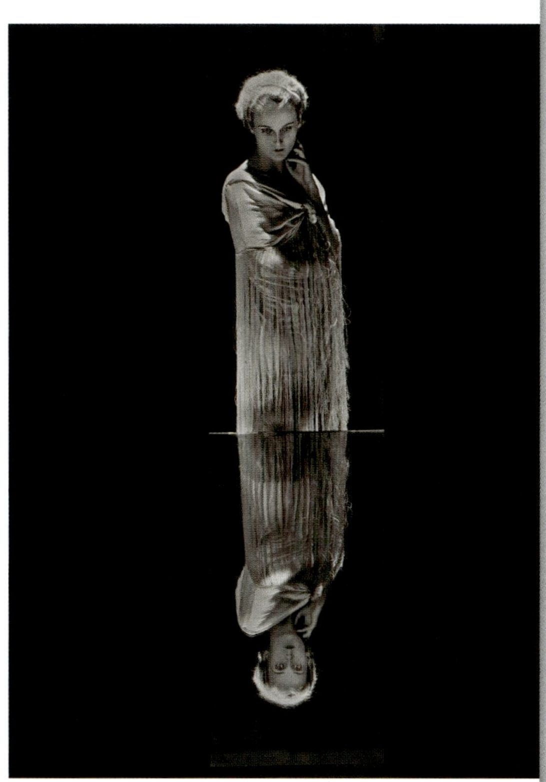

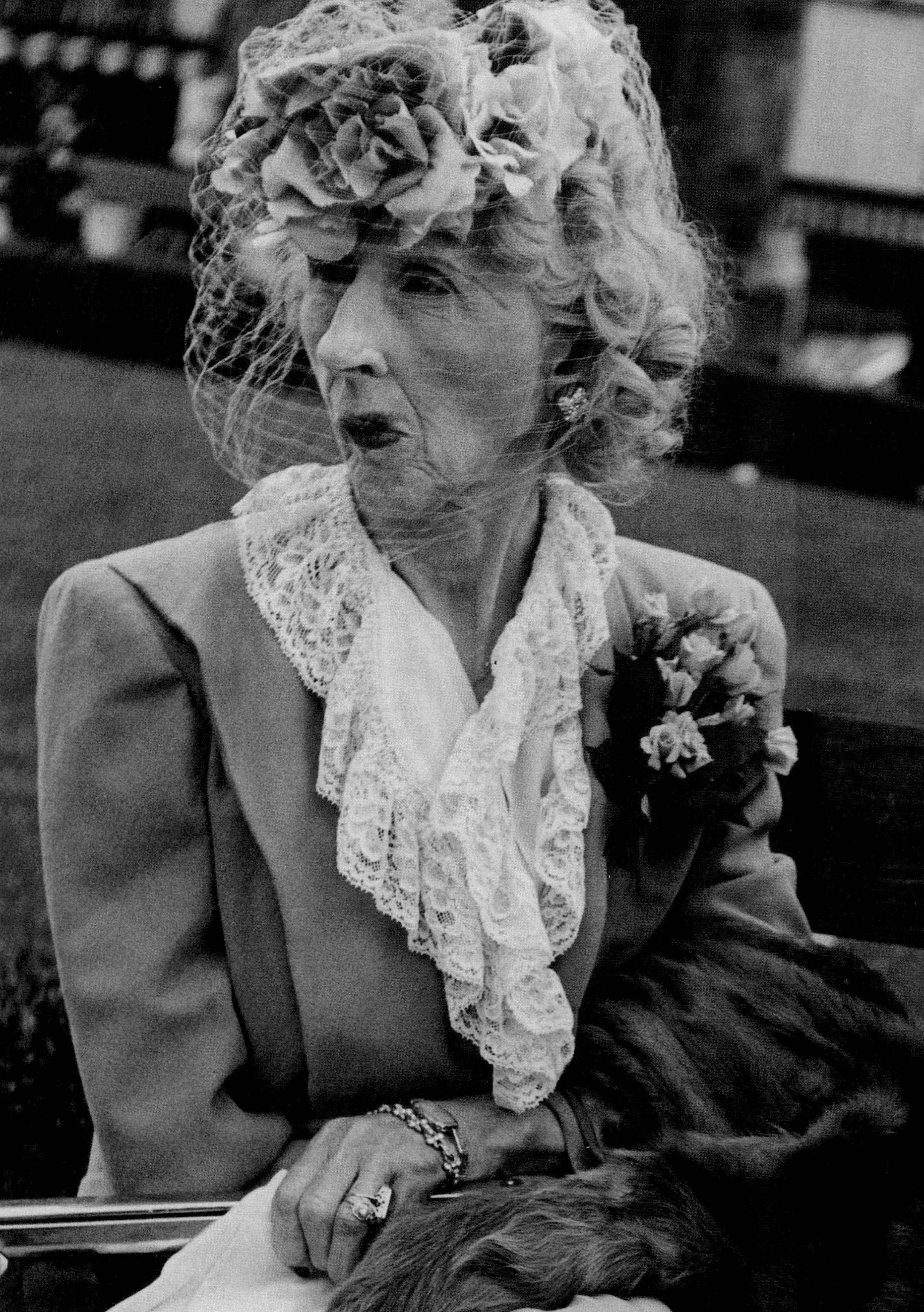

'Shoot from the gut!'

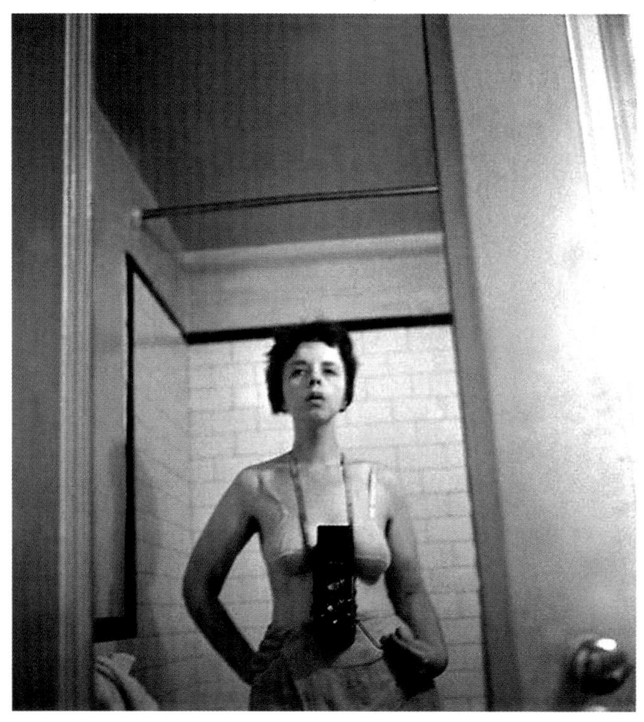

# Lisette Model

1901–1983

AUSTRIA

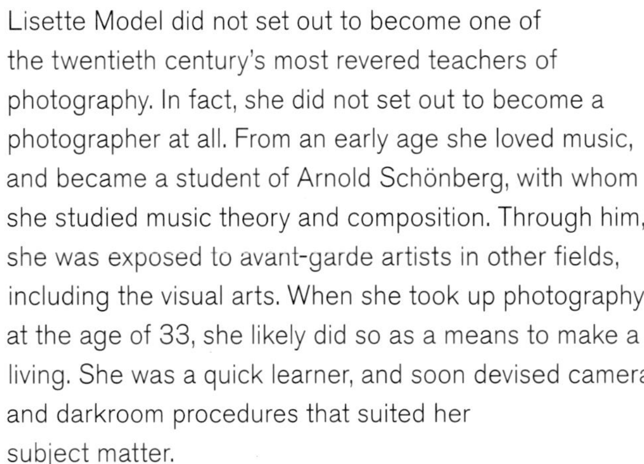

Lisette Model did not set out to become one of the twentieth century's most revered teachers of photography. In fact, she did not set out to become a photographer at all. From an early age she loved music, and became a student of Arnold Schönberg, with whom she studied music theory and composition. Through him, she was exposed to avant-garde artists in other fields, including the visual arts. When she took up photography at the age of 33, she likely did so as a means to make a living. She was a quick learner, and soon devised camera and darkroom procedures that suited her subject matter.

From the look of her finished prints, it seems she took literally her dictum 'Shoot from the gut'. In the so-called belly-button photography of the pre-war years, many cameras were held at waist-level because they had a focusing screen on top, which required the photographer to bow the head to see what the picture would look like. But Model's motto also meant that the photographer should make photographs that instigate a gut reaction in the viewer. That said, Model was more likely to get up close and personal with her subjects in the darkroom than in person. For her, the negative was a starting place within which she found pictures. She then cropped until she got the picture she wanted to enlarge into a final print.

Although Model did several series of street photographs, her strength was in street portraits that explored the coincidence of individualism and eccentricity. Her work shocked some of her colleagues, including Paul Strand (p. 52), who announced: 'You cannot photograph America that way.'

As a teacher, Model had many successful students, including Diane Arbus, Larry Fink, Bruce Weber, Peter Hujar and Eva Rubinstein. The gist of her teaching approach was her own philosophy of picture-making. She encouraged students to be grateful for other image-makers' work but not to imitate it. Moreover, she discouraged variety for its own sake. She urged her students to let themselves first be affected by a scene and then translate that feeling into a picture.

**Opposite** *Woman with Veil, San Francisco,* 1949.

**Above** Self-portrait, 1940s.

**Below** *Belmont Park Race Track, Arms*, 1956.

**Opposite top** *Westminster Kennel Club, Royal Poodle*, c. 1946.

**Opposite bottom** *Wall Street*, c. 1939.

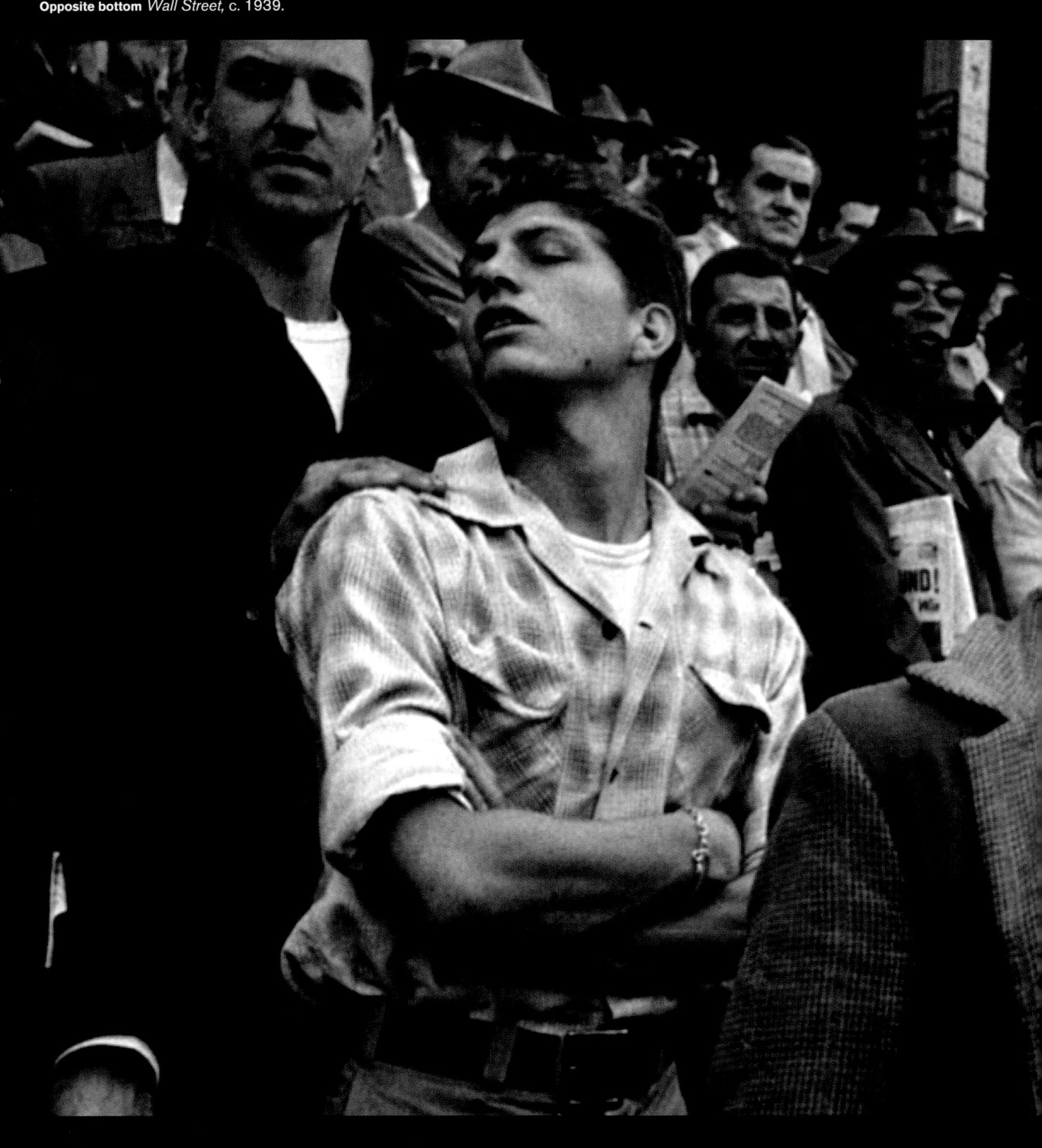

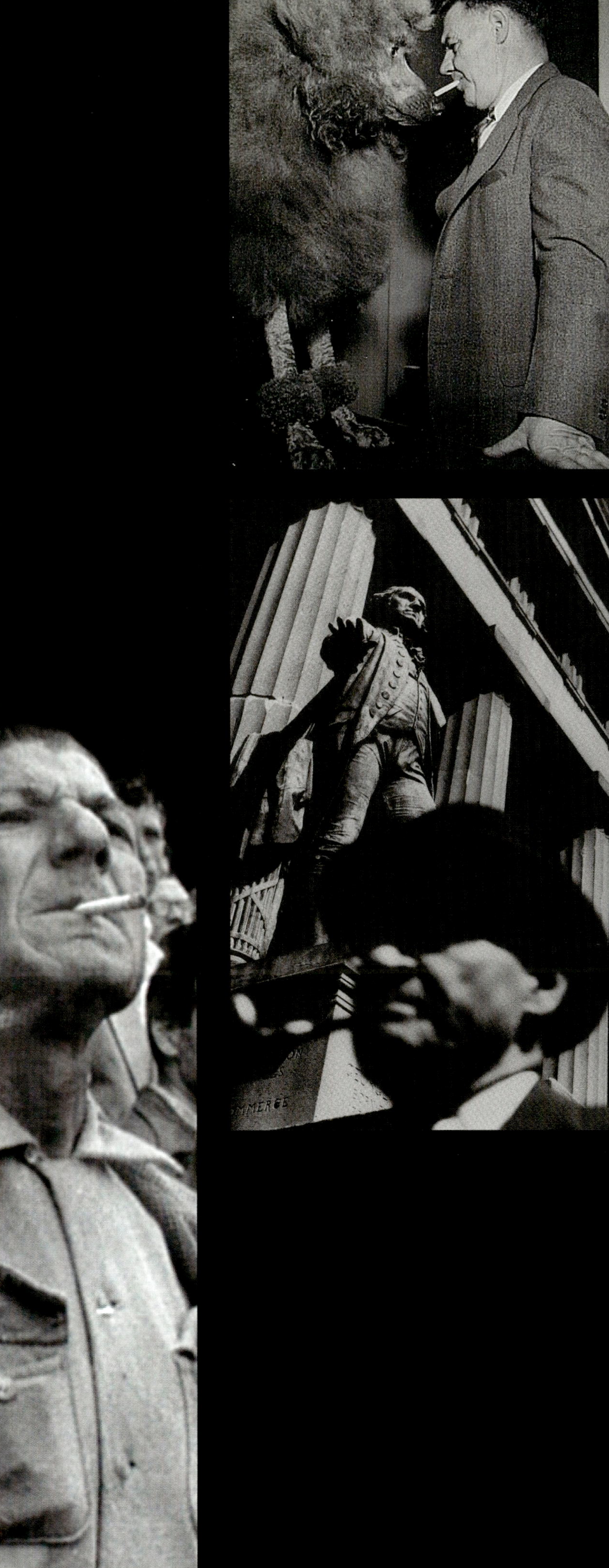

# Lisette Model

1890

1900

1901 Born Elise Amelie Felice Stern (called Lisette) in Vienna, Austria

1910

1920 Begins studying with composer Arnold Schönberg

1926 Moves to Paris; studies voice for several years

1930

1933 Takes up photography as a profession

1935 Produces 'Promenade des Anglais' series

1937 Marries Evsa Model

1938 Moves to New York, where she does magazine work as well as art photography

1941 Exhibits work at the Photo League

1949 Teaches at the New School for Social Research and offers private classes (to 1983)

1960

1970

1980

1983 Dies in New York, USA

*Moonrise and Half Dome, Yosemite Valley*, 1960.

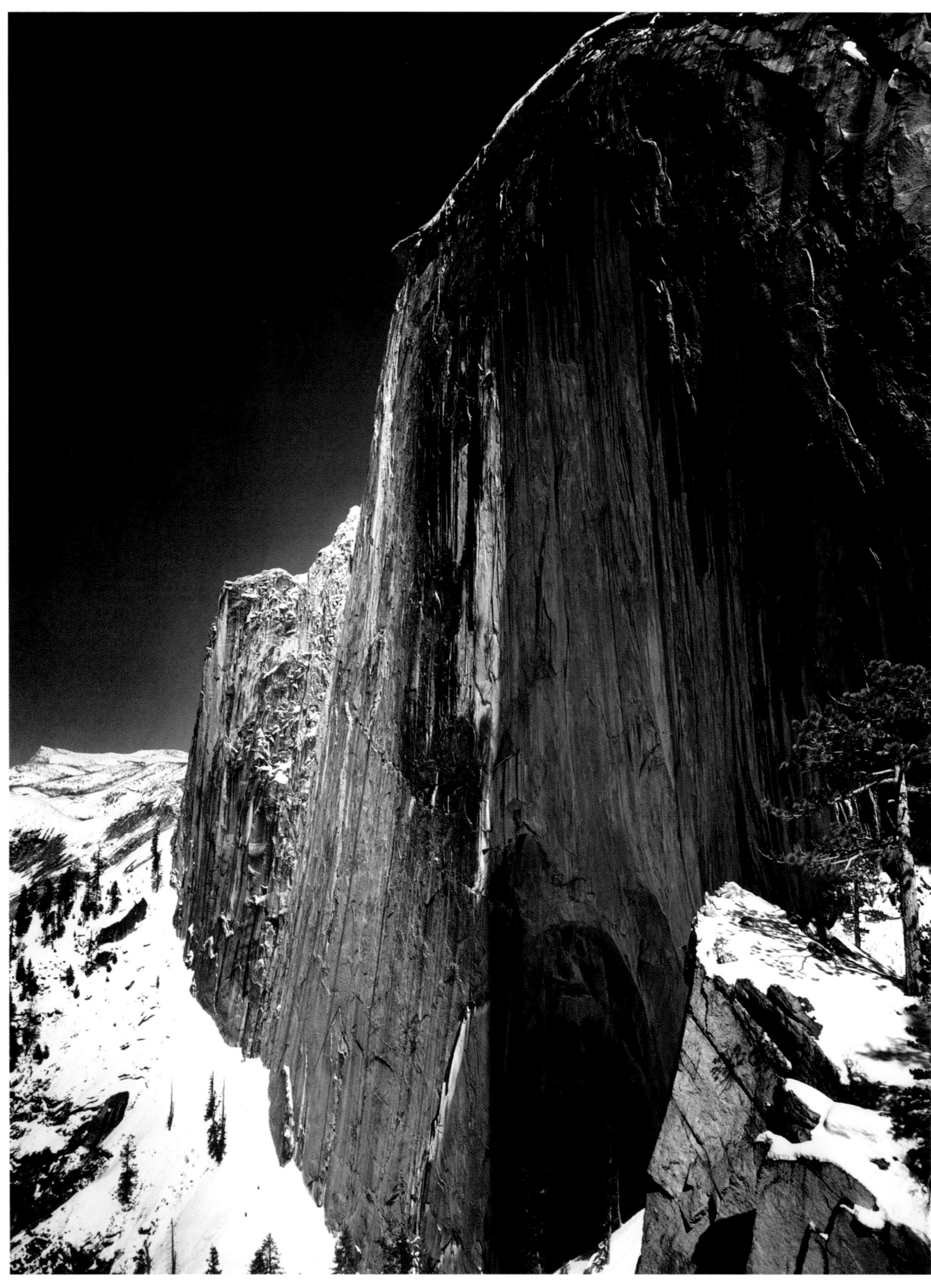

'There is nothing worse than a brilliant image of a fuzzy concept.'

# Ansel Adams

1902–1984

UNITED STATES

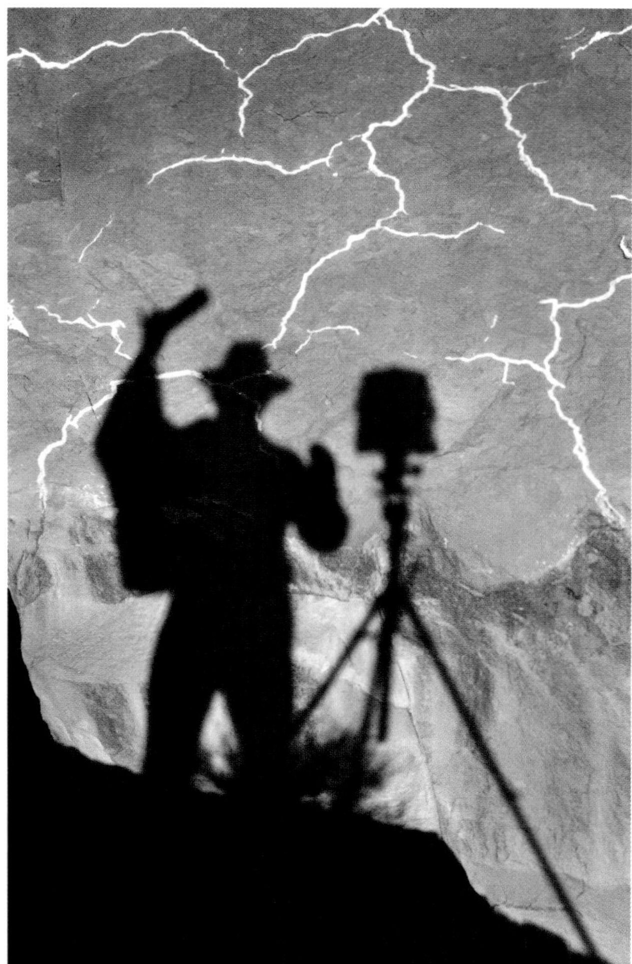

Ansel Adams's photographs of the American West are so well known that they seem to have summed up the man. Indeed, a mountain was named Mount Ansel Adams in the Sierra region of California, near Yosemite National Park, where he worked. His iconic images of pristine wilderness remain unsullied mental icons, even though some of the places they depict have become overcrowded with tourists and endangered by the effects of development and natural-resource recovery.

Adams believed that contact with unadulterated nature was tonic to the soul, and he created his pantheistic photographs with their scintillating silver tones to transmit his experience to viewers. His conservationism was unnuanced; he could not understand why increasing numbers of ecologists argued that to preserve endangered species, the people should be excluded from some public land. Similarly, he saw no contradiction in doing public relations work for mining and drilling companies, because he used the salary to support his nature photography.

In the Depression era, when some of his friends, including Dorothea Lange (p. 72), believed that the times endorsed social action and documentary photography, Adams demurred, favouring the high-minded spirituality of his adopted mentor, Alfred Stieglitz (p. 12). Yet he befriended anti-authoritarian artists, such as Mexican painter and political radical Diego Rivera. When Japanese Americans living on the West Coast were forcibly detained in internment camps during World War II, Adams photographed and wrote about them in a book he uncompromisingly titled *Born Free and Equal*.

An egalitarian streak informs his influential books intended to make the craft and chemistry of photography available to anyone who wanted to take the time to learn it. In theory, Adams's Zone System was thoroughly democratic. One 'previsualized' the final photograph by translating a scene into an elaborate declension of darks and lights, which could be achieved with lenses, filters and film, as well as in the darkroom. The Zone System was analogous to musical notation, which could be translated through the mind and skill of a musician into a greater entity.

*Self-portrait, Monument Valley, Utah,* 1958.

*Winter Sunrise, Sierra Nevada*, 1944.

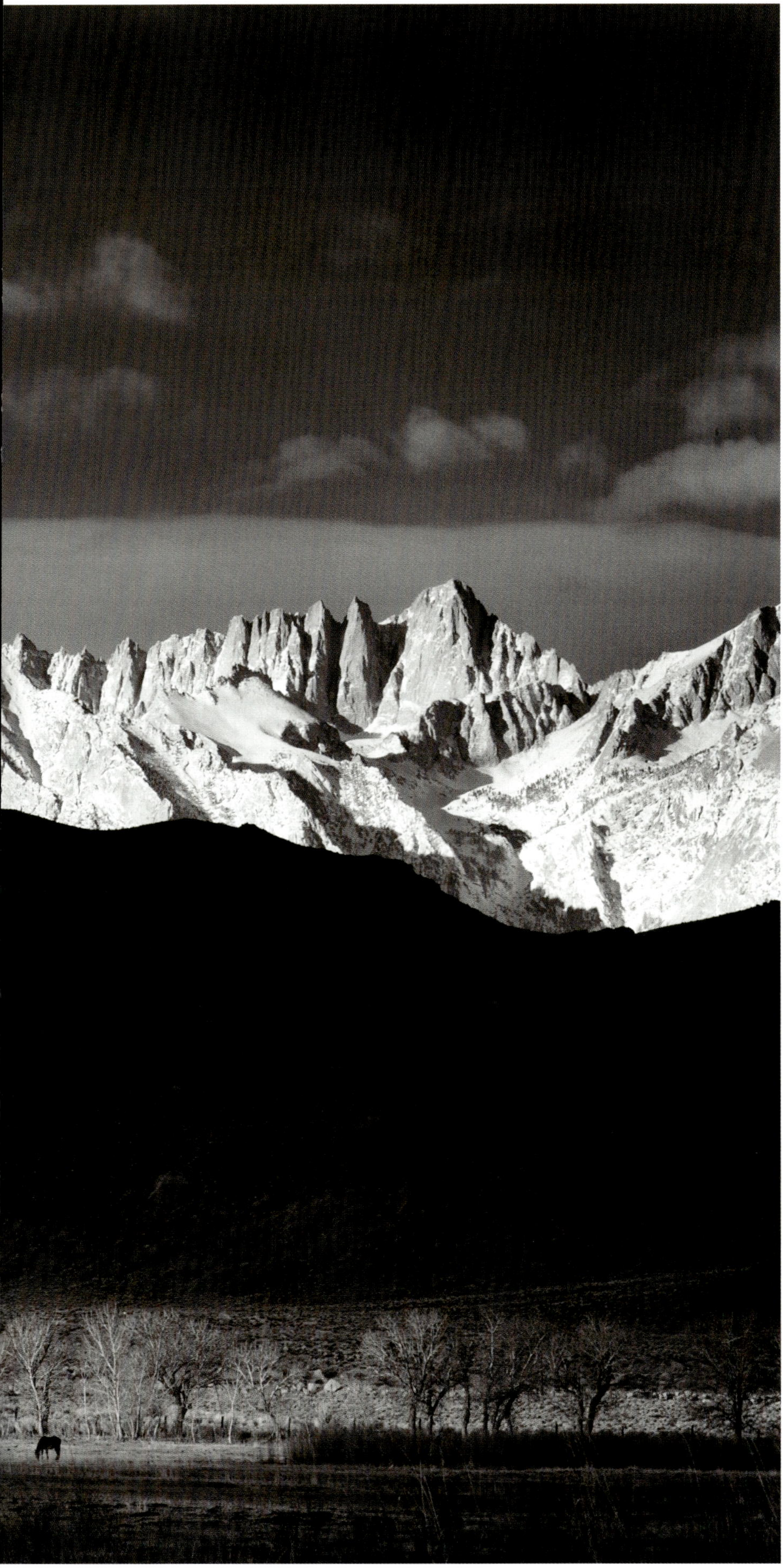

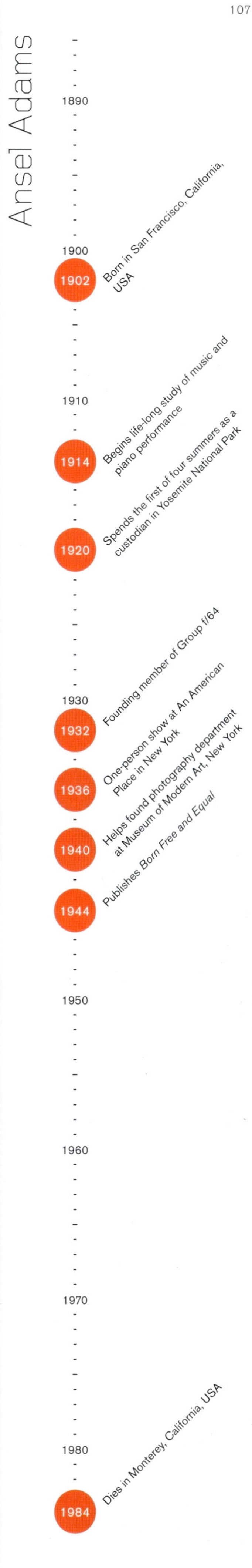

Ansel Adams
1890
1900
1902 Born in San Francisco, California, USA
1910
1914 Begins life-long study of music and piano performance
1920 Spends the first of four summers as a custodian in Yosemite National Park
1930
1932 Founding member of Group f/64
1936 One-person show at An American Place in New York
1940 Helps found photography department at Museum of Modern Art, New York
1944 Publishes Born Free and Equal
1950
1960
1970
1980
1984 Dies in Monterey, California, USA

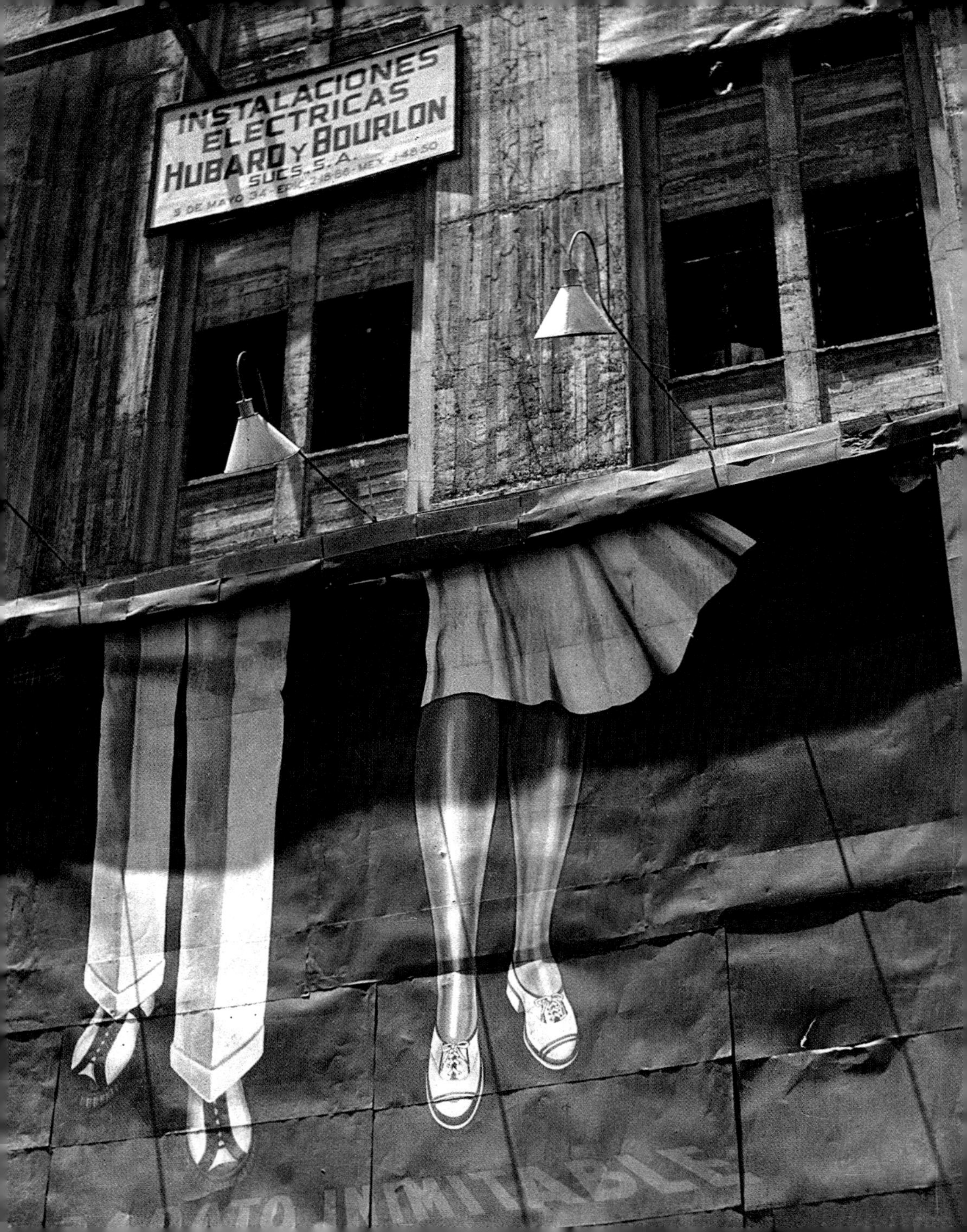
INSTALACIONES
ELECTRICAS
HUBARD y BOURLON
SUCS. S.A.
INIMITABLE

'I cannot say that I work, exactly. It is part of my life to take photographs, to develop.'

# Manuel Álvarez Bravo

1902–2002

MEXICO

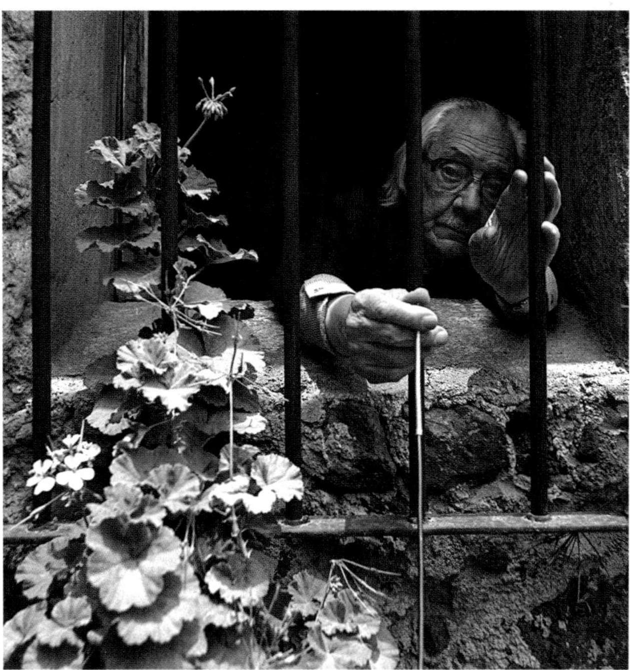

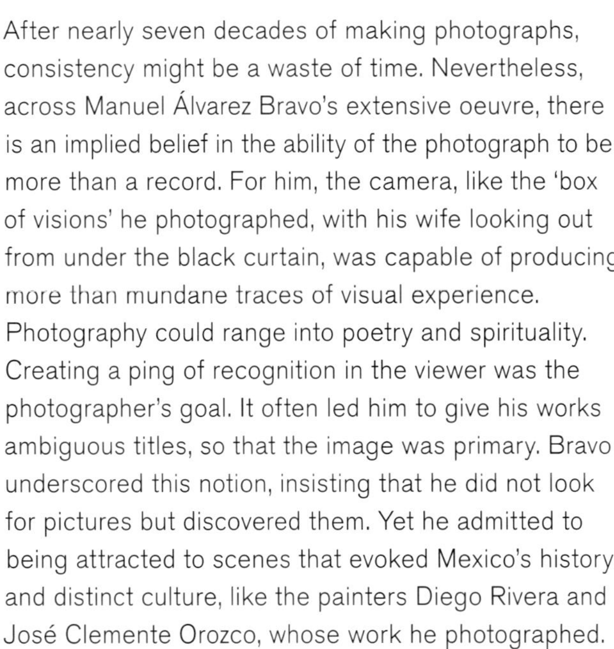

After nearly seven decades of making photographs, consistency might be a waste of time. Nevertheless, across Manuel Álvarez Bravo's extensive oeuvre, there is an implied belief in the ability of the photograph to be more than a record. For him, the camera, like the 'box of visions' he photographed, with his wife looking out from under the black curtain, was capable of producing more than mundane traces of visual experience. Photography could range into poetry and spirituality. Creating a ping of recognition in the viewer was the photographer's goal. It often led him to give his works ambiguous titles, so that the image was primary. Bravo underscored this notion, insisting that he did not look for pictures but discovered them. Yet he admitted to being attracted to scenes that evoked Mexico's history and distinct culture, like the painters Diego Rivera and José Clemente Orozco, whose work he photographed.

His photographs offer enigmas to be savoured, if not understood. Although resting only on a thin sheet covering a concrete slab, a seemingly sleeping young man does not come across as homeless but enviably enrapt in a dream or a vision. The light that outlines his figure is reminiscent of Baroque art, as is the suggestion of sexuality mixed with ecstasy. While many of Bravo's images, such as his street photographs, were found rather than created for the camera, he also took chance to mean that sometimes imagery could be constructed for the camera. *The Good Reputation Sleeping* was composed with elements understood in traditional Mexican culture, such as the protective qualities of some cacti and the role of dancers in ancient sculptural relief. Although the picture was admired by Surrealist André Breton, it was not created with Western Surrealism in mind. Bravo's indirect yet fervent attention to Mexican culture, including pre-Hispanic elements, influenced subsequent generations of Mexican photographers, who, regardless of their outlooks, have had to come to terms with his work.

**Opposite** *Two Pairs of Legs,* 1928–29.

**Above** *Self-portrait in a window,* 1982.

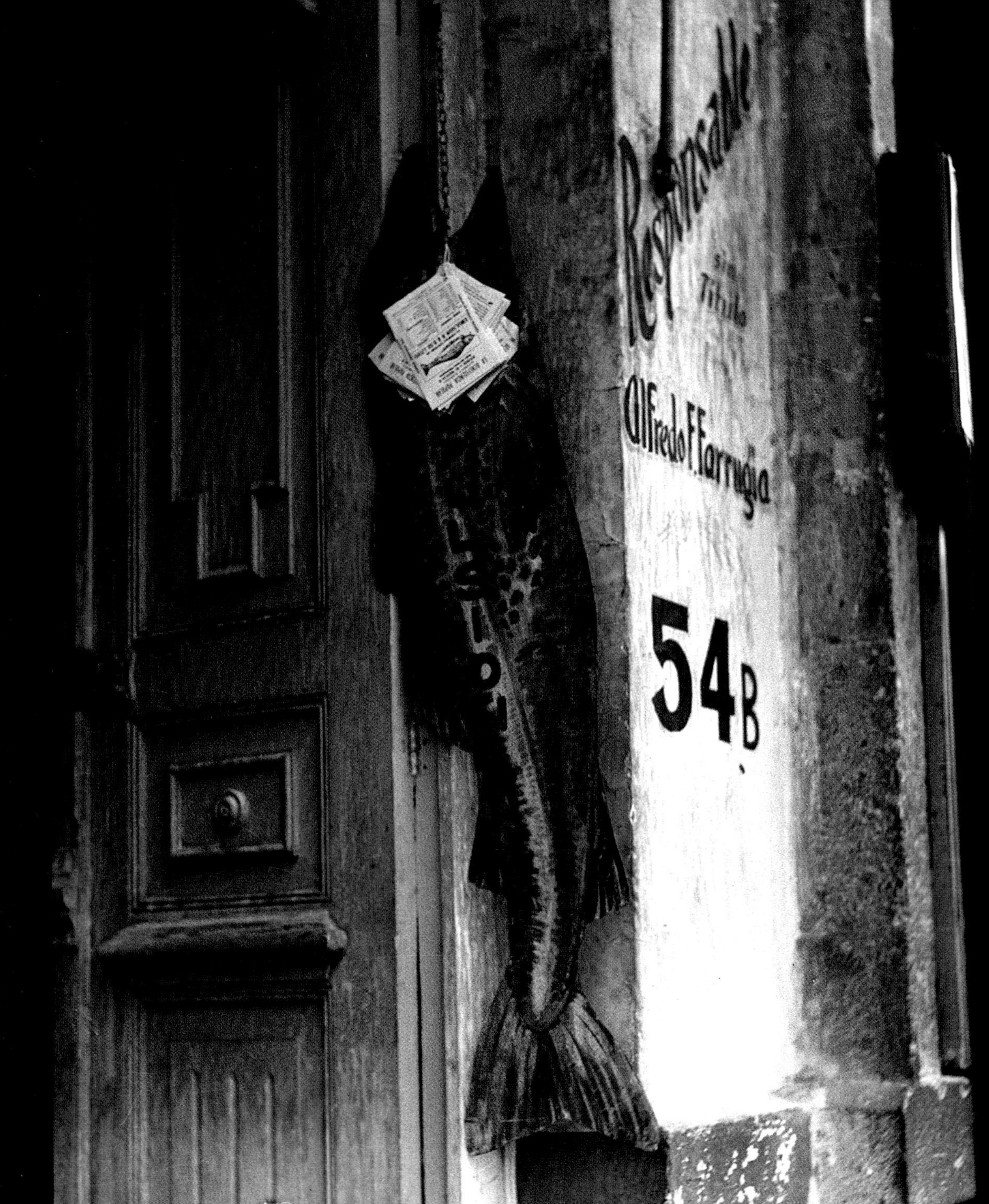
Responsabbli
Alfredo F. Farrugia
54 B

# Manuel Álvarez Bravo

**1902** Born in Mexico City, Mexico

**1923** Meets Tina Modotti and Edward Weston, who are living in Mexico, around this time

**1924** Gets his first camera

**1929** Begins to photograph the work of Mexican muralists, including Diego Rivera

**1933** Meets Paul Strand, who is filming *Redes*

**1935** Meets André Breton; exhibits in Mexico City Surrealist exhibition

**1955** Exhibits in 'The Family of Man', Museum of Modern Art, New York

**1984** Receives the Hasselblad Award in Sweden

**1997** Retrospective at the Museum of Modern Art, New York

**2002** Dies in Mexico City, Mexico

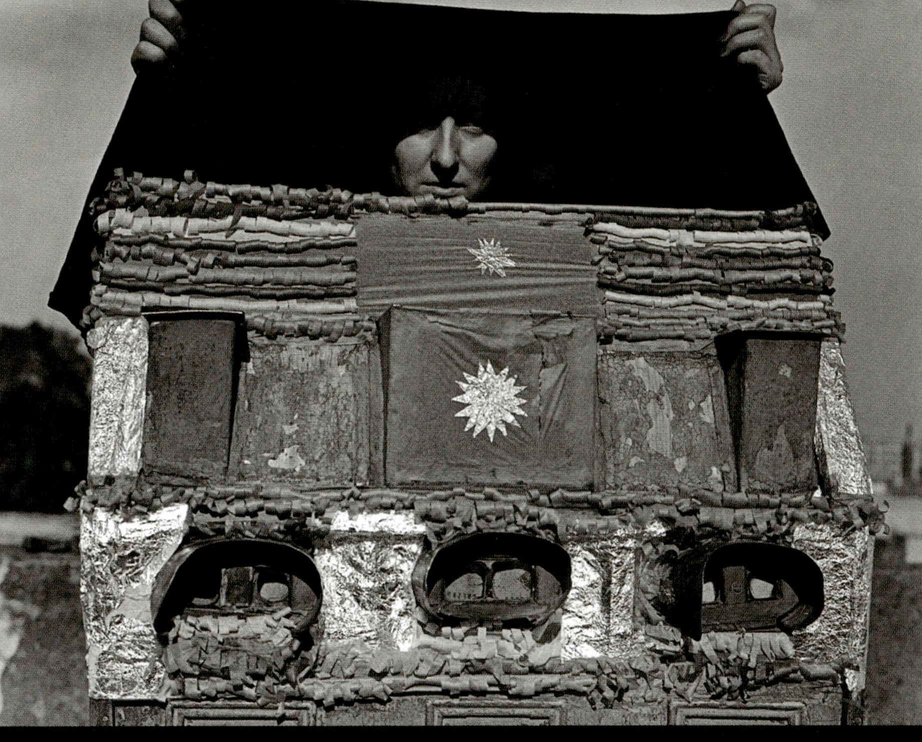

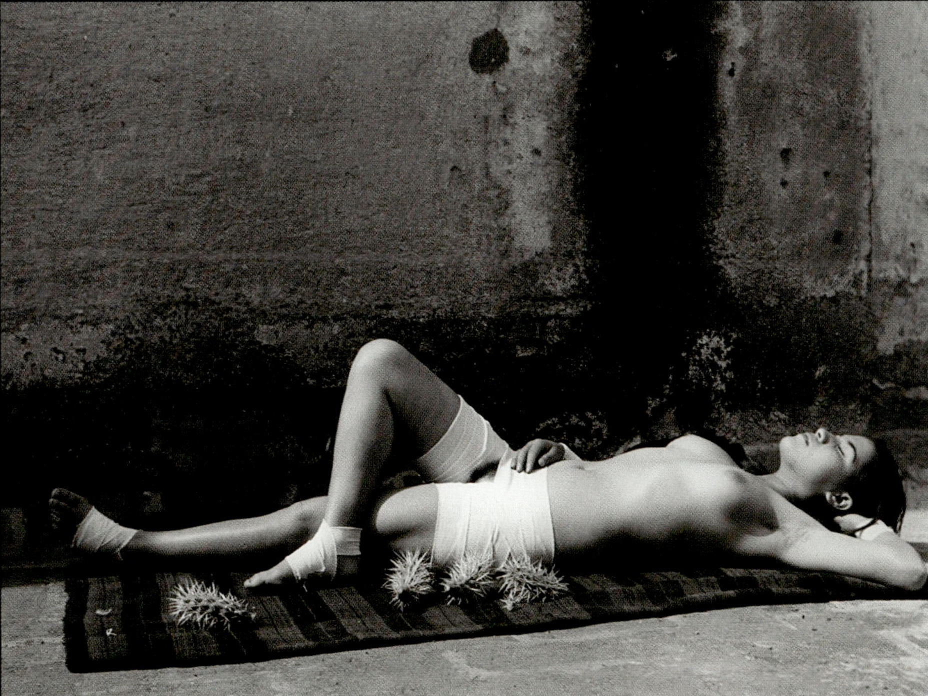

**Above top** *Box of Visions*, 1938.

**Above** *The Good Reputation Sleeping*, 1938–39.

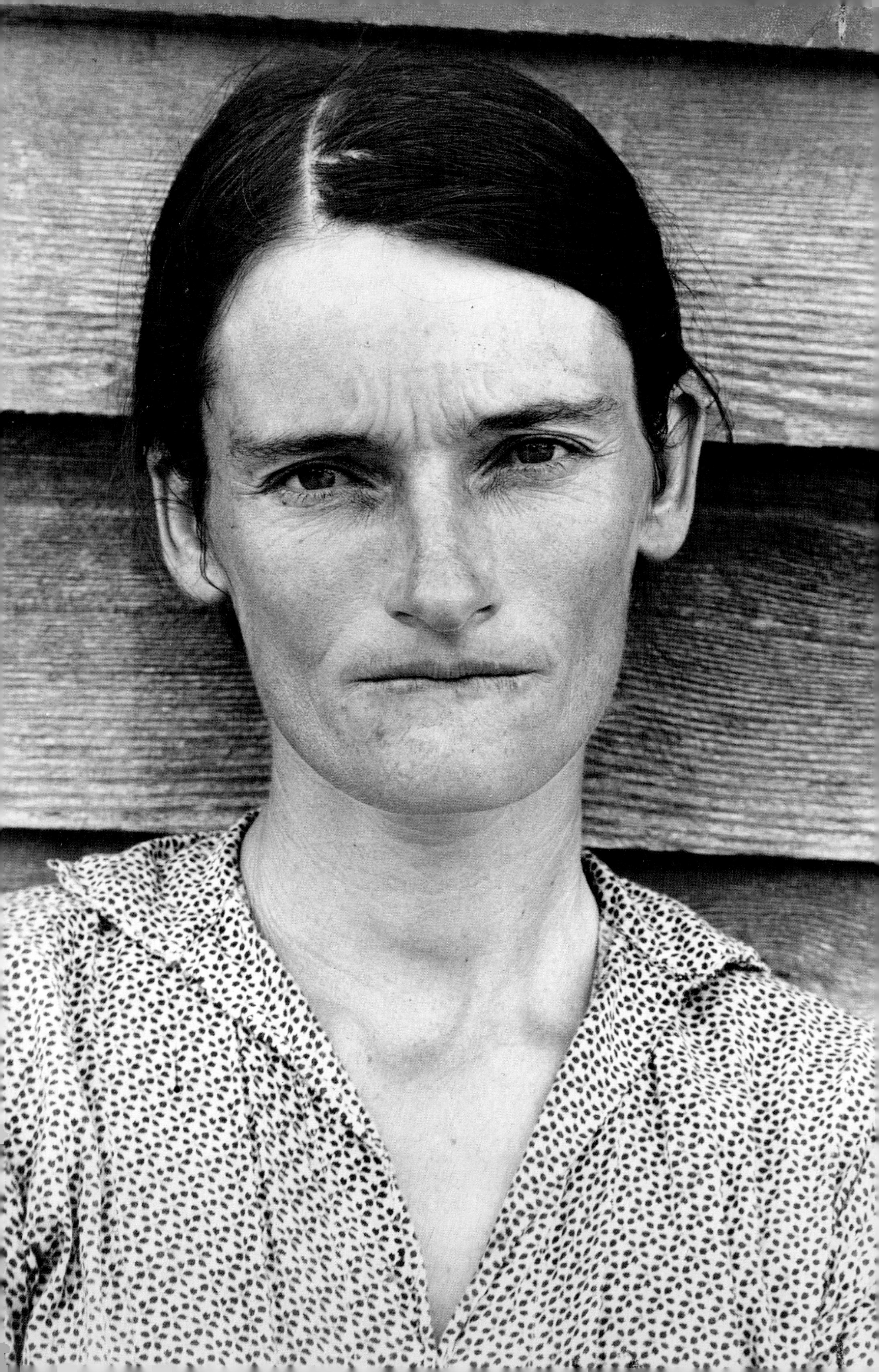

'You don't want your work to spring from art; you want it to commence from life, and that's in the street now.'

# Walker Evans

1903–1975

UNITED STATES

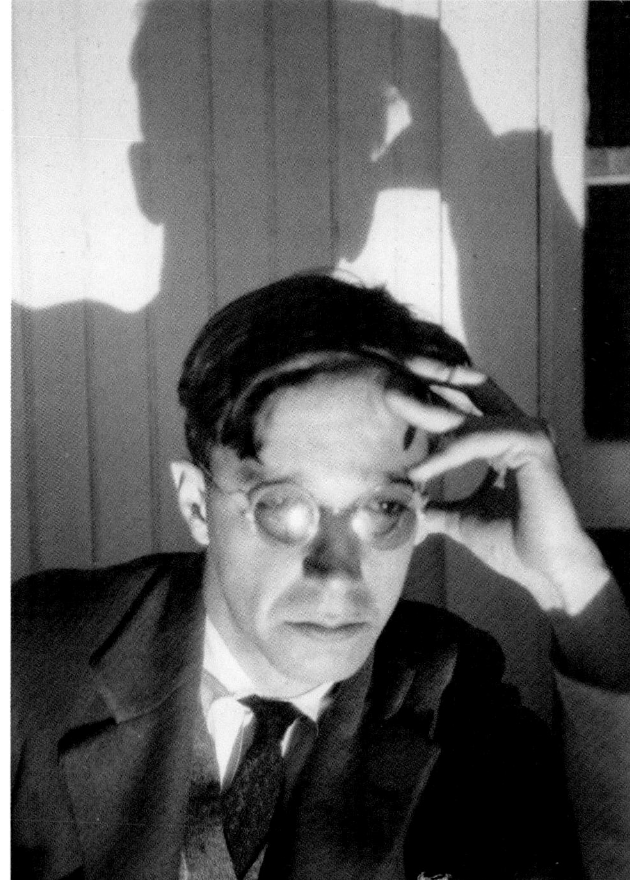

Although he attended some of the most prestigious schools in the United States, Walker Evans was largely self-taught. His passion was recent and contemporary poetry and fiction, with an emphasis on French literature. Photography came later, but with such force that he compared its arrival with an illness: 'Couldn't think about anything else. I just caught it, like a disease.' A devoted Francophile, he combined the ideas of the writer Charles Baudelaire, whom he read closely about becoming a connoisseur of scenes on the modern city street, with an appreciation for Eugène Atget's unsentimental visual chronicles of Paris neighbourhoods (p. 8).

His early work employed the sharp and disturbing angles of European Modernism and an experimental aspect. Using a right-angled lens that led those who might object to assume that he was shooting straight ahead, he began making photographs of people on the street.

Evans vacillated between simply observing and actively interpreting scenes before his camera. In his work for the Farm Security Administration during the Depression, he became a storyteller, condensing ideas in shots calculated to invite the viewer's participation. His belief that pictures should be understood as narratives compelled him to cluster unlabelled, undated photographs at the front of *Let Us Now Praise Famous Men,* the chronicle of tenant-farmer life that he and James Agee published in 1941. But in his extensive records of vernacular architecture, the building stands on its own, as do his many photographs of billboards and signs. Indeed, Evans was so fond of signs that he carried a tool kit with him so he could pilfer his favourites.

With photographer Helen Levitt as his willing co-conspirator, he brought his camera into what he called 'the swaying sweatbox' – that is, the New York City subway – where, with the camera lens peeking out of his coat, he stalked people unawares. A complicated, contradictory man, he deplored colour photography as vulgar: 'a bebop of electric blues, furious reds, and poison greens.' Yet this self-proclaimed 'grey man' produced lyrical colour photographs during two decades of working for *Fortune* magazine.

**Opposite** *Allie Mae Burroughs, Hale County, Alabama*, 1936.

**Above** Portrait of Walker Evans by Paul Grotz 1929.

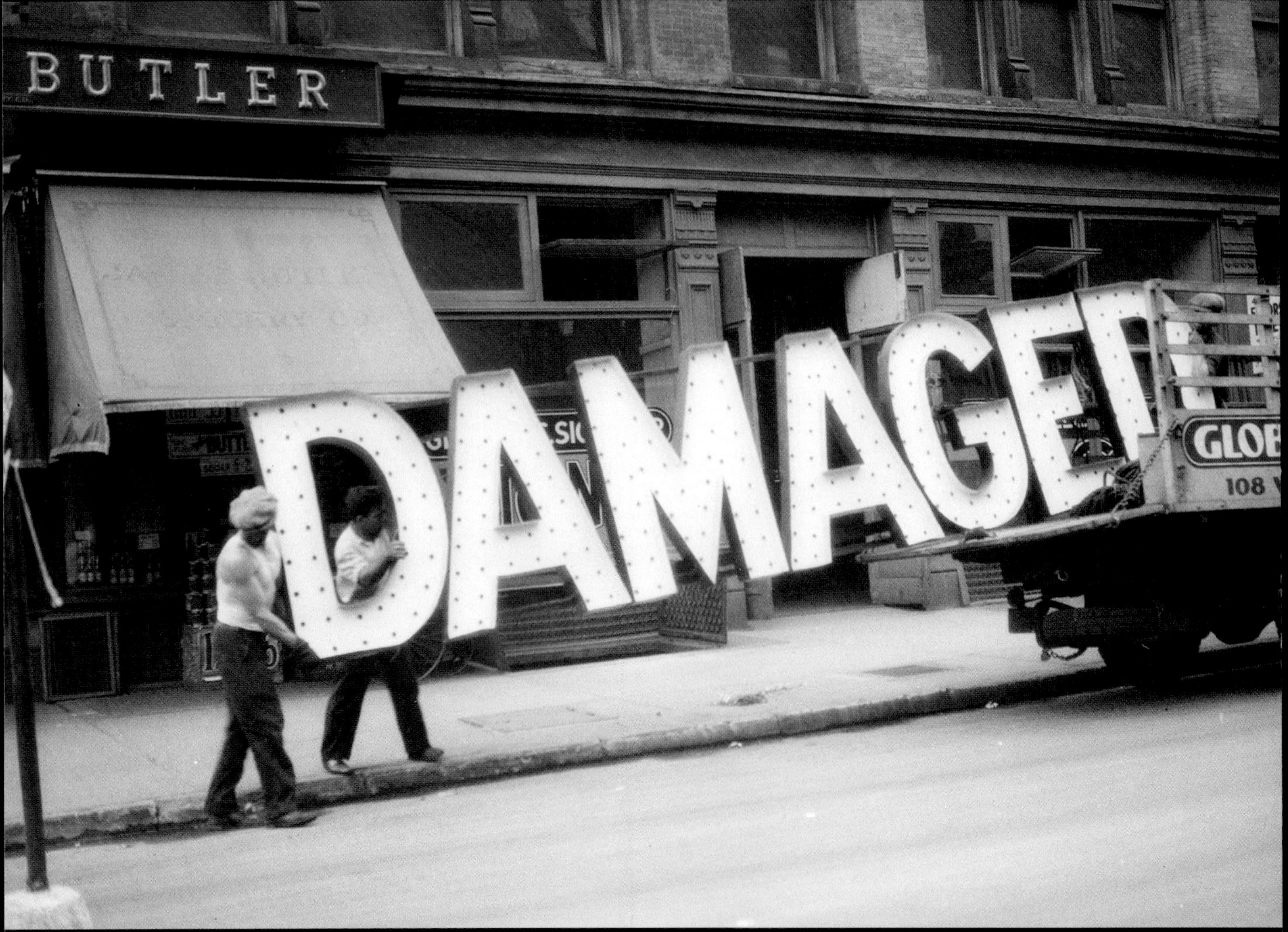

**Above** *DAMAGED*, 1928–30.

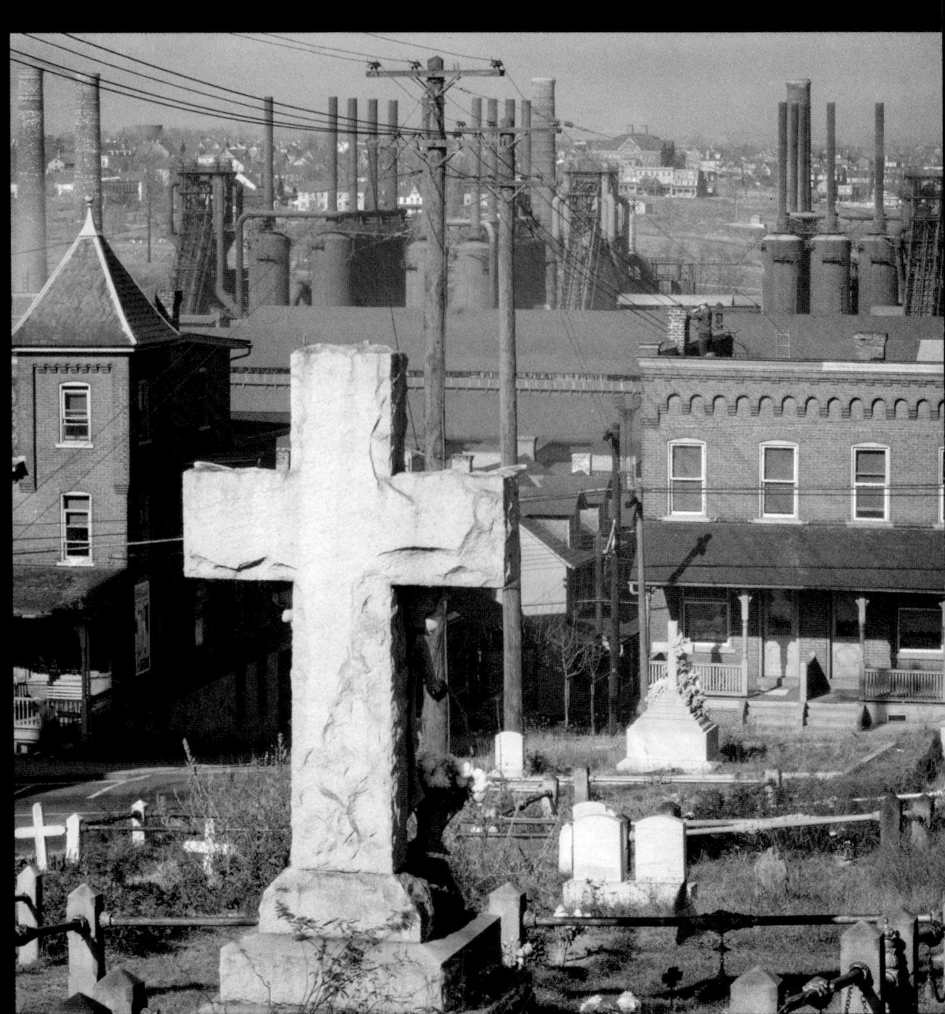

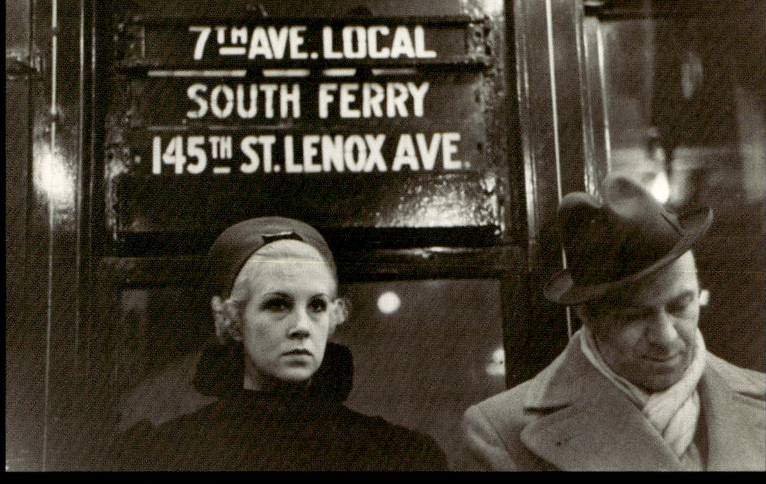


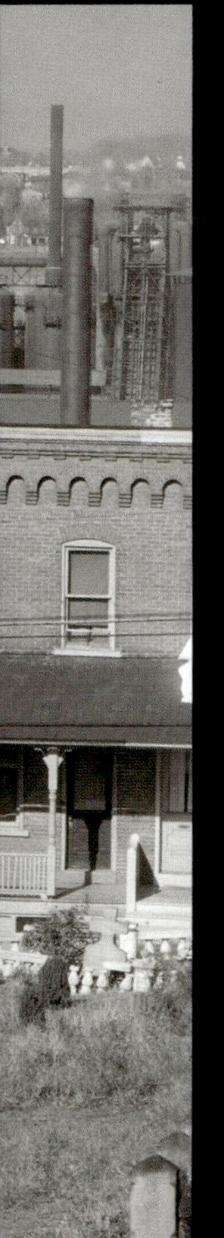

**Left** *Graveyard and Steel Mill*, 1935.

**Above** *Subway Passengers*, 1938–41.

## Walker Evans

1900

1903 Born in Saint Louis, Missouri, USA

1910

1920

1927 Takes up photography

1930

1933 Photographs in Cuba

1935 Photographs for the Farm Security Administration

1938 Publishes *American Photographs*; begins subway photographs

1941 Publishes *Let Us Now Praise Famous Men*, with James Agee

1945 Staff photographer at *Fortune* magazine (to 1965)

1950

1960

1970

1975 Dies in New Haven, Connecticut, USA

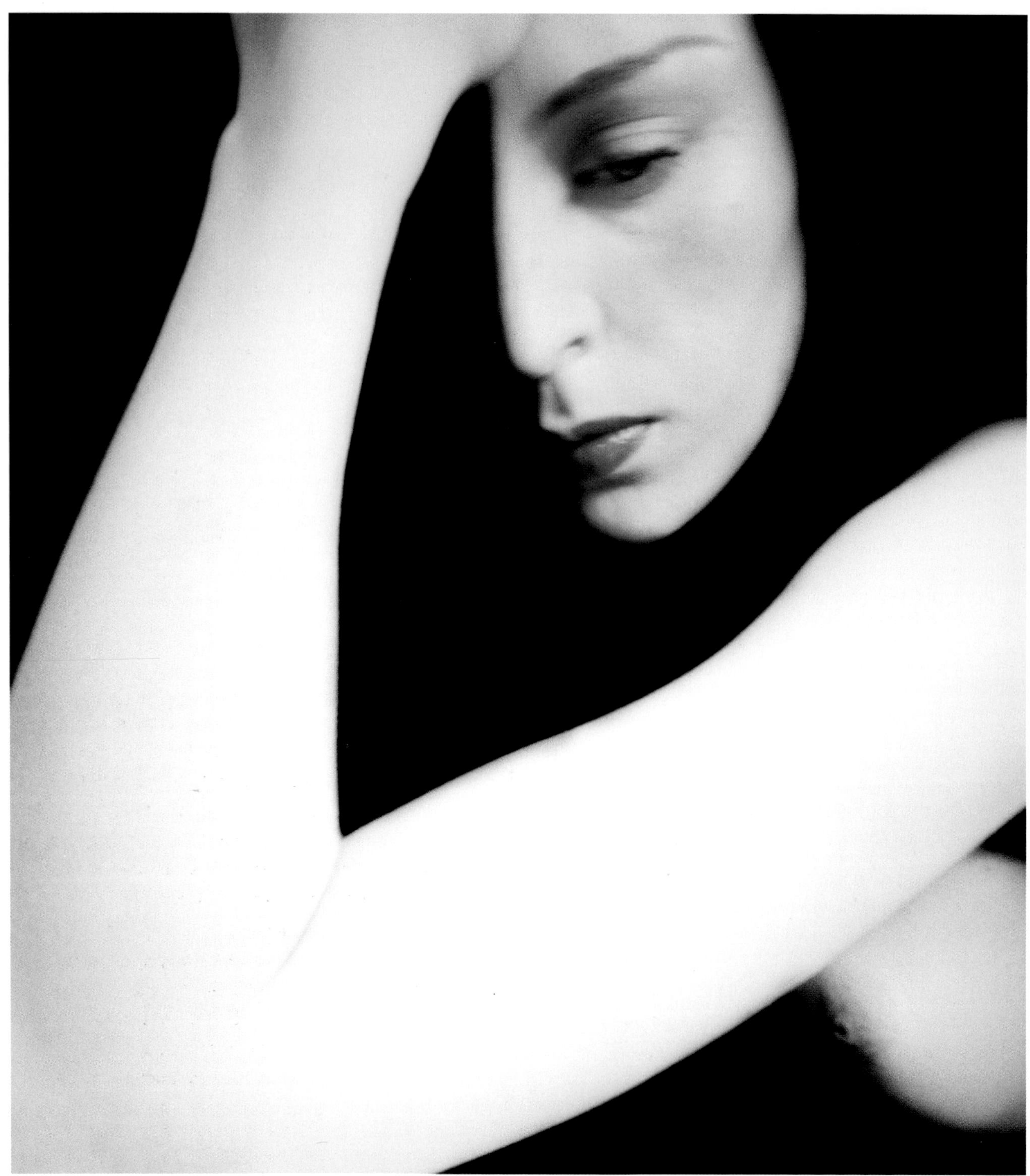

*Nude, London*, 1952.

'We are most of us too busy ... too obsessed with ideas, to stand and stare.'

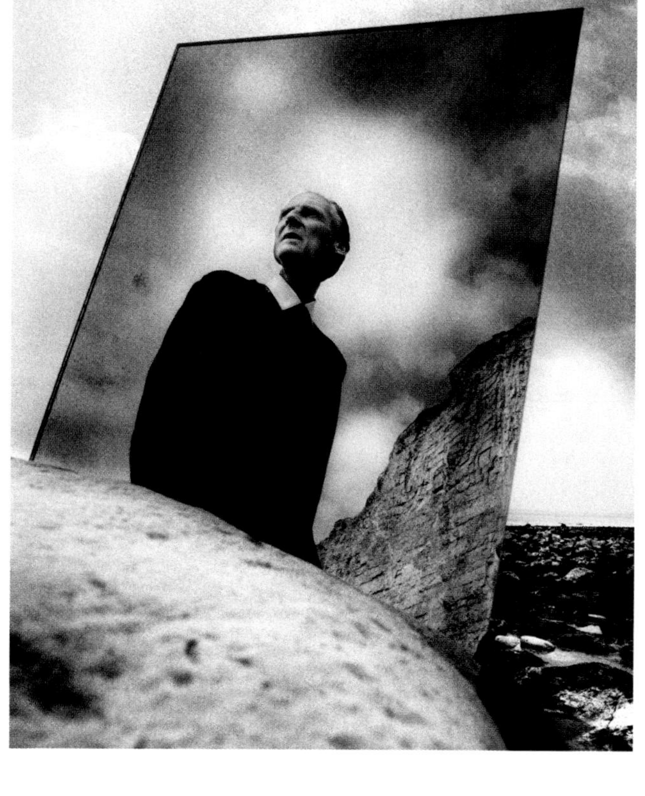

# Bill Brandt

1904–1983

GERMANY

Born in Germany, Bill Brandt enjoyed a cosmopolitan youth, living and studying in Switzerland, Austria and France. When he moved to London in 1932, he easily mingled with sophisticated artists and writers. Paradoxically, his photography was not international, either in style or in subject. In pre-World War II books and magazines, Brand studied British life, chronicling street life in cities as well as daily lives of coal miners, parlourmaids and the upper-classes. His scenes of people sleeping in Underground (subway) tunnels and air-raid shelters during the German bombardments of London were commissioned by the Ministry of Information and widely reproduced, as were Brandt's images of the war at home. He showed people sprawled on the floors trying to sleep, balancing stalwart resistance with evocations of death. These images later emerged as a cherished part of British visual history.

After the war, Brandt expanded on his experimental and Surrealist tendencies, which had been present, if more subtle, in his early work. Lighting always interested him, and he readily employed the newly invented flashbulb. He also experimented with unusual sources of light, such as car headlamps as they fleetingly revealed scenes in the dark night. Although he had spent several pre-war months in Paris and had access to Man Ray's studio, Brandt insisted that he learned little from the prominent Surrealist (p. 48) but learned a great deal from the poets, artists and photographers who were also in the city. For instance, his book *A Night in London* was consciously modelled on Brassaï's *Paris by Night* (p. 93). Brandt imported sinister qualities of Surrealism and the prickle of detective fiction to his early documentary efforts. From this perspective, his post-war nudes and darker tonalities are an intensification of his early work rather than a break with the past. The nudes were made in a period when he felt artistically exhausted. He rebelled by adjusting the camera's lens to produce pictures that mimicked human perception. Pure camera vision, which he tried to achieve in many of the nude studies, resulted in what the human eye judges to be distortions of form and perception, but which Brandt called photographing what the camera sees. He concluded that 'the lens produced anatomical images and shapes which my eyes had never observed'.

Self-portrait, 1966.

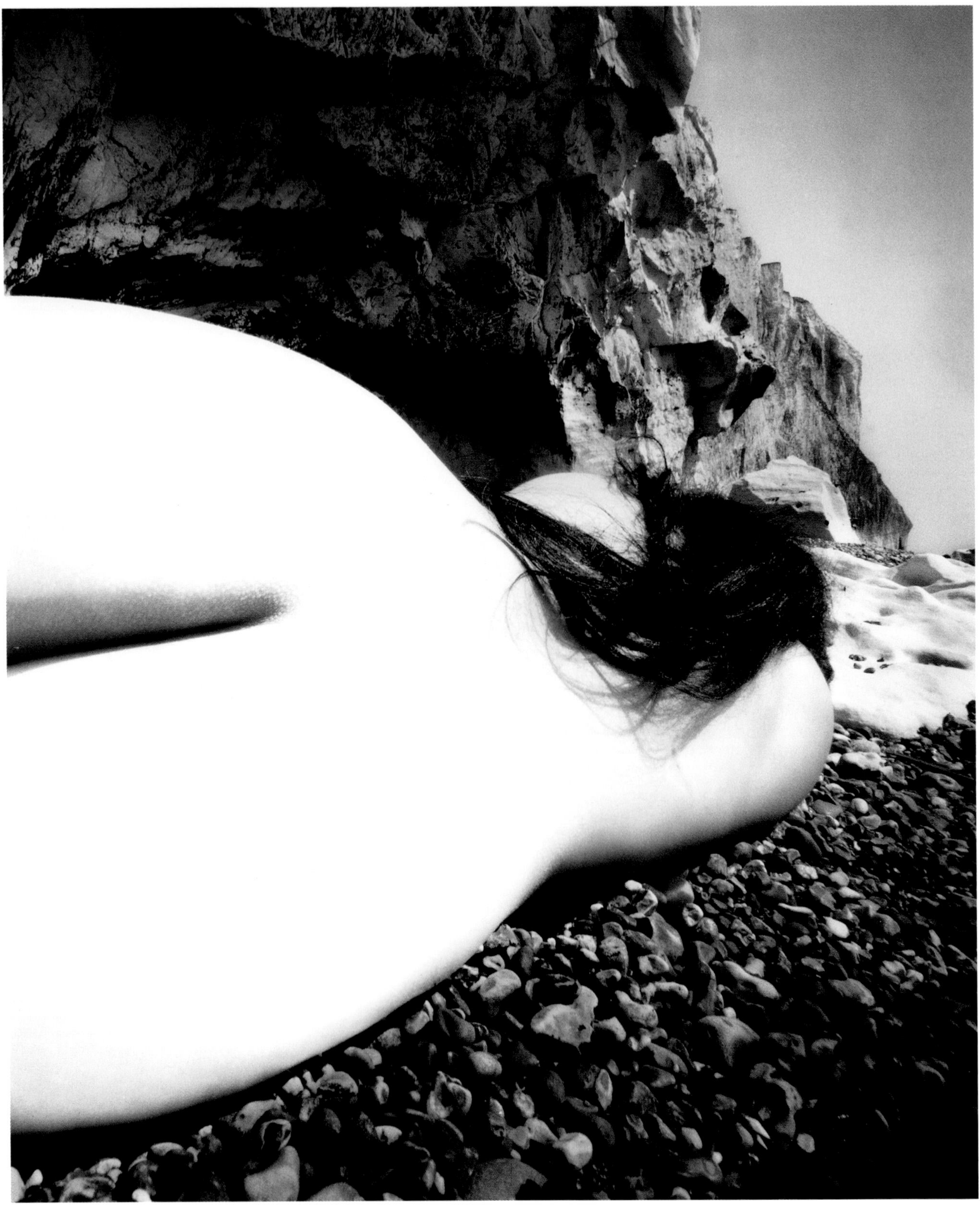

**Above** *Nude, East Sussex Coast,* 1953.

**Opposite top** *People Sheltering in the Tube, Elephant and Castle Underground Station,* 1940.

**Opposite bottom** *Street Scene,* 1936.

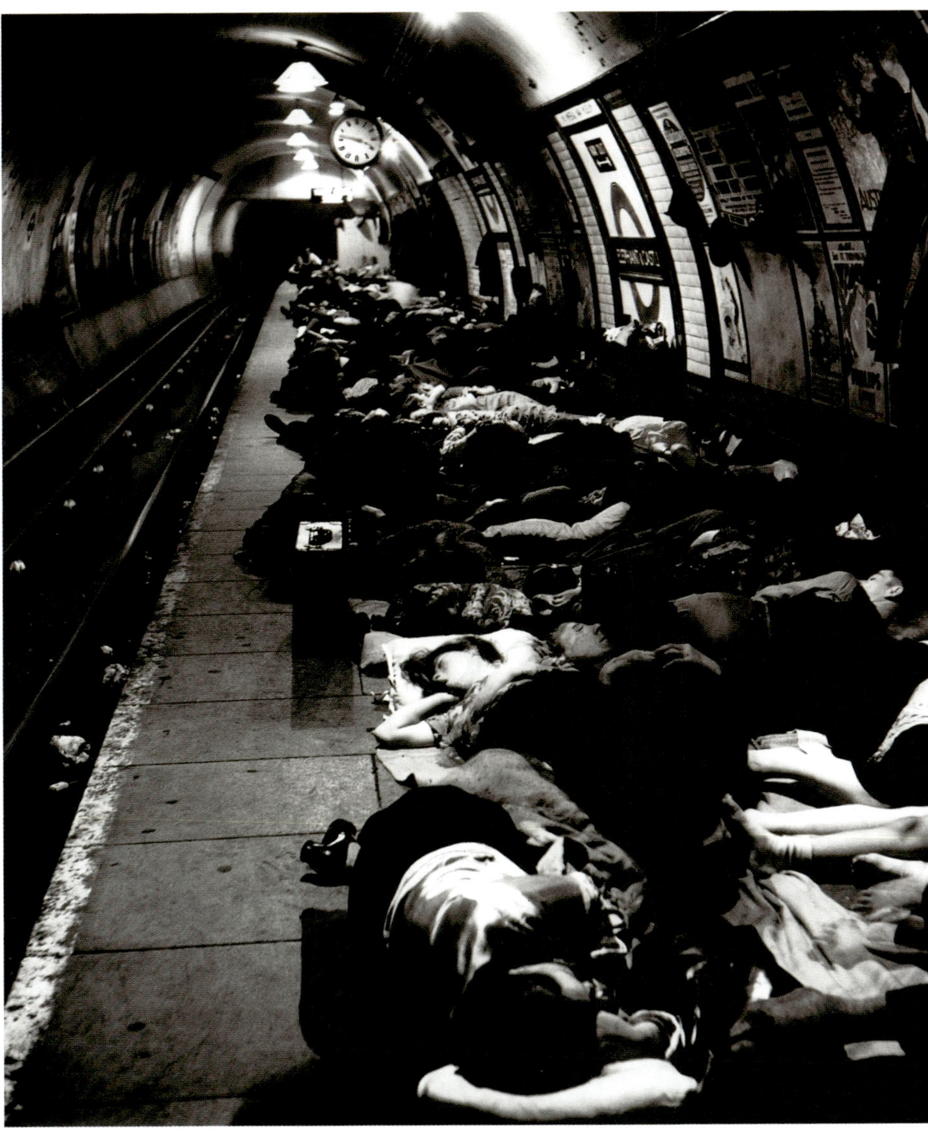

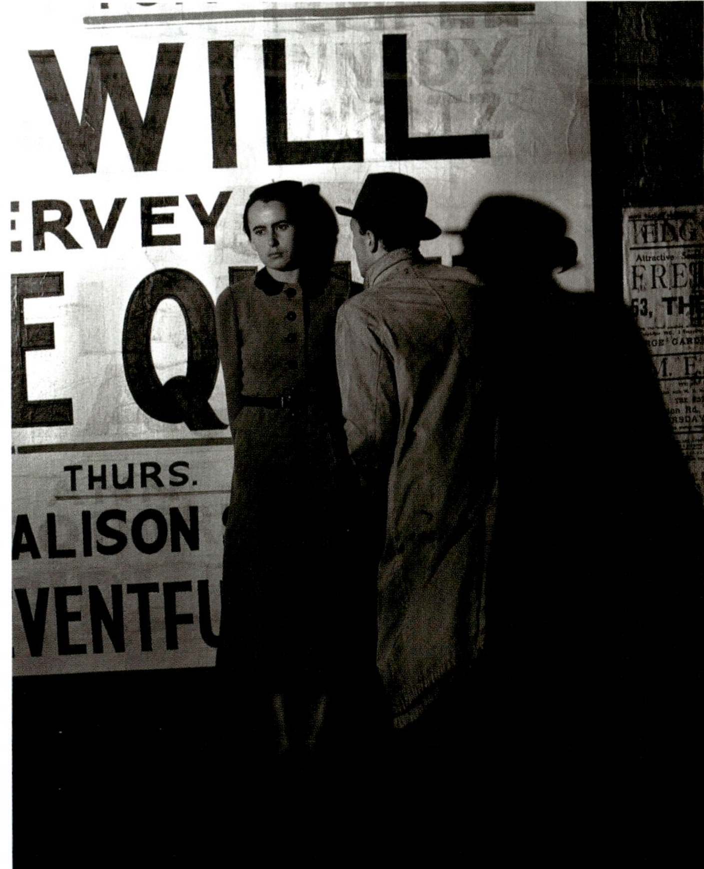
WILL
ERVEY
E Q
THURS.
ALISON
VENTFU

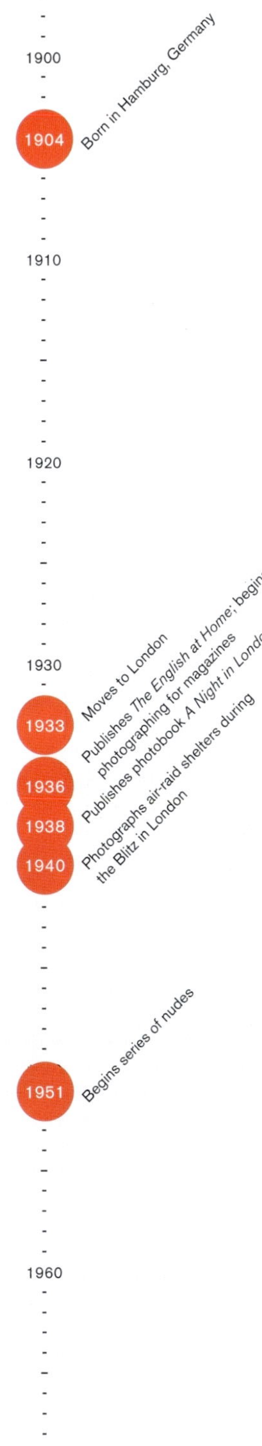
Bill Brandt
1900
1904 Born in Hamburg, Germany
1910
1920
1930
1933 Moves to London
1936 Publishes The English at Home; begins photographing for magazines
1938 Publishes photobook A Night in London
1940 Photographs air-raid shelters during the Blitz in London
1951 Begins series of nudes
1960
1970
1980
1983 Dies in London, UK

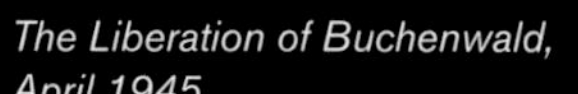

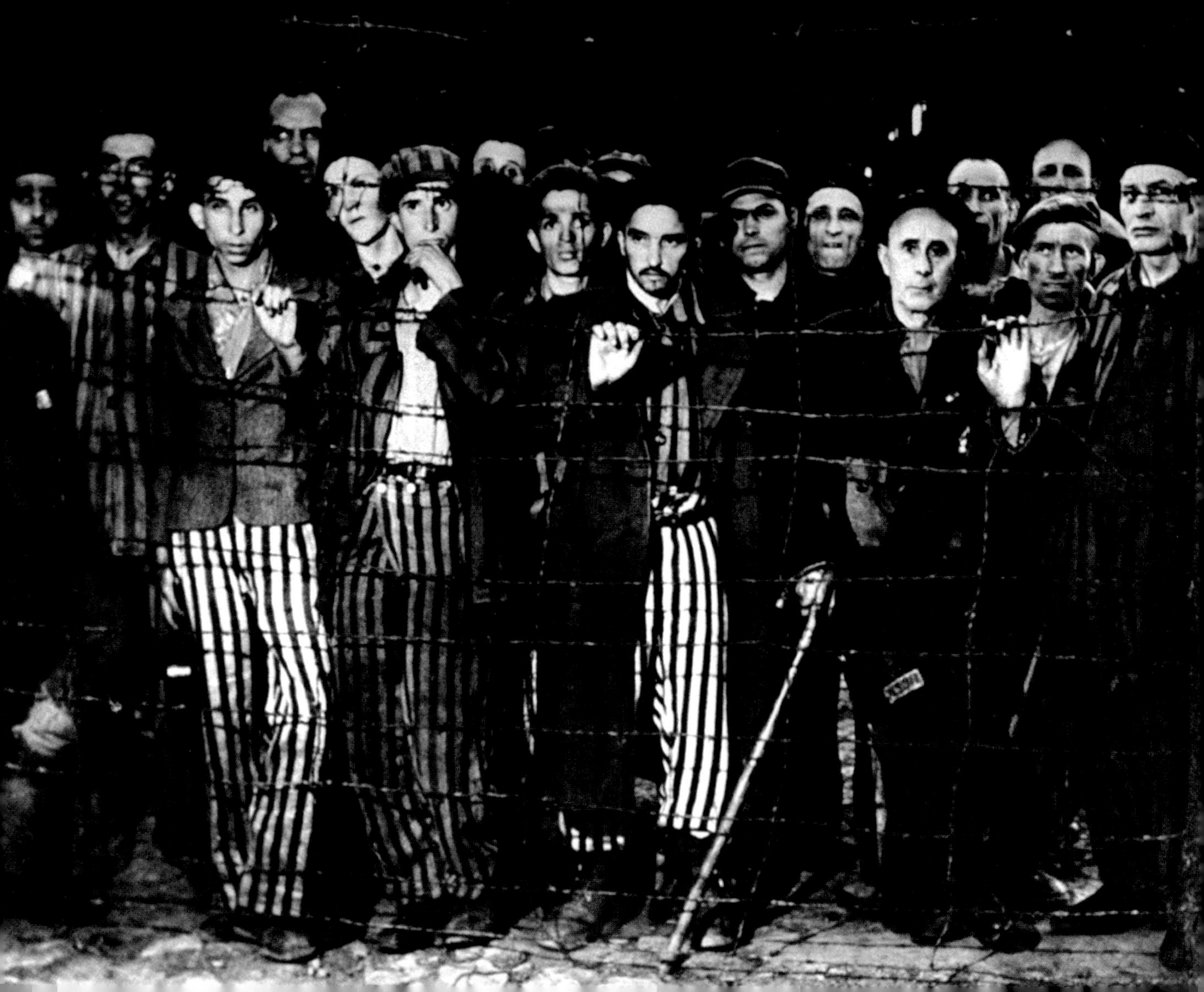

*The Liberation of Buchenwald,*
*April 1945.*

'The whole dynamic world of industry lay before me.'

# Margaret Bourke-White

1904–1971

UNITED STATES

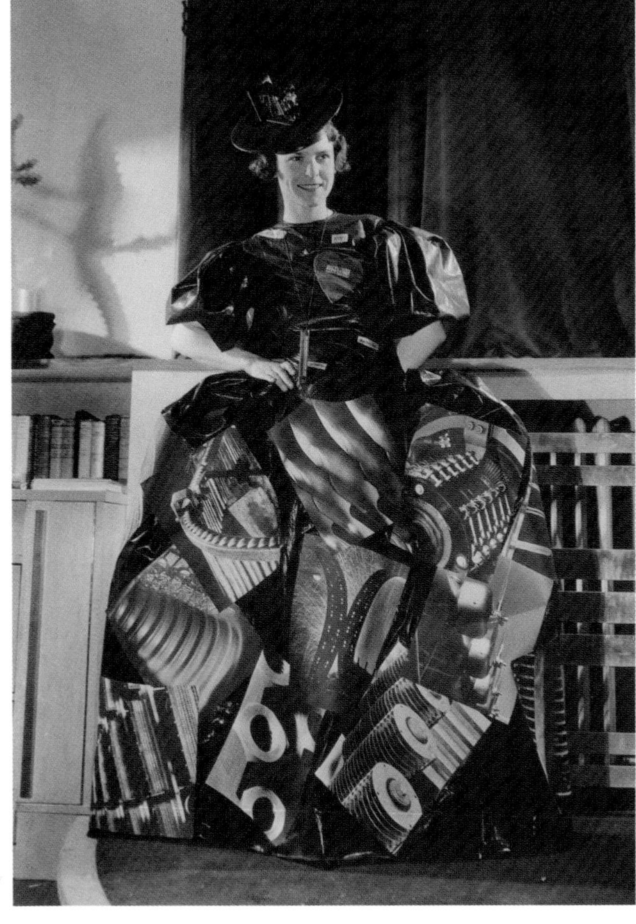

She was the woman of firsts – first foreign photographer allowed to take pictures of industry in the new Soviet Union; first female photographer at *Fortune* and *Life* and creator of *Life's* first cover; first woman to photograph in active combat zones during World War II. She not only covered the news, she was the news, with articles about her appearing in events and celebrity newspaper columns.

While she learned photography at an early age, it was not Margaret Bourke-White's foremost interest; natural history was, and she never gave it up. Regardless of her arduous schedule, she kept pet alligators and raised insects. She attended seven colleges before getting her bachelor's degree in biology. At Cornell University, she found that she could earn money by making souvenir shots of the campus. Not an auspicious beginning, but one that taught her to take a chance on herself. She moved to Cleveland, whose murky steel mills helped switch her soft-focus style for the clarity and pattern more suited to newspaper and magazine reproduction. She became not only a Modernist but also a proponent of photography's distinctive ability to communicate industrial forms.

Where other photographers might arrive at Modernism through theory or contemporary art, Bourke-White got there mostly through practice and a dogged determination to learn while doing. The geometric patterns she found and isolated in lathes, plough blades, suspension bridges, typewriter keys and even the Statue of Liberty's Greek garb delighted the eye, romanced industrialization as the great achievement of the early twentieth century and earned her corporate as well as print clients. Bourke-White coddled fame, but was never famous simply for being famous.

She recognized that her approach diminished the contribution and presence of people. When she worked on her own projects, or when distance diminished the force of directives from her clients or publishers, she taught herself how to move away from mechanical patterning of the picture's surface. Over time, she became more socially aware and politically astute. She employed the patience she learned in the Cleveland mills to wait for the right moment, and composed candid close-ups and group shots in which each individual was distinguished from the others.

Portrait of Margaret Bourke-White by Anthony Frederick Sarg, 1934.

*The Louisville Flood*, 1937.

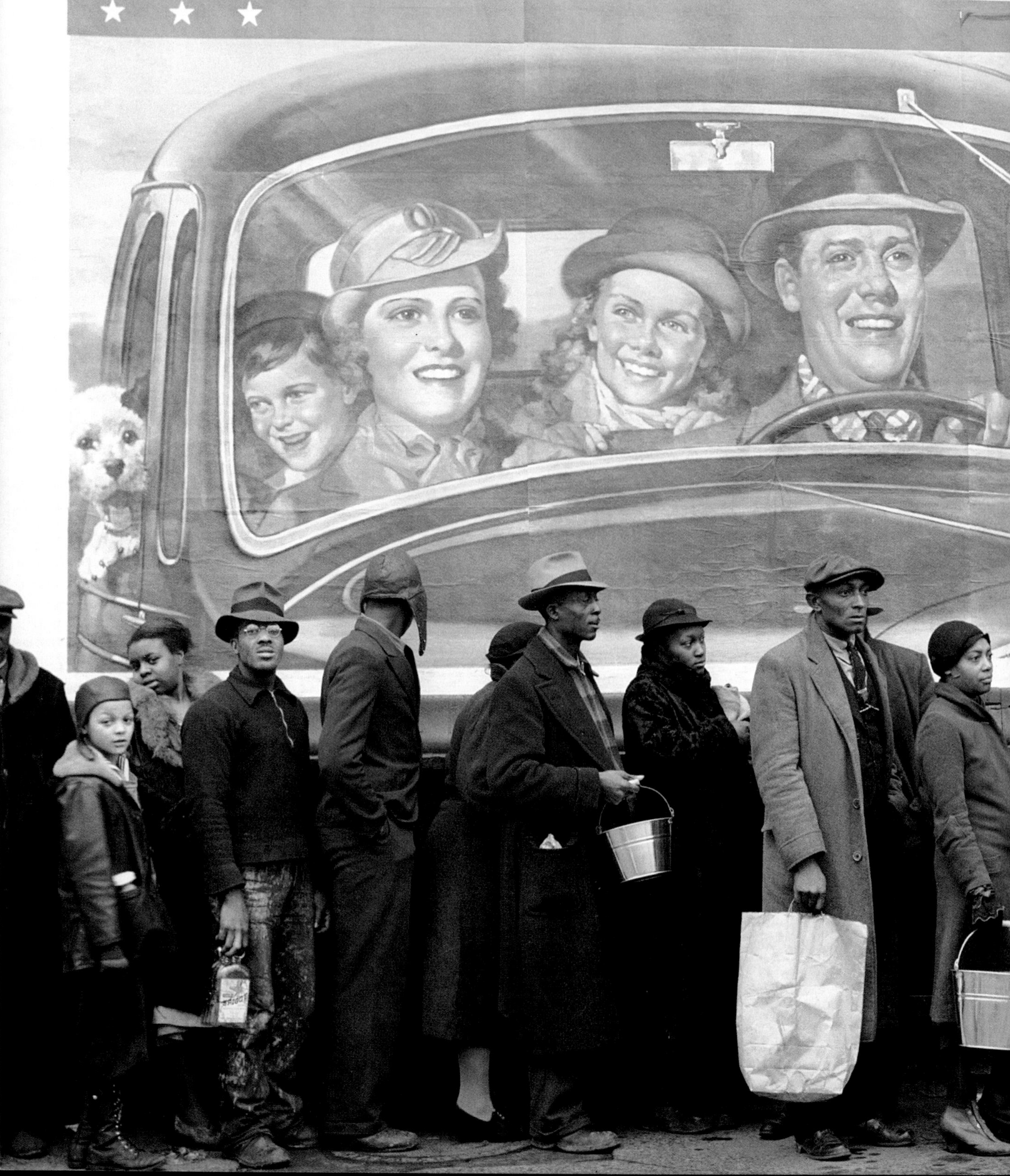

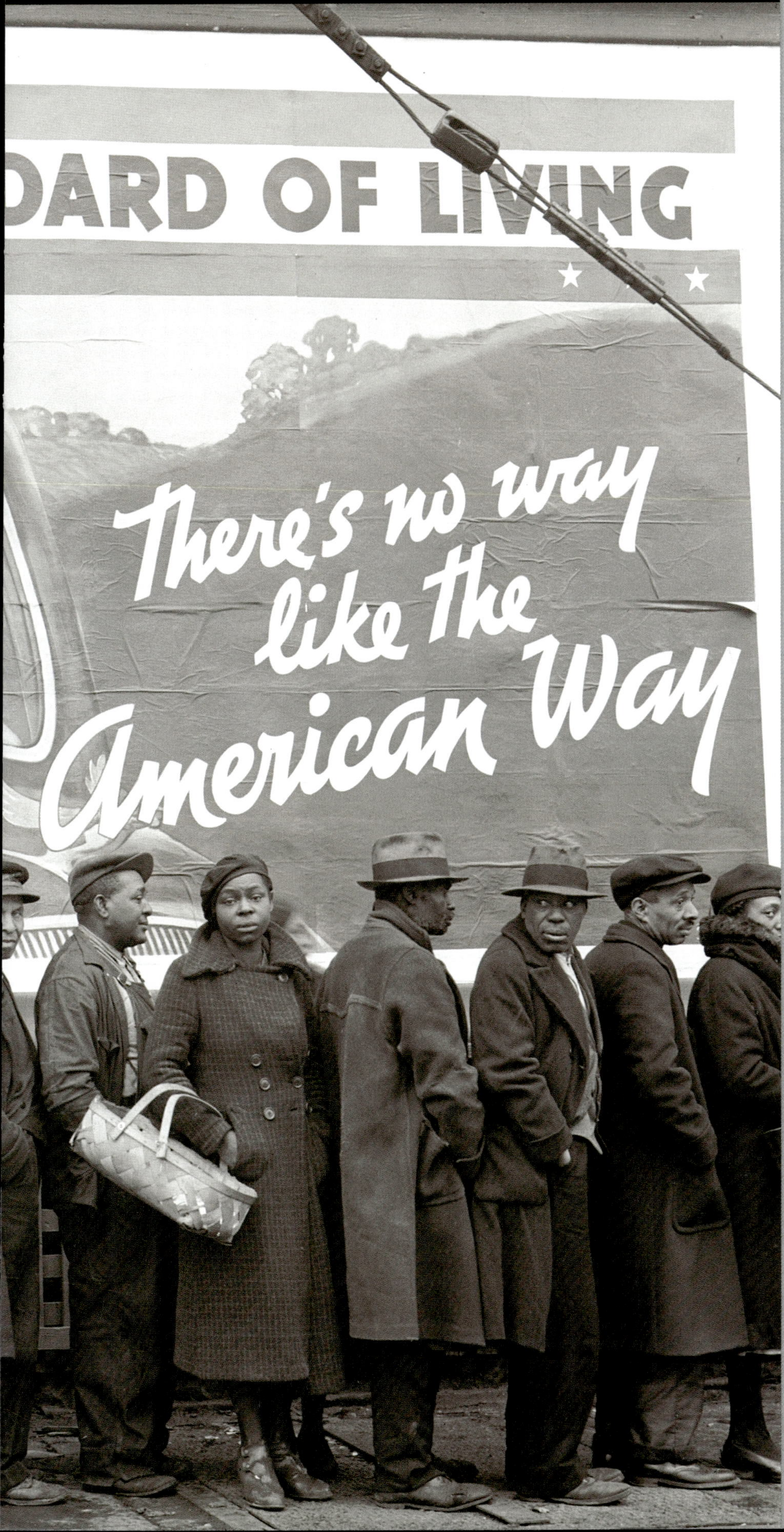

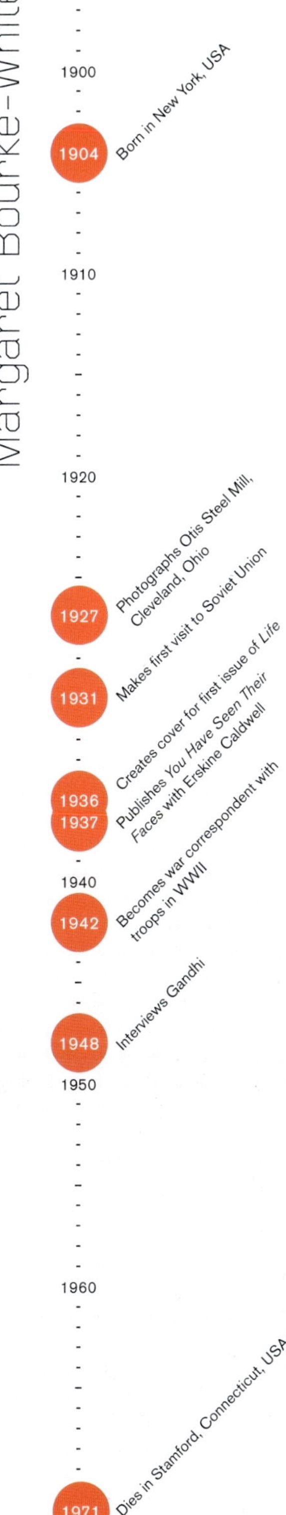

Margaret Bourke-White
1900
1904 Born in New York, USA
1910
1920
1927 Photographs Otis Steel Mill, Cleveland, Ohio
1931 Makes first visit to Soviet Union
1936 Creates cover for first issue of *Life*
1937 Publishes *You Have Seen Their Faces* with Erskine Caldwell
1940
1942 Becomes war correspondent with troops in WWII
1948 Interviews Gandhi
1950
1960
1971 Dies in Stamford, Connecticut, USA

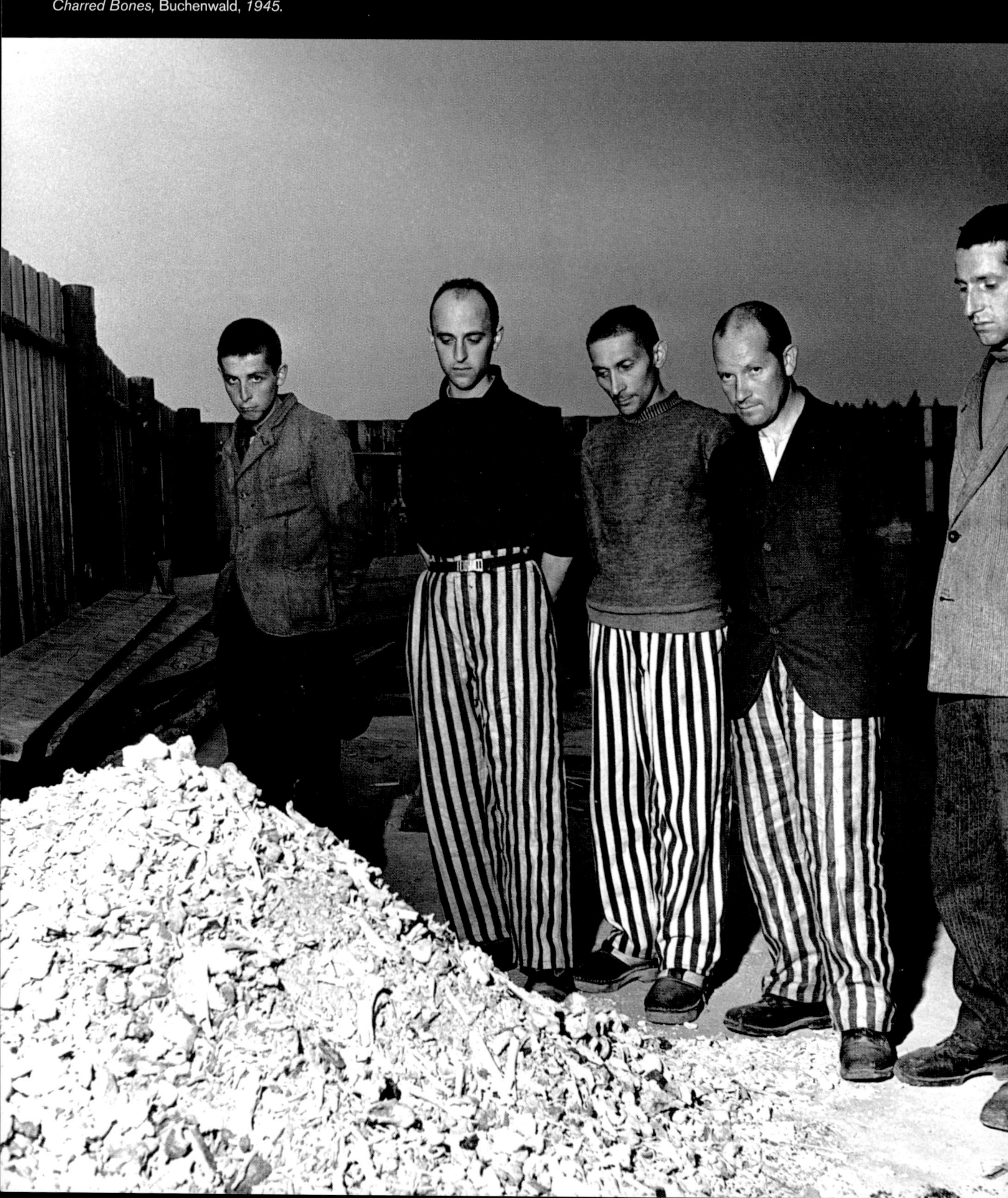

*Charred Bones*, Buchenwald, *1945.*

'The personality of the photographer... is really more important than his technical genius.'

# Lee Miller

1907–1977

UNITED STATES

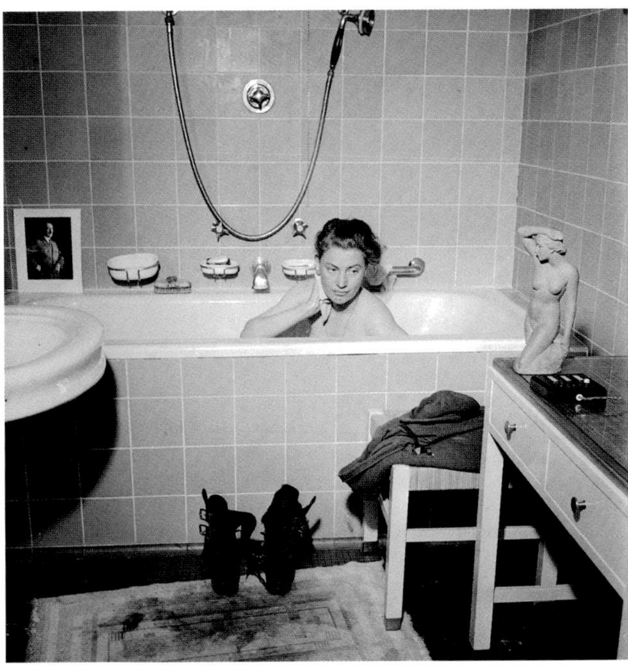

Lee Miller led the improbable, changeful life of those who are truly lucky. Soon after travelling to Paris with her French tutor, an impoverished Polish countess, she called off their arrangement and enrolled in a stage-design course. Returning home seven months later, she was saved from being run over in traffic by the founder and publisher of *Vogue*, Condé Nast. At the age of 19, she shone on the cover of the magazine and began posing for top photographers such as Edward Steichen (p. 28).

Although she had been familiar with photography since childhood, she decided to become a photographer only after spending two years on the other side of the camera, perhaps because of Steichen's coaching. When she returned to Paris, with a letter of introduction written by Steichen to Man Ray (p. 28), she had changed her first name, Elizabeth, to the more ambiguous Lee. She continued to model for French *Vogue.* Her intimate relationship with Man Ray included acquiring his unconventional approach to camera work and his tastes in art. While she soaked up Surrealism in his circle of friends, she came to appreciate the work of Eugène Atget (p. 8). Her photographs from that period are mostly street photographs with a tinge of mystery. All this before she was 25 years old.

Her life continued to oscillate, and her photography followed its fluctuations. She returned to New York after a break with Man Ray, but continued to create Surrealist photographs, advertising her new studio as adept in 'the Man Ray school of photography'. Her portraits of the rich and famous shimmered with solarization, a Surrealist technique achieved by applying light to a print or negative. She gave her advertising clients, such as Mary Chess cosmetics, edgy cosmopolitan images. When she married an Egyptian and moved to Cairo, her pictures took on a Modernist angularity, as if the fierce desert sunburned away the shadows required for a sly, uncanny Surreal picture. In wartime London, she continued fashion photography but also wrote about and photographed the war's effects. As a war correspondent for *Vogue*, she photographed bomb blasts and combat surgeons at work. Her photographs of German concentration camp victims illustrated her passionate articles and cables to the magazine. Her staged photograph of herself taking a bath in Hitler's tub at his Munich residence was a thumb-in-the-eye to his followers, whose hero committed suicide on the same day.

*Lee Miller in Hitler's Bathtub,* Munich, Germany by Lee Miller with David E. Scherman, 1945.

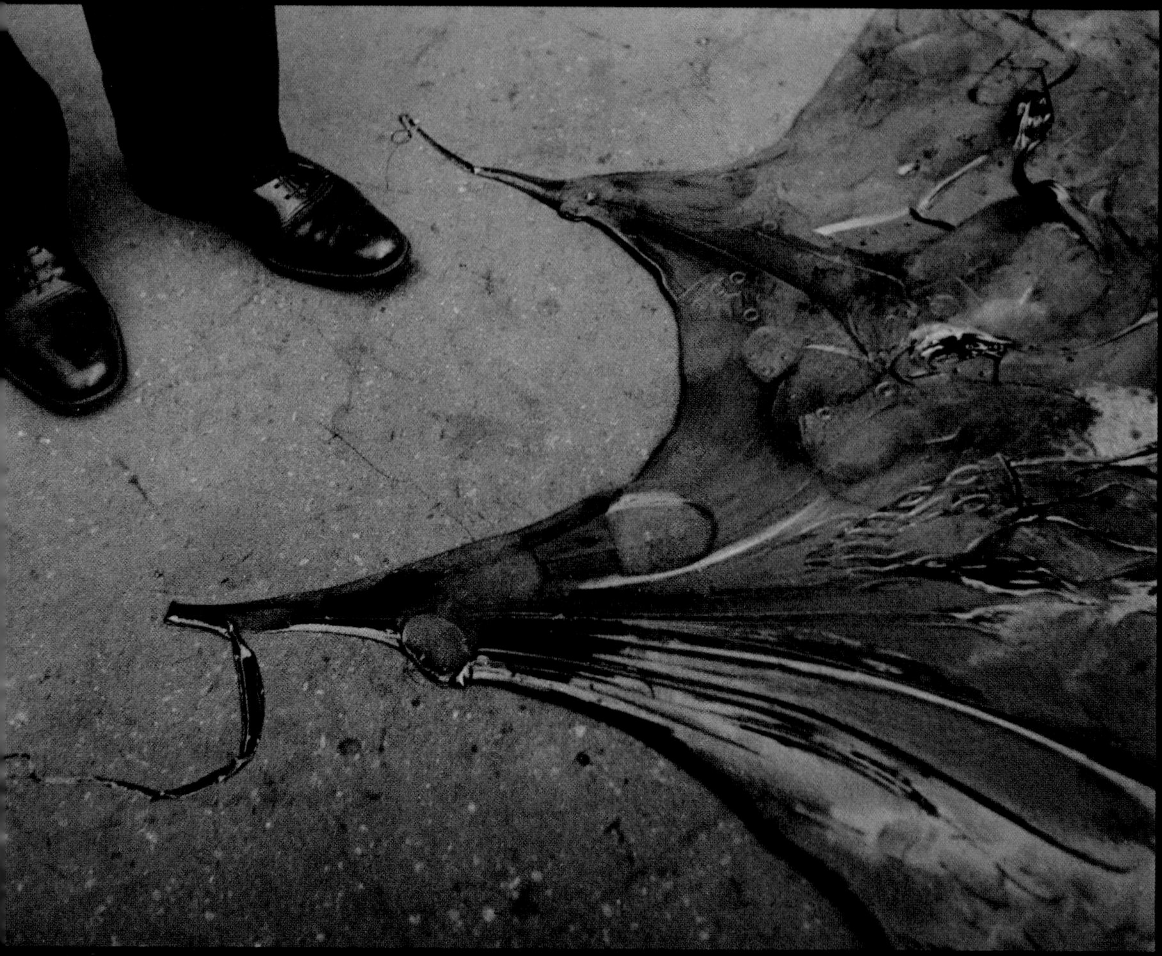

**Above** *Untitled, man and tar,* c. 1930.

**Below** *Mary Chess cosmetics shot,* 1933.

**Opposite** *Portrait of Space,* 1937.

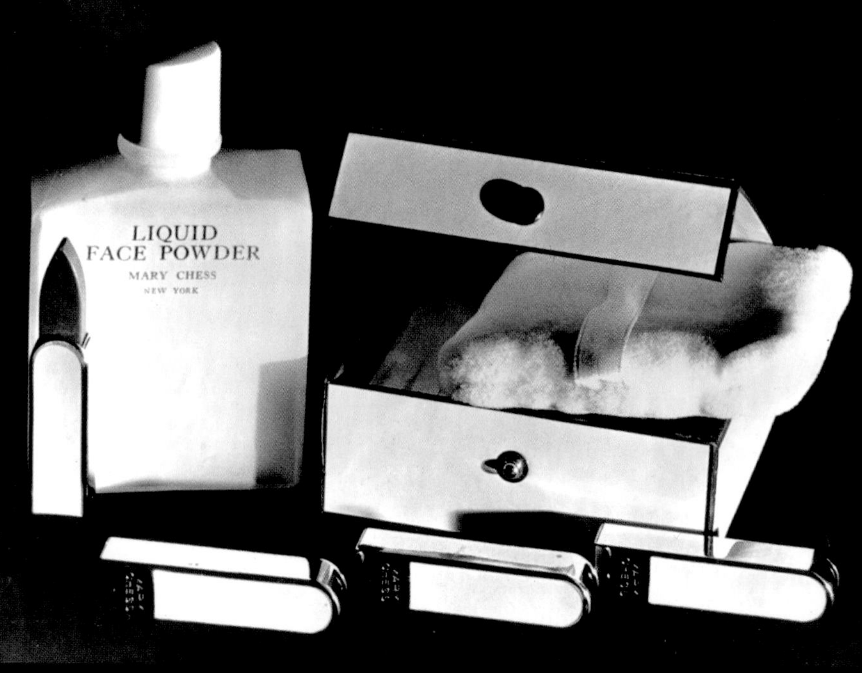

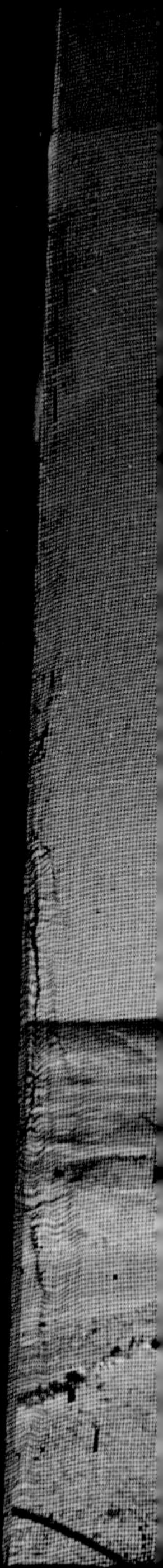

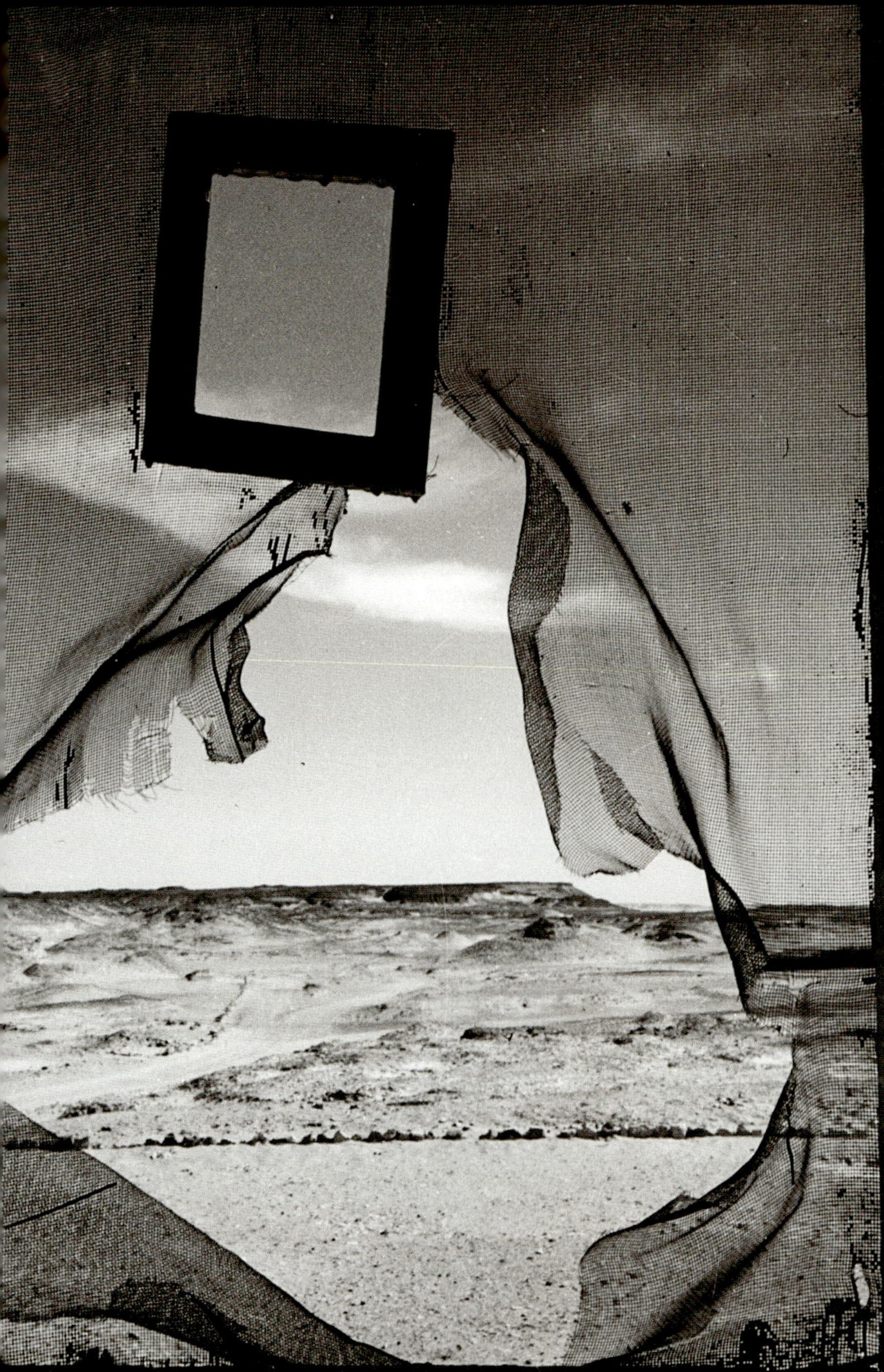

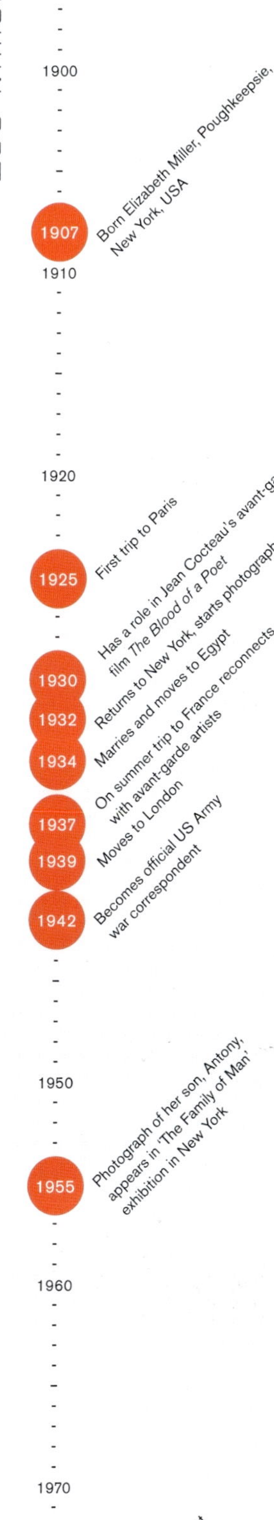
Lee Miller
1900
1907 Born Elizabeth Miller, Poughkeepsie, New York, USA
1910
1920
1925 First trip to Paris
1930 Has a role in Jean Cocteau's avant-garde film The Blood of a Poet
Returns to New York, starts photography studio
1932 Marries and moves to Egypt
1934 On summer trip to France reconnects with avant-garde artists
1937 Moves to London
1939 Becomes official US Army war correspondent
1942
1950
1955 Photograph of her son, Antony, appears in 'The Family of Man' exhibition in New York
1960
1970
1977 Dies in Chiddingly, East Sussex, England

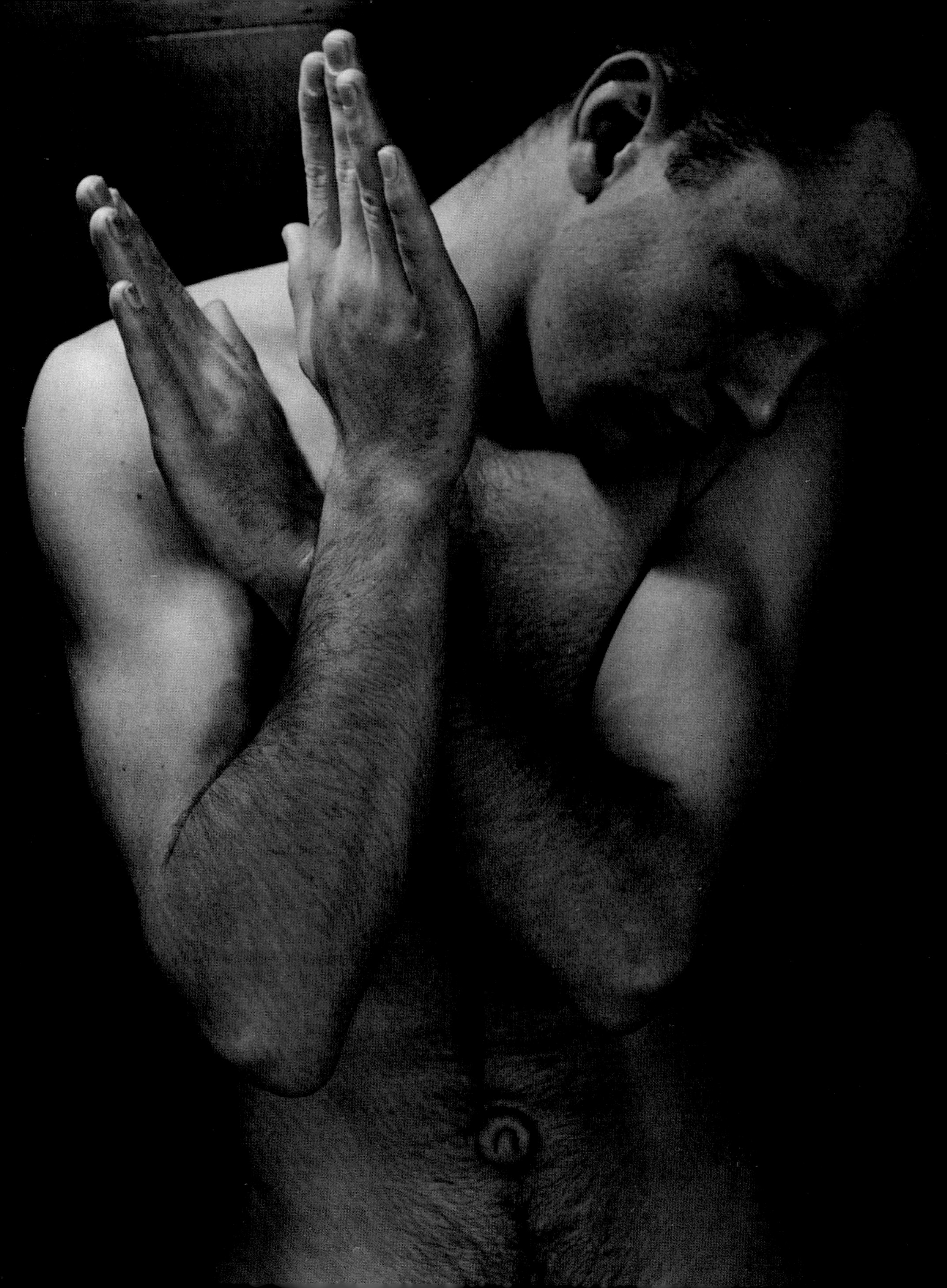

'The camera is first a means of self-discovery and then a means of self-growth.'

# Minor White

1908–1976

UNITED STATES

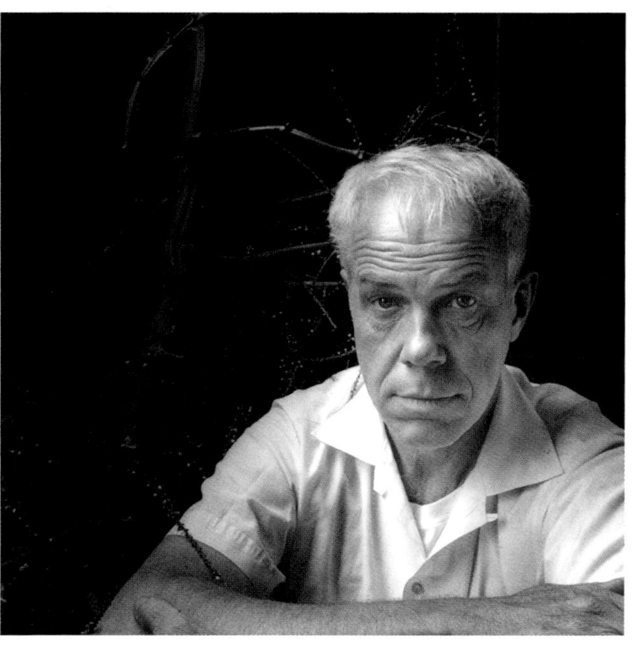

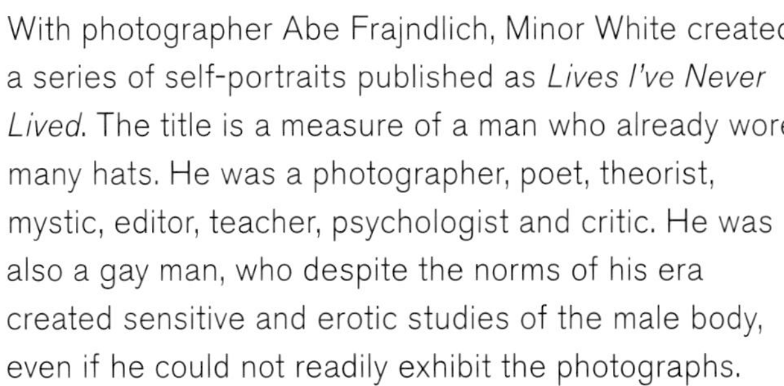

With photographer Abe Frajndlich, Minor White created a series of self-portraits published as *Lives I've Never Lived*. The title is a measure of a man who already wore many hats. He was a photographer, poet, theorist, mystic, editor, teacher, psychologist and critic. He was also a gay man, who despite the norms of his era created sensitive and erotic studies of the male body, even if he could not readily exhibit the photographs.

White discovered poetry as a young man, and its fruitful indirection informed his image-making throughout his life. 'In becoming a photographer,' he wrote, 'I am only changing medium.' His early work, such as his street photography in San Francisco, reveals a quick eye for composition. When he learned about Alfred Stieglitz's notion of the 'equivalent' (p. 12), he understood it to be a cross-cultural methodology for stimulating spiritual knowledge in the viewer.

Yet it was his interactions with Californian photographer Edward Weston (p. 36) that helped him focus on suggestive meanings. Beginning in the 1950s, White's photographs began to require the viewer to accept visual metaphor and symbolism. Over the course of his career, he experimented with serial works that he called sequences or a 'cinema of stills'. Unlike a written poem, with its permanent word order, sequences could be rearranged. His book *Mirrors Messages Manifestations* emphasized the last word of its title. Throughout his work, instantaneous and fleeting images attracted White. A glint of light on wet sand, the shadows created by a fluttering curtain, ice crystals on a winter window – such moments as these are among his best work.

Portrait of Minor White by Imogen Cunningham, 1963.

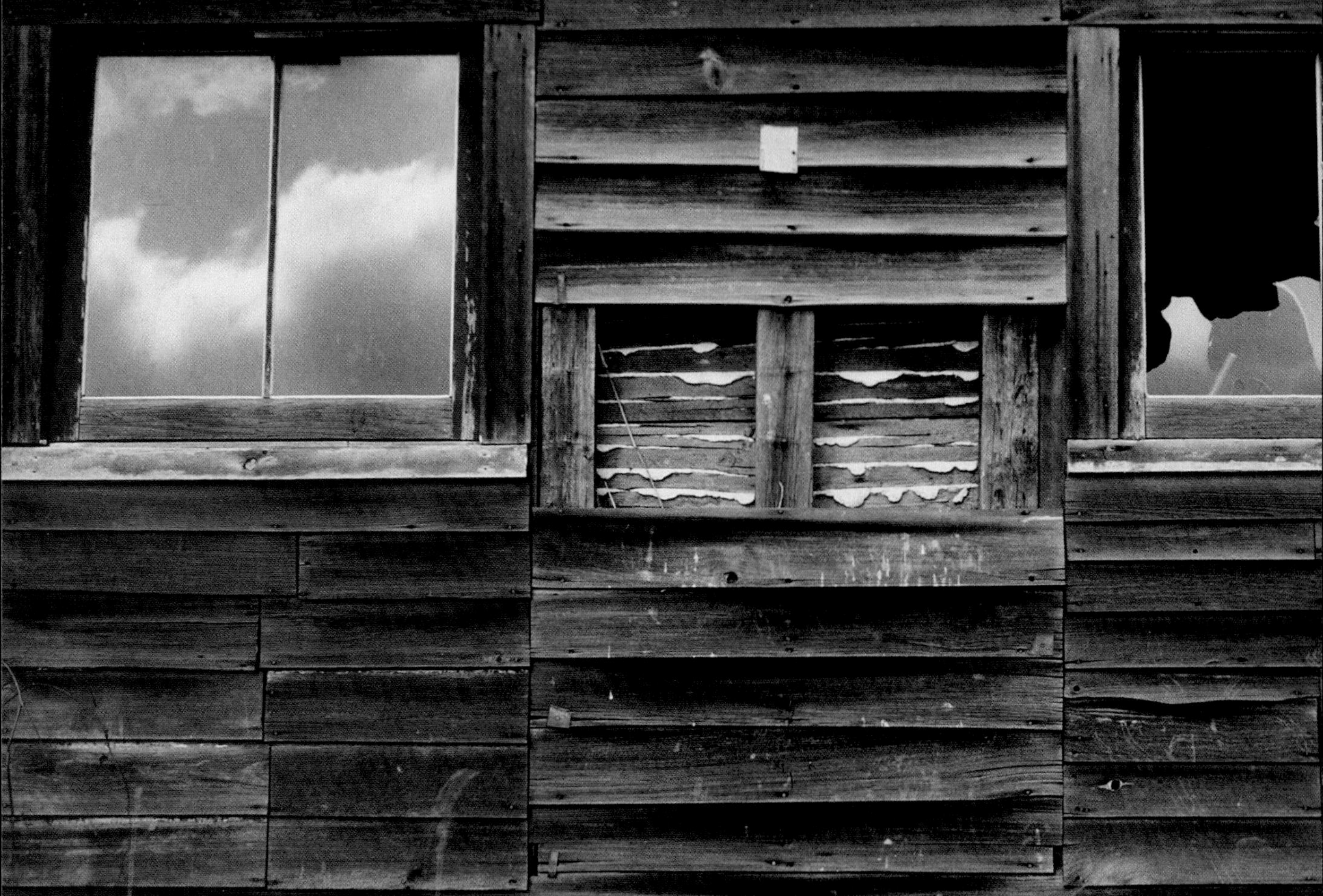

## Minor White

1900

**1908** Born in Minneapolis, Minnesota, USA

1910

**1915** Gets a Brownie camera

1920

1930

**1940** Starts commercial photography business in Portland, Oregon

**1945** Moves to New York; meets Alfred Stieglitz and Beaumont Newhall

**1947** Publishes *Song Without Words.*

1950

**1952** Co-founds *Aperture* magazine

**1953** Moves to Rochester, New York; works at George Eastman House (to 1956)

**1956** Starts teaching at Rochester Institute of Technology (to 1964)

1960

**1965** Appointed to a position at the Massachusetts Institute of Technology

**1969** Completes *Mirrors Messages Manifestations*

**1976** Dies in Boston, Massachusetts, USA

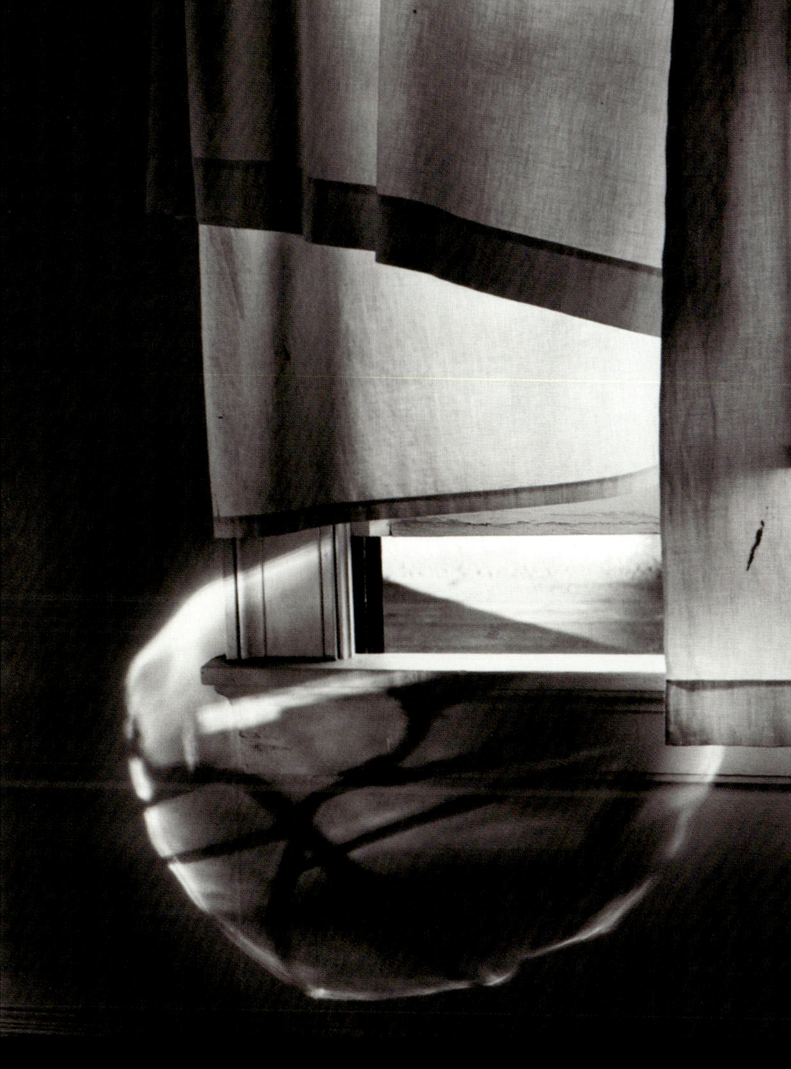

*Windowsill Daydreaming*, 1958.

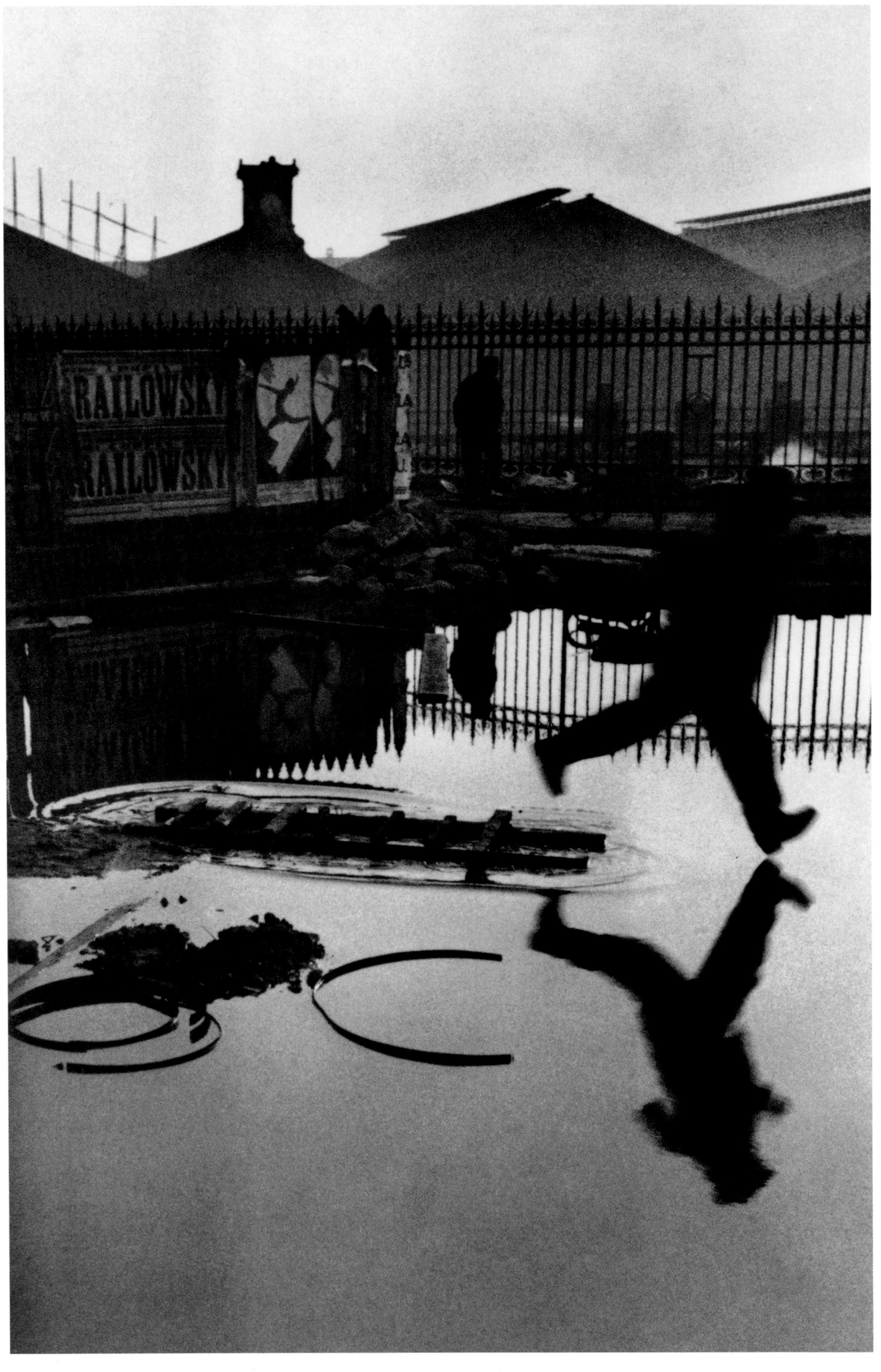
RAILOWSKY
RAILOWSKY

'With Magnum was born the necessity for telling a story.'

# Henri Cartier-Bresson

1908–2004

FRANCE

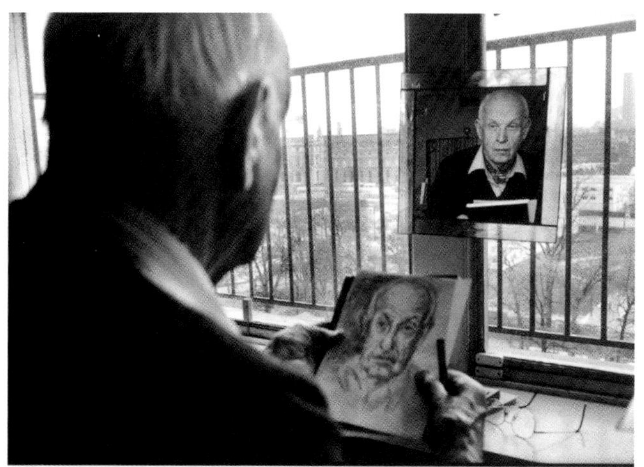

Henri Cartier-Bresson was not the first painter to switch careers to photography, but he may have been the most admired and influential. Especially for photographers and film-makers who lived through World War II and its prelude, Cartier-Bresson was known as a partisan who made anti-fascist films on the Spanish Civil War, for example *L'Espagne Vivra,* as well as an exposé on the French ruling class. When he disappeared early in the war, it was reasonable to think that he had been killed in battle or slain for his political beliefs. Indeed, towards the end of the conflict, the Museum of Modern Art in New York began planning a posthumous retrospective of his work. Distinctly alive after the war, Cartier-Bresson travelled to the United States to help complete the exhibition. While there, he and others created the Magnum photographic agency, which aimed at giving photojournalists increased control of their work and greater creative scope.

His film style, quickened by his admiration for Surrealism, also informed his photography. He moved through the world grasping moments in time that were geometrically arresting yet intimated more than compositional savvy. Like the movie-camera operator and director that he was, he asserted that 'the photographer's eye is perpetually evaluating'. He transferred that restless gaze to a small, lightweight Leica camera, which allowed him to be fast and unobtrusive. A luncheon partner recalled that he could leap up, take a picture and sit down in less than a minute, sure that he had got the shot he wanted.

Cartier-Bresson described his approach as 'the decisive moment', which he defined as 'the simultaneous recognition, in a fraction of a second, of the significance of an event as well as of a precise organization of forms which gave that event its proper expression'. The idea, which had engaged analogue photographers since its presentation in 1952, remains a force in the digital era.

**Opposite** *Behind the Gare Saint-Lazare*, 1932.

**Above** Henri Cartier-Bresson drawing his self-portrait by Martine Franck, 1999.

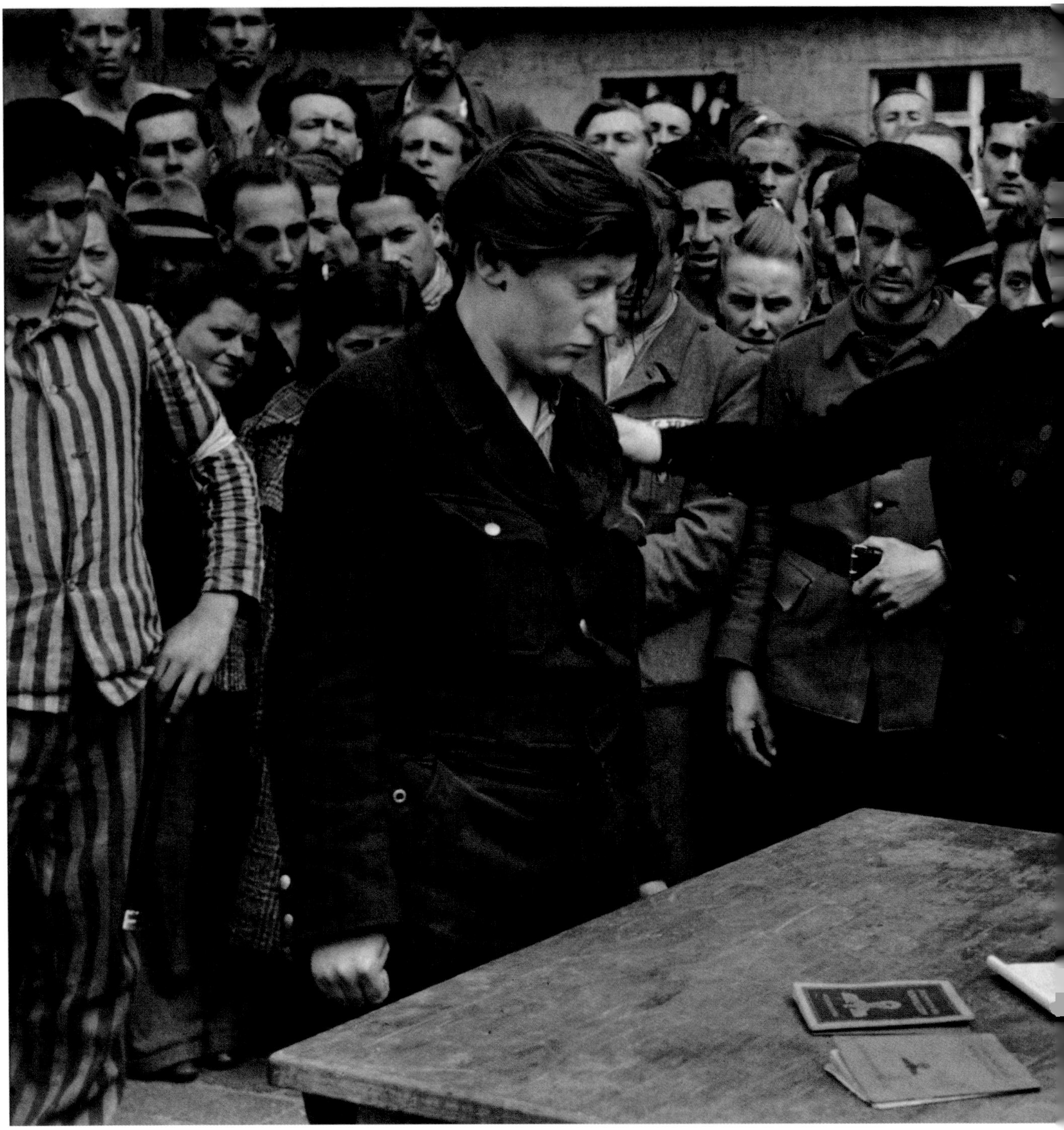

**Above** Gestapo informer, Dessau, April 1945.

**Right** Alicante, 1933.

**Opposite** Landscape, Brie, 1968.

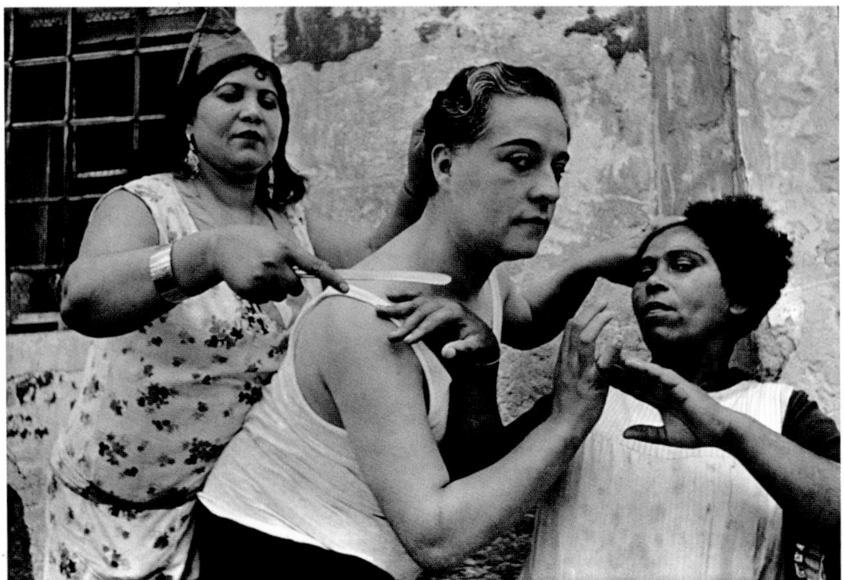

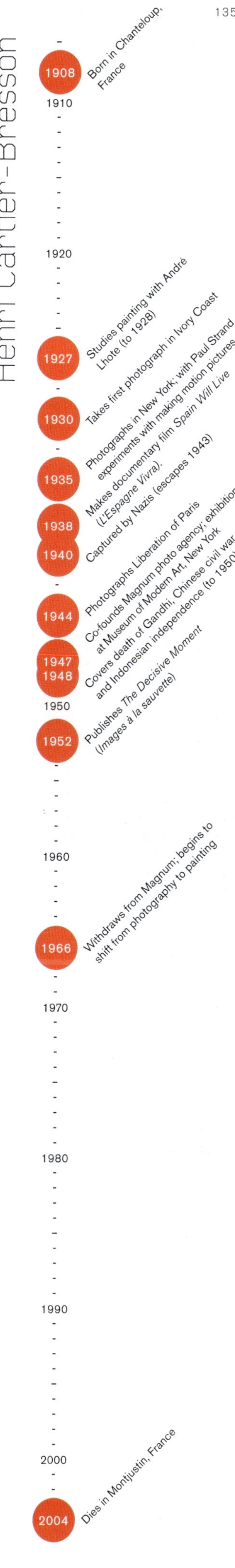
Henri Cartier-Bresson
1908
Born in Chanteloup, France
1910
1920
1927
Studies painting with André Lhote (to 1928)
1930
Takes first photograph in Ivory Coast
1935
Photographs in New York; with Paul Strand experiments with making motion pictures
1938
Makes documentary film Spain Will Live (L'Espagne Vivra).
1940
Captured by Nazis (escapes 1943)
1944
Photographs Liberation of Paris
1947
Co-founds Magnum photo agency; exhibition at Museum of Modern Art, New York
1948
Covers death of Gandhi, Chinese civil war, and Indonesian independence (to 1950)
1950
1952
Publishes The Decisive Moment (Images à la sauvette)
1960
1966
Withdraws from Magnum; begins to shift from photography to painting
1970
1980
1990
2000
2004
Dies in Montjustin, France

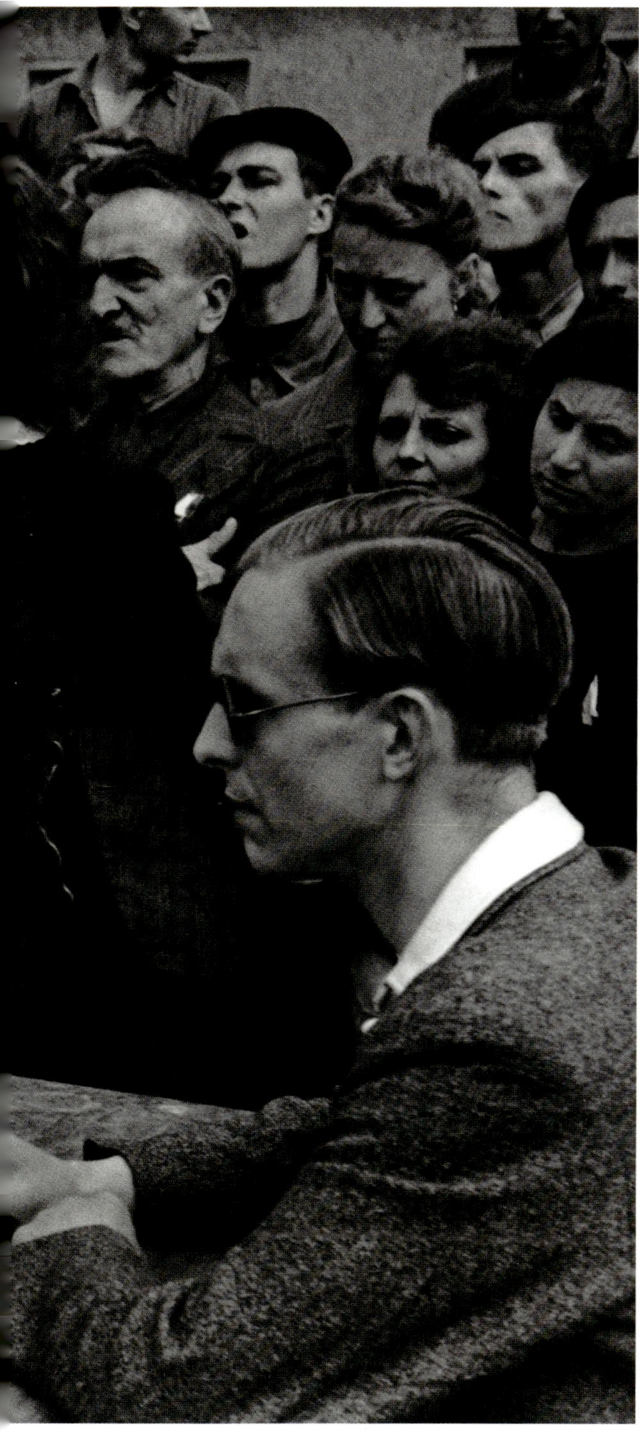

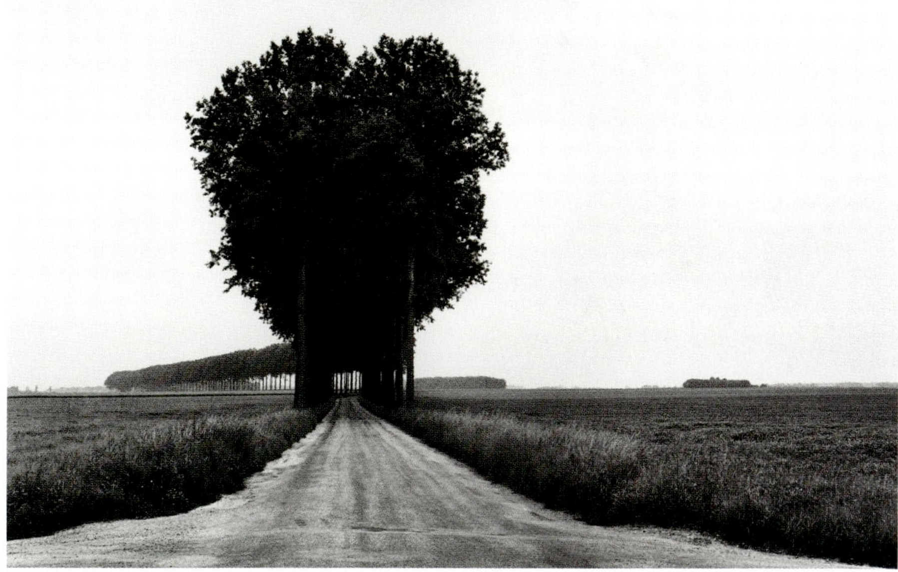

Muhammad Ali, c. 1970

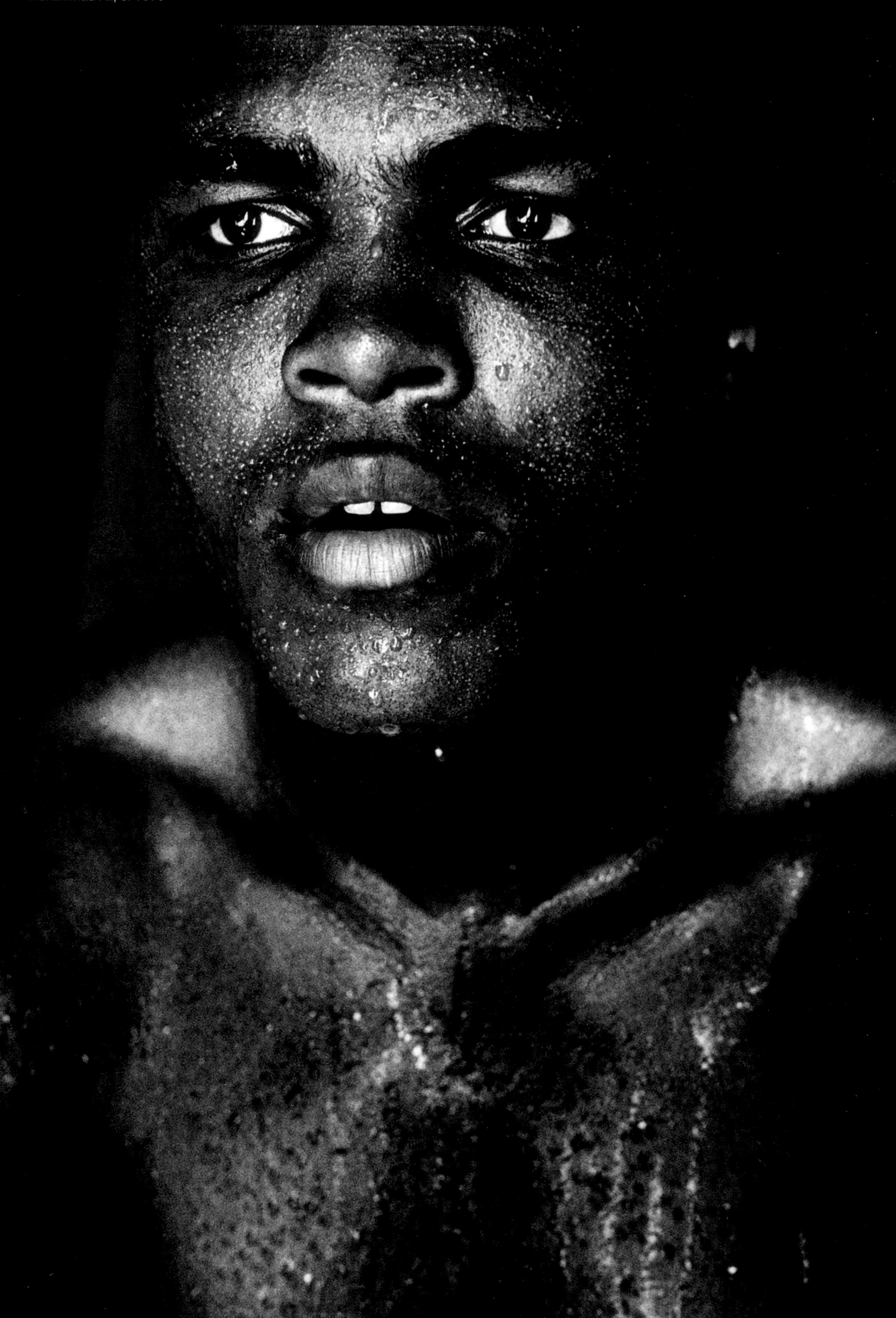

'I saw that the camera could be a weapon against poverty, against racism, against all sorts of social wrongs.'

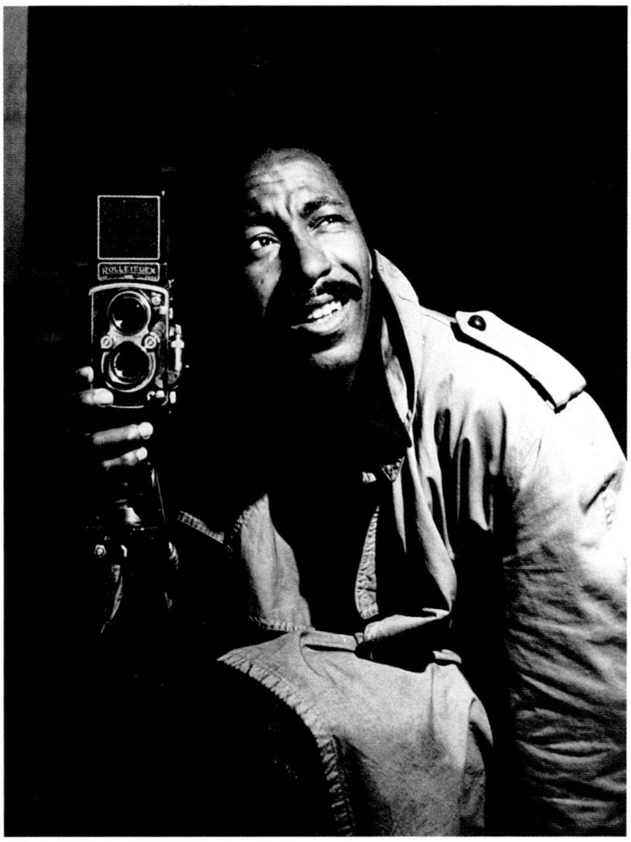

# Gordon Parks

1912–2006

UNITED STATES

Despite his long, productive life in the arts, polymath Gordon Parks is instantly recalled as the director of the film *Shaft,* featuring the too-cool-for-school private detective whose name is also a warning. Parks's anti-authoritarian spirit was evident nearly 30 years earlier, when, as a new hire at the Farm Security Administration (FSA), he enlisted Ella Watson, one of the building's cleaners, to pose with her broom and mop in front of an American flag. Against the tide of uncritical patriotism in August 1942, with the United States engaged in World War II, Parks's picture suggested that African-American life remained the same.

In the 1960s, few photographers who associated themselves with serious documentary work would risk loosing the aura of authenticity by shooting fashion photographs. But Parks shot fashion for both *Vogue* and *Life* magazines, and he was familiar with the style and approach taken by various fashion houses, including Chanel and Schiaparelli. Where other photographers chewed on their self-loathing for shooting fluff, Parks did a first-rate job regardless of subject. He recalled the contrast in assignments with Deborah Willis (p. 272), who curated his retrospective 'Half-Past Autumn': 'I had been given assignments I had never expected to earn... Some proved to be as different as silk and iron. Once, crime and fashion was served to me on the same day. The color of a Dior gown I photographed one afternoon turned out to be the same color as the blood of a murdered gang member I had photographed earlier that morning up in Harlem.'

Over his two decades with *Life* he shot iconic images of people, ranging from families in Harlem to such celebrities as Ingrid Bergman and Muhammad Ali. Many of these images are part of America's collective memory, while some, such as his images of Flavio da Silva from the *Life* magazine essay titled 'Freedom's Fearful Foe: Poverty', were famous for decades but now are in need of rediscovery.

Self-portrait, 1948.

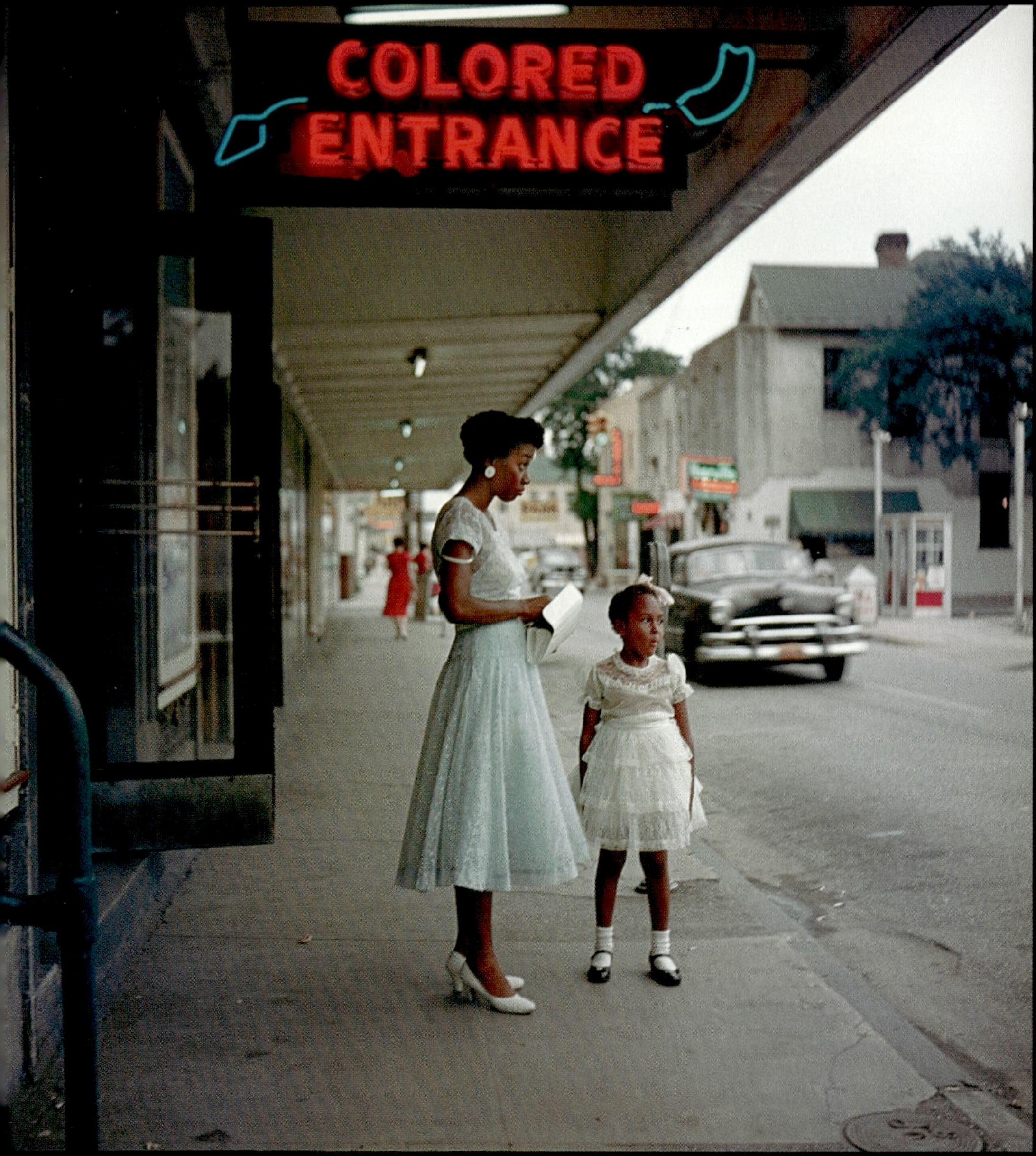

**Above** Jo Ann Thornton Wilson and Shirley Anne Kirksey in Mobile, Alabama, for *Life* magazine, 1956.

**Right** *Evening Wraps*, New York, 1956.

**Opposite** Flavio da Silva, Rio de Janeiro, 1961.

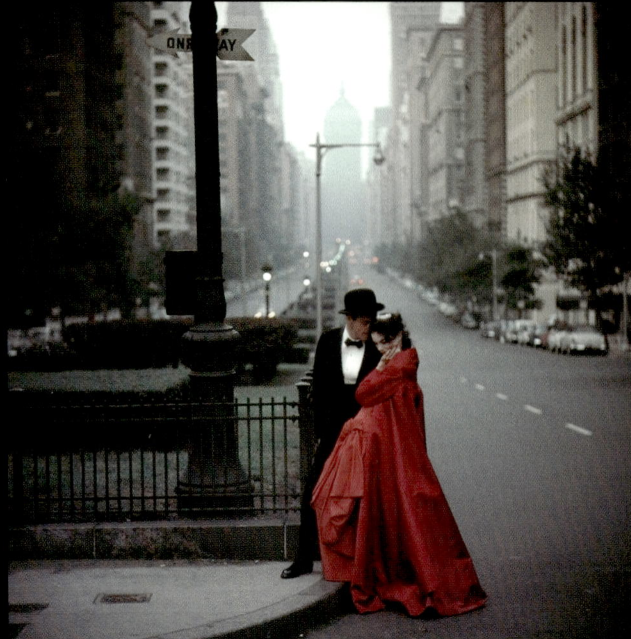

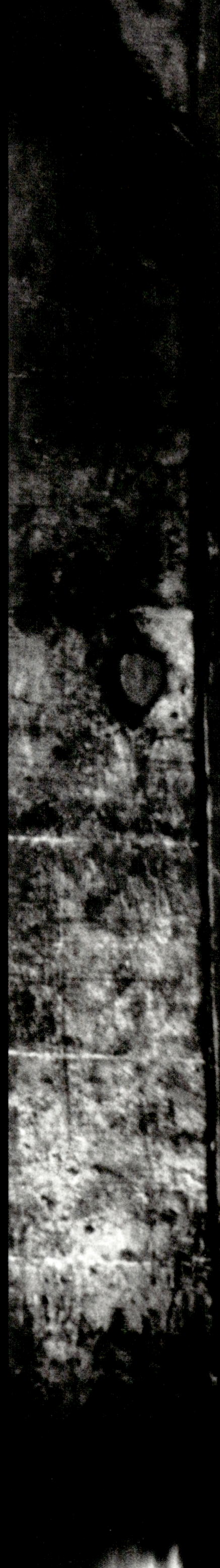

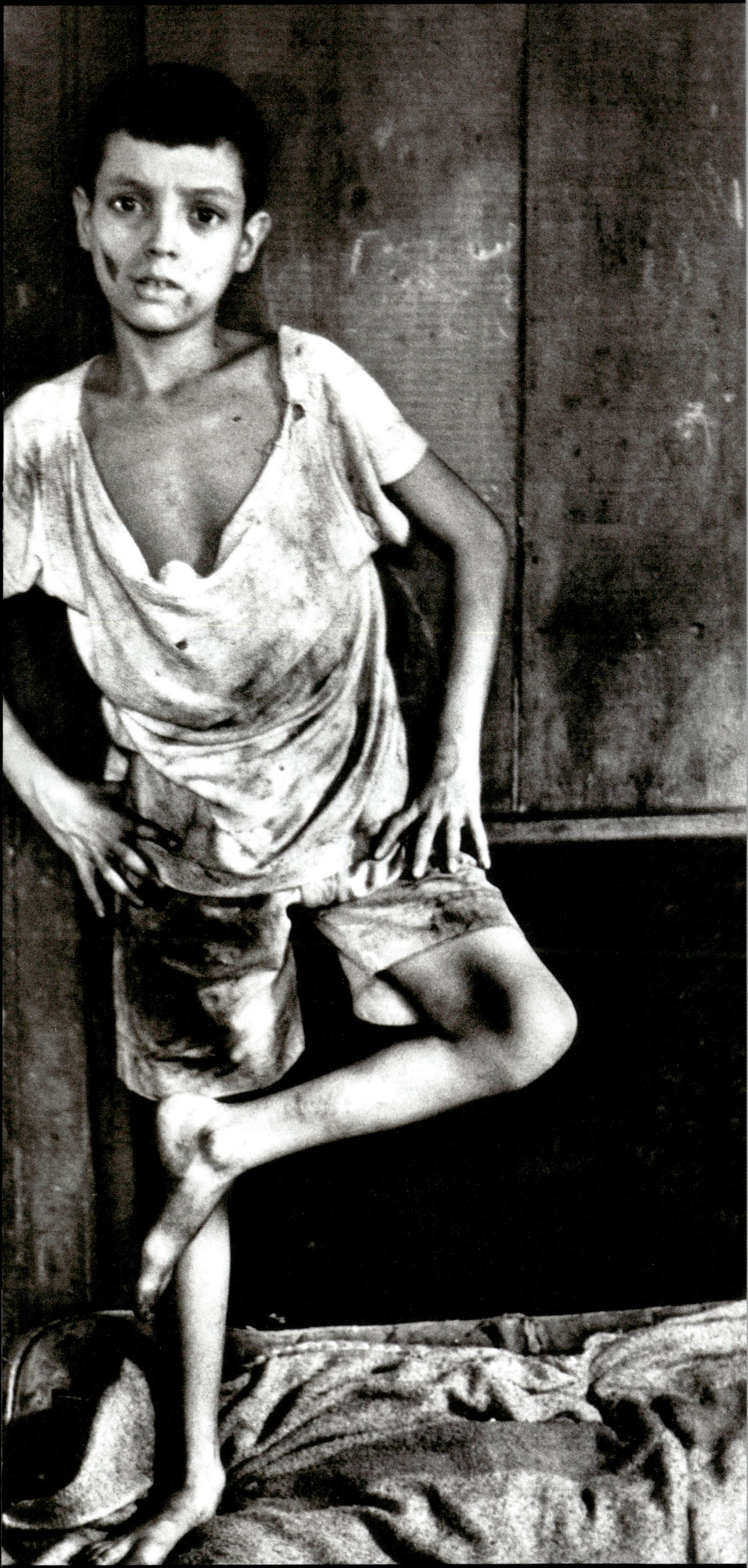

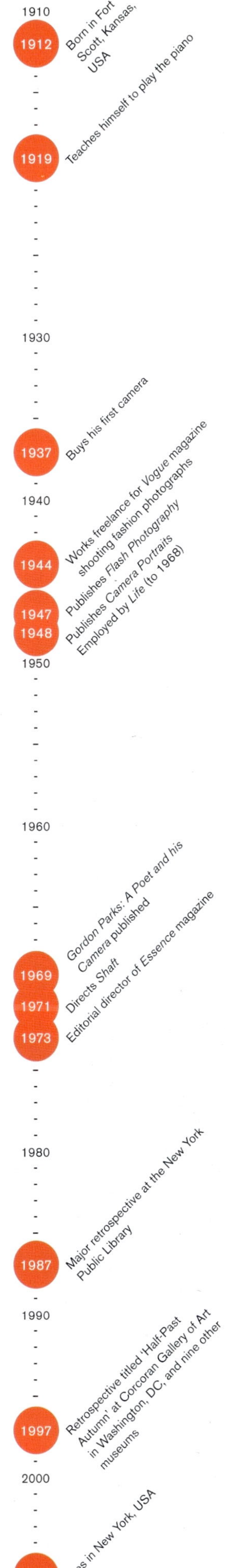
Gordon Parks
1910
1912 Born in Fort Scott, Kansas, USA
1919 Teaches himself to play the piano
1930
1937 Buys his first camera
1940
1944 Works freelance for Vogue magazine shooting fashion photographs
Publishes Flash Photography
1947 Publishes Camera Portraits
1948 Employed by Life (to 1968)
1950
1960
1969 Gordon Parks: A Poet and his Camera published
1971 Directs Shaft
1973 Editorial director of Essence magazine
1980
1987 Major retrospective at the New York Public Library
1990
1997 Retrospective titled 'Half-Past Autumn' at Corcoran Gallery of Art in Washington, DC, and nine other museums
2000
2006 Dies in New York, USA

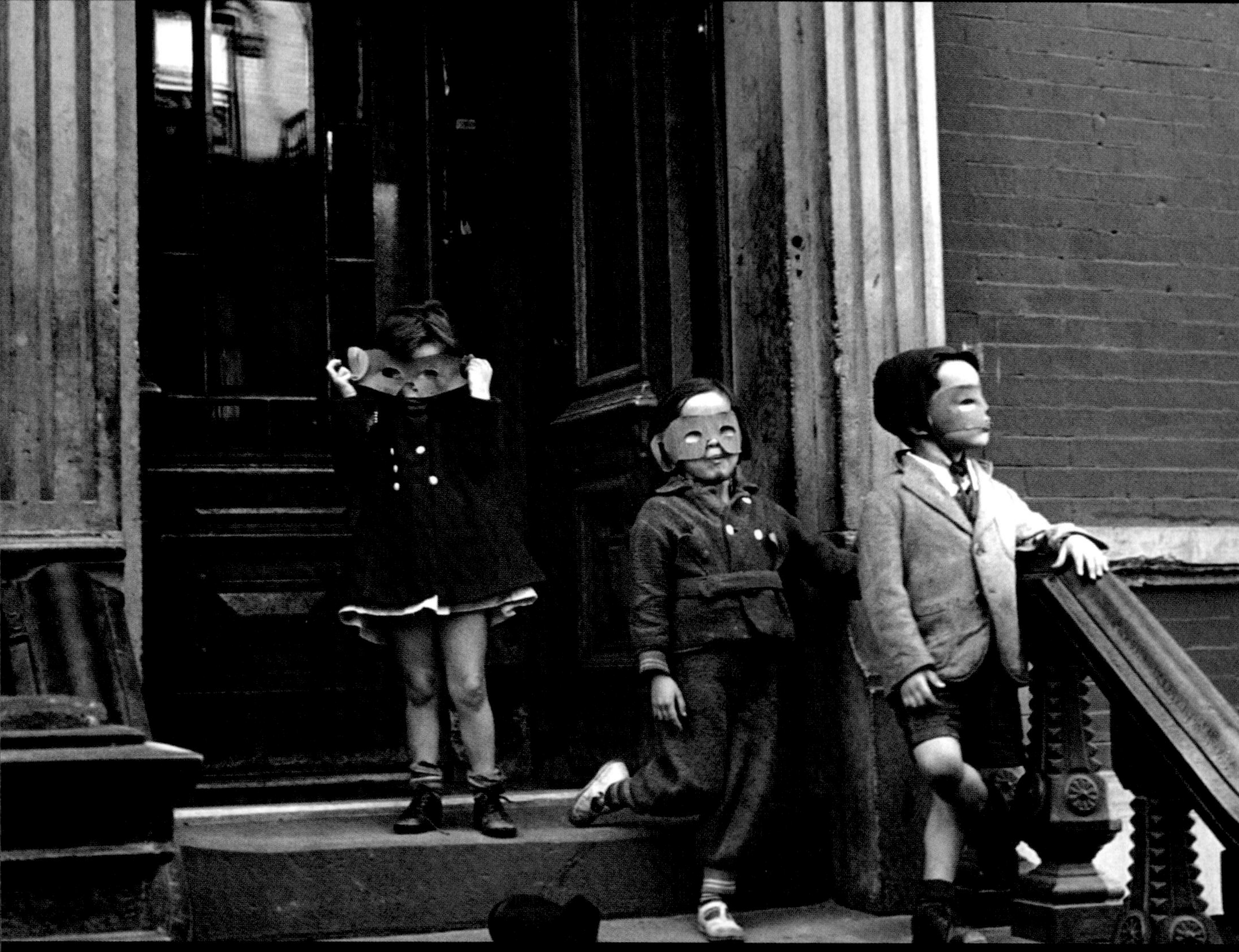

New York, c. 1942.

'Since I'm inarticulate, I express myself with images.'

# Helen Levitt

1913–2009

UNITED STATES

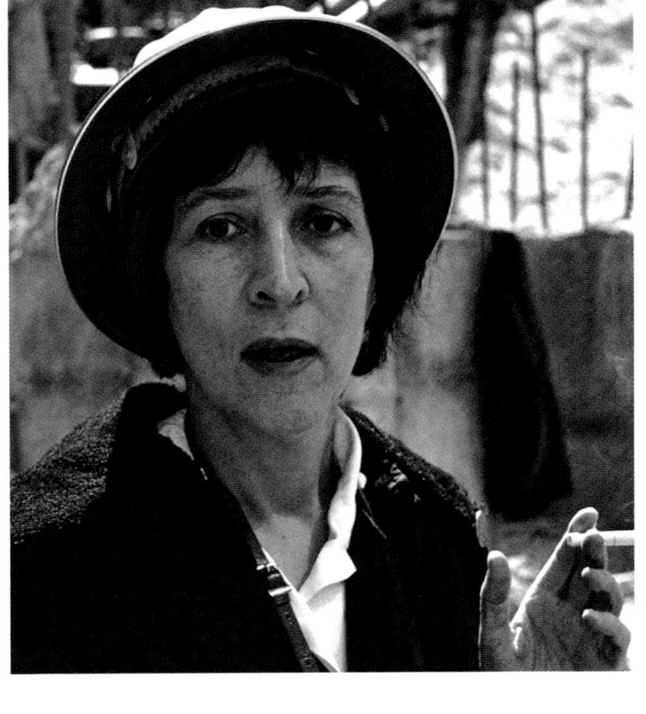

In a moment of brutal candour, Walker Evans (p. 112) announced that he did not admire Ansel Adams (p. 104), Paul Strand (p. 52) or Edward Weston (p. 36). The only photographers he thought had something original to say – apart from himself – were Henri Cartier-Bresson (p. 132) and Helen Levitt.

Levitt, who knew Cartier-Bresson when he was making photographs in New York, learned from him that a picture did not have to have social meaning, but 'could stand up by itself'. Levitt was soon admired for her instantaneous street compositions, which led to her work being included in the Museum of Modern Art's inaugural 1937 photography exhibition, and in a 1939 edition of *Fortune* magazine, then a hotbed of photographic talent. Her solo exhibition at MoMA, 'Photographs of Children by Helen Levitt', was not the sort of thing you would take the kids to at the weekend. Levitt's pictures were of children playing out their own fantastic games and identities, stuff more akin to Surrealism than Sunday school. Some found the photographs lyrical and poetic, but no one thought them appropriate for story hour.

Levitt's pictures did not change greatly when she took up colour photography in the 1950s, but the audience that found children to be fascinating wild things faded. Moreover, there was less play in the streets as kids moved inside to watch television. Also, Levitt was not as well known to intellectuals or discussed as much as she had been in the 1930s and 1940s. Her photographs appeared in the historic 1955 'Family of Man' show, where they were drained of their uniqueness and made to speak of human goodness. Eventually, though Levitt's work had its fans, it was also criticized because its subject was deemed to be the province of snap-shooters and department store photographers.

Today, Levitt's early work has shaken off its 1950s sugar coating, in part because of her dynamic colour work, which she began well before colour was taken seriously in the art world. Children appear in this later work, but she also photographed a variety of adults. The range of her colour work is likely never to be known, because most of her work from the 1960s was stolen in a burglary at her home.

Self-portrait, 1963.

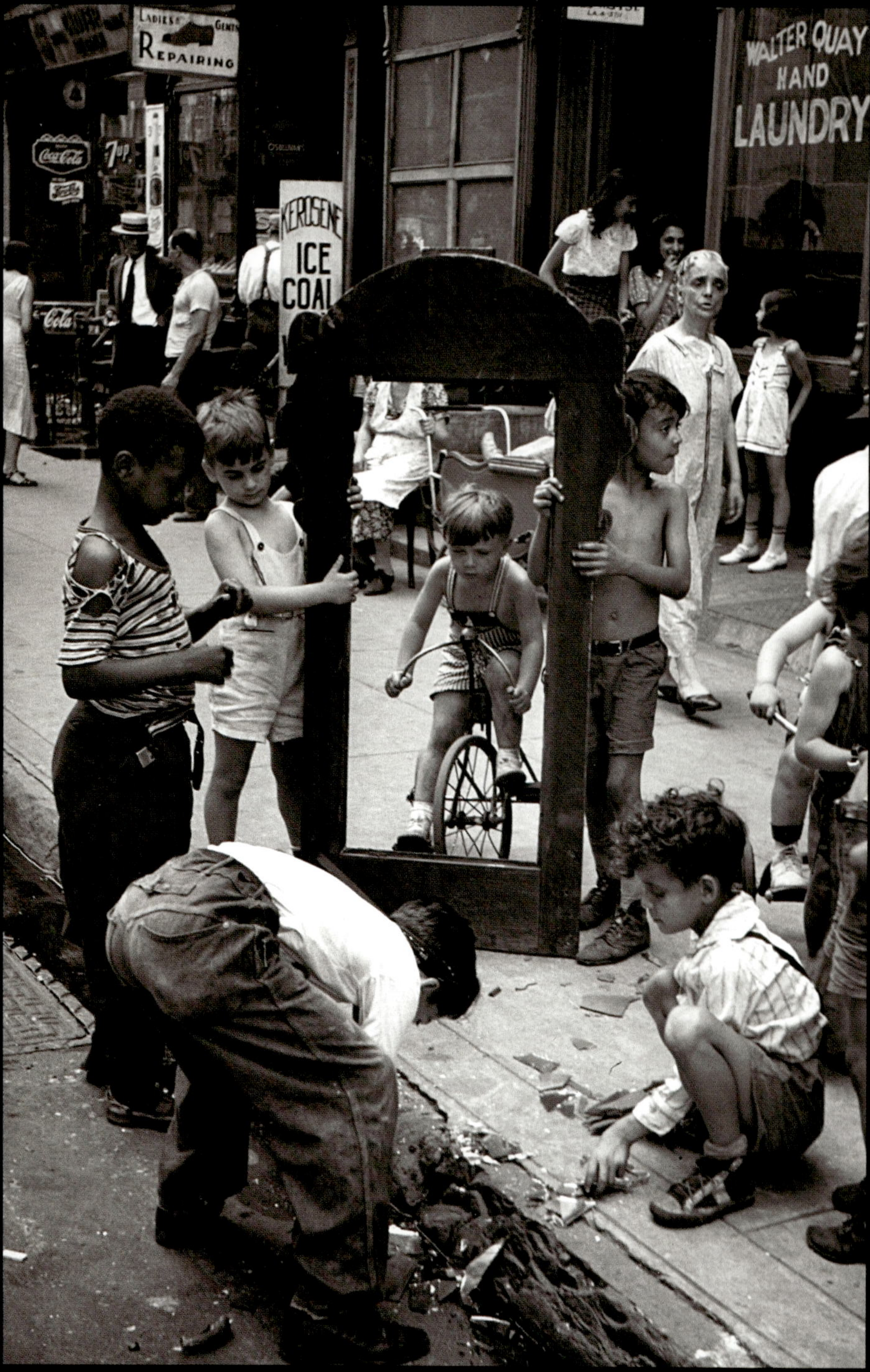

New York, c. 1945.

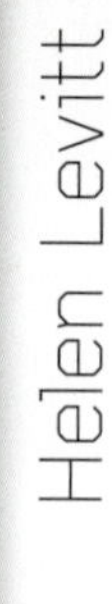


1910

**1913** Born in New York, USA

1920

**1931** Works for a commercial portraitist, where she learns darkroom techniques

**1936** Begins photographing children on the streets of New York

**1939** Images reproduced in *Fortune* magazine

**1943** One-person exhibition at Museum of Modern Art, New York

**1948** With painter Janice Loeb, collaborates on independent films *Spanish Harlem* and *The Quiet One*

1950

**1955** Images appear in 'Family of Man' exhibition at Museum of Modern Art

1960

**1965** Publishes *A Way of Seeing*, started in the 1940s with James Agee

**1970** Burglar makes off with most of her colour work from the 1960s

1980

**1991** Retrospective at the Metropolitan Museum in New York and the San Francisco Museum of Modern Art

**1997** Retrospective at the International Center for Photography, New York

**2001** Publishes *Crosstown*, a collection of her photographs

**2009** Dies in New York, USA

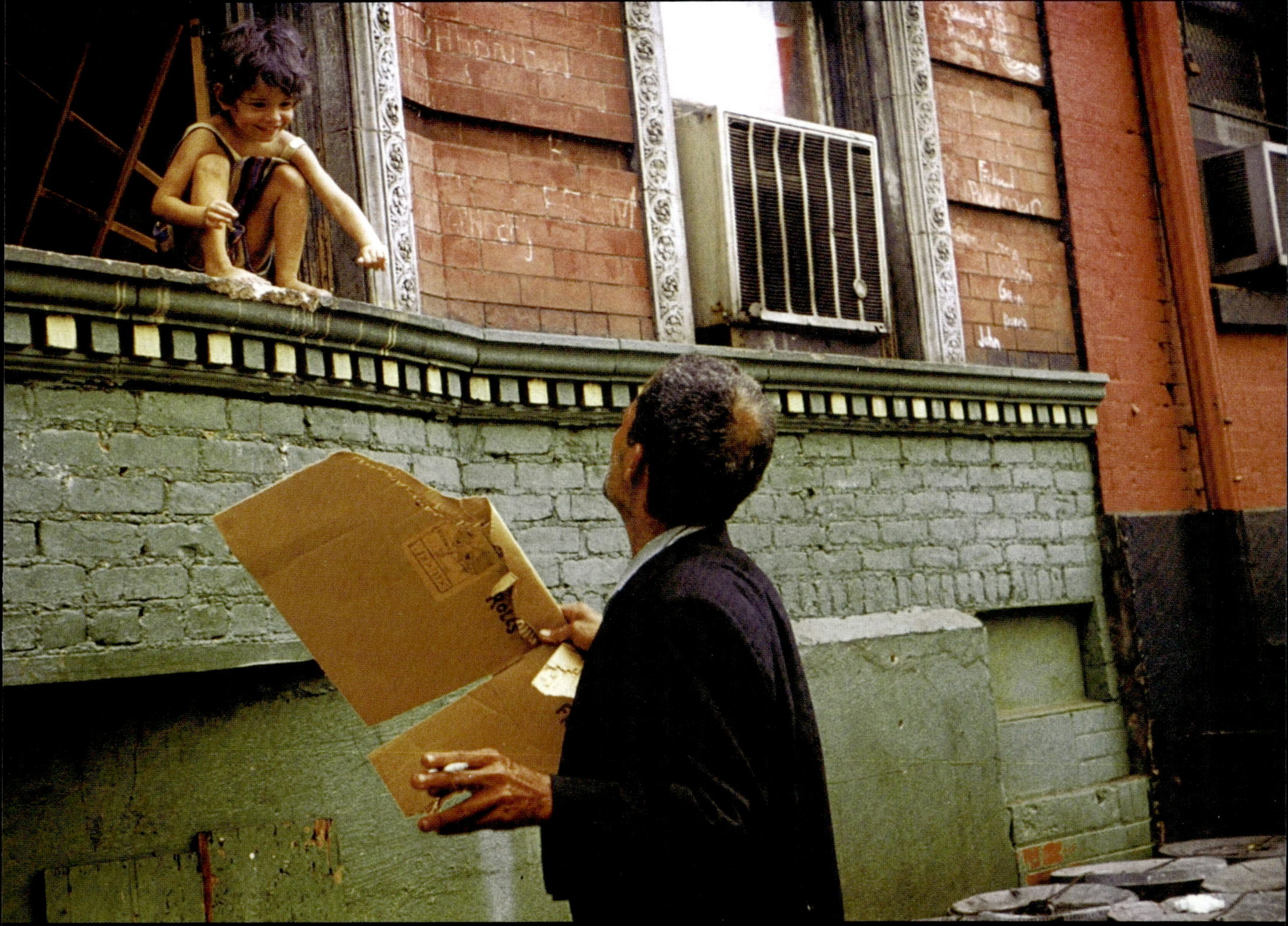

**Above** New York, 1972.

**Below** New York, 1971.

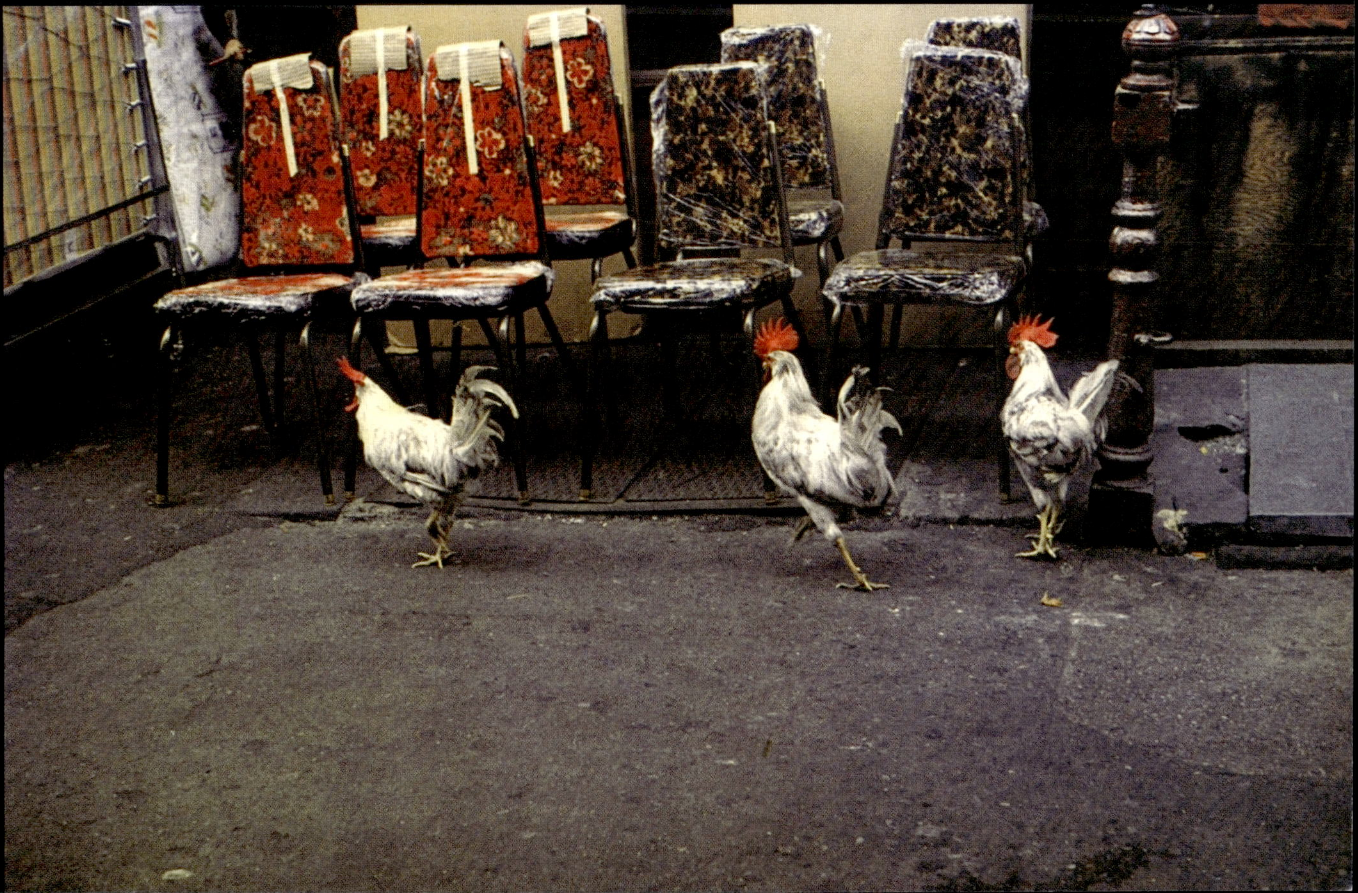

American soldier killed by
German snipers, Leipzig, Germany,
18 April, 1945.

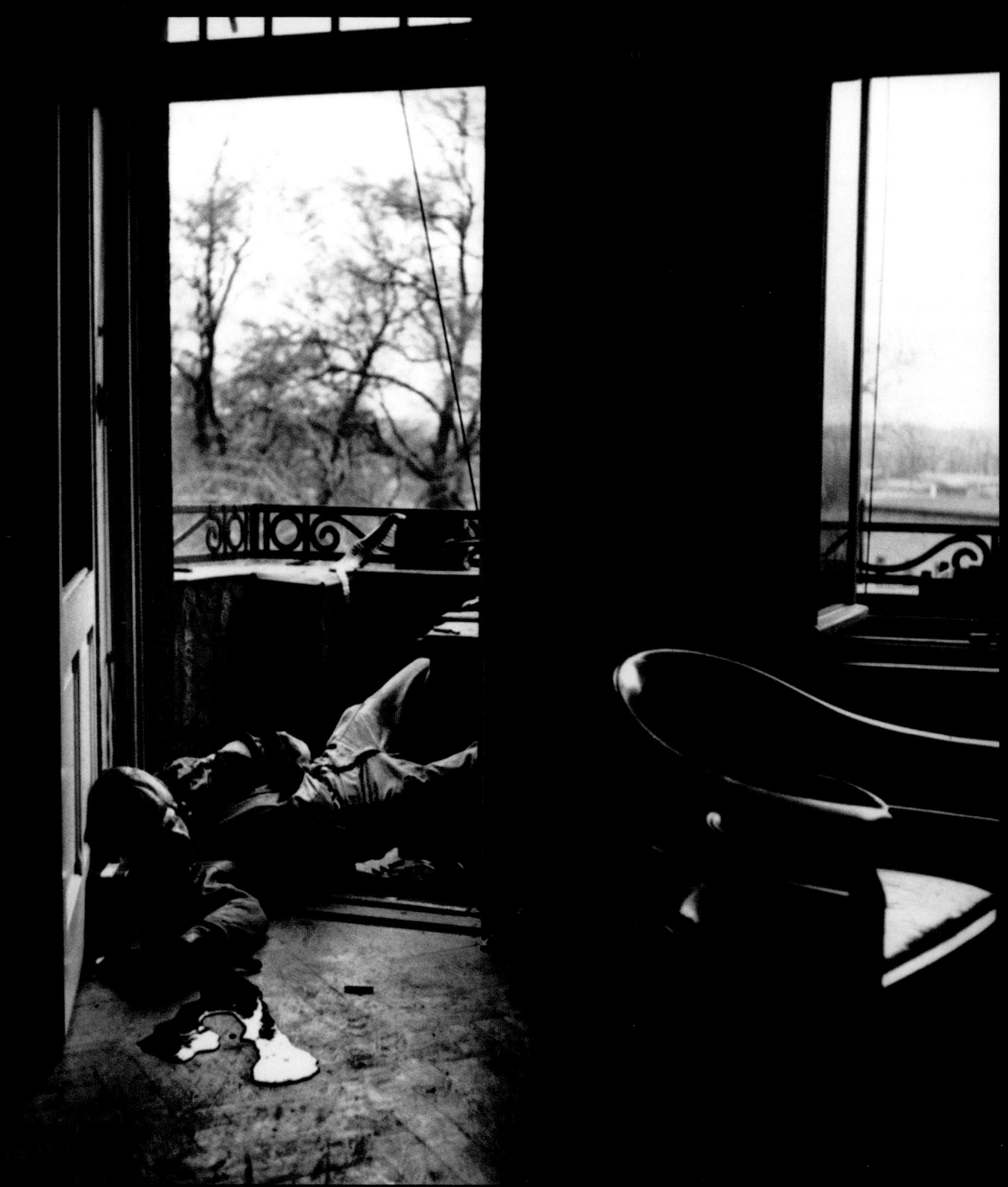

'The war correspondent has his stake – his life – in his hands.'

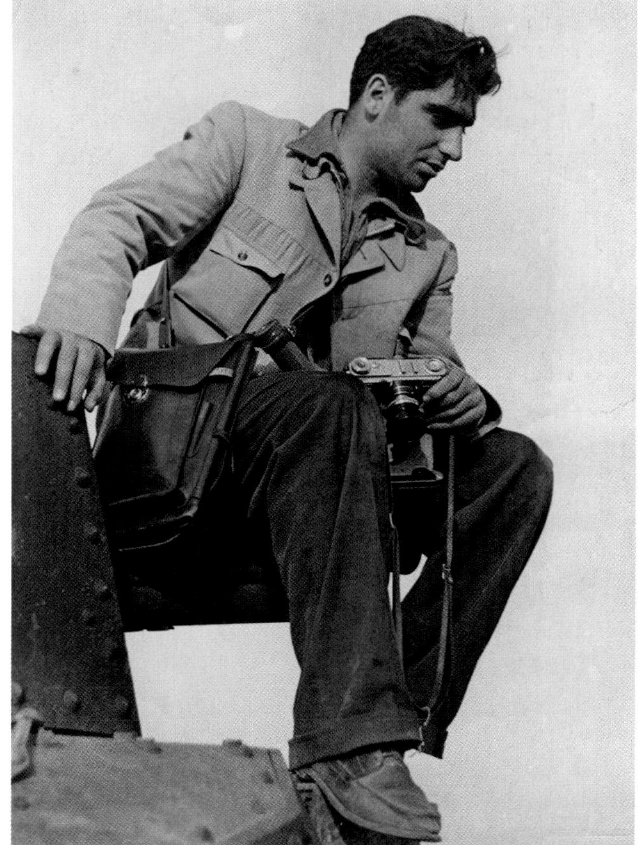

# Robert Capa

1913–1954

HUNGARY

When Robert Capa went to Hollywood after World War II, he began to write his war memoirs, with an eye to turning them into a screenplay. It was never made into a film. From time to time, there are big-budget biopics about Capa under consideration, but none has appeared, suggesting that Hollywood does not dislike Capa so much as find him difficult to dramatize. Capa himself was self-invented – he created the fascinating if illusive photographer 'Robert Capa' in order to sell his photographs in Paris during the 1930s. Before he left to cover the Spanish Civil War, he adopted the name and claimed his doppelganger's fame.

The life of the man whose legendary catchphrase was 'If your pictures aren't good enough, you're not close enough' might better fit in the realm of video games and superheroes, though his name seems to have come from the movies. Possibly from the now classic *It Happened One Night,* he adapted 'Capa' from the director's name, Frank Capra. 'Robert' seems to have come from popular leading man Robert Taylor.

However fictitious the name, Robert Capa the photographer lived up to his motto. One picture from the Spanish Civil War, which seems to show the instant that a Loyalist soldier is mortally wounded, was challenged in the 1970s and has been a source of speculation ever since. In a lost radio interview recorded in 1947 but rediscovered in 2013, Capa told interviewers that he took the picture by holding the camera over his head and never saw the photo until after it was published. Capa's decision to go in with the first wave of soldiers to reach Omaha Beach was motivated by the belief that a photographer needed to be in the thick of the action. The pictures' silvery blur and graininess was not intentional, but exacerbated by a mistake made by a darkroom assistant who used too much heat and melted the film.

Over time, Capa's venturesome attitude towards war photography has become a norm for both still and moving image coverage of conflicts, making war photography one of the world's most deadly occupations.

Self-portrait, China, 1938.

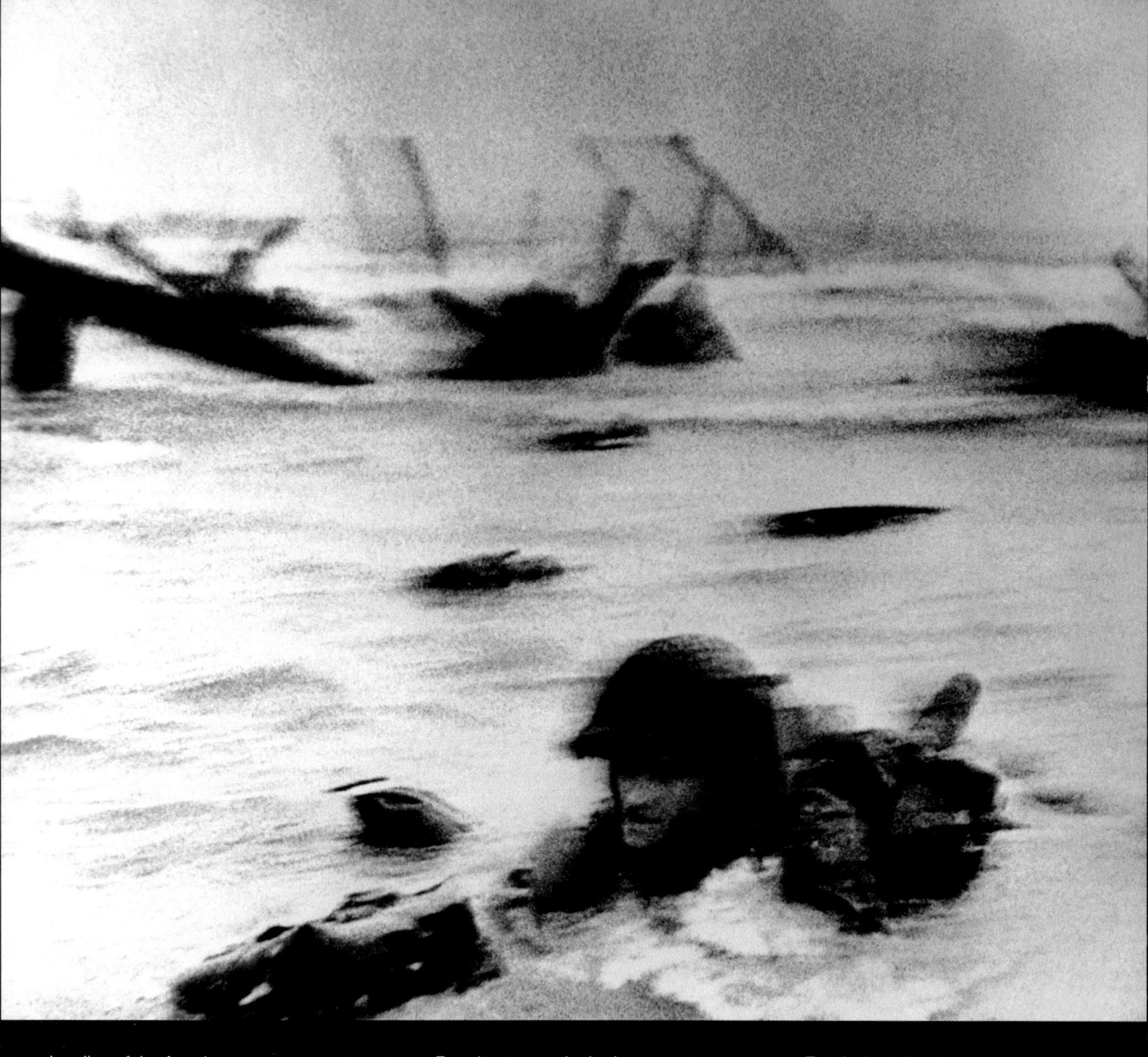

**Above** Landing of the American troops on Omaha Beach, Normandy, France,

**Opposite top** French woman who had a baby with a German soldier, Chartres,

**Opposite bottom** Trotsky lecturing in Copenhagen, 1932.

# Robert Capa

1910

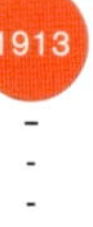

1913 Born Endre Friedmann in Budapest, Hungary

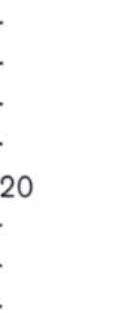

1920

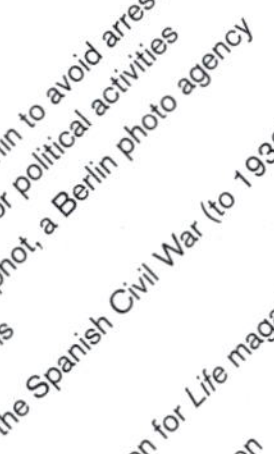

1931 Moves to Berlin to avoid arrest in Hungary for political activities

1932 Works at Dephot, a Berlin photo agency

1933 Moves to Paris

1936 Photographs the Spanish Civil War (to 1939)

1940 Photographs Mexican election for *Life* magazine

1944 On D-Day, lands with American troops on Omaha Beach in Normandy, France

1946 Attempts to write a war chronicle

1947 Founds Magnum photo agency with other photographers

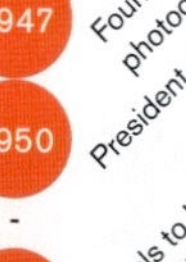

1950 President of Magnum (to 1953)

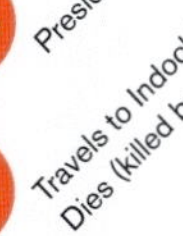

1954 Travels to Indochina for *Life*
Dies (killed by landmine) in Thai Binh, Vietnam

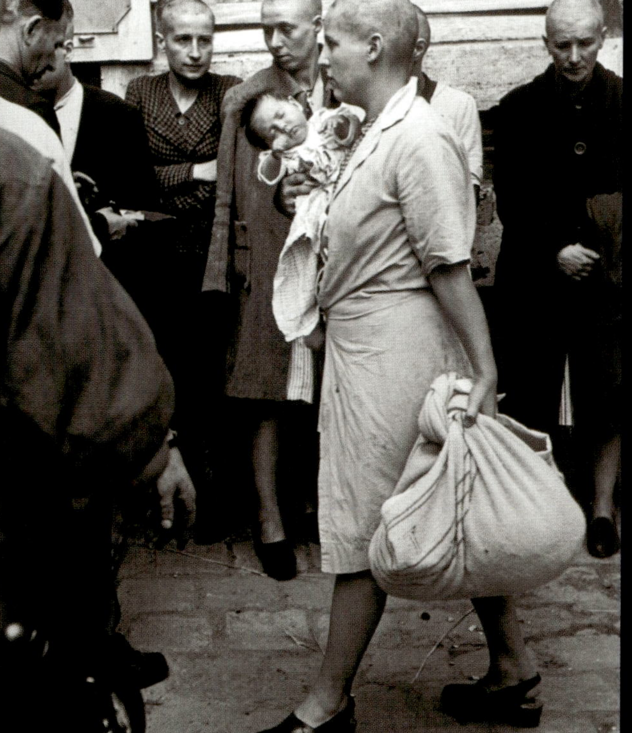

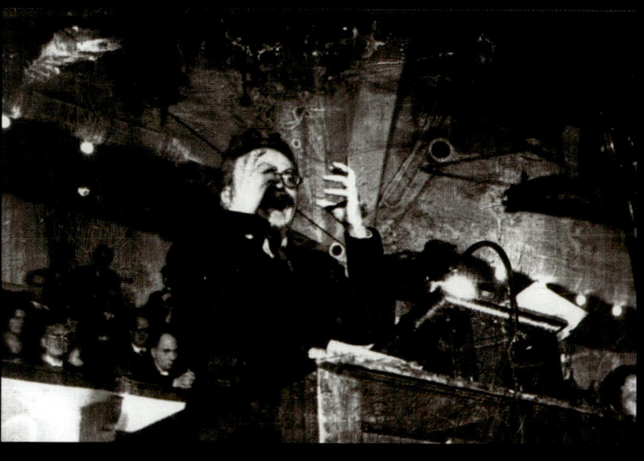

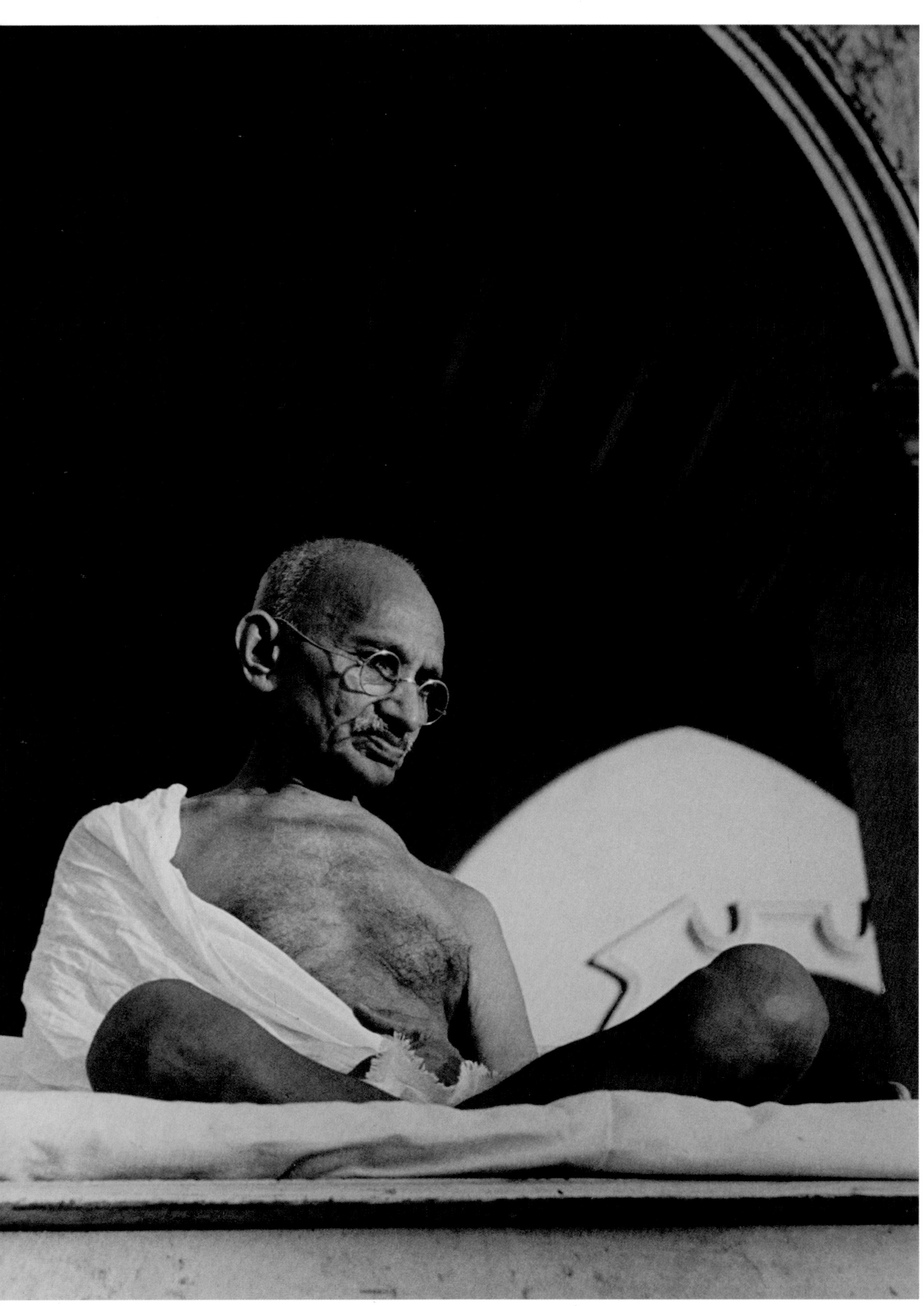

'A photograph should at least have clarity.'

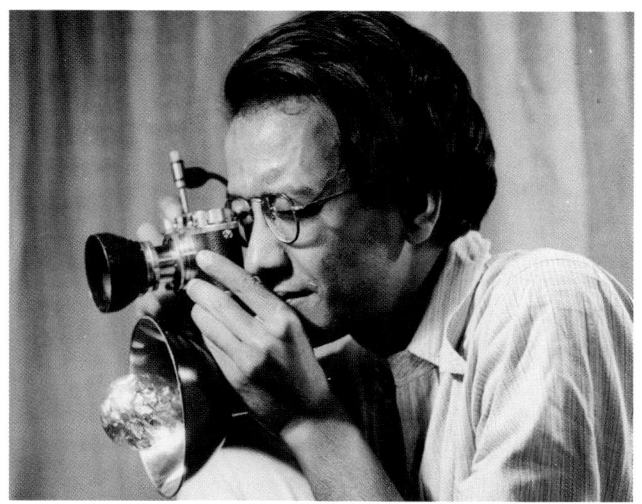

# Sunil Janah

1918–2012

INDIA

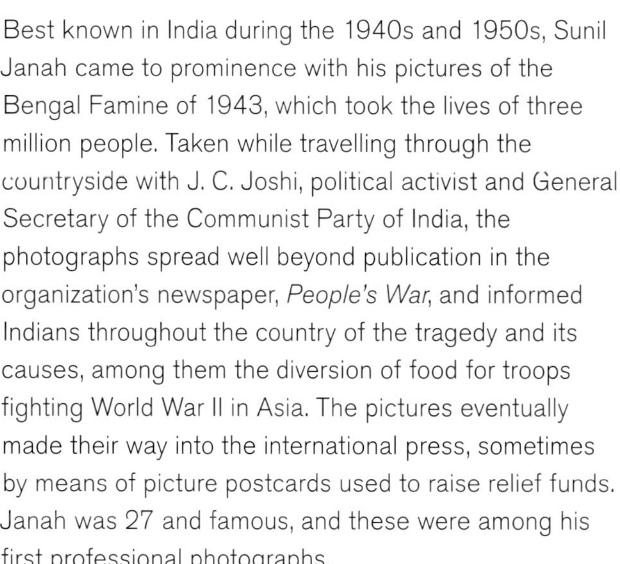

Best known in India during the 1940s and 1950s, Sunil Janah came to prominence with his pictures of the Bengal Famine of 1943, which took the lives of three million people. Taken while travelling through the countryside with J. C. Joshi, political activist and General Secretary of the Communist Party of India, the photographs spread well beyond publication in the organization's newspaper, *People's War*, and informed Indians throughout the country of the tragedy and its causes, among them the diversion of food for troops fighting World War II in Asia. The pictures eventually made their way into the international press, sometimes by means of picture postcards used to raise relief funds. Janah was 27 and famous, and these were among his first professional photographs.

Janah turned his back on his academic pursuit of English literature and law degrees, and became a full-time photographer. Yet he did not take advantage of his reputation to work in mainstream photojournalism. With a small stipend from the Communist Party, he travelled through the country, recording hardship as well as the distinctive tribal people of India.

Margaret Bourke-White (p. 120), who worked in India from 1945 to 1948, asked him to accompany her to photograph famines in the south, and they worked on and off together while she was in India. She was staying in Janah's family home in Calcutta when Gandhi was assassinated, and they both photographed the subsequent uproar in the streets. When Janah grew disillusioned with politics, he became a portrait photographer, making likenesses of Indian artists, scientists and dancers, as well as of temple sculpture. With film-maker Satyajit Ray, who designed Janah's first book, and others, he also formed the Calcutta Film Society.

Two contrasting bodies of work occupied his time in post-independence India. He took assignments to photograph the creation of large steel plants, aluminium works and power stations, while his photographs of tribal people and their lives expanded. His work is an unparallelled record of Indian cultural history and of the era of independence and modernization in the mid-twentieth century.

**Opposite** Mohandas K. Gandhi at a meeting in Birla House, Bombay (now Mumbai), Maharashtra, 1946.

**Above** Portrait of Sunil Janah by Ramesh Bellare, 1940s.

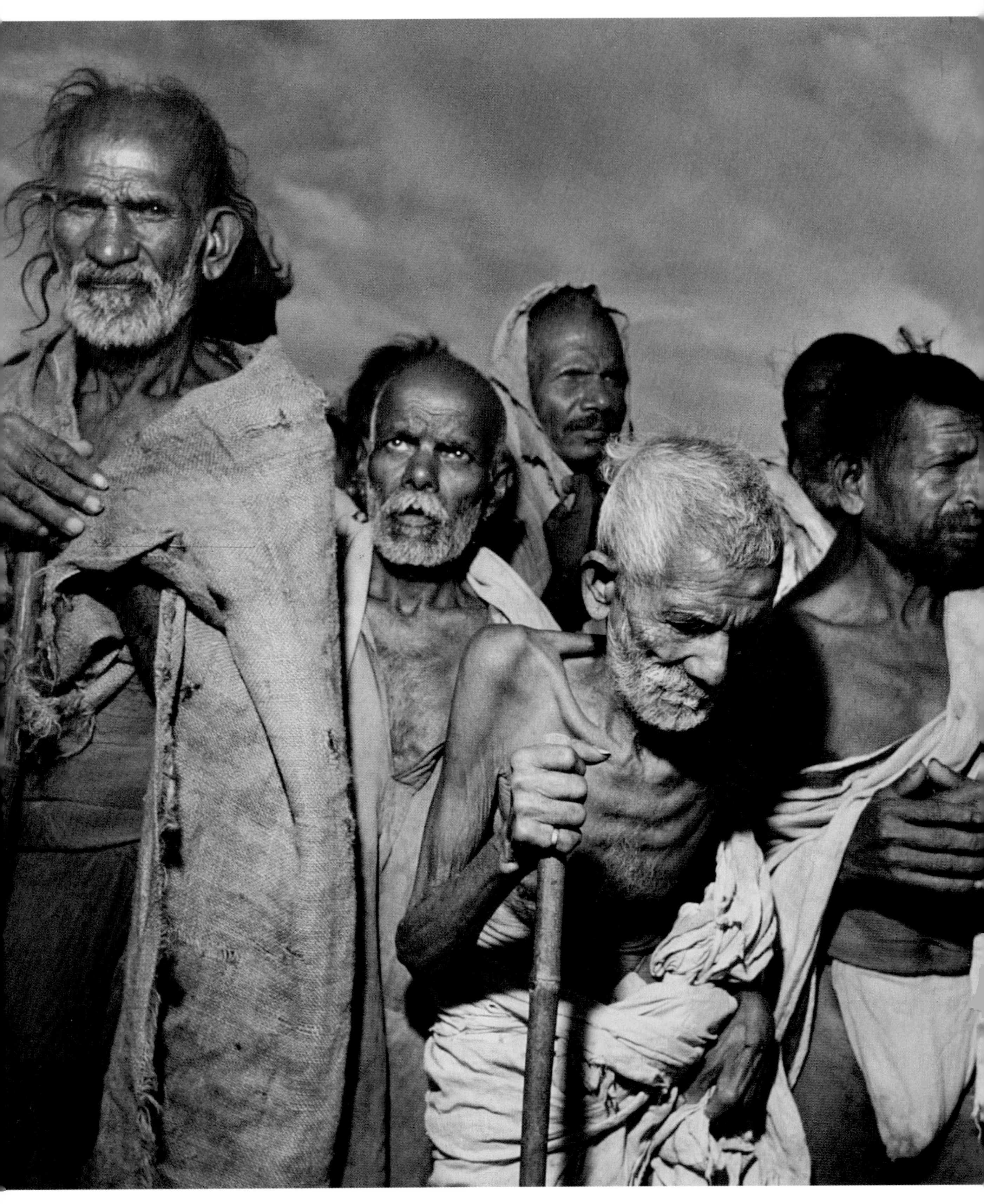

**Opposite** Starvation victims arriving at a relief centre in the Rayalaseema region, 1945.

**Below** Muria boy in front of the decorated mud wall of a ghotul, Bastar, Chhattisgarh, India, 1950s.

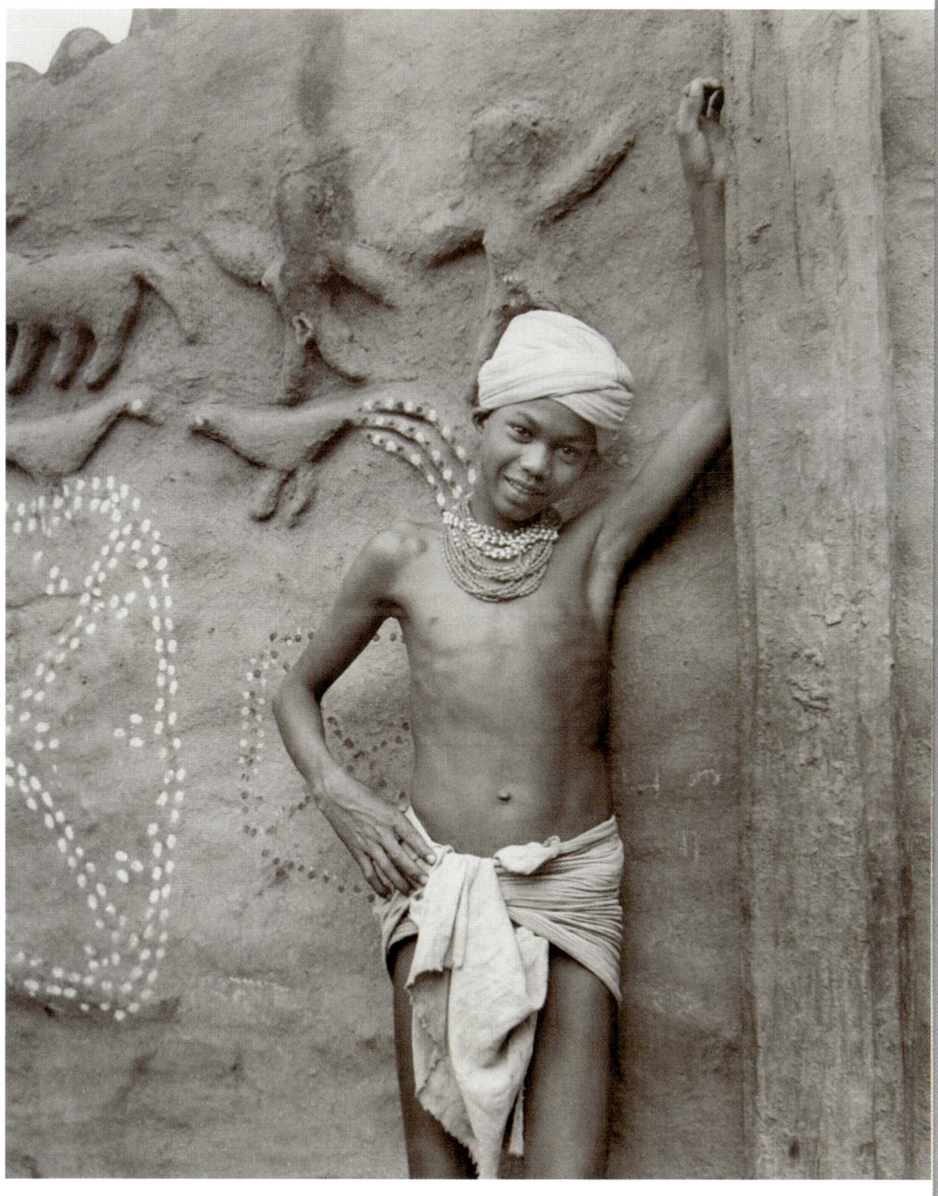

## Sunil Janah

- **1918** Born in Dibrugarh, Assam, India
- **1925** Receives his first camera
- **1943** Photographs the Bengal Famine; photo editor of the *People's War*/*People's Age* newspaper (to 1946)
- **1945** Covers the South India famine, with Margaret Bourke-Whitte
- **1949** Publishes *The Second Creature*, a book on women in India
- **1958** Head of the Department of Photography at the Calcutta School of Printing Technology (to 1967)
- **1967** Works in Delhi (to 1979)
- **1972** Awarded the Parma Shri outstanding achievement award by the Government of India
- **1979** Publishes *Dances of the Golden Hall*, with an introduction by Indira Gandhi
- **1993** Publishes *The Tribals of India*
- **2003** Moves to the USA
- **2012** Dies in Berkeley, California, USA
- **2013** *Photographing India* published

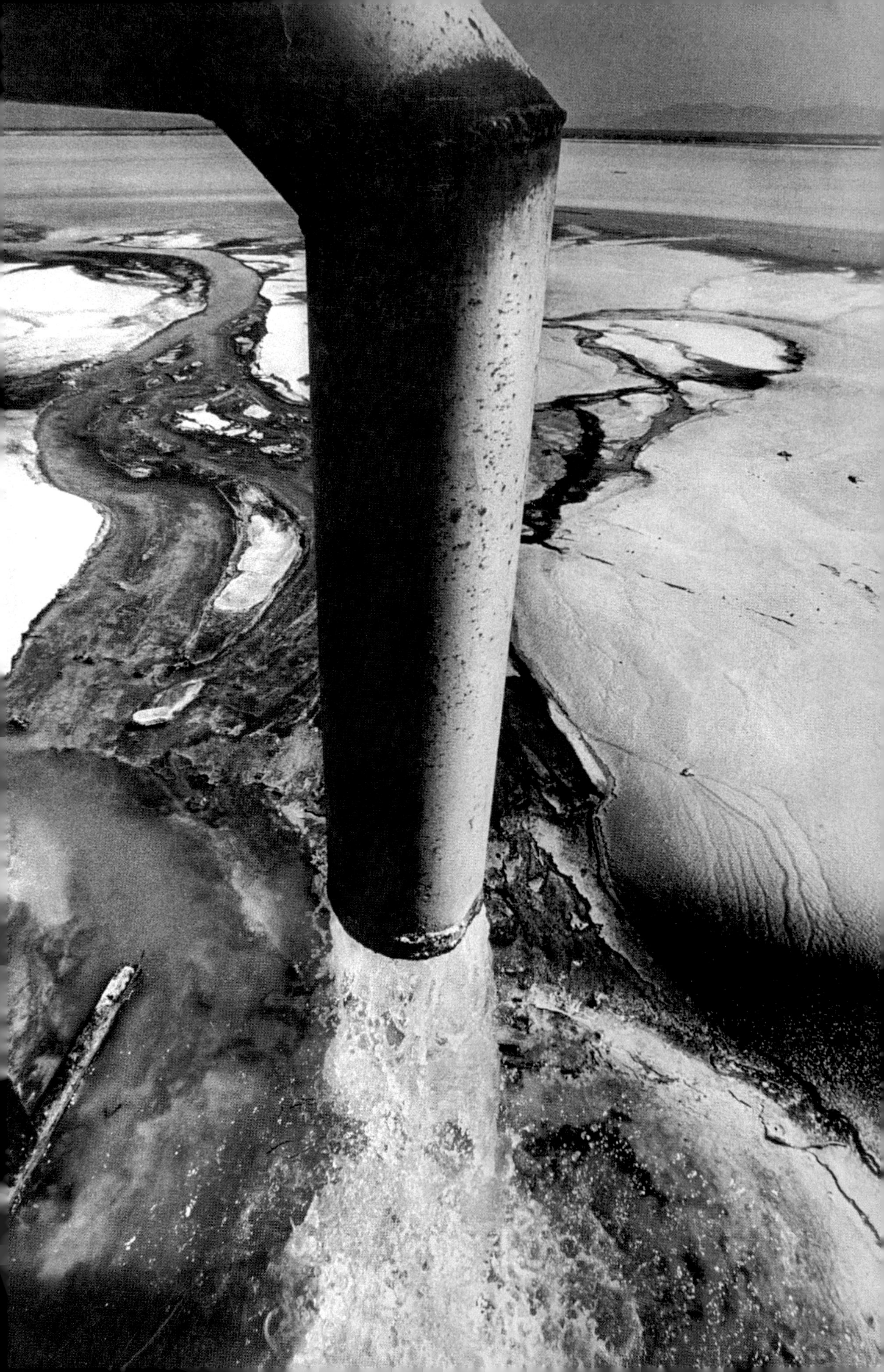

'Photography is a small voice, at best, but sometimes one photograph ... can lure our sense of awareness.'

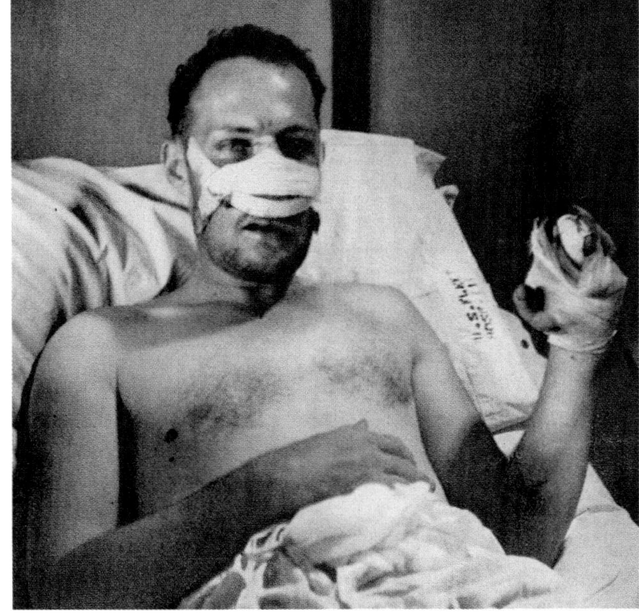

# W. Eugene Smith

1918–1978

UNITED STATES

Gene Smith, as he was called, learned photography at his mother's knee, and again when he learned how to pitch assignments to photo-editors in New York. But the advent of World War II made him disdain the frivolous pictures he had made and, with the invulnerability of youth, he proclaimed: 'I will find a way to be in this war – I must! ... I must bring my cameras to this war.' When he was hired by the publishing firm of Ziff-Davis to be a naval correspondent, he quickly prepared for the assignment that would ultimately make him despise war.

The photographs that Smith took during combat on the islands of Saipan and Iwo Jima were published as a photo-essay in *Life* magazine. They have endured, both as historical accounts of the devastation wreaked on combatants and inhabitants, and as symbols of wartime excess. Smith suffered the continuing effects of combat injuries for the rest of his life.

While his strongest work appeared in his photo-essays for *Life,* such as 'The Country Doctor' and 'Man of Mercy' (a description of Albert Schweitzer's hospital near Lambaréné, now in Gabon, Africa), Smith's personal and visual style did not always coincide with that of his editors. Smith preferred inky blacks and bright highlights that eliminated detail, and he wanted to be in charge of the layout and sequence of his images. Tonal areas in his photos sometimes resemble those of woodblock printing, a look that did not sit well with editors struggling for an emotionally and visually balanced publishing approach that would work well with advertisements. Disagreements about such matters as this led to Smith's resignation from *Life.*

When he was given relatively free rein to work with writer-photographer Stefan Lorant in the creation of a book to celebrate the hundredth anniversary of Pittsburgh, Pennsylvania, in 100 prints, Smith shot more than 22,000 negatives. In these pictures, his dark patches remained, but the formerly flat lights became luminous. A similar luminosity gave a religious tone to pictures of Tomoko Uemura and other Japanese victims of mercury poisoning that Smith made during three years in Japan. These were collected in the book *Minimata,* named for the city where many were made ill. Smith also joined protest marches against a company accused of malfeasance and suffered injuries, including one to his left eye. At the end of his life, his body bore many marks testifying to his work.

**Opposite** Industrial Waste from the Chisso Chemical Company, 1972.

**Above** Portrait of an injured W. Eugene Smith by Carl Mydans, 1945.

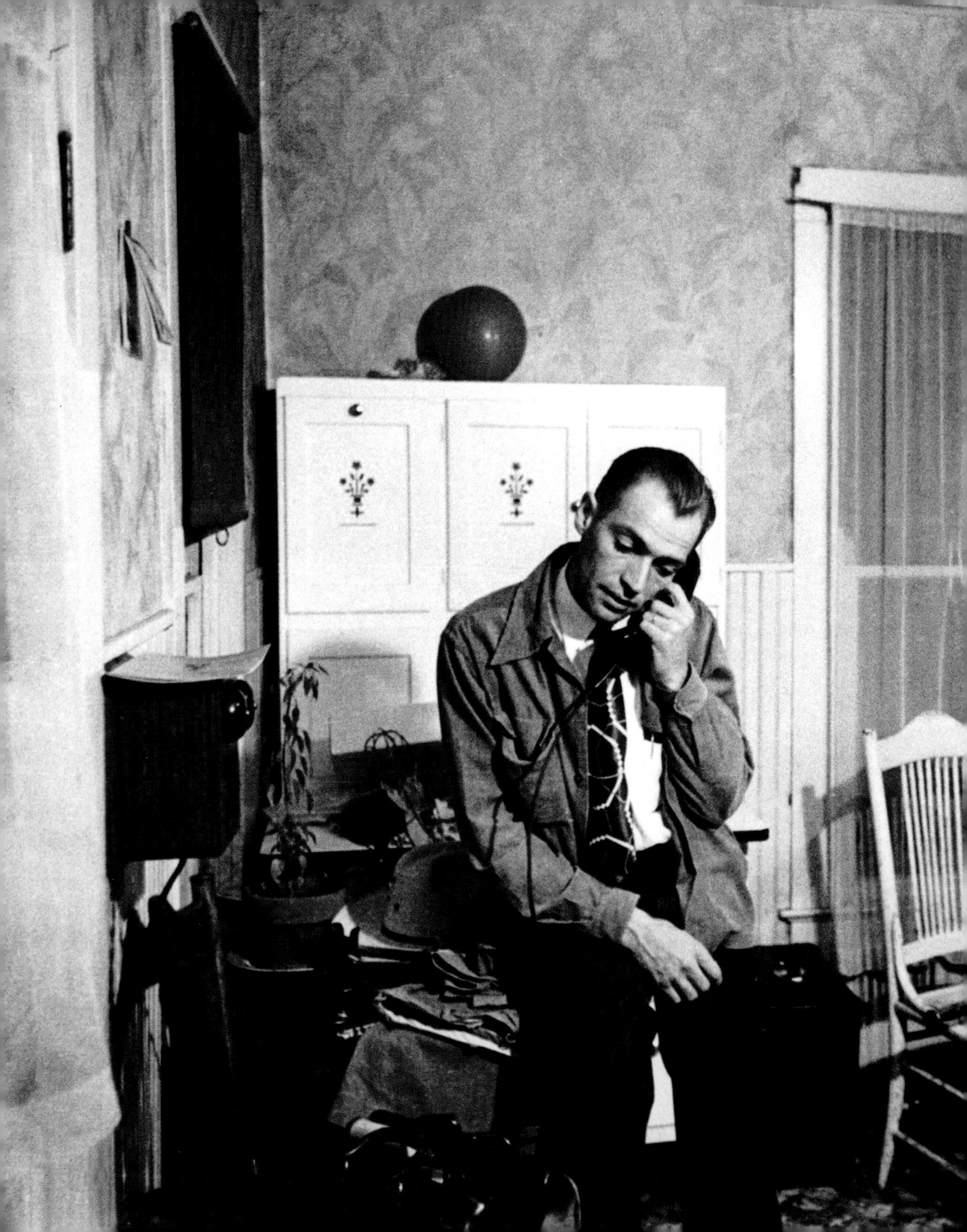

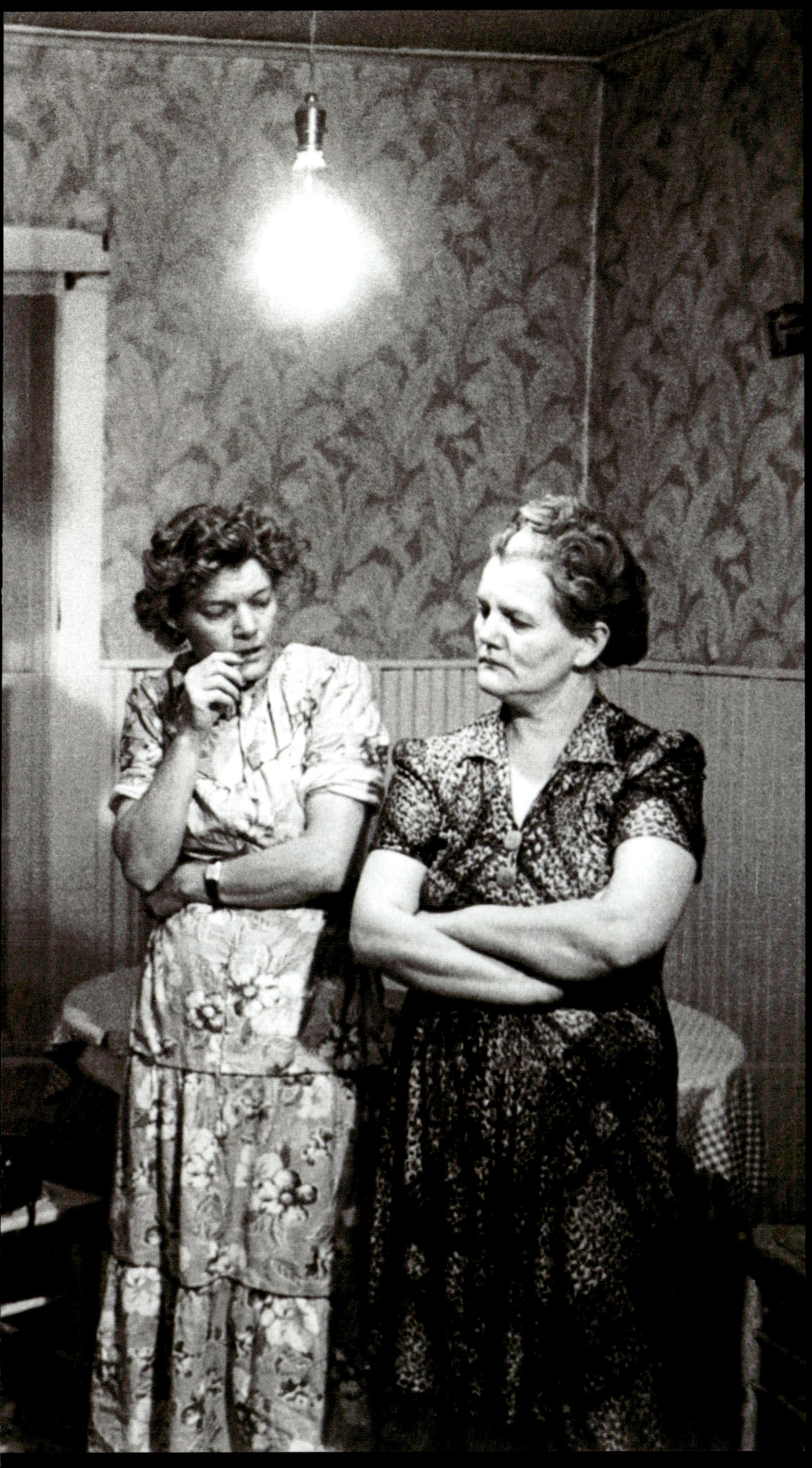

## W. Eugene Smith

1910

1918 Born William Eugene Smith in Wichita, Kansas, USA

1920

1930

1937 Moves to New York

1939 Gets his first assignment with *Life* magazine; also publishes work with *Newsweek*, *Colliers* and *Look*

1943 Photographs WWII in the Pacific (to 1945)

1947 Starts publishing photo-essays for *Life*

1950

1955 Leaves *Life* magazine; joins Magnum photo agency; begins project to make visual record of Pittsburgh, Pennsylvania

1960

1970

1974 'Let Truth Be the Prejudice' at the Jewish Museum in New York and the National Gallery of Art in Washington, DC

1975 Publishes *Minamata*

1978 Dies in Tucson, Arizona, USA

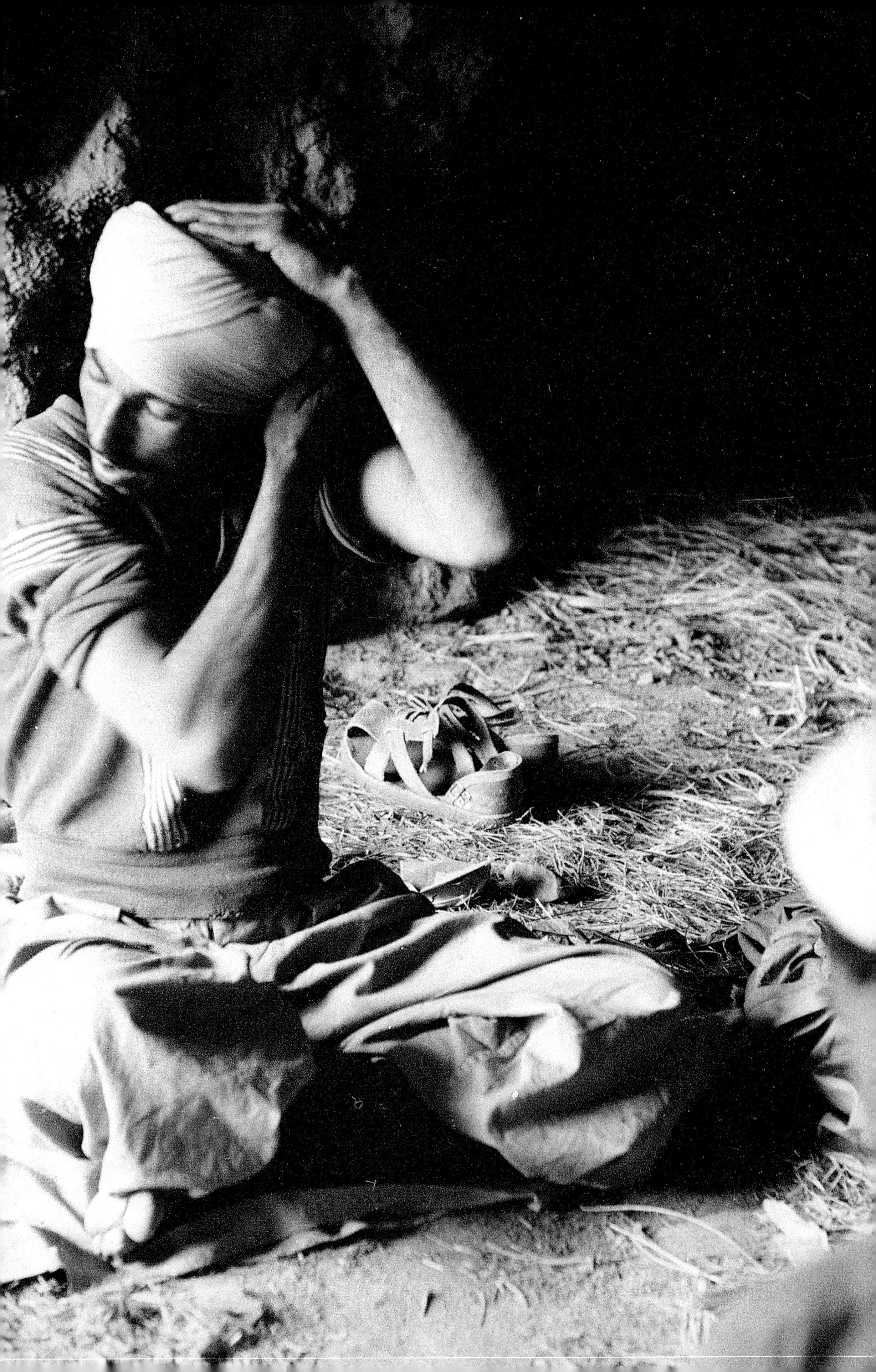

'I wish I knew what was expected of me ... I have a fine incipient case of split personality.'

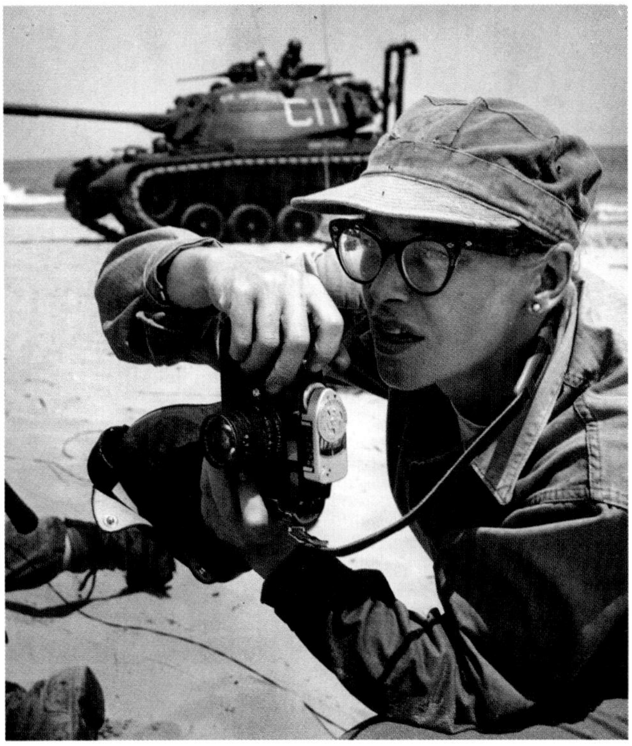

# Dickey Chapelle

1919–1965

UNITED STATES

Young Dickey Chapelle had a passion for aeroplanes. She published her first magazine article, 'Why We Want to Fly', when she was 14. Rejecting her given name, she dubbed herself Dickey after the explorer Admiral Richard Byrd. When, at 17, she received a full scholarship to the Massachusetts Institute of Technology to study aeronautics, her future seemed clear. But she was an indifferent student, and left MIT after one year, earning a living from jobs at air shows and writing articles; she called herself 'Boston's flying girl reporter'. She took up photography not because she had a calling, but because there were more jobs for photographers than for writers. When she met and later married photographer Tony Chapelle, he taught her the refinements of the craft.

Her sputtering photography career veered towards aviation and, as World War II approached, military operations. She took Margaret 'Peggy' Bourke-White's celebrity to heart (p. 120) and set her goal to be the first woman to photograph a place or an event. She liked to point out that during the war she was the first accredited woman correspondent to accompany Marines into a jungle. In the midst of the fighting on Iwo Jima, she had a chance to move up to the front, a position strictly forbidden to women correspondents. 'Let Peggy tie that!' she exclaimed.

Chapelle fought against the post-war notion that women should return to hearth and home by working abroad for relief agencies. With author James Michener, she made clandestine trips into Communist Hungary to aid fleeing refugees, earning her a mention in his book *The Bridge at Andau.* Imprisonment in Budapest for seven weeks did not lessen her nerve, and she soon found a way to accompany the anti-French rebels in Algeria. As she did in Hungary and would do in Cuba, she identified with the rebels. Setting aside the notion of objective journalism, she used her writing and photography to promote their activities. Her Algerian efforts finally convinced her colleagues that she was a capable combat journalist and photographer, and made her known to the general public. She gave lectures, sometimes driving from place to place in a 1957 'puke pink Chevrolet' provided by the lecture agency.

After working in Laos and Vietnam, she wrote a report on her own initiative to the Marine Commandant General asking that more American advisers be sent in. Dickey Chapelle died on patrol in Vietnam, when a mortar exploded while she was not wearing a flak jacket. She was the first war correspondent killed in the Vietnam War. Brigadier General S. L. A. Marshall remarked: 'No male war correspondent in our time has a comparable record. Most of the time, the men got the glory and the bylines, while she was doing it the hard way.'

**Opposite** *Algerian Man Adjusting a Turban*, 1957.

**Above** Self-portrait, 1959.

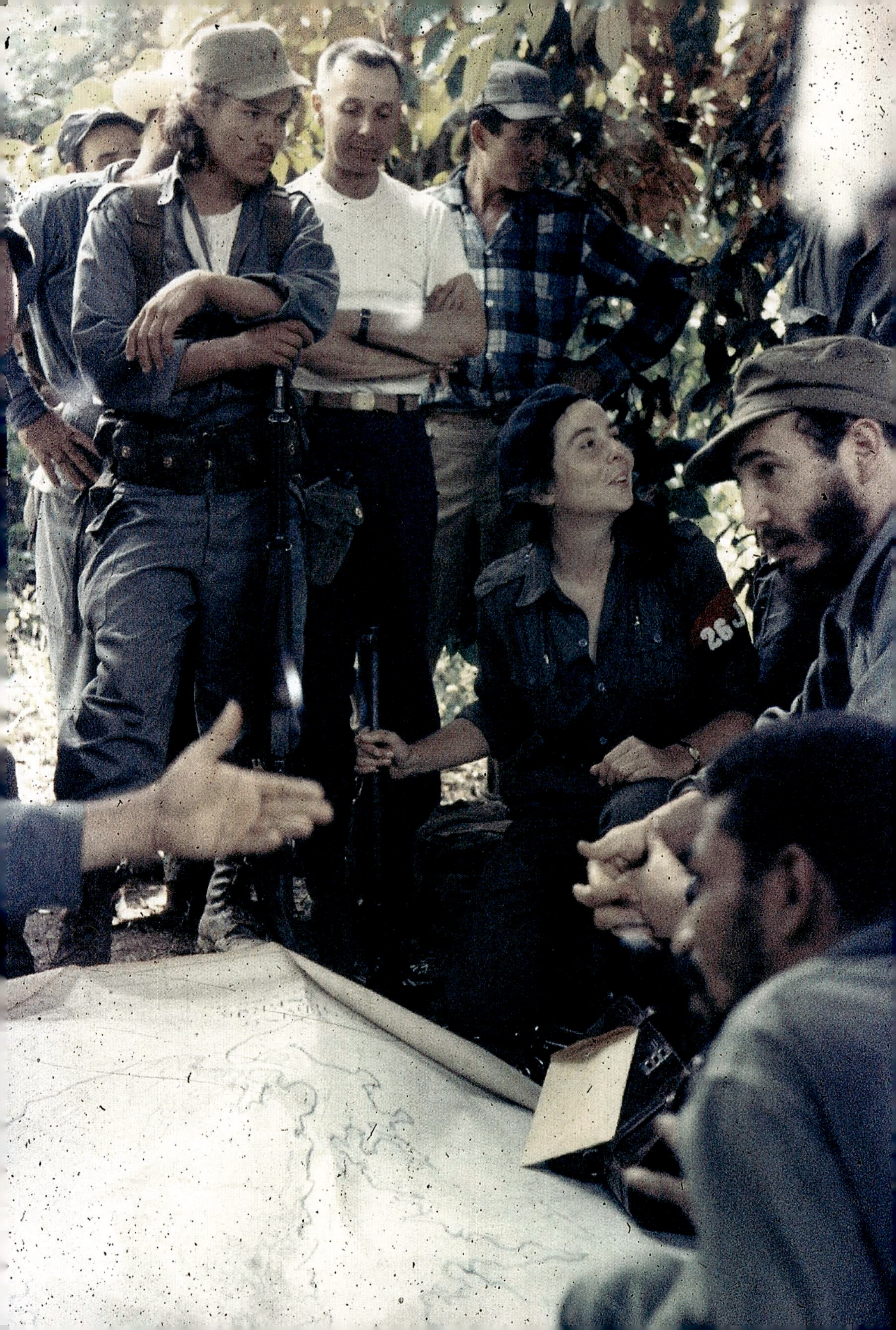
26J

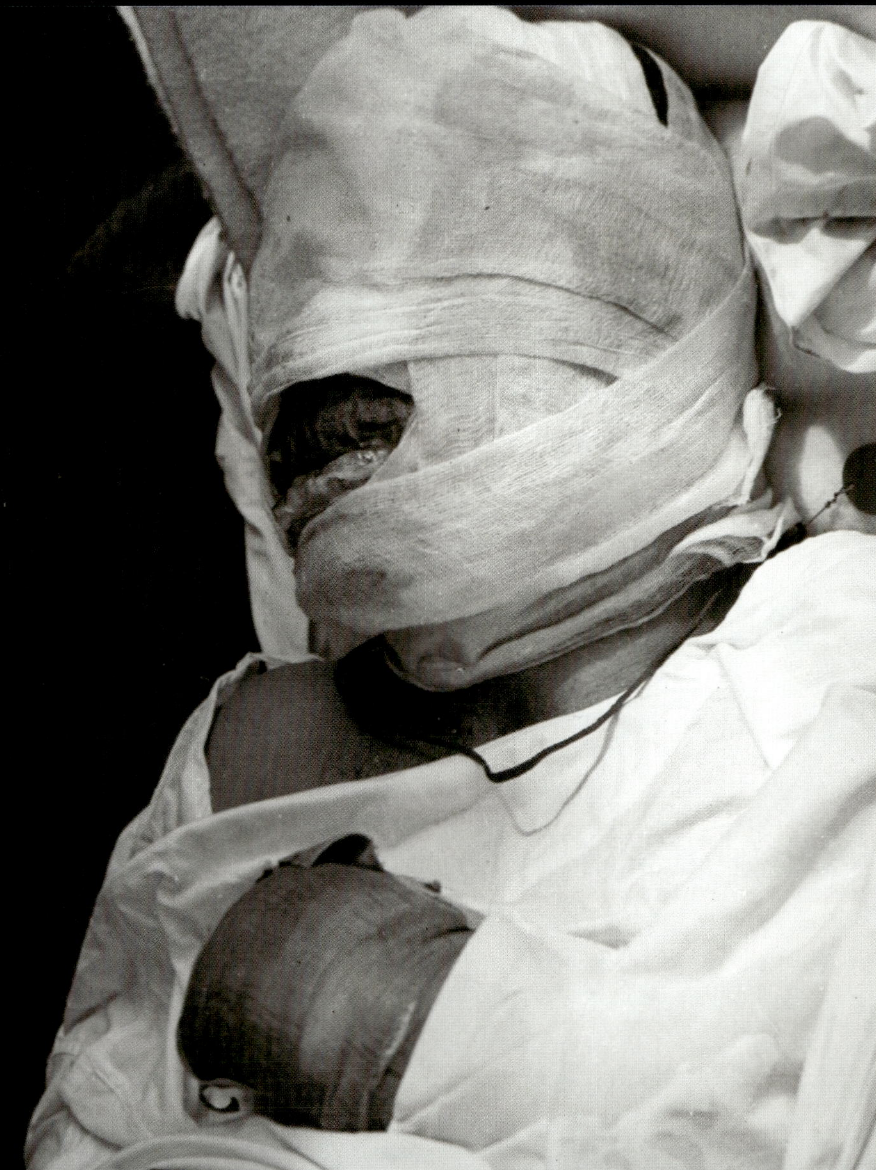

Opposite *26th of July Meeting in Oriente Province*, 1958.

Above *Injured Soldier*, 1945.

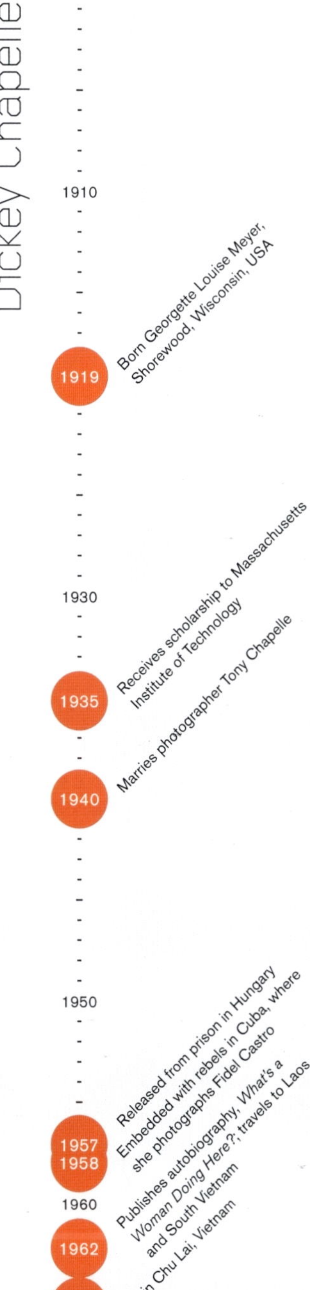

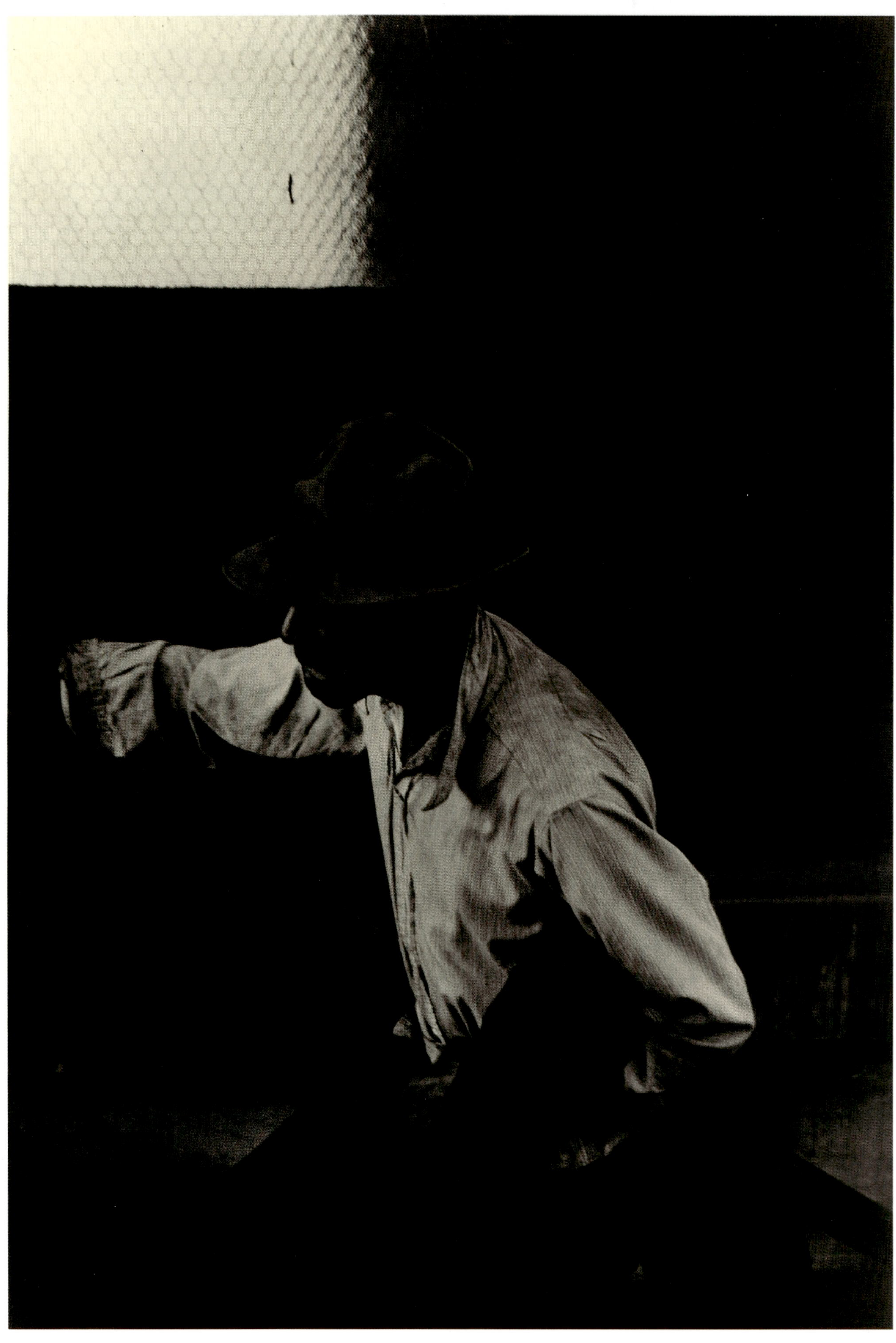

*Man Coming up Subway Stairs*, 1952.

'People – their well-being and survival – are the crux of what's important to me.'

# Roy DeCarava

1919–2009

UNITED STATES

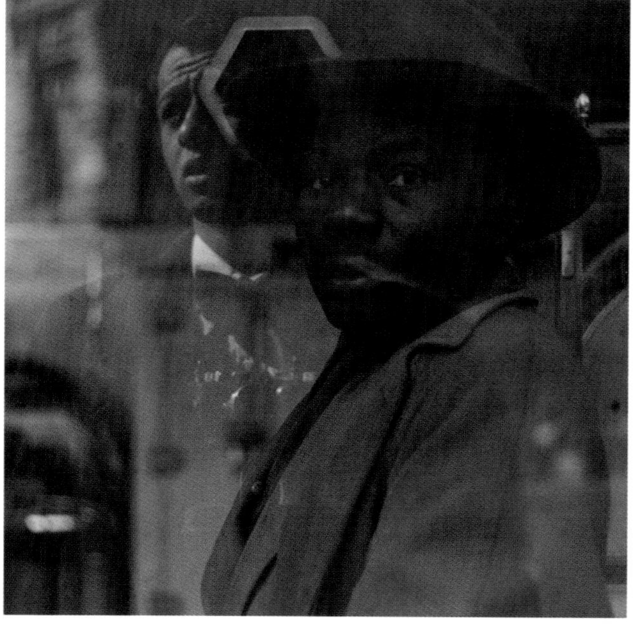

Although Roy DeCarava bought a camera to record ideas for his printmaking and painting, he soon realized that photography was more than a means for making notes. Close to 30 years old, he began to concentrate solely on camera work. He came to photography with a philosophy of picture-making that included a desire to express himself through interaction with photography's graphic properties of light and dark. He stated that documentary photography was often too coldly factual, and he never viewed himself as a street photographer because the genre frequently dwelled on crowds to the detriment of individual identity. In his own work, he often focused on single persons or small groups. That emphasis informed his application to the Guggenheim Foundation, where he wrote that for this early project he wanted to concentrate on showing 'the strength, the wisdom, and the dignity of the Negro people'.

DeCarava had a keen sense of formal experimentation. He loved working with available light as much as possible. Consequently, his pictures tend to be dark, with a multitude of values inhabiting what he decribed as the 'infinite range of tonalities' possible within photography. He insisted that 'each image has its own fingerprints, its own dynamic'.

DeCarava's interest in experimentation and preference in portraying individuals worked well when he collaborated with poet Langston Hughes for a book that became *The Sweet Flypaper of Life.* His photographs were the source for and enlarged Hughes's observations through the imaginary character, Sister Mary Bradley, an African-American grandmother, who narrates the text with her impressions of the people in the Harlem area and beyond. Soon after the book was published, DeCarava envisioned another volume, a compendium of his jazz photographs and poems, to be called *the sound i saw*, a title that astutely plays with the concept of synesthesia, the phenomenon of experiencing one of the human senses through another, in this case, seeing through hearing, and vice versa. Despite the success of *Sweet Flypaper*, he was unable for some time to find a publisher for a decade's worth of intimate and improvisational photographs. When the book was finally published in 2001, it contained jazz photographs and DeCarava's prose poems, along with a creative montage of his earlier pictures, forming a broad summa for his life in photography.

*Self-portrait through a Window*, 1956.

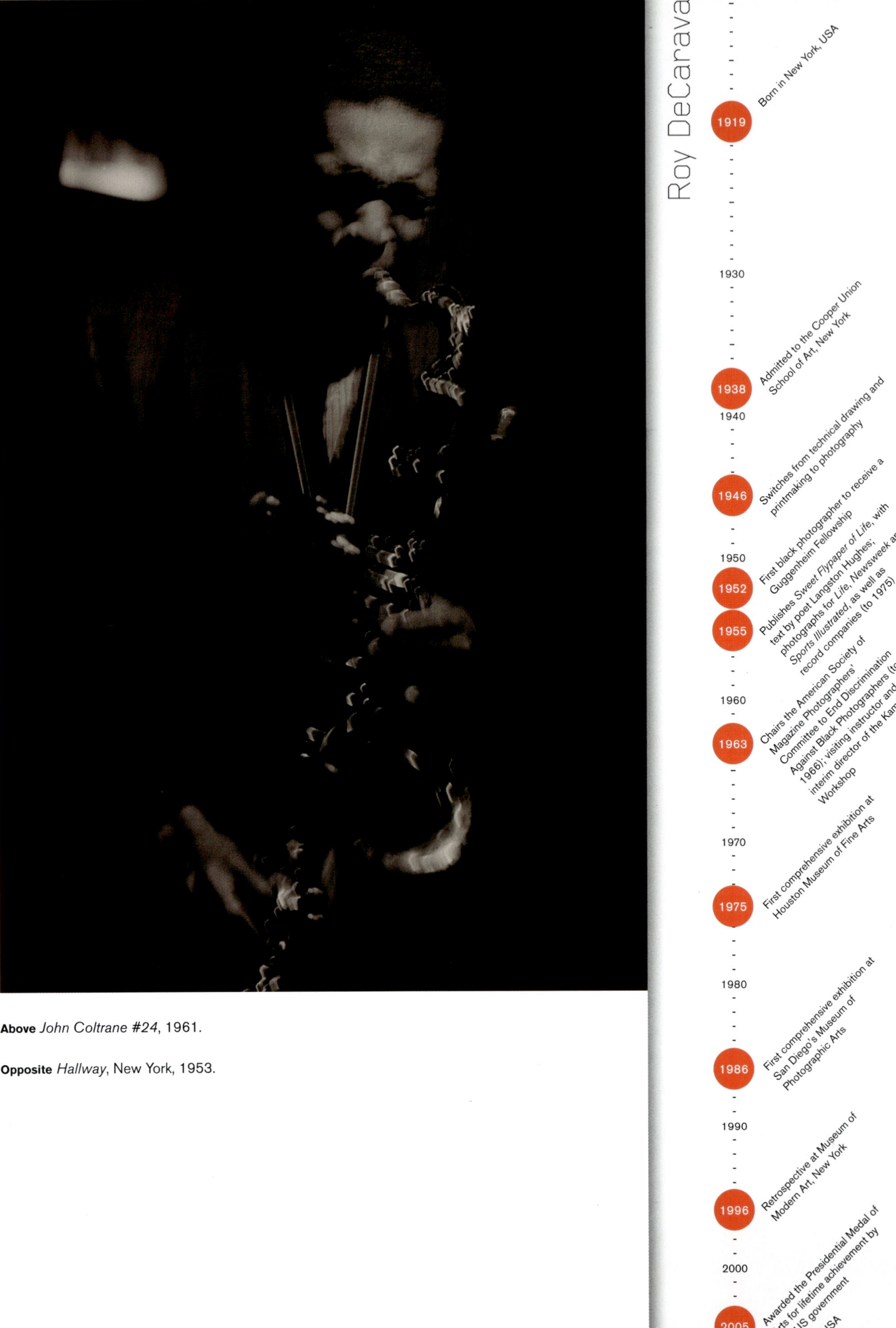


**Above** *John Coltrane #24*, 1961.

**Opposite** *Hallway*, New York, 1953.

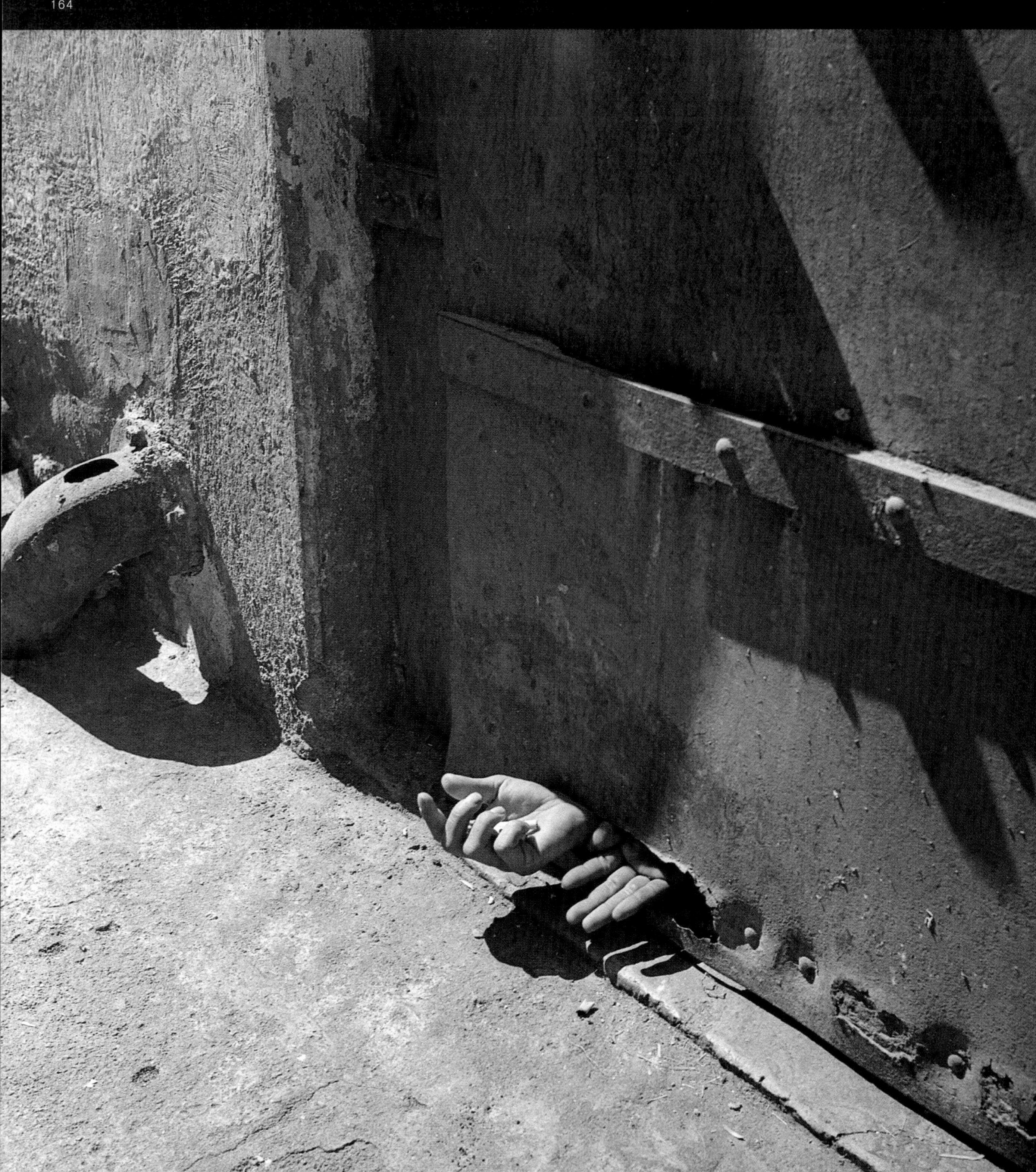

Hands with cigarettes under cell door, Lecumberri Penitentiary, Mexico City, from the series '*Prisión de Sueños*' ('Prison of Dreams'), 1950.

'The best photographers … master their job as personal expression and to earn their daily bread.'

# Nacho López

1923–1986

MEXICO

Self-portrait, c. 1950.

During an extraordinarily prolific period in the 1950s, Nacho López merged the aesthetic concerns of Mexican Modern photography with the topical imperatives of photojournalism. At the same time, he softened the sharp angularity of art photography and rejected the enigmatic Surrealism of his mentor, Manuel Álvarez Bravo (p. 108). When Mexico was going through an era of modernization that affected everything from cars to clothes, López refused to produce self-congratulatory paeans to progress.

In photo-essays that he shot and for which he sometimes created text and captions, he centred on everyday life, as it was available for all to see, in the streets, markets, churches and public buildings particularly of Mexico City and its environs. He struggled with prevailing ideas about indigenous people and the urban and rural poor, evolving relationships with his subjects and visual strategies that honoured difference. With text by journalist Carlos Arguelles, López's chronicle of prison life appeared in an issue of *Mañana,* showing the daily lives of the inmates, including outstretched hands below a rusty door. His strategy for portraying the poor in popular picture magazines often involved showing desperately inadequate dwellings. Even though his photographs may be shocking, they are not lurid.

López frequently posed his subjects and, indeed, created scenarios for shoots, in the manner of the film director he would become. He hired an attractive female model to walk populated streets while he recorded the expressions of men as they watched her. In another gag, he had a man walk through crowded streets carrying a female mannequin, setting it down occasionally, while López photographed. Although he mostly rejected the popular picturesque photographs that made poverty quaint, he was aware of the cruel irony that the subjects of his photographs would likely never see his published images, which appealed to comfortable middle-class readers. However chauvinistic, these scenes of popular humour may have served as a counterweight to his images that critiqued social conditions, increasing López's street creds at a time when some thought that his pictures denigrated Mexico.

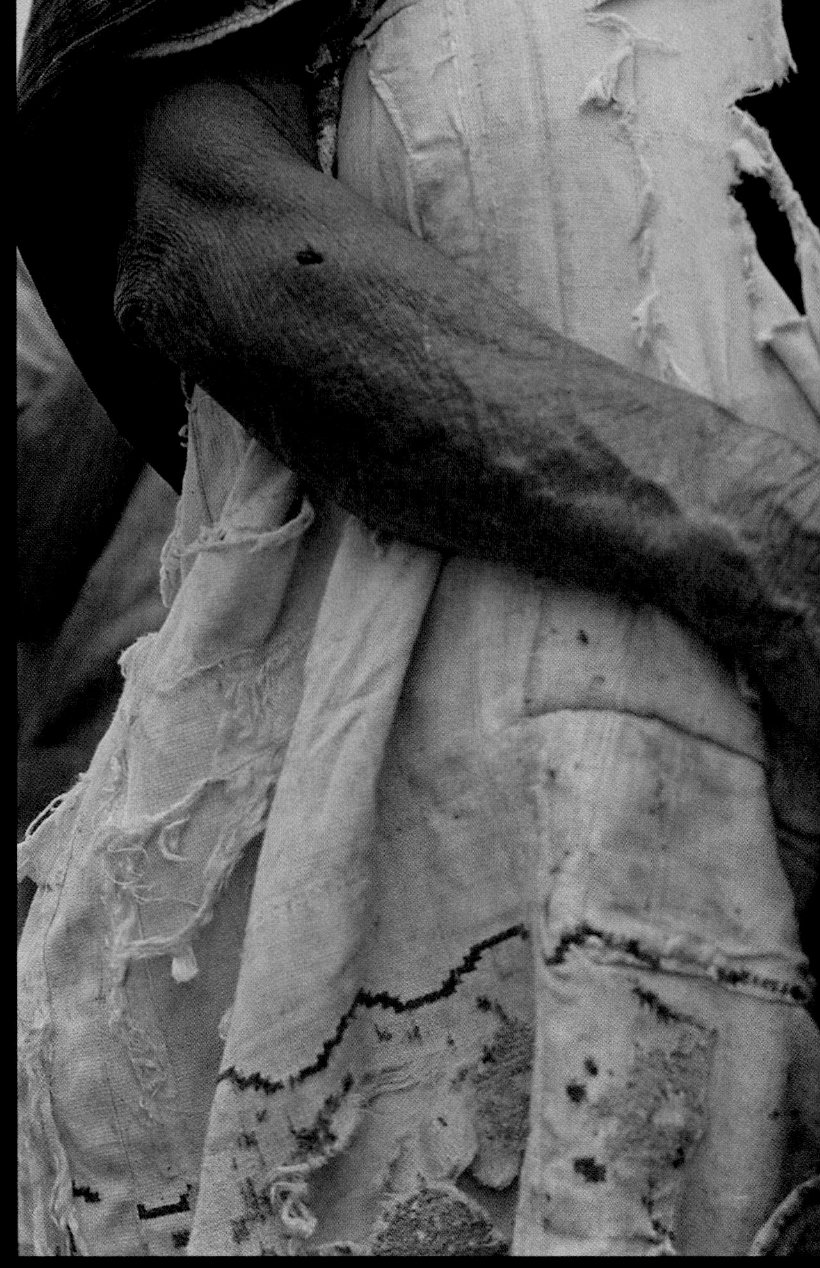

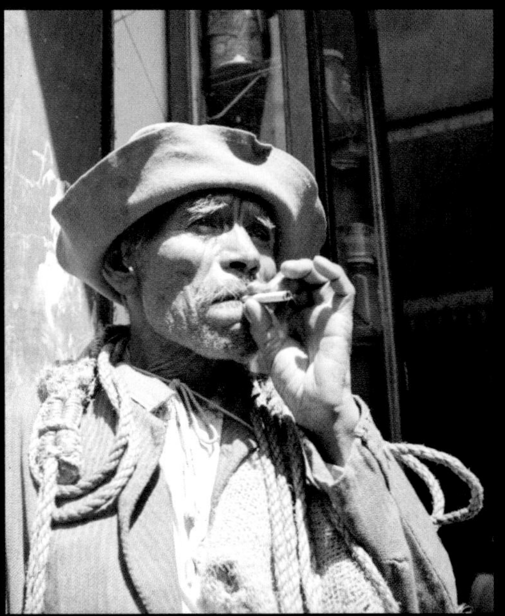

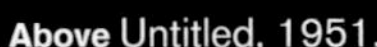

**Above** Untitled, 1951.

**Above right** From the 'María Sabina' series. Huatla de Jímenez, Oaxaca, 1980.

**Right** *Pachuco* or *Gigolo*, c. 1950.

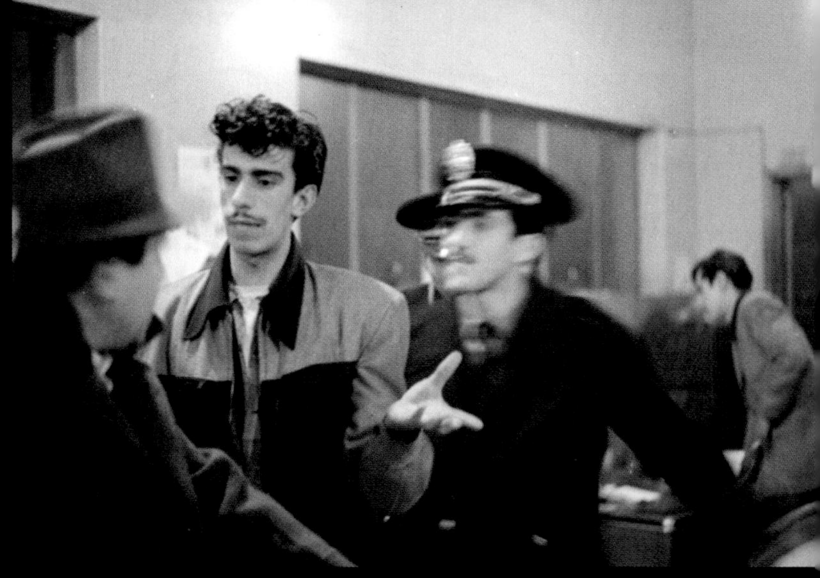

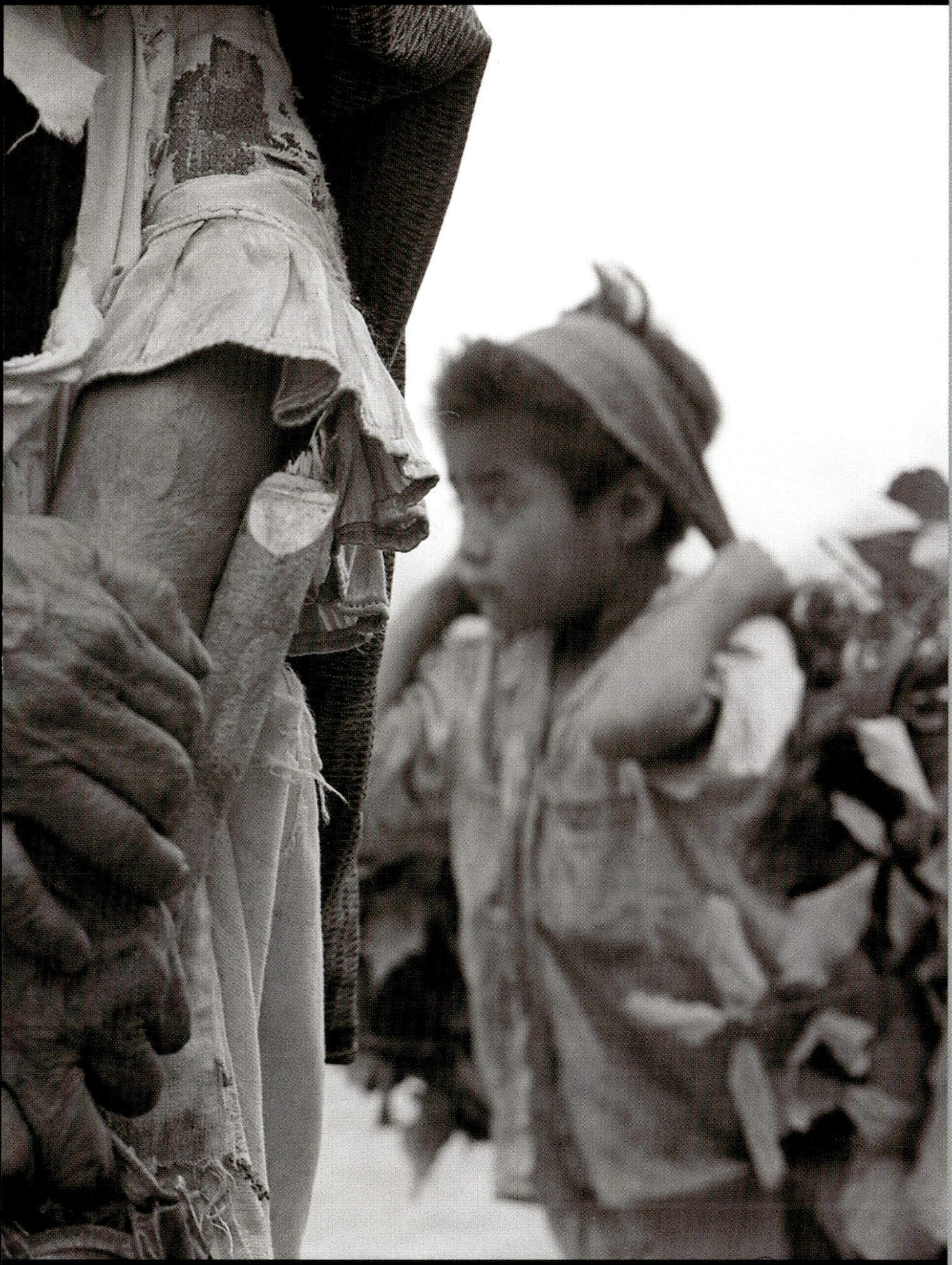

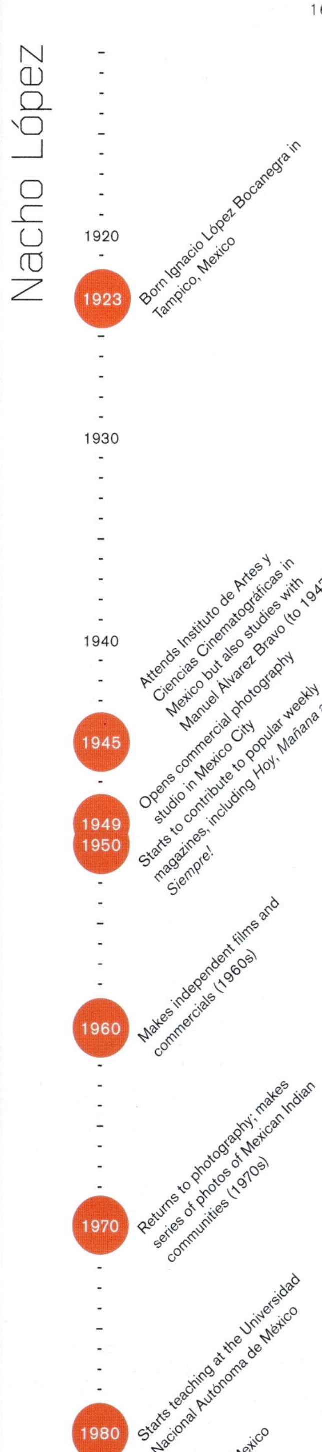

Nacho López
1920
1923
Born Ignacio López Bocanegra in Tampico, Mexico
1930
1940
1945
Attends Instituto de Artes y Ciencias Cinematográficas in Mexico but also studies with Manuel Álvarez Bravo (to 1947)
1949
Opens commercial photography studio in Mexico City
1950
Starts to contribute to popular weekly magazines, including *Hoy*, *Mañana* and *Siempre!*
1960
Makes independent films and commercials (1960s)
1970
Returns to photography; makes series of photos of Mexican Indian communities (1970s)
1980
Starts teaching at the Universidad Nacional Autónoma de México
1986
Dies in Mexico City, Mexico

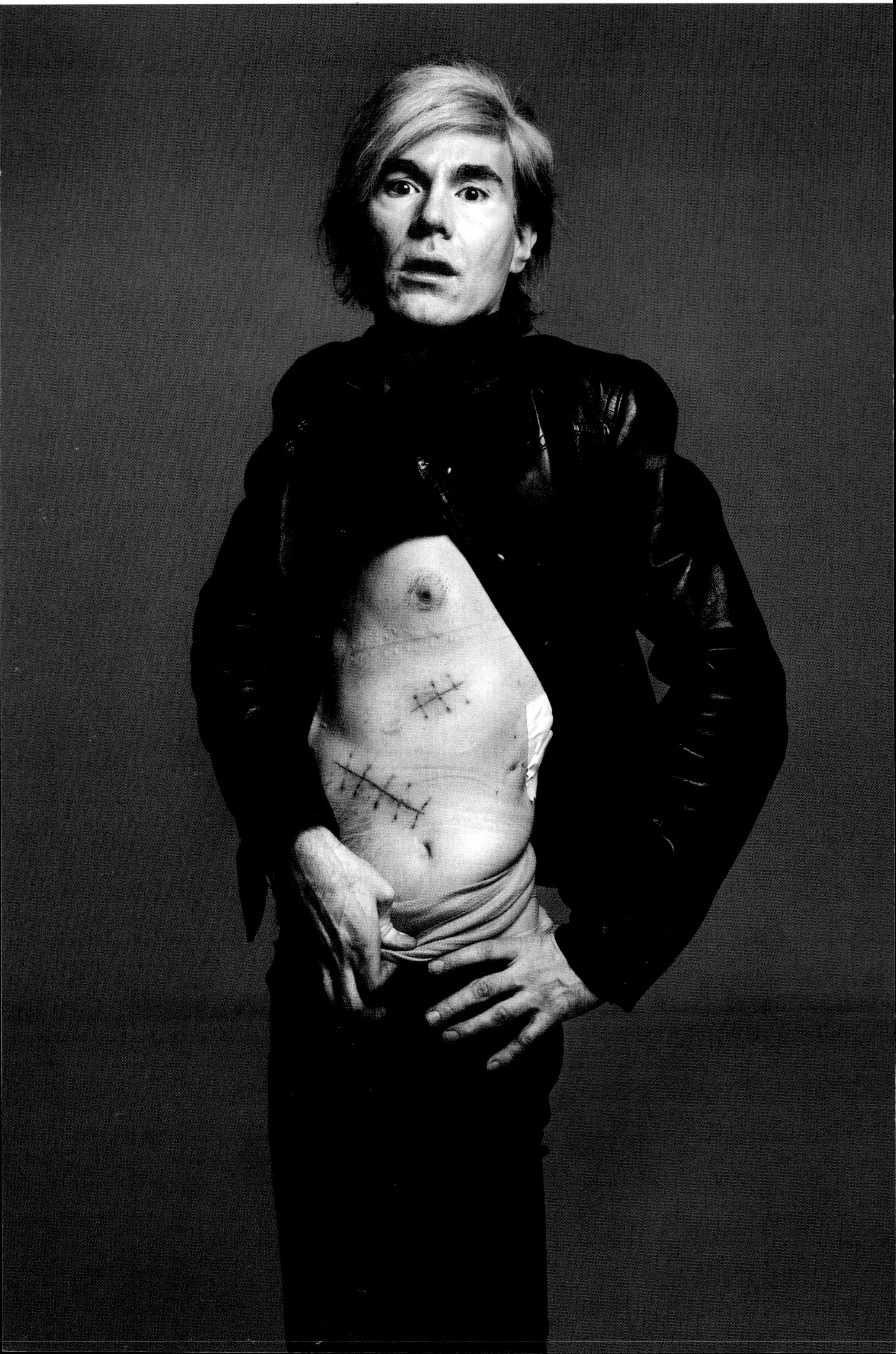

'All photographs are accurate. None of them is the truth.'

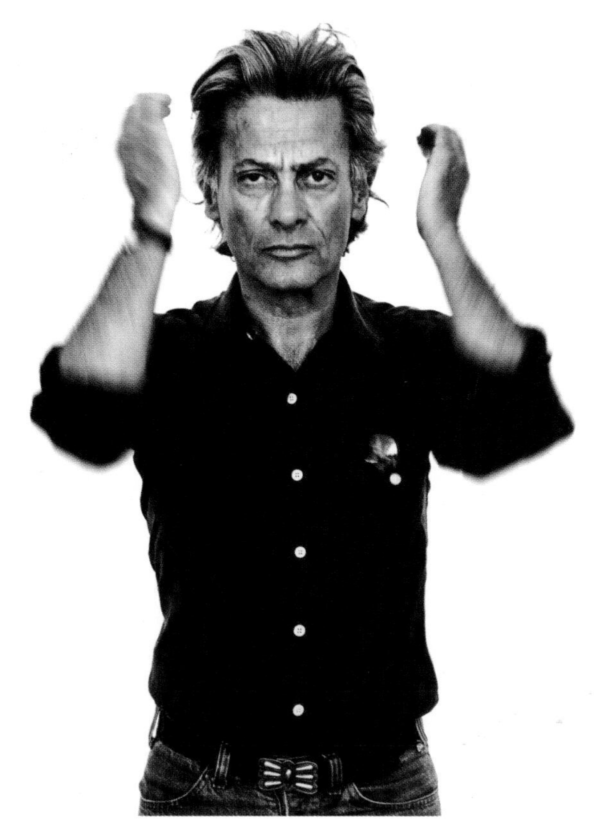

# Richard Avedon

1923–2004

UNITED STATES

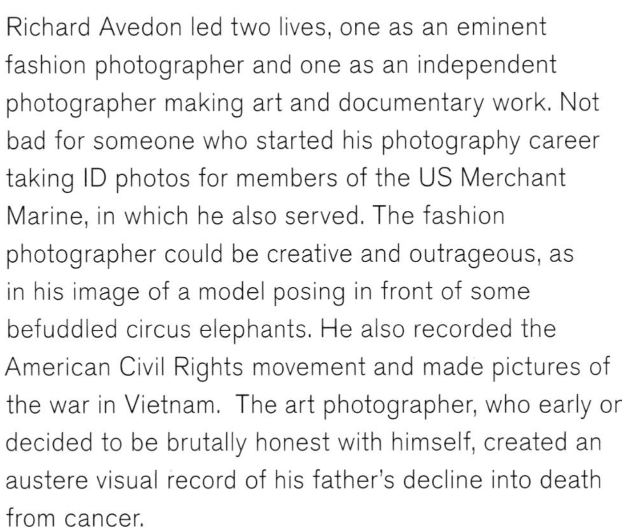

Richard Avedon led two lives, one as an eminent fashion photographer and one as an independent photographer making art and documentary work. Not bad for someone who started his photography career taking ID photos for members of the US Merchant Marine, in which he also served. The fashion photographer could be creative and outrageous, as in his image of a model posing in front of some befuddled circus elephants. He also recorded the American Civil Rights movement and made pictures of the war in Vietnam. The art photographer, who early on decided to be brutally honest with himself, created an austere visual record of his father's decline into death from cancer.

In post-war Paris, he took his models outside the studio, where they interacted him, and with the settings. Over time, he developed a signature style that persists today: photographing in front of a white background – sometimes called seamless, for the paper sheet it used. He used it in fashion shoots and in his reportage. As fashion became more democratic and demotic, Avedon moved with the trend. His long-lived photographs and television commercials for Calvin Klein jeans showed a sultry teenage model, Brooke Shields, who asked the audience: 'You want to know what comes between me and my Calvins? Nothing.' The image Avedon made of a recumbent and naked Nastassja Kinski with a Burmese python crawling through her legs and towards her face has become iconic.

Avedon also made it a point to photograph ordinary people as well. The stark images from 'In the American West' question the unique designation of the West as the land of independence and second chances in America. How much did the people who posed for him know about how they would be represented, literally and symbolically? Even before 'In the American West', critics such as Arthur Danto and Harold Rosenberg described what Rosenberg called Avedon's 'objective cruelty'. Ironically, Avedon's 'pursuit of what has befallen his subjects and what they have done to themselves' is the negative corollary of fashion photography, in which the models seem to exist in a state of grace. Avedon was not the first artist to use these approaches, but his celebrity amplified them into questions that are still discussed.

**Opposite** Andy Warhol, artist, New York, 20 August, 1969.

**Above** Self-portrait, Provo, Utah, 20 August, 1980.

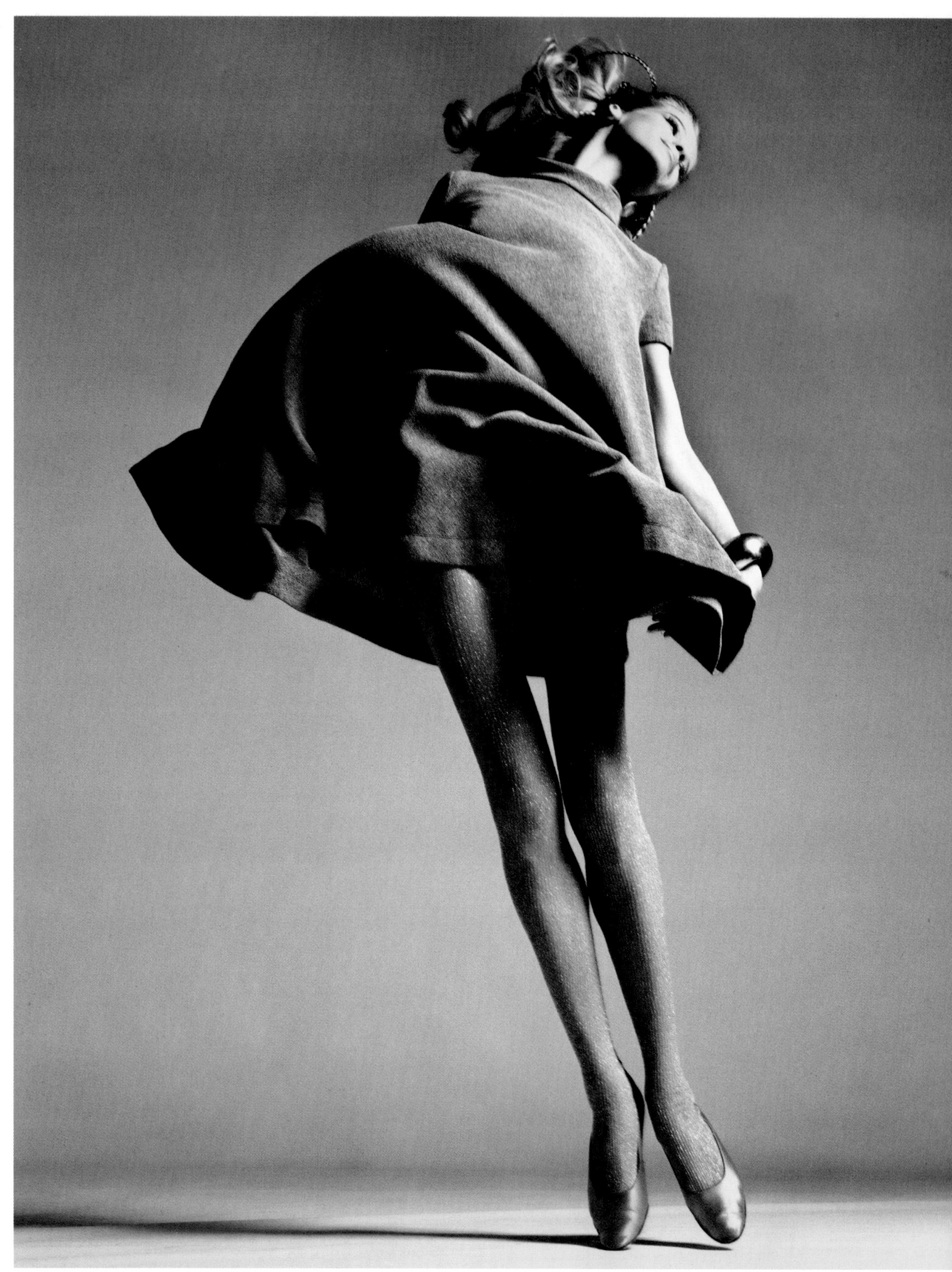

Veruschka, dress by Bill Blass,
New York, 4 January, 1967.

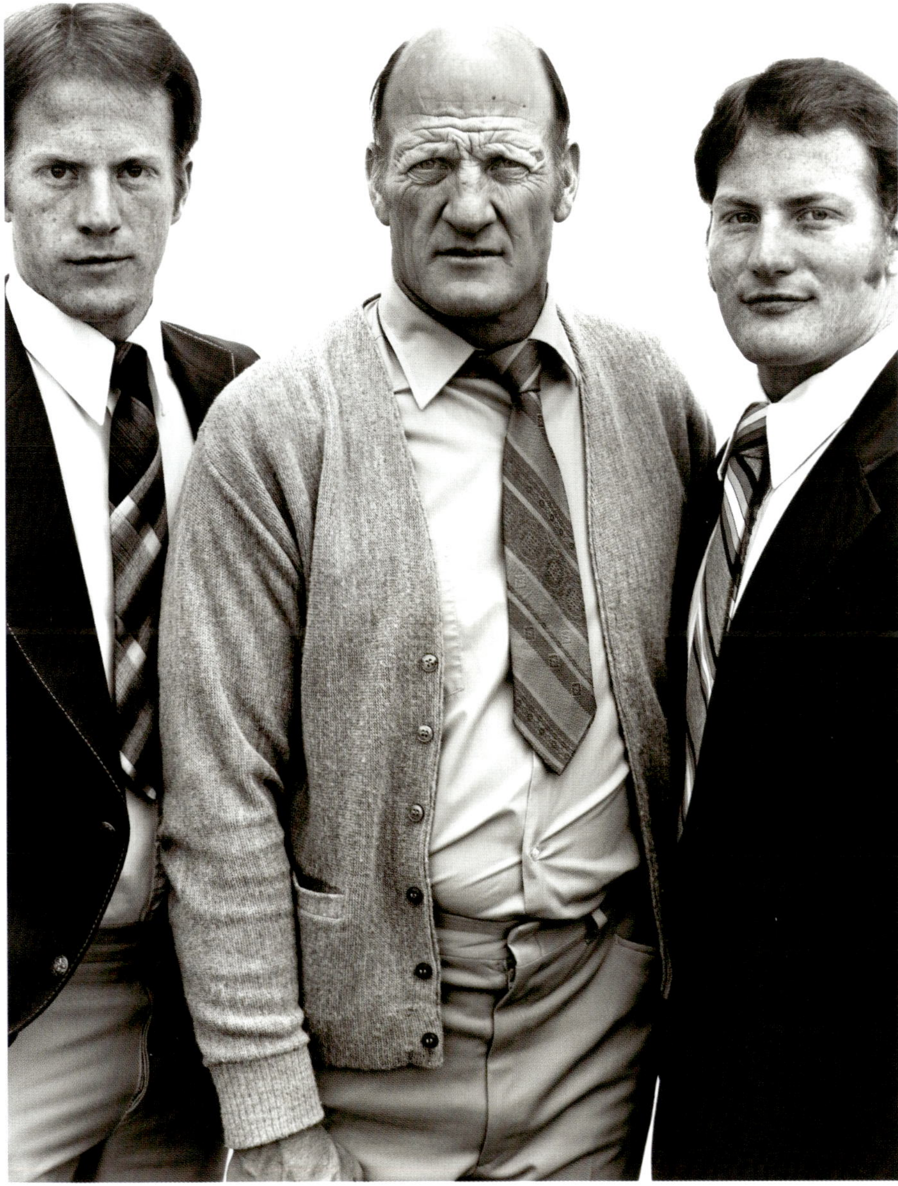

Lyal Burr, coal miner, and his sons Kerry and Phillip, The Church of Jesus Christ of Latter-Day Saints, Koosharem, Utah, 7 May , 1981.

## Richard Avedon

1920

**1923** Born in New York, USA

1930

1940

**1945** Staff photographer at *Harper's Bazaar* (to 1965)

1950

**1959** Publishes *Observations*

**1963** Photographs the Civil Rights movement in the American South

**1966** Staff photographer at *Vogue* (to 1990)

**1969** Photographs anti-war movement in the USA; also photographs in Vietnam

1980

**1985** 'In the American West' opens at the Amon Carter Museum of American Art, Fort Worth, Texas, and then six other museums

1990

**1992** First staff photographer for *The New Yorker* magazine

2000

**2002** Publishes *Richard Avedon: Portraits*

**2004** Dies in San Antonio, Texas, USA

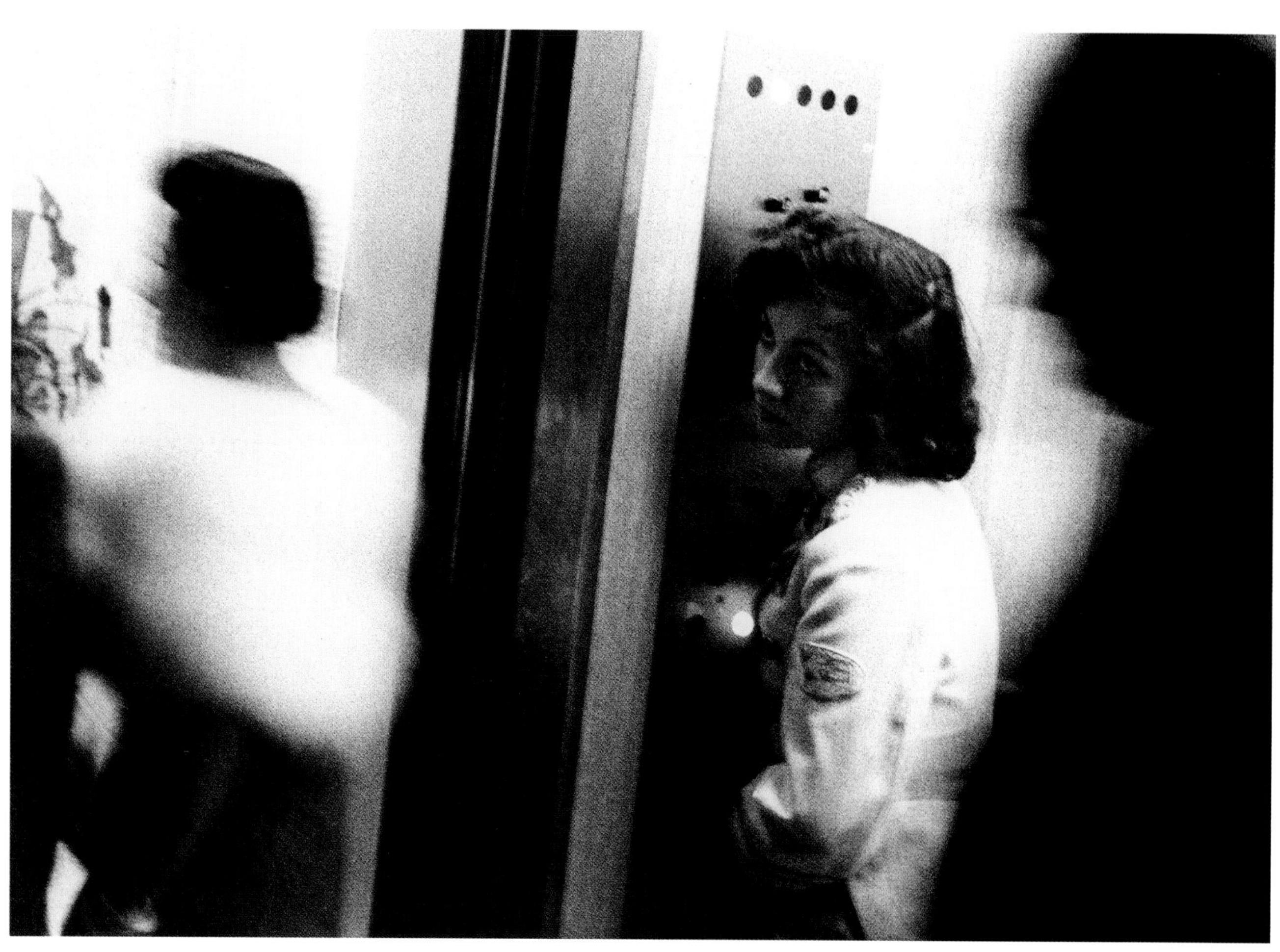

*Elevator – Miami Beach*, 1955.

'It was myth that the sky was blue and that all photographs were beautiful.'

# Robert Frank

b. 1924

SWITZERLAND

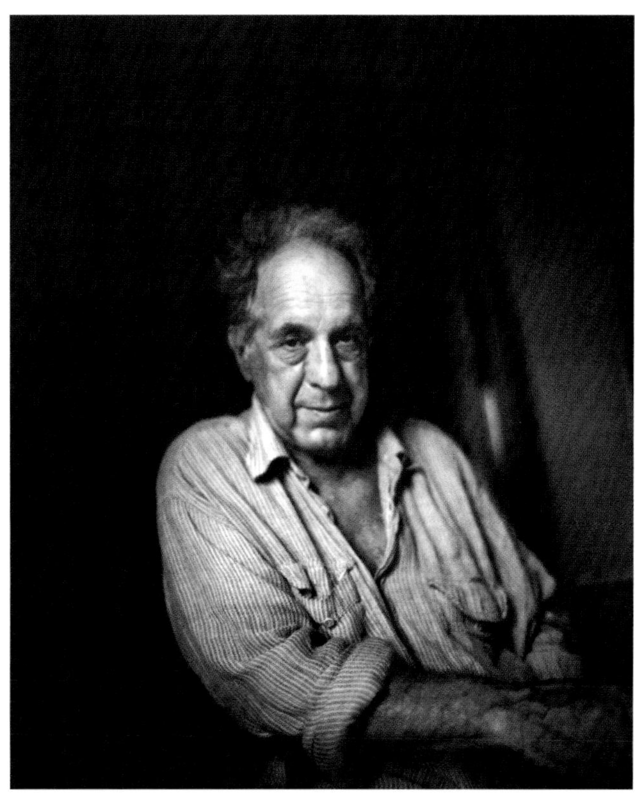

Portrait of Robert Frank by Dodo Jin Ming, undated.

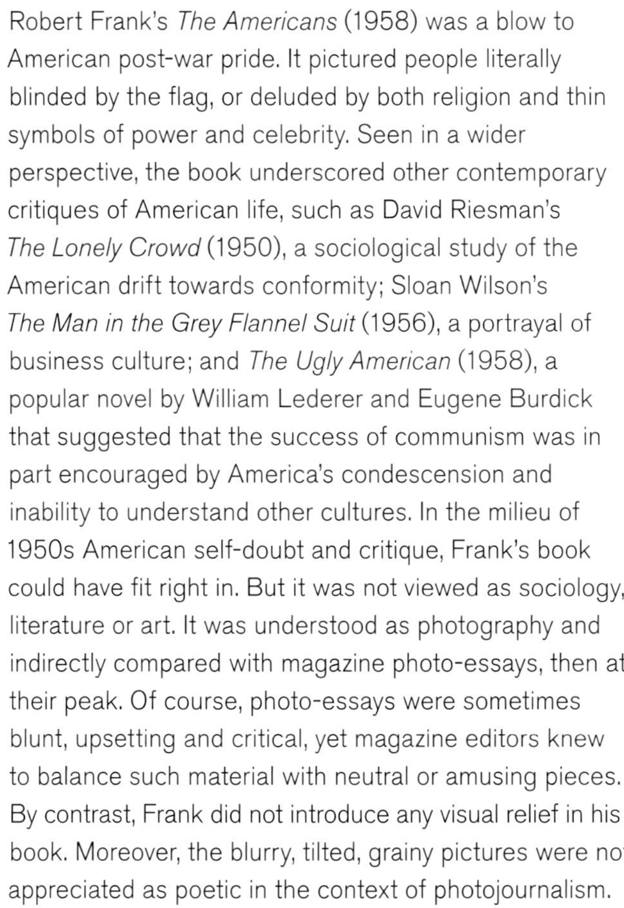

Robert Frank's *The Americans* (1958) was a blow to American post-war pride. It pictured people literally blinded by the flag, or deluded by both religion and thin symbols of power and celebrity. Seen in a wider perspective, the book underscored other contemporary critiques of American life, such as David Riesman's *The Lonely Crowd* (1950), a sociological study of the American drift towards conformity; Sloan Wilson's *The Man in the Grey Flannel Suit* (1956), a portrayal of business culture; and *The Ugly American* (1958), a popular novel by William Lederer and Eugene Burdick that suggested that the success of communism was in part encouraged by America's condescension and inability to understand other cultures. In the milieu of 1950s American self-doubt and critique, Frank's book could have fit right in. But it was not viewed as sociology, literature or art. It was understood as photography and indirectly compared with magazine photo-essays, then at their peak. Of course, photo-essays were sometimes blunt, upsetting and critical, yet magazine editors knew to balance such material with neutral or amusing pieces. By contrast, Frank did not introduce any visual relief in his book. Moreover, the blurry, tilted, grainy pictures were not appreciated as poetic in the context of photojournalism.

As understanding and admiration for the book grew in the 1960s, *The Americans* became a touchstone for aspiring photographers, who saw it not as documentary work, but as a new avenue of art that could, and eventually did, inform photojournalism and documentary work. Its influence has never waned.

Frank turned his talents to film soon after *The Americans* was published, having determined that film was his 'first choice'. In 1972, when the book *The Lines in My Hand* was first released in limited edition, it contained a few photographs from *The Americans* but was an insistently personal and autobiographical volume. In the twenty-first century, Frank returned to *The Americans* as both its author and its editor. He reinterpreted the tonal values of images and their size, as well as participating in several retrospectives.

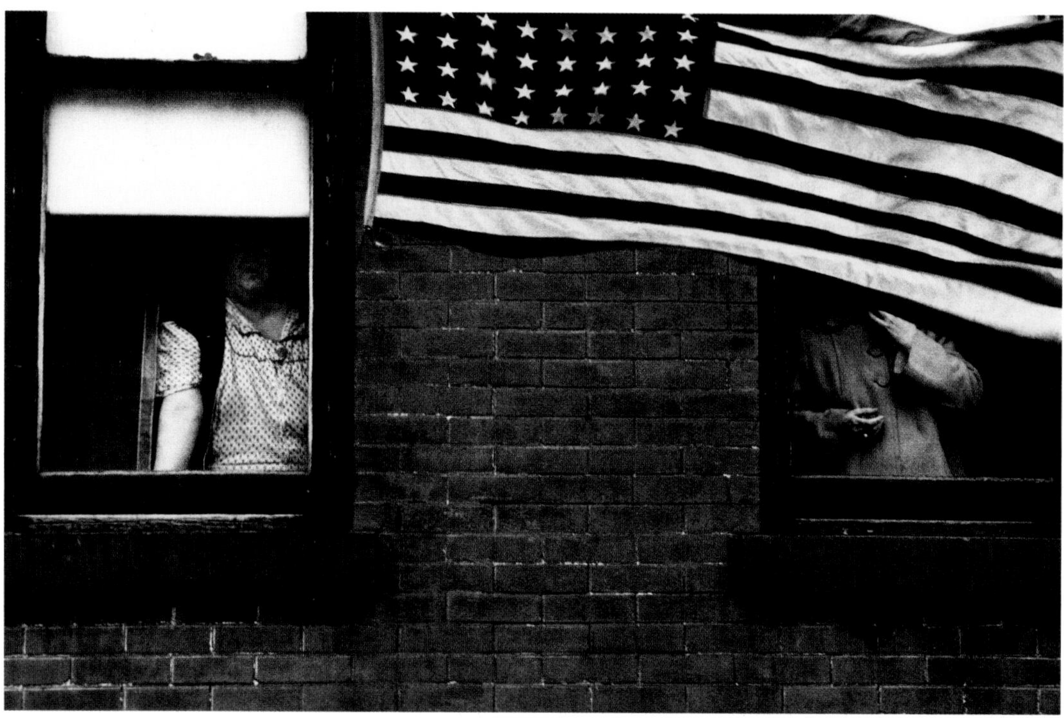

*Parade – Hoboken*, New Jersey, 1955.

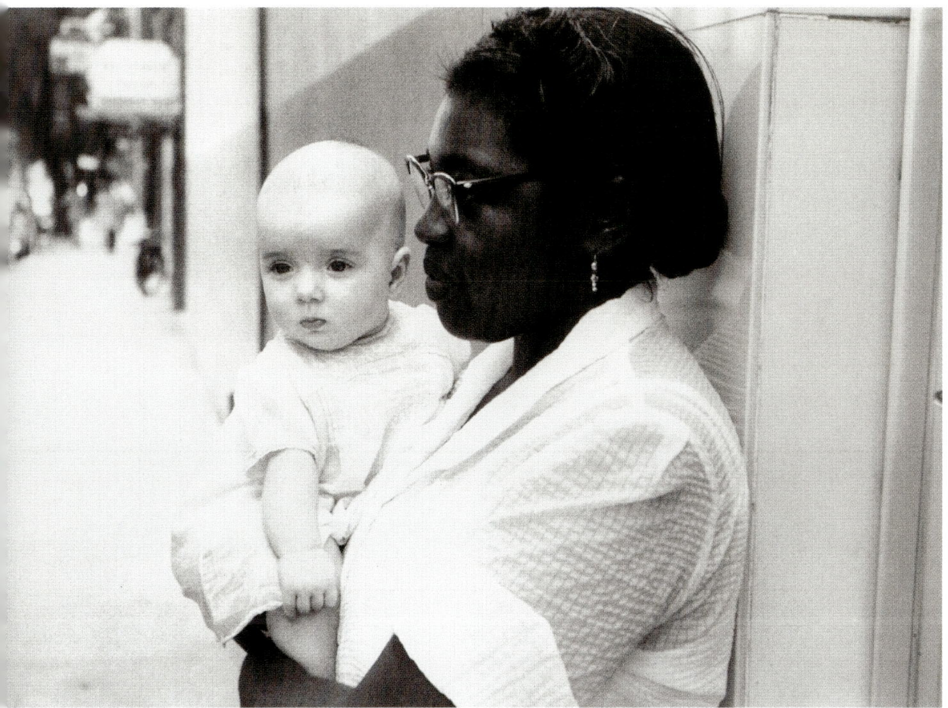

*Charleston,* South Carolina, 1955.

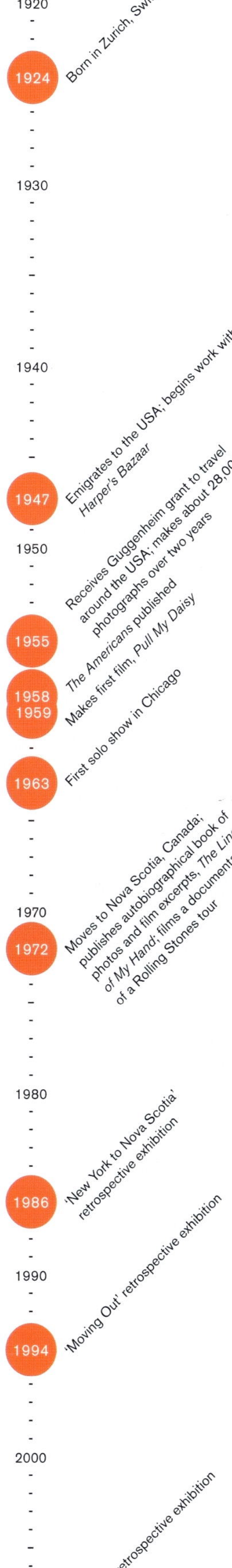

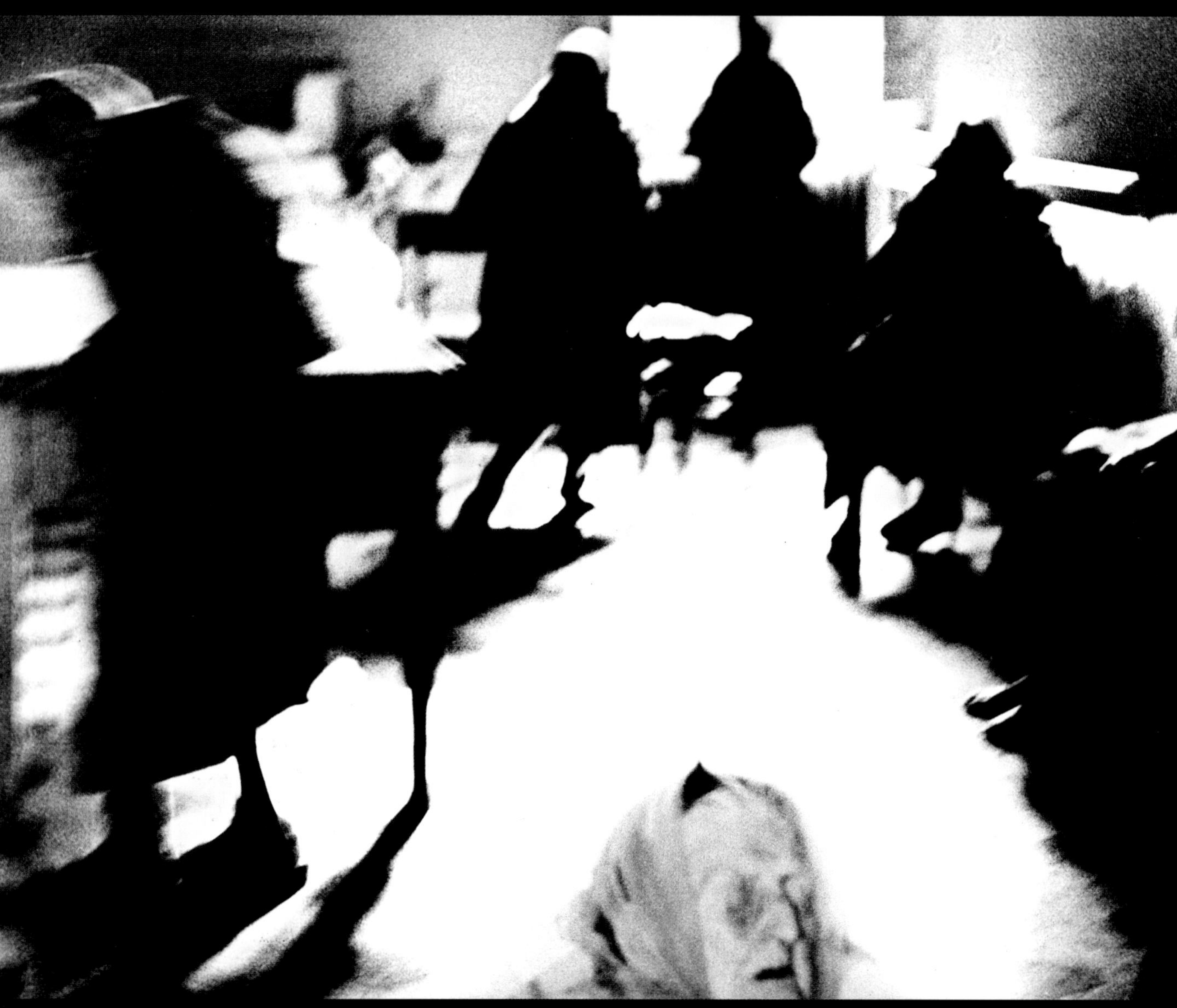

From '*Verrà la morte e avrà i tuoi occhi*'
('Death will come and it will have your
eyes'), 1966–68.

'I can nearly always see a photo before I make it.'

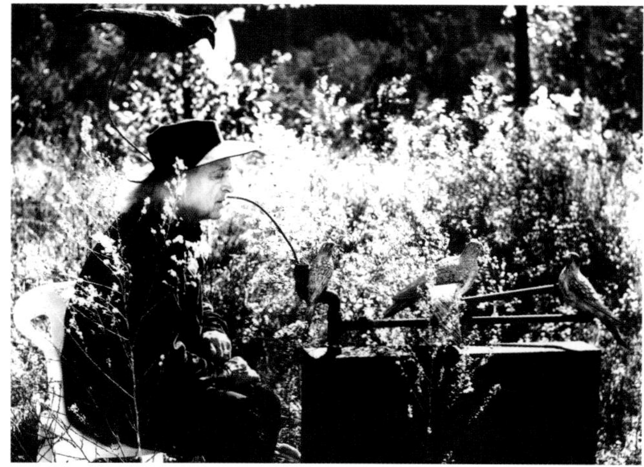

# Mario Giacomelli

1925–2000

ITALY

Mario Giacomelli's visual accomplishment is so improbable that it invites speculation. To account for the depth of feeling in his work, one is tempted to play the 'may have' game: he 'may have' seen Federico Fellini movies, he 'may have' known the work of Bill Brandt (p. 116) ... Giacomelli was bemused by the 'may haves', commenting: 'Some university academic came to see me and wrote that this photograph is all about Cézanne. What do they know?'

Born in a small historic seaside city, impoverished at the age of 9 by the death of his father and beginning work as a typesetter at the age of 13, he stayed in the printing business for the rest of his life, and he seldom left his home town. A hobbyist weekend painter, he bought his first camera – an inexpensive one – in 1952. From the beginning, the camera and the darkroom served as his eccentric and permissive tutors, letting him freely explore the visual effects he could produce rather than striving for fidelity to optical experience. Giacomelli used out-of-date film, over- and under-exposed his prints and drew freely on his negatives. His contrasty or bleached-out-looking work was a poor example of conventional practice, but it emerged as an expressive medium.

The titles of his photographs and series emerged after the work was done, and were often derived from the poets he read, such as Jorge Luis Borges and Edgar Lee Masters. His themes are ancient: youth and age, work and leisure, memory and desire. For nearly 30 years, he photographed the residents in a home for the aged, sometimes making their skin appear so thin that their souls seemed to show through. It was, for him, his 'truest' series, because it showed what he called 'my disgust at the price one has to pay for one's life'. Another ongoing series, begun about the same time, involved using a tractor to make shapes and lines in farmers' fields after the harvest, and then photographing the result from an aeroplane or an elevation. It was a godlike act to create the earth in his own imagination.

Self-portrait, undated.

**Below** From '*Io non ho mani che mi accarezzino il volto*' or '*I Pretini*' ('I don't have hands that caress my face' or 'The Little Priests'), 1957.

**Opposite** From 'Presa di coscienza sulla natura' ('Becoming aware of nature'), Sant Angelo di Senigallia, 1955–68.

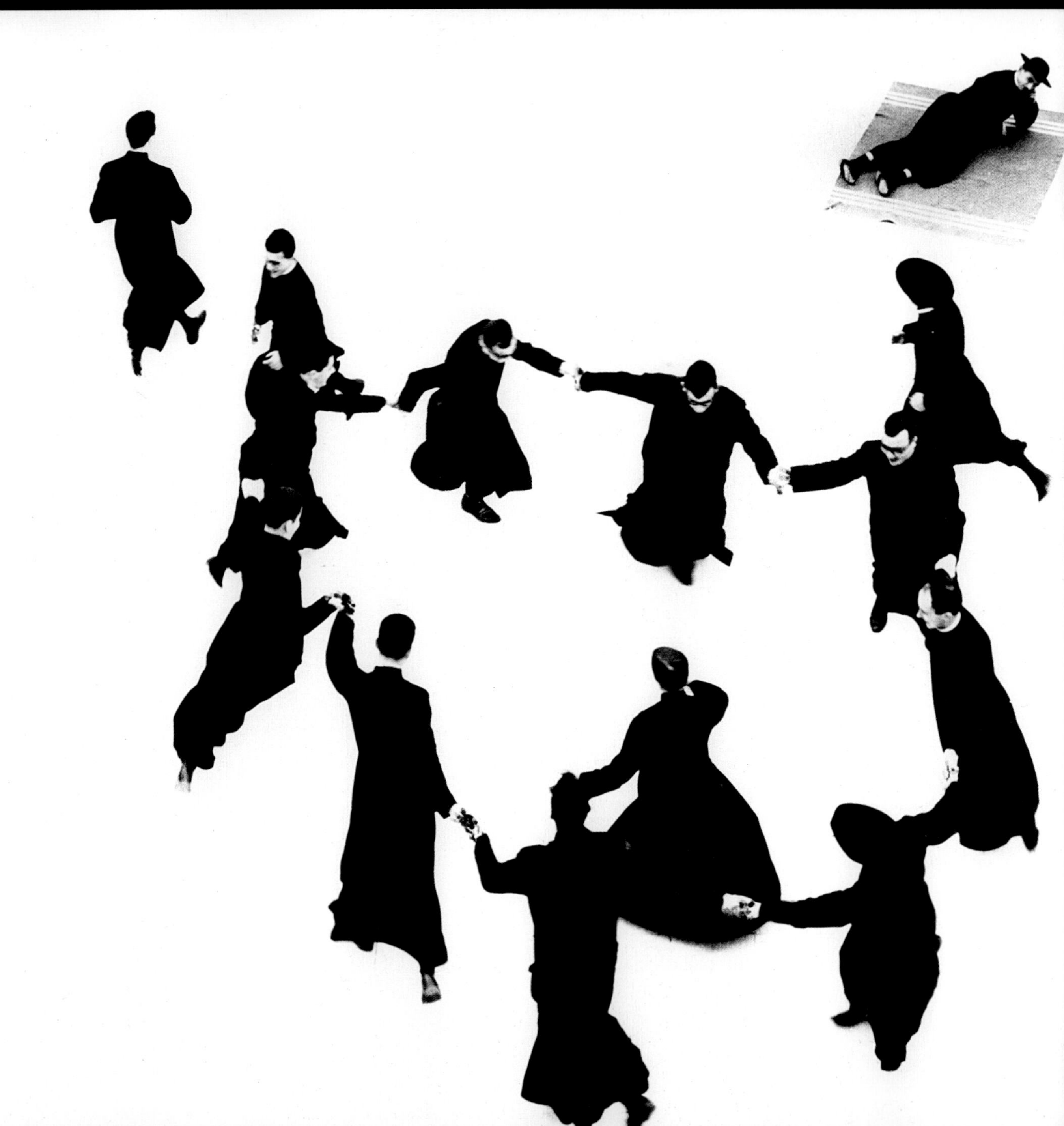

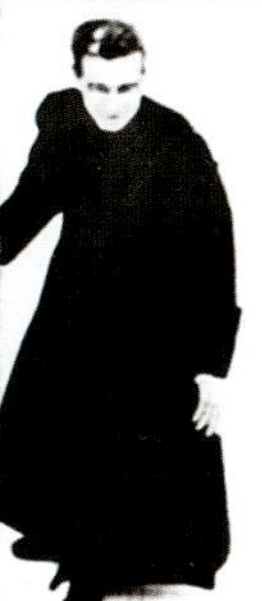

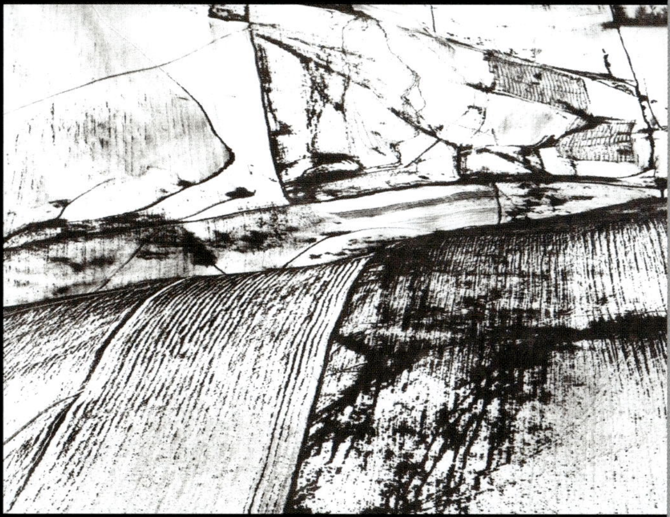

# Mario Giacomelli

1920

1925 Born in Senigallia, Italy

1930

1940

1950

1954 Begins photographing Marche landscape

1955 Publishes first picture in the *Rivista Fotografica Italiana*; begins landscape images and writing poetry

1960

1963 Work appears in 'Looking at Photographs', Museum of Modern Art, New York

1970

1972 Begins 'Homage to Spoon River'

1980

1990

2000 Dies in Ancona, Italy

*American Legion Convention,* Dallas, Texas, 1964.

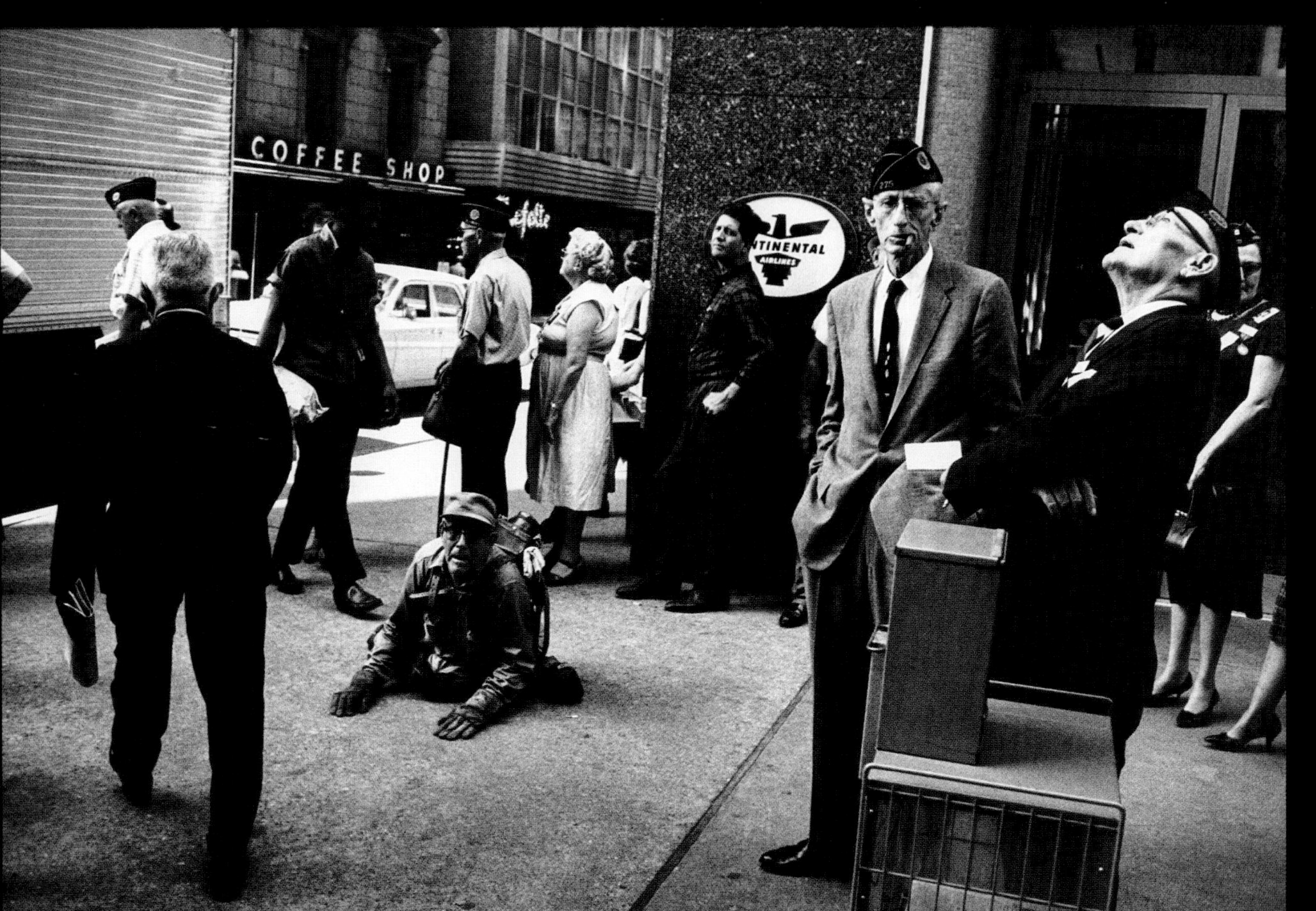

'A photograph can look any way.'

# Garry Winogrand

1928–1984

UNITED STATES

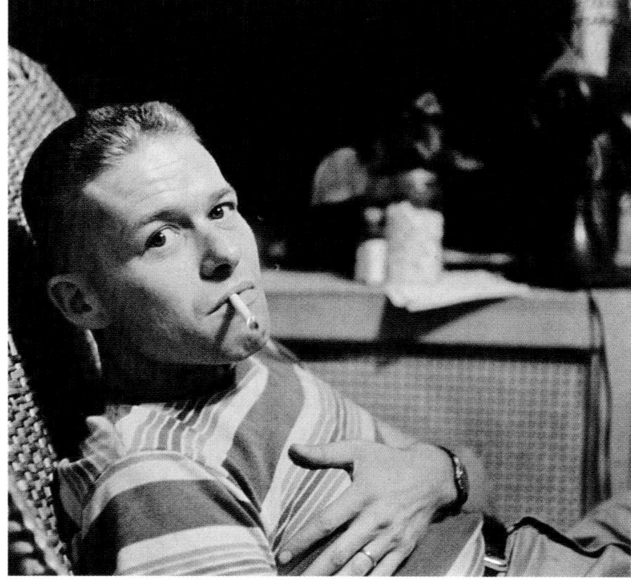

Can one make too many photographs? In the digital era, that question is now moot, because, unlike with analogue photographs, storage capacity and instant access have allowed muchness. Moreover, digital photographs do not need extensive darkroom development and processing. Likewise, photographs can be erased almost as quickly as they are created.

The quantity question beleaguered Garry Winogrand during his life. Winogrand loved to take pictures: 'The more I do, the more I do,' he remarked. Developing rolls of films, which were accumulating in desk drawers and plastic bags during his life, was laborious for him, and he also found examining contact sheets and choosing what to print taxing. When he died, he left about 300,000 images undeveloped or unedited. Figures vary, but his lifetime total of images may be as much as half a million.

His best-known work for the general public shows John F. Kennedy accepting the presidential nomination at the Democratic convention in 1960. It is not typical of his antipathy to established harmonies of visual design, even if it does visually comment on Kennedy's superior media skills by including a television monitor. Winogrand's more experimental early photojournalism was done as contract work, including shots of President Dwight Eisenhower and his vice-president, Richard Nixon, in a moment when they have dropped their public faces despite the throng of cameras.

Winogrand thrived on the street, rapidly patrolling and shooting, trading comments with those who passed by. He was, as his friend Lee Friedlander (p. 200) recalled, 'a bull of a man and the world was his china shop'. Winogrand flouted Henri Cartier-Bresson's reigning notion of the decisive moment (p. 132), insisting that it contradicted the chaos of visual life. While he could make instant decisions of what to photograph, he was stymied by the time-consuming tedium of choosing images for books and exhibitions.

What we know of Winogrand's photography has been sifted by other minds, and it is fair to say that editors and curators created the contemporary understanding of Winogrand. How close that appreciation agreed with Winogrand's is impossible to judge, since he maintained, 'I don't have anything to say in any picture. My only interest in photography is to see what something looks like as a photograph. I have no preconceptions.'

Portrait of Garry Winogrand by Lee Friedlander, 1957.

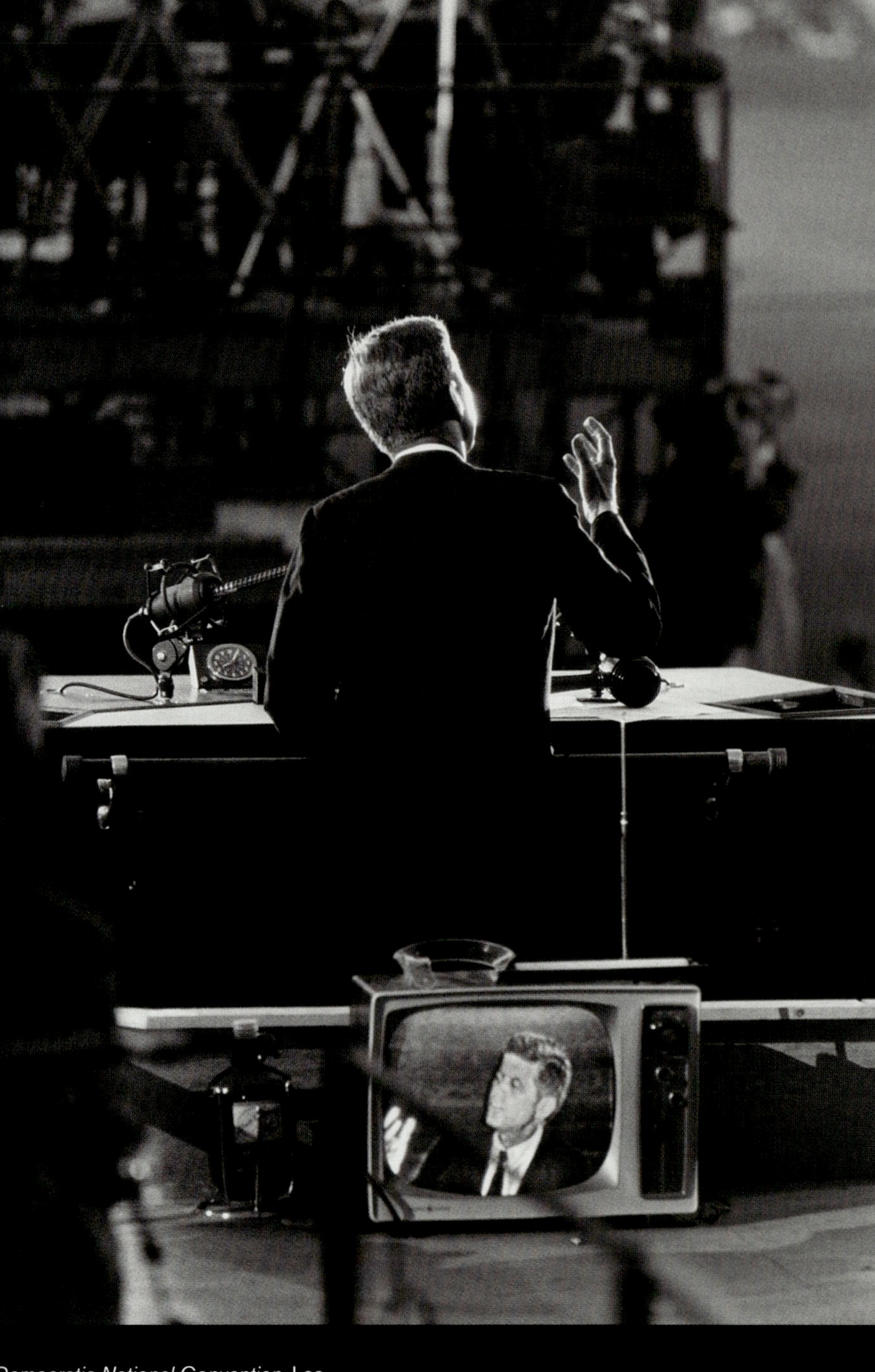

*Democratic National Convention,* Los Angeles, 1960.

# Garry Winogrand

- **1928** Born in New York, USA
- **1955** Included in 'Family of Man' exhibition at the Museum of Modern Art, New York
- **1964** Included in the exhibition 'The Photographer's Eye', MoMA
- **1966** Included in 'Toward a Social Landscape', Eastman House, Rochester, New York
- **1969** Published *The Animals*
- **1978** Included in 'Mirrors and Windows', MoMA
- **1981** Retrospective exhibition at Fraenkel Gallery, San Francisco
- **1984** Dies in Tijuana, Mexico
- **2013** Retrospective at San Francisco Museum of Modern Art and the National Gallery of Art in Washington, DC

1920 · 1930 · 1940 · 1950 · 1960 · 1990 · 2000 · 2010

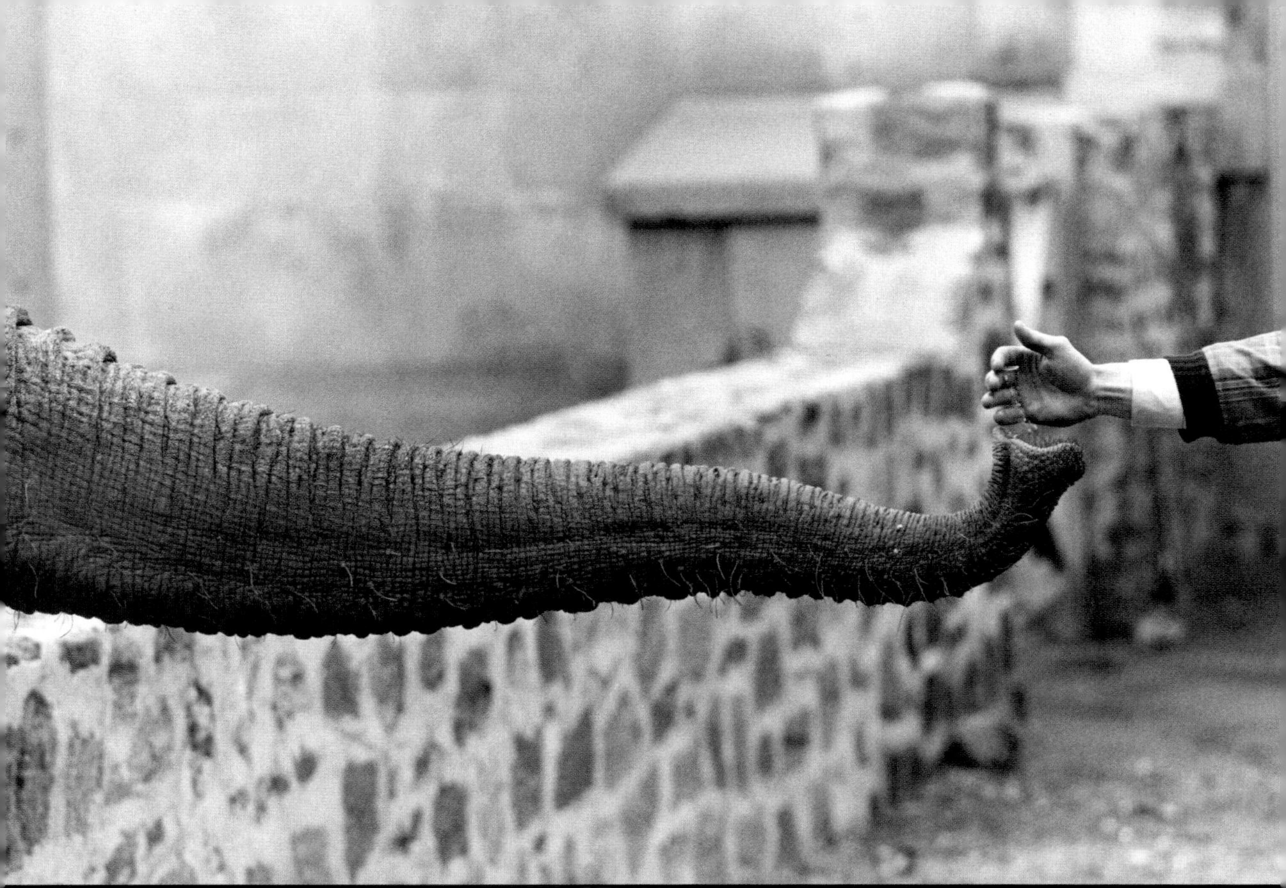

Location unknown, 1963.

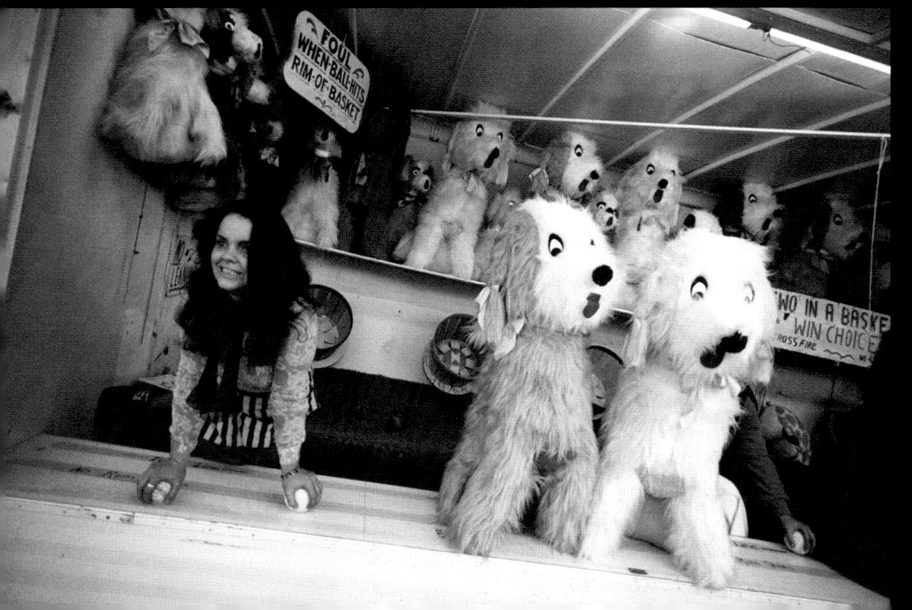


Fort Worth, Texas, 1975.

*Bottle Melted and Deformed by Atomic Bomb Heat, Radiation and Fire*, Nagasaki, 1961.

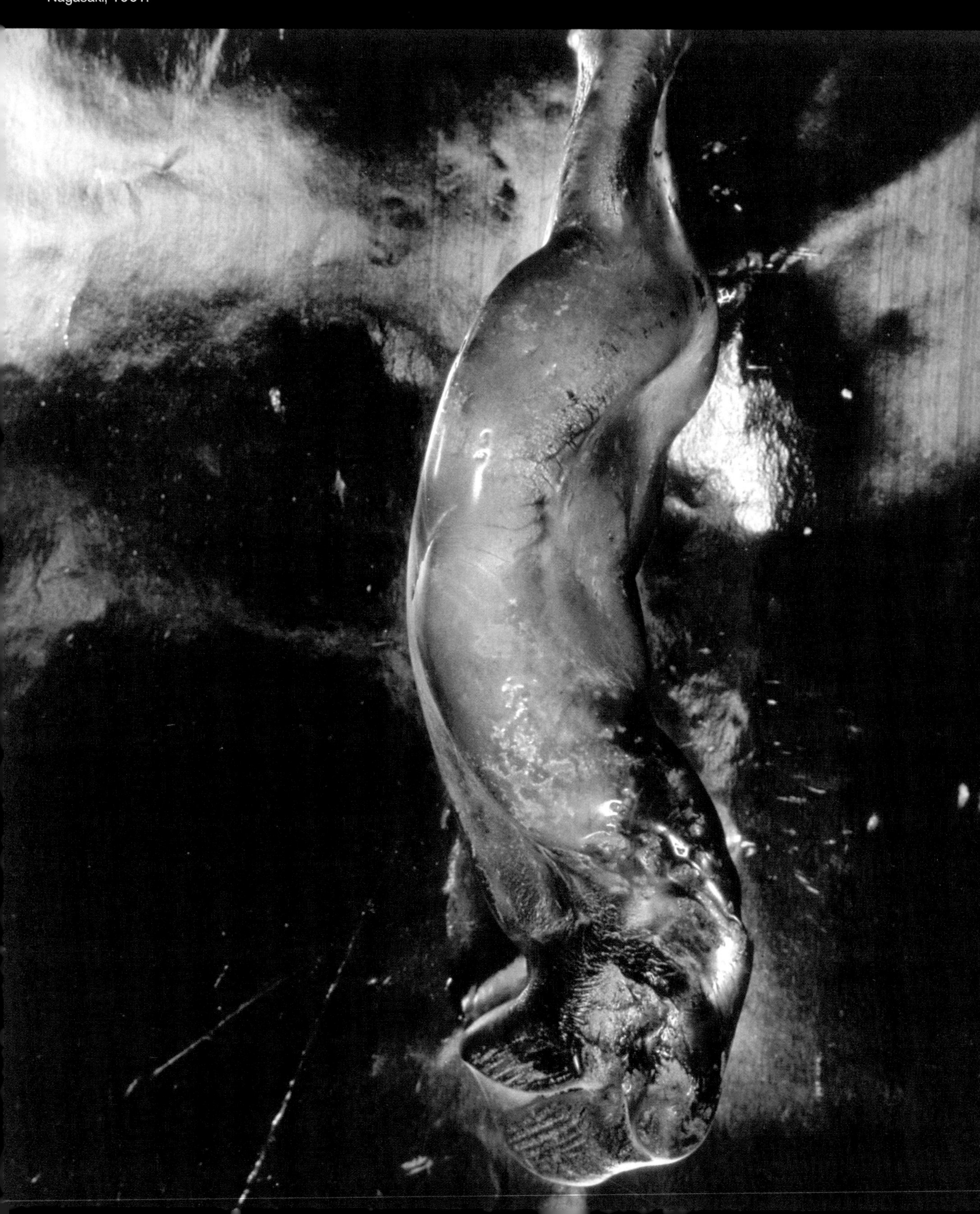

'In short, [photography] is a matter of turning loneliness into thoughts.'

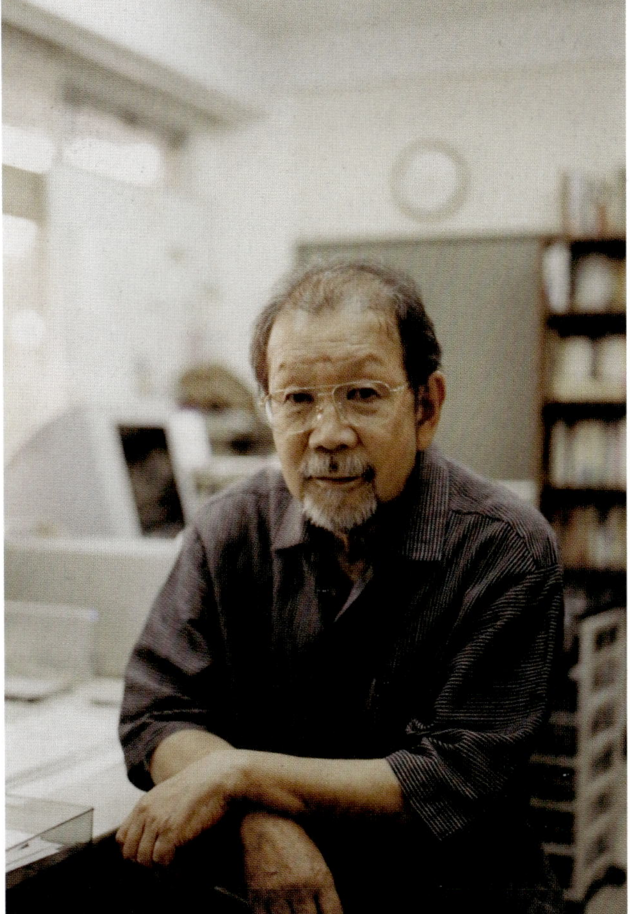

# Shōmei Tōmatsu

1930–2012

JAPAN

Few photographers have the range to create trenchant images of hope as well as searing pictures of despair. Tōmatsu could combine them in a single image, perhaps because he rejected simple pictures. The effect is restless meaning – images that resolve only to question themselves. For many photographers in post-war Japan, photography was a book art that used printer's ink rather than photographic chemicals to secure final visual effects. Tōmatsu's experiments with tonalities, especially rich, deep midnight blacks, worked to emphasize form rather than to clarify meaning.

In his series 'Floods and the Japanese' Tōmatsu challenged the norms of intelligibility and edification prevalent in photojournalistic accounts of disasters. His pictures pitch the beauty of the sun reflected in rippling water and the sway of rice plants against the viewer's knowledge of the tragedy. Lost boots glimmer attractively in shimmering mud. The wide tonal range, from the darkest black to pure white, gives the images a disturbing intensity.

In Japan, Tōmatsu is best known for his 'Nagasaki 11:02' series, created 16 years after the atomic bomb was dropped on that city. While the compilation produced memorable images of the lasting effects on people, the startling image of a bottle softened and distorted suggestively into a monstrous anthropomorphic shape in the blast has become a national icon of the moment.

Other series display what Tōmatsu called Americanization, which he saw as seeping from the military bases in the country and destroying Japan's cultural values. 'Chewing Gum and Chocolate', ironically named for the foods that American GIs passed out to children hungry for real nourishment, shows the invasion of American music, clothing, cars and ideas. His concern with prostitution and public eroticism also made implicit contrasts with traditional life. Through cropping, lighting and staging in pictures such as *Coca-Cola, Tokyo*, he presented a sort of frenzied end time. Ironically, in Okinawa, the site of intense fighting, and later, of an American military base, Tōmatsu found areas where village life persisted: he photographed it, sometimes even in colour.

Portrait by unknown, undated.

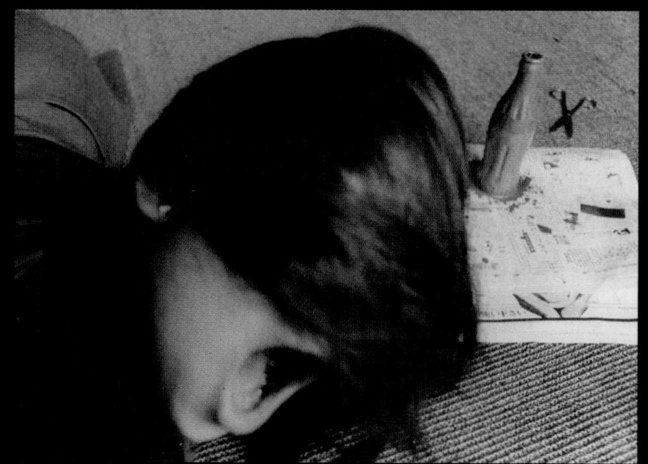

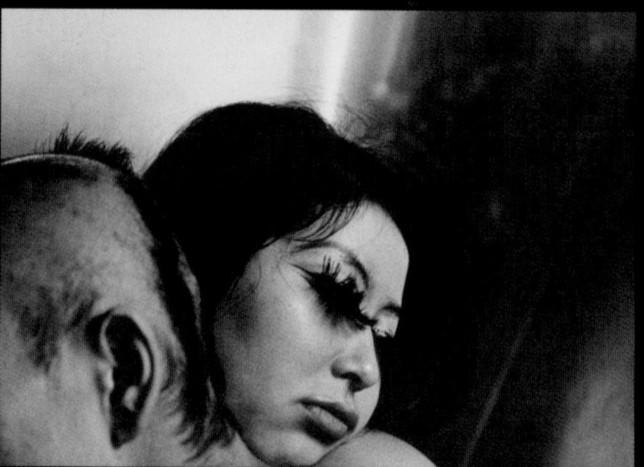

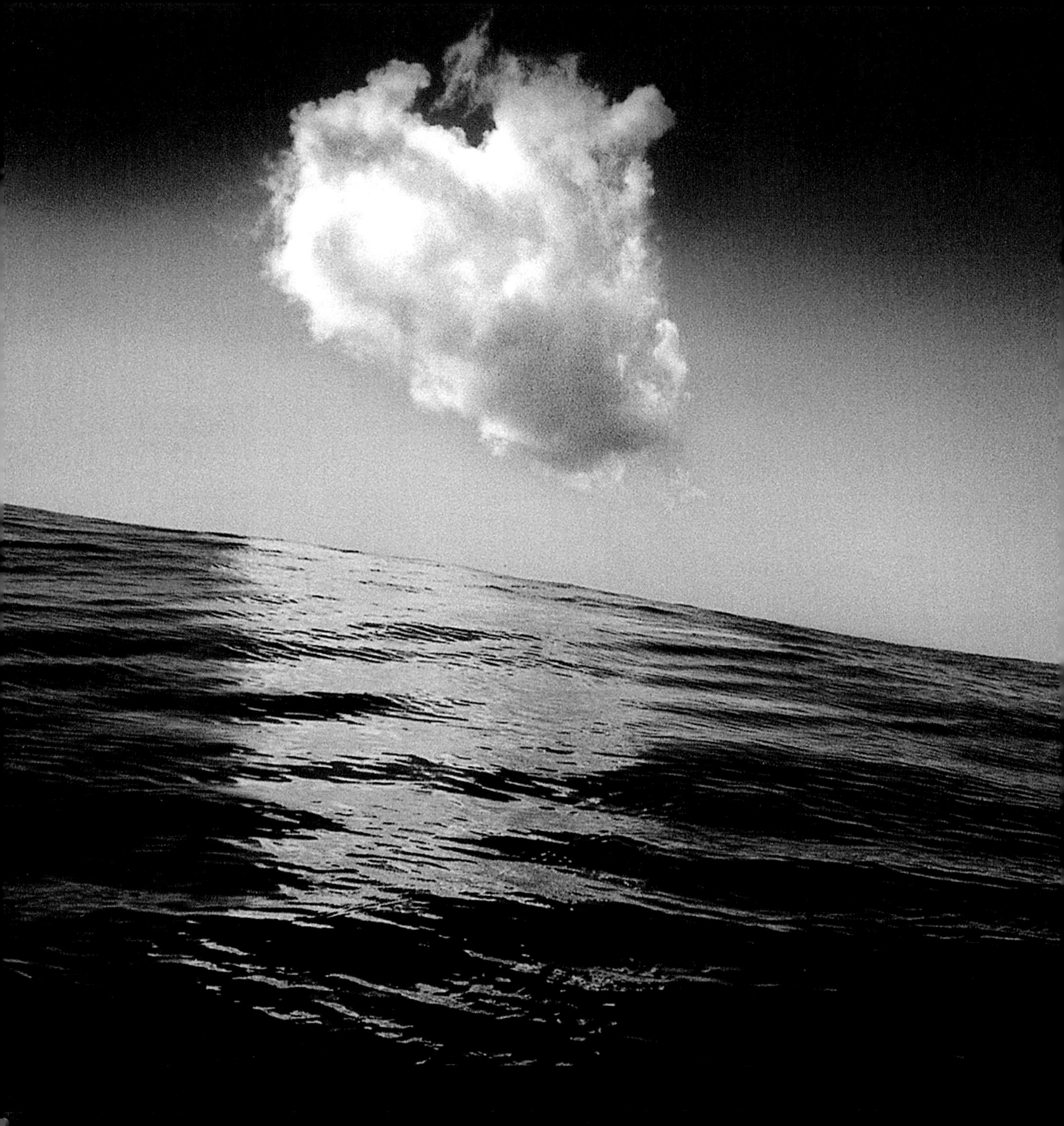

**Opposite left** *Coca-Cola*, 1969.

**Opposite right** *Eros*, Tokyo, 1969.

**Left** Untitled from 'The Pencil of the Sun', 1973.

# Shōmei Tōmatsu

1920

1930 Born Teruaki Tōmatsu in Nagoya, Japan

1940

1950 Takes first photographs

1954 Graduates from Aichi University; begins working in series and publishes *Floods and the Japanese*

1959 Starts series on American occupation of Japan and Nagasaki

1966 Publishes *Nagasaki 11:02*

1968 Curates exhibition 'One Hundred Years of Photography'

1970

1975 Publishes *The Pencil of the Sun: Okinawa and South-East Asia*

1980

1990

2000

2010

2012 Dies in Naha, Okinawa, Japan

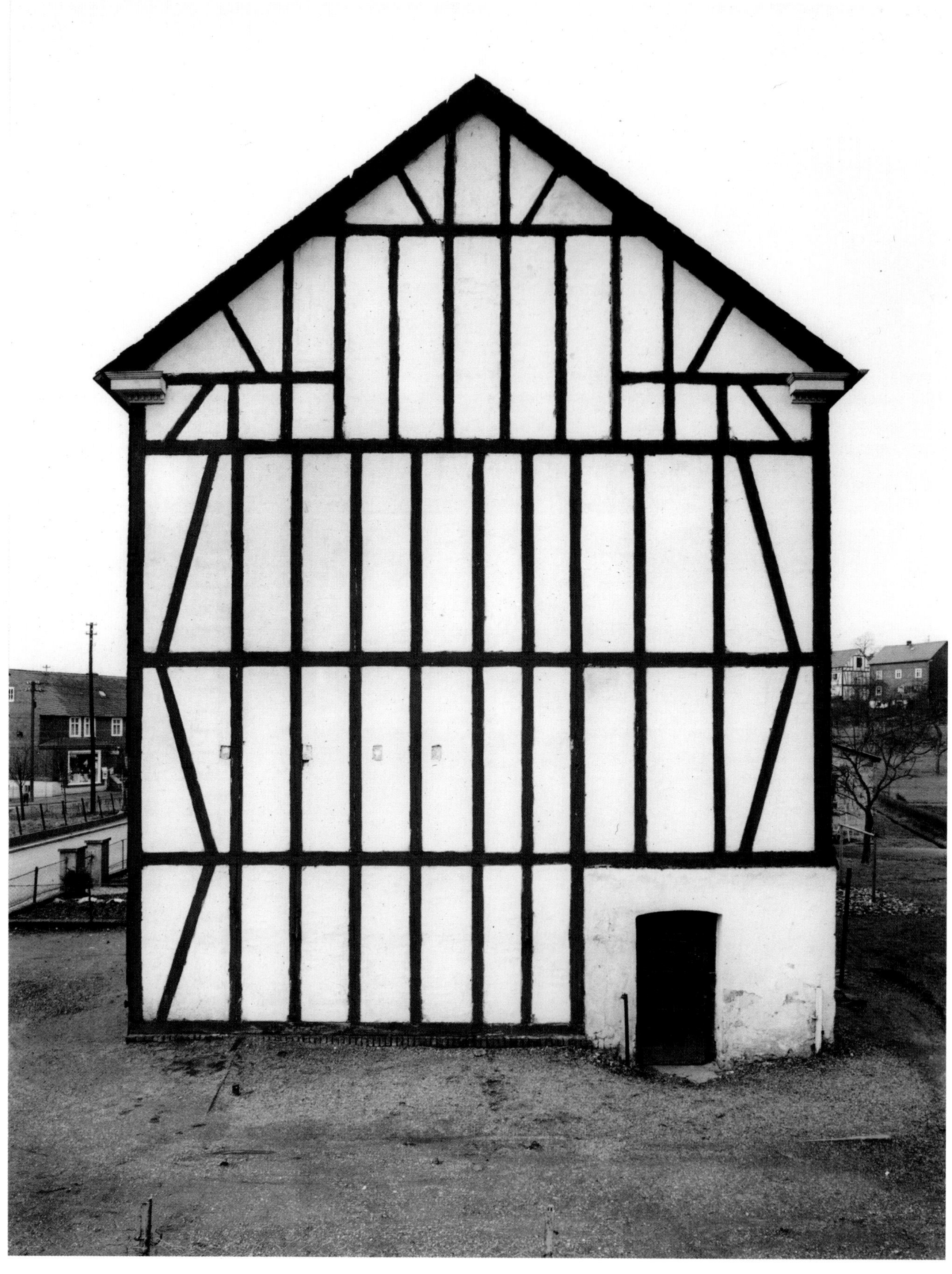

'The question "is this a work of art or not?" is not very interesting for us.'

# The Bechers

Bernhard Becher 1931–2007

Hilla Wobeser Becher b. 1934

GERMANY

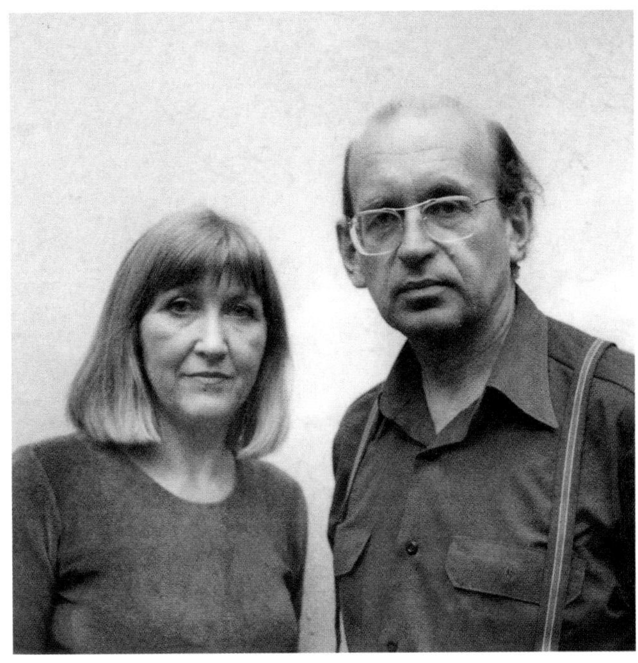

When Bernhard 'Bernd' Becher was hired in 1976 to teach photography at the Kunstakademie (Art Academy) in Düsseldorf, Germany, he and his wife Hilla had been working together for nearly two decades. They were widely known for their distinctive series of photographs of what they called 'anonymous sculpture': vernacular architecture, such as half-timbered houses, and utilitarian industrial buildings, such as water towers, gas tanks and blast furnaces.

Anonymity is increased by the absence of people. Many of the so-called 'dead tech' buildings were scheduled to be demolished. The Bechers' pictures were not only related by building type but also connected by their tight cropping-out of immediate environs, and long exposures that drank in detail. The Bechers preferred the diffuse light of overcast days, which worked to eliminate shadows. They created time and place ambiguity, in part by not including people in their images. In addition, they were fond of presenting their photographs in grids, which suggested interrelationships and allowed them to reorder and replace individual pictures.

Although the Kunstakademie's employment policy prevented Bernd and Hilla being hired at the same time, she co-taught photography with her husband. Until his death, they were photography's power couple, recognized for their distinctive and deceptively simple photographs as well as for their lasting influence on a generation of students, including Andreas Gursky (p. 296). The first generation of Becher students found individual approaches while under the couple's tutelage, and, in turn, they passed the Bechers' ideas about photography on to contemporary photography students around the world.

While their efforts were quickly recognized internationally, the images had a particular oppositional resonance in post-war Germany, where a nearly abstract, subjective photography held sway. For some Germans, the Bechers' work harkened back to the documentary work of pre-World War II artists, such as August Sander (p. 24). Outside Germany, their work was frequently discussed as participating in two art movements, Minimalism and Conceptualism. Hilla Becher responded by dismissing the idea that she and her husband made art at all, and suggesting that their work was situated between established categories. However much the Bechers wanted their work understood as not being a form of art photography, their wide, international influence has been to promote the medium as a serious art form.

**Opposite** *Half-timbered House*, 1959.

**Above** Self-portrait, 1985.

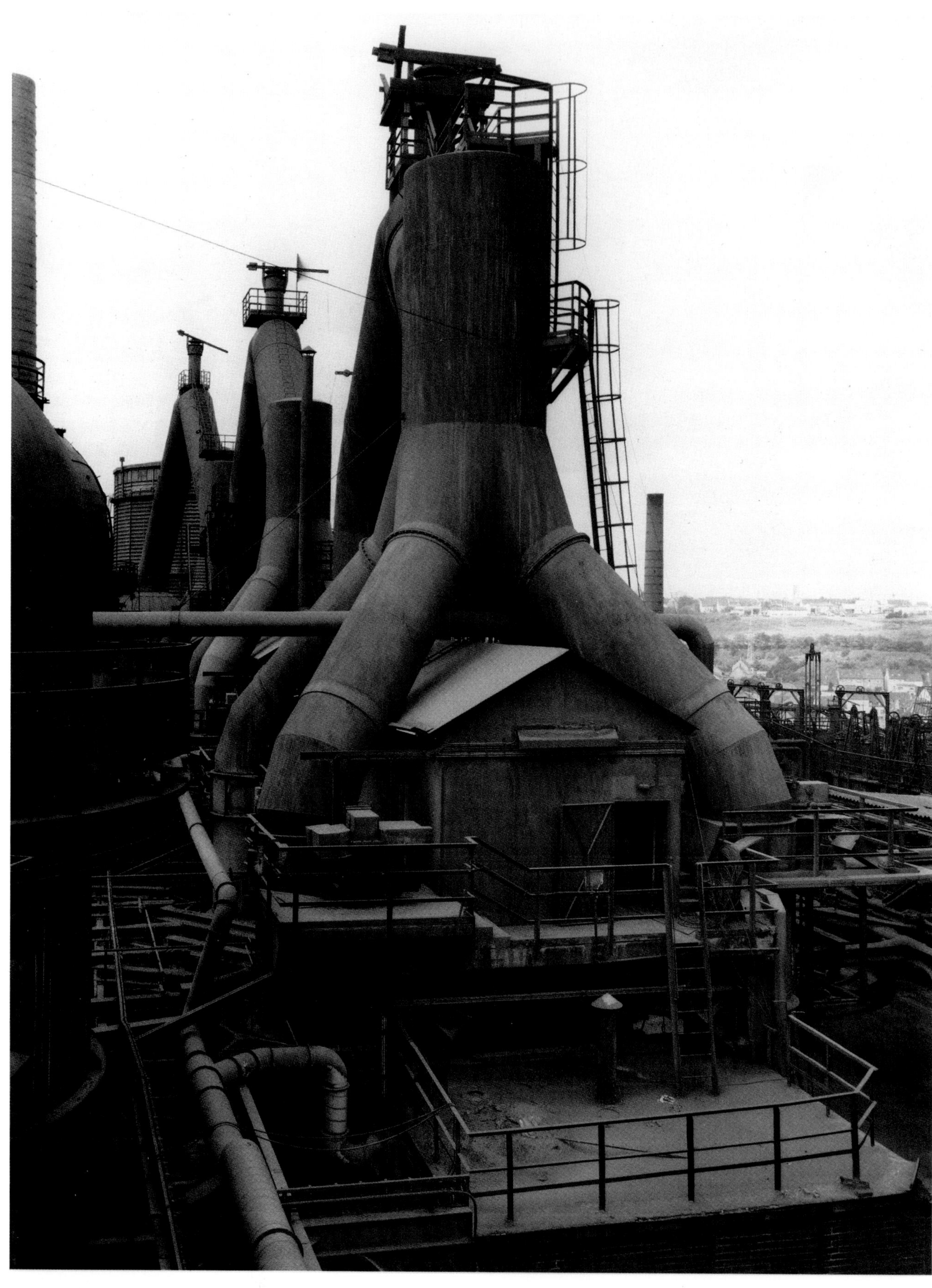

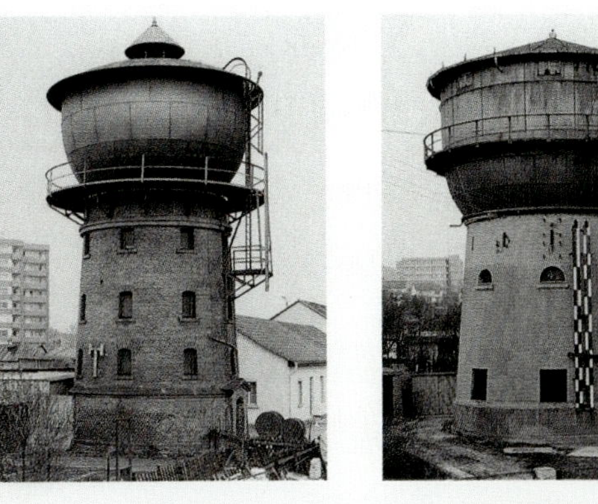

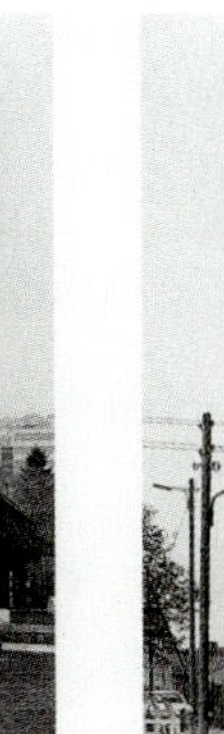

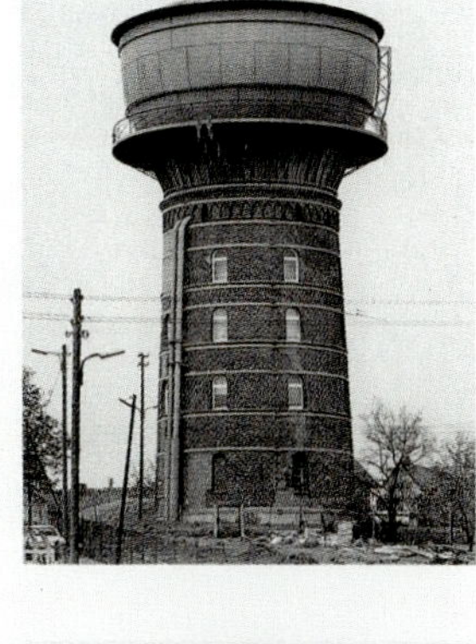

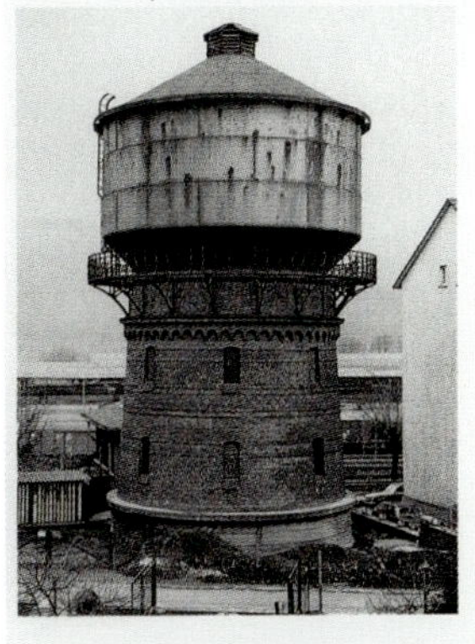

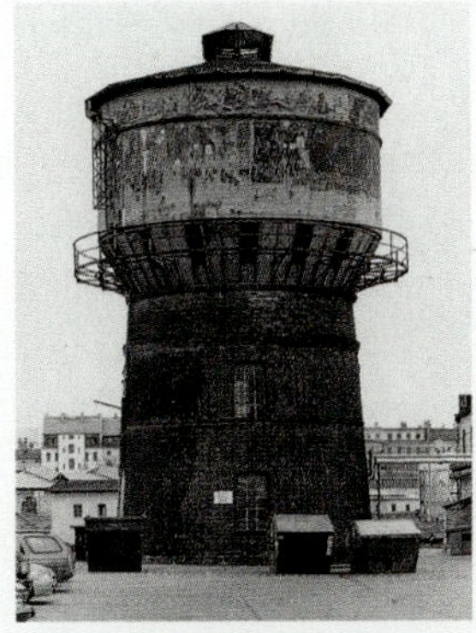

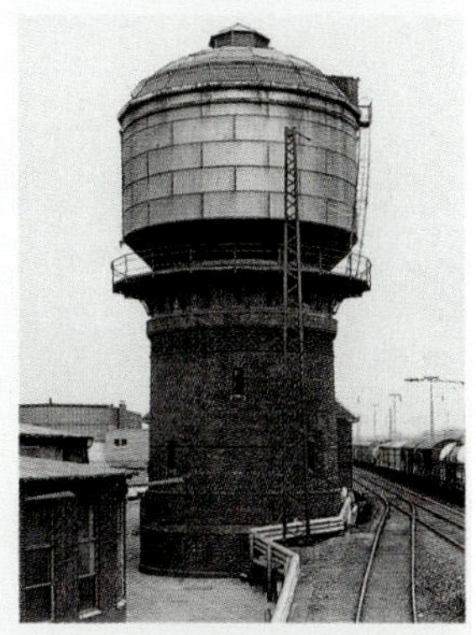

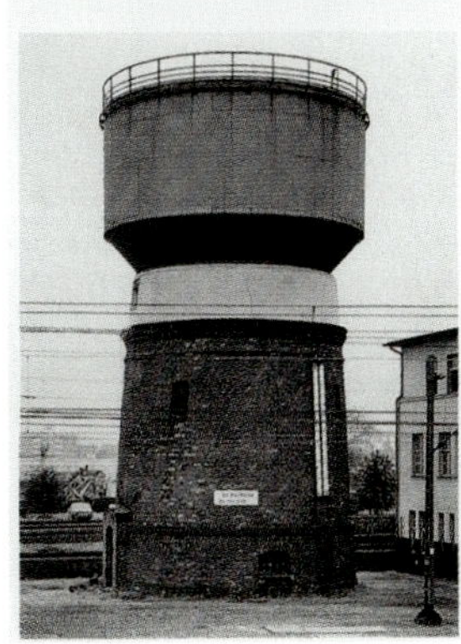

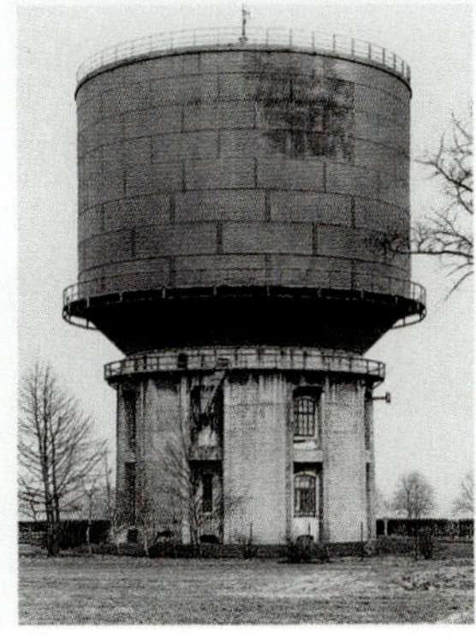

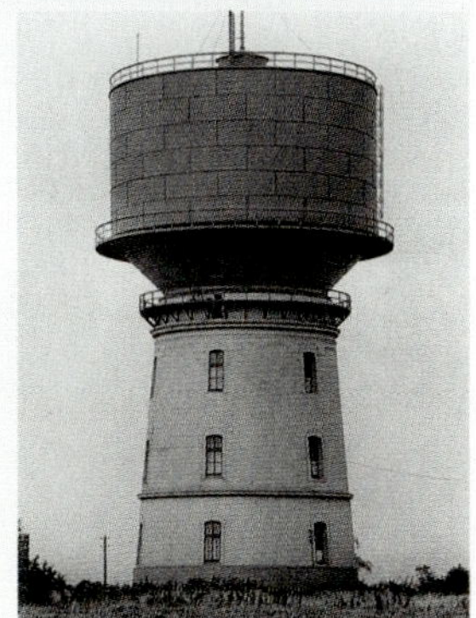

**Opposite** *Blast Furnace View*, Volkingen, Saar, Germany, 1989.

**Above** *Watertowers*, 1967–80; printed 1980.

## The Bechers

1920

1931 Bernhard Becher born in Siegen, Germany

1934 Hilla Wobeser born in Potsdam, Germany

1940

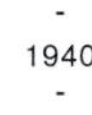

1950

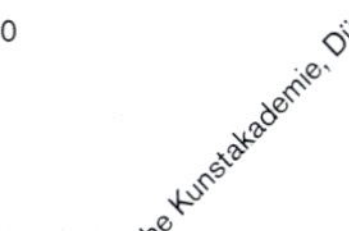

1957 Meet at the Kunstakademie, Düsseldorf

1960

1963 Hold their first show in a bookstore in Siegen, Germany

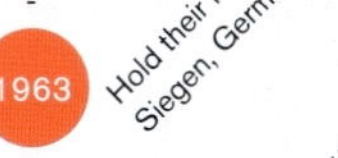

1969 Marriage

1970 Publish *Anonymous Sculptures: A Typology of Technical Construction*

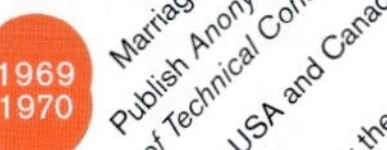

1974 Travel to the USA and Canada

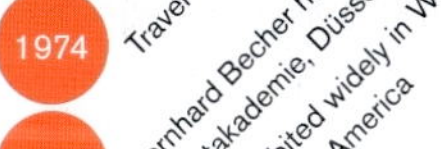

1976 Bernhard Becher hired by the Kunstakademie, Düsseldorf

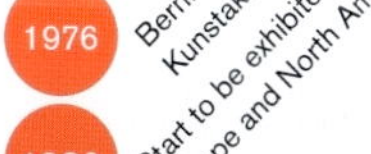

1980 Start to be exhibited widely in Western Europe and North America

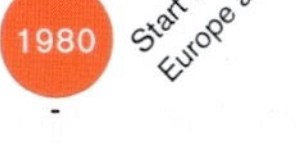

1991 Awarded the Golden Lion at the Venice Biennale, in the category of sculpture

2000

2002 Erasmus Prize awarded to both for excellence in teaching

2004 Receive Hasselblad Award

2005 Retrospective at the Centre Pompidou, Paris

2007 Bernhard Becher dies in Rostock, Germany

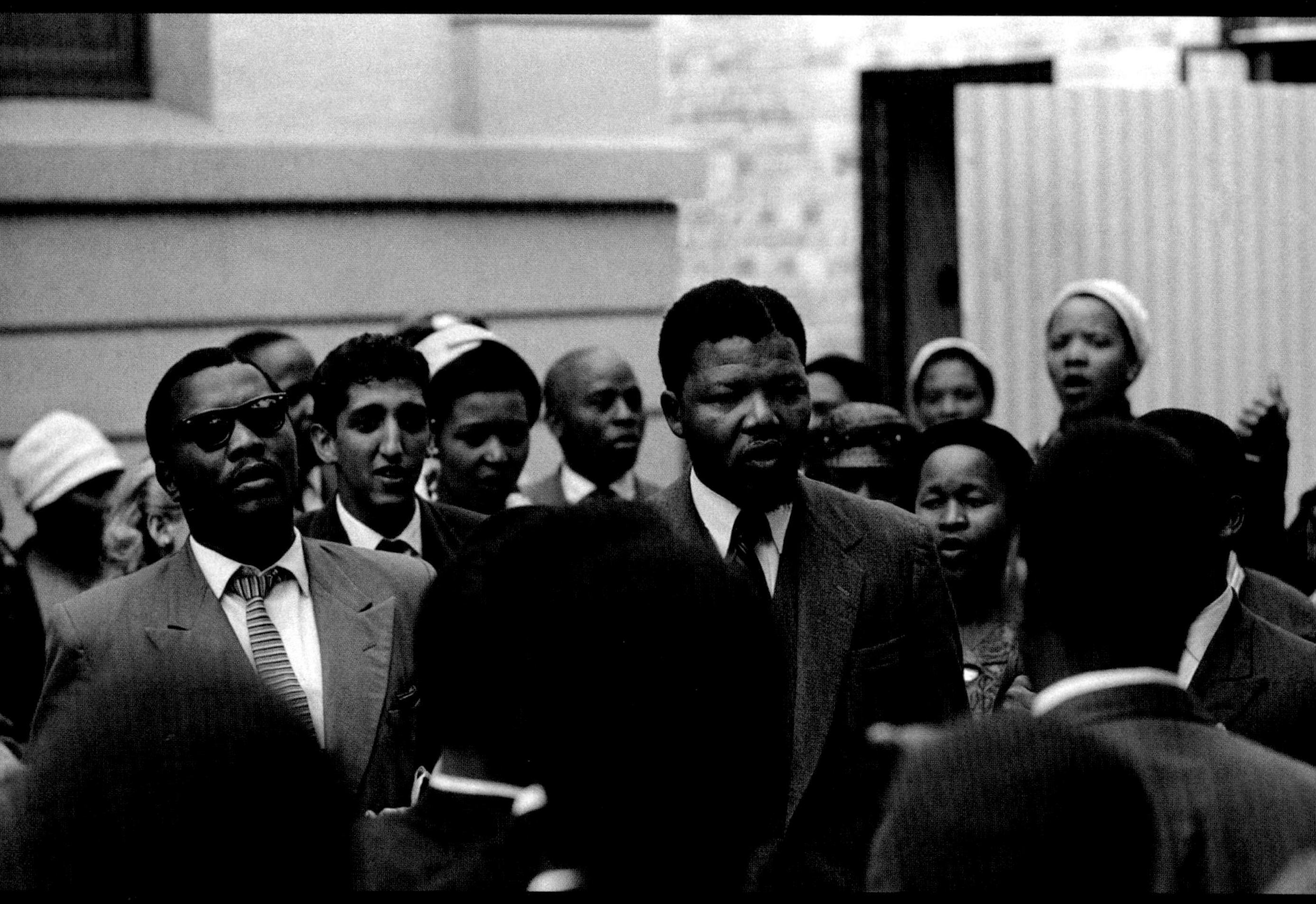

Nelson Mandela with co-accused and supporters during a treason trial in Johannesburg, in 1956.

'If you want a picture, you get that picture, under all circumstances.'

# Peter Magubane

b. 1932

SOUTH AFRICA

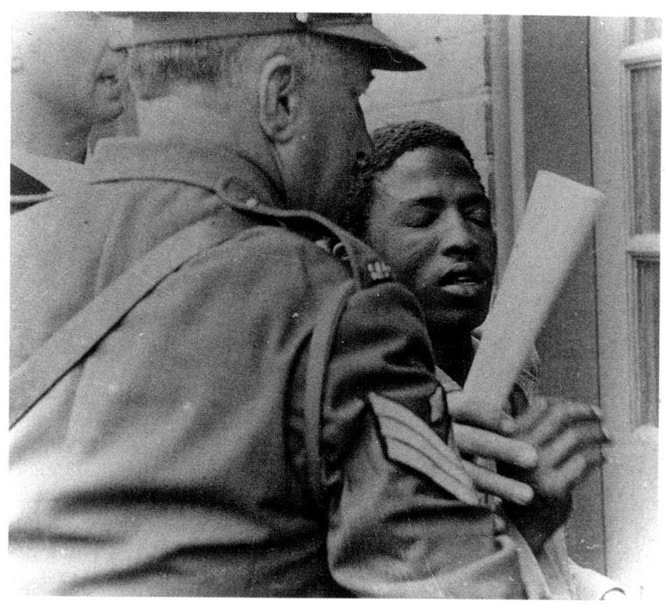

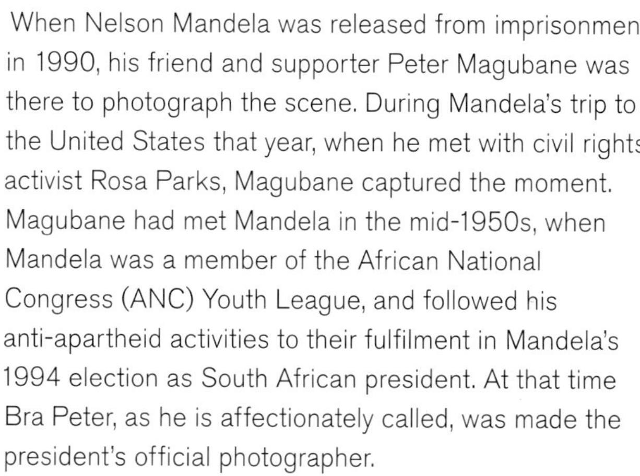

When Nelson Mandela was released from imprisonment in 1990, his friend and supporter Peter Magubane was there to photograph the scene. During Mandela's trip to the United States that year, when he met with civil rights activist Rosa Parks, Magubane captured the moment. Magubane had met Mandela in the mid-1950s, when Mandela was a member of the African National Congress (ANC) Youth League, and followed his anti-apartheid activities to their fulfilment in Mandela's 1994 election as South African president. At that time Bra Peter, as he is affectionately called, was made the president's official photographer.

Magubane's accomplishments and suffering during the anti-apartheid struggle are recognized in South African history. Indeed, he seems to have had a keen sense that his work, which found its immediate outlet in the picture press, at home and abroad, would also become an important national archive. Once, when he was forced to open his camera, thus exposing the film to light and erasing his work, he felt it as a crime against history. Magubane's books, such as *Black Child*, published outside of South Africa, illustrated the social conditions behind the news.

Magubane's pictures have an immediacy that is still poignant. Part of that effect is due to the way Magubane put himself and his camera in the middle of things, and shot from a relatively low position. Literally, he would not look down on people. His risky efforts to get close to the action are legend. A list of the materials with which he camouflaged his camera includes a loaf of bread, a newspaper, a milk carton and a Bible. He devised a system whereby he could keep his camera beneath his jacket, only exposing it for the instant he needed to make a picture.

In recent years, Magubane turned his attentions towards another sort of history, that of traditional African cultural practices. 'I'm sick and tired of taking pictures of dead people,' he explained.

Peter Magubane arrested, *Rand Daily Mail*, 1956.

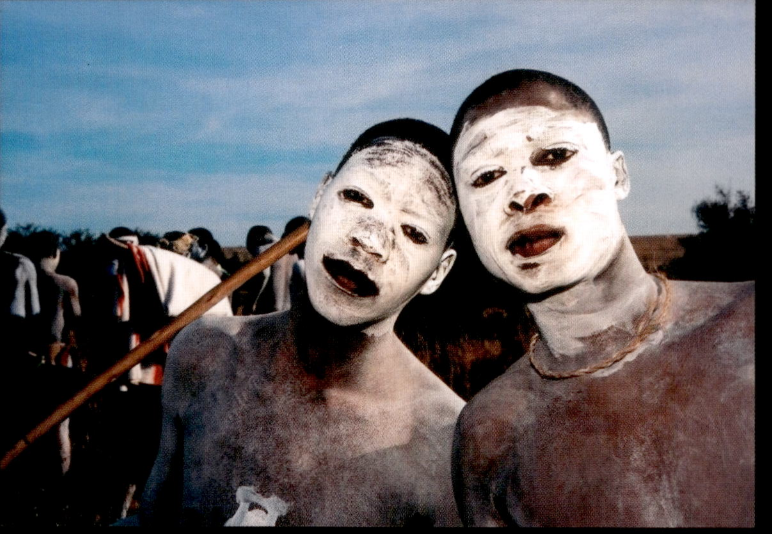

**Above** From *Ceremonies*, 2003.

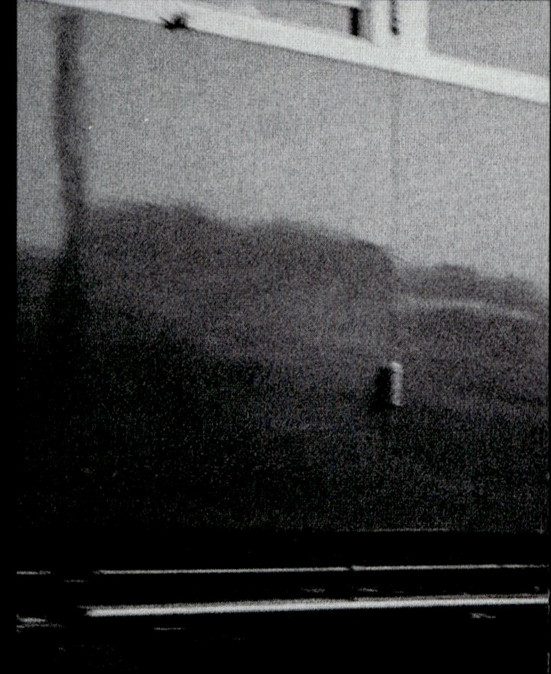

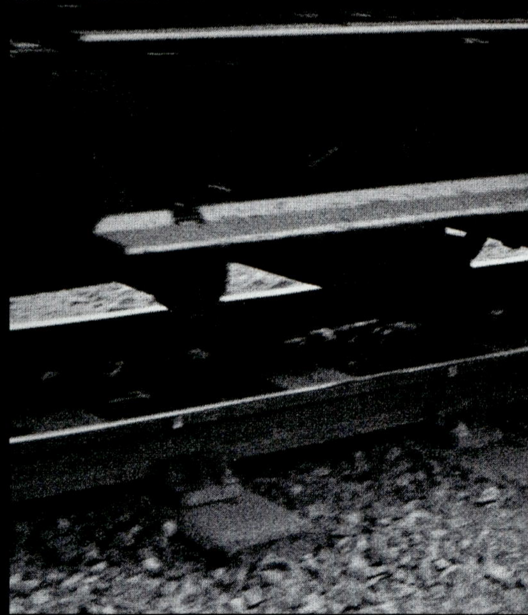

**Right** 'Staff riders' on a train leaving Soweto, 1970s.

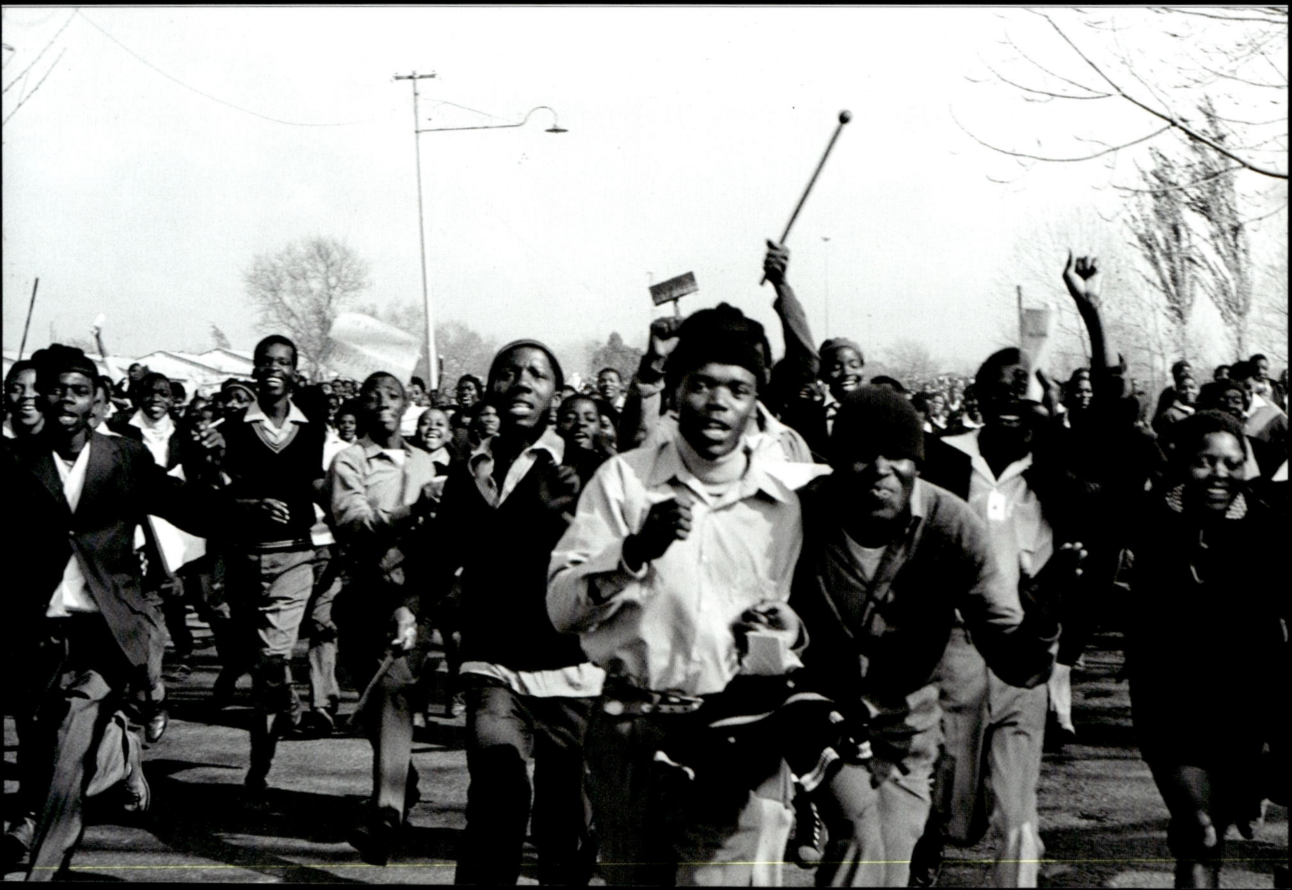

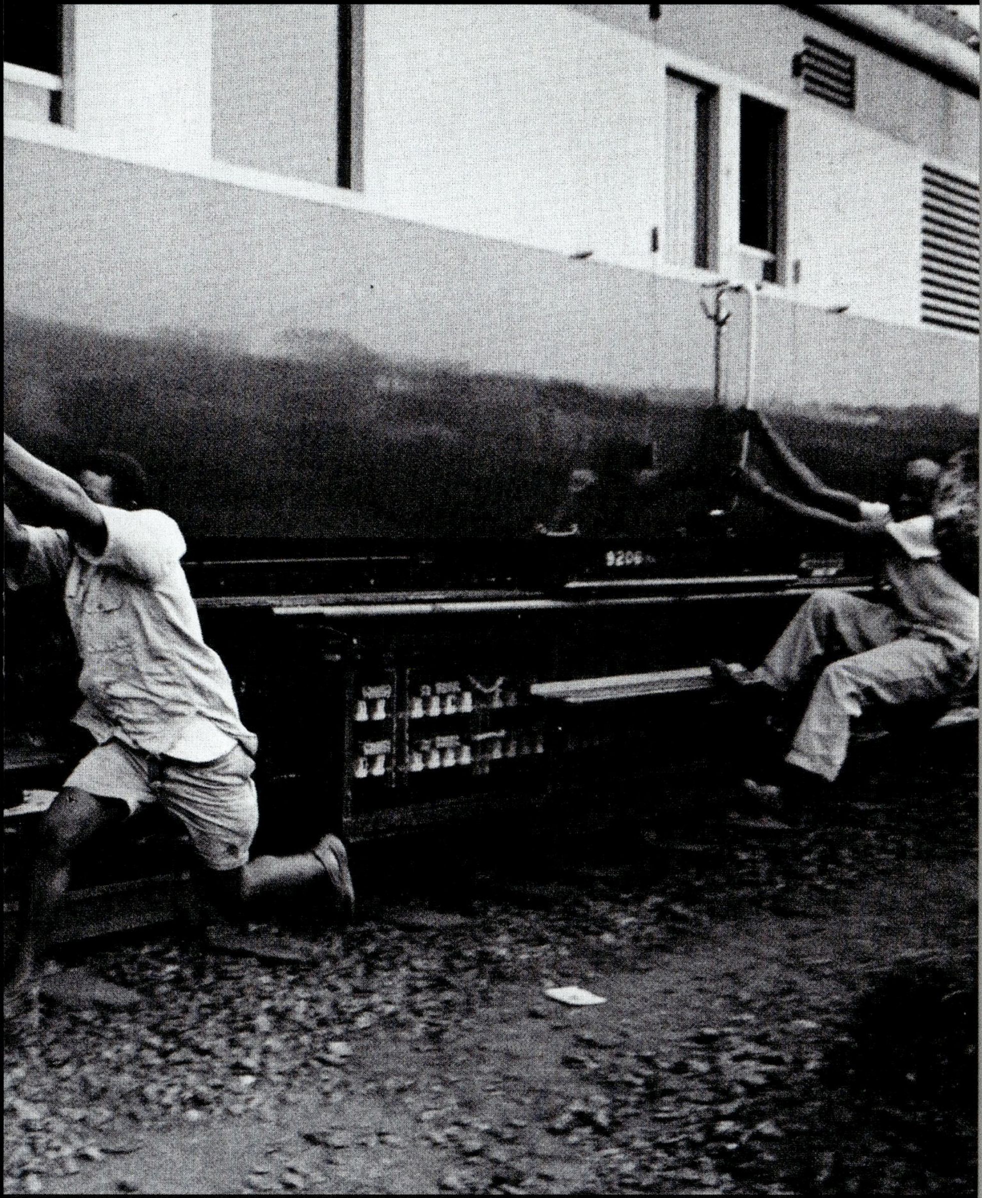

Soweto uprising, 1976.

# Peter Magubane

1920

1930

**1932** Born in Vrededorp, now Pageview, near Johannesburg, South Africa

1940

**1945** Receives his first camera, a Kodak Brownie, around this time

1950

**1954** Joins *Drum* magazine (originally as a driver)

**1958** First black South African to win a photographic prize

**1960** Double-page coverage of Sharpeville massacre in *Time* magazine

**1969** Begins imprisonment in solitary confinement for 586 days, and banned from making photographs for five y

**1972** Re-imprisoned for breaking ban

**1978** Works for *Time* magazine (to 1988)

1980

**1985** Shot with buckshot 17 times in police crossfire, while attending a funeral

1990

**c.1998** Begins publishing books of photographs on South Africa's art and culture

2000

**2006** Awarded Honorary Fellowship by Royal Photographic Society, UK

**2010** Receives the Robert Capa Infinity Award in New York

'To me photography can be simultaneously both a record and a mirror or window of self-expression.'

# Eikoh Hosoe

b. 1933

JAPAN

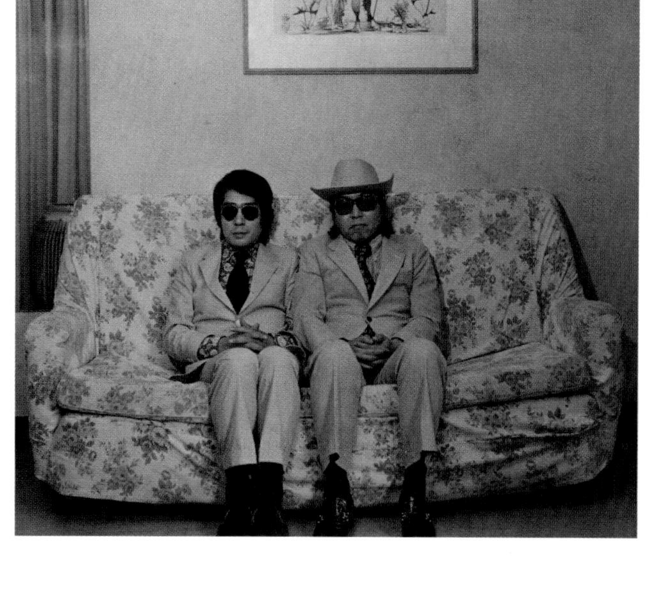

Eikoh Hosoe's interactions with other arts, such as poetry and dance, not only created vibrant hybrid forms of photography but also elevated the relatively new medium through fruitful interaction with arts that enjoyed long and valued histories in Japanese culture. His pictures mix contemporary events and ideas with pre-modern concepts and legends. The result is often a seamless blend of avant-garde and tradition.

With Tatsumi Hijikata, an inventor of Butoh, a heretical, sometimes improvisational, highly athletic form of dance, Hosoe created a spontaneous series of images that were brought together in the book *Kamaitachi (Sickle-toothed Weasel),* centred on a mythical demon from folklore who lurks in rice fields waiting to terrorize farmers and villagers. For Hosoe and Hijikata, both of whom had personal memories of the Japanese countryside, the *kamaitachi* encapsulated the fear and unpredictability of life they had known during the war years. The grainy quality of the images dramatized anxiety.

Hosoe's 'Simon: A Private Landscape' is an ongoing series about personal identity and desire. His best-known and most frequently translated work, *Ordeal by Roses,* was created with writer Yukio Mishima, who, like Hosoe, blended the avant-garde and the traditional. As in his other work, Hosoe considered that impulse was a form of insight. Seeing an unattended garden hose, he wrapped it around Mishima, creating one of the writer's most well-known portraits. Together Hosoe and Mishima, who seems to have prepped for the photographer's visits by stockpiling sets and costumes, created what are now considered to be homoerotic images but which also incorporate the ideals of physical culture in Japan. For Hosoe, who recalled Mishima's ritual suicide in a later edition of the book, the images capture 'the perfect body of Mishima, who never admitted the decay of the flesh'.

**Opposite** *Kamaitachi #31*, 1968.

**Above** Portrait of Daidō Moriyama and Eikoh Hosoe in the latter's studio by Hitoshi Fugo 1973.

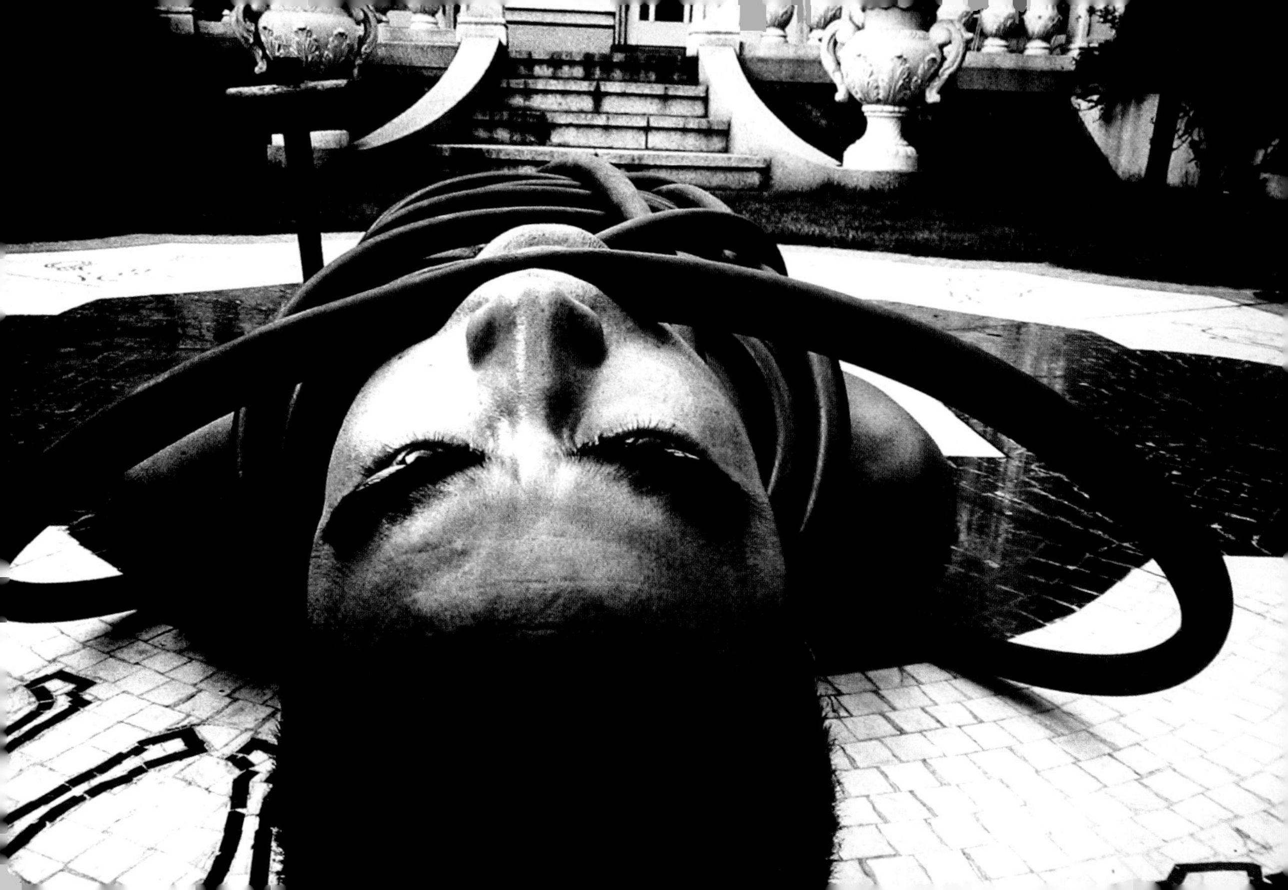

# Eikoh Hosoe

- **1933** Born Toshihiro Hosoe in Yonezawa, Yamagata Prefecture, Japan
- **1947** Changes first name to Eikoh
- **1954** Graduate from Tokyo College of Photography
- **1956** First solo show, 'An American Girl in Tokyo'
- **1957** Participates in 'Eyes of Ten' exhibition, Tokyo
- **1959** With others, forms the Vivo photo agency
- **1963** Publishes *Barakei* (*Killed by Roses*), later retitled *Ordeal by Roses*
- **1969** *Kamaitachi* published; 'Man and Woman' exhibition at Smithsonian Institution, Washington, DC
- **1975** Accepts professorship at Tokyo College of Photography
- **1990** 'Eikoh Hosoe: Photographs 1955–1988' at FotoFest, Houston, Texas
- **2003** Receives Royal Photographic Society's Centenary medal
- **2006** 'Spherical Dualism of Photography: The World of Eikoh Hosoe,' Tokyo Metropolitan Museum of Photography
- **2013** 'Eikoh Hosoe: Curated Body 1959–1970' at Miyako Yoshinaga Gallery, New York

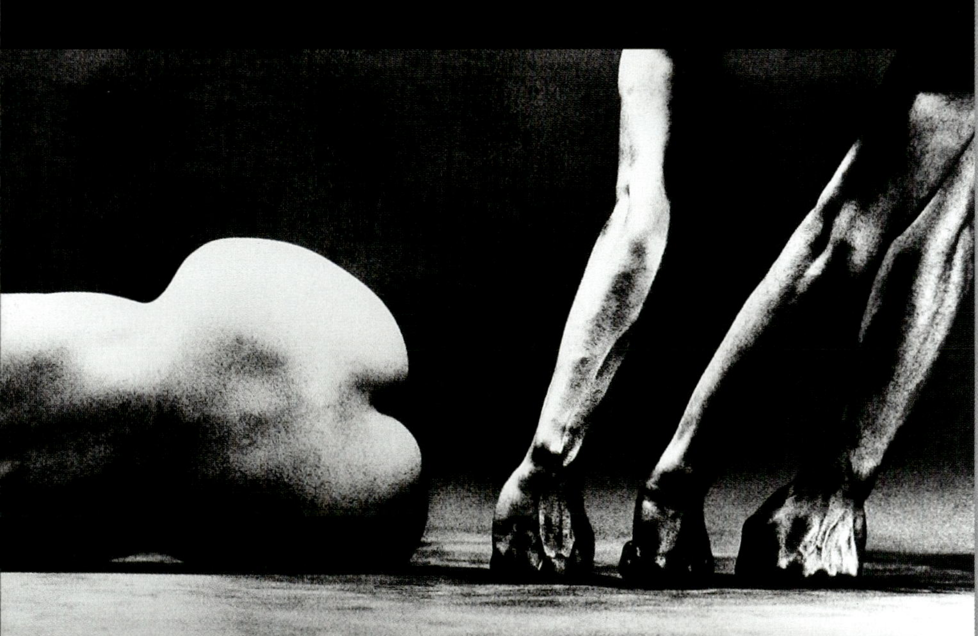

**Opposite** Yukio Mishima, *Ordeal by Roses #6*, 1961–62.

**Above** *Man and Woman # 24*, c. 1960.

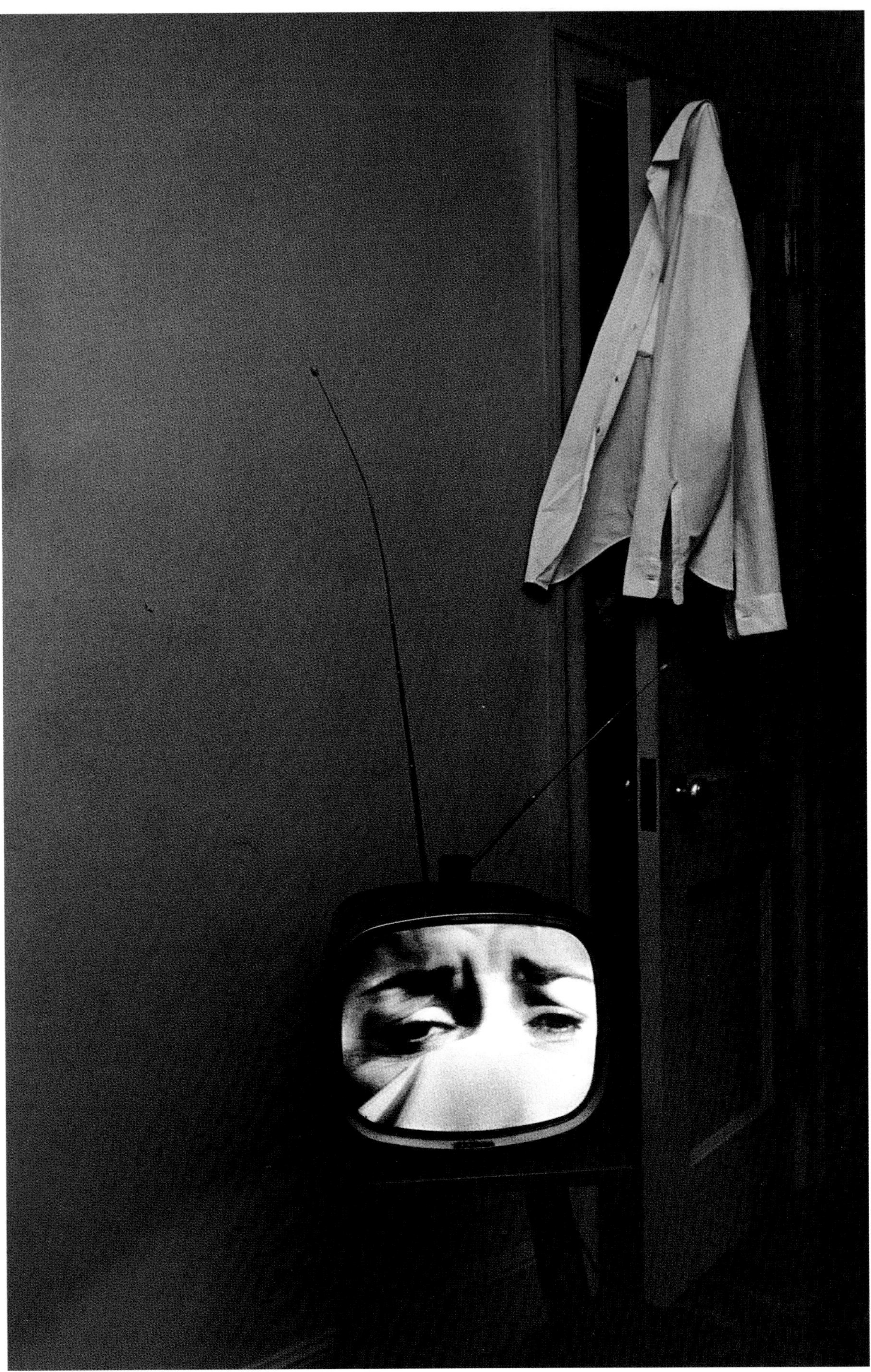

'I don't have messages in my pictures ... The true business of photography is to capture a bit of reality.'

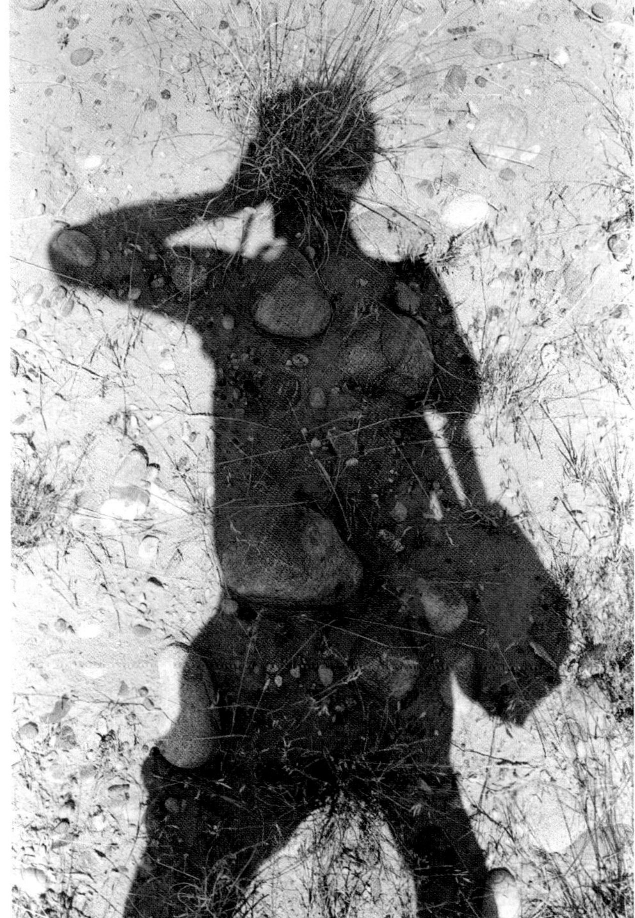

# Lee Friedlander

b. 1934

UNITED STATES

Although Lee Friedlander and his friend Garry Winogrand (p. 180) sometimes photographed on the opposite side of the same New York city street, their street photographs are dissimilar. Friedlander regularly shot from a position that would put an obstruction between him and the scene. Trees, lamp-posts, signs, doors and window frames break up urban scenes into a careless geometry, as if the viewer were chugging by in a slow bus with frequent stops. Add to the visual barriers his predilection for putting himself in his pictures, via a cast shadow or a reflection, and the pictures seem at cross purposes. Indeed, Friedlander has taken so many self-portraits since the 1960s that the sometimes geometrically intricate, often tongue-in-cheek images have been presented in print and in exhibitions solely devoted to them.

The documentary mode, in which the photographer becomes the all-seeing eye, swooping in on moments when meaning is expressed through visual representation, has been banished in Friedlander's work. He may have famously remarked that he wanted to photograph the social landscape, but Friedlander does best what Winogrand described as photographing 'to see what the world looks like in photographs'.

Friedlander took a different approach in other projects. His series on televisions makes them look like glowing portals to Hades, while his nudes balance sensuality and realism, not unlike the bordello photographs of E. J. Bellocq (1873–1949), the New Orleans photographer whom Friedlander admired so much that he reprinted Bellocq's negatives and published the results. Friedlander's 'American Monument' series indirectly plays on *American Photographs,* Walker Evans's photographic survey of the Depression era (p. 112), and on Robert Frank's *The Americans,* a raw critique of pettiness and decline (p. 172). 'The American Monument' is exactly as advertised, a pictorial review of those mostly forgotten statues and plaques celebrating people and events as marooned in the public imagination as they are in their physical settings. The influence of Friedlander's genre-breaking work continues to be embraced by younger photographers who favour his expanded, idiosyncratic and personal critique of documentary.

**Opposite** From 'The Little Screens', Nashville, 1963.

**Above** Self-portrait, Canyon de Chelly, Arizona, 1983.

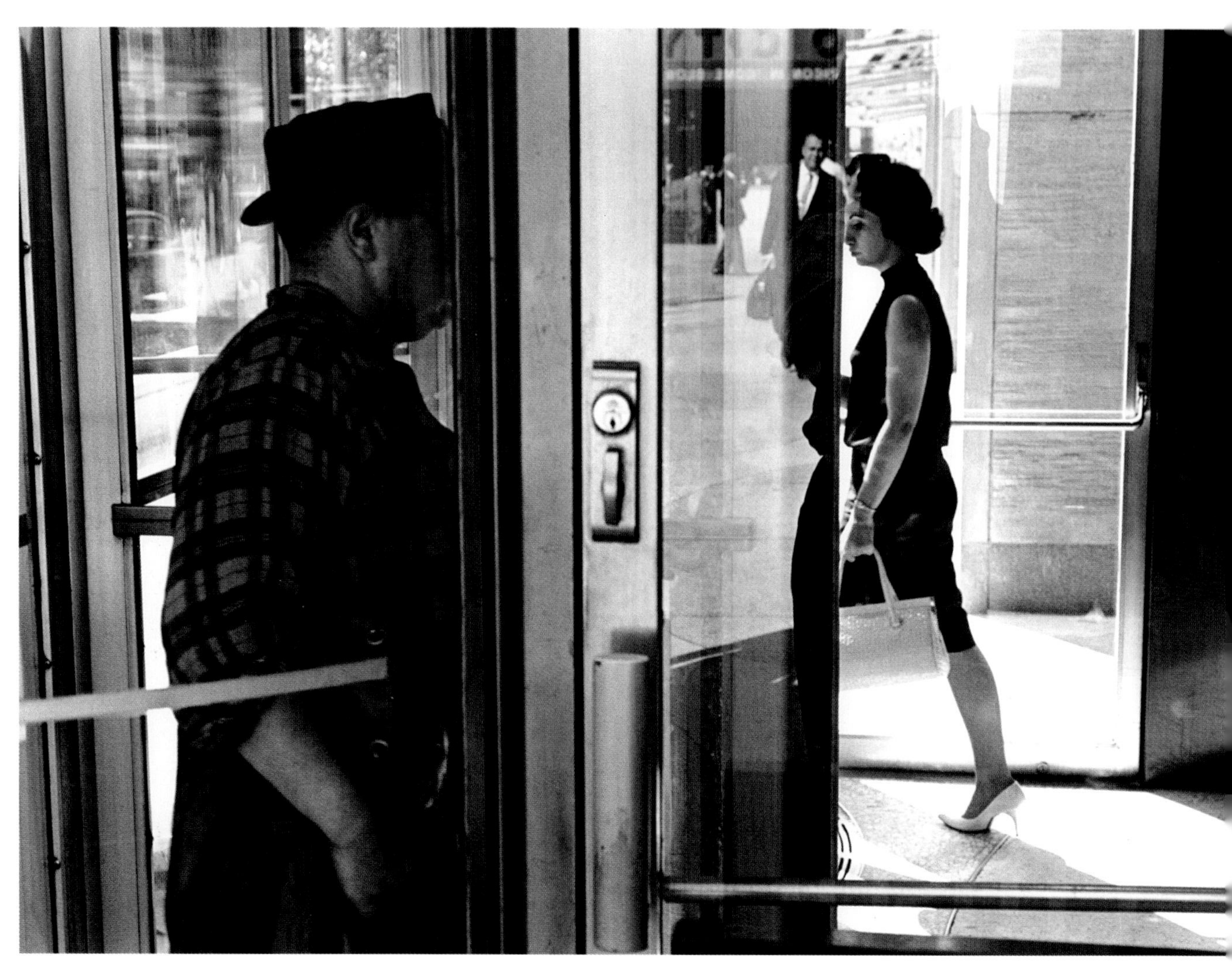

# Lee Friedlander

1934 Born in Aberdeen, Washington, USA

1960 Receives first of three Guggenheim Foundation Fellowships (also 1962 and 1977)

1963 Solo exhibition at George Eastman House, Rochester, New York

1964 Work appears in 'The Photographer's Eye' at the Museum of Modern Art, New York

1976 *The American Monument* published

1978 Included in John Szarkowski's influential book and exhibition, *Mirrors and Windows: American Photography since 1960*

1990 Receives a MacArthur Foundation Fellowship

2003 'Lee Friedlander: At Work' exhibition travels widely in Europe and the USA

2005 Retrospective at Museum of Modern Art, which also publishes the book *Lee Friedlander: Self Portrait*

**Opposite** New York, 1963.

**Below** Chicago, 1968.

**Bottom** Texas, 1997.

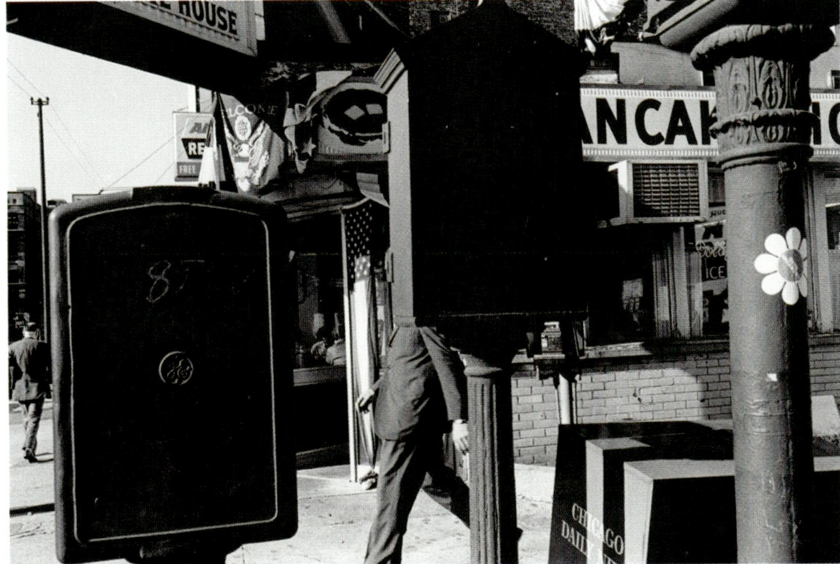

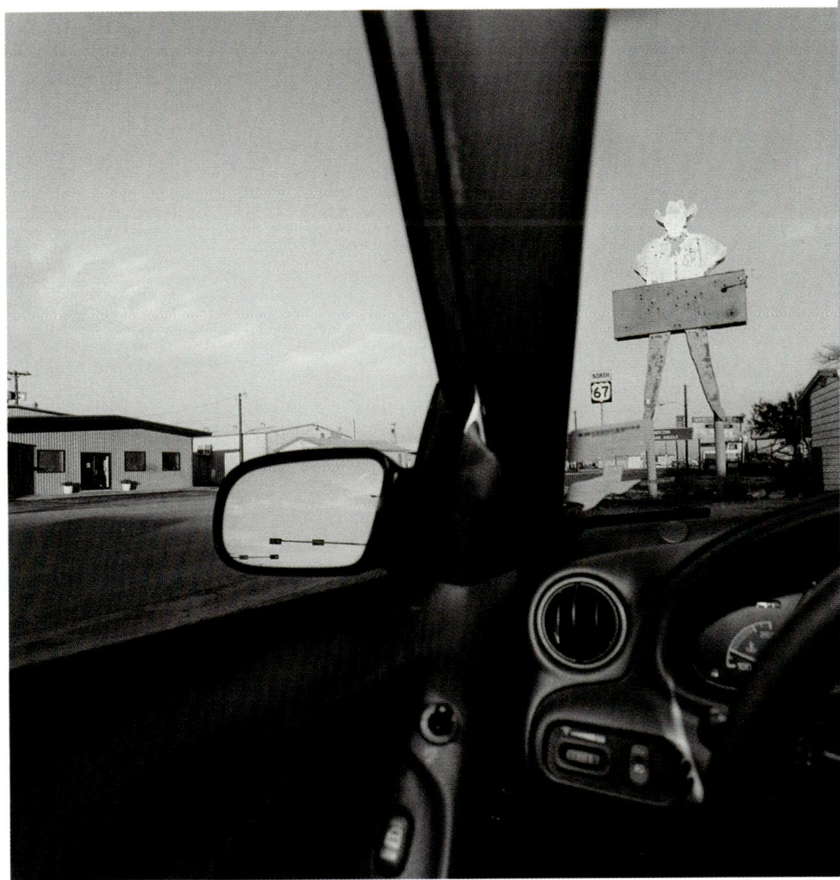

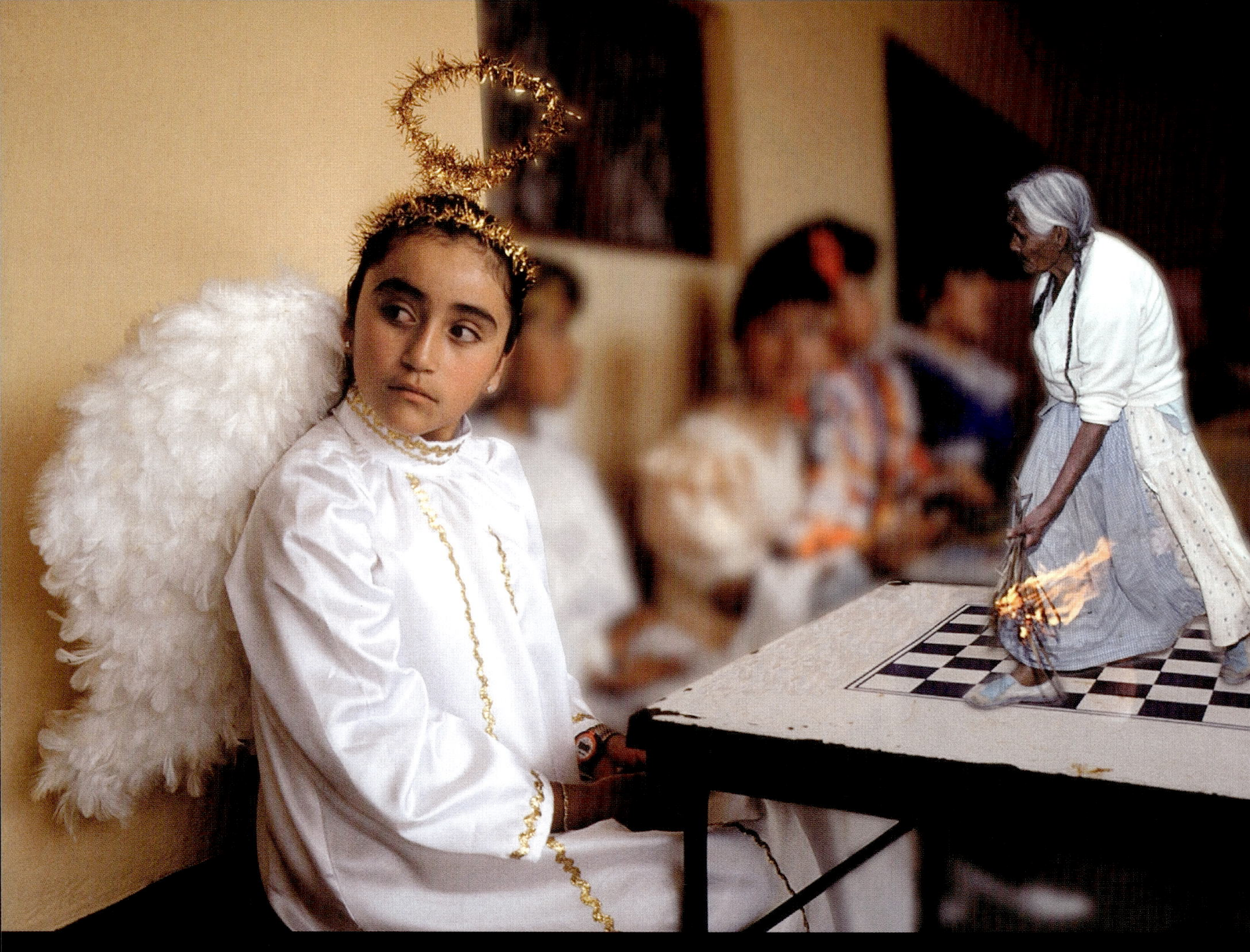

*The Temptation of the Angel*, 1991.

'I have always questioned everything: education, the obligation to memorize, authority.'

# Pedro Meyer

b. 1935

SPAIN

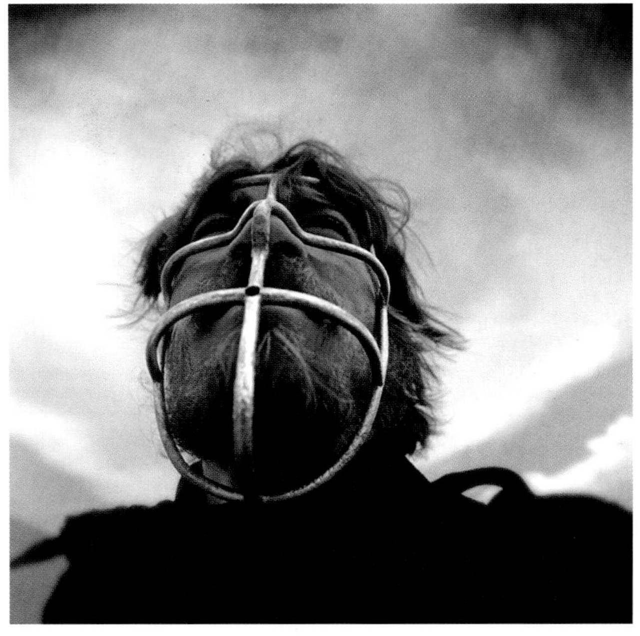

Photographic practice caught up to Pedro Meyer in the late 1990s, when the scales tipped away from analogue cameras to the interface of digital cameras and computers equipped with photo-editing software. These pairings changed the production and distribution of both professional and amateur photography. It was a long wait.

A largely self-taught photographer, who had taken a correspondence course in the subject, Meyer was a full-time businessman. As his interest in photography deepened, he took photographs of current events, such as the Mexican student movement of 1968. He moved heavily into street photography, and used his business skills to promote Latin American photography through conferences and networks for image-makers, creating a regional identity for image-making despite differences in cultural experience.

When he acquired his first computer – said to be the first Apple sold in Mexico – its primitive interactivity quickly inspired him to integrate photography into digital platforms. He began to refer to all prior photographic work as BC, before computers, and was the first to put photographs on a CD, along with sound. As Meyer's experience of digital complexity grew, he began to refer to photographs as fiction: that is, as constructed realities, capable of conveying truths beyond appearances, just as literature is capable of doing. He has argued that photo-manipulation has a long history in the medium and controversially suggested that photojournalism should also be permitted more freedom in creating images through digital manipulation.

Unlike many art photographers who work digitally, Meyer usually prefers to create the illusion of deep space in his work, regardless of the size or coloration of the figures and things he places in these constructed environments. Photographer-critic Joan Fontcuberta invented the term *vrai-faux* (true-false) and applied it to Meyer's distinctive use of the illusion of three-dimensional space. Meyer also continues to work as an organizer and promoter of photography through the popular website zonezero.com, which presents photographers' work as well as ideas.

Self-portrait as a heretic, 1975.

**Below left** Untitled from '*Hecho en Latinoamérica*' ('Made in Latin America') exhibition, 1978.

**Below** *Destroyed Somoza*, Nicaragua. 1979.

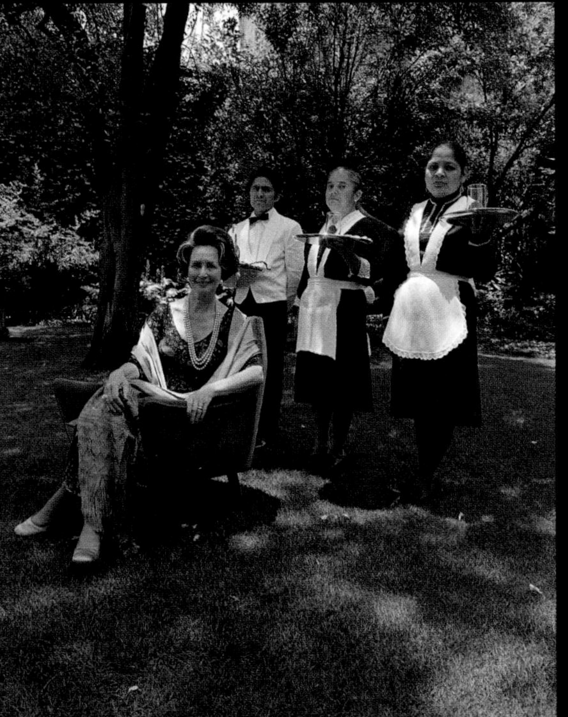

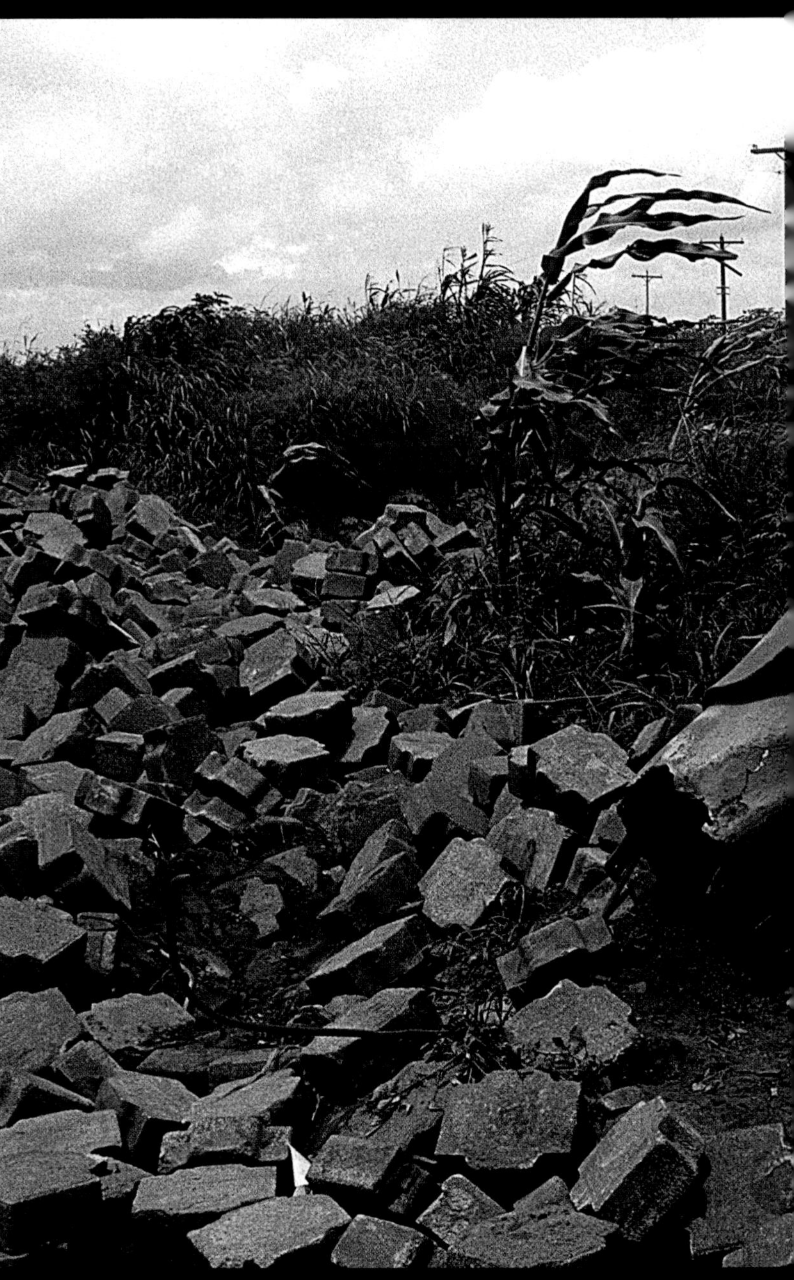

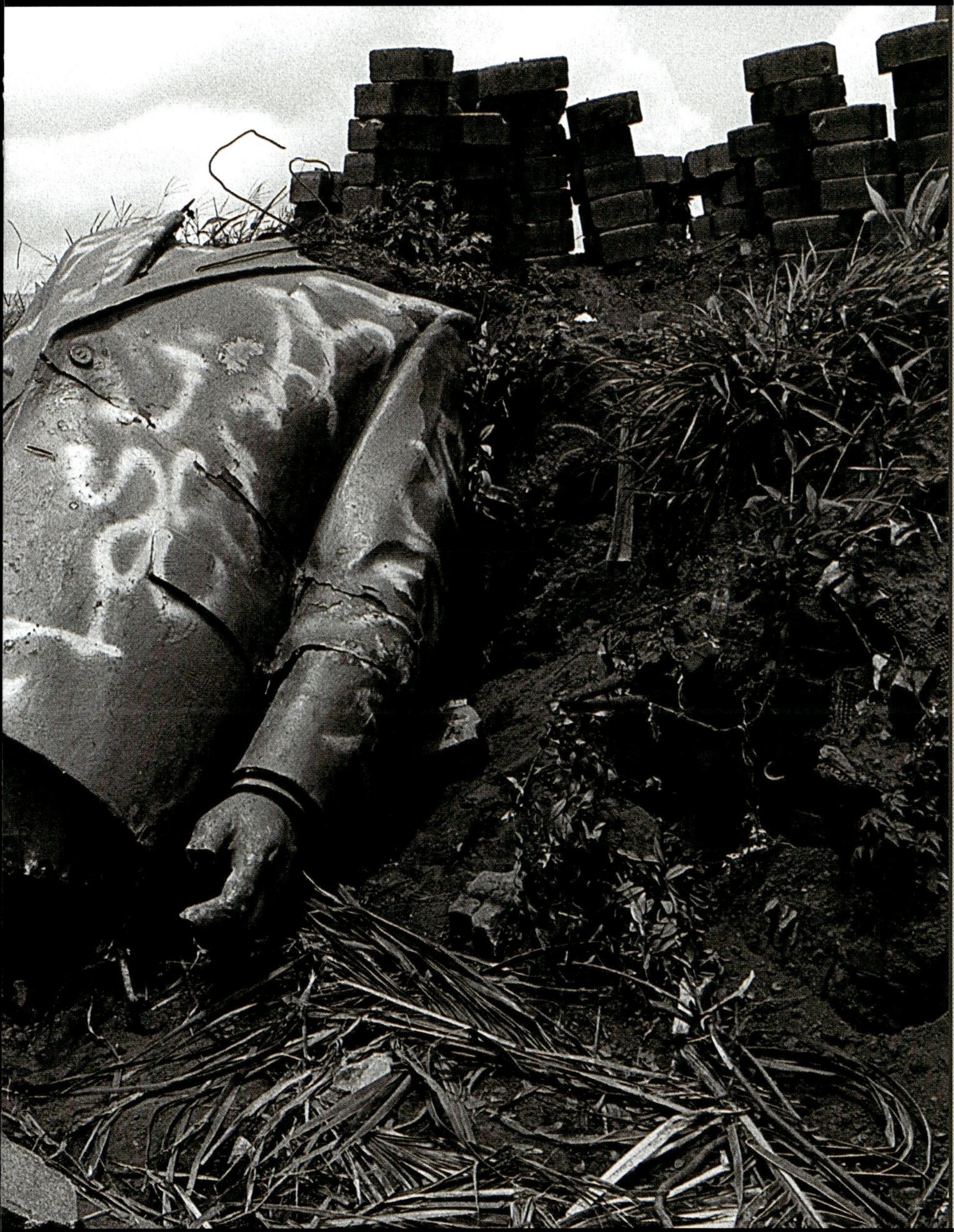

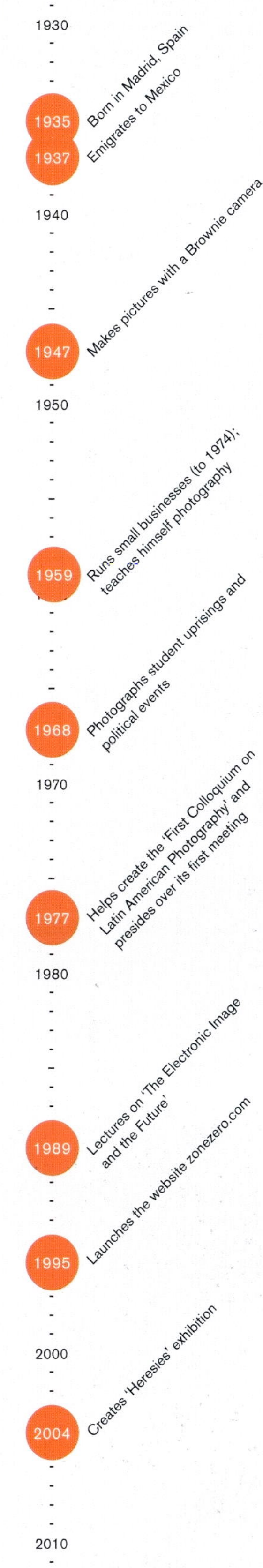
Pedro Meyer
1930
1935 Born in Madrid, Spain
1937 Emigrates to Mexico
1940
1947 Makes pictures with a Brownie camera
1950
1959 Runs small businesses (to 1974); teaches himself photography
1968 Photographs student uprisings and political events
1970
1977 Helps create the 'First Colloquium on Latin American Photography' and presides over its first meeting
1980
1989 Lectures on 'The Electronic Image and the Future'
1995 Launches the website zonezero.com
2000
2004 Creates 'Heresies' exhibition
2010

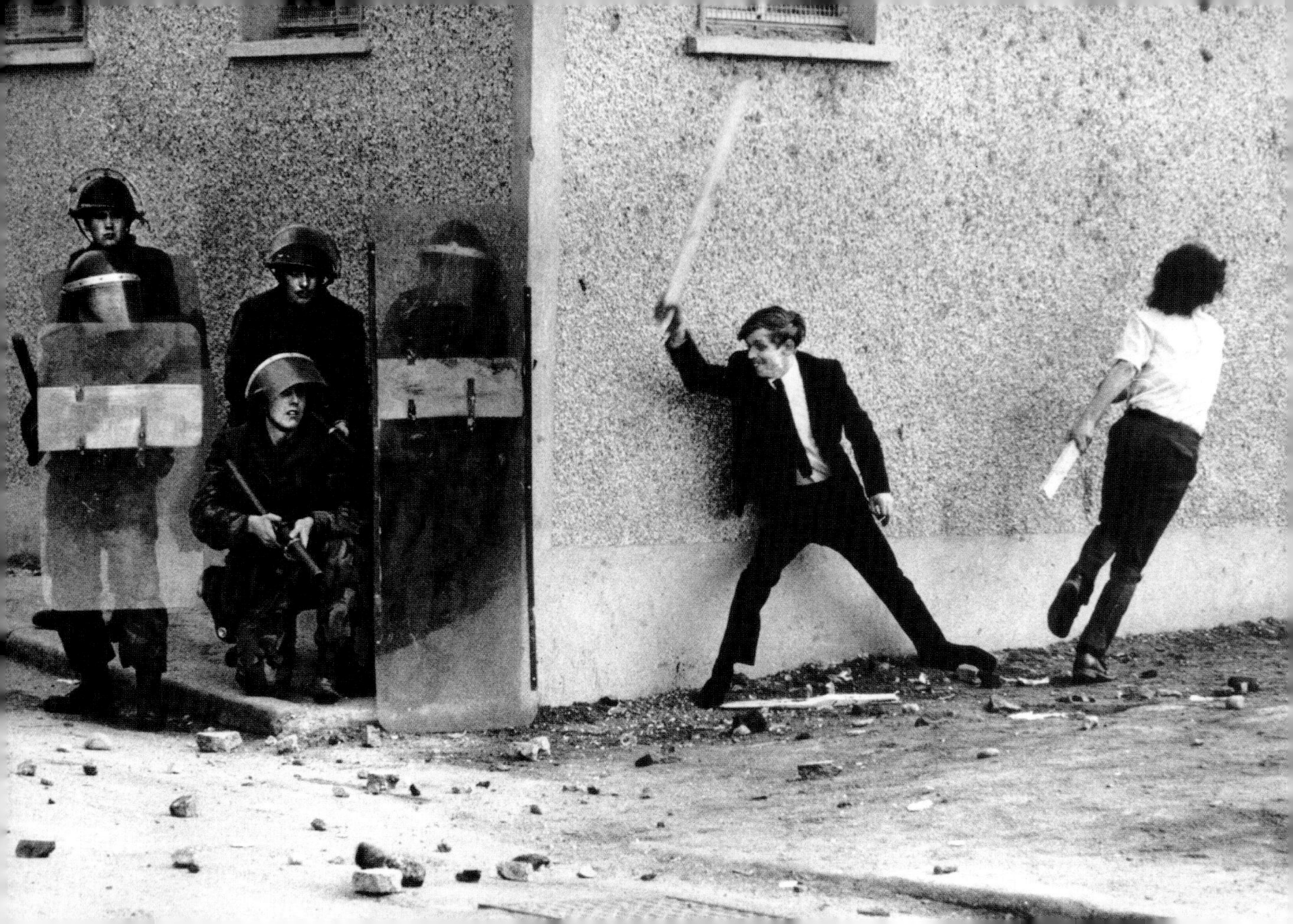

'I could have gone on photographing wars all my life, but what kind of person would it have made me?'

# Don McCullin

b. 1935

UNITED KINGDOM

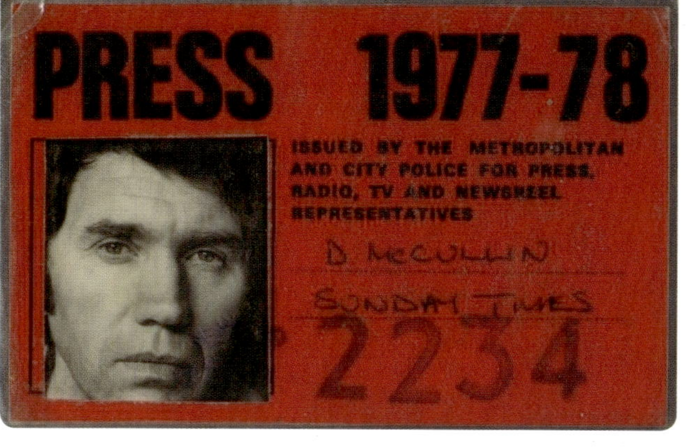


Don McCullin's war photographs have heroic gestures and art-historical references. Minutes after he made the picture of a US Marine hurling a grenade, looking like an ancient Greek statue of an athlete, the soldier was shot. The picture points to the ironic dynamics that drive McCullin's work: circumstances are always changing and the photographer is often between warring parties, as he was during the Troubles in Northern Ireland. His pictures balance conflict with suffering and outrage.

Assigned to photograph the tragic famine in Biafra, Nigeria, where the attempt by Christian people in the oil-rich south-eastern part of the country to secede was met with a blockade of food supplies, McCullin was grieved by what he saw: 'Sometimes it felt like I was carrying pieces of human flesh back home with me, not negatives. It's as if you are carrying the suffering of the people you have photographed.' He felt responsible for maintaining the dignity of the people he photographed, however dire their situations. To that end, he refused to photograph with a long lens, preferring to be close to his subjects.

Like many who have experienced it, McCullin admits to the exhilaration of combat. Yet he also feels a palpable responsibility to his subject to make the pictures as good as they can be. As a result, he continues to do his own printing and retouching, to perfect the image. He seldom photographs large crowds, preferring small groups and individuals to whom viewers can more easily relate. Sensitive to facile terms, he does not want to be called a war photographer, which he finds reductive. He describes his recent landscape studies, often done near his home in Somerset, as a form of rest, but could not resist travelling to Aleppo, Syria, in late 2012, to shoot pictures of the conflict-torn city for *The Times* of London.

Press pass, 1977–78.

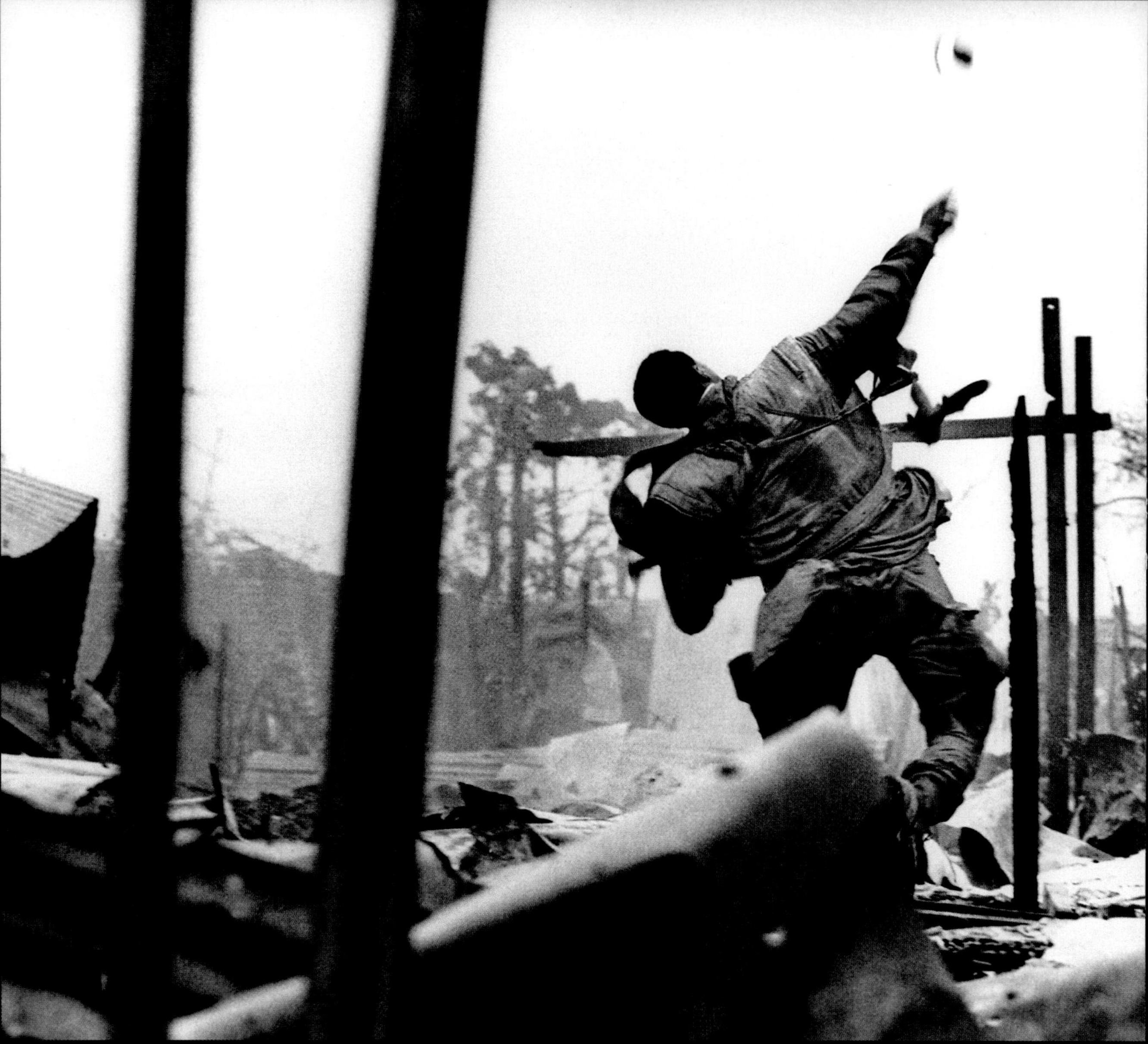

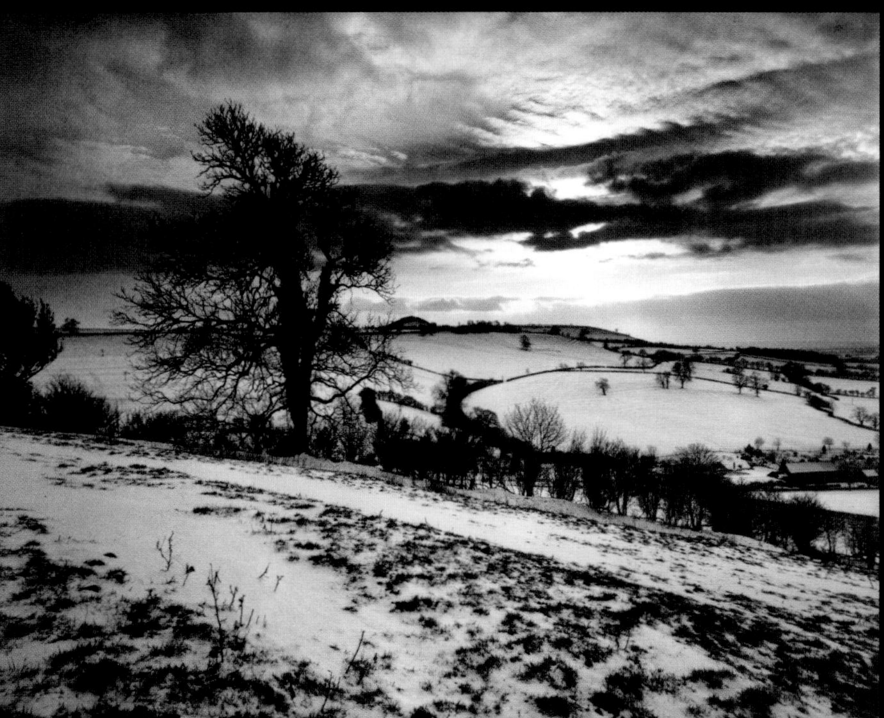

**Above** US Marine hurling a grenade, Hue, Vietnam, 1968.

**Opposite** Shellshocked US Marine, Hue, Vietnam, 1968.

**Left** Landscape in Somerset, 1991.

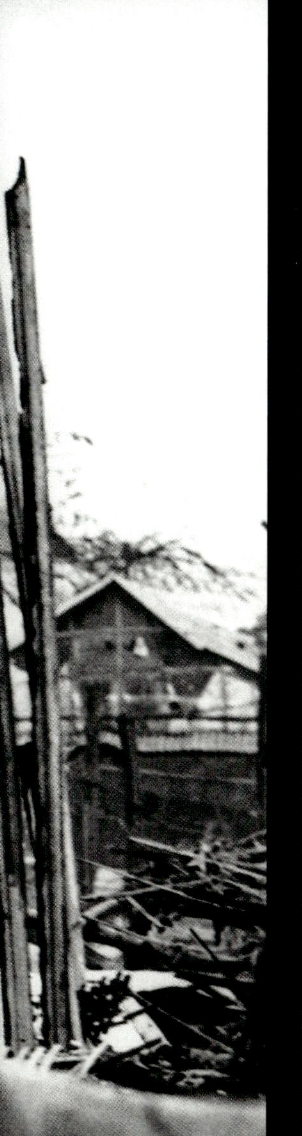

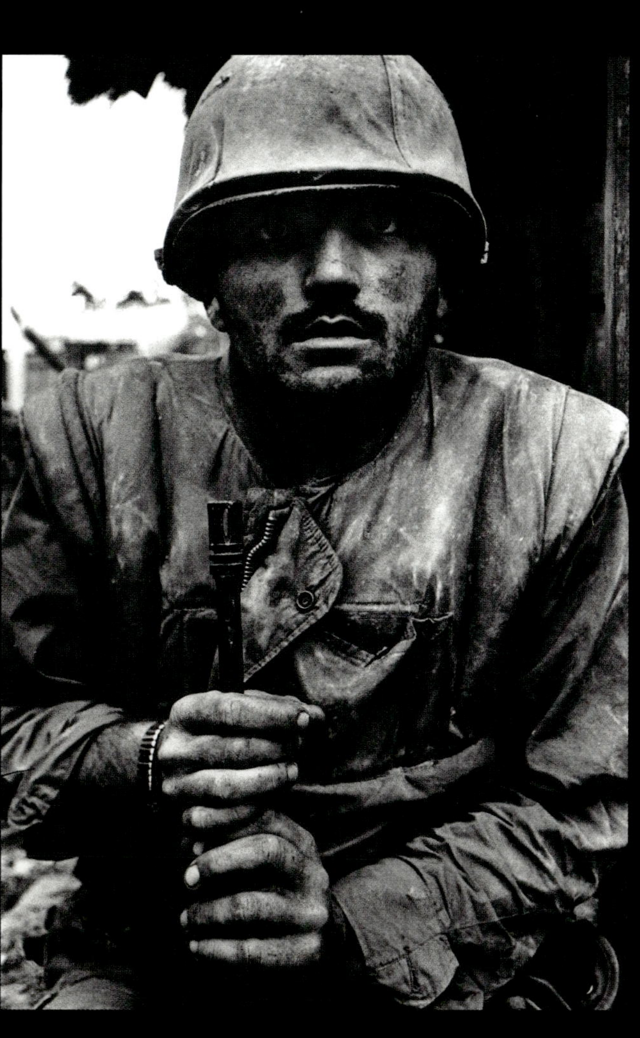

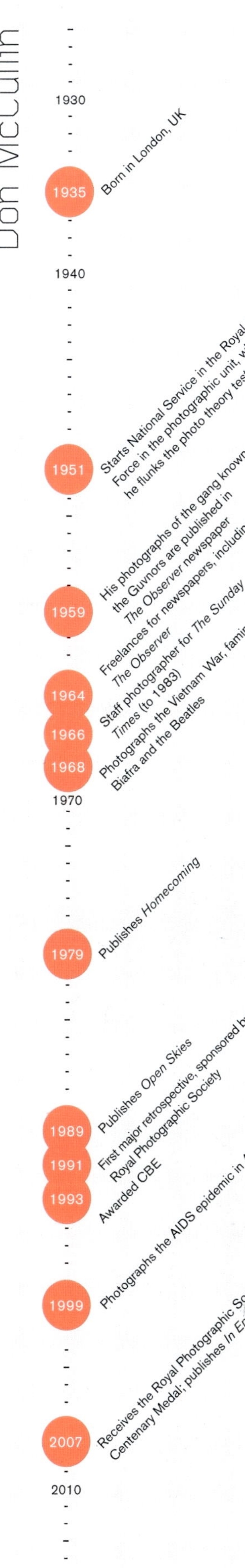
Don McCullin
1930
1935 Born in London, UK
1940
1951 Starts National Service in the Royal Air Force in the photographic unit, where he flunks the photo theory test
1959 His photographs of the gang known as the Guvnors are published in *The Observer* newspaper
1964 Freelances for newspapers, including *The Observer*
1966 Staff photographer for *The Sunday Times* (to 1983)
1968 Photographs the Vietnam War, famine in Biafra and the Beatles
1970
1979 Publishes *Homecoming*
1989 Publishes *Open Skies*
1991 First major retrospective, sponsored by the Royal Photographic Society
1993 Awarded CBE
1999 Photographs the AIDS epidemic in Africa
2007 Receives the Royal Photographic Society's Centenary Medal; publishes *In England*
2010

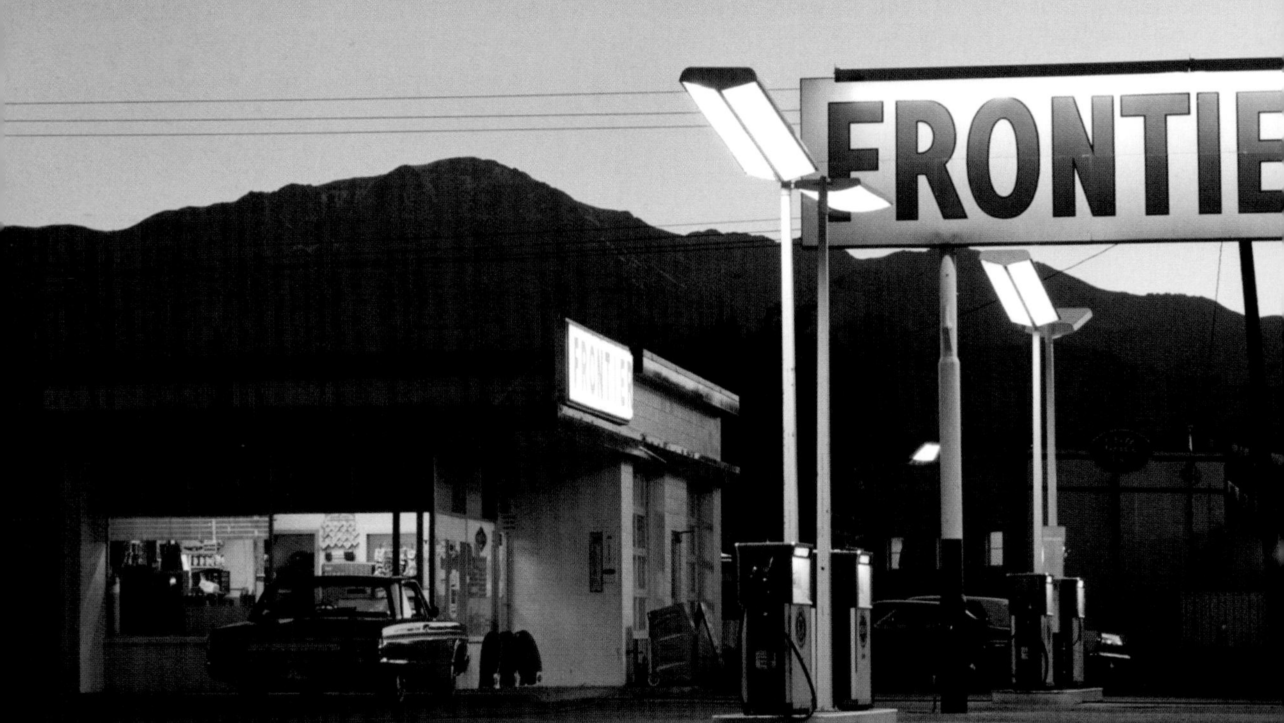
FRONTIE
FRONTIER

'Are there affirmable days or places in our deteriorating world?'

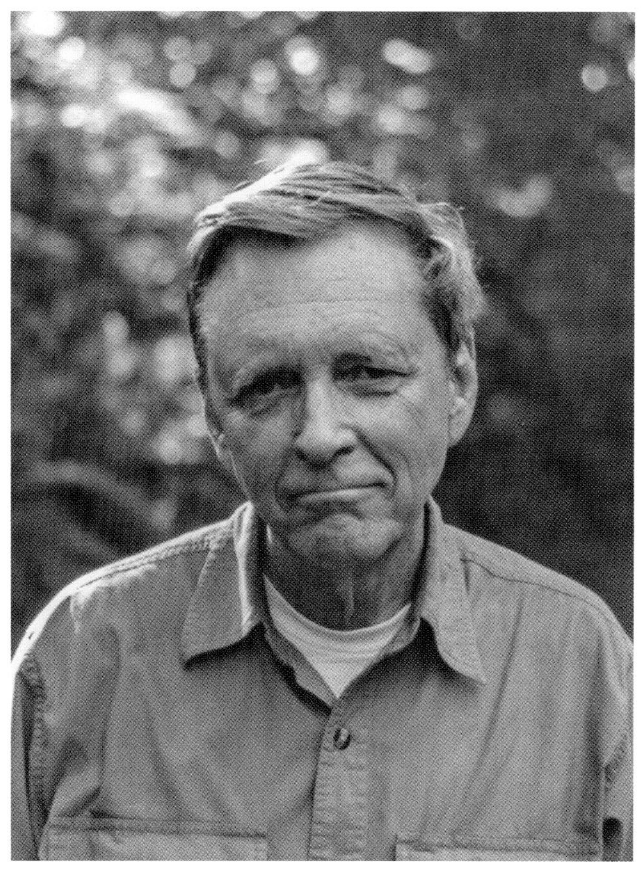

# Robert Adams

b. 1937

UNITED STATES

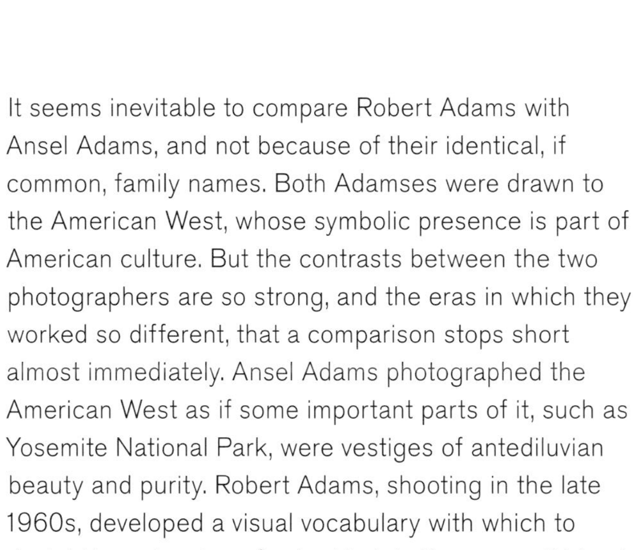

It seems inevitable to compare Robert Adams with Ansel Adams, and not because of their identical, if common, family names. Both Adamses were drawn to the American West, whose symbolic presence is part of American culture. But the contrasts between the two photographers are so strong, and the eras in which they worked so different, that a comparison stops short almost immediately. Ansel Adams photographed the American West as if some important parts of it, such as Yosemite National Park, were vestiges of antediluvian beauty and purity. Robert Adams, shooting in the late 1960s, developed a visual vocabulary with which to depict the extension of suburbia into the once wild land.

His early work was recognized as part of a 'new topographics' and was included in the seminal exhibition of that name in 1975. 'New Topographics' brought together post-World War II photographers, such as Lewis Baltz (p. 260), Stephen Shore (p. 268) and Bernd and Hilla Becher (p. 188), whose work combined a sense of emotional defeat with the energy of new imagery.

Of that assortment of photographers – who were never a group – Robert Adams is the most literary and, perhaps, the one who most readily looks for moments of spiritual conciliation. His book *Beauty in Photography* oriented readers to the small and fleeting instants of aesthetic exhilaration that can occur in humble and even disturbing visual moments. For Adams, photographs can offer moments that are more true than conventionally beautiful. 'We rely on landscape photography,' he wrote, 'to make intelligible to us what we already know.' In groups of photographs, such as those in *Summer Nights*, overlooked scenes emerge as transformative.

Portrait of Robert Adams by unknown, Manzanita, Oregon, 2004.

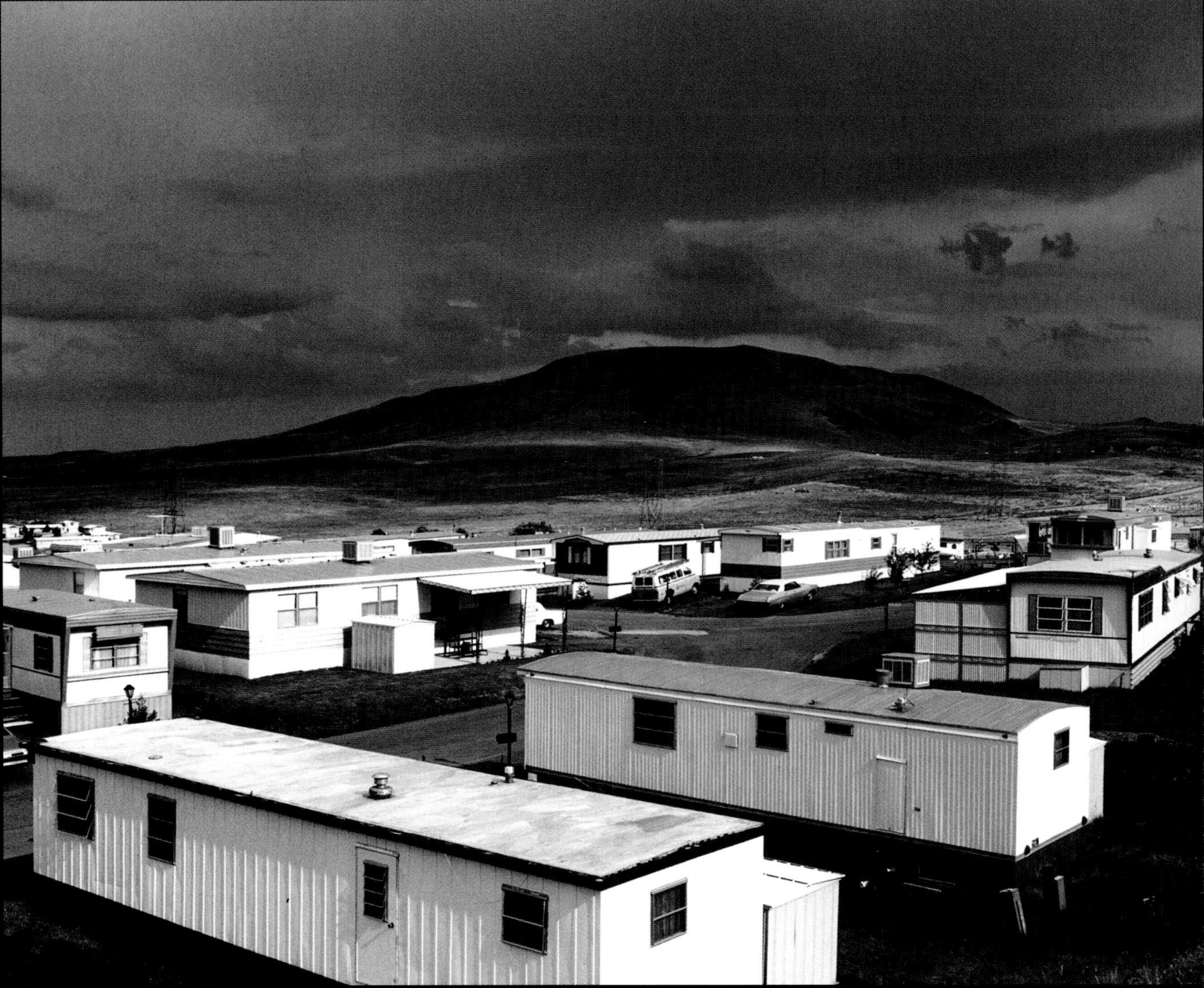

**Above** Colorado, c. 1973.

**Right** Signal Hill overlooking Long Beach, California, 1983.

**Opposite** *Aurora*, Colorado, c. 1980.

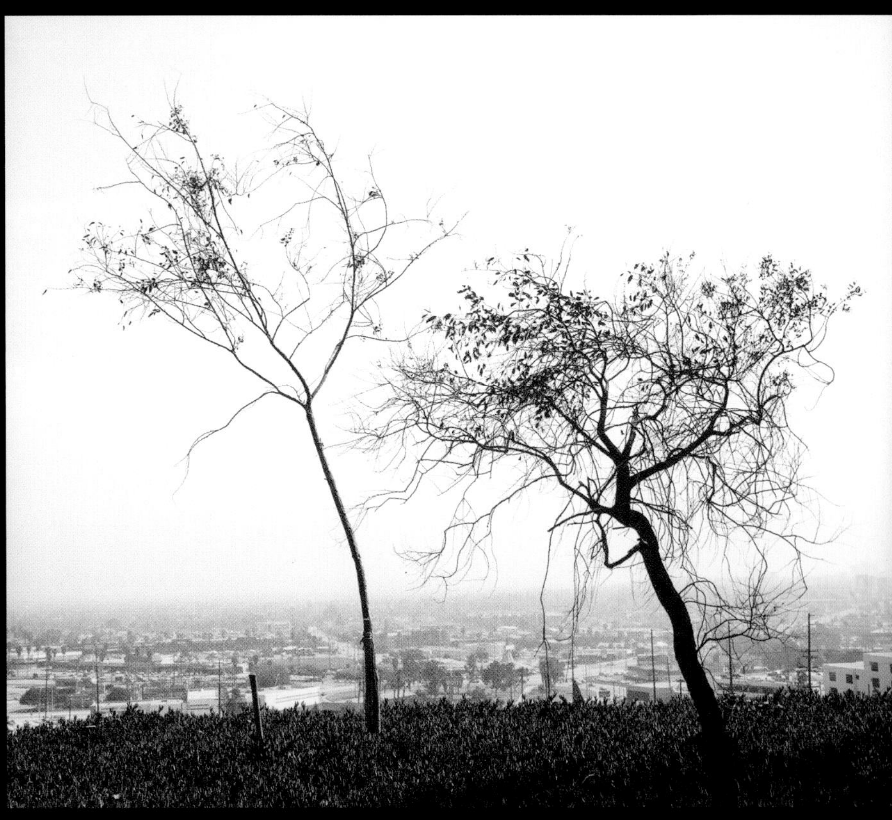

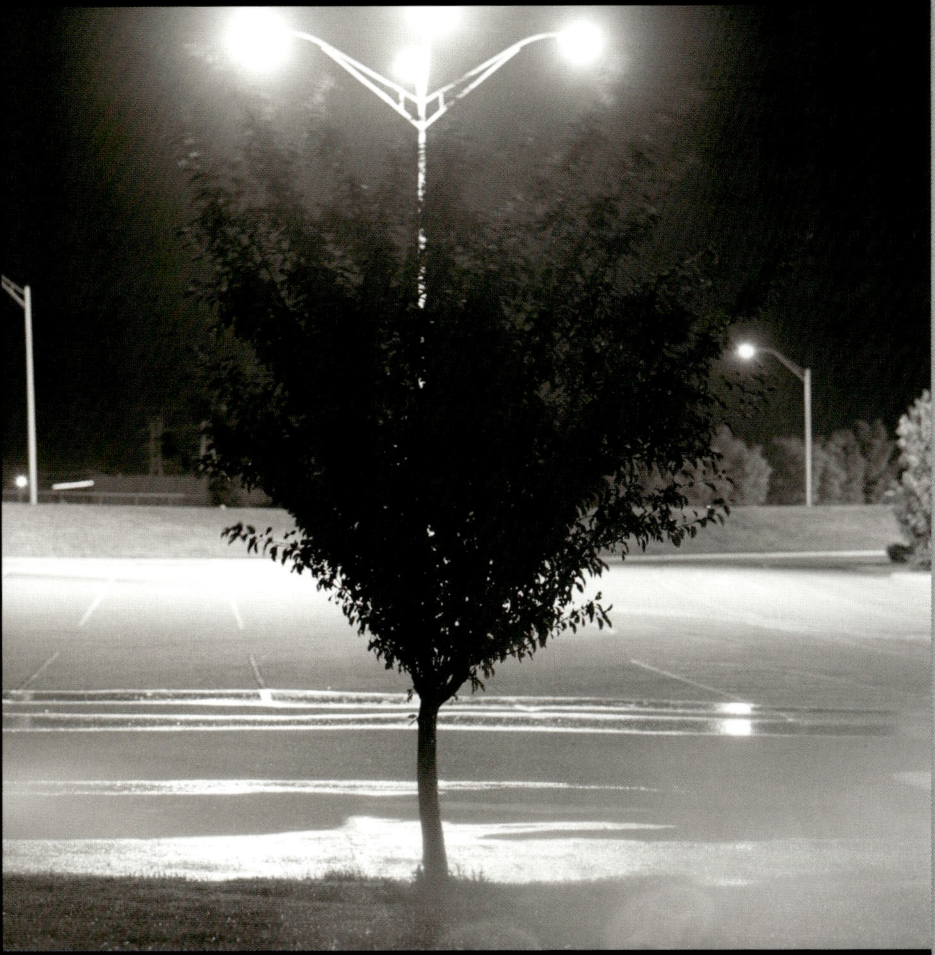

# Robert Adams

1930

**1937** Born in Orange, New Jersey, USA

1940

1950

**1956** Begins teaching at Colorado College

1960

**1963** Starts taking black-and-white photographs

**1968** Begins photographing suburban development near Denver, Colorado

**1970** Leaves teaching; publishes *White Churches of the Plains*

**1975** 'New Topographics' exhibition, George Eastman House, Rochester, New York

**1978** 'Mirrors and Windows: American Photography since 1960' at the Museum of Modern Art

**1981** Publishes *Beauty in Photography*

**1985** Publishes *Summer Nights*

**1989** Retrospective 'To Make It Home: Photographs of the American West 1965–1986' at the Philadelphia Museum of Art

**1994** Receives MacArthur Fellowship; publishes *Why People Photograph*

2000

**2004** 'Turning Back' exhibition at the Haus der Kunst, Munich, and the San Francisco Museum of Art

**2011** 'Robert Adams: The Place We Live: A Retrospective' at Denver Museum of Fine Arts

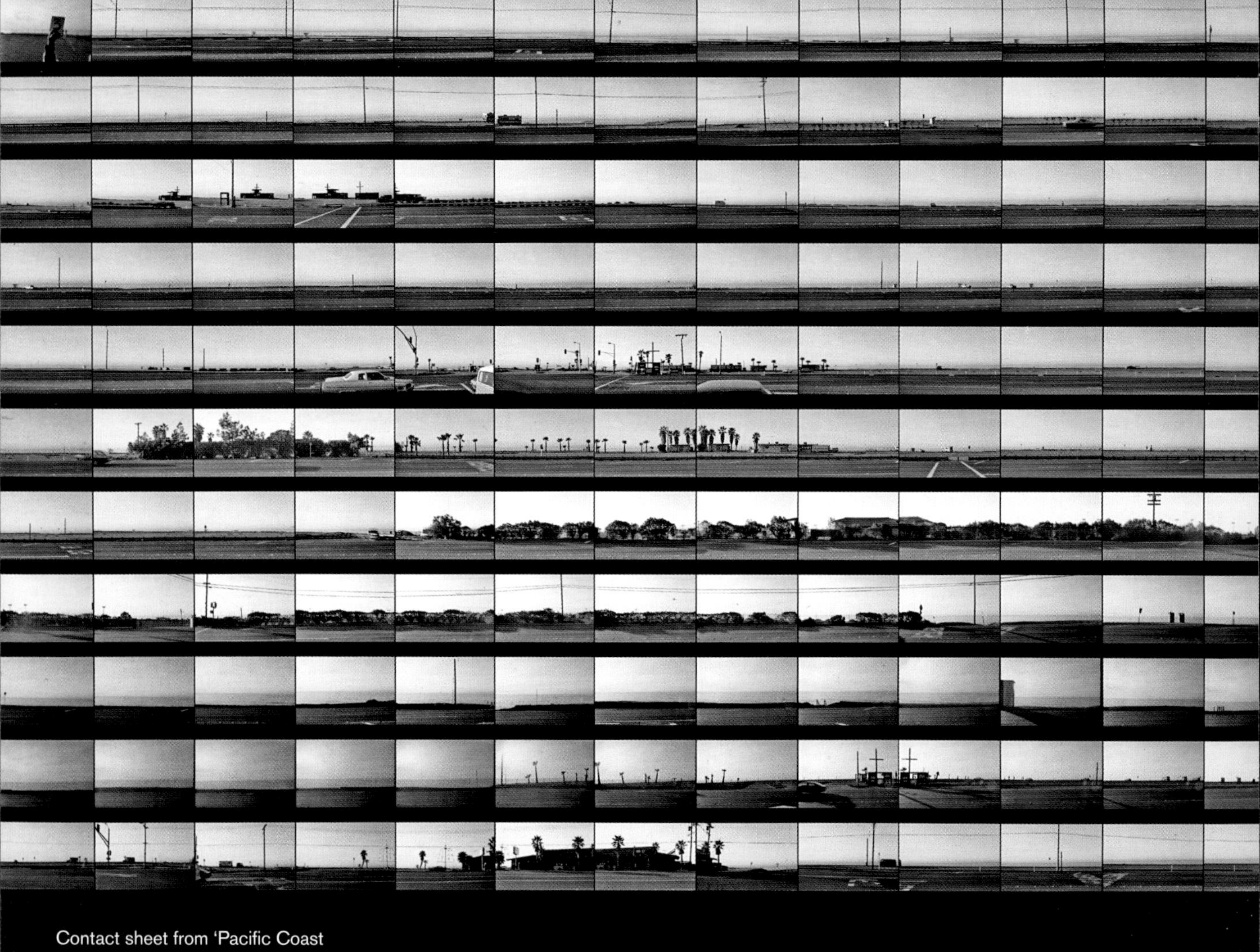

Contact sheet from 'Pacific Coast Highway', 1974–75.

'I have no interest in photography as a medium.'

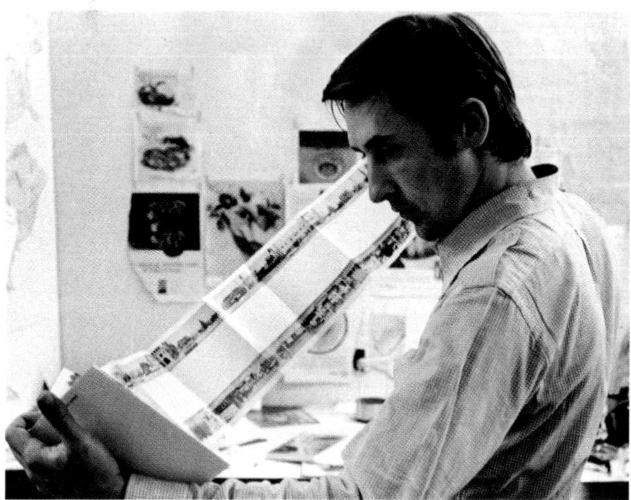

# Ed Ruscha

b. 1937

UNITED STATES

Why *Every Building on the Sunset Strip,* but only *Twentysix Gasoline Stations*? Ed Ruscha's photographs raise more questions than their insistently banal and monotonous imagery might suggest. A sliver of humour appears in Ruscha's work, tracing back to his childhood interest in cartooning and his adult love of wordplay. But he credits Jasper Johns's paintings of targets and flags for the idea that popular and commercial iconography could be used to make art. That Pop perception endures in his work in the many media he utilizes, accompanied by the deadpan photography he created in the 1960s.

Ruscha did photograph every building on the Sunset Strip, a piece of highway in West Hollywood, California. Shot from his car, the distant, unremarkable buildings are indistinctly rendered in black-and-white film, spooled along in a motorized camera. Linked together like folding postcards, the photographs became the basis for a book of the same name. Individually or collectively, they could not be said to do the job of documentary photography, nor to offer the aesthetic interpretation of art photography. Neither were they expressions of thoughts or fine feelings. They were, in sum, the photographic equivalent of Andy Warhol's *Campbell's Soup Cans*, minus the colour: slices of ubiquitous banality, delivered without comment or beauty, using media associated with indifferent design concepts. Why *Twentysix Gasoline Stations,* or *Nine Swimming Pools*? The numbers are as empty as the pictures.

With his other early photobooks, Ruscha's work influenced a generation of artists to take up photography precisely because it could be shorn of expressiveness in a way that gestural art could not – like painting, unable to rid itself of the human touch.

Portrait of Ed Ruscha by Jerry McMillan, 1967.

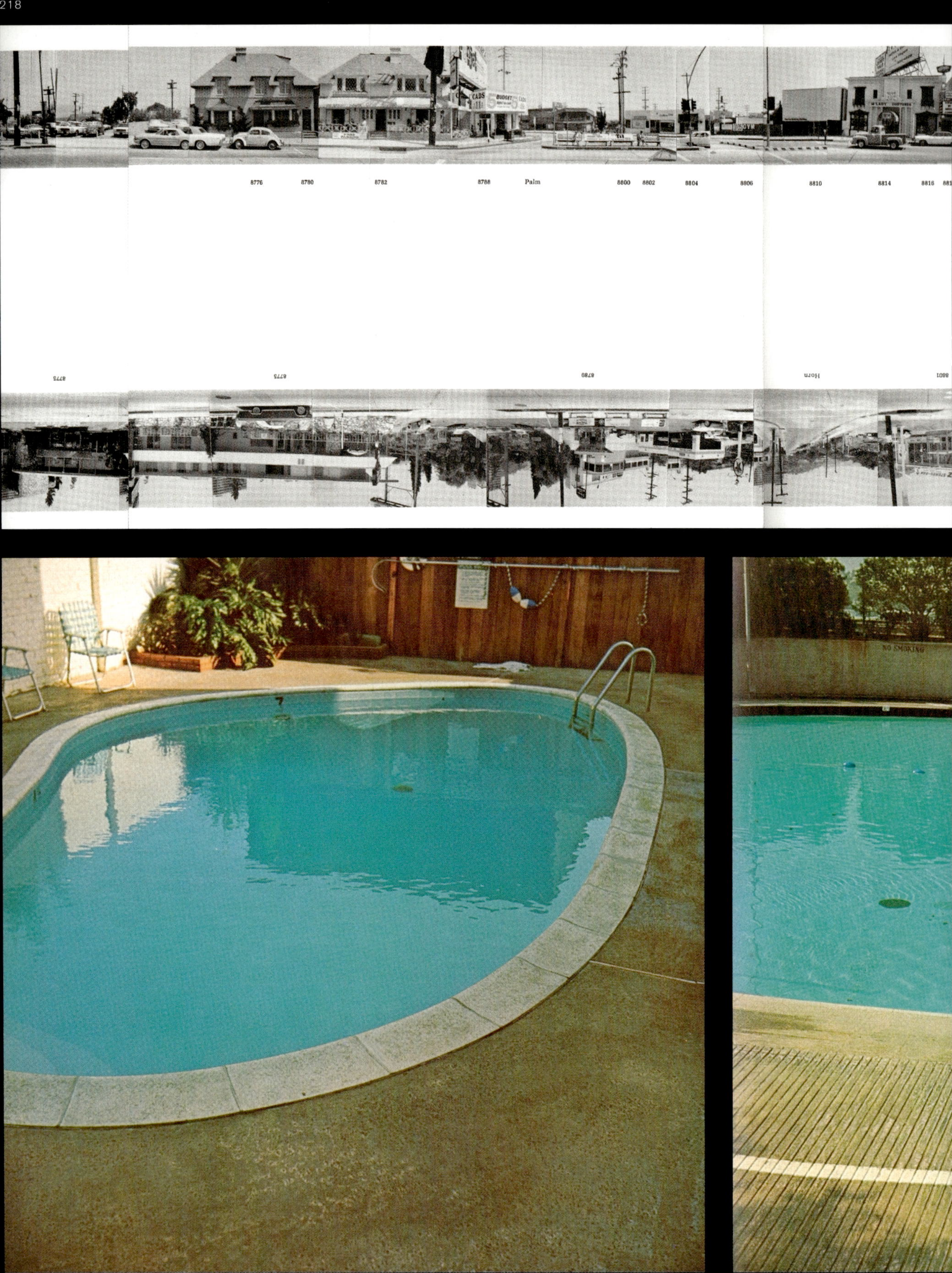
8776
8780
8782
8788
Palm
8800
8802
8804
8806
8810
8814
8816
CADS
BUDGET
8775
8775
8789
Horn
8801
NO SMOKING

# Ed Ruscha

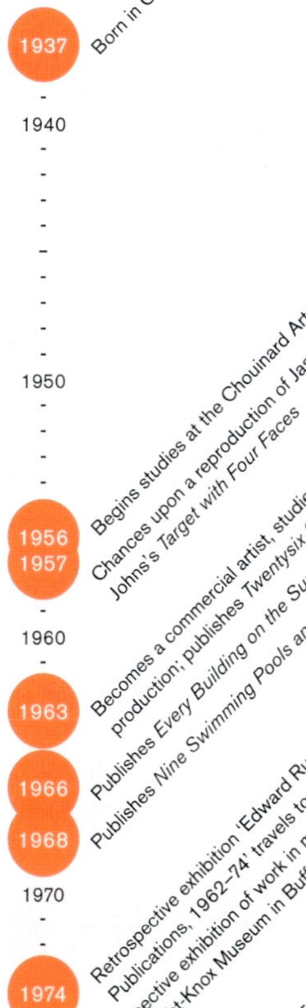


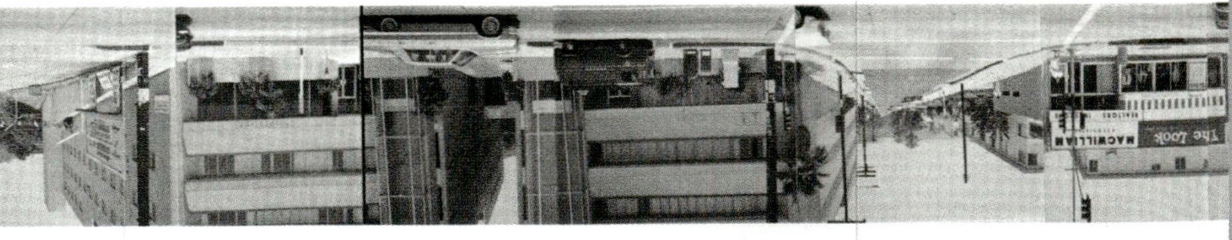


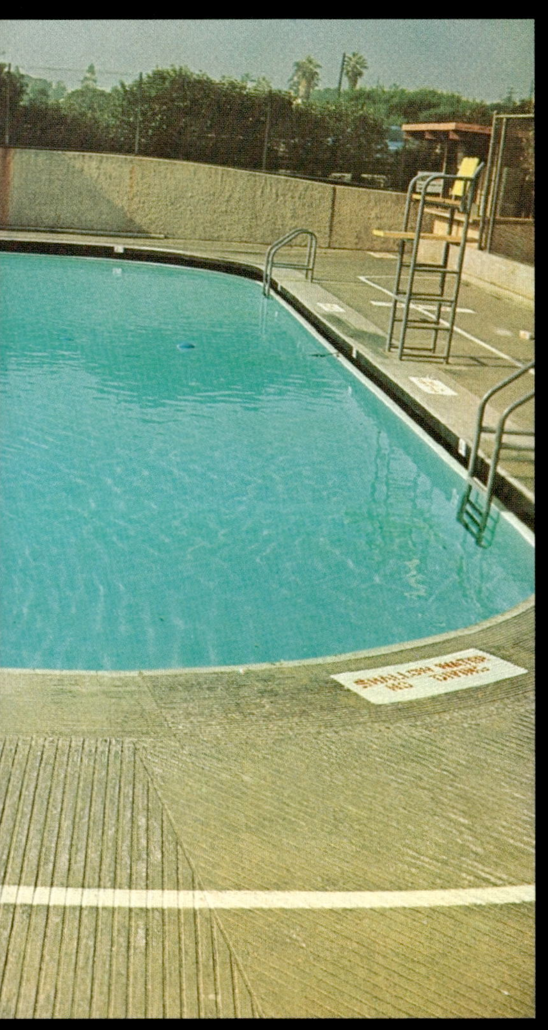

**Above** Camera-ready maquette for *Every Building on the Sunset Strip*, 1966.

**Left** From *Nine Swimming Pools and a Broken Glass*, 1968.

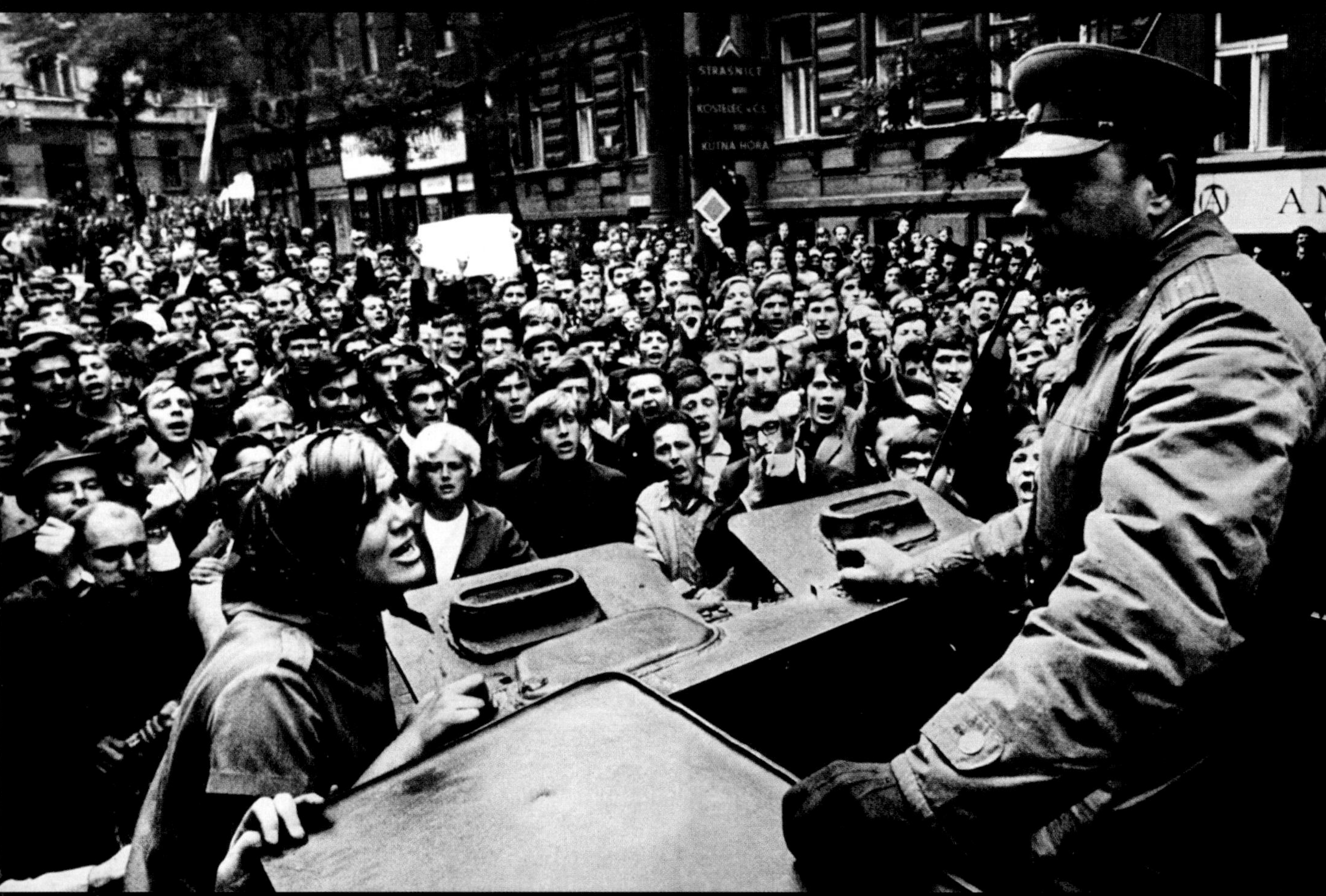


Soviet invasion of Czechoslovakia,
Prague, 1968.

'I only carry things that are needed – my cameras, film and a spare pair of glasses.'

# Josef Koudelka

b. 1938

CZECHOSLOVAKIA

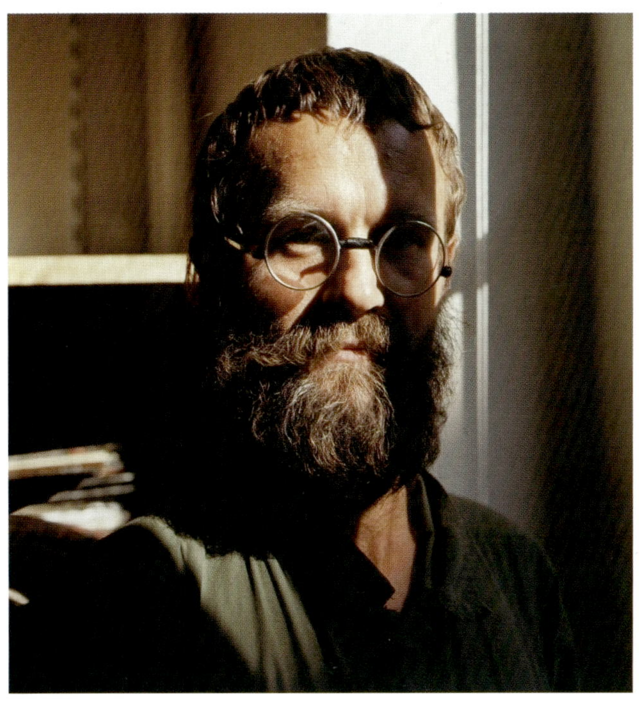

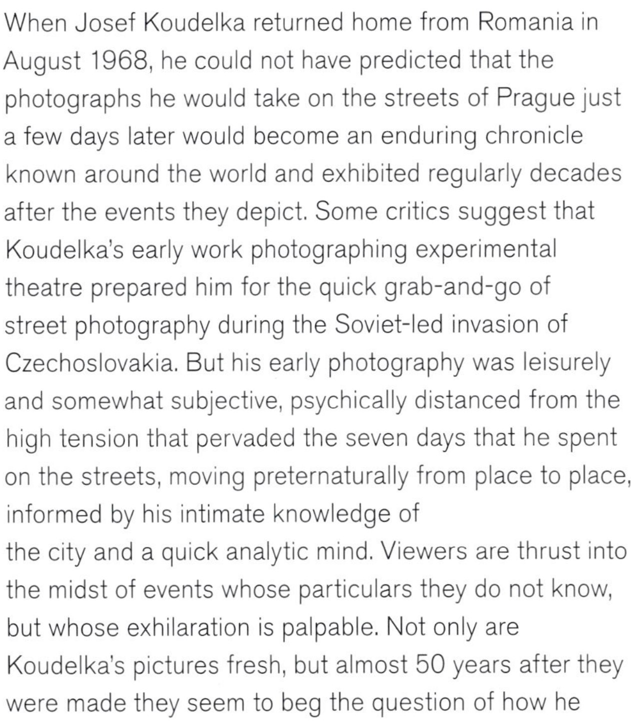

When Josef Koudelka returned home from Romania in August 1968, he could not have predicted that the photographs he would take on the streets of Prague just a few days later would become an enduring chronicle known around the world and exhibited regularly decades after the events they depict. Some critics suggest that Koudelka's early work photographing experimental theatre prepared him for the quick grab-and-go of street photography during the Soviet-led invasion of Czechoslovakia. But his early photography was leisurely and somewhat subjective, psychically distanced from the high tension that pervaded the seven days that he spent on the streets, moving preternaturally from place to place, informed by his intimate knowledge of the city and a quick analytic mind. Viewers are thrust into the midst of events whose particulars they do not know, but whose exhilaration is palpable. Not only are Koudelka's pictures fresh, but almost 50 years after they were made they seem to beg the question of how he knew where to be before the age of mobile phones and Twitter.

Koudelka's photographs of the Roma in various Central European countries, including Romania, are as still as the Prague photographs are jittery. Taken before the Soviet-led invasion, and afterwards, when Koudelka left Czechoslovakia and became a stateless person for 17 years, the pictures indicate a calm comradeship born of living among people for extended periods.

Not all of Koudelka's post-1968 work is as stoical as the Roma images. Most of the pictures that were eventually published in the book *Exiles* exude melancholy and alienation. One, a photograph of a dog in a park near Paris, presents itself as an animated medieval gargoyle or beast that has just smelled fresh prey in the direction of the viewer. Yet Koudelka also made pictures with a panoramic camera that display an enlivened curiosity for what the world looks like photographed, even if that world is a landscape devastated by coal mining.

Portrait of Josef Koudelka by unknown, 1974.

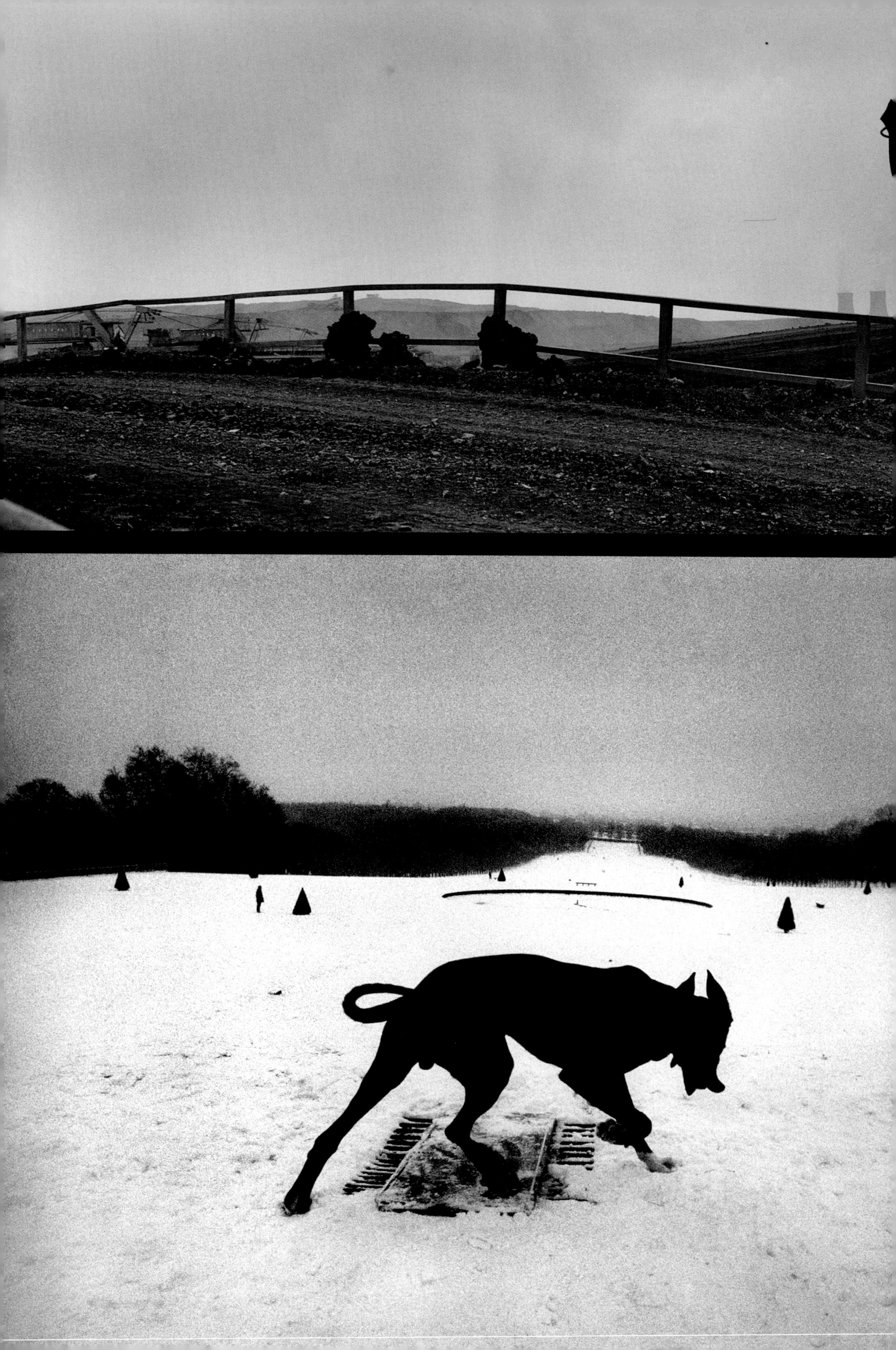

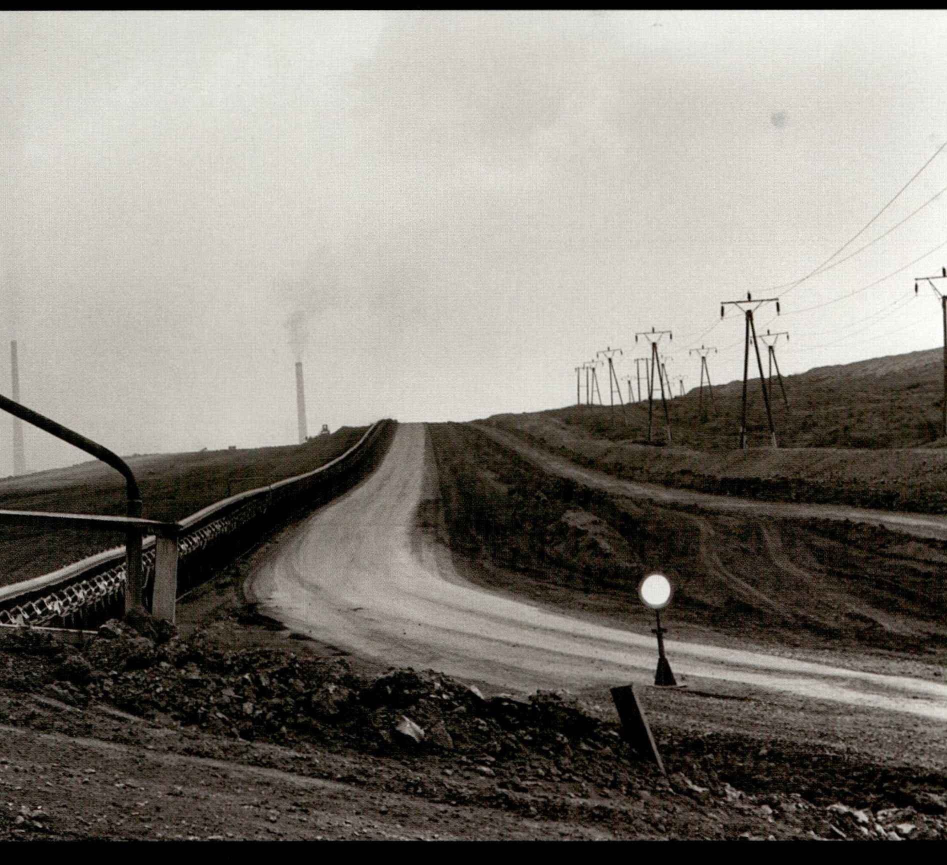

**Above** The Foothills of the Ore Mountains from *Black Triangle*, 1994.

**Left** Hauts-de-Seine. Parc de Sceaux, France. 1987.

## Josef Koudelka

1930

1938 Born in Boskovice, Czechoslovakia

1940

1950

c.1952 Makes first photographs

1961 Begins photographing Roma people in Czechoslovakia
Works as an aeronautical engineer until resigning to become a full-time photographer

1968 Photographs the August invasion of Soviet-led troops into Prague

1970 Leaves Czechoslovakia and becomes stateless; granted asylum in Britain

1971 Joins Magnum photo agency

1975 Solo exhibition at Museum of Modern Art in New York; *Gypsies* published

1980 Moves to France; becomes French citizen in 1987

1988 Two large exhibitions of his work travel in Europe and North America; *Exiles* published

1990 Returns to Prague for first time

1994 Publishes *The Black Triangle*

1999 Publishes *Chaos*

2004 Given Cornell Capa Infinity Award

2010

*Lips 15*, 1989.

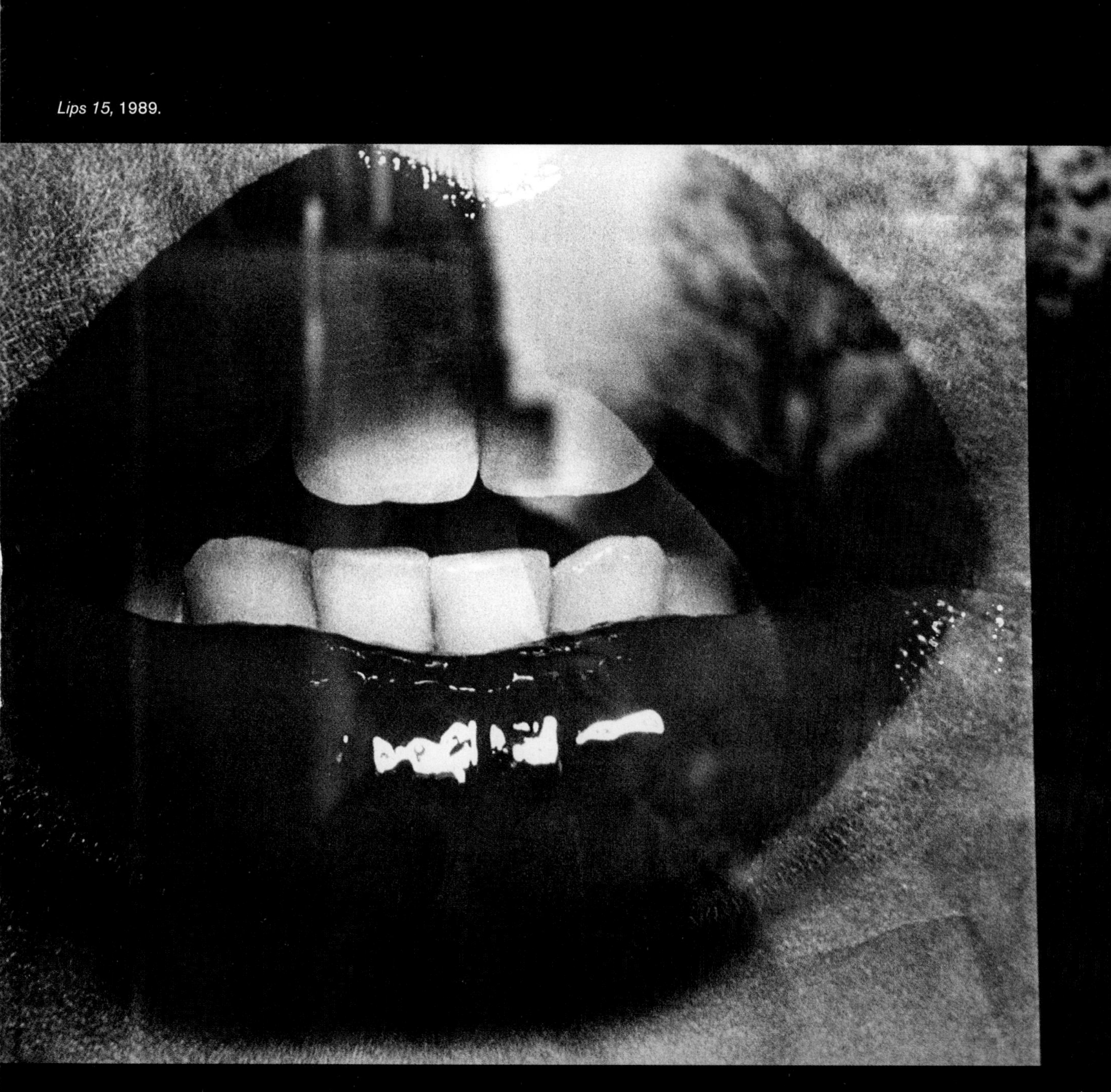

'Photographs are fossils of light and memory, and photographs are the history of memory.'

# Daidō Moriyama

b. 1938

JAPAN

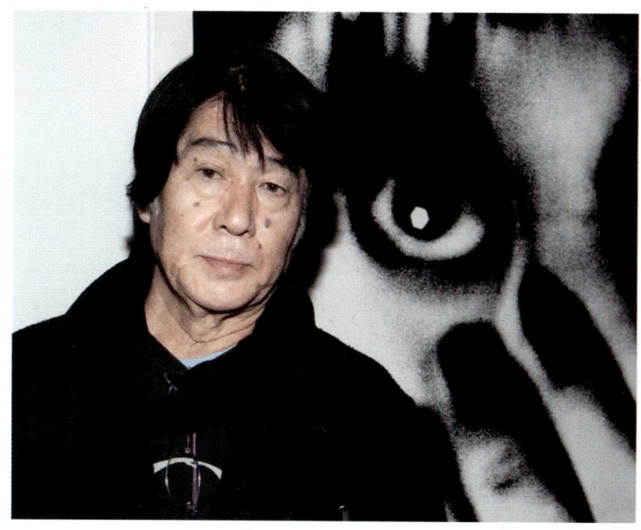

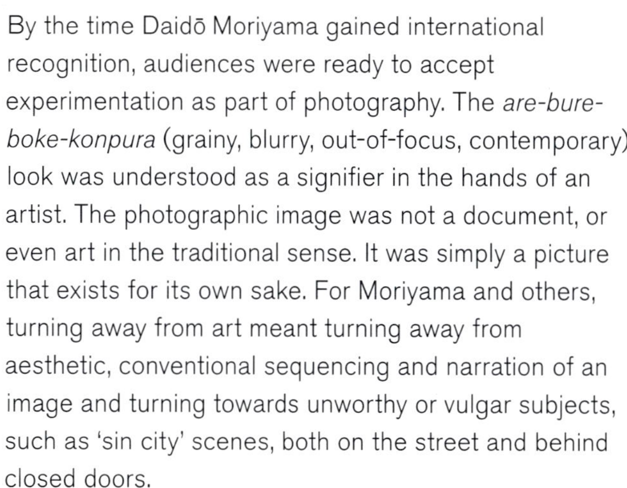

By the time Daidō Moriyama gained international recognition, audiences were ready to accept experimentation as part of photography. The *are-bure-boke-konpura* (grainy, blurry, out-of-focus, contemporary) look was understood as a signifier in the hands of an artist. The photographic image was not a document, or even art in the traditional sense. It was simply a picture that exists for its own sake. For Moriyama and others, turning away from art meant turning away from aesthetic, conventional sequencing and narration of an image and turning towards unworthy or vulgar subjects, such as 'sin city' scenes, both on the street and behind closed doors.

Occasionally, Moriyama has pushed the virtue of vice by printing his work on cheap, rough paper, as if it, too, were disposable. He has also used the tradition of the Japanese photobook against itself by using high-speed presses, like those used to print newspapers, and letting his work be printed for billboards. His spontaneous and neutral picture-taking is reminiscent of the motives behind action painting, in which the artist's gestures and impulses are at the core of the work, rather than some after-effect deduced by the viewer. Moriyama insists that he has 'no intention of explaining anything with my photographs. Those who look at them are free to interpret them how they like.' In other words, representation of optical reality is not the point. Media artist and critic Akira Hasegawa recalled that Moriyama was perhaps the first Japanese photographer to have been called scandalous. There had been scandals involving photographic subjects before, but never extremely negative reactions to, nor staunch support of, photographic technique per se.

That said, there are locales that attract Moriyama, particularly Tokyo's Shinjuku district. This civic and commercial district, which has resisted gentrification and also contains some raunchy nightlife, has been his beat since the 1960s. Despite his claims about impartial picture-taking and not thinking in sequences, Moriyama seems drawn to the contrast of propriety and impropriety. He admits that his work is prompted by the ping of inchoate desire. Yet he credits his audience with making the image *Stray Dog* a worldwide success, a development he never foresaw.

Portrait of Daidō Moriyama by unknown, 2011.

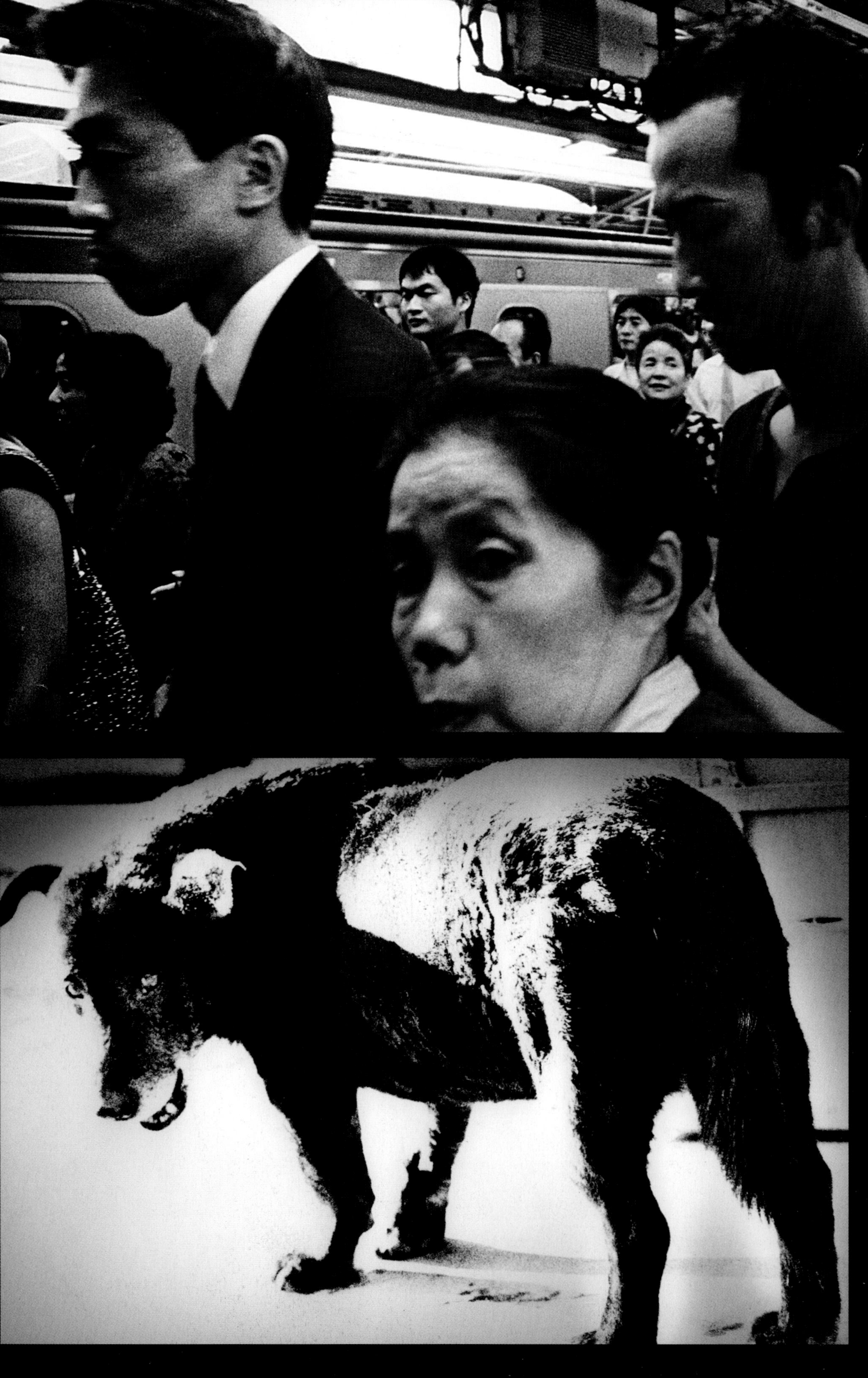

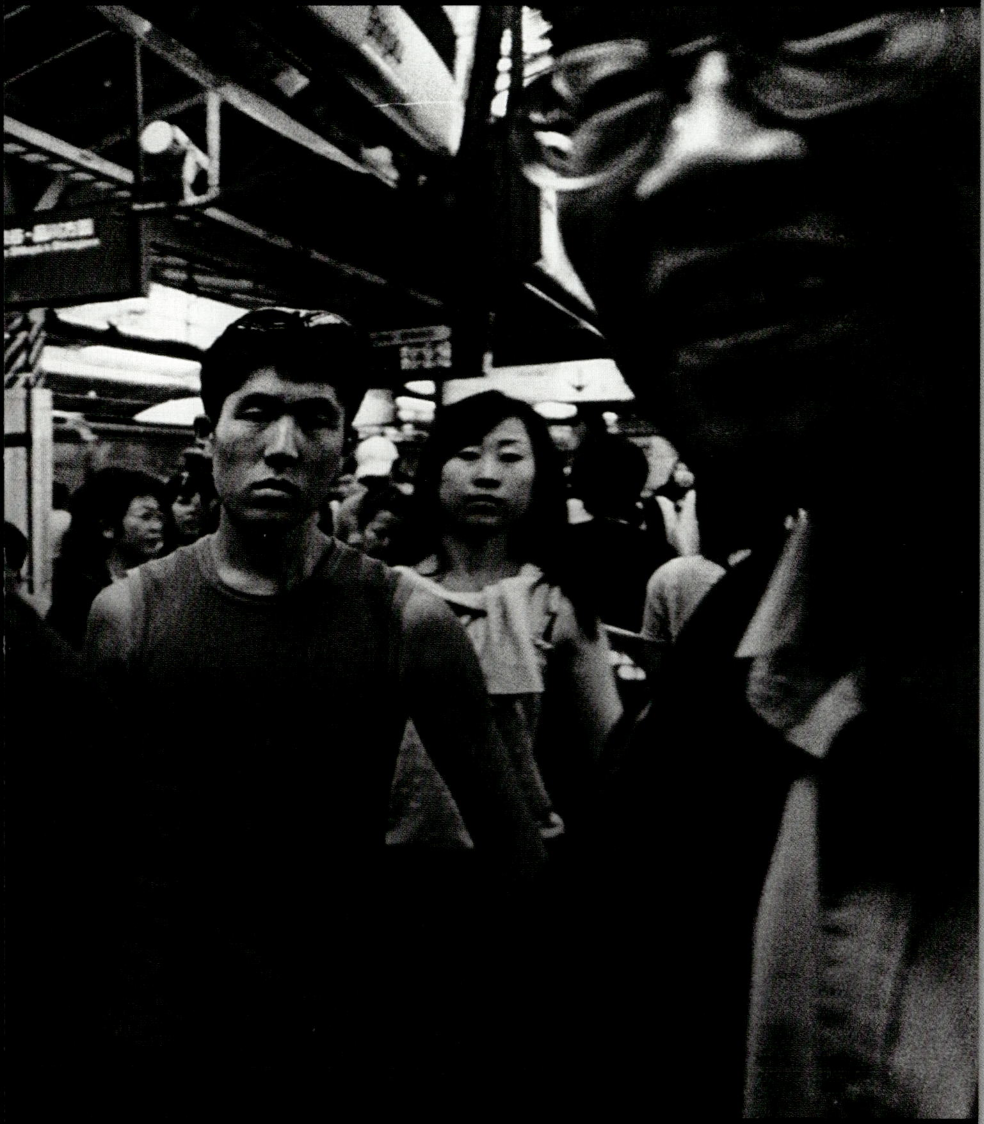

Above Shinjuku, 2001.

Left *Stray Dog*, Misawa, 1971.

Below *Shinjuku Station* from *Japan: A Photo Theatre*, 1968.

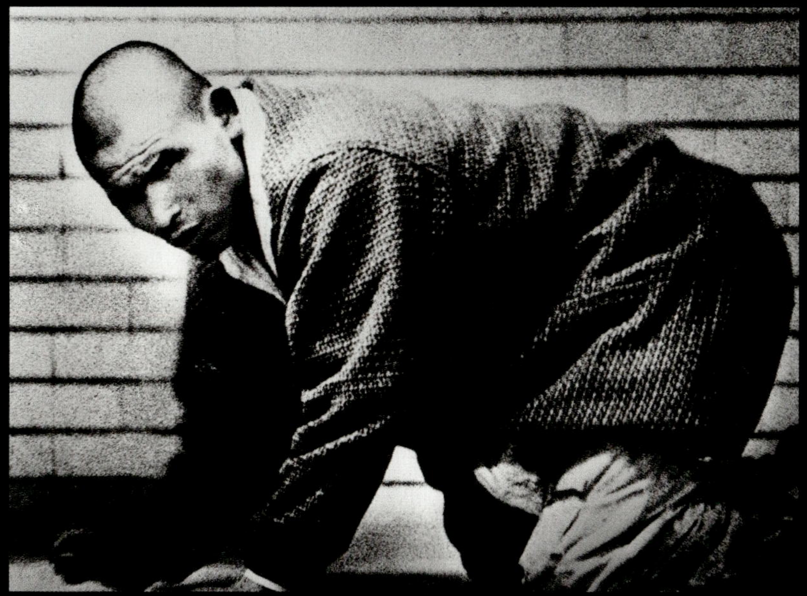

## Daidō Moriyama

- **1938** Born Hiromichi Moriyama in Ikeda, Osaka, Japan
- **c.1957** Develops an interest in photography
- **1961** Moves to Tokyo, joins Vivo group of independent photographers and meets Eikoh Hosoe and Shōmei Tōmatsu
- **1968** Appears in influential magazine *Provoke*
- **1969** Publishes *Nippon Gekijo Shashincho* (*Japan: A Photo Theatre*)
- **1972** Publishes *Shashin yo Sayonara* (*Farewell Photography*)
- **1985** Publishes influential essay 'A Dialogue with Photography'
- **1999** Retrospective at San Francisco Museum of Modern Art
- **2008** Retrospective at Tokyo Metropolitan Museum of Photography

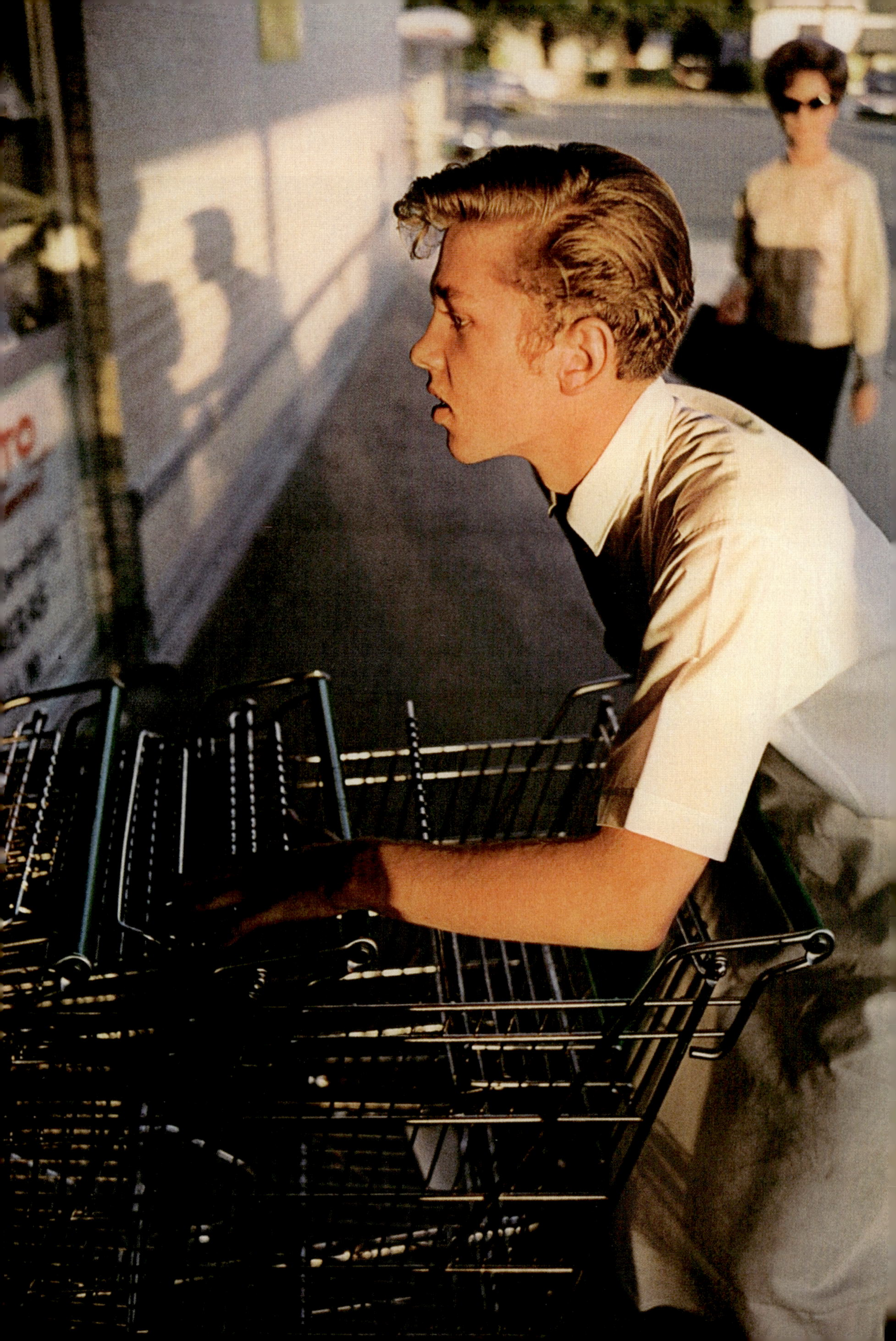

'I am at war with the obvious.'

# William Eggleston

b. 1939

UNITED STATES

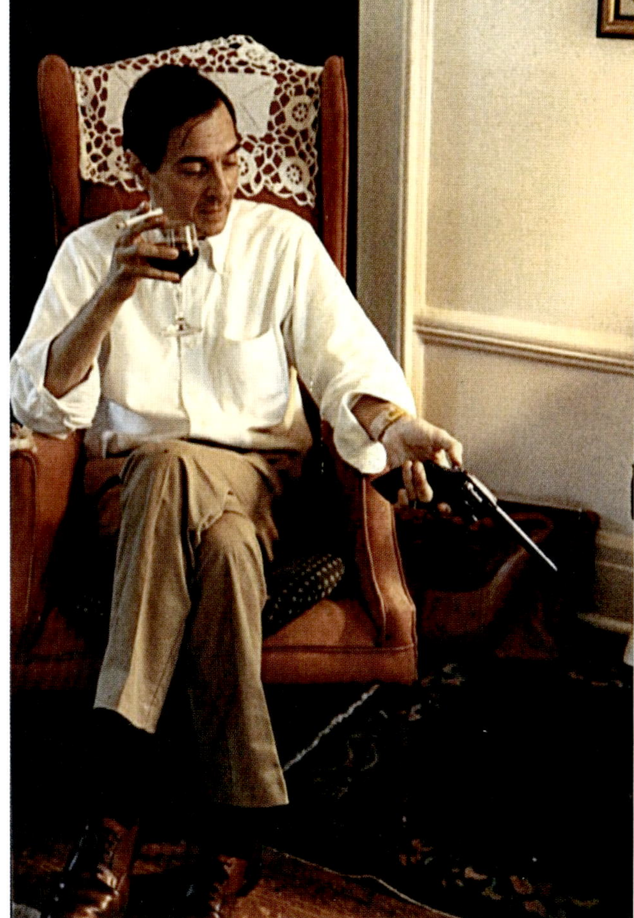

Several times, William Eggleston was the right person in the right place. New to photography, he came across a college friend's copy of a book containing images by French photographer Henri Cartier-Bresson (p. 132). He ardently absorbed Cartier-Bresson's book *The Decisive Moment,* with its central idea that a photographer must become attuned to the often sudden and fleeting elements of a good picture, and then refined it as a way of looking at everyday life. He recalled that he 'had this notion of what I called a democratic way of looking around, that nothing was more or less important'. That attitude persisted throughout his images of sights we mostly ignore: kerbside trash, crusty barbeque grills, various manifestations of mud. However much he is devoted to the quotidian, there is also beauty in his work. It often comes from colour in unexpected places, such as a kitchen sink or electric wires crossing a ceiling.

Before Eggleston, photographers including Helen Levitt (p. 140) and Stephen Shore (p. 268), experimented in colour, but most believed that photography was a graphic black-and-white art. Colour was for snapshots and advertising. Just as iconoclastic was Eggleston's attitude towards shooting. Where other photographers would take many pictures, hoping to find the special one on a contact sheet, he would make one exposure and move on, 'democratically photographing', as he calls it.

Eggleston's lucky streak continued when he stumbled across an advertisement for the dye-transfer process, which he would come to love for its ability to render colour as different from the scene photographed. Another auspicious aspect of Eggleston's life was his home near the Deep South, an area that had yielded many icons of American imagery during the Great Depression. It offered him detachment from current photographic trends, and a landscape ready to be reinterpreted. But his greatest good fortune was to live in a period when photographers could bring their work to be viewed by John Szarkowski at the Museum of Modern Art in New York. Szarkowski recognized a unique attitude in his work, observing that Eggleston's images were not social documentary but closer to a diary. They 'are simply present: clearly realized, precisely fixed, themselves, in the service of no extraneous roles'. In photographic circles, the acceptance of colour in art photography is dated from Eggleston's meeting with Szarkowski.

**Opposite** From 'Los Alamos', 1965–68 and 1972–74.

**Above** Portrait of William Eggleston by Alan Ulmer, 1993.

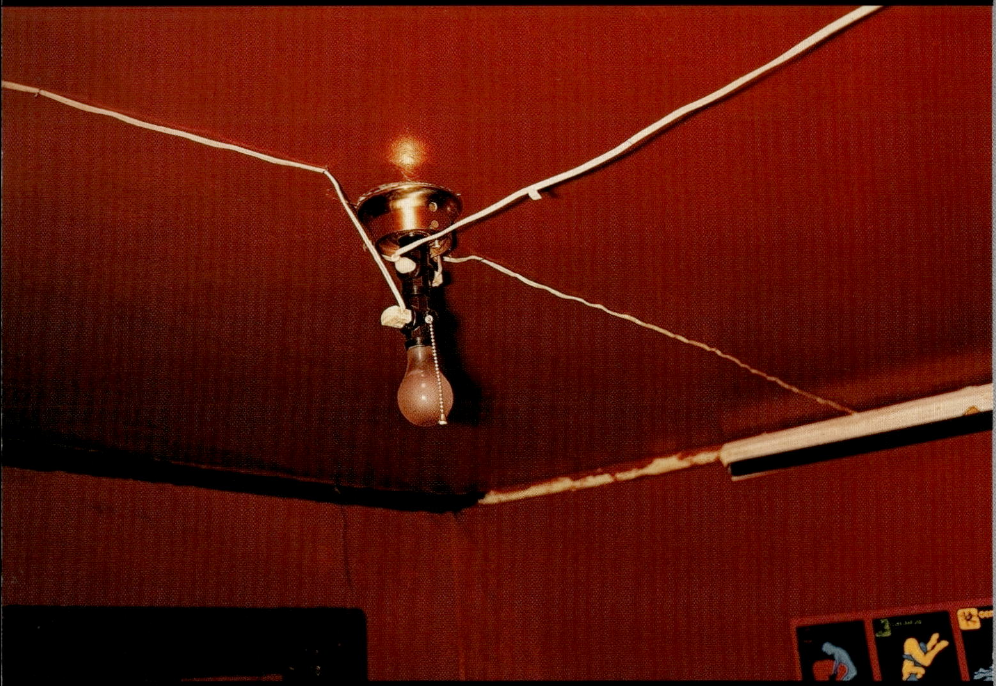

**Above** *The Red Ceiling*, Greenwood, Mississippi, 1973.

**Opposite top** Untitled, 1970.

**Opposite bottom** From 'Los Alamos', Louisiana, c. 1971–74.

## William Eggleston

- **1939** Born in Memphis, Tennessee, USA
- **1965** Begins making colour slides
- **1967** Meets John Szarkowski, head of the Photography Department at the Museum of Modern Art, New York
- **1973** Discovers the colour qualities of the dye-transfer method
- **1976** Gets his first solo colour photography show at the Museum of Modern Art. *William Eggleston's Guide* is published
- **1983** Commissioned to photograph Elvis Presley's house, Graceland
- **1990** *The Democratic Forest* exhibition and book
- **2003** Publishes *Los Alamos*

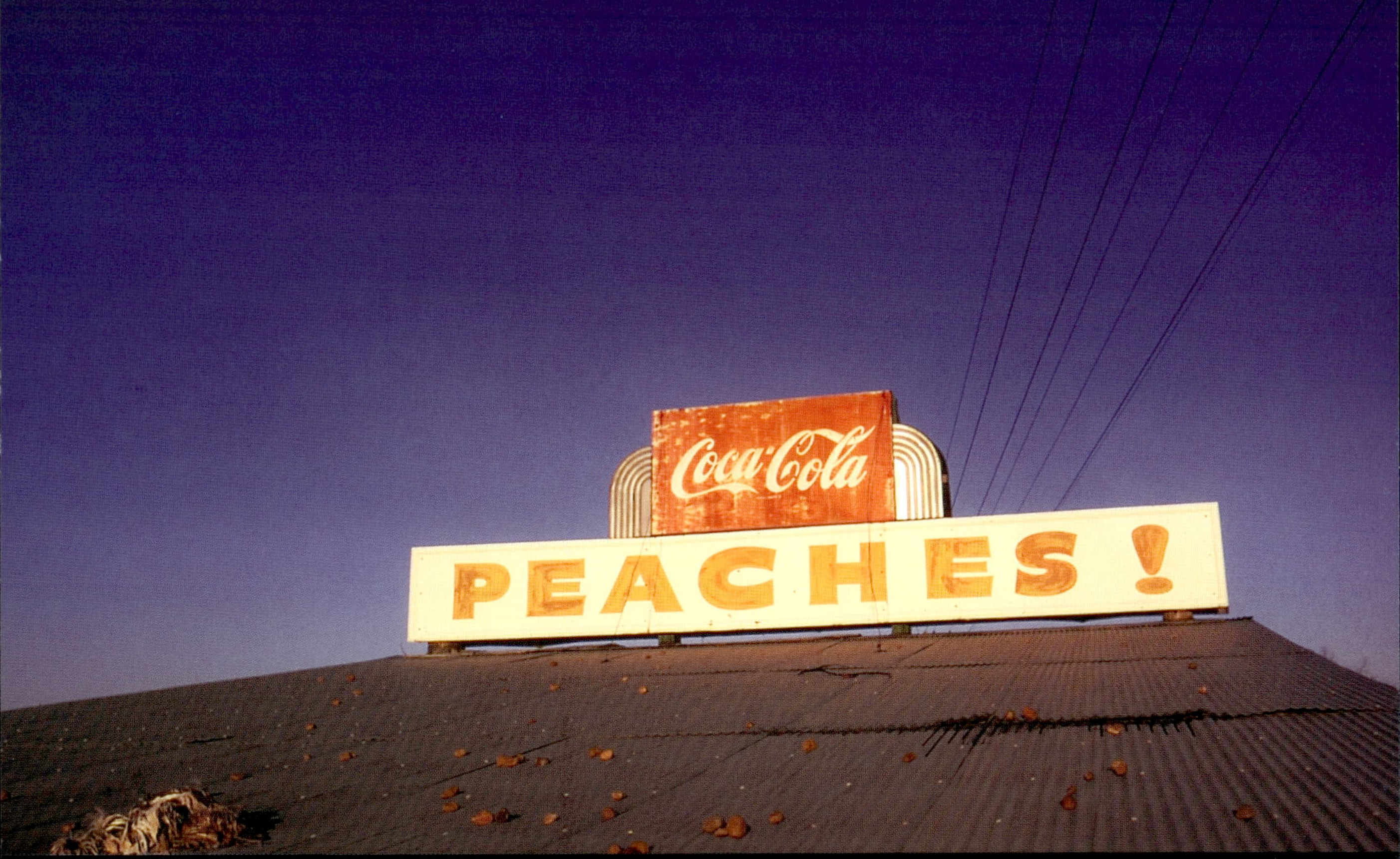
Coca-Cola
PEACHES !

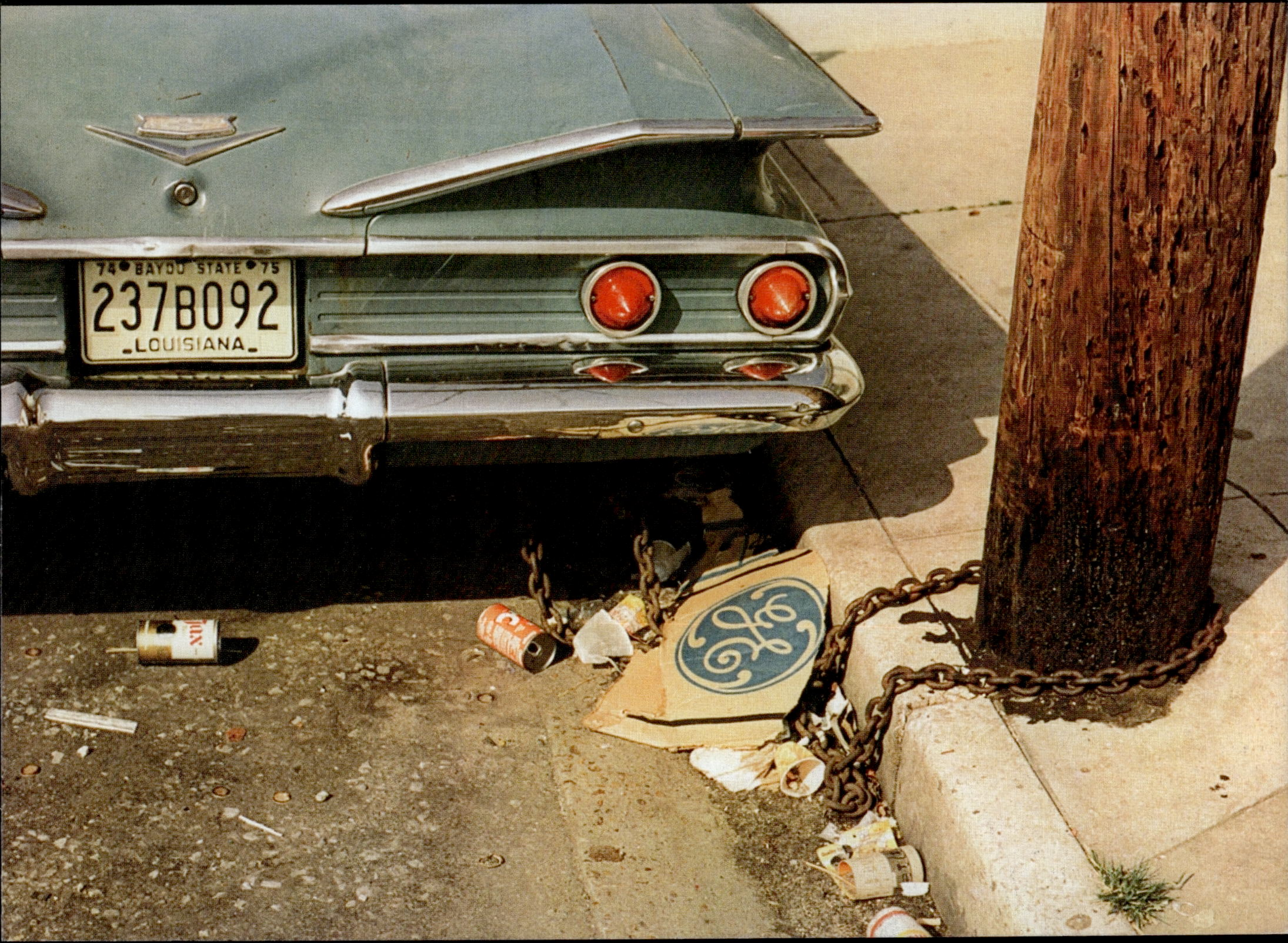
74 BAYOU STATE 75
237B092
LOUISIANA

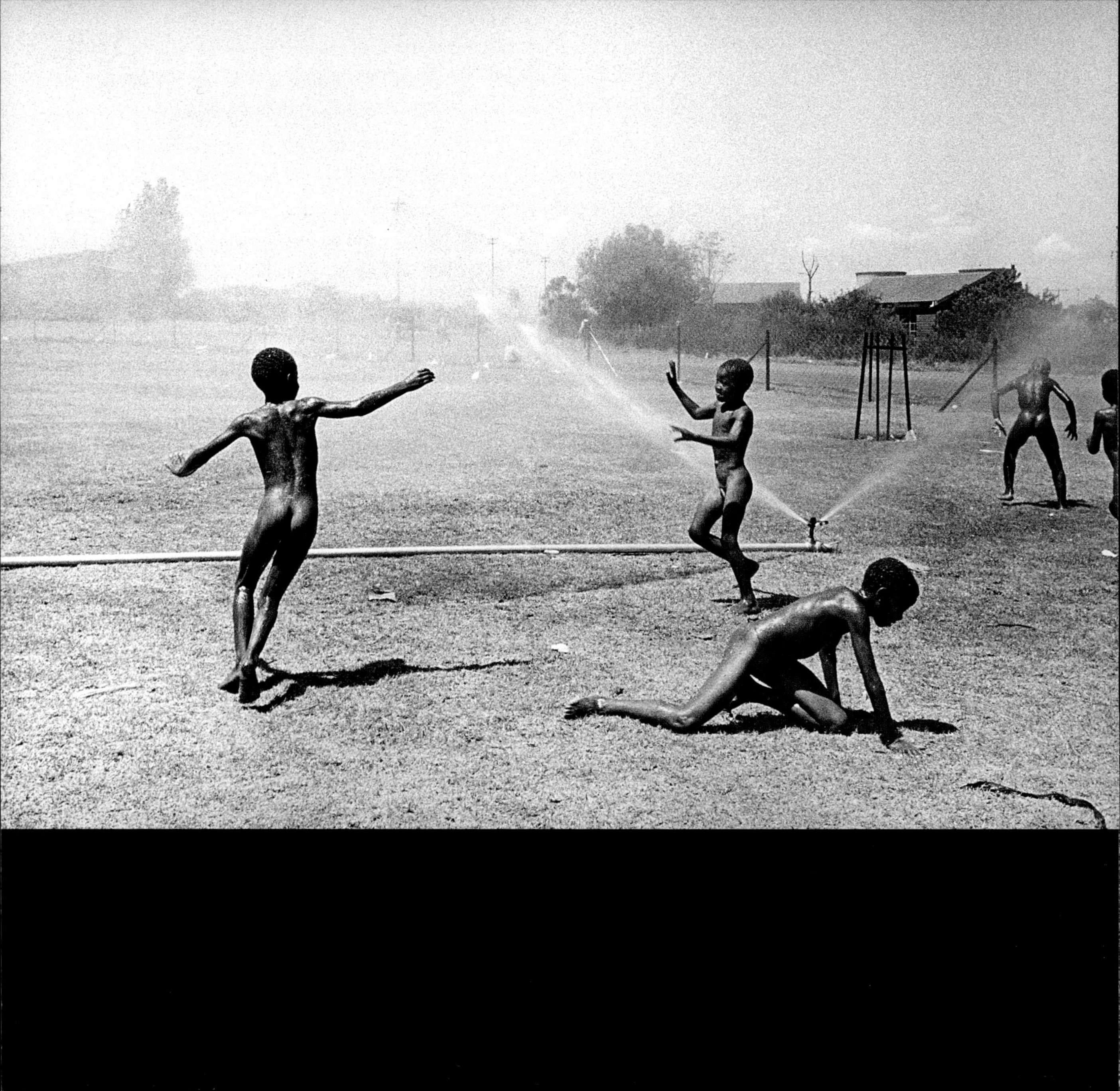

'Three hundred years of white supremacy in South Africa has placed us in bondage.'

# Ernest Cole

1940–1990

SOUTH AFRICA

As much as Ernest Cole admired the photographic books and ideas of Henri Cartier-Bresson (p. 132), he was not able to fully exploit the Frenchman's notion of the decisive moment, always scanning the scene for that moment when meaning and composition come together to form a picture. A black photographer in South Africa during the period of apartheid needed to be surreptitious, clever and quick. Cole learned, literally, to shoot from the hip, because he hid his camera inside his jacket, with the settings already established. To photograph black workers in gold mines, he secreted his camera in a paper bag, beneath a sandwich and an apple. To picture children in jail, he had himself arrested. To photograph *tsotsis* – youth who had turned to crime – he hung out with them. He even managed to convince officials he was not black but coloured: that is, of mixed race, and therefore able to gain employment and to walk the streets with greater freedom.

Although he worked for magazines and newspapers aimed at black Africans, Cole's goal was to create a volume like Cartier-Bresson's books of the 1950s, which offered a broad range of pictures and text describing the daily lives of people. *House of Bondage*, Cole's only book, is encyclopedic, following the lives of manual and domestic workers as well as the separate and unequal schools, hospitals and penal system. He was there when black freeholders, like his family, were removed from their land and transported to inferior housing.

*House of Bondage*, which could not be published in South Africa, inadvertently made Cole an exile at the age of 26. It was published in the United States and Britain with a text by Thomas Flaherty, and remains a model for subsequent advocacy books and websites. In the short term, the searing portrayal of apartheid benefited Cole, who was able to secure funds from the Ford Foundation for another project, an in-depth study of the black migration from the South to the North in the United States, on which Cole seems to have made little progress. His peripatetic life in the United States and Sweden may indicate that his heart was not in the day-to-day work of an assignment-driven photojournalist outside his country. He began to spiral down into physical and mental illness, losing his cameras along the way. Since he died, some of his missing negatives have been located, but many seem to have been lost.

Portrait of Ernest Cole by Struan Robertson, undated.

*Bondage*, 1960–66.

**Below right** Segregated bus from *House of Bondage*, 1960–66.

**Opposite** Boy squats and strains to follow lesson in heat of packed classroom, from *House of Bondage*, 1960–66.

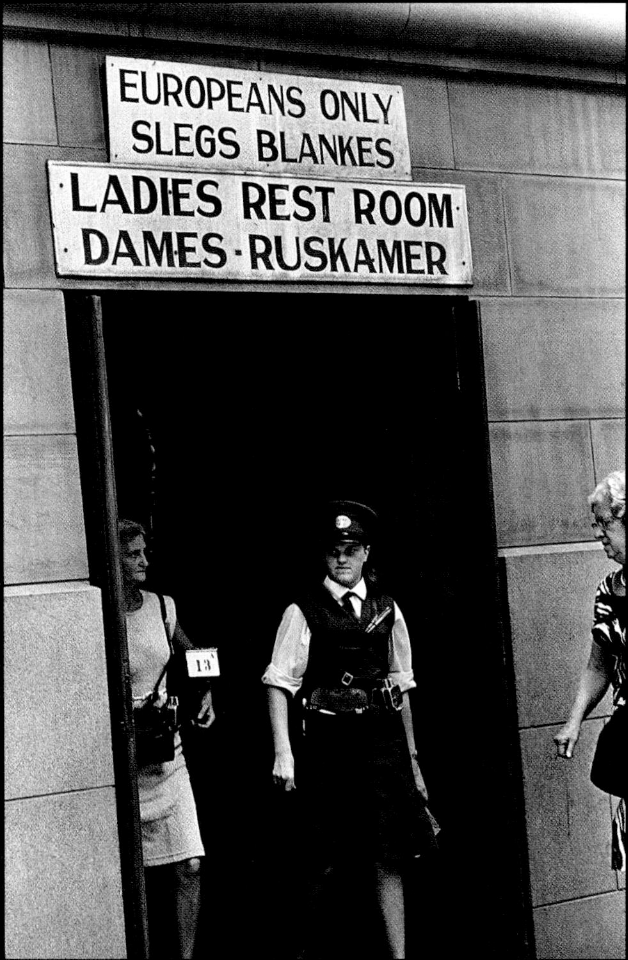

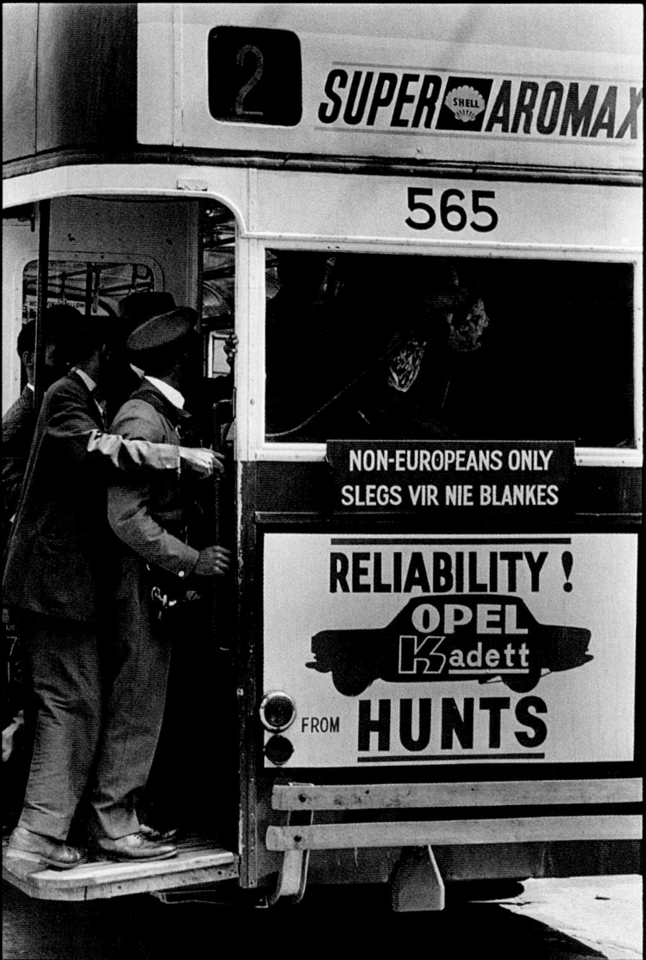

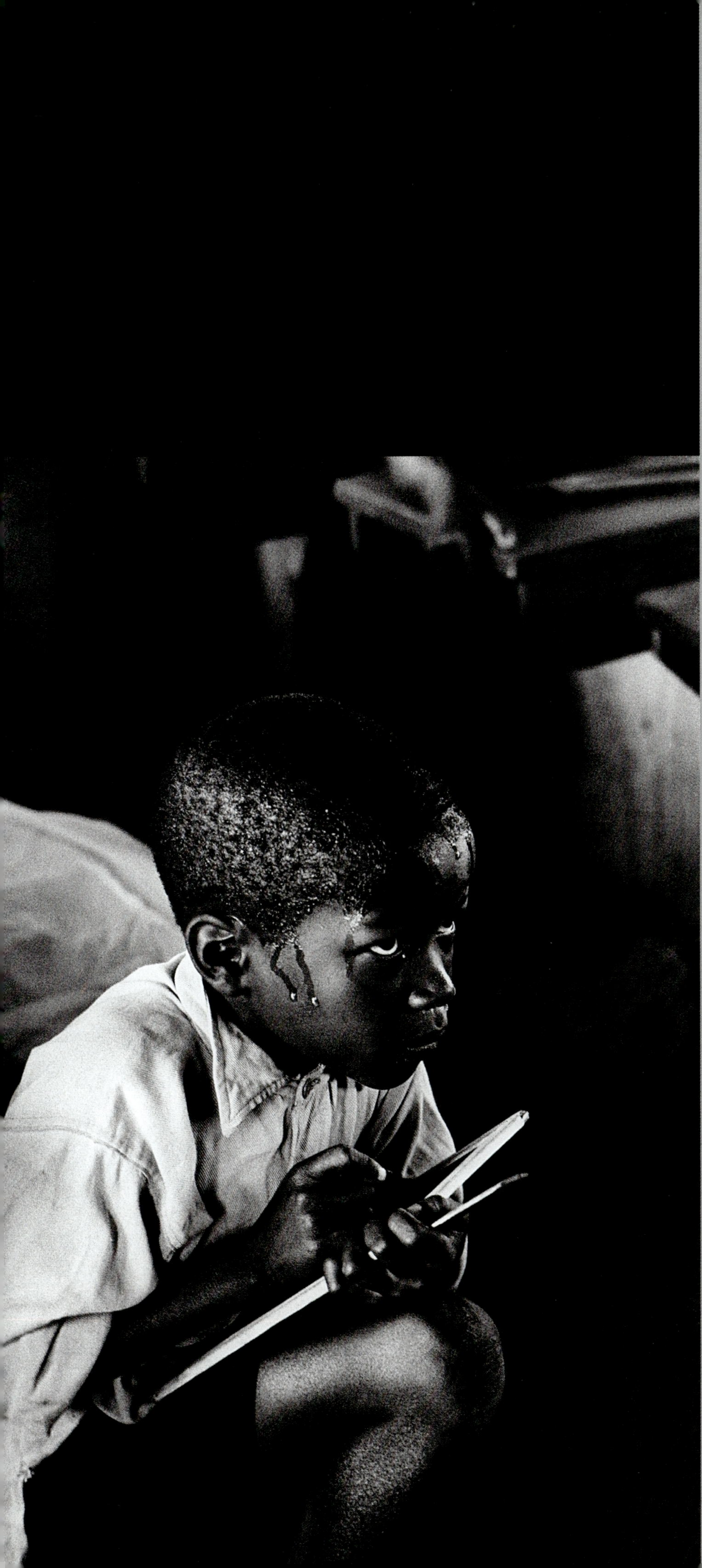

# Ernest Cole

1930

**1940** Born Ernest Levi Tsoloane Kole in Eersterust, Pretoria, South Africa

1950

**1958** Joins *Drum* magazine as assistant; later works for *Bantu World*

1960

**1966** Moves to New York

**1967** *House of Bondage* published

**1970** Moves to Sweden, where he works for *Tio fotografer*, a photography association (to c. 1975)

**1976** Returns to the USA

1980

**1990** Dies in New York, USA

2000

**2010** Major retrospective in South African and American cities

*The Damm Family in Their Car*, Los Angeles, California,, 1987.

'You are a voyeur – you're stealing something from people. And you have to live with it.'

# Mary Ellen Mark

b. 1940

UNITED STATES

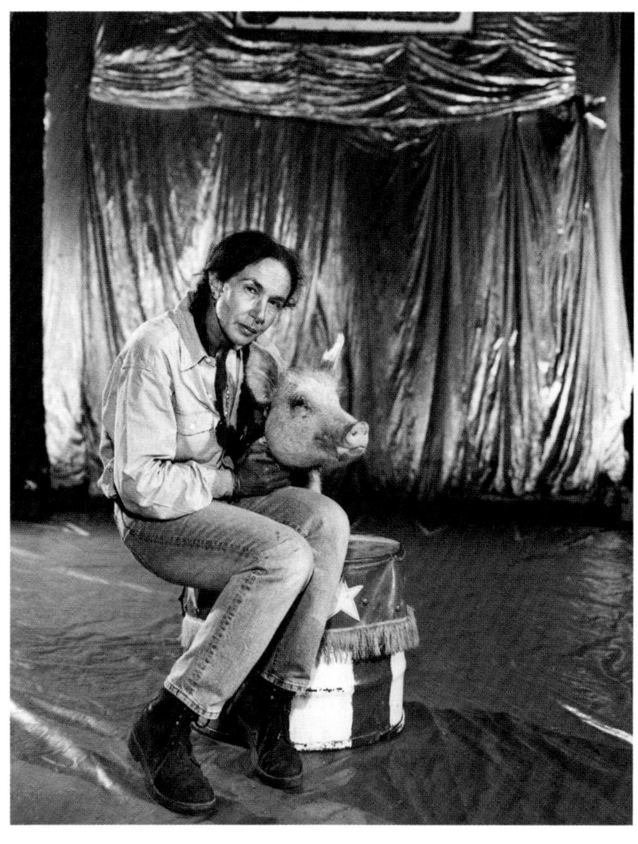

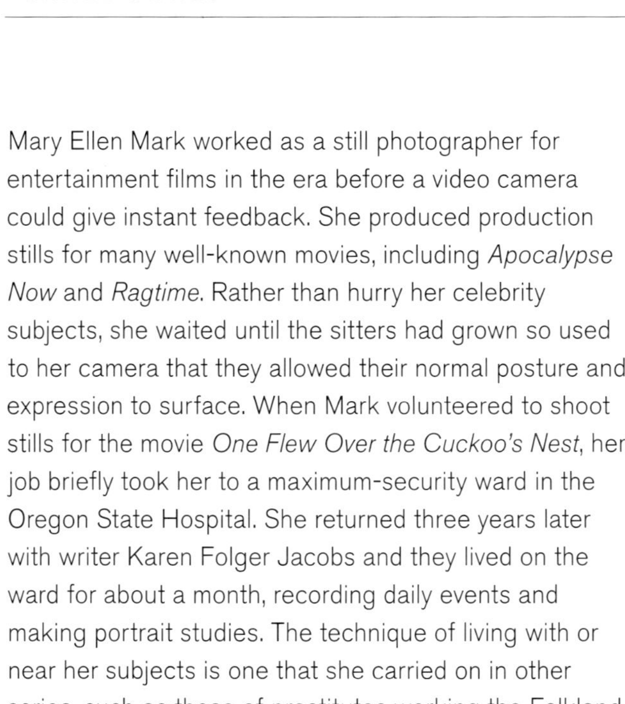

Mary Ellen Mark worked as a still photographer for entertainment films in the era before a video camera could give instant feedback. She produced production stills for many well-known movies, including *Apocalypse Now* and *Ragtime*. Rather than hurry her celebrity subjects, she waited until the sitters had grown so used to her camera that they allowed their normal posture and expression to surface. When Mark volunteered to shoot stills for the movie *One Flew Over the Cuckoo's Nest*, her job briefly took her to a maximum-security ward in the Oregon State Hospital. She returned three years later with writer Karen Folger Jacobs and they lived on the ward for about a month, recording daily events and making portrait studies. The technique of living with or near her subjects is one that she carried on in other series, such as those of prostitutes working the Falkland Road area in Mumbai, India.

Unlike the film stars she photographed, the women of Falkland Road and Ward 81 were unlikely to understand the full extent of their photographs' circulation in both galleries and print. Mark's portrayals of outsiders who manage to live and work on the edges of a majority culture – a staple theme of print photojournalism in the age of picture magazines such as *Life* – were fiercely criticized as voyeuristic in the late 1970s, when Postmodern critics demanded that photographers take a more activist approach to inequality.

Mark turned that critique upside down, asking, 'Why does a celebrity deserve to be recognized and made known more than someone struggling on the edges of our society? Why should they just be ignored?' Interestingly, while some of her photographs heroicize subjects, such as children afflicted with cancer, most images are visually complex and emotionally ambivalent, for example her studies of runaway teenagers in Seattle. Not only does Mark spend extended time with her subjects, she also tends to stay in contact with them over long periods of time, creating personal relationships and photographs that avoid clichés by emphasizing personal interactions. Her extensive series of performers who work in small travelling circuses is tender and surprisingly funny at times.

Because she puts in more interpretive time than photojournalists with deadlines, some of whom cut corners by pre-planning their shots, Mark characterizes herself as a documentary photographer. Today that genre, which was endangered by the end of weekly news and public interest magazines, is growing, mostly by means of websites that collect and present work by professionals and amateurs. They are rephrasing outsiders as heroic contributors to a vital chronicle of global diversity.

Portrait of Mary Ellen Mark by Jon Naiman, undated.

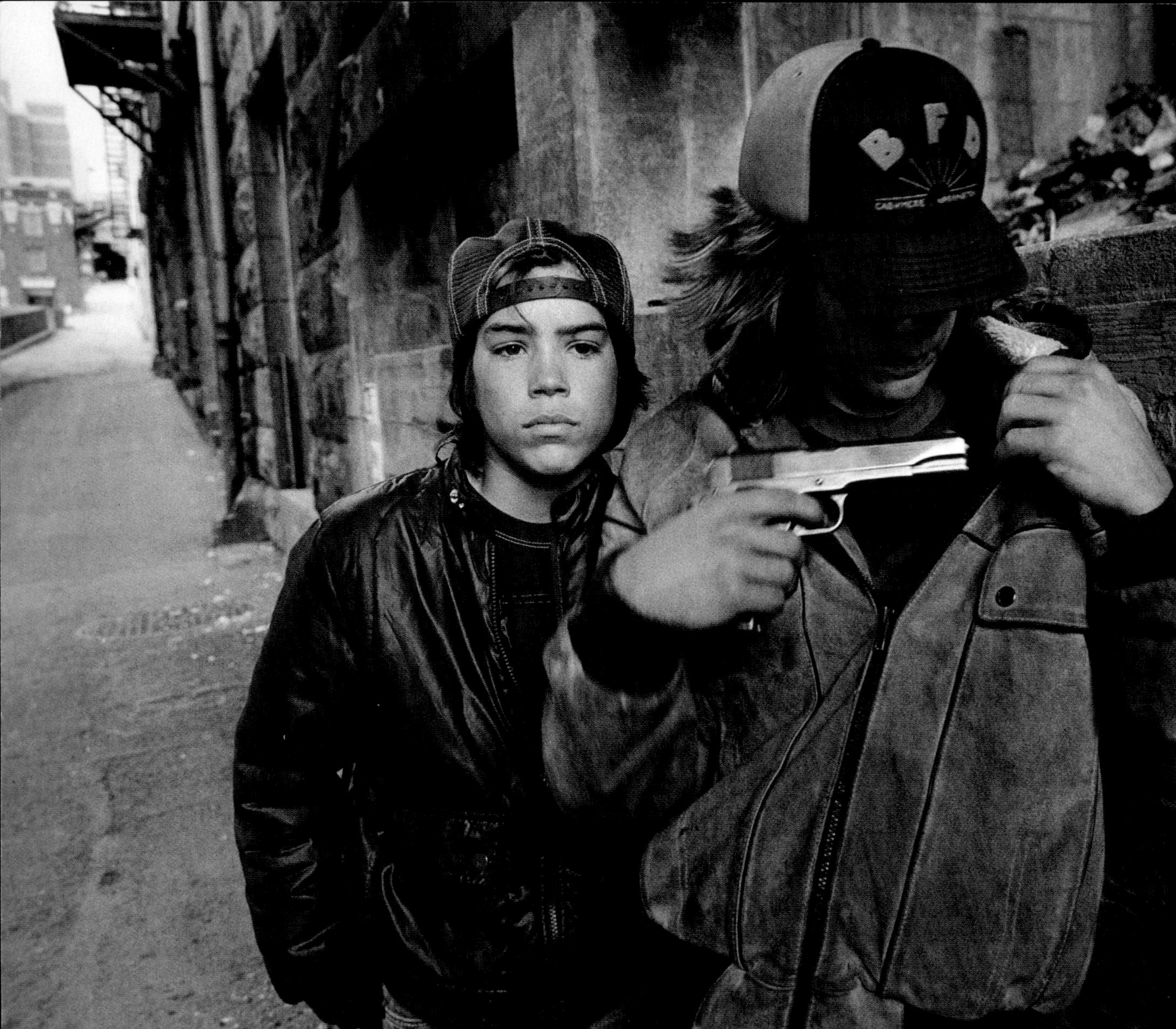


**Above** *'Rat' and Mike with a Gun*, Seattle, Washington, 1983.

**Opposite top** *Mary Frances in the Bathtub, Ward 81*, Salem, Oregon, 1976.

**Opposite bottom** *Marlon Brando fascinated by a dragonfly, Apocalypse Now*, Pagsanjan, Philippines, 1976.

# Mary Ellen Mark

1930

**1940** Born in Philadelphia, Pennsylvania, USA

**c.1949** Receives a Brownie camera

1960

**1965** Begins work as a freelance photographer

1970

**1976** First solo show in London presents the women in Ward 81, Oregon State Hospital; joins Magnum photo agency

**1981** Publishes *Falkland Road* and begins her series on Mother Teresa

**1982** Leaves Magnum

**1988** Publishes *Streetwise*

1990

**1992** 'Mary Ellen Mark: 25 Years' exhibition travels worldwide

**2001** Receives Cornell Capa Infinity Award

**2006** Starts the project *Prom*

2010

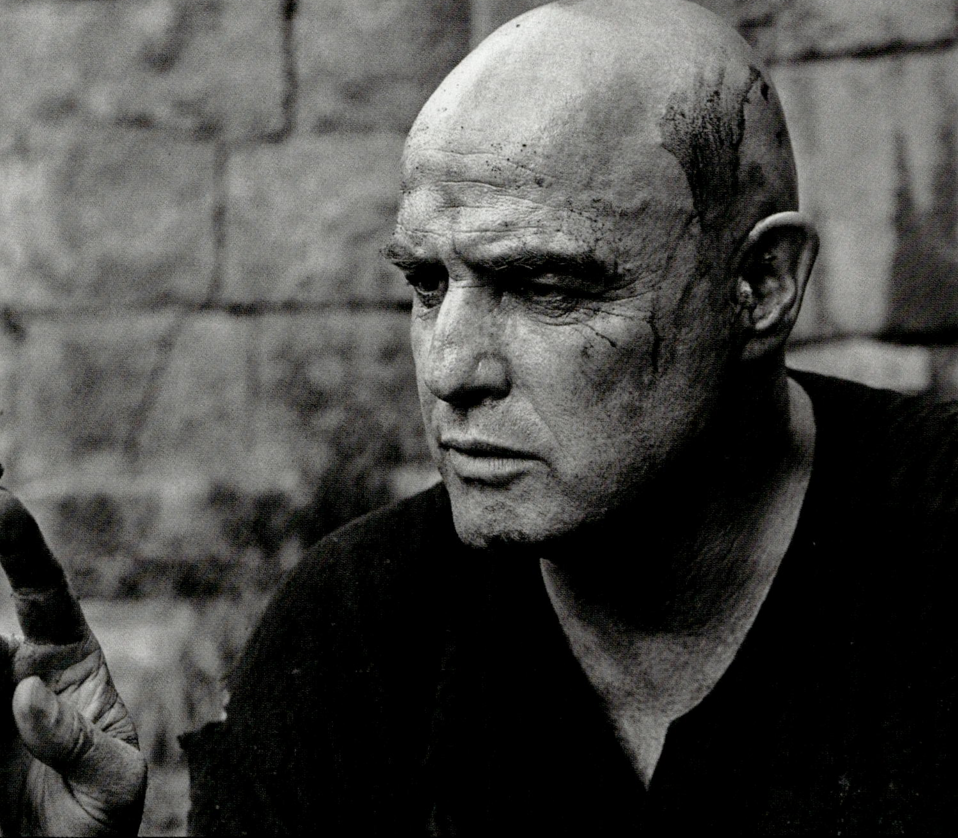

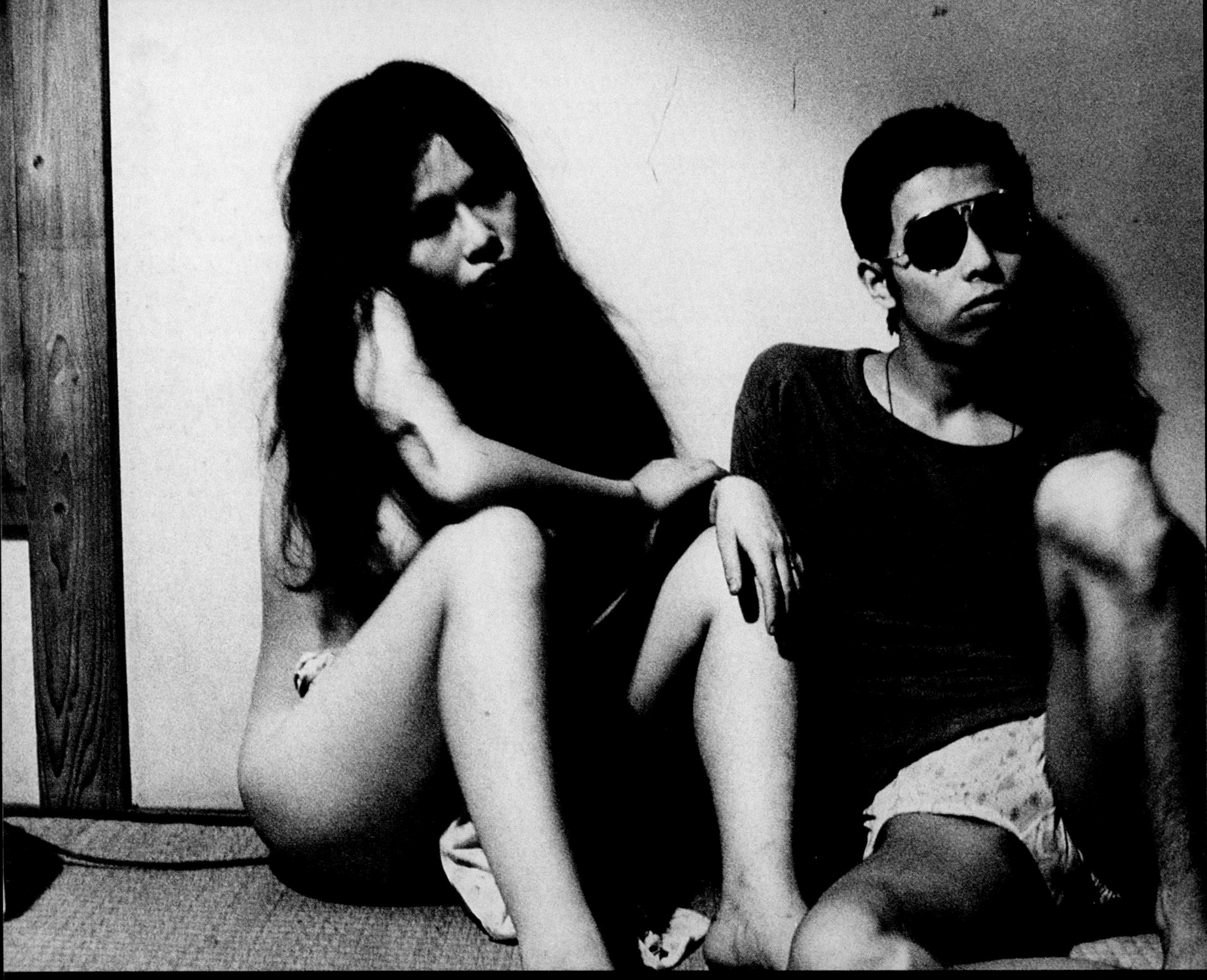

*Tokyo Blues 1977*, 1977.

'I will take my own photo from the coffin by using a digital camera for the first time.'

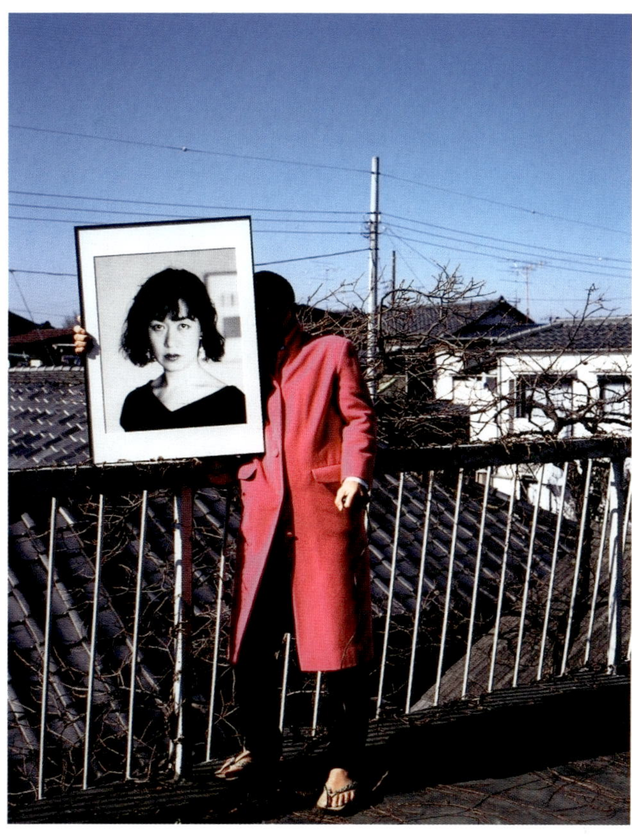

# Nobuyoshi Araki

b. 1940

JAPAN

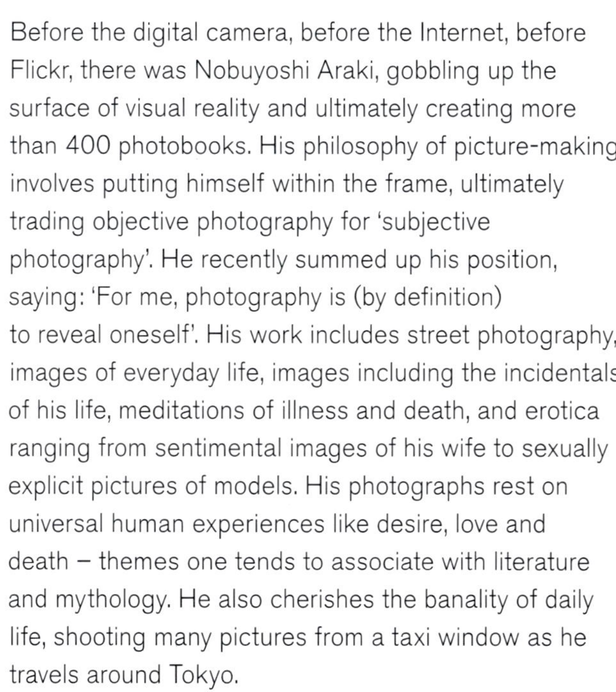

Before the digital camera, before the Internet, before Flickr, there was Nobuyoshi Araki, gobbling up the surface of visual reality and ultimately creating more than 400 photobooks. His philosophy of picture-making involves putting himself within the frame, ultimately trading objective photography for 'subjective photography'. He recently summed up his position, saying: 'For me, photography is (by definition) to reveal oneself'. His work includes street photography, images of everyday life, images including the incidentals of his life, meditations of illness and death, and erotica ranging from sentimental images of his wife to sexually explicit pictures of models. His photographs rest on universal human experiences like desire, love and death – themes one tends to associate with literature and mythology. He also cherishes the banality of daily life, shooting many pictures from a taxi window as he travels around Tokyo.

Though something of a prolific marvel in the analogue age, he could not be further from the indiscriminate street-security cameras or orbiting satellites that have become mines for material and for style for several twenty-first-century photographers. In fact, Araki has rejected digital photography, insisting that 'digital cameras are for stupid people. Pictures taken by a digital camera only show the instant moment'.

Although he has made efforts to disguise his craft, it is obvious that with so much experience behind the lens he is particularly adept at quick focusing and composing – as is evident in his urban photography and in thematic images of sex workers. Araki's influence in Japan is different from his international sway. In Japan, his carnal images have a partial cultural precursor in the woodblock prints genre referred to as 'shunga' – that is, erotic art. Shunga became popular in the 1600s and continued to be printed and copied until the early twentieth century. Araki, a fan of the genre, stated that he would like to take photographs like shunga but had not reached the level of 'bashful boldness' he admired in the work.

In Japan, his insistence on making the personal public, as he did with his honeymoon photographs in *Sentimental Journey*, helped to initiate alternatives to conventional photography categories, such as art and documentary work. For example, in the case of some young Japanese women photographers, he has been a supporter of women's diaristic image-making, often centred on the body. Thus, while his international reputation often points to his insistence on the personal, in Japan, Araki's work has come to stand for the importance of self-exploration amidst rapidly changing societal values.

Self-portrait from '*Shikikei*' ('Colourscapes'), 1991.

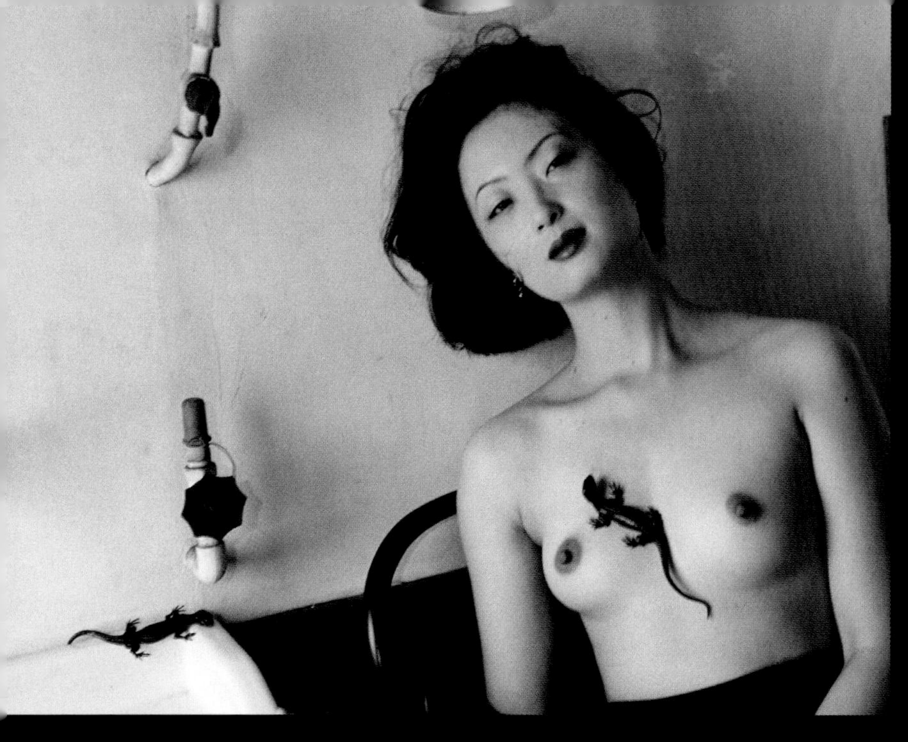

**Left** *Tokyo Comedy*, 1997.

**Below** Yoko Araki, from *Sentimental Journey*, 1971.

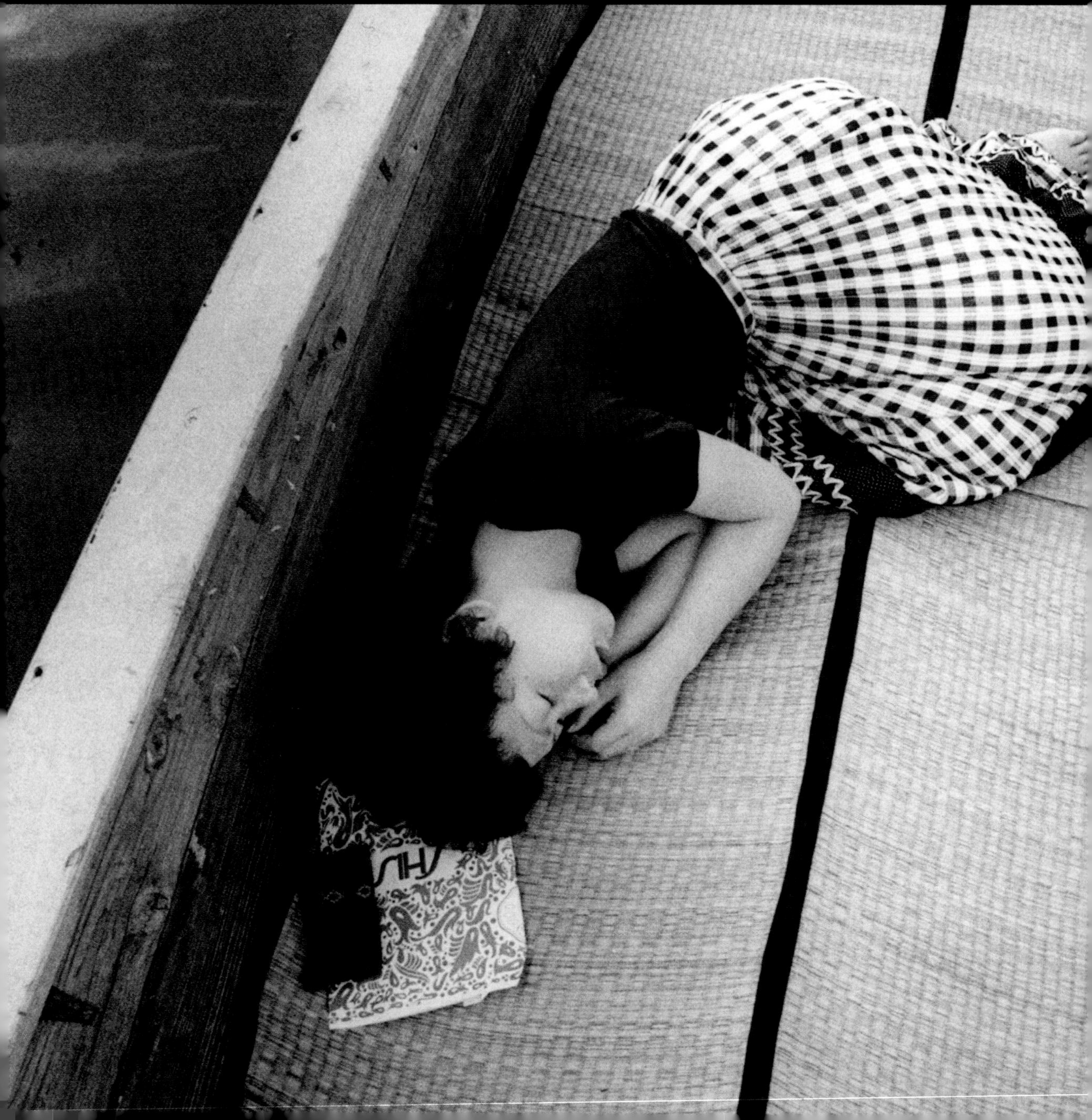

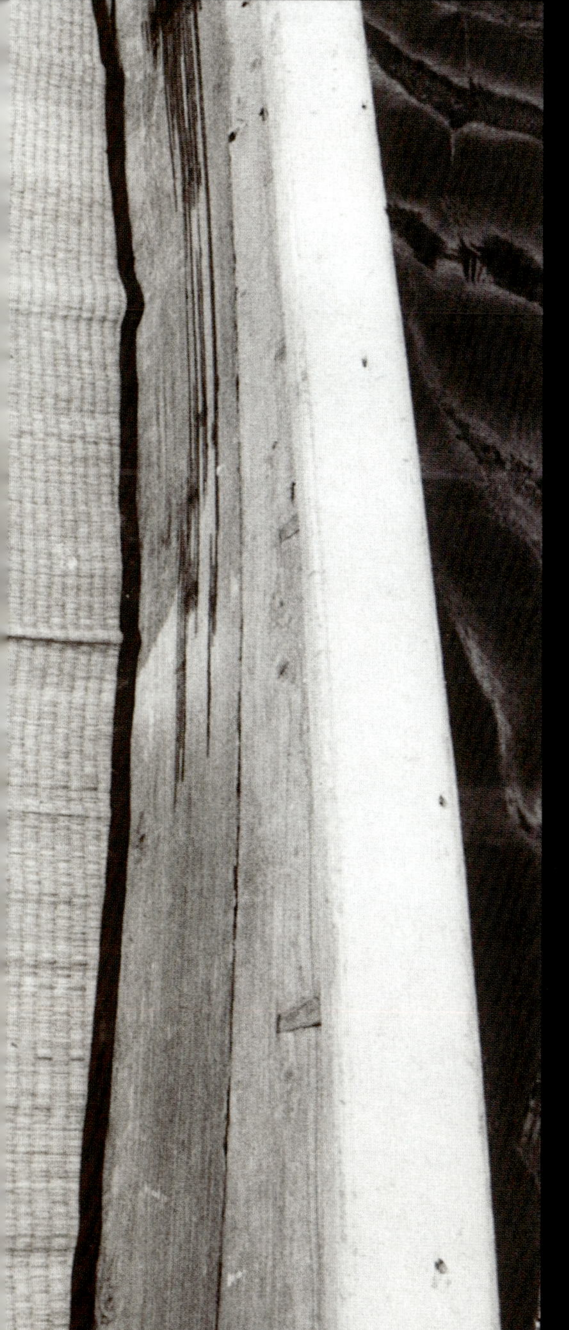

# Nobuyoshi Araki

1930

1940 Born in Tokyo, Japan

1952 Gets first camera

1960

1963 Graduates from college, where he studied photography and film; takes job in advertising agency

1971 Publishes images from his honeymoon in *Sentimental Journey*

1974 Creates photography school with others including Shōmei Tōmatsu, Daidō Moriyama and Eikoh Hosoe

1979 Travels internationally

1981 Makes first bondage photographs

1992 Fined for exhibition deemed pornographic

2001 Retrospective exhibition, 'Tokyo Still Life', Ikon Gallery, Birmingham, UK

2005 'Nobuyoshi Araki: Self, Life, Death', Barbican Art Gallery, London

2013 Major retrospective at Michael Hoppen Gallery, London

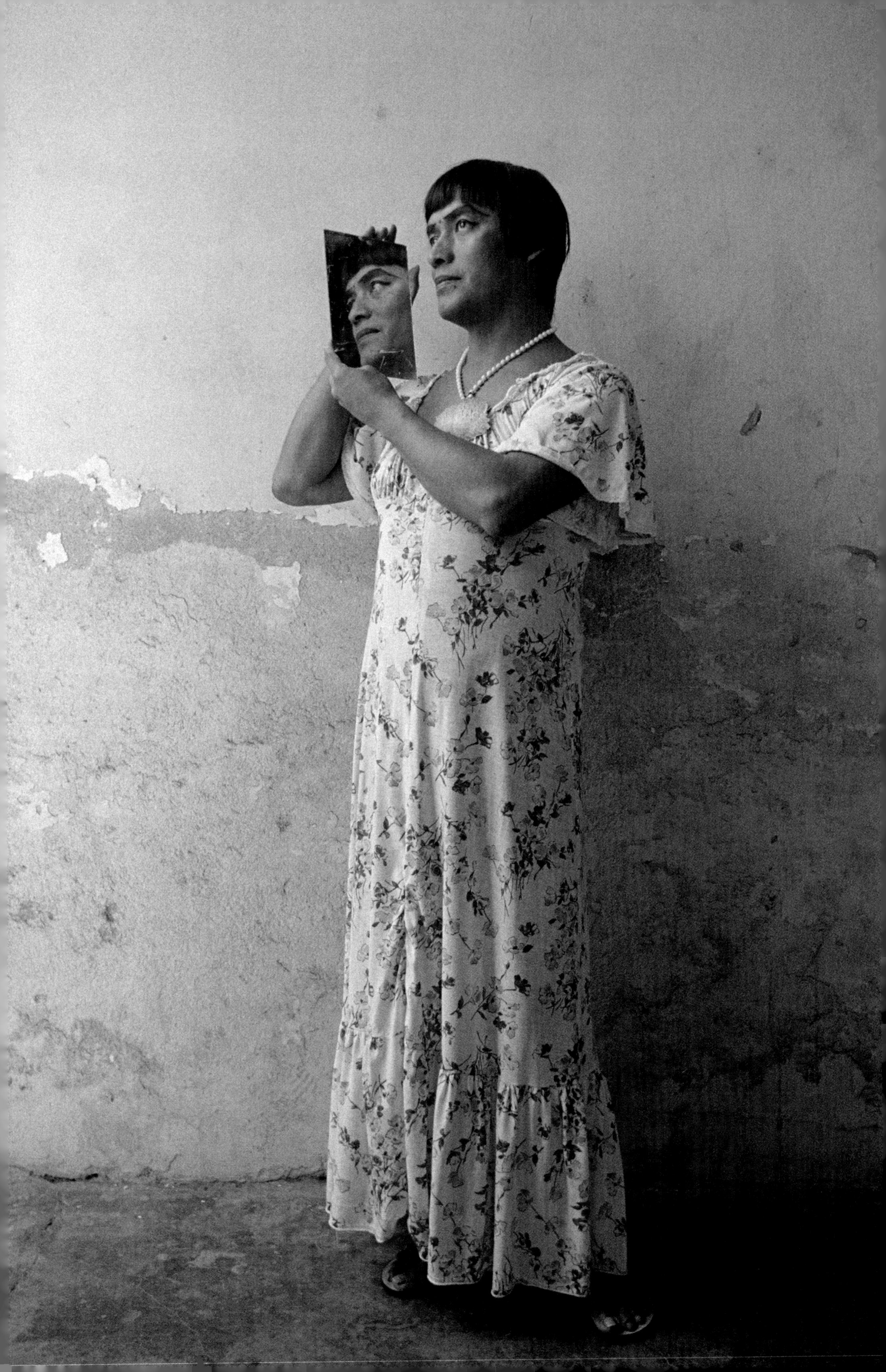

'I like to be close to people.
I need their complicity.'

# Graciela Iturbide

b. 1942

MEXICO

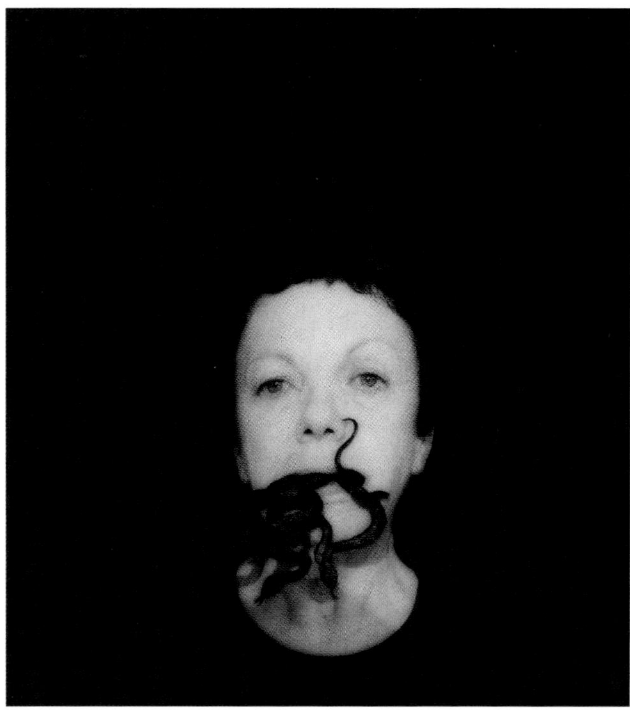

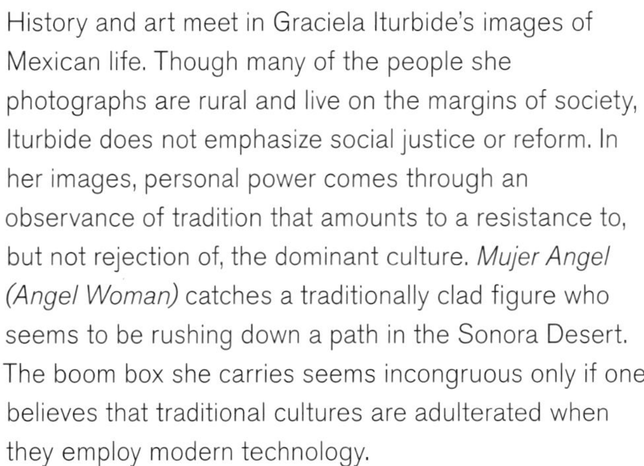

History and art meet in Graciela Iturbide's images of Mexican life. Though many of the people she photographs are rural and live on the margins of society, Iturbide does not emphasize social justice or reform. In her images, personal power comes through an observance of tradition that amounts to a resistance to, but not rejection of, the dominant culture. *Mujer Angel (Angel Woman)* catches a traditionally clad figure who seems to be rushing down a path in the Sonora Desert. The boom box she carries seems incongruous only if one believes that traditional cultures are adulterated when they employ modern technology.

Iturbide prefers to make photographs with minimal equipment. Rejecting a tripod, lights or a flash, she finds that using only a camera allows her to respond more immediately to intuitive visual ideas. She thinks in black-and-white film, and produces her work in the darkroom.

Unlike former teacher, Manuel Álvarez Bravo (p. 108), she prefers to work in series. Iturbide pictures the persistence of the past in the present, but entertains no illusion that traditional lives should remain unchanged. However, she does believe that local cultures are resilient and inventive. Her photographs of people of Mexican descent in gang culture and living in Los Angeles depict them as creating a local culture with roots, however attenuated, in Mexico.

For nearly ten years, she got to know the people who live in and around the city of Juchitán, where women dominate politics, business and culture, and where cross-dressing by men is not remarkable. Nevertheless, she photographed rituals in which only men may participate, such as a procession in Chalma. Iturbide describes herself as working 'in complicity with the people', a word that suggests mutual cooperation as well as a bit of norm-breaking.

**Opposite** *Magnolia*, Juchitán, Oaxaxa. c. 1986.

**Above** Self-portrait, Oaxaca, 2006.

*Mujer Angel* (*Angel Woman*), Sonora Desert, 1979.

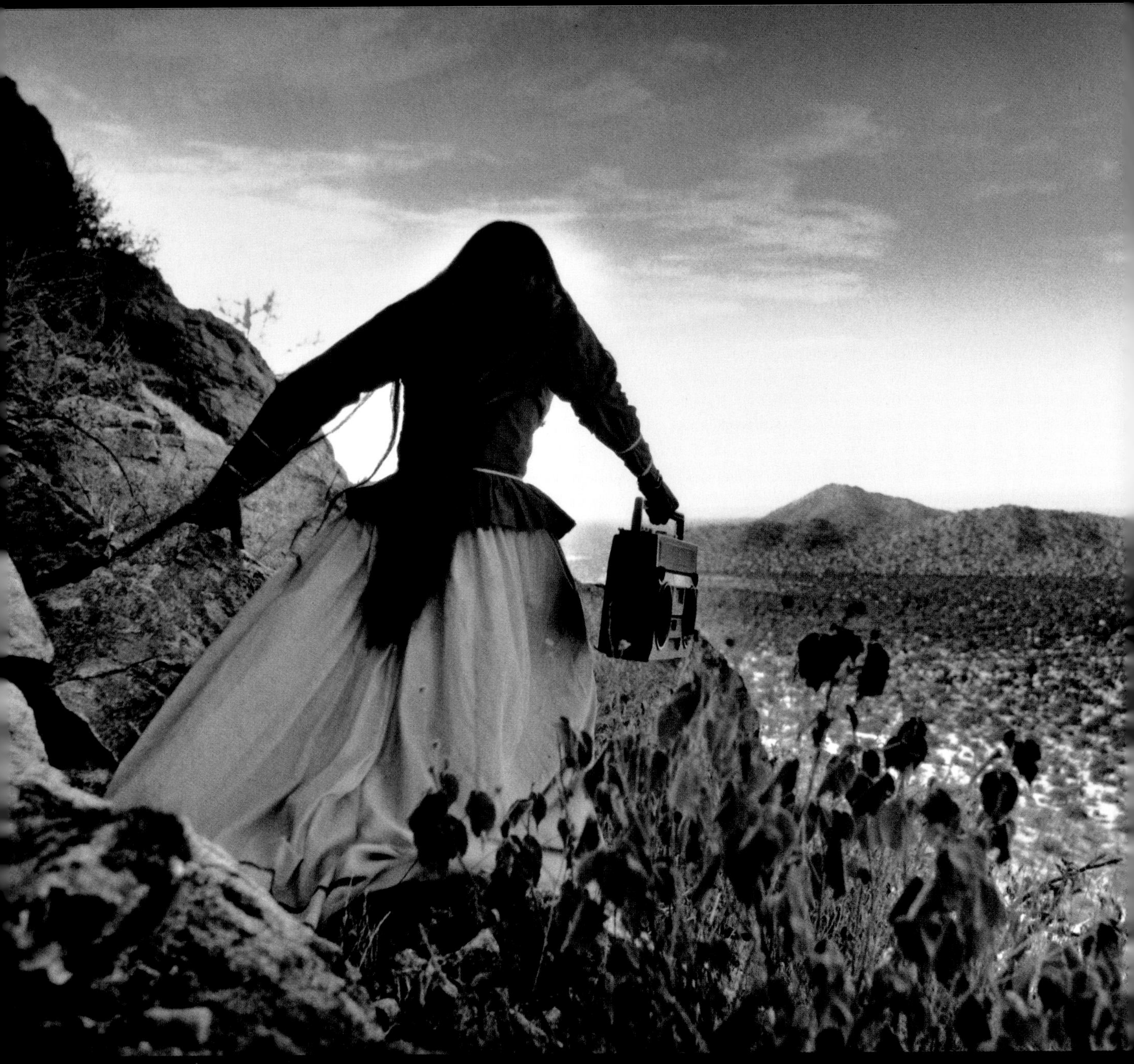

**Below** *Nuestra Señora de las Iguanas* ('Our Lady of the Iguanas'), Juchitán, México, 1979.

**Bottom** *Procesión* ('Procession'), Chalma, State of Mexico, 1984.

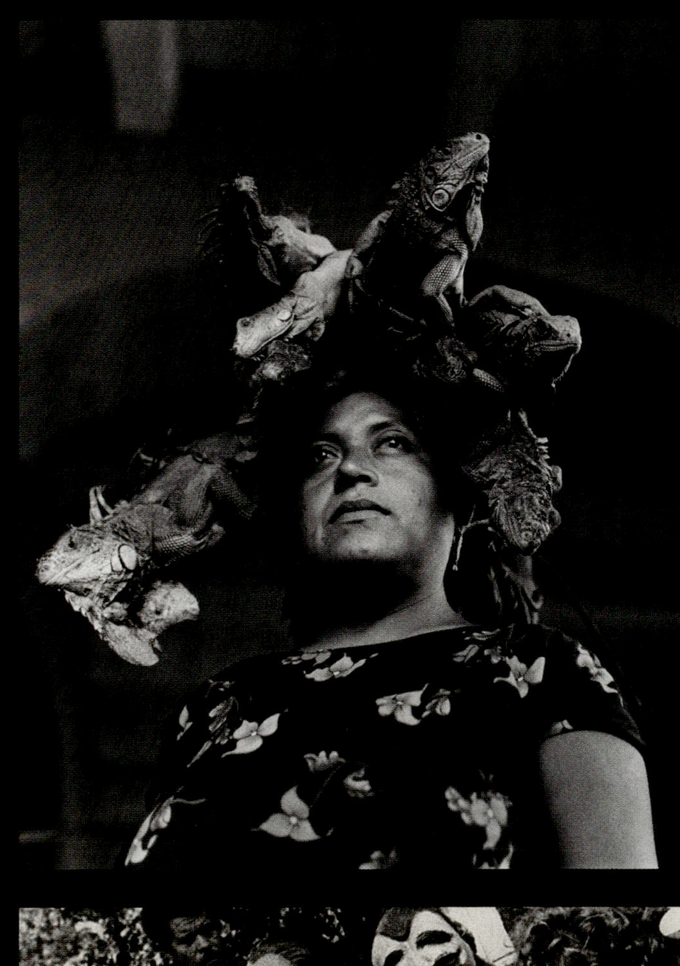

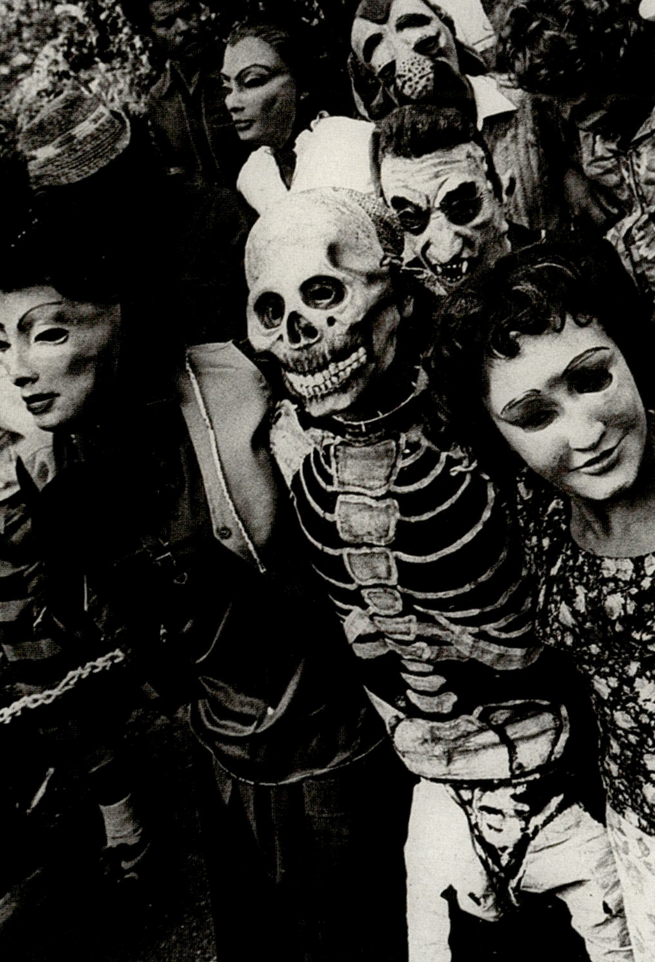

## Graciela Iturbide

1930

1940

**1942** Born in Mexico City, Mexico

1950

1960

**1970** While studying cinematography in college, she takes a class with Manuel Álvarez Bravo and becomes his assistant

**1978** Receives commission from the National Indigenous Institute of Mexico

**1979** Starts photographing in Juchitán, Mexico, from which she creates the series and book *Juchitán of the Women* (to 1988)

1980

**1986** Photographs people of Mexican descent in the White Fence barrio of East Los Angeles

1990

**1996** Publishes *Images of the Spirit*

**1999** 'Graciela Iturbide' exhibition at the Helsinki Museum, Finland

2000

**2006** Publishes *Eyes to Fly With*

**2007** 'The Goat's Dance' exhibition at the Getty Museum, Los Angeles

**2011** 'Graciela Iturbide' exhibition at the Museum of Modern Art, Mexico City

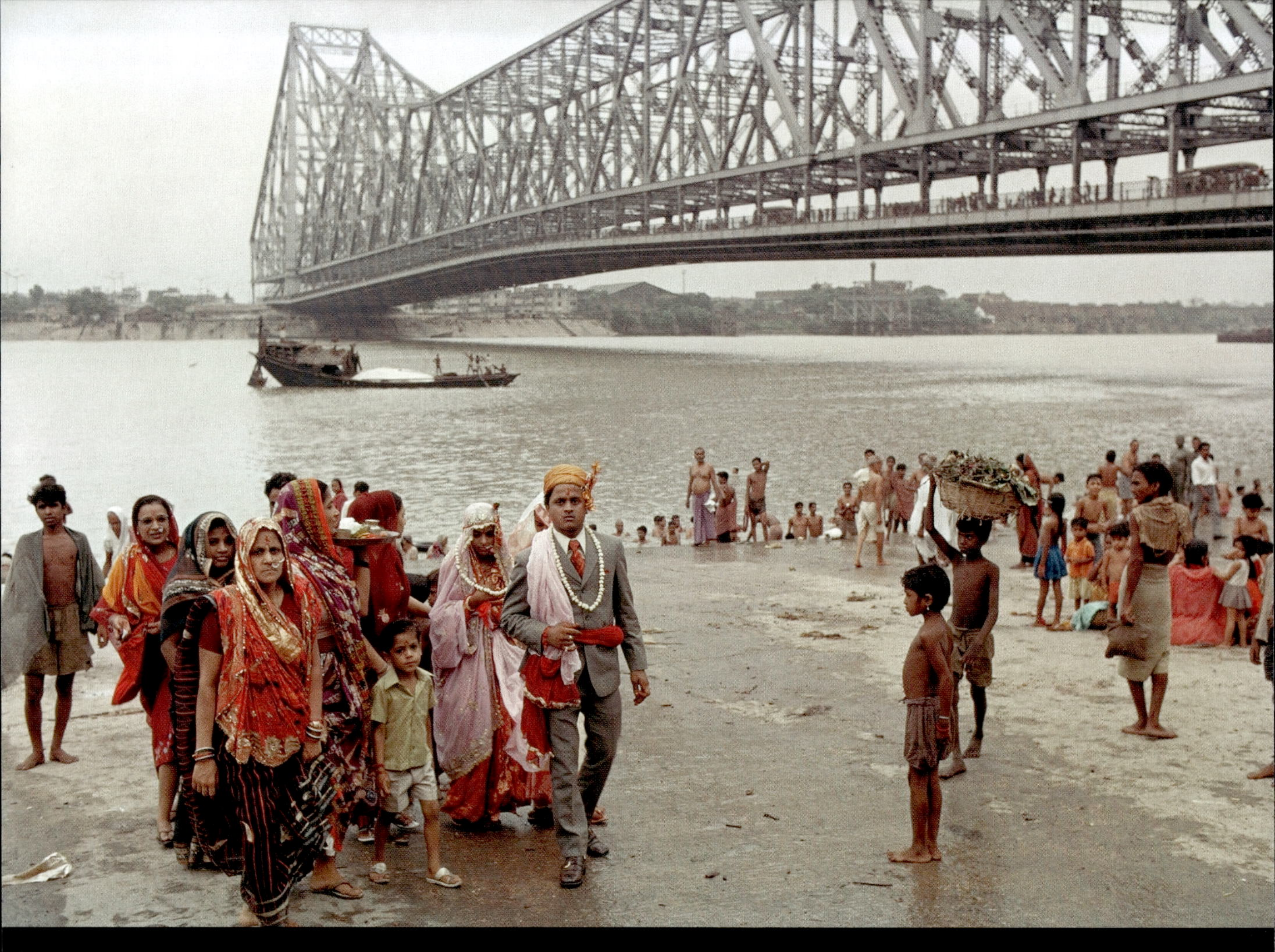

*Below the Howra Bridge a Marwari bride and groom after rites by the Ganges*, Calcutta, West Bengal, 1968.

'The true Indian artist cannot ignore the blessing of colour.'

# Raghubir Singh

1942–1999

INDIA

In the era after World War II, when colour photography processes became more reliable, black and white remained the dominant tones of serious photography. The popular picture magazines mixed photographically based colour advertisements and fluff pieces with sombre-toned images that reported on major social and political events. Raghubir Singh adopted colour photography relatively early on and like Satyajit Ray and Sunil Janah (p. 148), he emphasized Indian stories and themes in his work.

Singh recalled that he was steeped in a river of colour during his childhood. Indeed, for him, India was colour, and he was fortunate enough to find commercial clients such as *National Geographic* and *Time* magazine to commission his work. His first book, *Ganga*, a portrait of life along the Ganges River, appeared in colour, as did his other studies of Indian regions such as Kashmir, Kerala and Tamil Nadu, and of the Grand Trunk Road.

Singh complicated colour work in a variety of ways. Sometimes he sought out simple compositions, in which objects in colour, especially red, seem to radiate tones into the scene. However, his forte was composition, which he studied in the work of Henri Cartier-Bresson (p. 132), Bill Brandt (p. 116) and Robert Frank (p. 172). He activated the viewer's perception by finding scenes where he could array surfaces on various recessive planes. His pictures cannot be grasped instantly, but have to be examined and recomposed by the viewer. Throughout his career, Singh invited writers, journalists and film-makers including Eric Newby, Joseph Lelyveld, Satyajit Ray, Jean Deloche, R. K. Narayan and V. S. Naipaul, to contribute essays to his books, thereby augmenting his visual study.

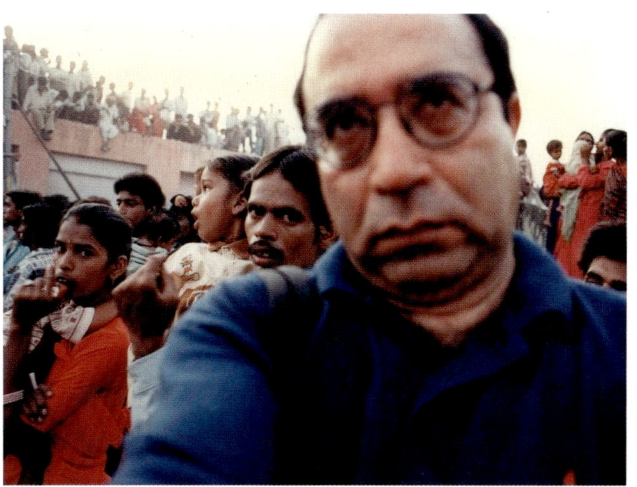

Self-portrait, 1998.

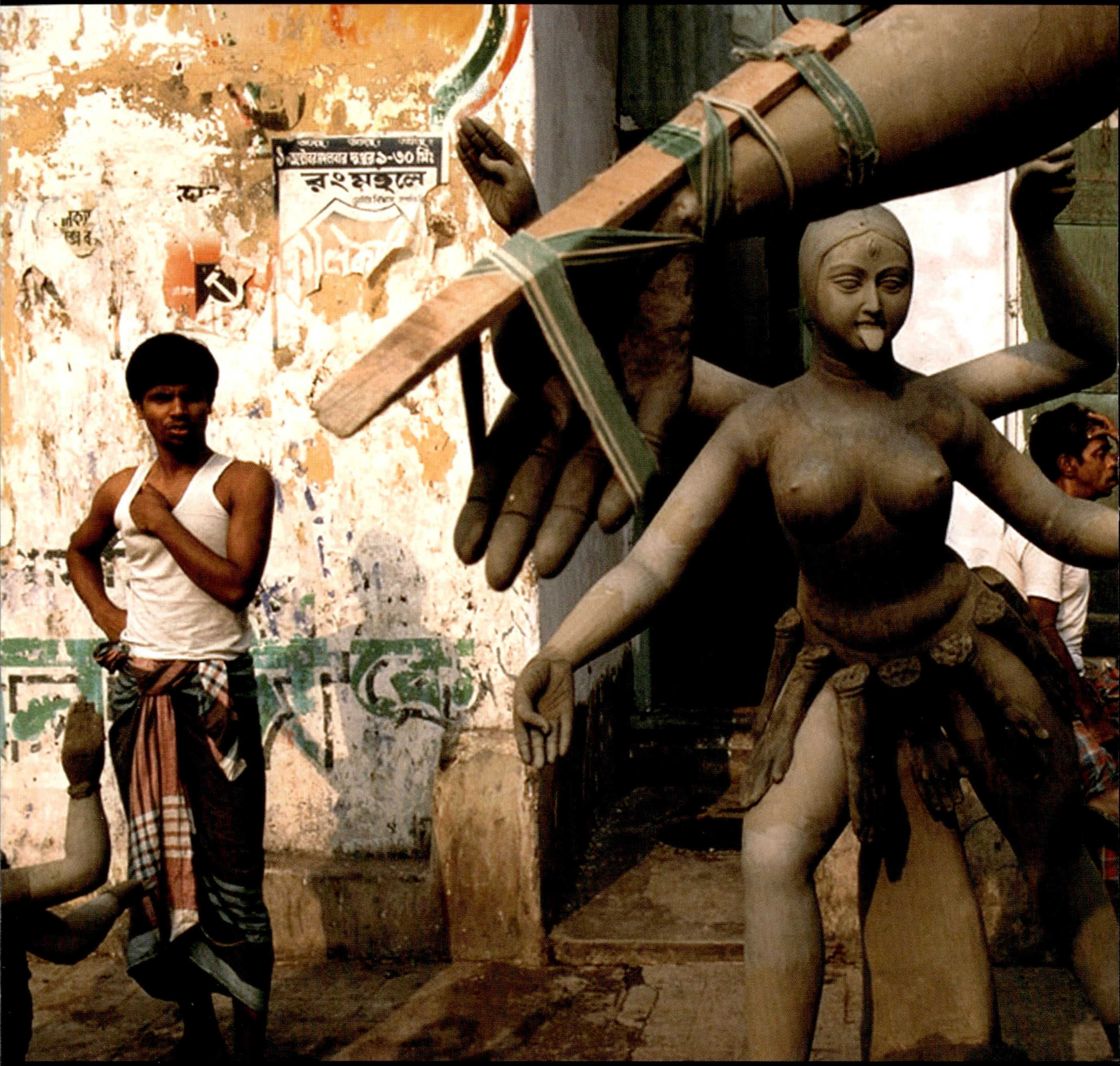

**Above** *Barber and Goddess Kali*, Calcutta, West Bvengal, 1987.

**Right** *The Pilgrim and Ambassador Car*, Kumbh Mela, Allahabad, 1977.

**Opposite** *Member of a middle-class family of North Calcutta and Two Servants Listen to Tagore Songs*, Calcutta, 1986.

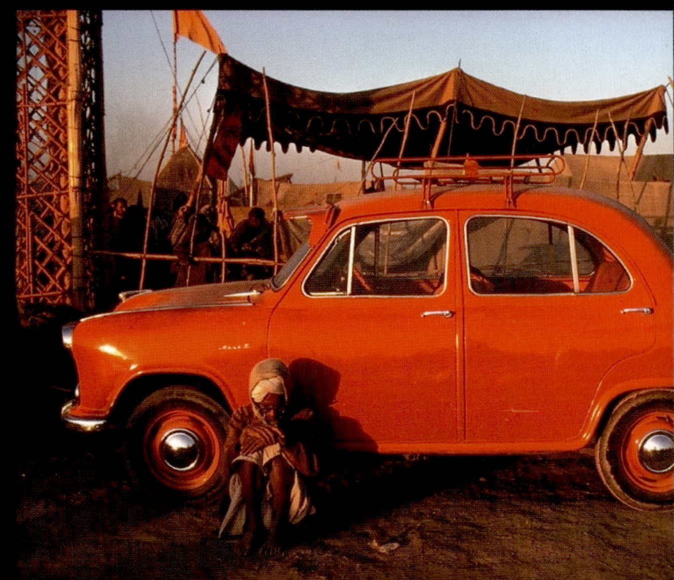

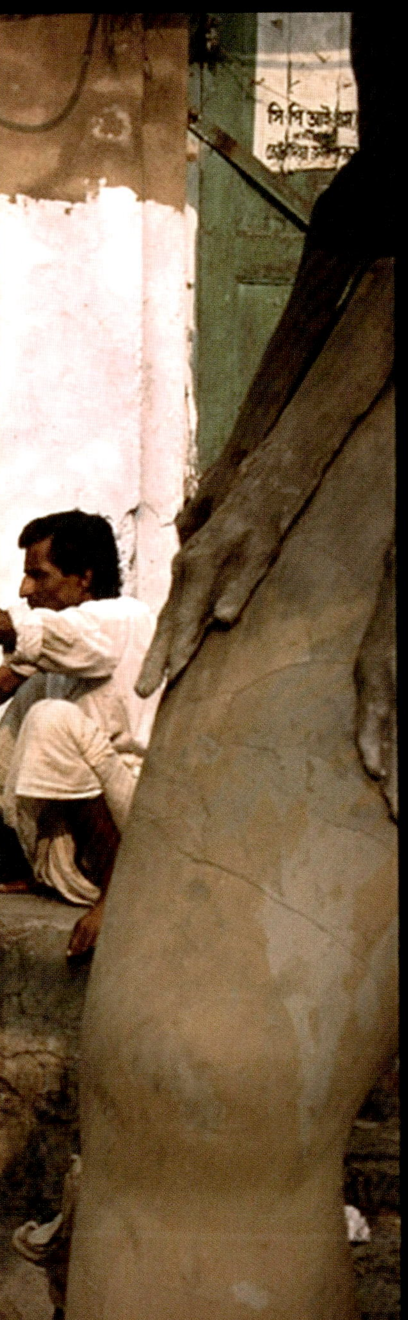

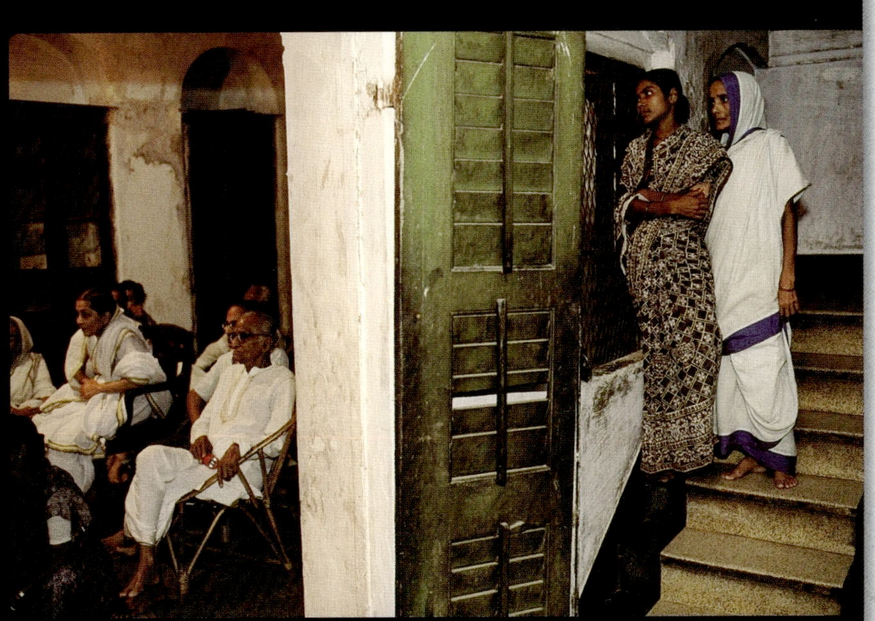

# Raghubir Singh

1930

1940

**1942** Born in Jaipur, India

1950

**1961** Leaves college and moves to Calcutta; meets film director Satyajit Ray

**1966** Meets Henri Cartier-Bresson

1970

**1974** Publishes *Ganga: Sacred River of India*

**1981** Publishes *Rajasthan: India's Enchanted Land*, with a foreword by Satyajit Ray

**1983** Publishes *Kashmir: Garden of the Himalayas*, which includes a conversation with V. S. Naipaul

1990

**1995** Publishes *The Grand Trunk Road*

**1998** Publishes *River of Colour*

**1999** Dies in New York, USA

*Saddam's Palace*, from 'House Beautiful: Bringing the War Home, New Series', 2004.

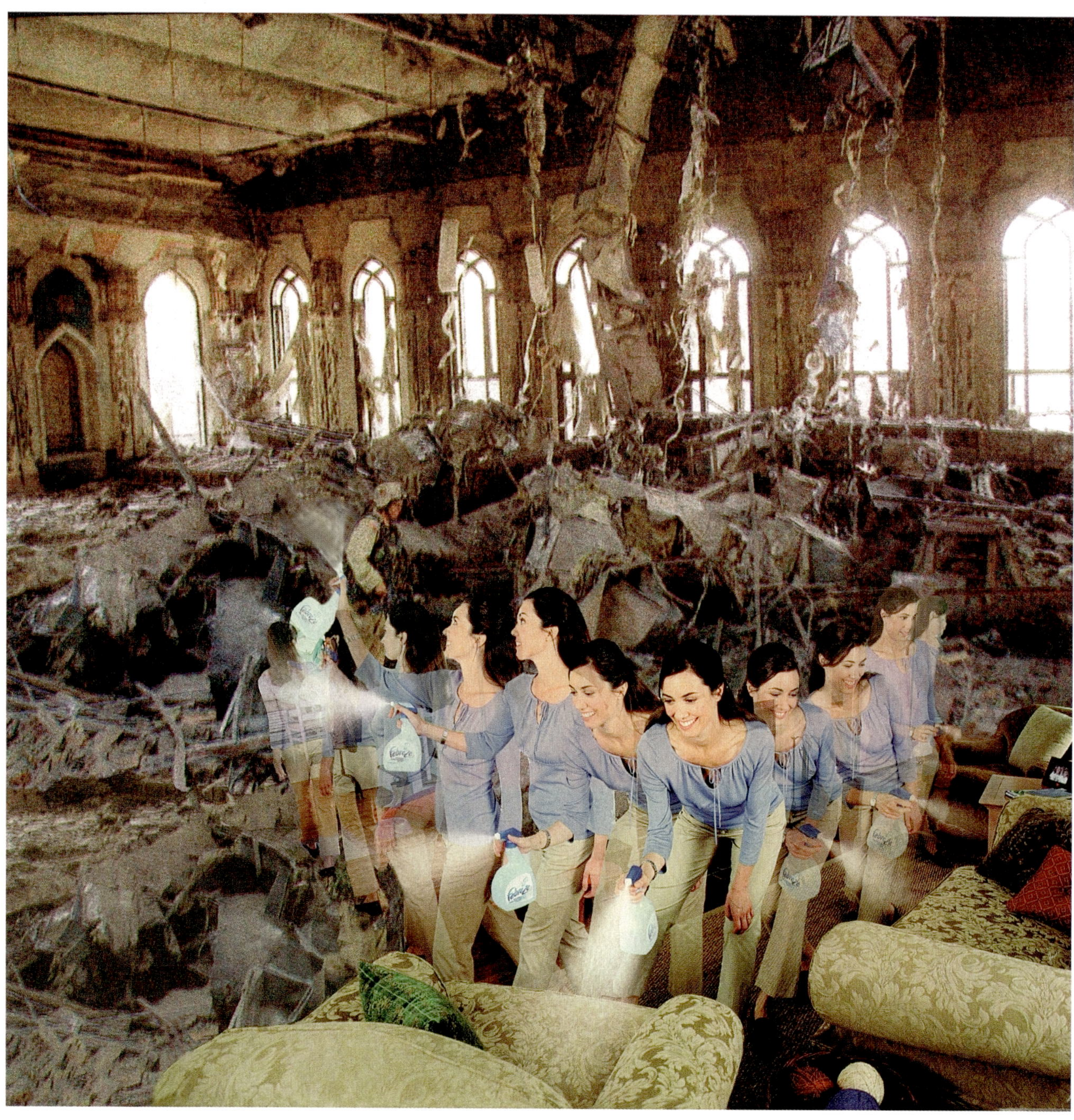

'I want to enlist art to question the mythical explanations of everyday life.'

# Martha Rosler

b. 1943

UNITED STATES

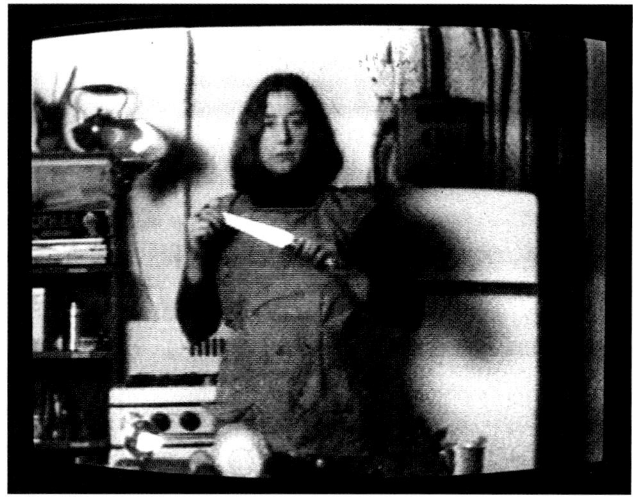

During the 1970s, Martha Rosler was one of the artist-scholars who reshaped photographic studies while creating an influential new social-documentary photography. Her photomontage series 'House Beautiful: Bringing the War Home' created a visual and intellectual clash between images from the Vietnam conflict taken from newspapers and magazines, and pictures taken from design and architectural magazines. Her picture-war brought elements of the visual spectacle of modern life into close proximity. Rosler's point was not simply to make an anti-war protest, but also to comment on the homogenization of mass-media imagery in the public imagination.

Rosler's 'The Bowery in two inadequate descriptive systems' was one of the most discussed photographic series in the 1970s and 1980s. It challenged the tradition of documentary photography by not showing people as victims. Instead, the comparison that Rosler's panels forced between inadequate words and inadequate pictures inadvertently brought together artists, critics and academics interested in semiotics, cultural criticism and political action. It meshed with the wider academic and artistic emphasis on what was called 'thinking photography', which, in turn, had the unexpected result of increasing interest in image-making as well as in the history of photography. Other Rosler works, such as those in her 'Body Beautiful' panels, connected to contemporary feminism with its emphasis on gender as a performance rather than an essence.

In more recent efforts Rosler, who works in many media, used photography to examine public spaces such as airports and highways, in photographs whose colours were both irritating and alienating. And, to the great delight of New Yorkers, she staged her 'Meta-Monumental Garage Sale', which was exactly that, minus the garage, in the large atrium of the Museum of Modern Art in 2012.

Self-portrait from 'Semiotics of the Kitchen', 1975.

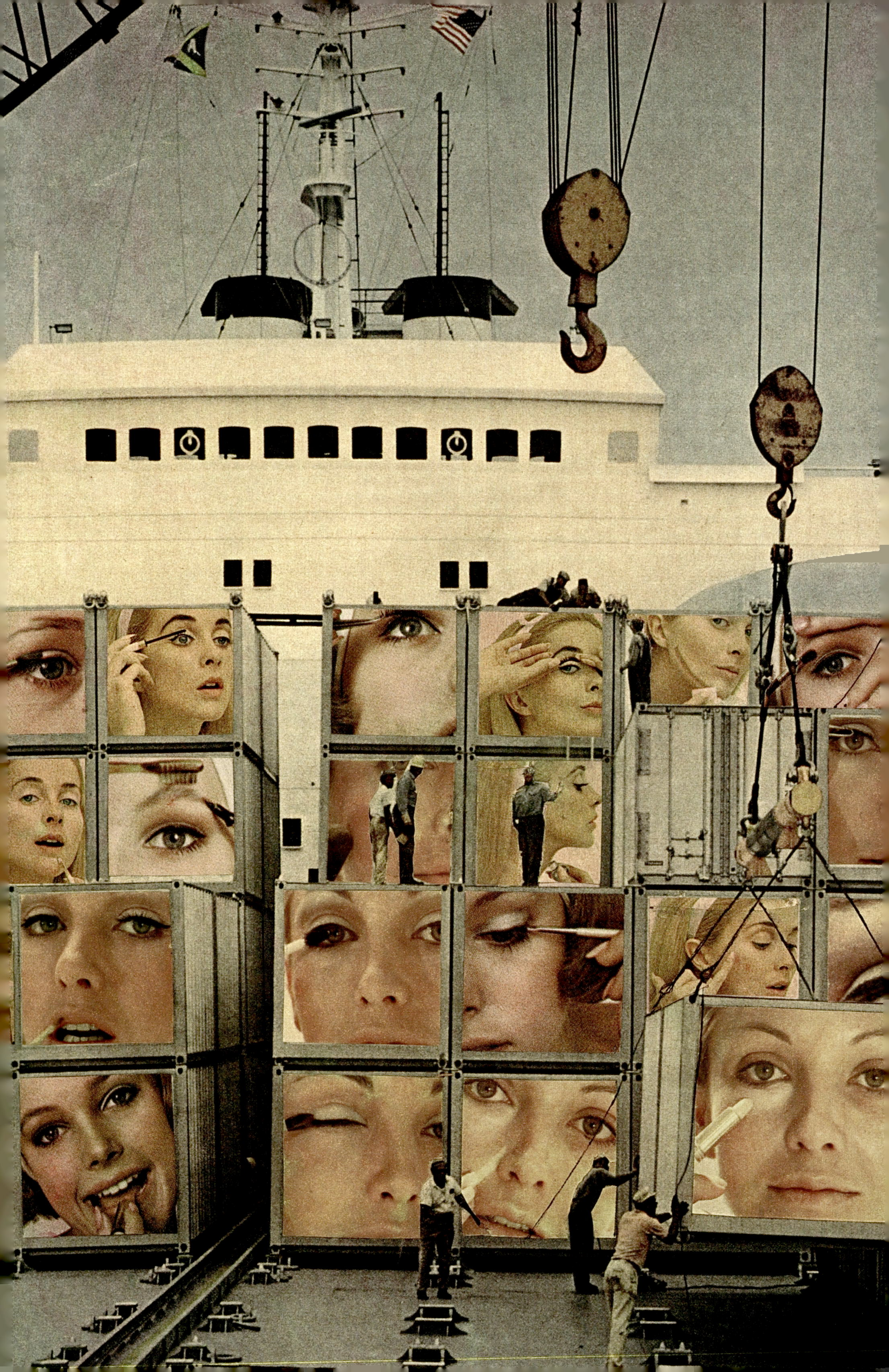

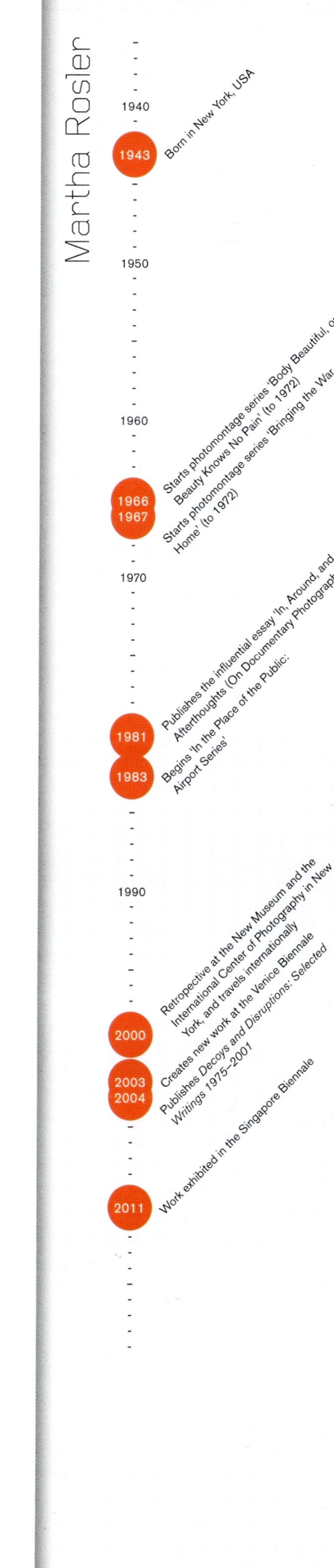


*Cargo Cult* from 'Body Beautiful, or Beauty Knows No Pain', 1966–72

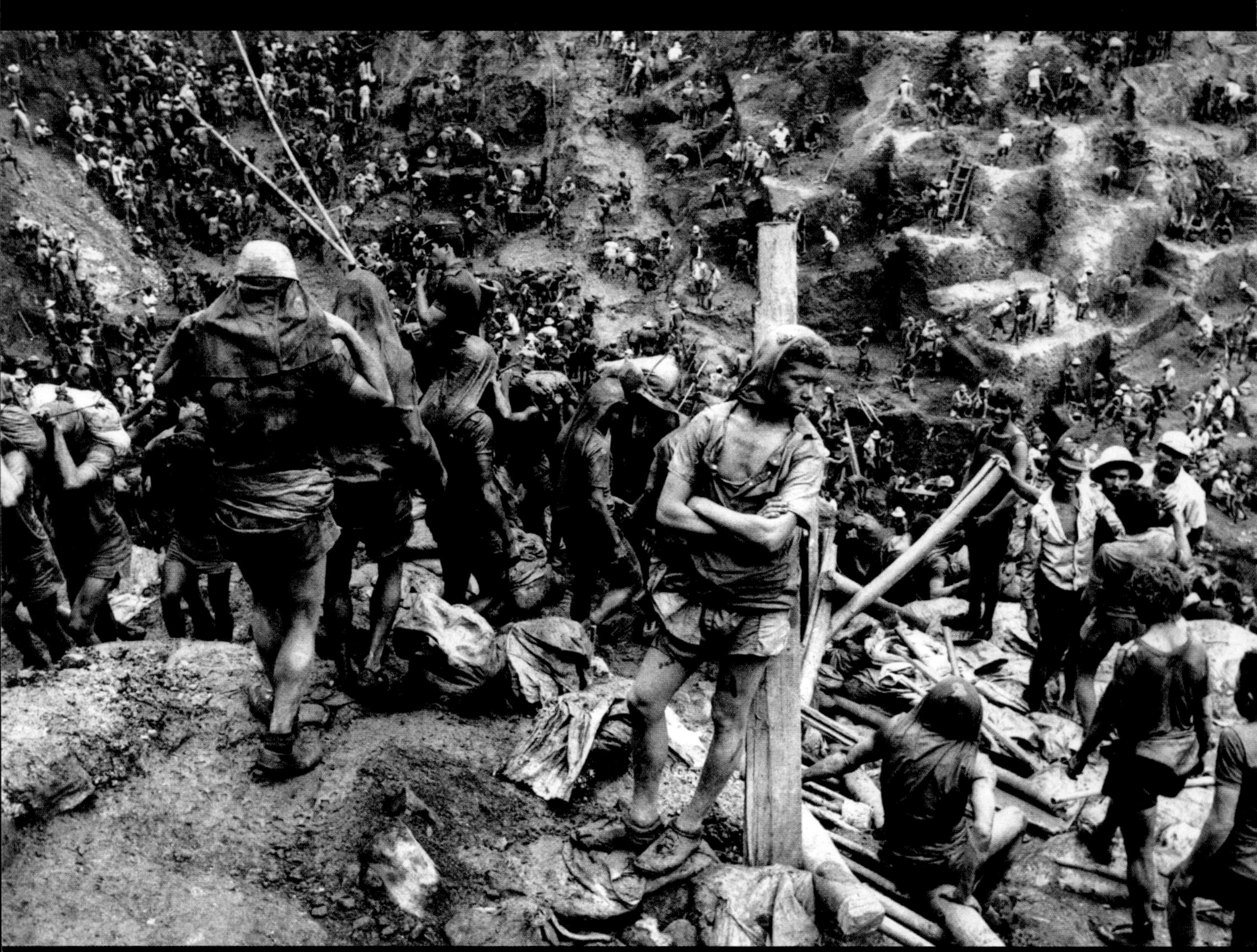

Serra Pelada Goldmine, Brazil, 1986.

'If you take a picture of a human that does not make him noble, there is no reason to take this picture.'

# Sebastião Salgado

b. 1944

BRAZIL

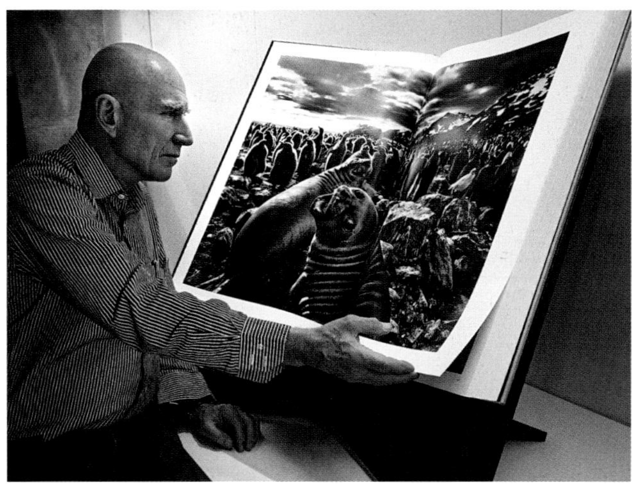

When he describes how he became a photographer at the age of 29, Sebastião Salgado uses the kind of language that usually alludes to religious conversion: 'One day photography made a total invasion of my life. I became a photographer. Abandoned everything and became a photographer.' In his youth, he was an activist and a Marxist, and when he had to leave Brazil because of his politics he took an economics degree at the University of Paris, where left-wing politics were freely discussed. Subsequent work and travel, as well as economic development work in Africa, may have hardened his resolve.

By 1973, he was sufficiently agile with the camera to begin a series on the lives of immigrant workers in Europe, and to interpret the effects of drought in Africa's Sahel, to which he would return when drought conditions reoccurred in the 1980s. Salgado's scope is global in every sense of the word. His interpretation of major displacements of peoples in the 1990s, whether seeking work or avoiding conflicts, took seven years as he travelled to three dozen countries.

Salgado's work springs from his belief that photographs can affect people – not simply urge them to make donations for good causes, but make them lastingly concerned about what is going on in the world. His work has been compared to the photographic efforts of W. Eugene Smith (p. 152), who also immersed himself in human predicaments. Like Smith, Salgado does not accept the grab-and-go approach of photojournalism. He spends years on each of his series. In addition, money from the sale of Salgado's photographs has been used to support such organizations as Médecins Sans Frontières (Doctors Without Borders) and to fund local factories that make artificial limbs for Cambodian children who have lost legs to land mines.

Salgado refuses to publish lurid pictures of abject human suffering. He tends to heroicize the daily lives of simple people and create aesthetically compelling images of nature, leading some critics to suggest that he is politically naïve about social change. Indeed, Salgado's work has become a trigger point for discussions about both global poverty and climate change.

Portrait of Sebastião Salgado by Frank Goerhardt, 2013.

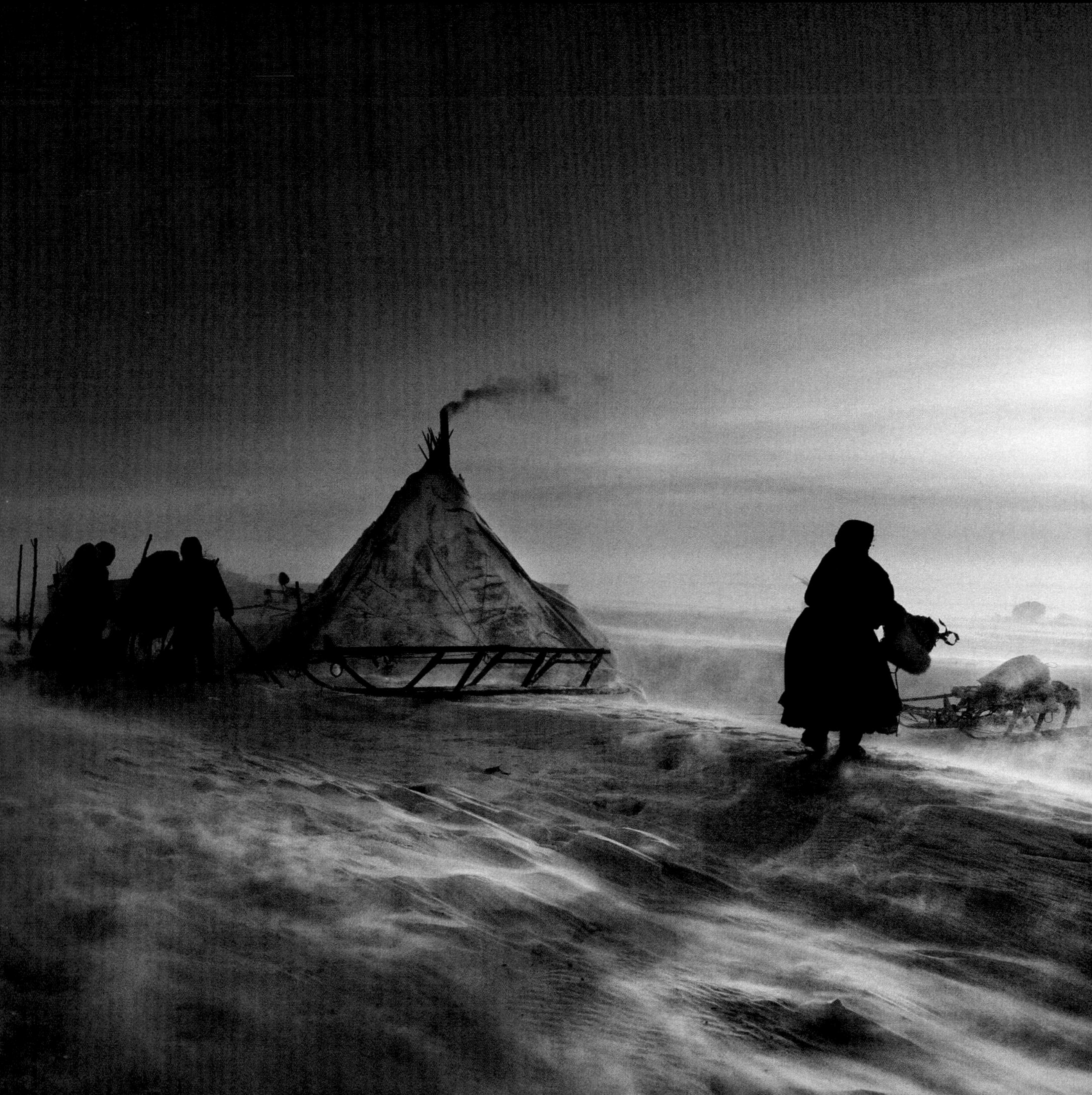

**Above** North of Ob River. Inside the Arctic Circle, Yamal Peninsula, Siberia, Russia. 2011.

**Opposite** From *Sahel: The End of the Road*, 1984.

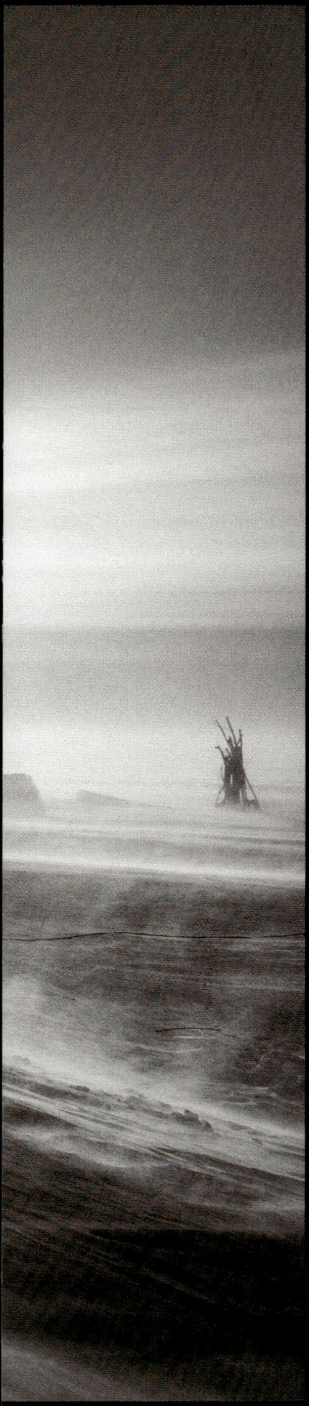

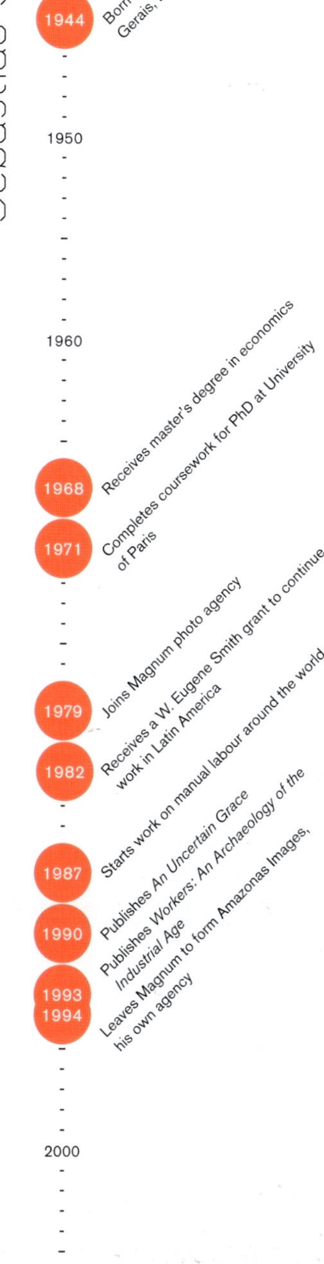
Sebastião Salgado
1940
1944 Born in Aimorés, Minas Gerais, Brazil
1950
1960
1968 Receives master's degree in economics
1971 Completes coursework for PhD at University of Paris
1979 Joins Magnum photo agency
1982 Receives a W. Eugene Smith grant to continue work in Latin America
1987 Starts work on manual labour around the world
1990 Publishes An Uncertain Grace
1993 Publishes Workers: An Archaeology of the Industrial Age
1994 Leaves Magnum to form Amazonas Images, his own agency
2000
2010
2013 Publishes Genesis

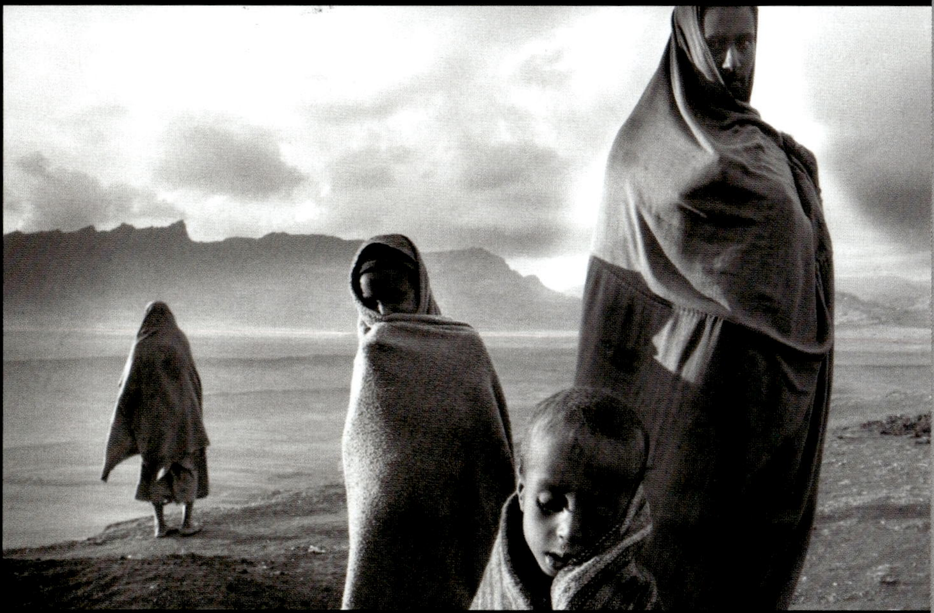

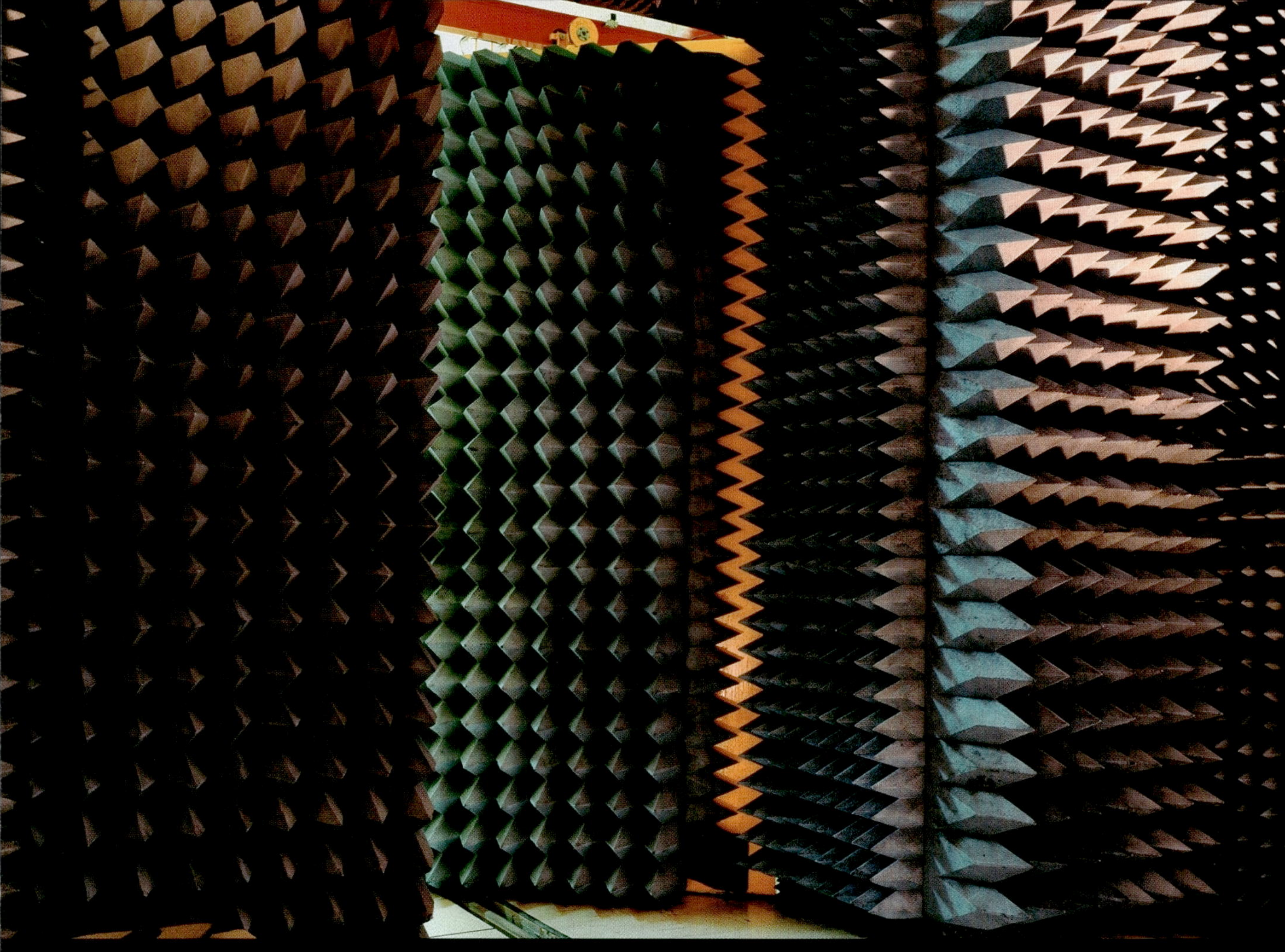

*Anechoic Chamber*, France Télécom Laboratories, Lannion, France, from the series 'Sites of Technology', 1989–91.

'Everything is photogenic once it has been photographed.'

# Lewis Baltz

b. 1945

UNITED STATES

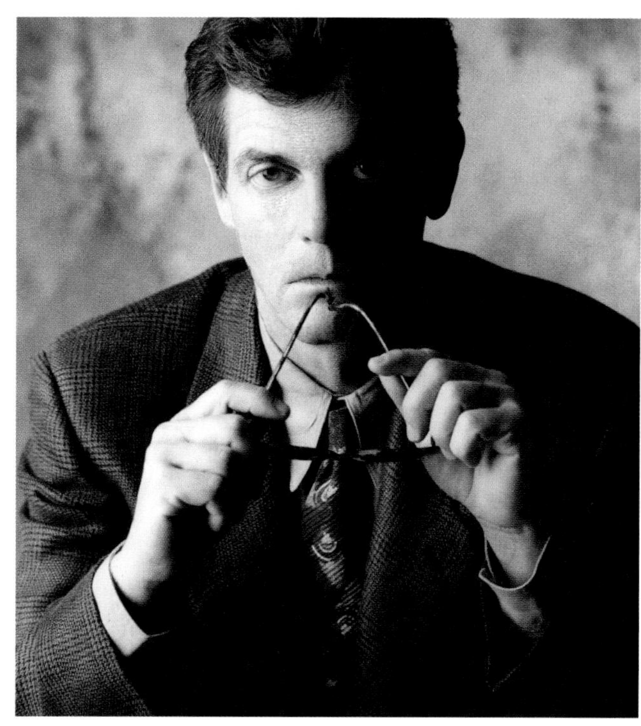

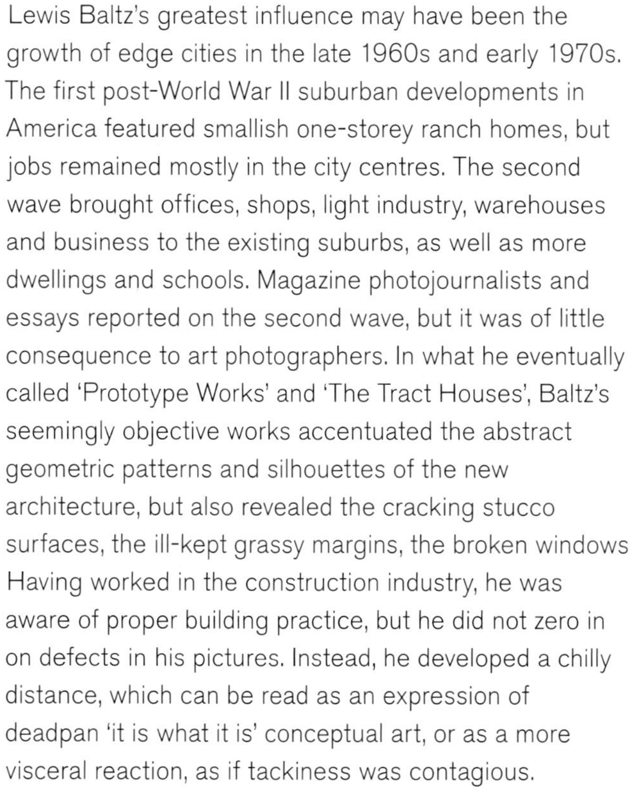

Lewis Baltz's greatest influence may have been the growth of edge cities in the late 1960s and early 1970s. The first post-World War II suburban developments in America featured smallish one-storey ranch homes, but jobs remained mostly in the city centres. The second wave brought offices, shops, light industry, warehouses and business to the existing suburbs, as well as more dwellings and schools. Magazine photojournalists and essays reported on the second wave, but it was of little consequence to art photographers. In what he eventually called 'Prototype Works' and 'The Tract Houses', Baltz's seemingly objective works accentuated the abstract geometric patterns and silhouettes of the new architecture, but also revealed the cracking stucco surfaces, the ill-kept grassy margins, the broken windows. Having worked in the construction industry, he was aware of proper building practice, but he did not zero in on defects in his pictures. Instead, he developed a chilly distance, which can be read as an expression of deadpan 'it is what it is' conceptual art, or as a more visceral reaction, as if tackiness was contagious.

Baltz's presentation of American life not as the triumph of the middle class but as a fall from grace, together with his routine production of series, put him in league with those who were identified as part of a disaggregated movement dubbed the 'New Topographics' in 1975. While his early work contributed to the acceptance of photography as a major medium in post-war art practice, Baltz's investigation of what he called 'sub-architecture' developed and maintained a social critique of the built environment. 'Candlestick Point', for instance, features construction debris and trees felled to allow development. Moreover, while he continues to photograph, he also creates installation, video and computer-based work. He readily embraces colour and digital photography, which are appropriate to his ongoing study of contemporary workplaces, themselves deeply dependent on information technology.

Portrait by Luciano Bonacini, 1991.

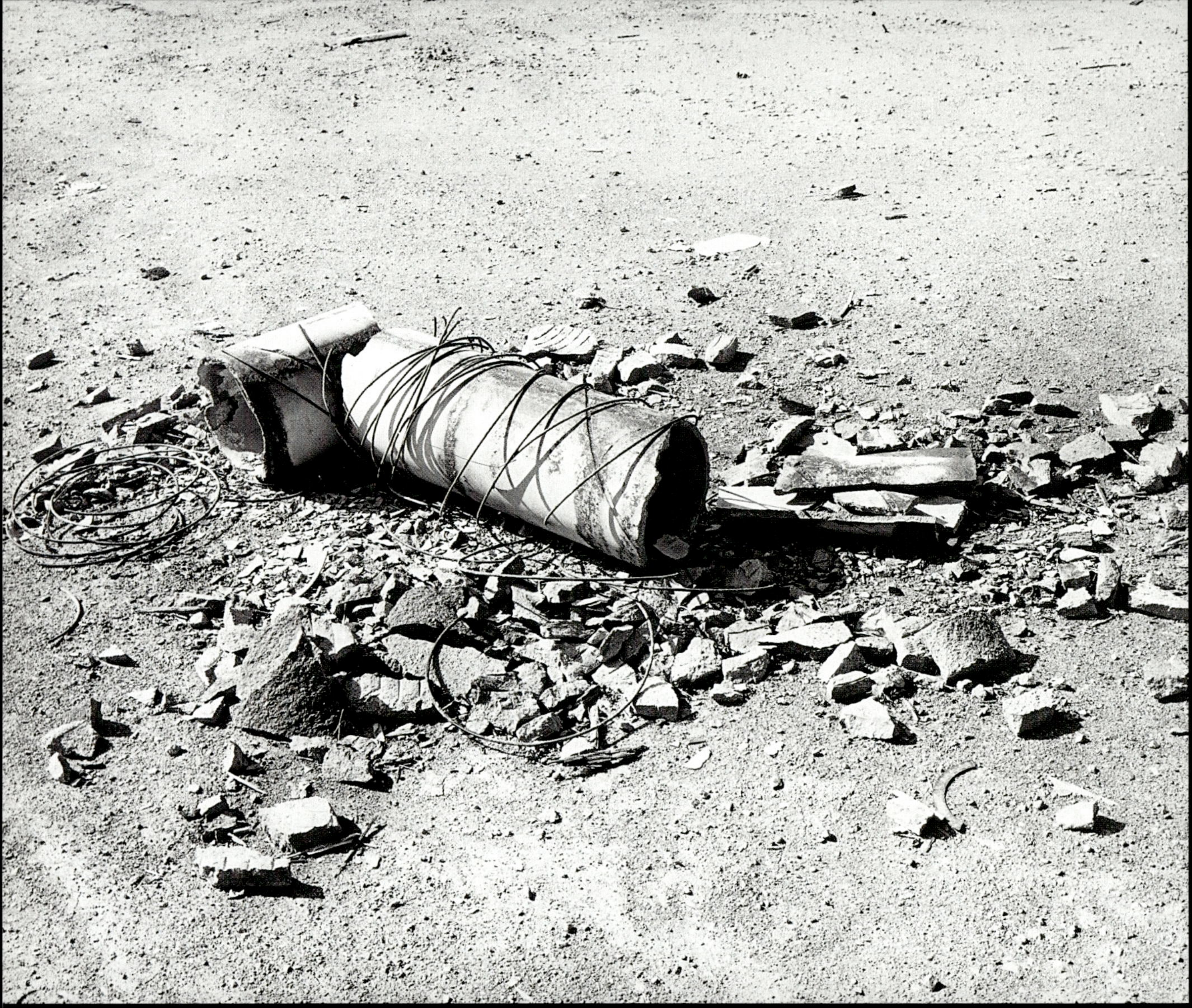

**Above** *San Quentin Point no. 41*, 1983.

**Opposite top** *Southwest Wall, Ware, Malcom & Garner* from *The New Industrial Parks Near Irvine, California*, 1974.

**Right** *National Centre for Meteorological Research, Grenoble*, from 'Sites of Technology', 1989–91.

**Opposite bottom** *Cray Supercomputer, CERN, Geneva*, from 'Sites of Technology', 1989–91.

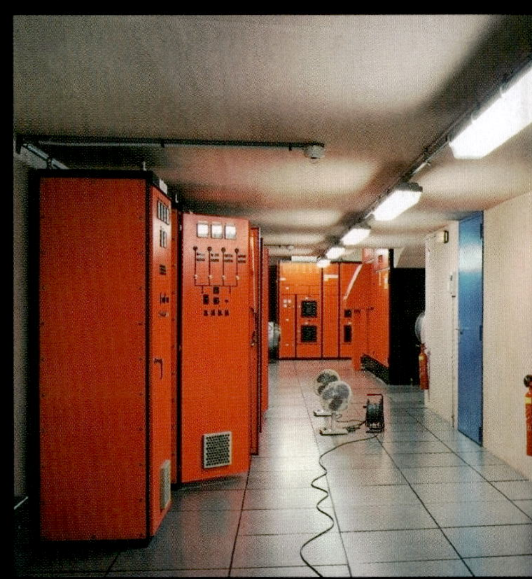

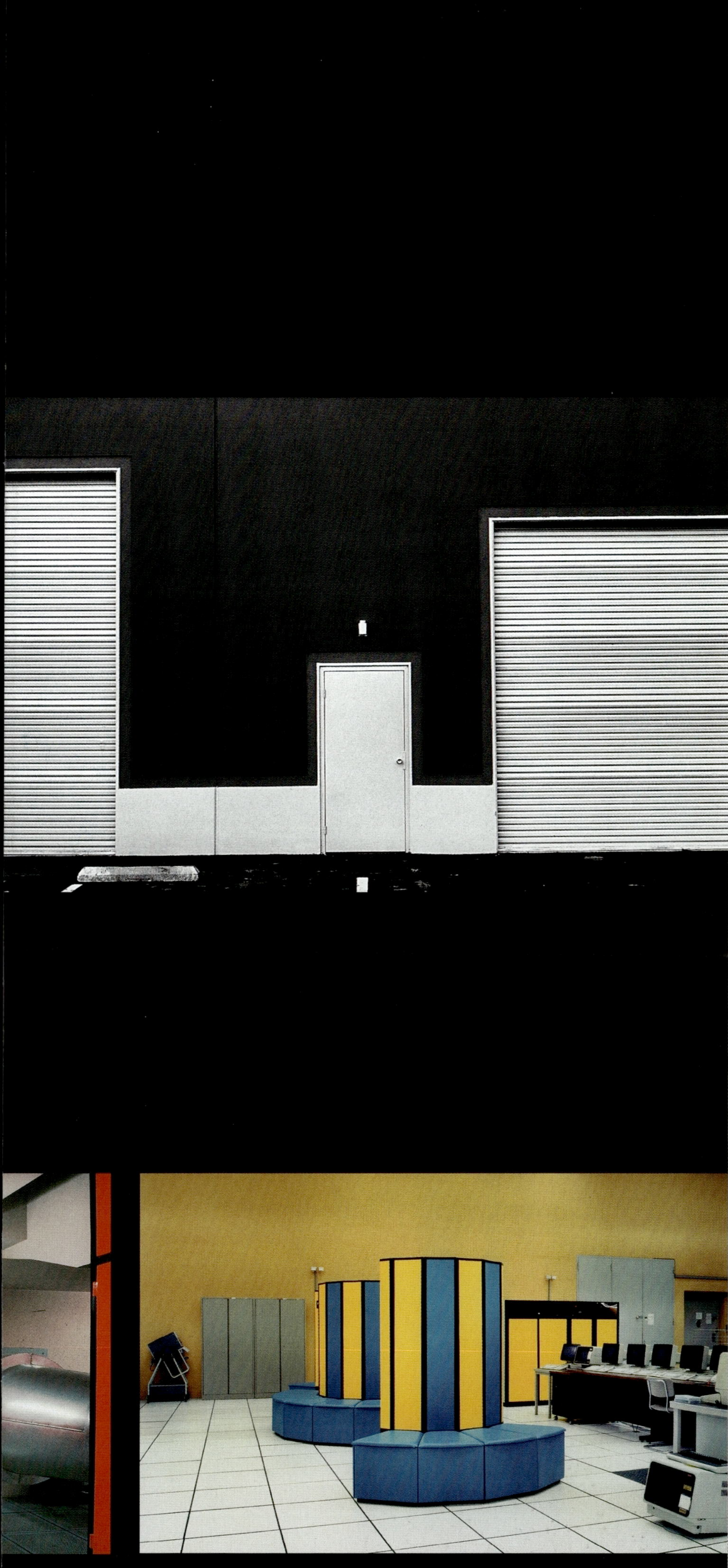

# Lewis Baltz

1940

**1945** Born in Newport Beach, California, USA

1950

**1956** Makes his first photograph

1960

**1967** Creates series now known as 'Prototypes' (to 1970)

1970

**1974** Publishes *New Industrial Parks near Irvine, California*

**1975** 'New Topographics' exhibition, George Eastman House, Rochester, New York

**1977** Publishes *Nevada*

1980

**1989** Publishes *Candlestick Point*
Starts to photograph the series 'Sites of Technology' (to 1991)

**1995** Moves to Europe

**1998** Publishes together the series 'Ronde de Nuit', 'The Politics of Bacteria' and 'Docile Bodies'

**2002** Begins professorship at the European Graduate School in Saas-Fee, Switzerland

2010

**2013** Exhibition titled 'Lewis Baltz' at the Albertina Museum, Vienna, Austria

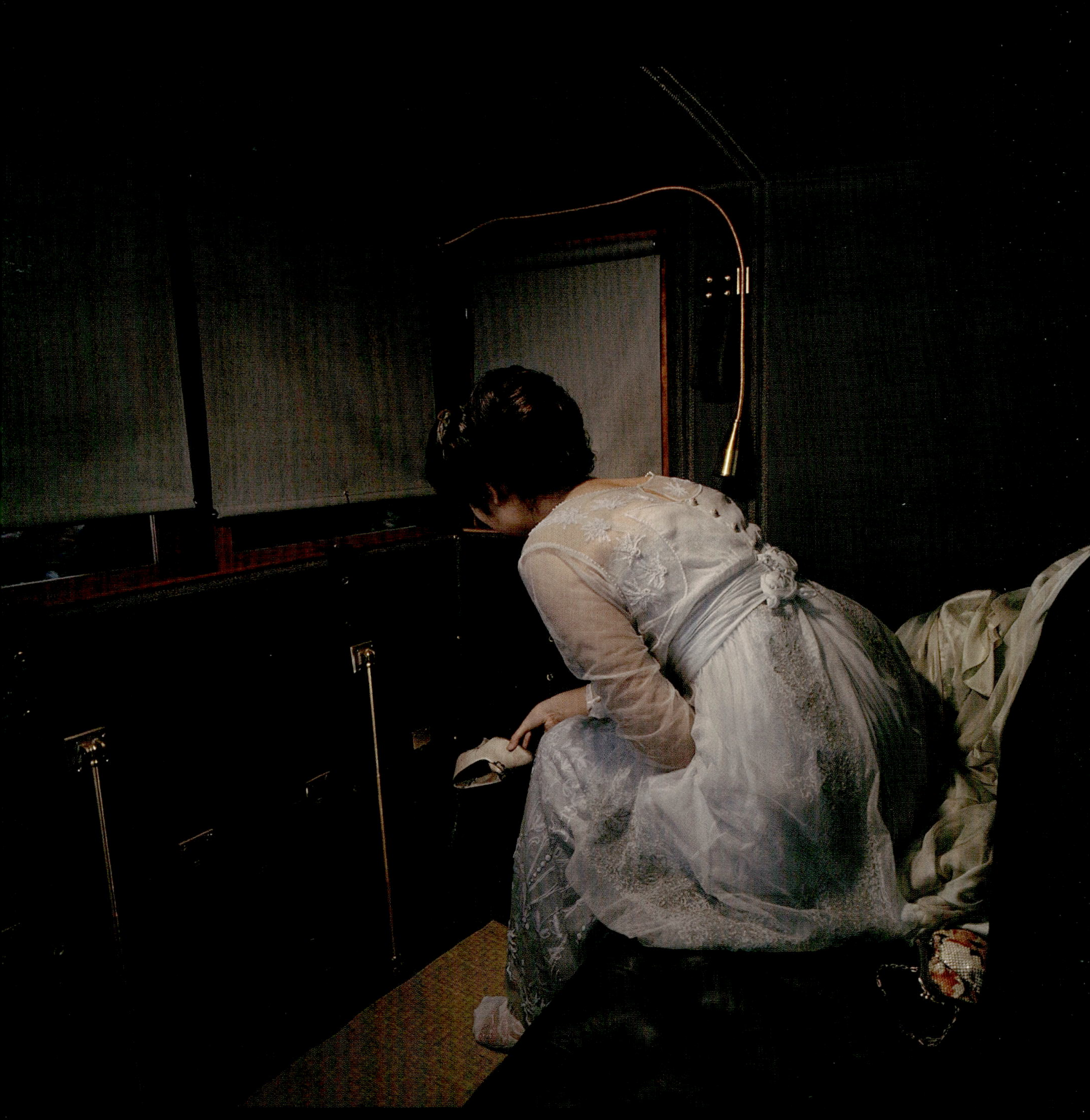

*After 'Spring Snow' by Yukio Mishima, chapter 34*, 2000–05.

'I'd like to be known as one of the good photographers, or good artists, or both.'

# Jeff Wall

b. 1946

CANADA

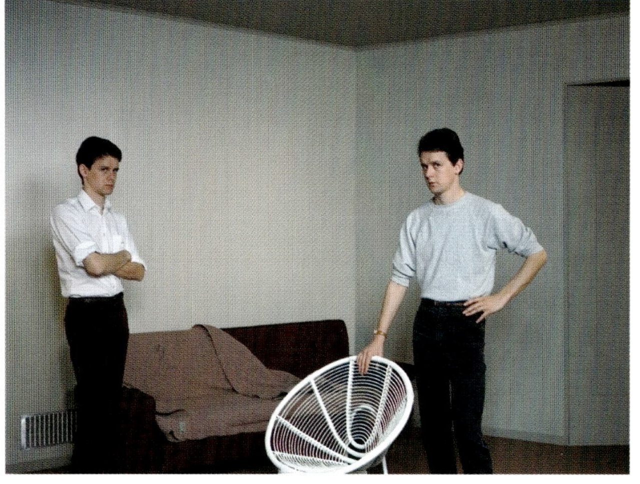

Throughout the twentieth century, as photographers gained confidence in the medium's abilities and stature, proud mantras like 'if you want to paint, pick up a brush' became more frequent. Jeff Wall, who was a committed exponent of conceptual art and Postmodern theory, came to the medium from another direction, principally through an extensive deliberation on how other media are valorized as high art. Almost as an intellectual puzzle, he seems to have deliberated on what qualities of photography seem to disqualify it from being rated as the equal to painting or sculpture. As he tells it – and one hopes the anecdote is as true as it is tasty – while travelling in Spain, after he saw masterworks by Velázquez and Goya at the Prado Museum, plus many backlit advertisements on bus stops, the two fused together in his mind: not in a camp way, but as a suggestion of how photography might be taken as seriously as the fine arts.

His first transparency, *The Destroyed Room*, is based on an analysis of Delacroix's painting *The Death of Sardanapalus*, yet it is not a copy of the work, nor a cynical send-up. It is an early example of what he would come to call 'emphatic picture making'. *The Destroyed Room* employs similar compositional elements, like the strong diagonal that bisects both works and the repoussoir devices that accentuate the feeling of recessive space. But in colours and historical references the works are unalike. One lives in the imagination of Western art and the other in the experience of a set-design of a trashed apartment, not a trashed apartment itself.

Much of Wall's subsequent work is built on occasional art-historical references, but it also references installation art and fabricated-to-be-photographed works that appeared in the late 1970s. Wall is the coordinator, or director, who designs and oversees the construction of a scene that may require actors, lighting experts and the other accoutrements of filmmaking. Indeed, he refers to his work as a kind of cinematic venture, but it is not limited to visual sources. He has built photographs from Japanese writer Yukio Mishima's novel *Spring Snow* (1969) and from Ralph Ellison's book *The Invisible Man* (1952), clearly acknowledging his sources, like painters in the nineteenth century whose images often derived from pivotal scenes in contemporary literature. Yet Wall is not dependent on sources outside of photography. He was an early adopter of digital editing, creating *Dead Troops Talk* in 1992. *In Front of a Nightclub* (2006) employed digital means to create a scene from picture pieces, confirming the capacity of photo-editing software to make contemporary fiction.

*Double Self-portrait*, 1979.

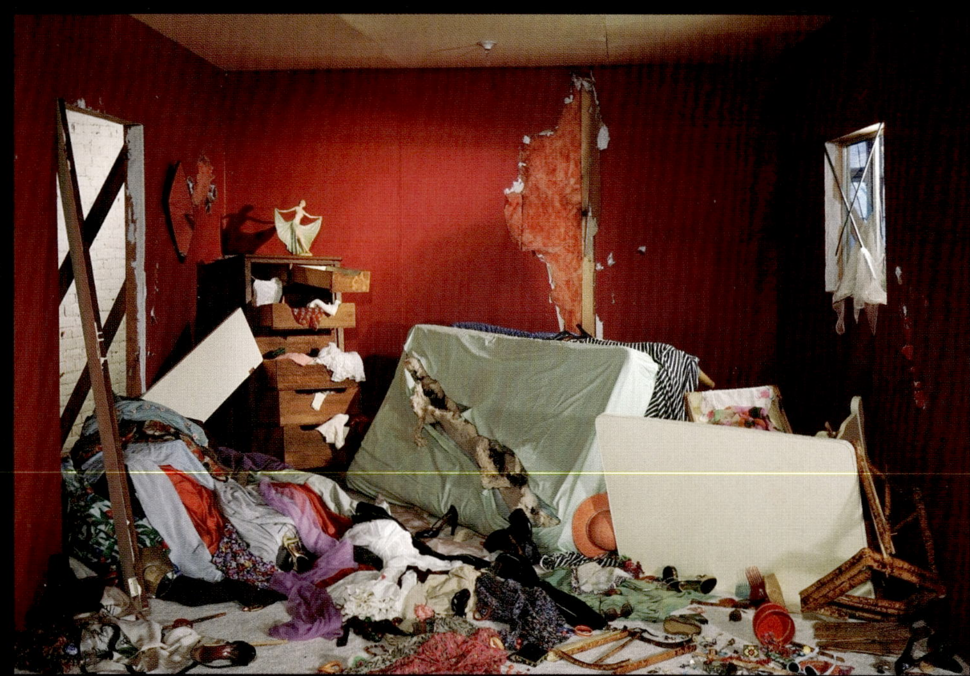

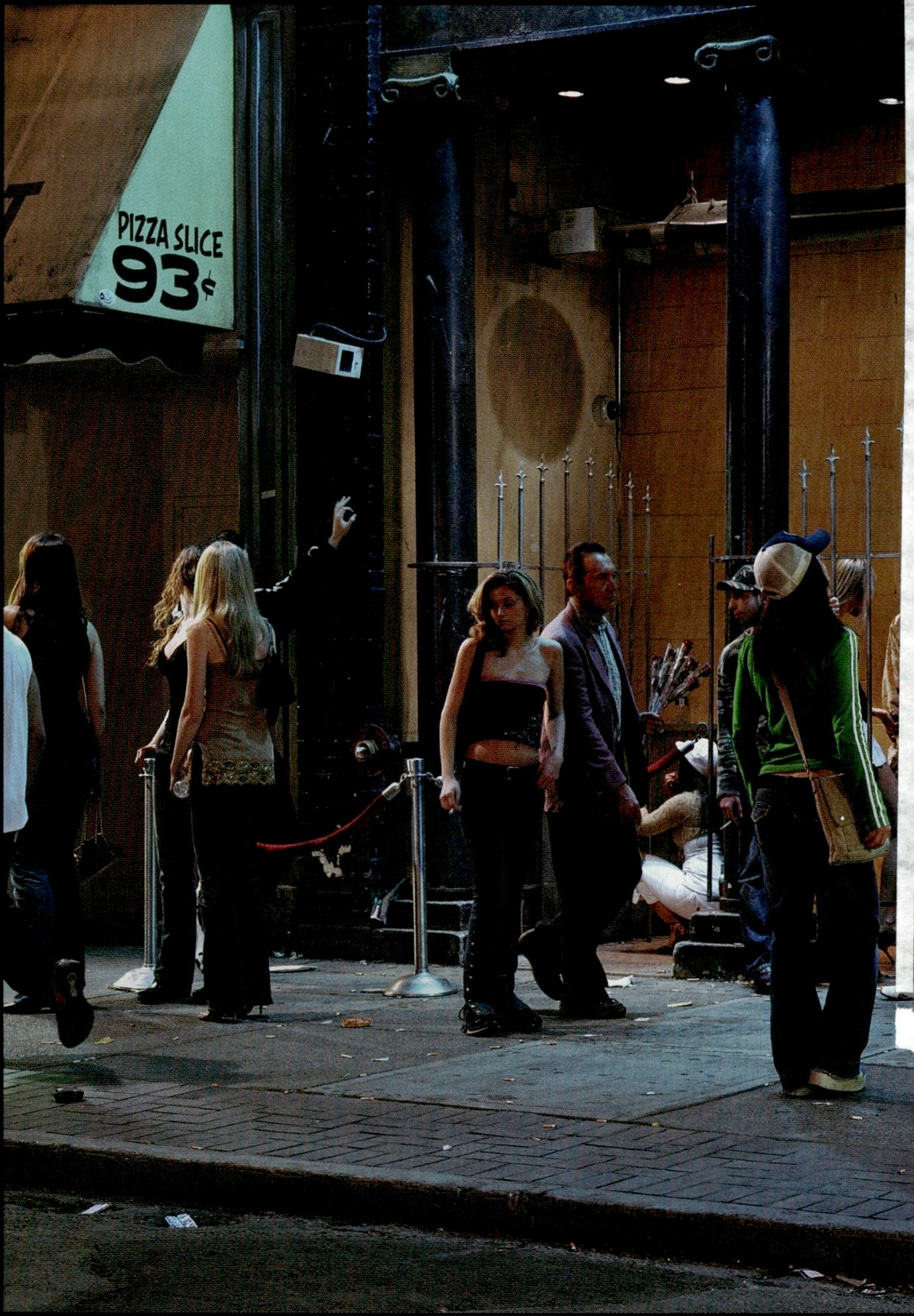

**Above** *The Destroyed Room*, 1978.

**Right** *In Front of a Nightclub*, 2006.

**Opposite** *'Invisible Man' by Ralph Ellison, the Prologue*, 1999–2001.

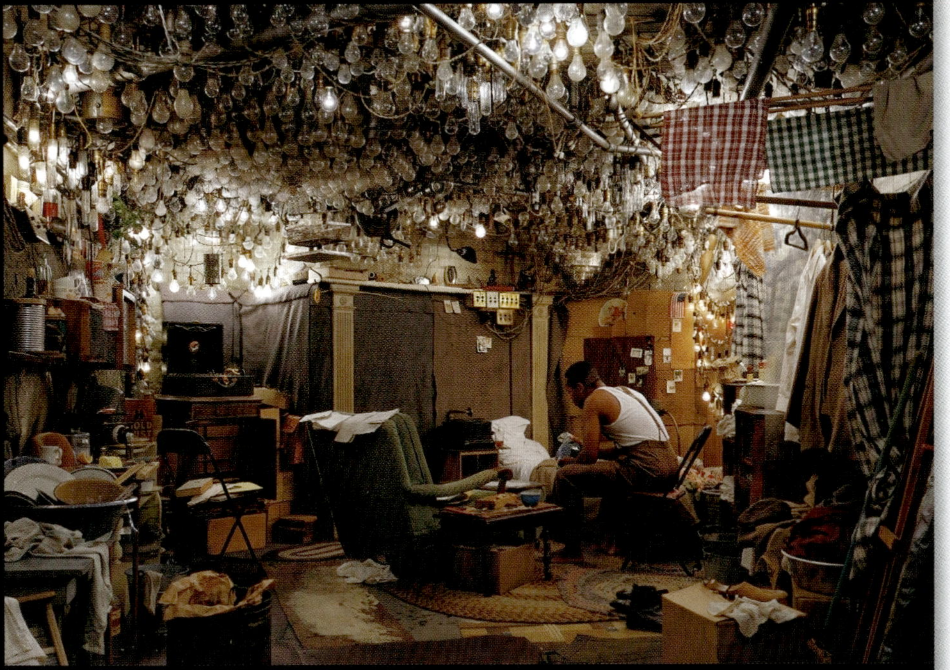

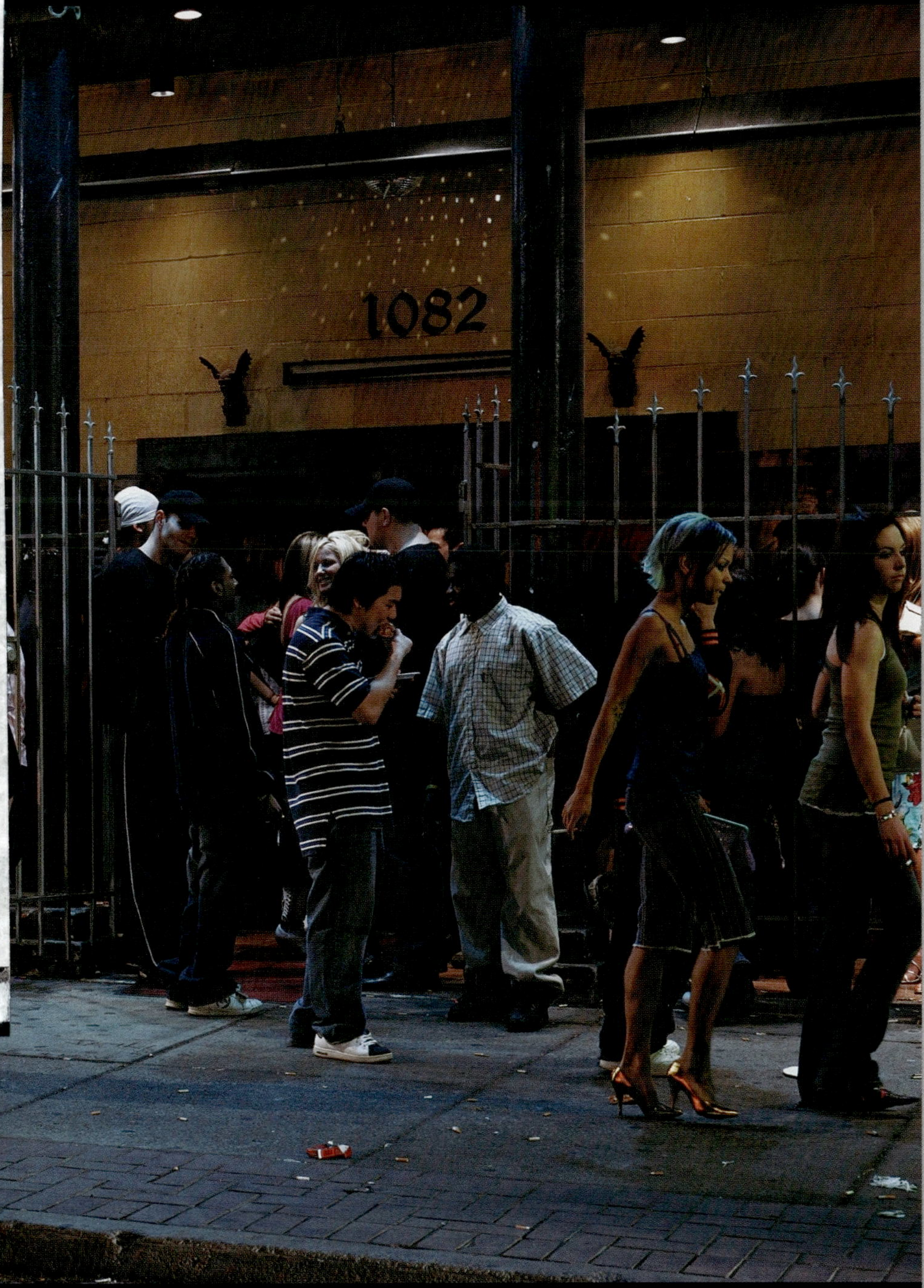

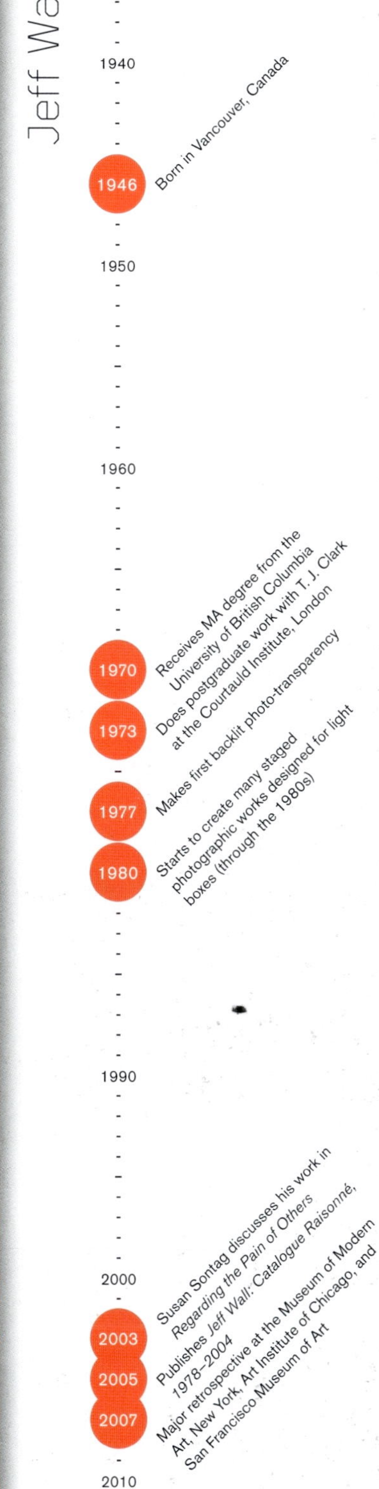

Jeff Wall
1940
1946 Born in Vancouver, Canada
1950
1960
1970 Receives MA degree from the University of British Columbia
1973 Does postgraduate work with T. J. Clark at the Courtauld Institute, London
1977 Makes first backlit photo-transparency
1980 Starts to create many staged photographic works designed for light boxes (through the 1980s)
1990
2000
2003 Susan Sontag discusses his work in *Regarding the Pain of Others*
2005 Publishes *Jeff Wall: Catalogue Raisonné, 1978–2004*
2007 Major retrospective at the Museum of Modern Art, New York, Art Institute of Chicago, and San Francisco Museum of Art
2010

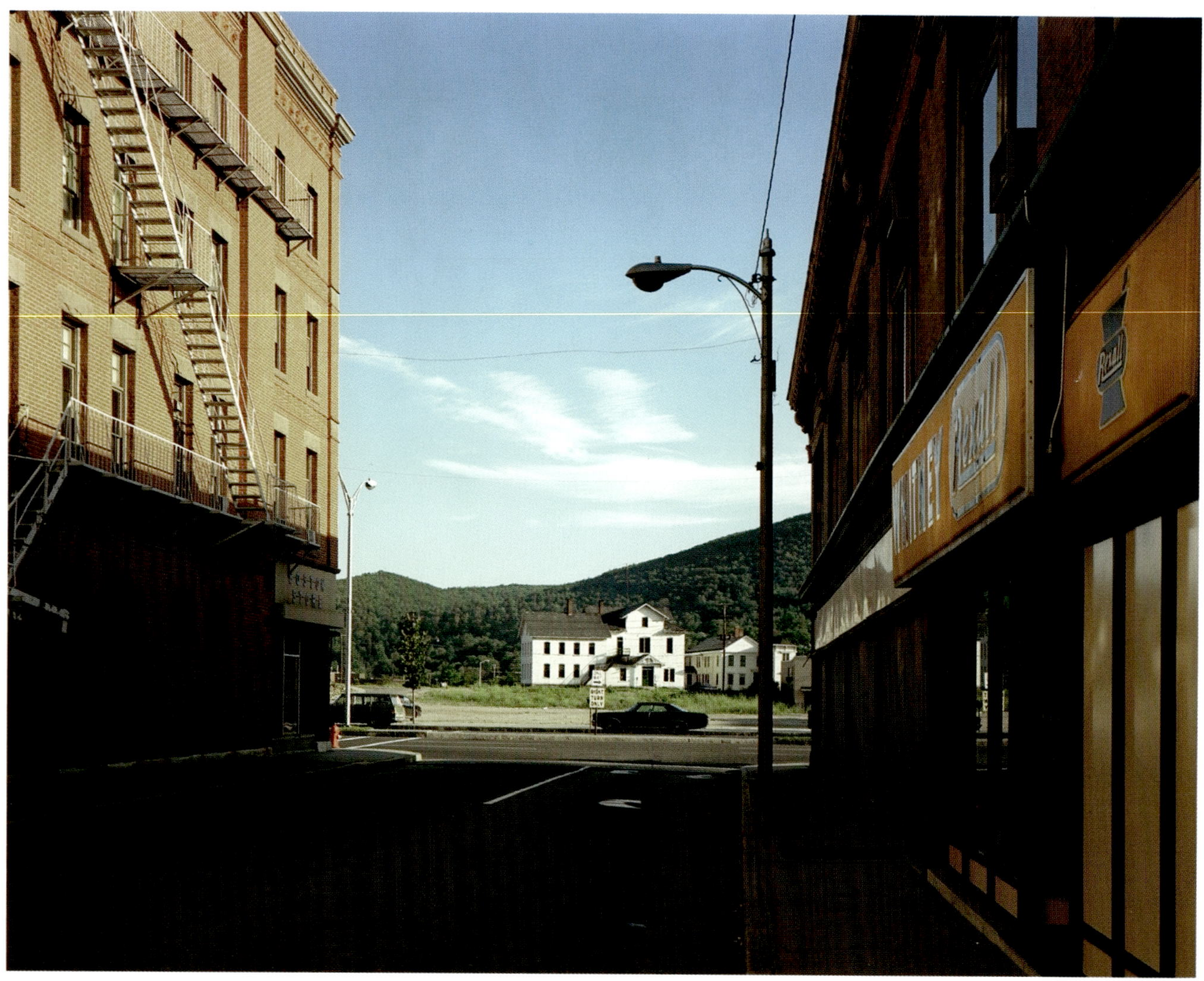


Holden Street, North Adams,
Massachusetts,1974.

'I was taking pictures that stripped away the artifice of visual convention. I wanted a more immediate experience.'

# Stephen Shore

b. 1947

UNITED STATES

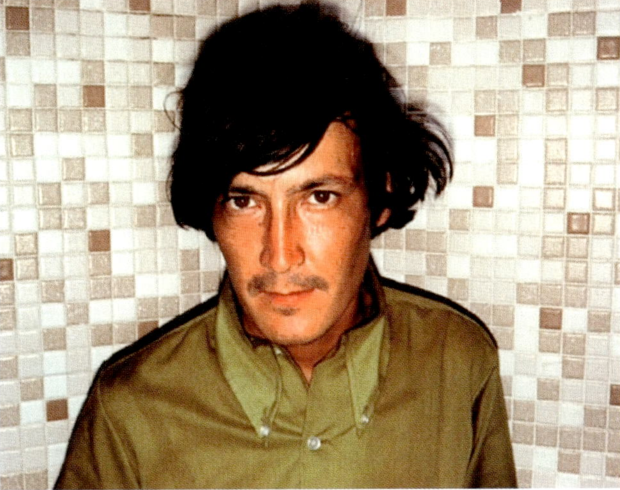

Maybe Stephen Shore acquired the patience to wait for a picture to suggest itself when he was a late teenager hanging out in Andy Warhol's studio, where the usual crowd loitered, hoping for something to happen. Shore has also suggested that fly fishing, of which he is a fan, might have something to do with his method: 'Fishing, like photography, is an art that calls for intelligence, concentration, and delicacy.'

Those qualities describe his work, which found expressions of colour in mundane American small cities and towns during his first road trip across the United States. Shore's pictures accept what poet Allen Ginsberg derisively called 'enoughness', a lack or curbing of ambition. Commonplace America with its ageing neon signs, discount grocery stores and patchy lawns is sufficient for Shore. Without irony or critique, he made pictures that are, in a curiously old-fashioned way, good to look at. Perhaps because he has stopped time in a setting with deep space, one can look with more leisure at ordinary scenes. Automobiles populate Shore's work. The variety of candy-coloured cars on streets and in parking lots in the past underscores the chromogenic monotony of contemporary vehicles.

Shore's work, along with that of nine other contemporaries, was exhibited in the 'New Topographics' exhibition of 1975, which recognized that a new sort of photography was being made by individuals who were not part of a group or movement. Subtitled 'Photographs of a Man-Altered Landscape', the exhibition outlined a trend in which sharp edge-to-edge clarity, combined with a physical and psychological detachment, challenged both the tradition of romantic landscape and the idea of socially engaged documentary. In retrospect, Shore's work, and that of the other New Topographics photographers, dovetailed with the arrival of conceptual art and its cerebral, impersonal, theory-driven, anti-commercial stance. This soft alliance of photography with the other arts was a crucial element in the acceptance of photography as a major cultural player and a field of academic study.

Self-portrait, 1972.

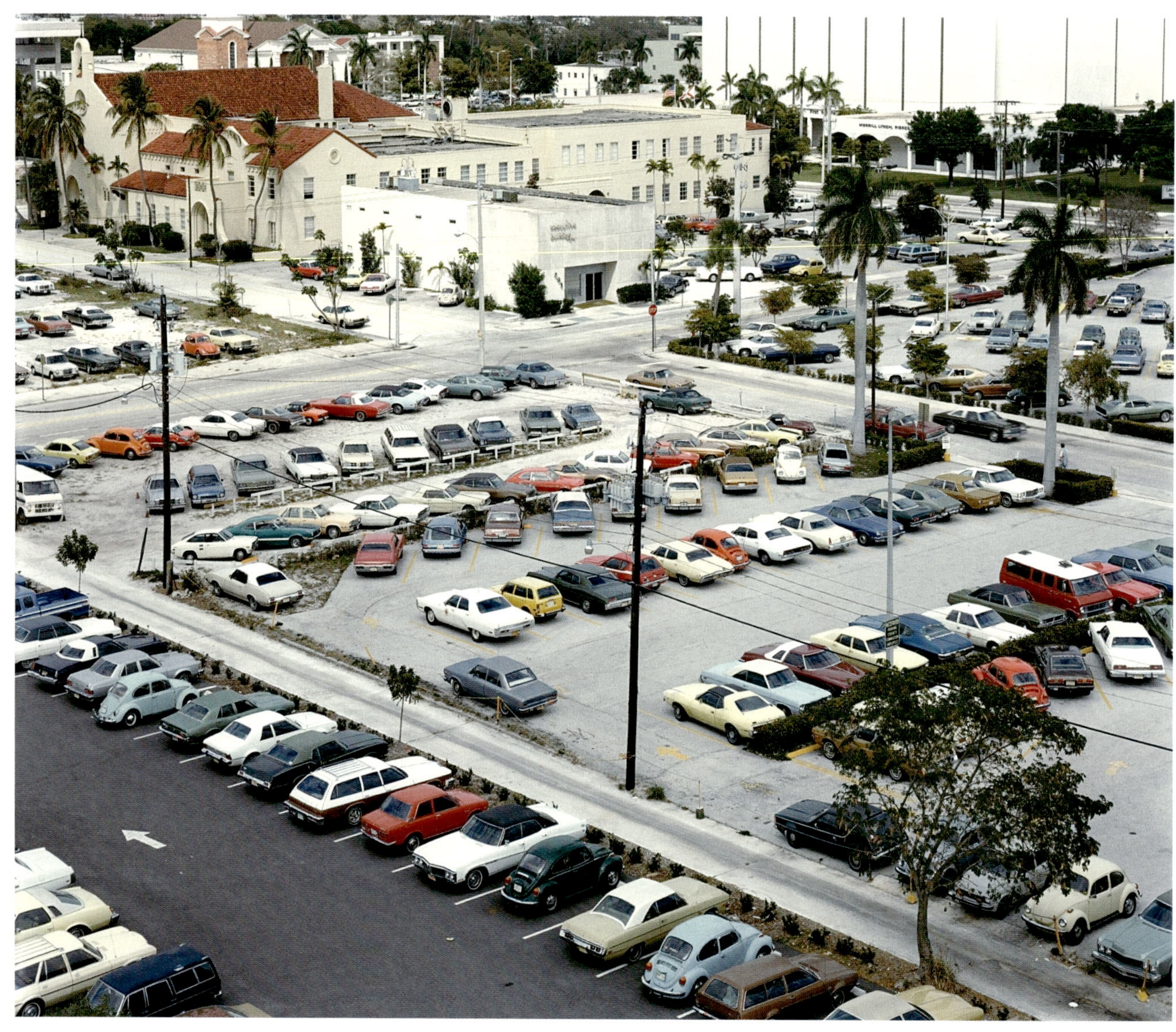

**Above** Fort Lauderdale, Florida, 1978.

**Opposite** Venice Boulevard, Los Angeles, California, 2006.

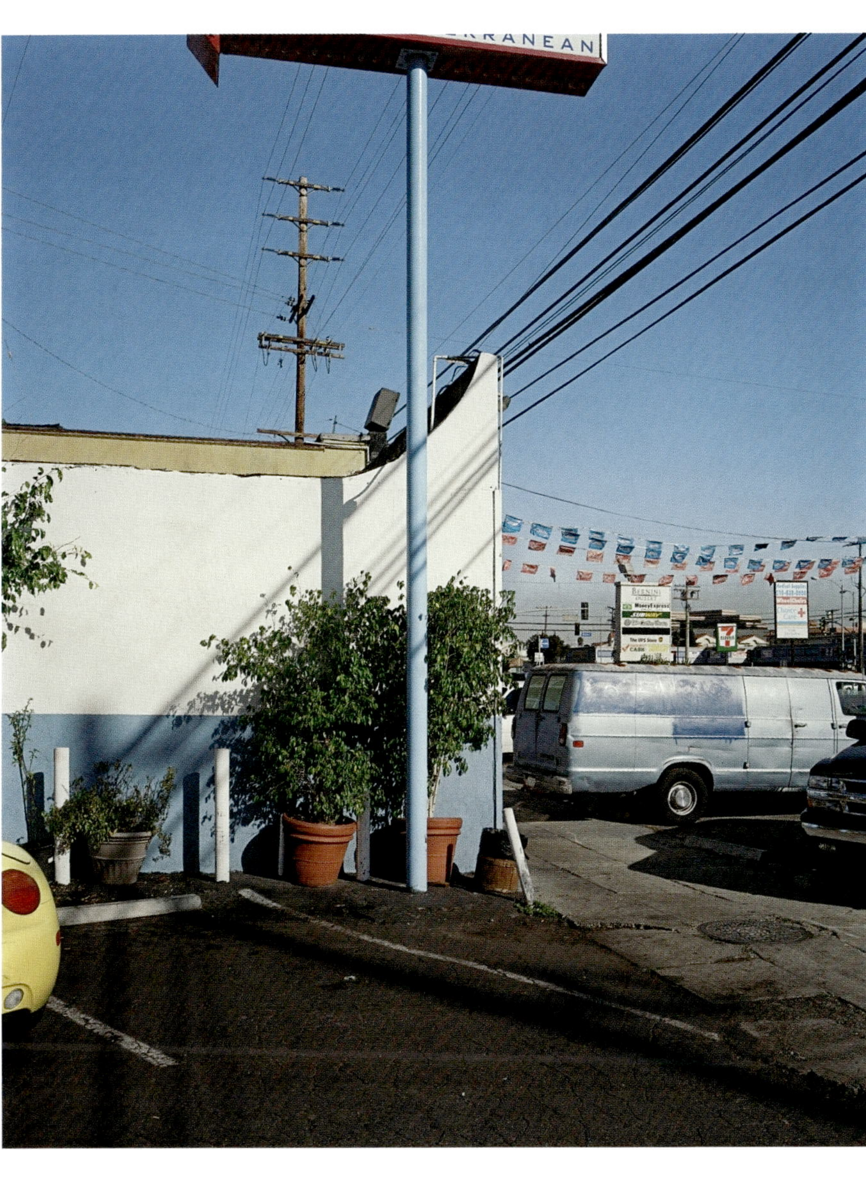

# Stephen Shore

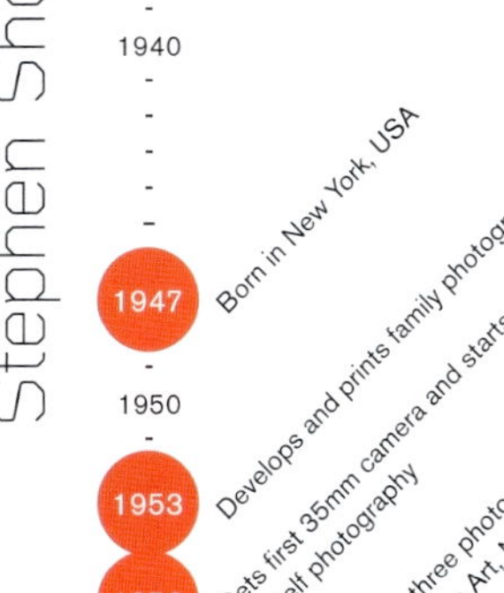

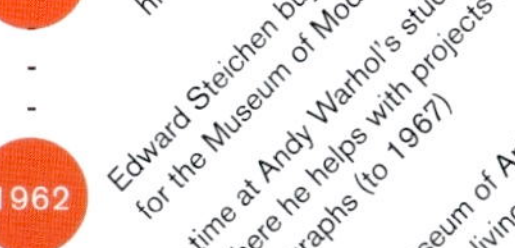

1940

**1947** Born in New York, USA

1950

**1953** Develops and prints family photographs

**1956** Gets first 35mm camera and starts to teach himself photography

**1962** Edward Steichen buys three photographs for the Museum of Modern Art, New York

**1965** Spends time at Andy Warhol's studio, The Factory, where he helps with projects and makes photographs (to 1967)

**1971** Exhibition at the Metropolitan Museum of Art, New York – only second show given to a living photographer. First road trip across the USA

**1975** 'New Topographics' exhibition, George Eastman House, Rochester, New York

**1982** Publishes *Uncommon Places*

1990

**1995** Publishes *The Velvet Years, Andy Warhol's Factory, 1965–1967*

**1999** Publishes *American Surfaces*

**2004** Publishes *Uncommon Places: The Complete Works*

**2006** Publishes *The Nature of Photographs*

2010

*To Catch a Lover*, from the 'The Mother Wit' 'Progeny', 2008.

To catch a lover, tape his picture behind your mirror.

'I put my own photography on the back burner because I decided to focus on finding and documenting.'

# Deborah Willis

b. 1948

UNITED STATES

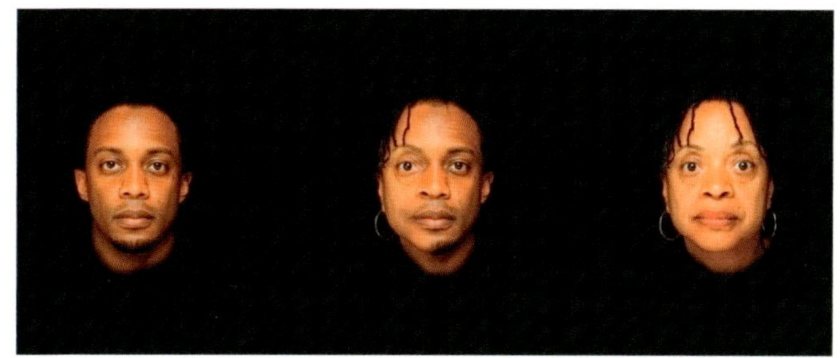

As the daughter of a serious amateur photographer, Deborah Willis became accustomed to being photographed. But the photographic process did not stop when the package of prints came back from the lab. She and her family reviewed, interpreted and arranged the pictures in albums that were frequently revisited. Of course, the remembrances and stories evoked by the photographs evolved over time.

As a young person, Willis learned enough photography to teach it to the neighbourhood kids, both in Philadelphia and later more formally at a youth centre in Brooklyn, New York. In her photography at the time, as well as in her teaching, she stressed the interrelationship of memory and images. During the years she worked with archival material and images at the Shomburg Center for Research in Black Culture in New York, she expanded her early experience of interpreting and revisiting family photos into a sophisticated understanding of photographs, particularly the vernacular and studio pictures that seldom reach the art gallery. She conceived a fluid network of reactions and interactions that emerged over time in the minds of individuals and in the collective experience of communities. In particular, she noticed how negative images commanded the public's visual imagination of black life, to the exclusion of photographs like those Roy DeCarava (p. 160) assembled in his photo-essay *The Sweet Flypaper of Life* (1955).

Putting her own photography aside for a time, she envisioned a historical compendium of photographs and interpretations stretching from 1840 to the present. Like an anthropologist, she focused on photography's role in individual, group and societal memories. The resulting exhibition and book, *Reflections in Black*, combined vernacular imagery, photojournalism and art: it became the first comprehensive history of African American photography. Lowery Sims, curator of New York's Museum of Art and Design, remarked: 'She is the person who has invented the art history of African-American photography almost singlehandedly.'

Her recent writing, such as *Posing Beauty*, employs this comprehensive analysis, allowing multiple and mingled notions and stories about beauty to emerge from a variety of image sources. In the past decade, Willis's own photography has also been varied and retrospective. For example, working with her son, the photographer Hank Willis Thomas, she created 'Progeny', a series on filial relationships. In the wake of the election of the first black American president, she edited photographic books on both Barack and Michelle Obama.

*Sometimes I See Myself in You*, from 'Progeny', 2008.

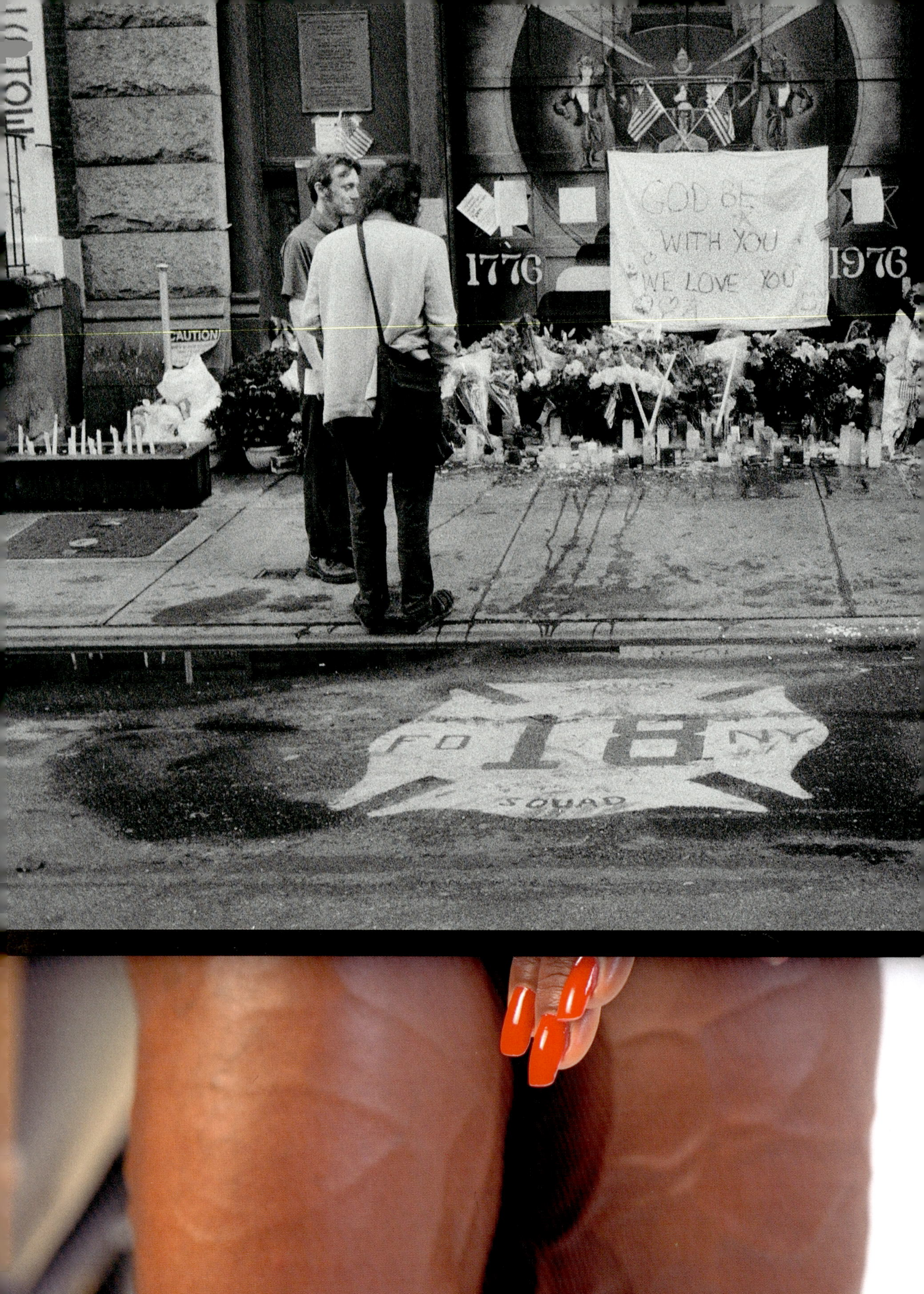
GOD BE
WITH YOU
WE LOVE YOU
1776
1976
CAUTION
FD 18 NY
SQUAD

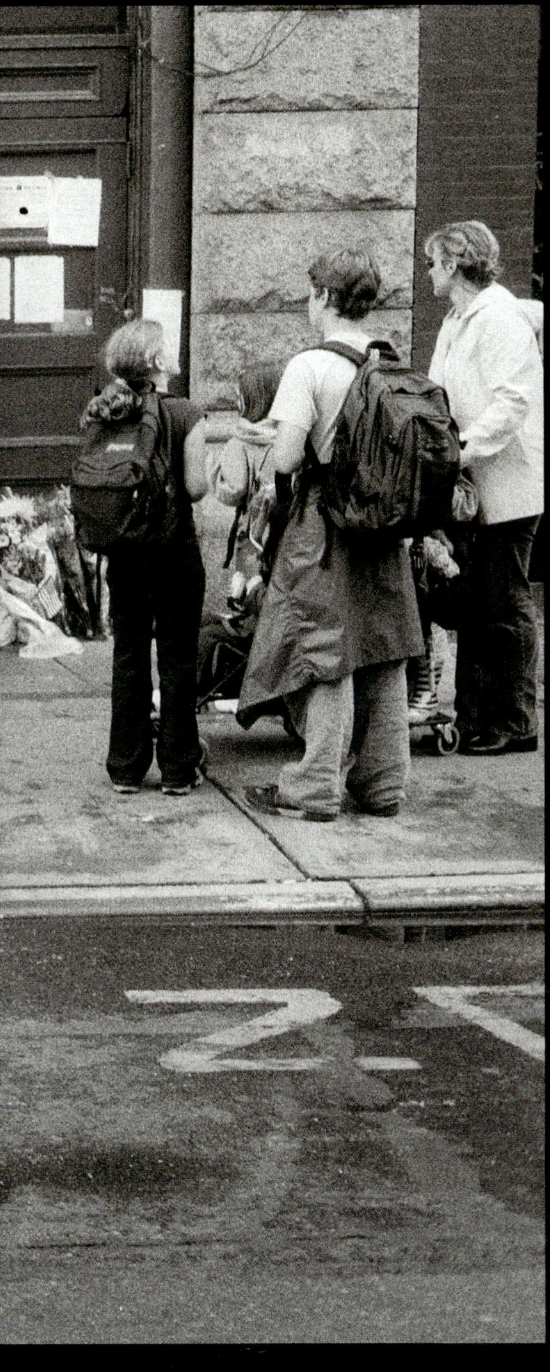

**Left** *Firehouse Memorial*, 2011.

**Opposite** From 'The Body Builder Series', 2001.

# Deborah Willis

1940

- **1948** Born in Philadelphia, Pennsylvania, USA

1950

1960

1970

- **1980** Curator of photography at the Shomburg Center for Research in Black Culture at the New York Public Library (to 1992)

1990

- **1992** Curator at the Anacostia Community Museum, Smithsonian Institution (to 2002)
- **1994** Publishes *Picturing Us: African American Identity in Photography*
- **2000** Publishes *Reflections in Black: A History of Black Photographers, 1840 to the Present*;
- **2002** Starts photographing for 'Embracing Eatonville' project
- **2008** Publishes *Obama: The Historic Campaign in Photographs* with Kevin Merida
- **2009** Publishes *Michelle Obama: The First Lady in Photographs* with Emily Bernard; publishes *Posing Beauty: African American Images from the 1890s to the Present*

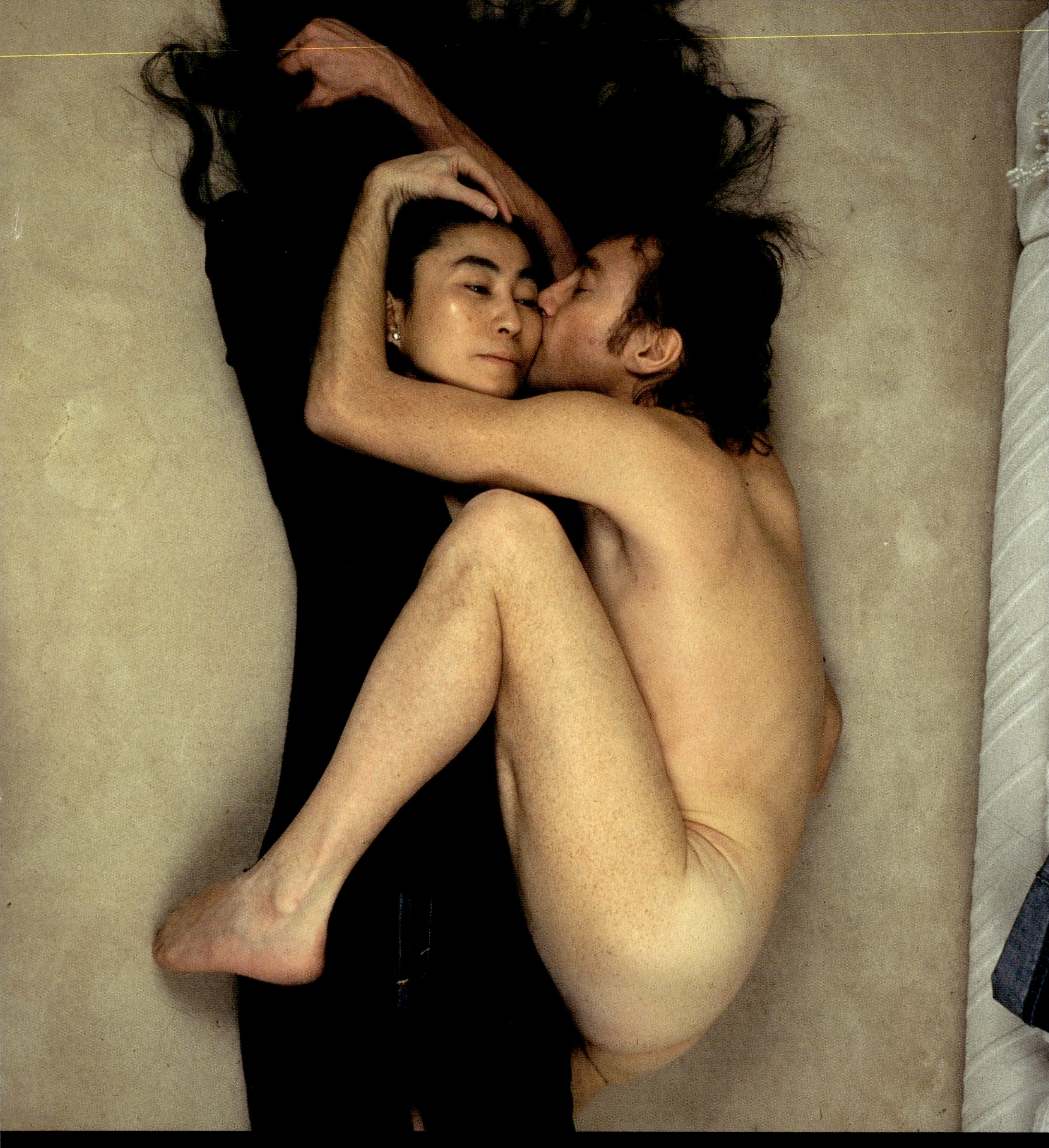

John Lennon and Yoko Ono, 1980.

'I'm more interested in being good than famous.'

# Annie Leibovitz

b. 1949

UNITED STATES

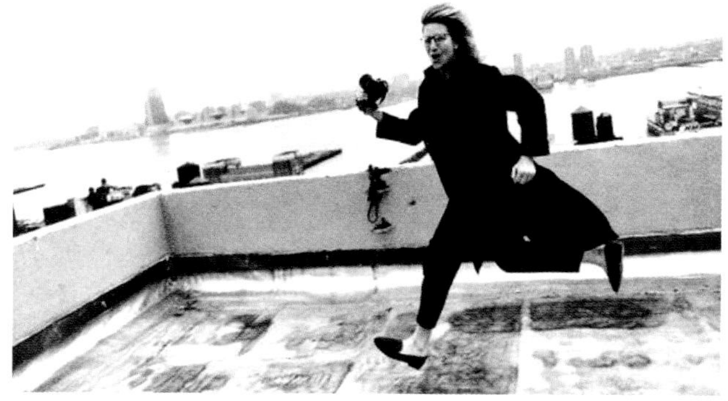

Some people think that Annie Leibovitz's celebrity portraits reveal the real person behind the publicist's hype and the stylist's brush. Other photographers, especially the paparazzi and people with cell phones in the right place at the right time, have made good money shooting stars at their boozy or weepy worst. But Leibovitz is not one of them, unless you think that Whoopi Goldberg regularly takes milk baths and Queen Latifah spends weekends surfing with her pet octopus.

Leibovitz not only plays on the notion that fame has its privileges, but also serves up expertly realized though seldom shocking fantasies from celebrity ingredients, like her photograph of actors from the television series *The Sopranos*. Models, actors, performers, politicians and others who regularly enact a public identity seem to respond to Leibovitz as a director. She has often said that many of her subjects open up to her unbidden. At the same time, Leibovitz has a keen sense of the serendipitous picture moment, when theme and composition and the subject's wishes come together. Her picture of Sting was taken when they were travelling in the desert and it was very hot. He wanted to take off his clothes.

Yet no photographer can completely control the public meaning of a photograph. Leibovitz's most famous image, that of John Lennon and Yoko Ono, in which he presses against her in a foetal position while she glances past him, has been reinterpreted by the public, in part because it was the last photograph taken of him before his death five hours later. When the image appeared on the cover of *Rolling Stone*, the right edge had been cropped away, leaving the couple to seem to float alone in space. But in her original picture, Leibovitz left in the details on the right side: the edge of a couch and the cuff of Lennon's recently shed jeans, which anchor the image in a particular moment.

Self-portrait, c. 1985.

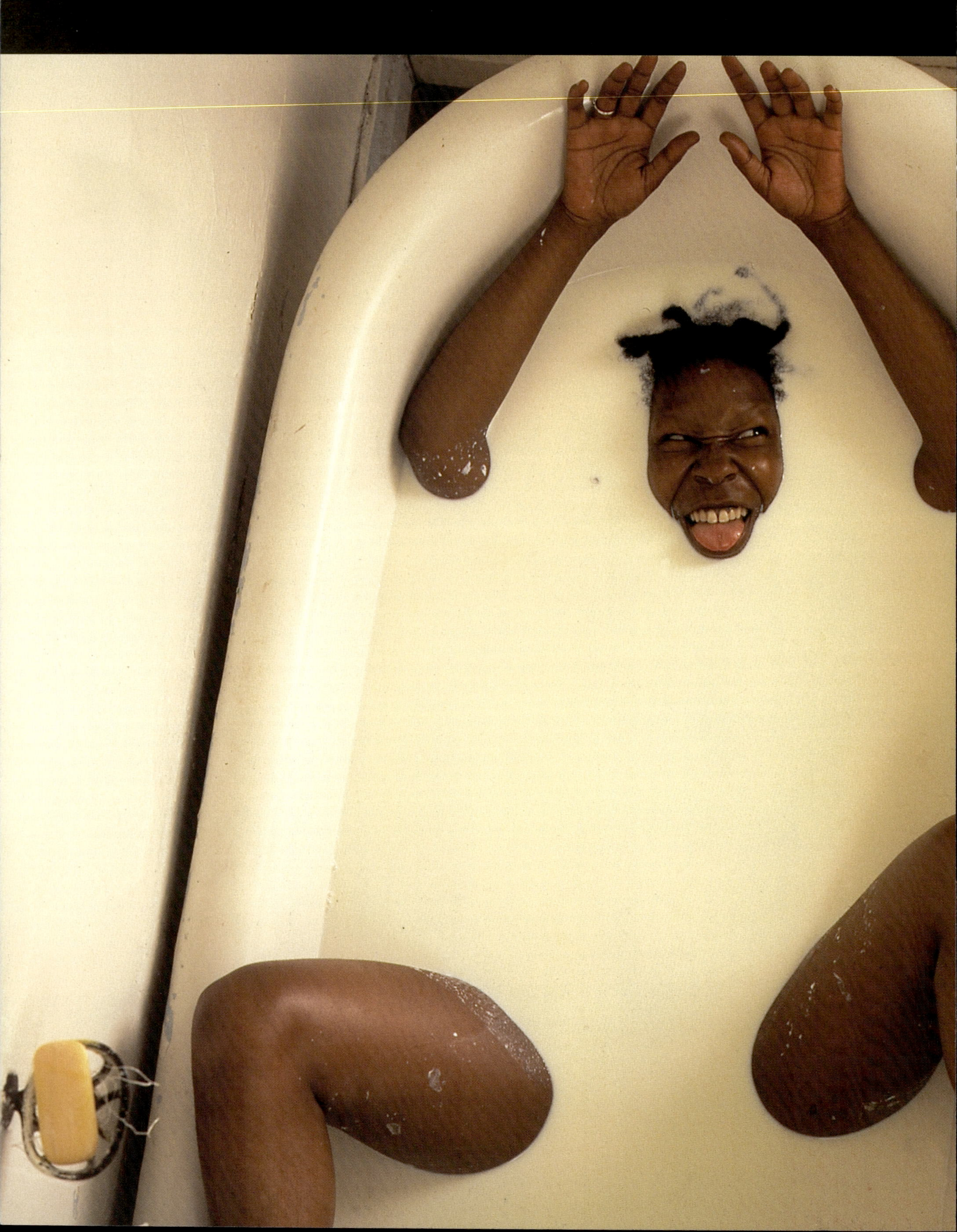

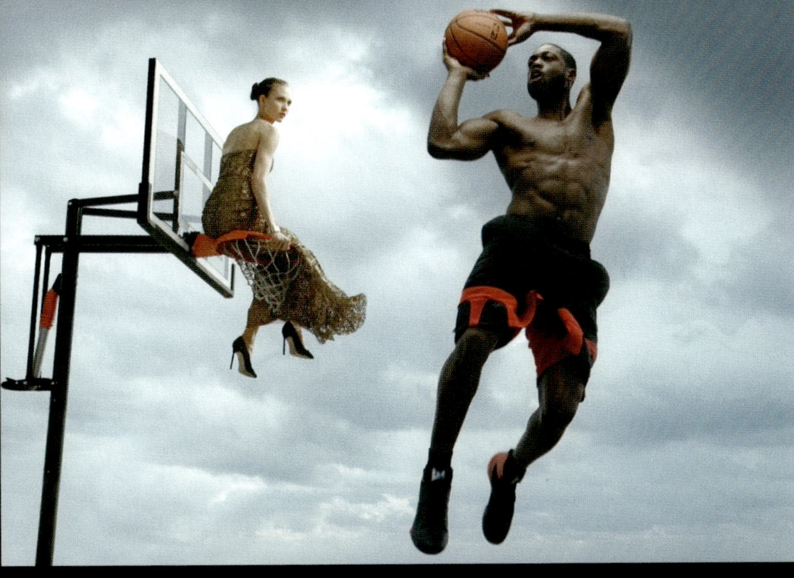

**Left** Whoopi Goldberg in a milk bath, 1984.

**Above** Dwyane Wade and Karlie Kloss for *Vogue*, 2012.

## Annie Leibovitz

1940

**1949** Born in Waterbury, Connecticut, USA

1960

**1970** Gets her first assignment with *Rolling Stone* and photographs John Lennon

**1973** Becomes the magazine's 'chief photographer'

**1975** Becomes official photographer for the Rolling Stones band

1980

**1983** Leaves *Rolling Stone* for *Vogue*

**1988** She and Susan Sontag become a couple

1990

**1994** 'Annie Leibovitz 1970–1990' exhibition at the National Portrait Gallery, Washington, DC

**1999** Exhibition titled 'Women' at the Corcoran Gallery of Art in Washington, DC

**2006** Retrospective at the Brooklyn Museum, New York

**2007** Photographs Queen Elizabeth II; Public Broadcasting System (PBS) programme on Leibovitz is broadcast

2010

**2013** Photographs Michelle Obama for the cover of *Vogue*

Sergeant F de Bruin, Department of Prisons Employee, Orange Free State, 1992.

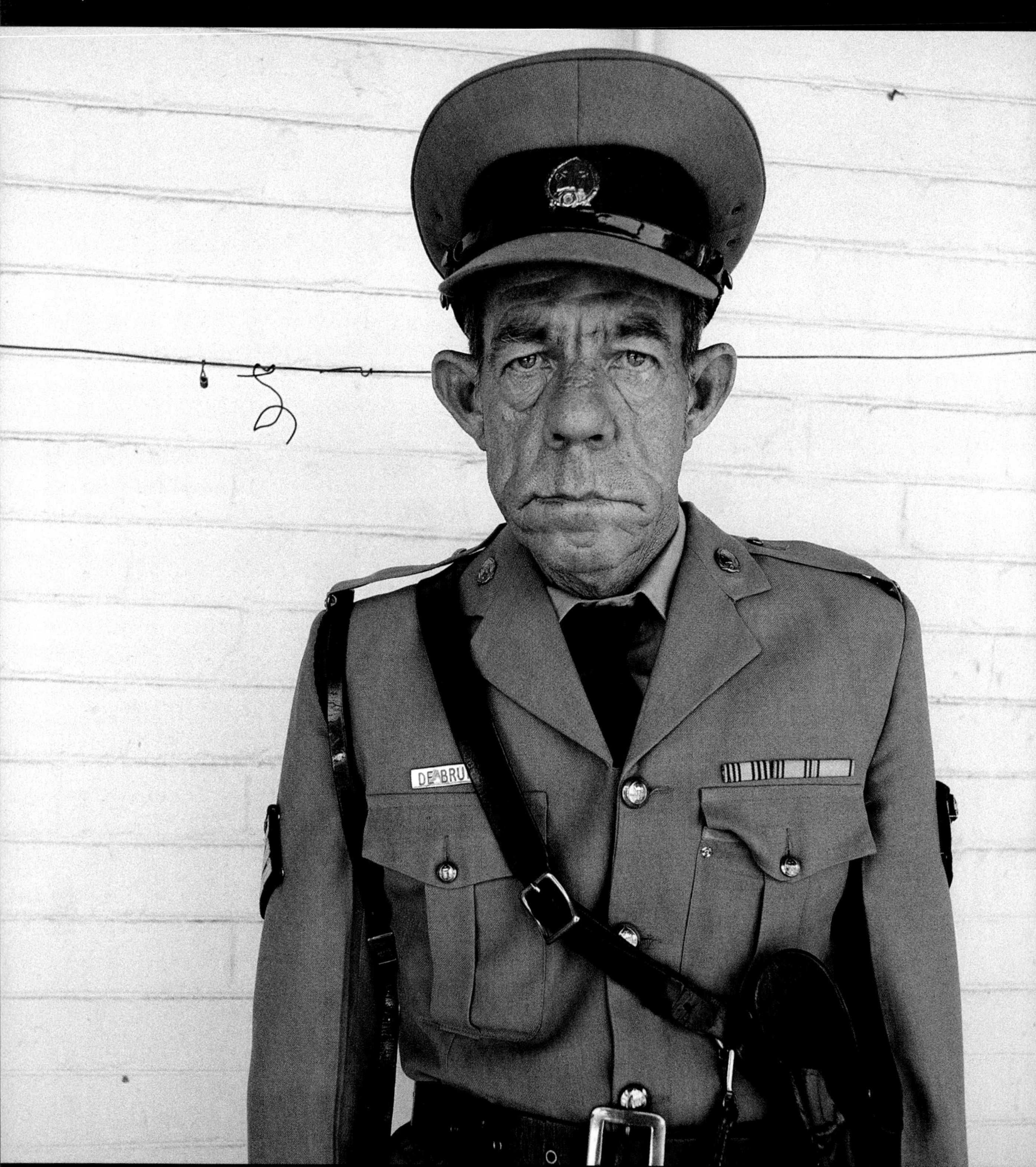

'I have eaten contemporary photography alive for the last fifty years.'

# Roger Ballen

b. 1950

UNITED STATES

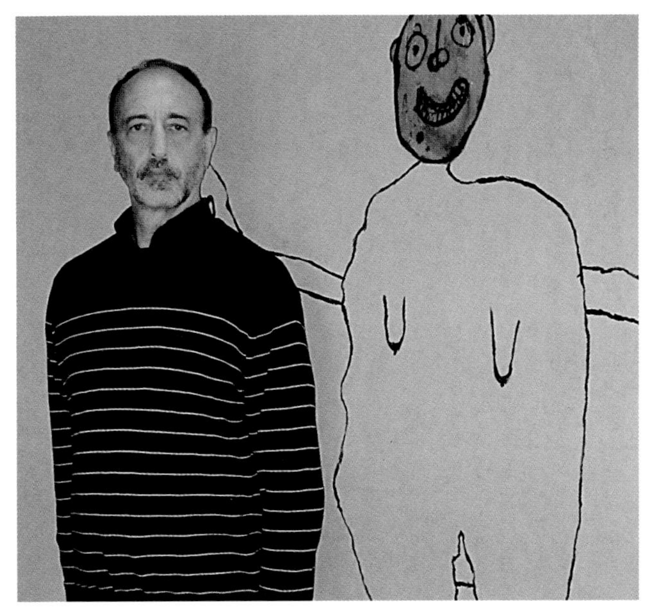

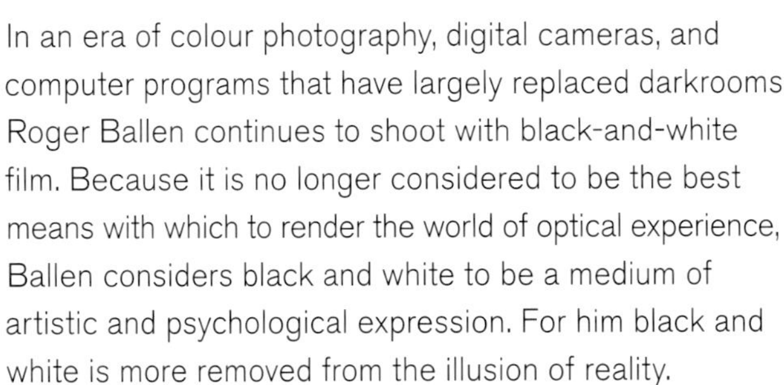

In an era of colour photography, digital cameras, and computer programs that have largely replaced darkrooms, Roger Ballen continues to shoot with black-and-white film. Because it is no longer considered to be the best means with which to render the world of optical experience, Ballen considers black and white to be a medium of artistic and psychological expression. For him black and white is more removed from the illusion of reality.

His early photographs dwelled on South Africans who live in areas relatively removed from modern life, like the remote small villages called 'dorps', and the rural areas known as the 'platteland'. Prime exteriors of historic churches and hotels give way to homes where wallpaper is crumbling and years of being down-at-heel have affected the human psyche. Ironically, these areas are composed mostly of Caucasians, who were once privileged psychologically and financially by apartheid. Now solitude and economic privation have taken their toll.

Over time, Ballen became a co-director with his subjects, allowing them to pose as they preferred. At the same time, he came to build more and more sets in which they might enact their presentations of self. These changes pushed what might earlier have been seen as investigative documentary into an exploration of psychic states meant to affect the viewer. In the late 1990s, wire of all kinds invaded Ballen's pictures. Antenna lines, electrical cords, twisted cable, baling wire, woven fence, coat hangers, and snippets of anonymous strands confound scenes, as do domestic and farm animals who appear increasingly. In a few instances the wire is menacing. But mostly it is there as an incongruous element, a sign that something is not right – or real. Similarly, sometimes walls are plain, and sometimes they exhibit primitive runic figures.

In the series called 'Asylum of the Birds', these background elements come to the foreground. The square format he used in his early work has become a shallow theatre. 'Asylum of the Birds' seems like an end point to the interpretive documentary Ballen began in the 1980s. The realism implied by spatial depth in the earlier work has receded to a more claustrophobic nearness, and people, when they appear, are merged with inscrutable signs and symbols, often roughly drawn on the walls.

Unlike earlier forays into photographic surrealism in the twentieth century, such as those by Man Ray (p. 48) and Manuel Álvarez Bravo (p. 108), Ballen's pictures are not technically experimental or erotic. Instead he is a master of disorder and dirt. From his earliest pictures to the most recent ones, stains infect surfaces, mildew climbs walls and artificial light accentuates soiled people and things. The indoor presence of animals like pigs, chickens and goats not only adds to the grime, it evokes physical and spiritual decay. But Ballen cautions: 'My purpose in taking photographs over the past forty years has ultimately been about defining myself. It has been fundamentally a psychological and existential journey.'

Portrait of Roger Ballen by Marguerite Roussow, 2013.

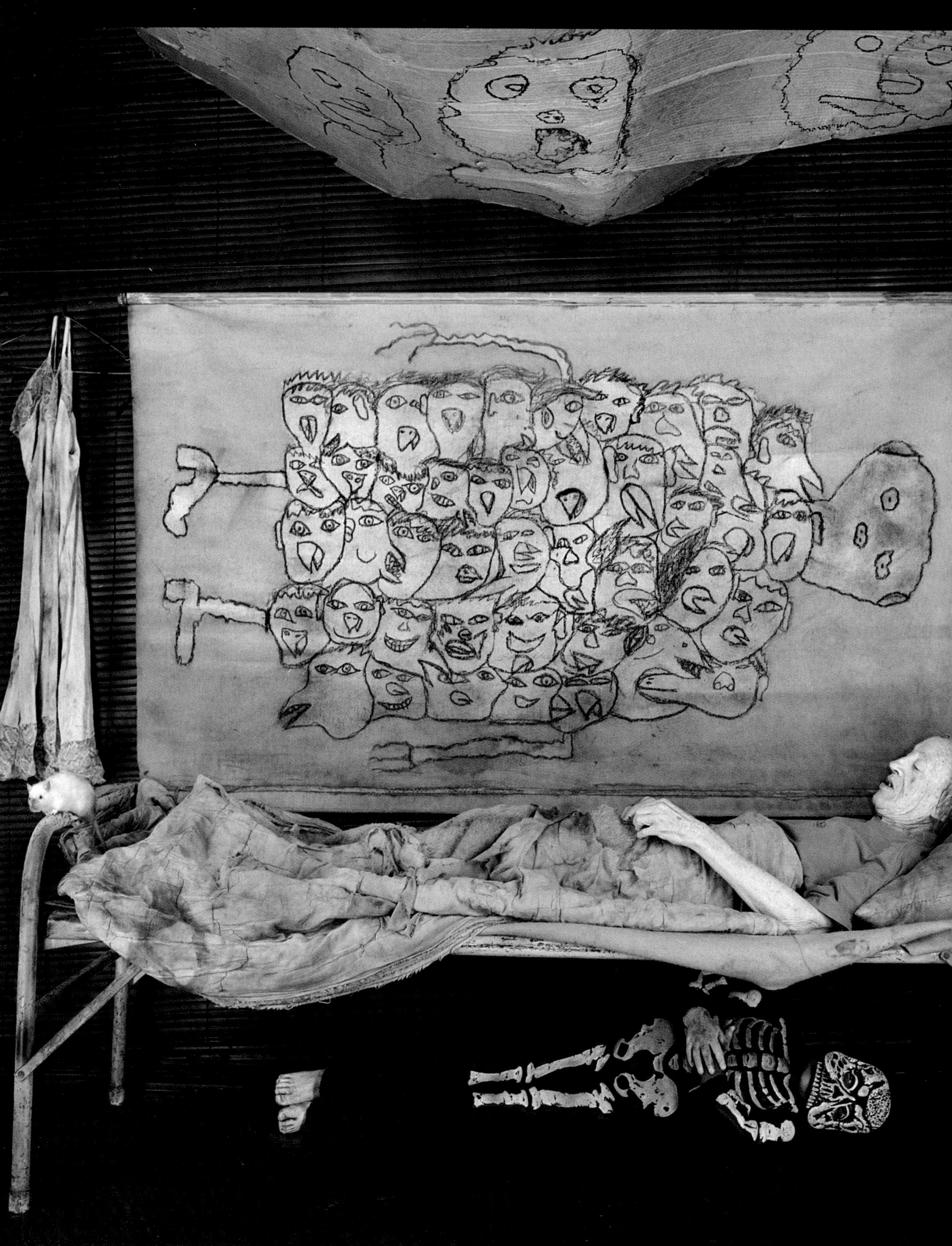

## Roger Ballen

1940

**1950** Born New York City, USA

1960

**1963** Buys first camera

**1968** Develops style of photographing individuals in crowds at Civil Rights and anti-Vietnam gatherings

1970

**1973** Travels extensively in Europe, Africa and Asia (to 1975)

**1982** Receives PhD. from the Colorado School of Mines; moves to South Africa

**1986** Publishes *Dorps: Small Towns of South Africa*

1990

**1994** Publishes *Platteland*

**2001** Publishes *Outlands*

**2002** Photographer of the Year, Rencontres d'Arles, France

**2008** Publishes *Boarding House*

2010

**2014** Publishes *Asylum of the Birds*

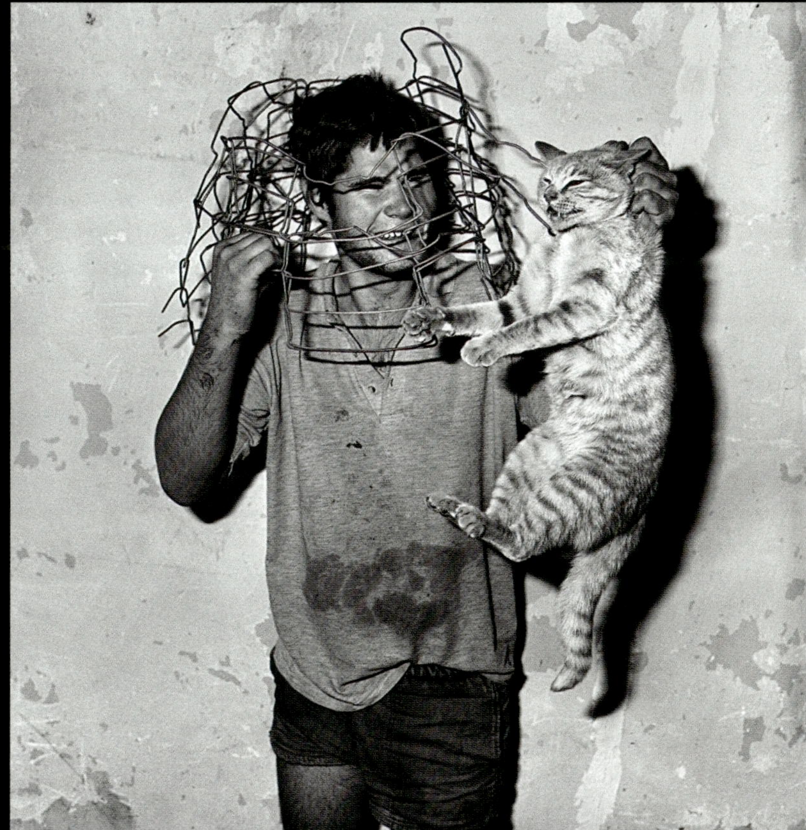

**Opposite** *Memento Mori*, 2005.

**Top** *Prowling*, 2001.

**Above** *Cat Catcher*, 1998.

From 'Eatonville', 2003.

Square toed and flat-footed
you appeared as my guardian angel
leading me along
the dust tracks in the road &
back to the meaning of myself

'Storytelling is fundamental to my work.'

# Carrie Mae Weems

b. 1953

UNITED STATES

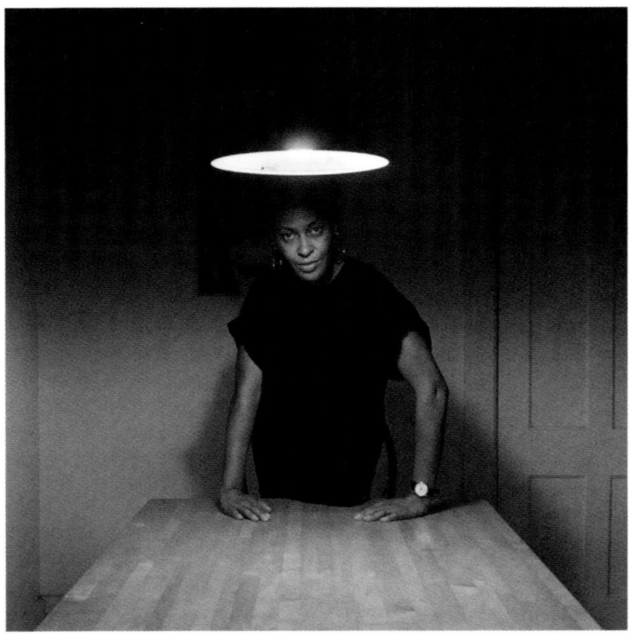

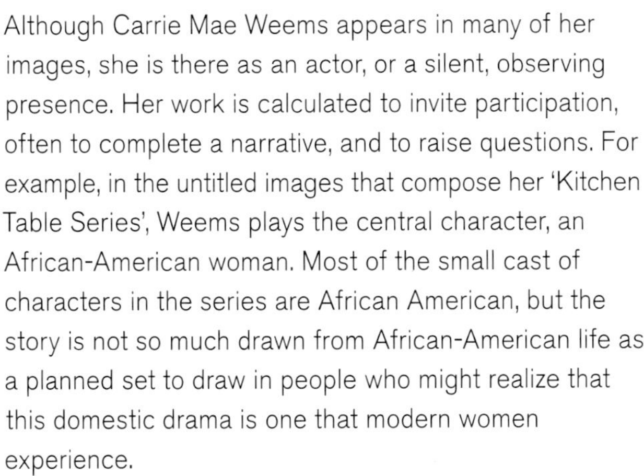

Although Carrie Mae Weems appears in many of her images, she is there as an actor, or a silent, observing presence. Her work is calculated to invite participation, often to complete a narrative, and to raise questions. For example, in the untitled images that compose her 'Kitchen Table Series', Weems plays the central character, an African-American woman. Most of the small cast of characters in the series are African American, but the story is not so much drawn from African-American life as a planned set to draw in people who might realize that this domestic drama is one that modern women experience.

In other work, Weems interpreted the experience of African-American history. 'From Here I Saw What Happened and I Cried', conjoins historical photographs, including some bits of racial pseudo-science, with Weems's comments etched into the glass plate covering the image. She took a similar approach using photographs taken by Frances Benjamin Johnston (p. 16) at Hampton Institute. Presenting them as images printed on long panels of semi-transparent muslin (calico), Weems could not only arrange multiple contrasts and comparisons, but also give them physicality by requiring visitors to walk among the panels.

When she was a graduate student, Weems discovered *Their Eyes Were Watching God* (1937), Zora Neale Hurston's brilliant integration of folklore, local dialect and African-American life, set in Eatonville, Florida, where Hurston spent some of her childhood. Hurston's inventiveness encouraged Weems to explore intersections of folklore and image-making. In 2003 she joined other photographers, including Deborah Willis (p. 272), in creating a photographic interpretation of Eatonville, a town founded by African Americans.

Self-portrait, from 'Kitchen Table Series', 1990.

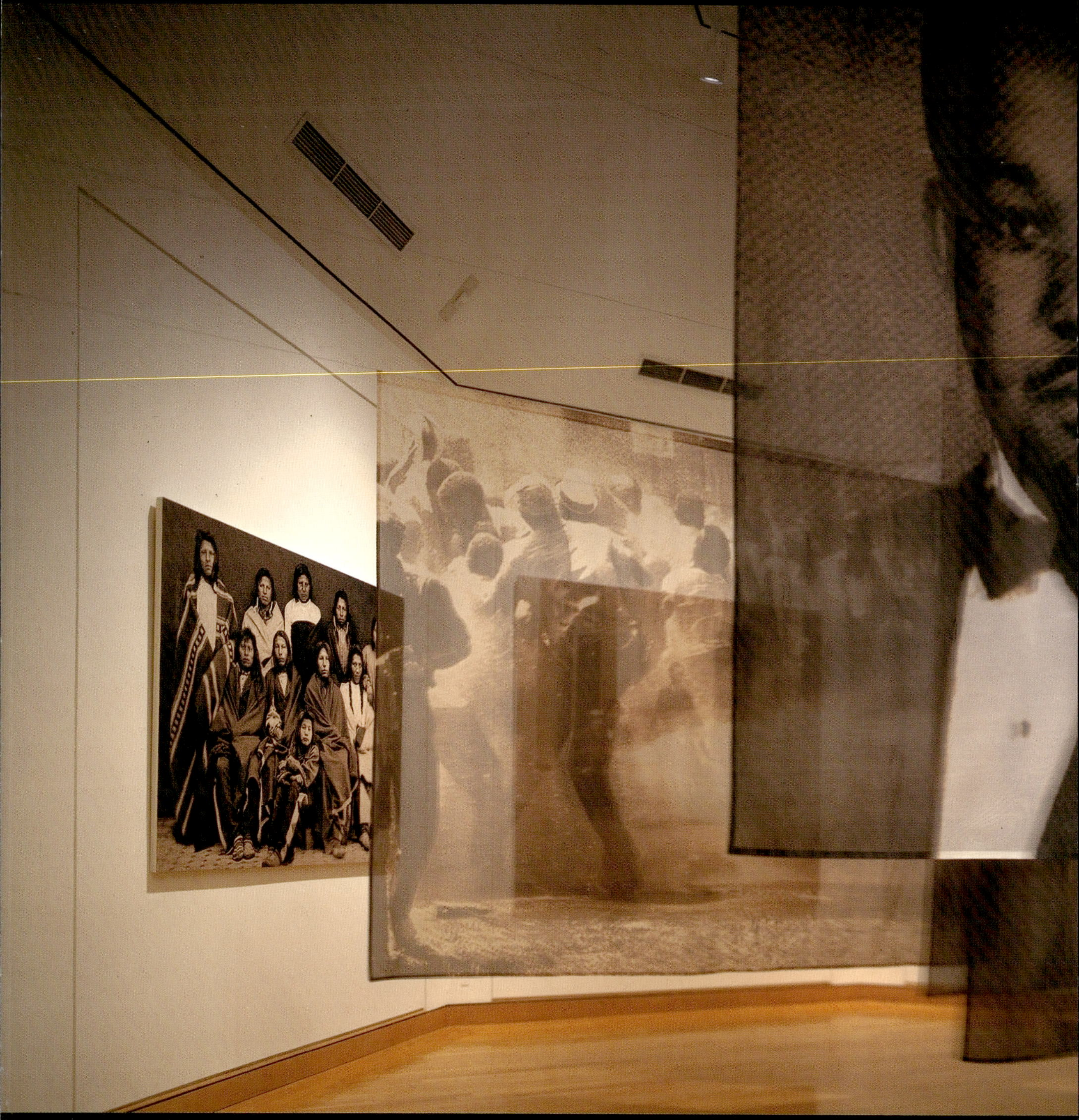

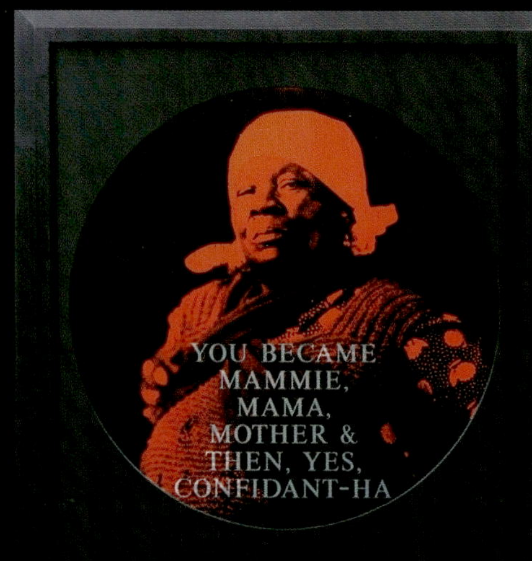
YOU BECAME
MAMMIE,
MAMA,
MOTHER &
THEN, YES,
CONFIDANT-HA

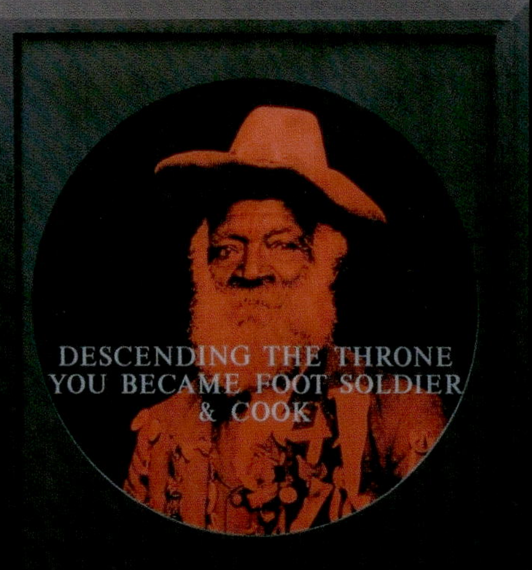
DESCENDING THE THRONE
YOU BECAME FOOT SOLDIER
& COOK

Left Installation from 'Carrie Mae Weems: The Hampton Project', William College Museum of Art, 2000.

**Opposite left** *You Became Mammie, Mama, Mother & Then, Yes, Confidant-ha,* from 'From Here I Saw What Happened and I Cried', 1995–96.

**Opposite right** *Descending the Throne You Became Foot Soldier & Cook*, from 'From Here I Saw What Happened and I Cried', 1995–96.

## Carrie Mae Weems

1950

- **1953** Born in Portland, Oregon, USA

1960

1970

- **1973** Receives first camera
- **1978** Starts to make photographs, text and audio for 'Family Pictures and Stories' as part of MFA thesis (to 1984)
- **1981** Receives BFA from California Institute of the Arts
- **1984** Receives MFA from the University of California, San Diego; enrols in graduate programme in folklore at the University of California, Berkeley (to 1987)
- **1990** Creates 'Kitchen Table Series'
- **1991** Studies and makes art reflecting the island lives of Gullah communities in the southern USA (to 1992)
- **1993** Makes first trip to Africa
- **1998** Prints photos on muslin cloth for installation *Ritual and Revolution*
- **2000** Makes *The Hampton Project*, repurposing images by Frances Benjamin Johnston
- **2003** Creates *The Louisiana Project*

2010

- **2013** Awarded a MacArthur Fellowship

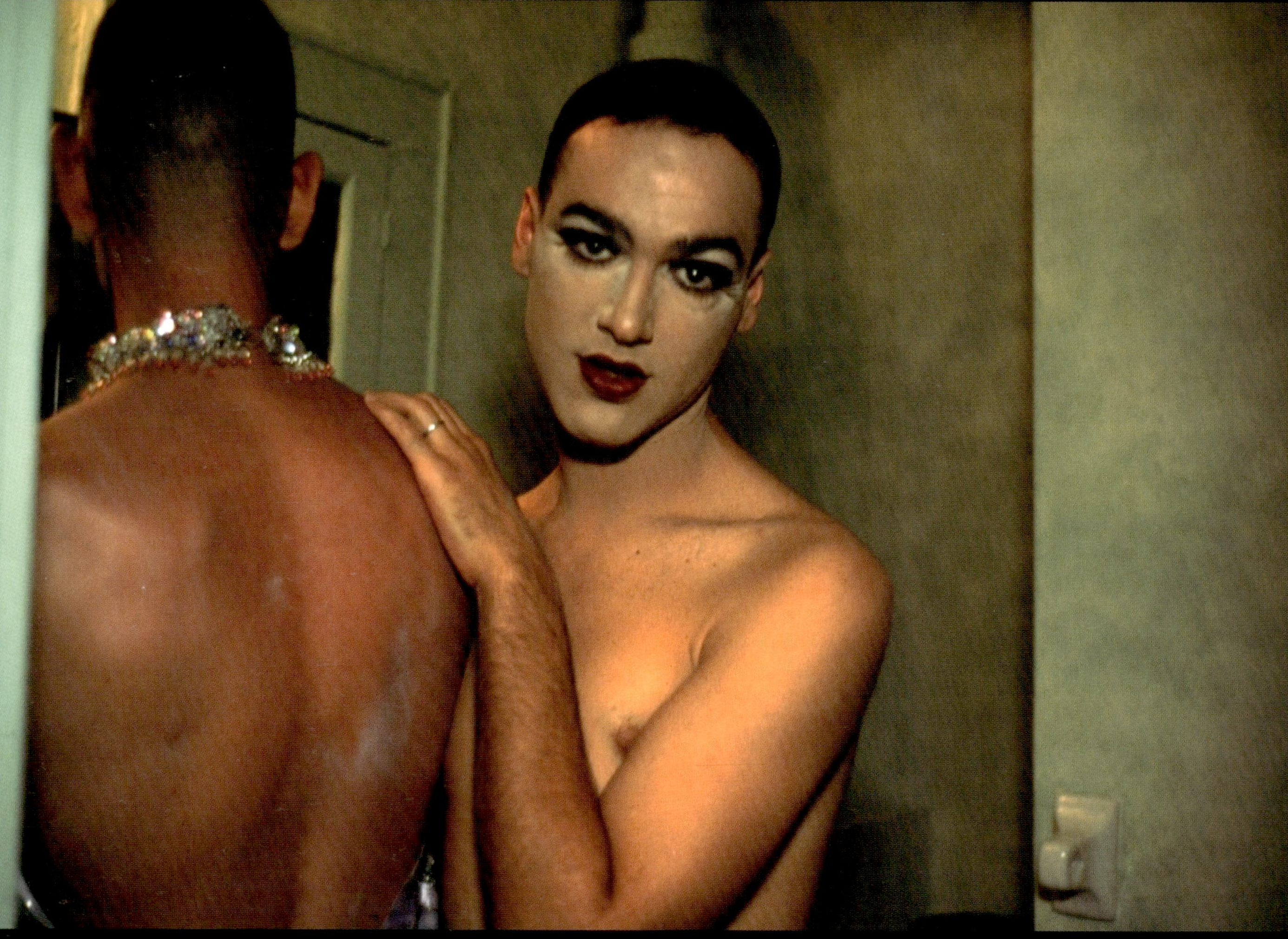

*Jimmy Paulette and Taboo! in the Bathroom*, New York, 1991.

'I used to think I couldn't lose anyone if I photographed them enough.'

# Nan Goldin

b. 1953

UNITED STATES

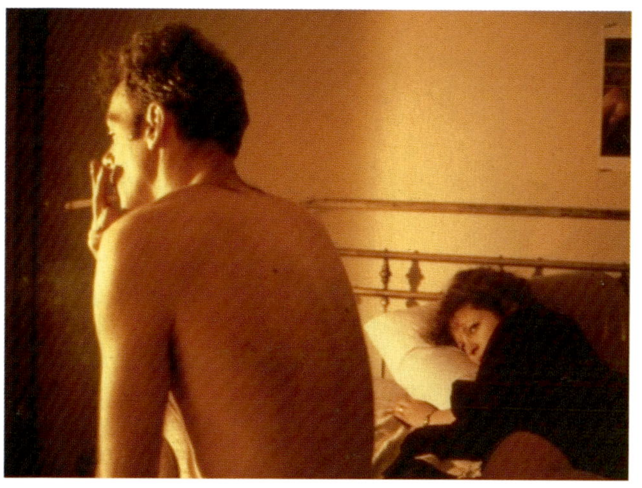

During the 1960s, small colour transparencies, or slides, were a common feature in households for recording and displaying family events and travel, via small projectors. Slides were also used in schools and colleges. While slides were not art, they were used to make art when Photorealist painters projected them on to canvases. In the 1960s slides were picked up by conceptual artists, who wanted to use media distinctly not associated with art. But on the eve of the digital age, which would edge slides into the dustbin, Nan Goldin produced a now legendary sound and slide show. 'The Ballad of Sexual Dependency', shot from 1981 to 1986, consisted of 700 to 800 slides detailing the intimate lives of Goldin and her friends, her 're-created family'.

Well before cell phone cameras made life an extended photo shoot punctuated by selfies, Goldin was a careful chronicler of her friends and their excesses, including her own. An AIDs activist, she included in her 1996 book *I'll Be Your Mirror* personal interviews with, as well as pictures of, friends who were HIV-positive.

What strikes one today about her work, particularly when compared to cell phone intimacies, is her adroit composition and, especially, how attuned she is to the palette of Cibachrome film, especially its blues and greens. Her quick use of the flash reminds some of Weegee (p. 88), but she is far from brutally intrusive. Her work validated the use of photography as a diary of daily life well before cell phone cameras, and her insistence on making uncompromised pictures of outsiders, especially people in the LGBT (lesbian, gay, bisexual and transgender) communities, contributed to their wider acceptance in the twenty-first century.

Goldin's recent work pairs her photographs with images of art-historical paintings and objects, suggesting the value of utopian interludes and the pleasures of just looking.

*Nan and Brian in Bed,* New York, 1983.

**Below** *Swan-like Embrace*, Paris, 2010.

**Bottom** *Sisters*, 2010.

**Opposite** *The Hug*, New York, 1980.

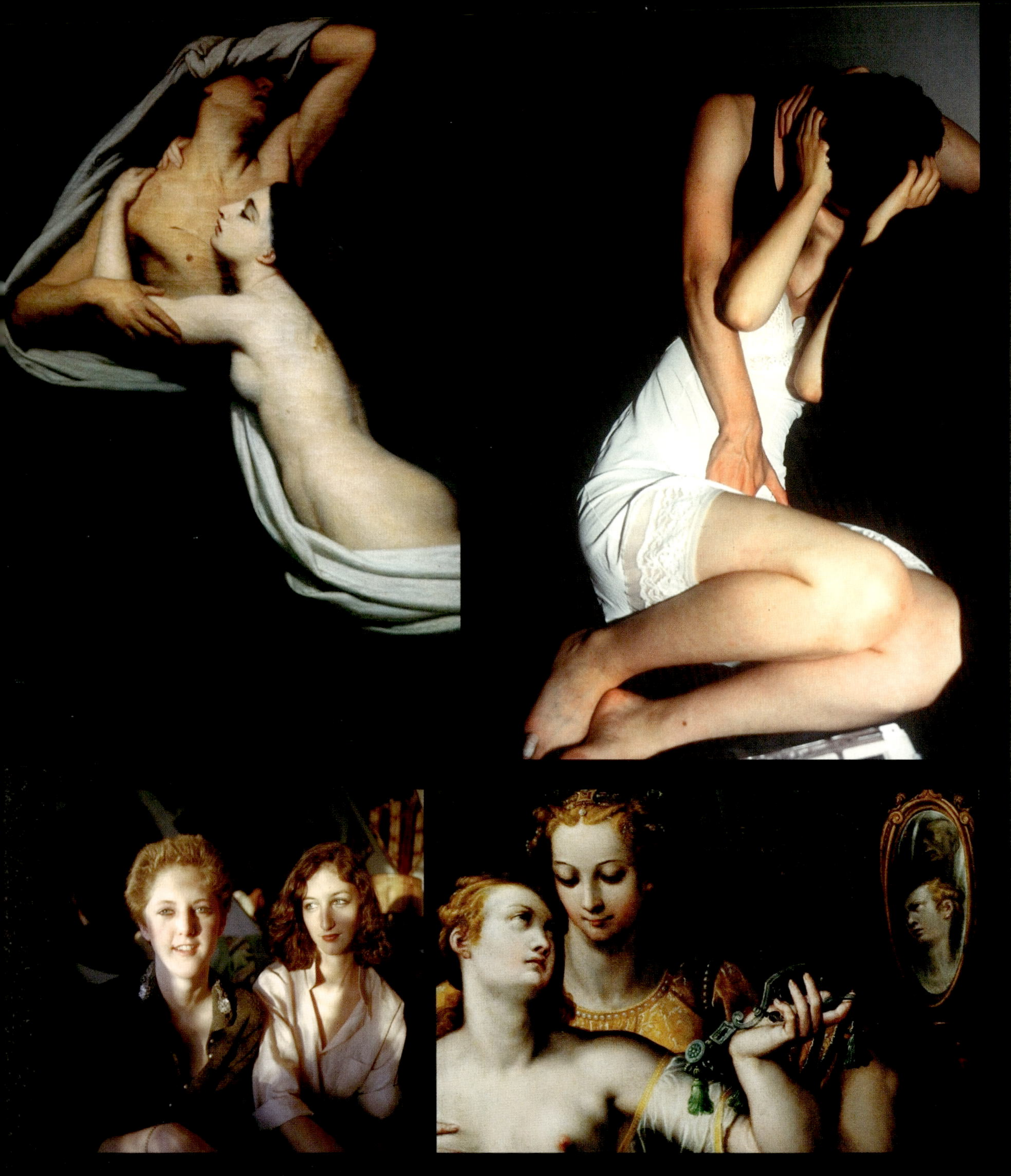

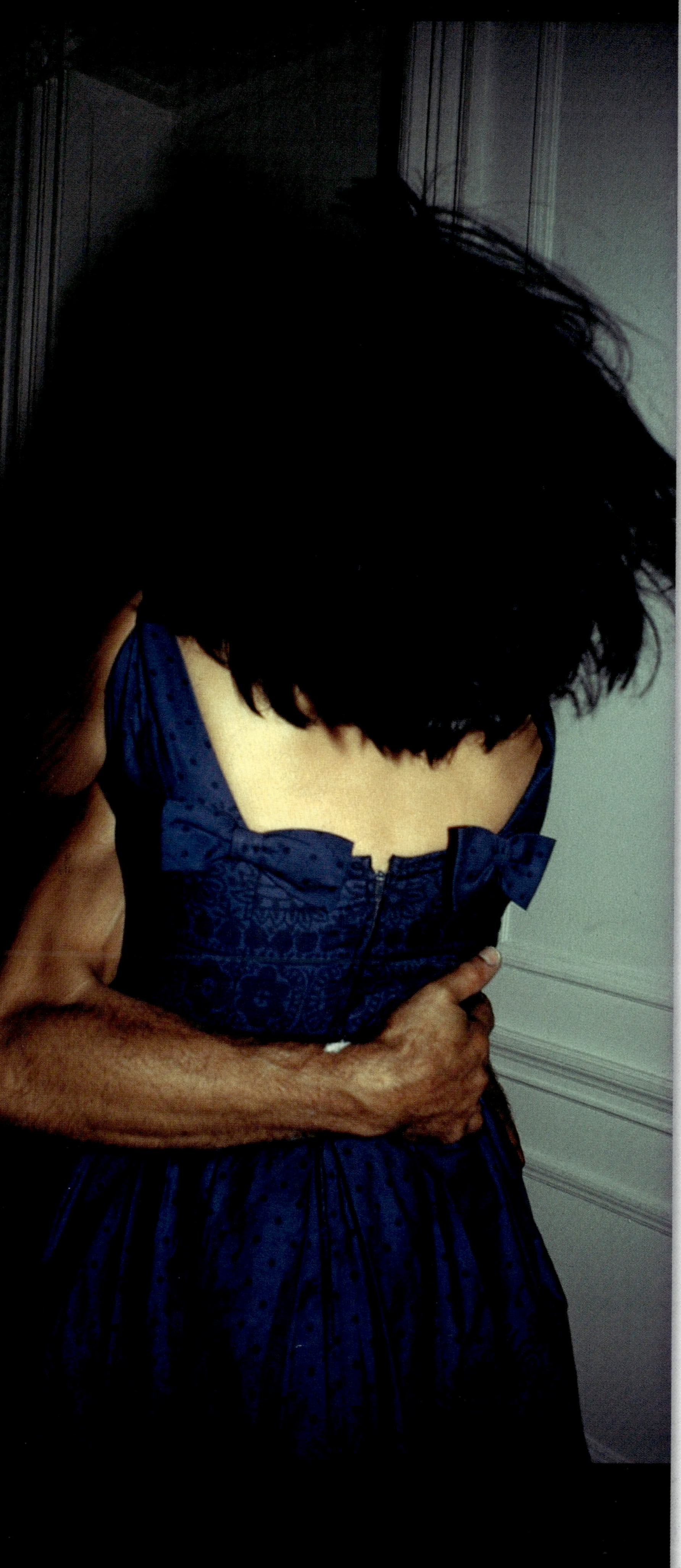

# Nan Goldin

1950

**1953** Born Nancy Goldin, Washington, DC, USA

1960

**1969** Takes up photography

**1978** Moves to New York, and begins creating 'The Ballad of Sexual Dependency'

1980

**1986** Publishes *The Ballad of Sexual Dependency*

**1989** Curates exhibition on the effects of AIDS at Artists Space in New York

**1992** Publishes *The Other Side*, photographs of transvestites and transsexuals

**1994** Publishes *Tokyo Love*

**1996** Retrospective exhibition at the Whitney Museum, New York

2000

**2006** Admitted to the French Legion of Honour

**2007** Receives the Hasselblad Foundation International Award

**2011** Work entitled 'Scopophilia' shown at Matthew Marks Gallery in New York

*Untitled #193*, 1989.

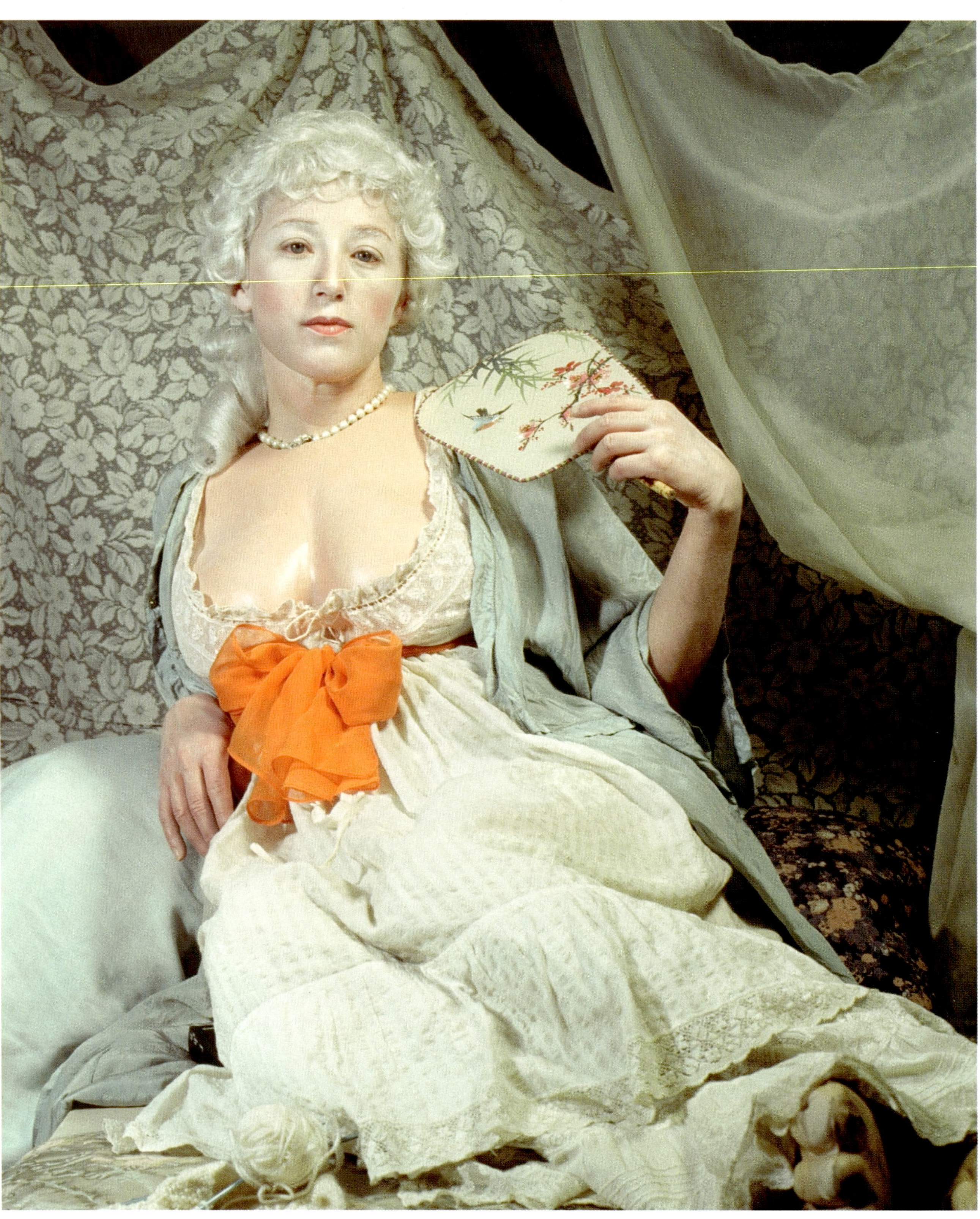

'I wanted the story to come from the face. Somehow the acting just happened.'

# Cindy Sherman

b. 1954

UNITED STATES

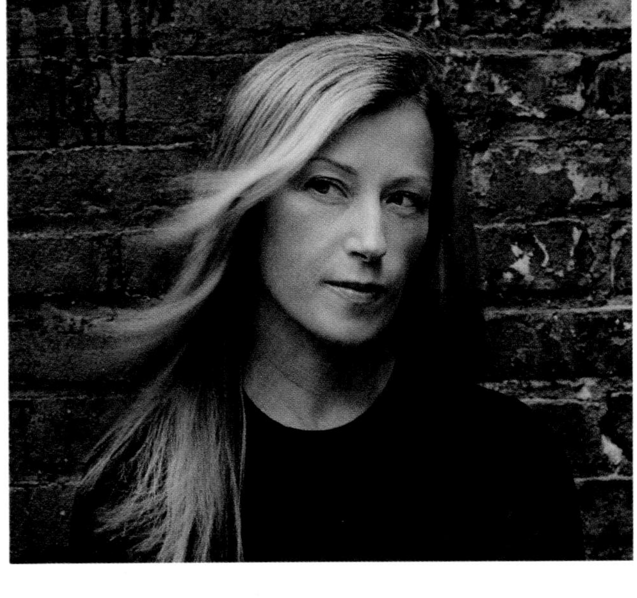

People who do not care much about art or photography may yet recognize the photographs of Cindy Sherman. Though few know what she really looks like, her interpretive portraits caught on in popular culture during the early 1980s. It was no surprise when Madonna sponsored her 1997 exhibition of the complete 'Untitled Film Stills'. Where prior photographers might photograph unconventional people on the streets or in gathering places, Sherman uses her body as the medium upon which she constructs likeness drawn from conventional imagery in mass media, especially film.

Particularly in her early work, she photographed herself as anxious, beleaguered women, who were, or sensed they were, threatened by some situation or entity just off-camera. The pictures alluded to the film stills – actually specially posed photographs – used in cinema lobbies to advertise coming attractions, and to the films themselves. Her subsequent series, 'Rear Screen Projection', referenced the technique common in low-budget films in which actors work in front of a projected background. Through costumes, wigs, make-up and poses contrived to indicate fretfulness or fright, Sherman enacted media stereotypes of women. Her work both derived from and helped shape that part of the Postmodern era of the 1970s and early 1980s that was concerned with appropriated images and the social saturation of media-derived ideas. In an era that doubted the notion of originality, Sherman's images served as illustrative evidence.

When she moved from black-and-white photographs to colour in the 1980s, the intensity and variety of images increased. Her pictures got larger, indirectly referencing that scale of painting, as other artists, such as Jeff Wall (p. 264), were doing. In the 'History Portraits' series the allusion to paintings is clear, and Sherman portrays a few male sitters, as she had rarely done in other series. In addition, digital technology gave Sherman what she has called 'artistic licence' to add backgrounds and alter images, as well as to quickly experiment with appearance.

While purists questioned Sherman's use of photography, photography students were enrapt, making their own interpretations of her work. Her insistence on self-representation brought women into a field that had been male-dominated. Ironically, Sherman's pictures, based as many of them were on mass-media sources, had an unexpected influence on art markets, which did not conflate her work with photography but treated it more like painting. Her photograph *Untitled #96* (1981) sold in 2011 for just under four million dollars.

Portrait of Cindy Sherman by Mark Seliger, 2012.

**Below** *Untitled #224*, 1990.

**Opposite** *Untitled #74*, 1980.

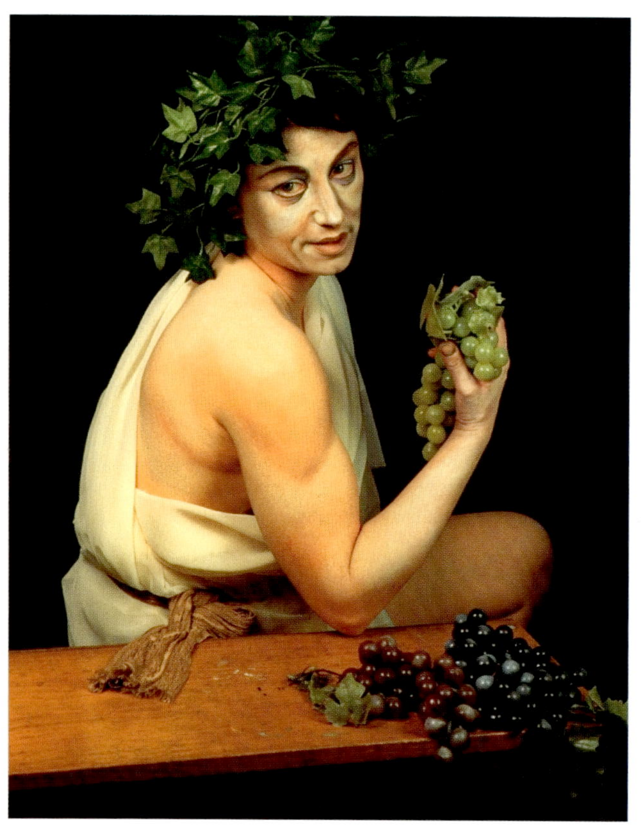

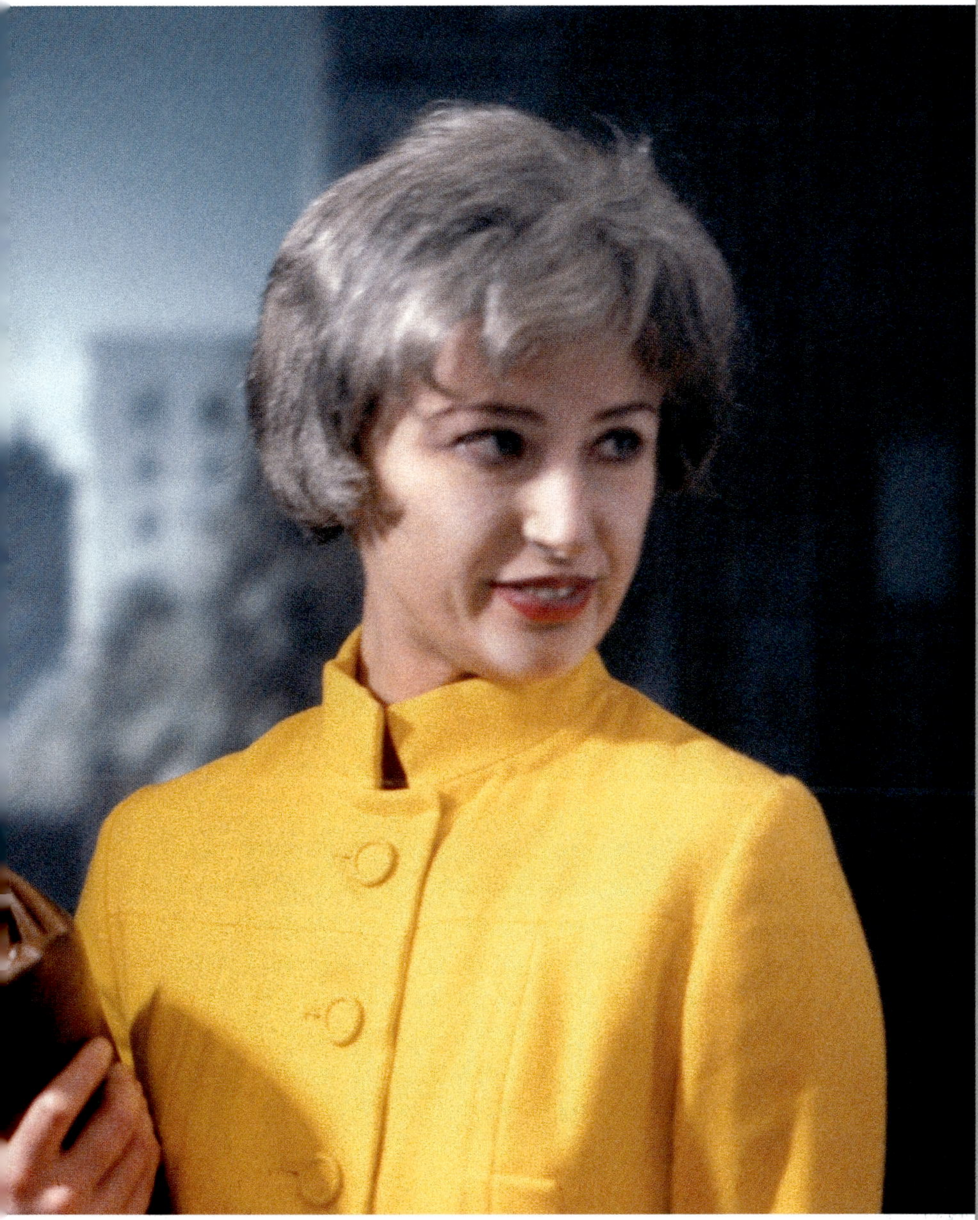

# Cindy Sherman

- **1954** Born in Glen Ridge, New Jersey, USA

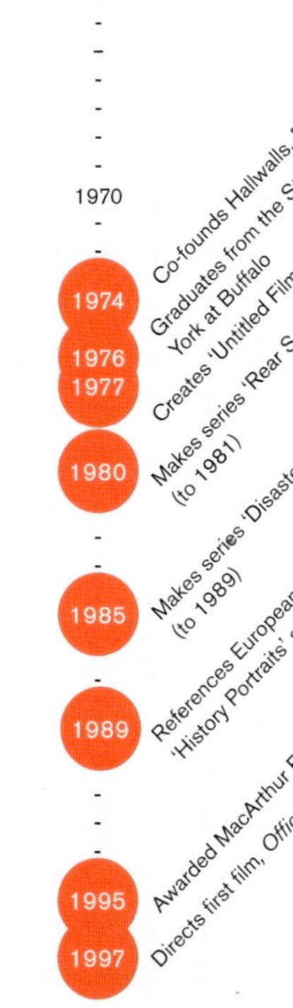

- **1974** Co-founds Hallwalls, Buffalo
- **1976** Graduates from the State University of New York at Buffalo
- **1977** Creates 'Untitled Film Stills' (to 1980)
- **1980** Makes series 'Rear Screen Projections' (to 1981)
- **1985** Makes series 'Disasters and Fairy Tales' (to 1989)
- **1989** References European old master paintings in 'History Portraits' series (to 1990)
- **1995** Awarded MacArthur Fellowship
- **1997** Directs first film, *Office Killer*
- **2012** Retrospective exhibition at Museum of Modern Art, New York

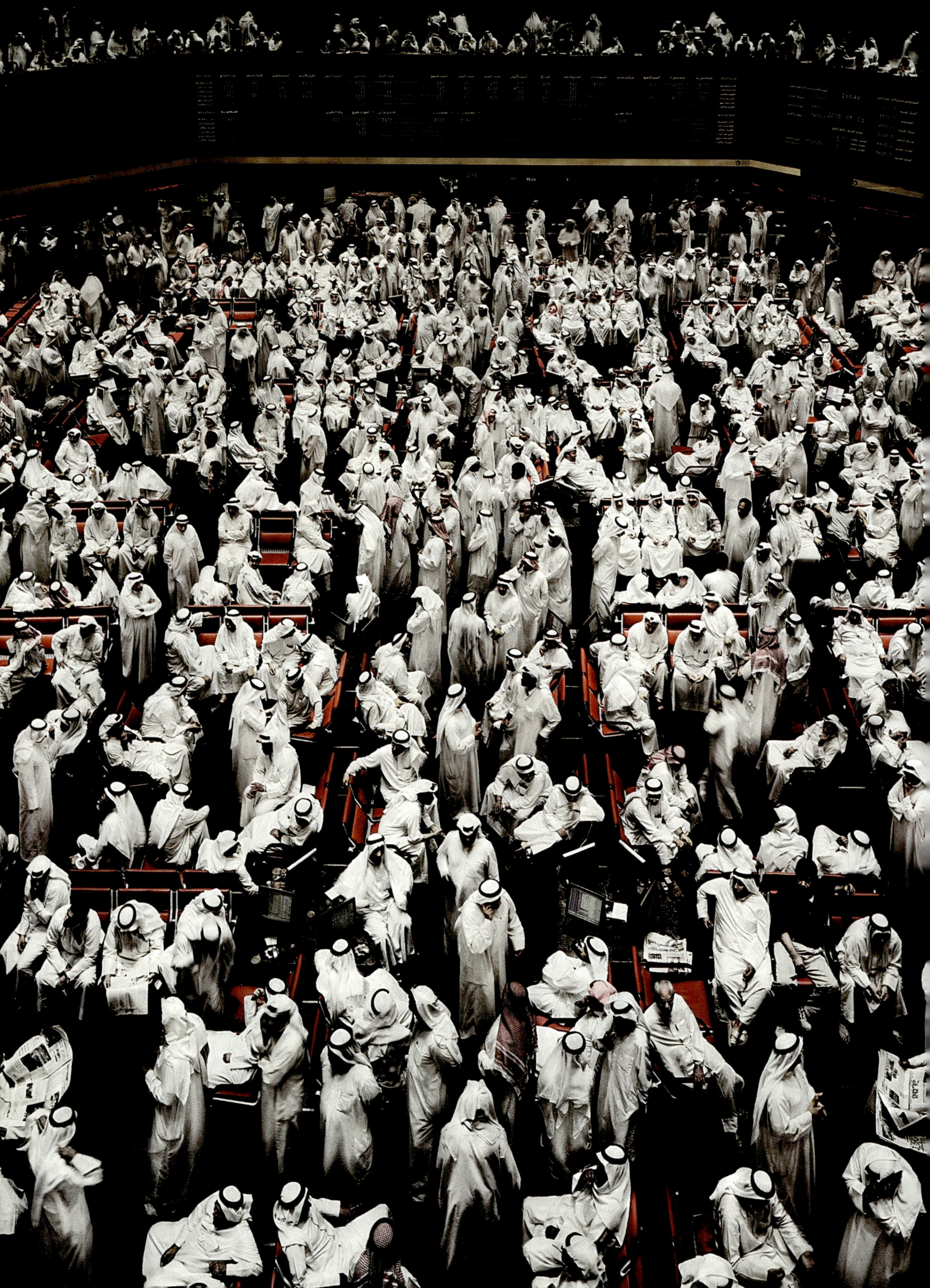

'I am never interested in the individual, but in the human species and its environment.'

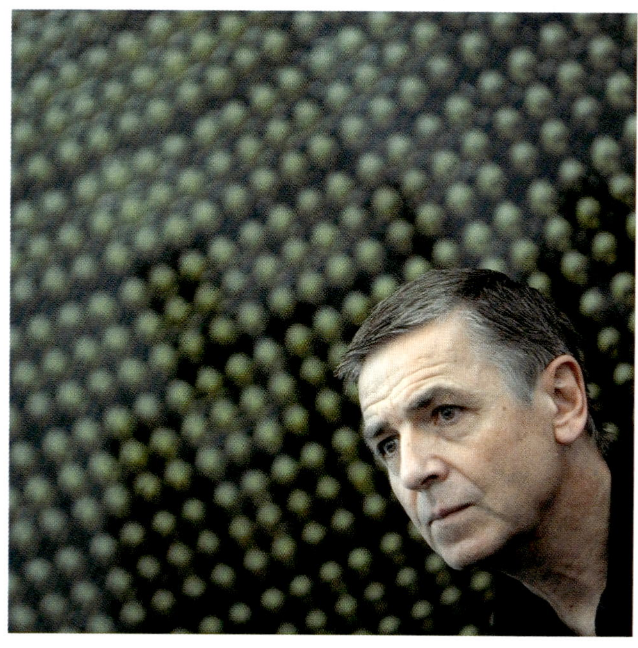

# Andreas Gursky

b. 1955

GERMANY

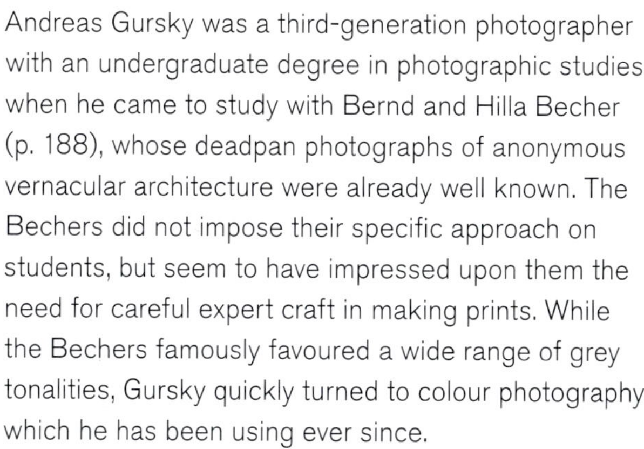

Andreas Gursky was a third-generation photographer with an undergraduate degree in photographic studies when he came to study with Bernd and Hilla Becher (p. 188), whose deadpan photographs of anonymous vernacular architecture were already well known. The Bechers did not impose their specific approach on students, but seem to have impressed upon them the need for careful expert craft in making prints. While the Bechers famously favoured a wide range of grey tonalities, Gursky quickly turned to colour photography, which he has been using ever since.

From the Bechers, he may have taken up the idea of typologies – that is, gathering images in categories, such as building security agents or salespersons – but his point of view was, and is, usually a position slightly above the subject. In his early work, Gursky employed film and darkroom techniques, but he became an early adopter of digital photography. Following the path that many photographers took in the late 1980s, he went from tweaking and cleaning up analogue photographs with photo-editing software to employing a digital camera and elaborate software capable of creating images that did not exist in front of the camera. Over time he developed what he called observing like 'an extraterrestrial being', that is, visually unknowing what was going on in a picture or where exactly to look.

Gursky travelled widely in the 1990s, and photographed industrial sites, high-tech offices, posh hotels and large crowds of people – from those gathering at the opening of the new German parliament to late-night raves. His international picture-making coincided with the increase of global goods and services. Before the fall of the financial markets, Gursky created large images with intensely saturated colour, showing stock exchanges around the world. Pictures of trading floors and traders in New York, Chicago, Kuwait, Tokyo, Hong Kong, Singapore and elsewhere are so wide and tall that viewers must change position, walking about and moving their heads to focus on any one section. Akin to the eye-of-god vantage point in early printmaking, Gursky's high angles imply power over the array presented. His photographs pleased high-rollers, who in turn paid top dollar to purchase Gursky's work.

To some observers, he seems to be challenging the primacy of painting, photography's long-lived nemesis. But Gursky maintains that he is interested in the potentials of photography, not in emulating other media. Ironically, unlike the world's stock markets, Gursky's photographs have held and increased their value. *Rhein II* sold for $4,338,500 in 2011, surpassing work by contemporary artists such as Cindy Sherman (p. 292) and elite historical figures such as Alfred Stieglitz (p. 12).

**Opposite** Kuwait Stock Exchange, 2010.

**Above** Portrait of Andreas Gursky by Federico Gambarini, 2012.

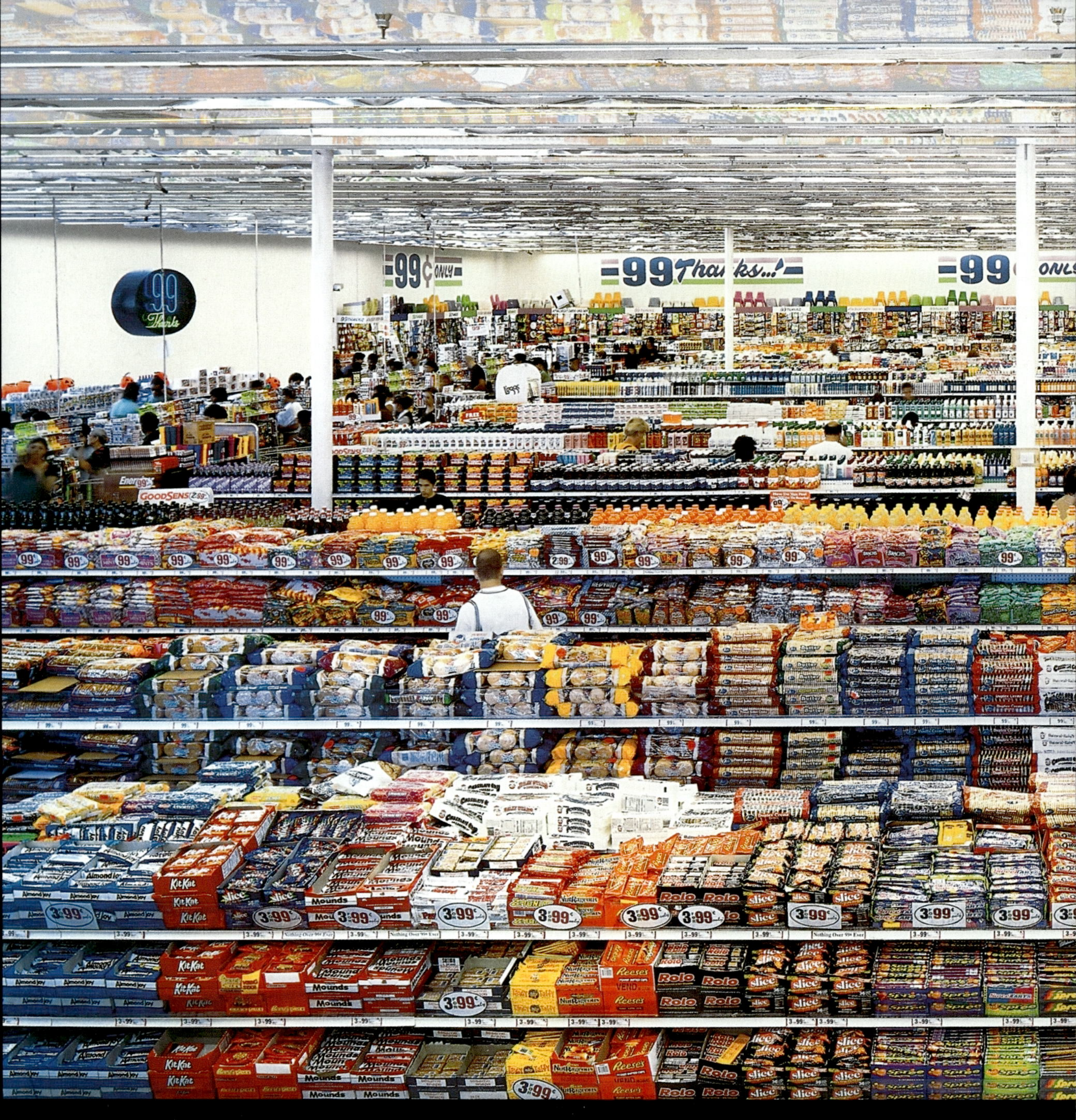
99¢ ONLY
99 Thanks...!
99 Thanks
GOODSENS
Kit Kat
Almond Joy
Mounds
Rolo
Reeses
slice
NutRageous

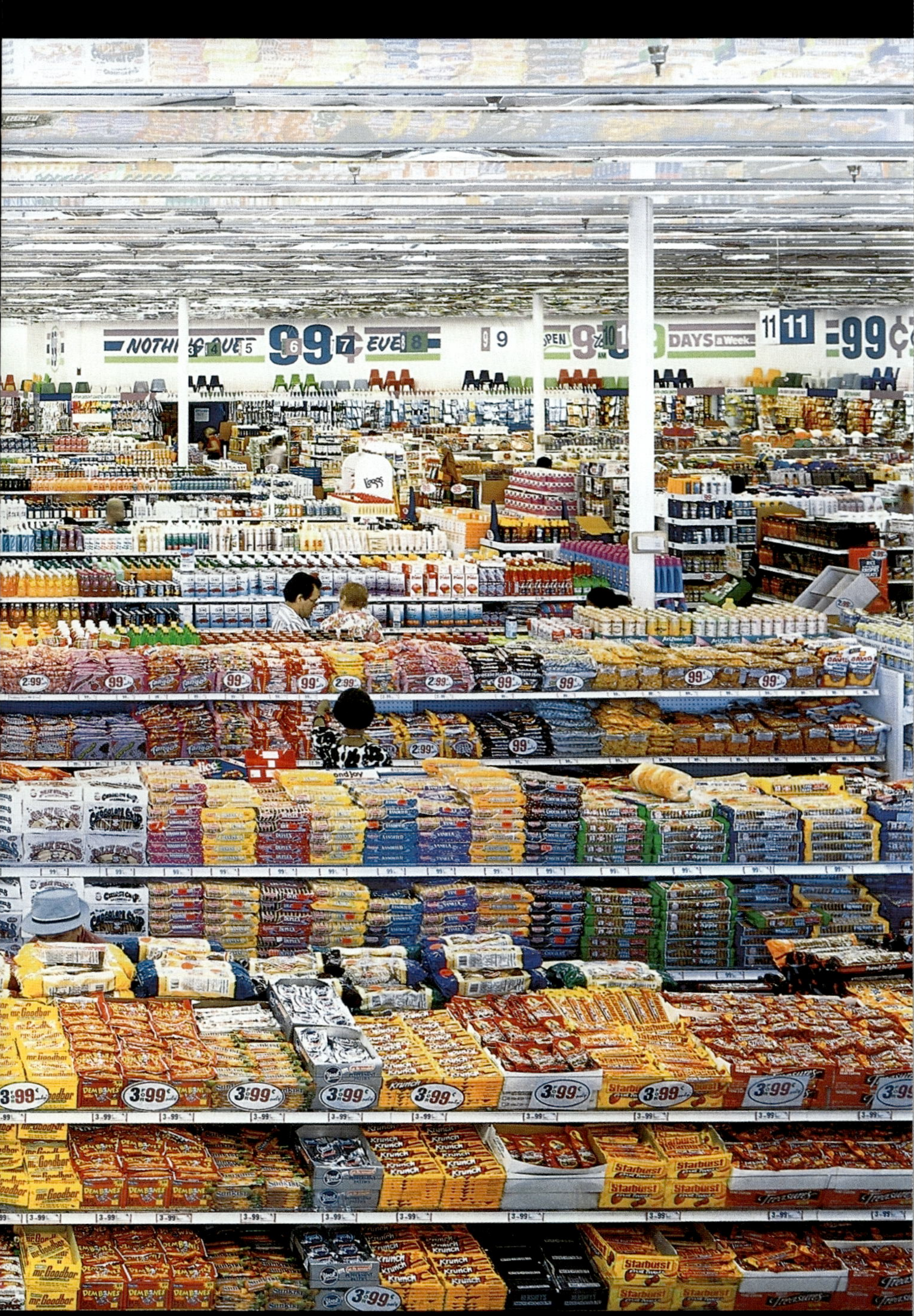


# Andreas Gursky

1950

**1955** Born in Leipzig, Germany

1960

1970

**1978** Studies photography at the Folkwangschule, Essen (to 1981)

**1981** Studies with Bernd and Hilla Becher at the Kunstakademie, Düsseldorf (to 1987)

**1982** Produces the 'Pförtner' series, featuring pairs of porters in office building entrances

**1990** Exhibits at the Venice Biennale

**1994** Retrospective exhibitions in Hamburg and Amsterdam

**1998** Second retrospective travels to several European museums

**2001** Retrospective at the Museum of Modern Art, New York

2010

**2013** First retrospective in Japan at the National Museum of Art in Osaka

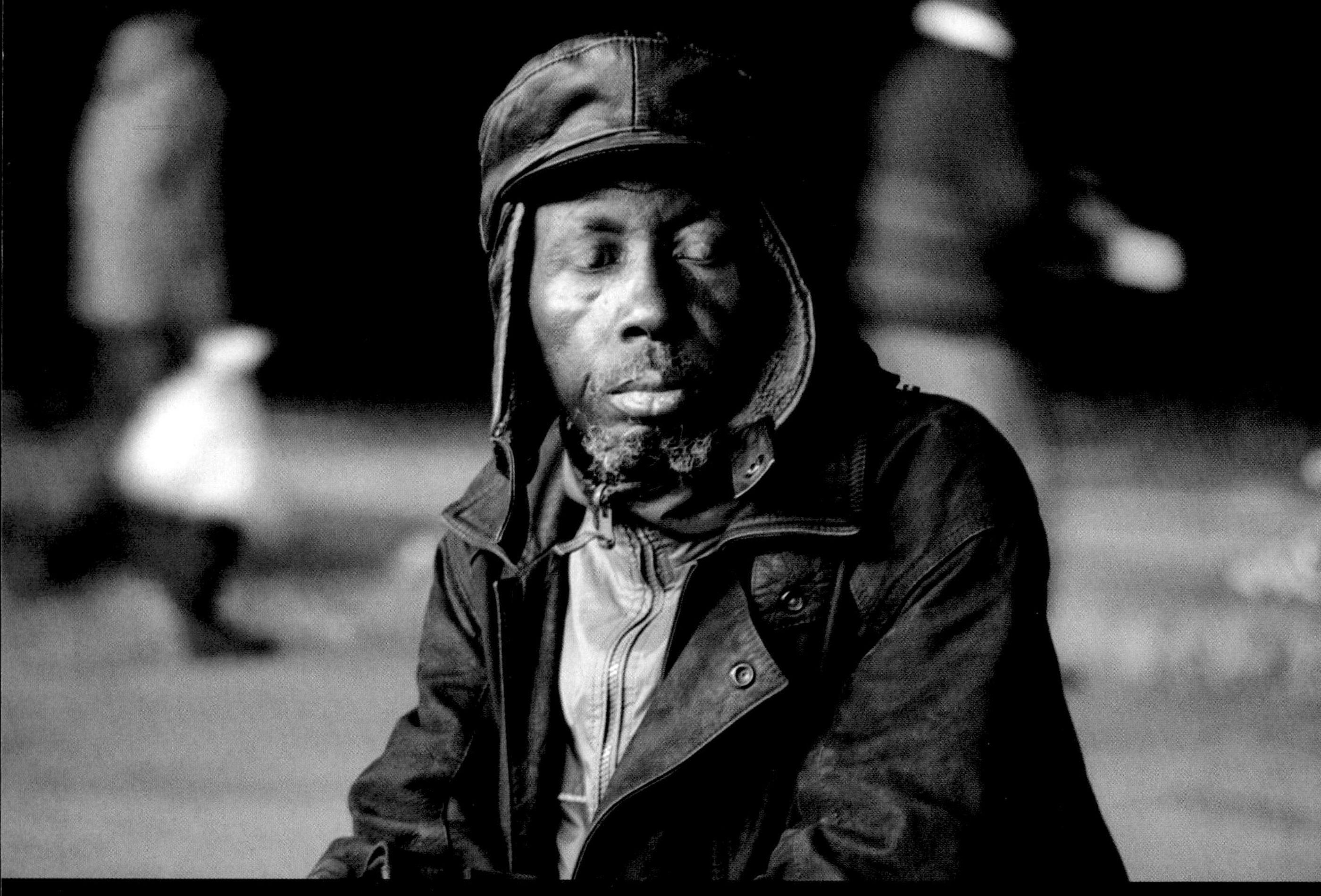

*Ishmael: Eyes Wide Shut*, 2004.

'The only way I could show both the good and the bad was in an essay.'

# Santu Mofokeng

b. 1956

SOUTH AFRICA

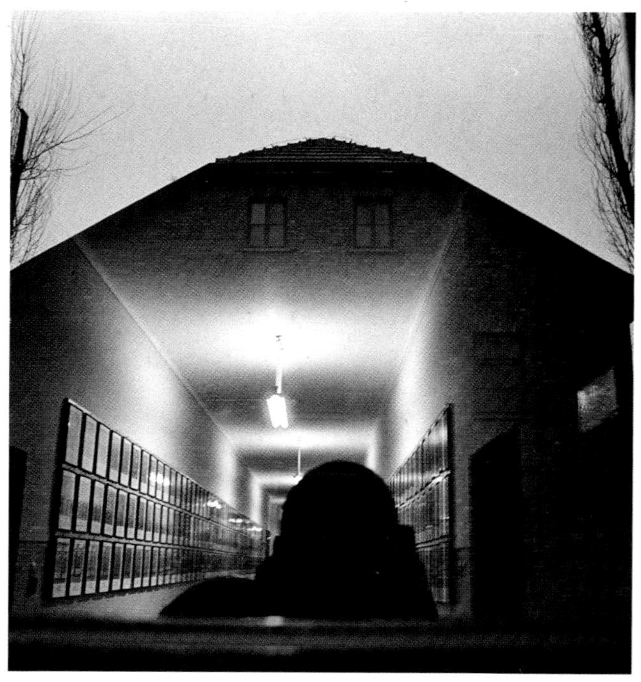

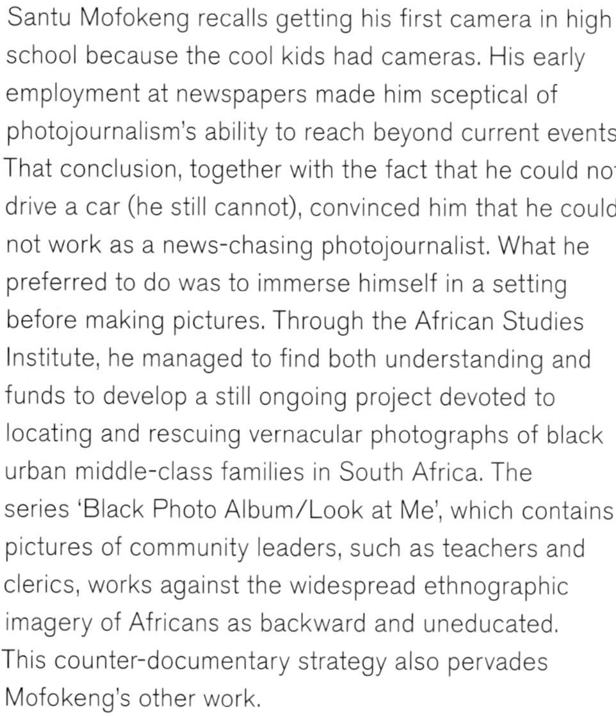

Santu Mofokeng recalls getting his first camera in high school because the cool kids had cameras. His early employment at newspapers made him sceptical of photojournalism's ability to reach beyond current events. That conclusion, together with the fact that he could not drive a car (he still cannot), convinced him that he could not work as a news-chasing photojournalist. What he preferred to do was to immerse himself in a setting before making pictures. Through the African Studies Institute, he managed to find both understanding and funds to develop a still ongoing project devoted to locating and rescuing vernacular photographs of black urban middle-class families in South Africa. The series 'Black Photo Album/Look at Me', which contains pictures of community leaders, such as teachers and clerics, works against the widespread ethnographic imagery of Africans as backward and uneducated. This counter-documentary strategy also pervades Mofokeng's other work.

From the first, Mofokeng accompanied his pictures with descriptive, historical or sociological texts, which he contends frame and inform them for the viewer and act as a counterweight to received ideas. In one text, Mofokeng argues that photojournalism, including television, has created an unnuanced and partial international understanding of such towns as Soweto as places of unmitigated misery. Another photo–text duo recounts how the spread of AIDs produced households headed by children.

Not all of Mofokeng's texts are straightforward. His exhibition 'Chasing Shadows' begins with an 'Invoice' that speaks to a spiritual insecurity that haunts post-apartheid South Africa. Indeed, religion and spirituality have been vital in his work, from the early photographs of commuter trains turned into impromptu churches for people making long commutes to work in cities, to images of the wide-ranging types of religious groups that practise in the Mantsopa caves in the eastern Free State.

Self-portrait, 1997.

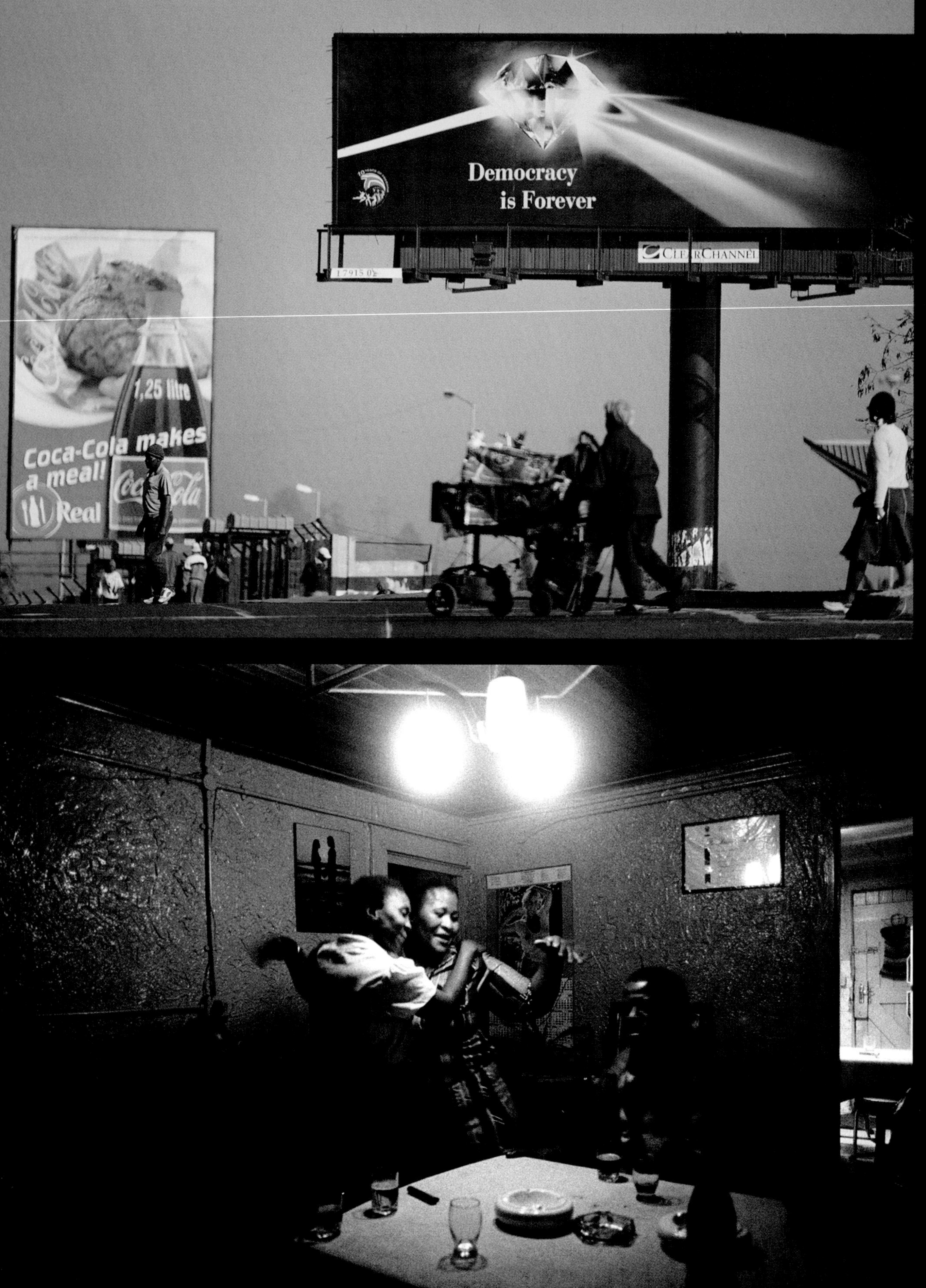
Democracy
is Forever
1,25 litre
Coca-Cola makes
a meal!
Real
Coca-Cola

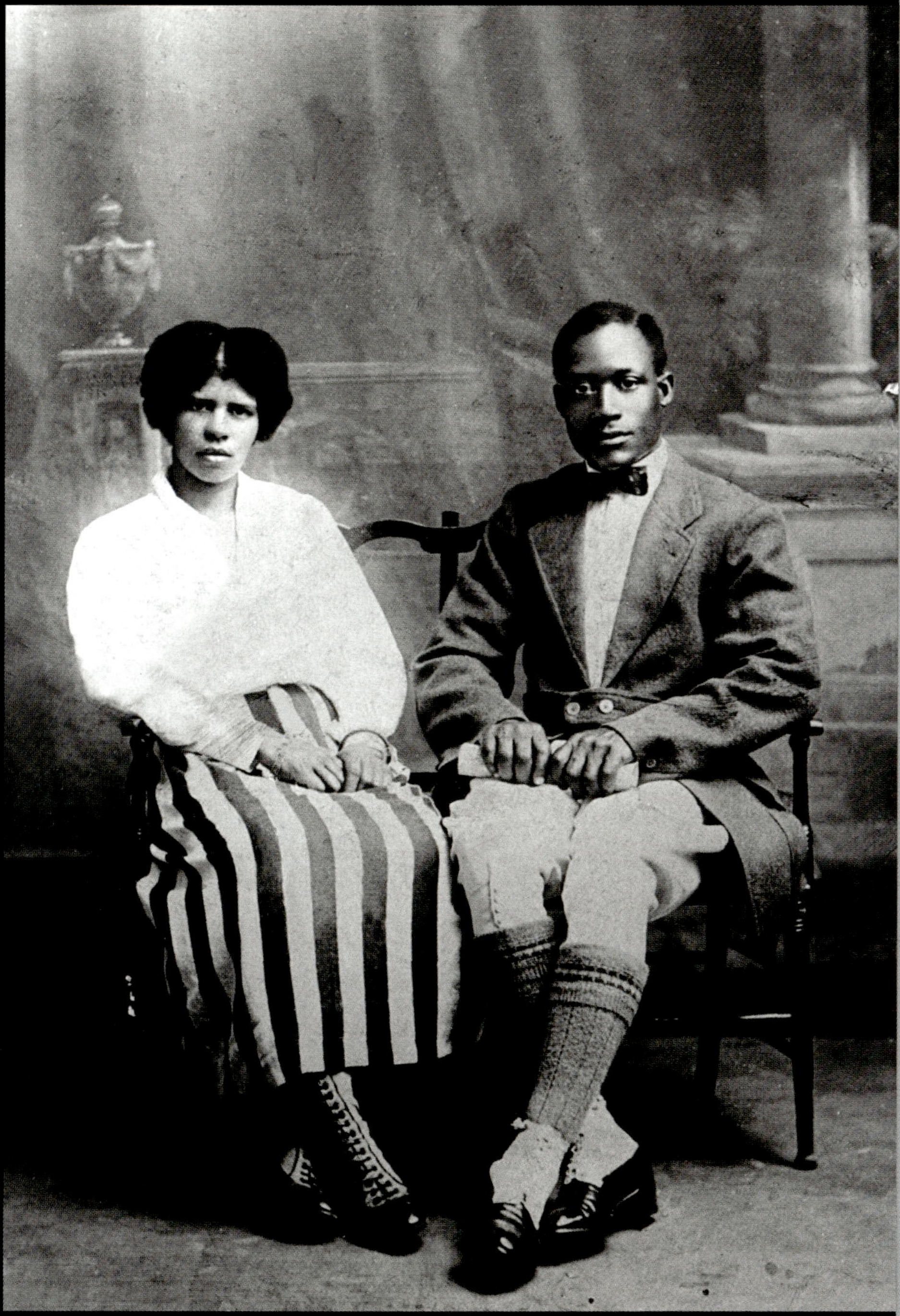

**Opposite top** *Democracy is Forever*, Pimville, 2004.

**Opposite bottom** *Sheeban, White City,* 1987.

**Above** *Slide 4/80*, from 'The Black Photo Album / Look at Me', 1997.

# Santu Mofokeng

1950

**1956** Born in Johannesburg, South Africa

1960

1970

**1975** Makes his first photographs about this time

**1981** Begins working as a darkroom assistant at a newspaper

**1985** Joins the Afrapix photo agency; shoots for alternative newspaper the *New Nation*

**1986** Creates series 'Train Church'

**1988** Works at African Studies Institute

1990

**1996** Begins series 'Trauma Landscapes' and 'Landscapes and Memory'

**1998** 'The Black Photo Album/Look at Me'

2000

**2007** Begins series 'Child-headed Households'

**2011** Retrospective international exhibition 'Chasing Shadows' and book of same name. Starts new series, 'Radiant Landscapes'

*Two Miners*, Datong, Shanxi Province, 1996.

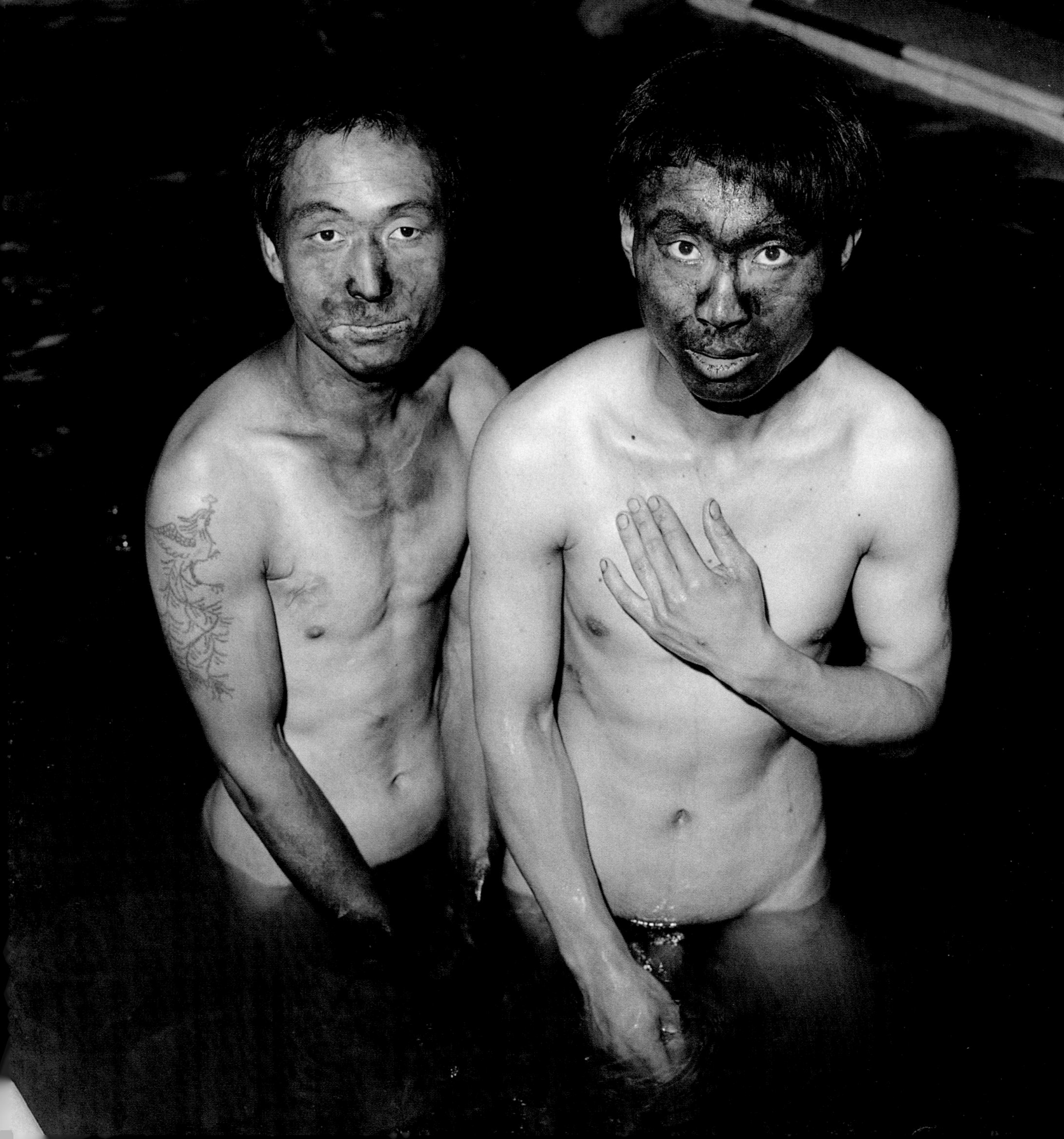

'I have no intention of moving out of China.'

# Liu Zheng

b. 1969

CHINA

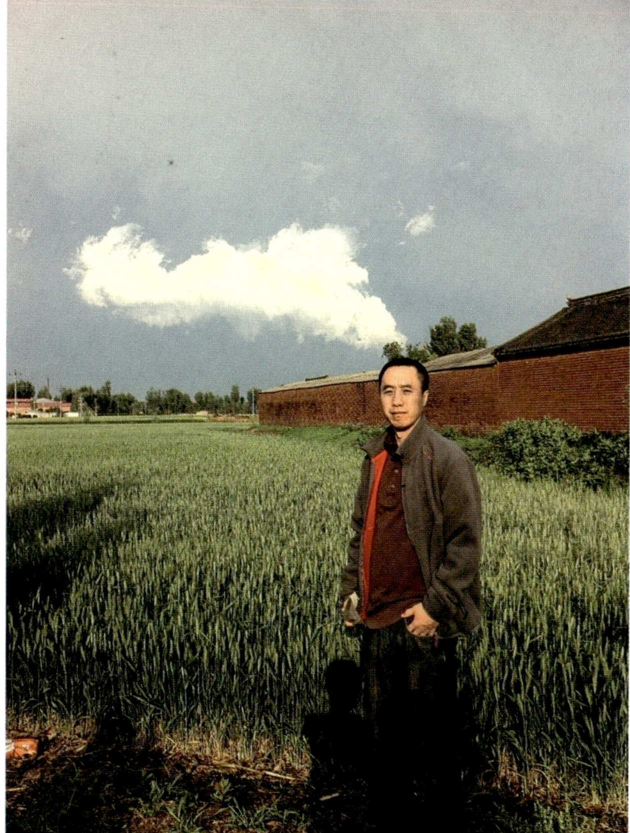

Self-portrait, undated.

Until the mid-1970s, control of photography in China was judged to be central to the maintenance of power. Despite upheavals such as the Cultural Revolution, photographic subjects remained mostly the same. Some historians argue that the first time after the 1949 Chinese Revolution that Chinese could personally photograph and thereby interpret events was during a protest in Tiananmen Square in April 1976.

By emphasizing the panoply of Chinese people and activities, Liu's photographs challenge the public memory of the past that was vested in homogenized, ideal representations of cheerful, patriotic Chinese workers and peasants. What may look to Western eyes like conventional documentary photography has been appreciated in China differently, where it is considered to be aesthetically avant-garde and politically charged. When Liu photographed a group of convicts as they stood in line to get drinking water, he broke established decorum by representing people who had been visually banished from the realm of mass-media images. Liu has photographed people with disabilities, ethnic minorities, transsexuals, cancer patients, beggars, the dying and the dead. His photographs are carefully illuminated and printed, enhancing their visual power but also granting a professional look to subjects previously not considered worthy of illustration.

In addition, Liu has photographed representations of the past that have formed Chinese memory. At the Nanjing Massacre Memorial Museum, he photographed lifelike waxworks that contributed to the public memory both as objects and as visual material referenced in other media, such as film. By photographing these representations, Liu attempts to show that they are invented documents.

Liu has been called the Diane Arbus and the August Sander (p. 24) of China. Framing his work with those associations suggests that he was working to categorize occupational groups, or that he deliberately photographs people who, at least in the moment that they are photographed, look confused and unkempt, which the photographer makes into a symbol of the fragile or damaged human psyche. But Liu seems to be pointing out that human differences, so long airbrushed away by propaganda, are a constant that China must acknowledge.

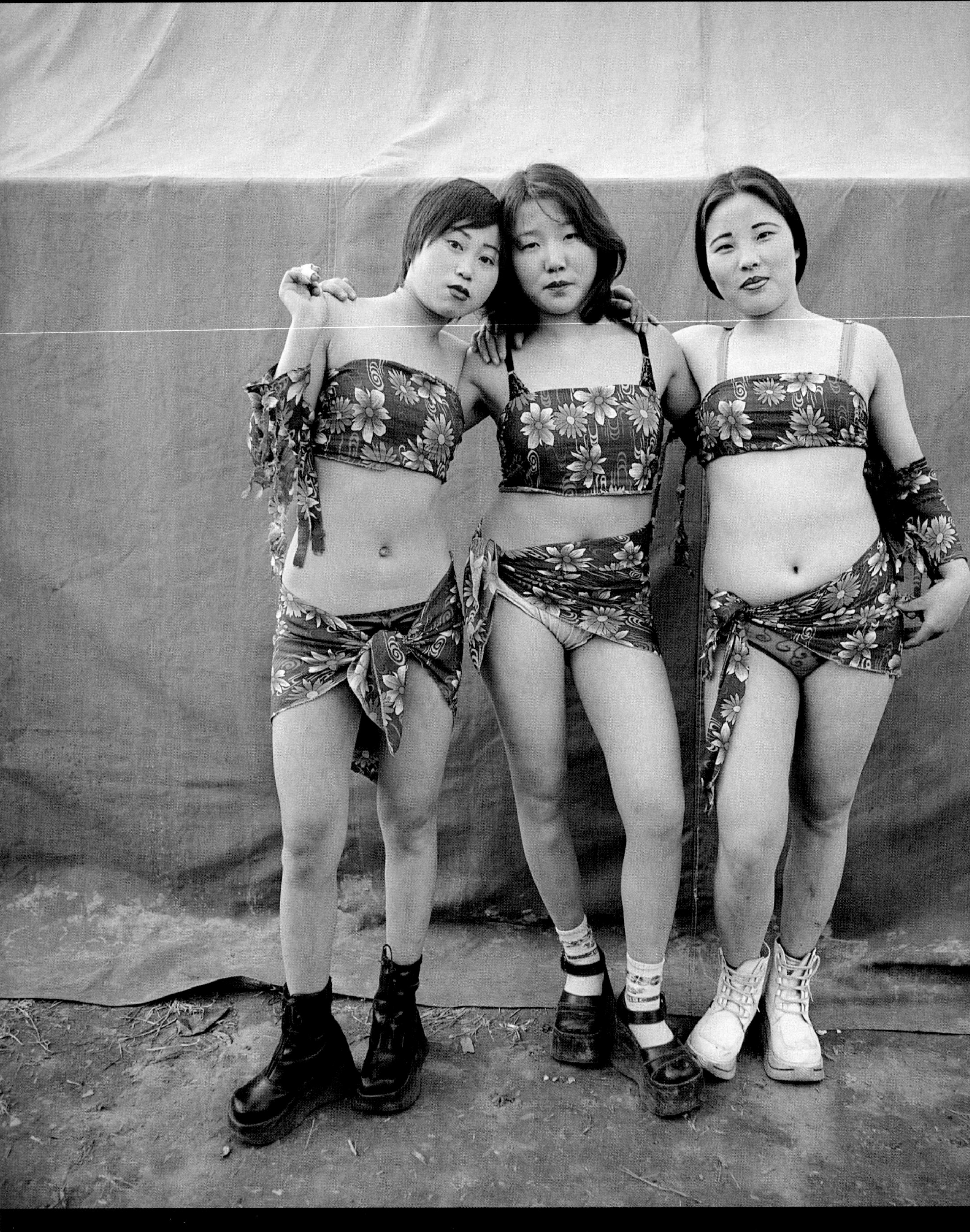

**Opposite** *Three Country Strippers*, Huoshentai, Henan Province, from 'The Chinese', 2000.

**Below** *Three Women at a Country Funeral*, Longxian, Shaanxi Province, from 'The Chinese', 2000.

**Bottom** *Convicts Fetching Water*, Baoding, Hebei Province, from 'The Chinese', 1995.

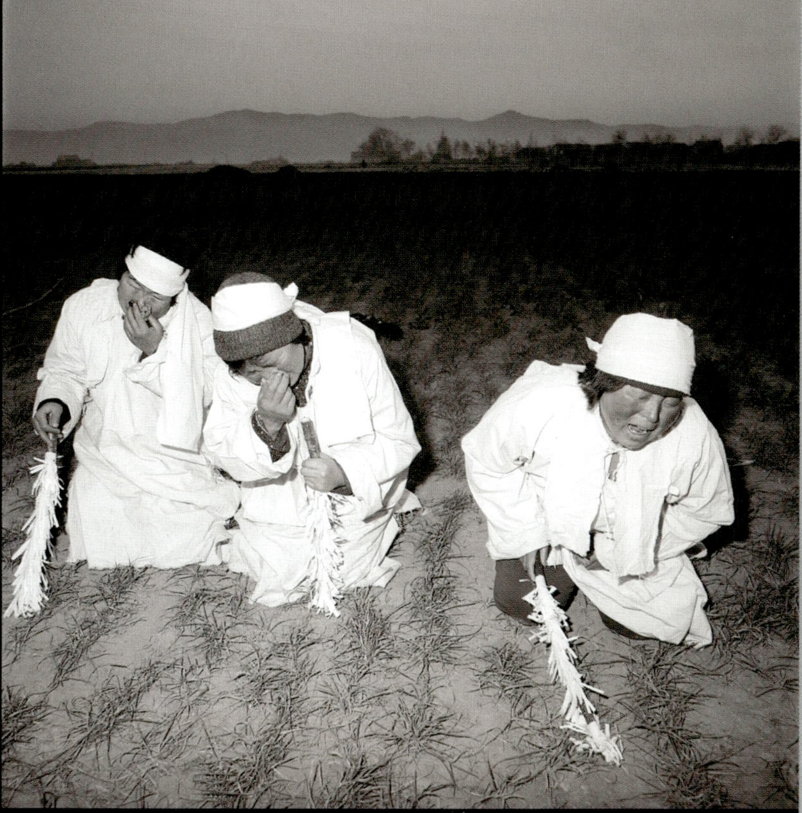

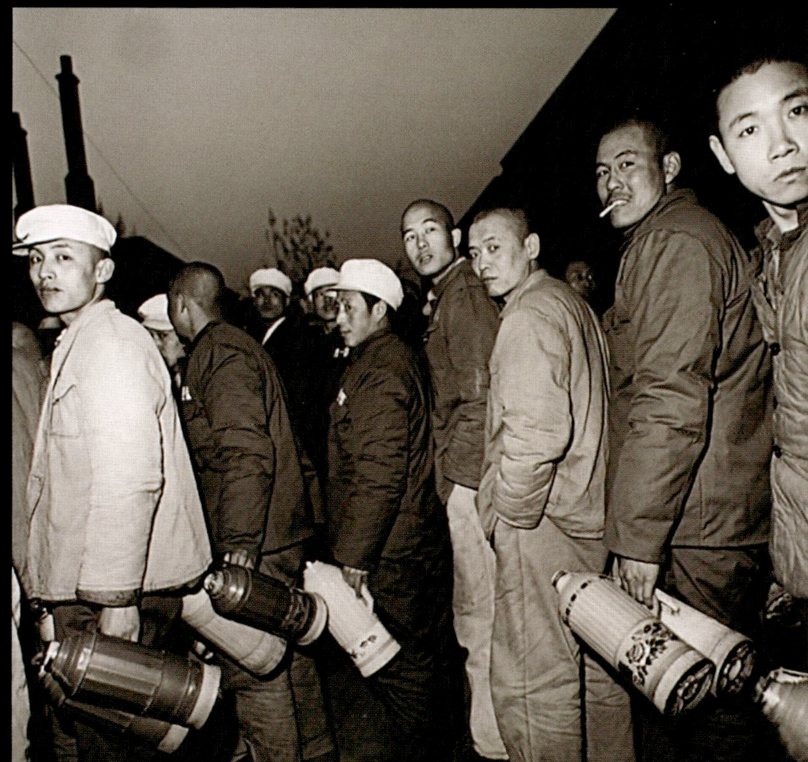

## Liu Zheng

1960

1969 Born in Wuqiang County, Hebei Province, China

1980

1991 Photojournalist for *Worker's Daily* (to 1997)

1995 Participates in 'Topic '95 Five Person Exhibit', Beijing

2000

2002 Work shown in First Guangzhou Triennial, China

2003 Solo exhibition at Rencontres Internationale de la photographie, Arles; exhibits at the 50th Venice Biennale and at the International Center of Photography, New York

2010

2013 Exhibits work titled 'Farewell to Photography' at the Three Shadows Photography Art Centre, Beijing

## Further Reading


Billeter, Erika. *A Song to Reality: Latin American Photography, 1860-1993* (Barcelona: Lunweg Editores, 1998).

Bright, Susan. *Art Photography Now*, 2nd ed. (London: Thames & Hudson, 2011).

Campany, David, ed. *Art and Photography* (London: Phaidon 2003).

Cotton, Charlotte. *The Photography as Contemporary* Art, 3rd ed. (London: Thames & Hudson, 2014).

Debroise, Olivier. *Mexican Suite: A History of Photography in Mexico*, trans., Stella de Sá Rego (Austin, TX: University of Texas Press, 2001).

Dehejia, Vidja. *India Through the Lens: Photography 1980–1911* (Munich: Prestel, 2001).

Dickerman, Leah. *Dada, Zurich, Berlin, Hannover, Cologne, New York, Paris* (Washington, D.C.: National Gallery of Art, 2008).

Enweazor, Okwui, ed. *The Short Century: Independence and Liberation Movements in Africa, 1945–1994* (Munich: Prestel, 2001).

Eskildsen, Ute. *Street and Studio: An Urban History of Photography* (London: Tate Publishing, 2008).

Fraser, Karen M. *Photography and Japan* (London: Reaktion Books, 2011).

Frizot, Michel, ed. *A New History of Photography* (Cologne: Könemann, 1998).

Gresh, Kristen. *She Who Tells the Story: Women Photographers from Iran and the Arab World* (Boston: Museum of Fine Arts Publications, 2014).

Hacking, Juliet, ed. *Photography: The Whole Story* (New York: Prestel, Ltd./Verlagsgruppe Random House, 2012).

Haney, Erin. *Photography and Africa* (London: Reaktion Books, 2010).

Honnef, Klaus. Rolf Sachsee, and Karin Thomas, eds. *German Photography 1870–1970: Power of a Medium* (Cologne: DuMont Buchverlag, 1997).

Jeffrey, Ian. *How to Read a Photograph* (New York: Abrams, 2008).

Kaneki, Ryuichi and Ivan Vartanian. *Japanese Photography Books of the 1960s and '70s* (New York: Aperture, 2009).

Lahs-Gonzales, Olivia, and Lucy Lippard. *Women Photographers of the Twentieth Century* (St. Louis: St. Louis Art Museum, 1997).

Lebeck, Robert, and Bodo von Dewitz. *Kiosk: A History of Photojournalism* (London: Steidl, 2002).

Marien, Mary Warner. *Photography: A Cultural History*, 4th edition (London: Laurence King Publishing, 2014).

Mraz, John. *Looking for Mexico* (Durham and London: Duke University Press, 2009).

Orville, Miles. *American Photography* (New York: Oxford University Press, 2003).

Parr, Martin, and Gerry Badger. *The Photobook: A History* vols. 1, 2 (London: Phaidon, 2004, 2006); Gerry Badger, *The Photobook: A History* vol. 3 (London: Phaidon, 2014).

Pelizzari, Maria Antonella. *Traces of India: Photography, Architecture, and the Politics of Representation* (Montreal and New Haven, CT: Canadian Centre for Architecture and Yale Center for British Art, 2003).

Pelizzari, Maria Antonella. *Photography and Italy* (London: Reaktion Books, 2011).

Pinney, Christopher. *Photography and Anthropology* (London: Reaktion Books, 2011).

Ritchin, Fred. *Bending the Frame: Photojournalism, Documentary, and the Citizen* (New York: Aperture, 2013).

Roberts, Claire. *Photography and China* (London: Reaktion Books, 2012).

Rosenblum, Naomi. *A World History of Photography*, 4th edition (New York: Abbeville Press, 2008).

Salvesen, Britt. *New Topographics* (Gottengen, Germany and Tucson, AZ Steidl and the Center for Creative Photography, 2010).

Soutter, Lucy. *Why Art Photography?* (London: Routledge, 2013).

Stepan, Peter, ed. *Icons of Photography: The 20th Century* (Prestel: Munich, 2005).

Squires, Carol, ed. *What is a Photograph?* (New York: Prestel, Ltd./Verlagsgruppe Random House, 2014).

Stott, William. *Documentary Expression and Thirties America* (New York: Oxford University Press, 1973).

Thomas, Anne. *Beauty of Another Order: Photography in Science* (New Haven, CT: Yale University Press, 1997).

Wells, Liz, ed. *Photography: A Critical Introduction*, 4th ed. (London: Routledge, 2009).

Wilder, Kelly. *Photography and Science* (London: Reaktion Books, 2009).

Witkowsky, Matthew S. *Light Years: Conceptual Art and Photography, 1964–1977* (Chicago: Art Institute of Chicago, 2011).

# Index

Figures in **bold** refer to main entries and figures in *italics* refer to photographs.

A
Abbott, Berenice 11, **8–47**
portrait of Eugène Atget *9*
*Jean Cocteau* 85, *87*
*Janet Flanner 84*
Adams, Ansel 7, 15, 75, **104–7**, 141, 213
*Moonrise and Half Dome, Yosemite Valley 104*
*Self-portrait, Monument Valley, Utah 105*
*Winter Sunrise, Sierra Nevada* 106–7
Adams, Robert **212–5**
*Aurora*, Colorado, *215*
Agee, James 142
*Let Us Now Praise Famous Men* 113
Ali, Muhammad *136*, 137 (Parks)
American Academy of Arts and Letters 87
American Place, An, New York 15, 107
*Aperture* magazine 35, 75
Araki, Nobuyoshi **240–3**
*Tokyo Blues 1977 240*
*Tokyo Comedy 242*
Araki, Yoko *242* (N. Araki)
Arbus, Diane 25, 89, 101
Arguelles, Carlos 165
Armory Show, New York (1913) 15, 51
Atget, Eugène **8–11**, 87, 113, 125
Avedon, Richard 97, **168–71**

B
Bain News Service (USA) 17
Ballen, Roger **280–3**
*Cat Catcher 283*
*Memento Mori 282*
*Prowling 283*
*Sergeant F. de Bruin 280*
Baltz, Lewis 213, **260–3**
'Candlestick Point' 261
*San Quentin Point no. 41 262*
*Santa Cruz 263*
'Sites of Technology' *260, 262–3*
Baudelaire, Charles 113
Bauhaus, Germany 78
Becher, Bernhard (Bernd) and Hilla Wobeser **188–91**, 213, 297
*Blast Furnace View... 190*
*Half-timbered House 188*
*Watertowers 191*
Bellare, Ramesh: *Sunil Janah 149*
Bellocq, E. J. 201
Bengal Famine (1943) 149
Benjamin, Frances Antoinette 17
Benjamin, Walter 9
Bergman, Ingrid 137
Biafra Famine (1968) 209
Borges, Jorge Luis 177
Bourke-White, Margaret 7, **120–3**, 149, 157
*The Liberation of Buchenwald 120*
*The Louisville Flood 122–3*
Bovington, John *32*, 33 (Cunningham)
Brando, Marlon *239* (Marks)
Brandt, Bill 6, **116–9**, 177, 249
*Nude, East Sussex Coast 118*
*Nude, London 116*
*People Sheltering in the Tube...* 117, *119*
*Street Scene 119*
Brassaï **92–5**, 117
*Group in Dance Hall* 92
Bravo, Manuel Álvarez 55, **108–11**, 165, 245, 281
*The Big Fish Eats the Little One 110*
*Box of Visions 111*
*The Good Reputation Sleeping* 109, *111*
*Two Pairs of Legs 108*
Brecht, Bertolt 47
Breton, André 109, 111
Bruin, Sergeant F. de *280* (Ballen)
Burroughs, Allie Mae *112* (Evans)

C
Cahun, Claude **68–71**
*Aveux non avenus 68*, 69, *71*
*C.M.C. 71*
*H.U.M. 68*
Calcutta Film Society 149
Caldwell, Erskine: *You Have Seen Their Faces* 123
*Camera Work* (journal) 13, 55
Capa, Robert **144–7**
Cartier-Bresson, Henri 7, 65, **132–5**, 141, 181, 229, 233, 249
*Behind the Gare Saint-Lazare 132*
Castro, Fidel 159
Cézanne, Paul 13
Chanel, Coco 85, 137
Chapelle, Dickey 7, **156–9**
*Algerian Man Adjusting a Turban 156*
*Injured Soldier 159*
*26th of July Meeting in Oriente Province 158*
Chapelle, Tony 157
Cocteau, Jean 85, *87* (Abbott)
*The Blood of a Poet* 127
Cole, Ernest **23–5**
*Boys Playing 232*
Coltrane, John *162* (DeCarava)
Conceptualism/conceptual art 189, 265, 269
Corcoran Gallery of Art, Washington, DC 139, 279
Cubism 13, 65
Cunningham, Imogen **32–5**, 73
*John Bovington 2 32*, 33
portrait of Minor White *131*
*Triangles 32*, 33
Curtis, Edward S. 35
Czechoslovakia, Soviet invasion of (1968) *220*, *221*

D
Dada 41, 49
Dalí, Salvador 93
Danto, Arthur 169
da Silva, Flavio 137, *139* (Parks)
DeCarava, Roy **160–3**, 273
*Hallway, New York 163*
*John Coltrane #24 162*
*Man Coming up Subway Stairs 160*
Deloche, Jean 249
Depression, the 21, 73, 113, 229
Dewey, Admiral George 17
Dixon, Maynard 73
Dodo Jin Ming: portrait of Robert Frank *173*
Downes, Bruce 89
*Drum* magazine 195, 235
Düsseldorf, Germany: Kunstakademie School of Photography 25, 189, 297, 299

E
Eastman House, Rochester, New York 131, 203
'New Topographics' (1975) 213, 263, 269
'Toward a Social Landscape' (1966) 182
Eggleston, William **228–31**
*The Red Ceiling 230*
Eisenhower, President Dwight 181
Ellison, Ralph: *The Invisible Man* 265, *266*
*Essence* magazine 139
Evans, Walker 7, **112–5**, 141, 201
*Allie Mae Burroughs 112*
*DAMAGED 114*
*Graveyard and Steel Mill 114*
*Let Us Now Praise Famous Men* (with Agee) 113
*Subway Passengers 115*

F
f/64 group 35, 39, 107
Farm Security Administration (USA) 73, 113, 137
Federal Art Project (USA) 85
feminism/feminists 7, 17, 45, 69, 253
*Fighting Lady, The* (film) 29
'Film und Foto' exhibition, Stuttgart (1929) 35, 39, 67, 99
Fink, Larry 101
Flaherty, Thomas: *House of Bondage* 233
Flanner, Janet *84* (Abbott)
Fontcuberta, Joan 205
*Fortune* magazine 113, 121, 141
Frajndlich, Abe 129
Franck, Martine: portrait of Henri Cartier-Bresson *133*
Frank, Robert 89, **172–5**, *173* (Dodo Jin Ming), 201, 249
*Charleston, South Carolina 175*
*Elevator 172*
*Parade – Hoboken, New Jersey 174*
Friedlander, Lee 181, **200–3**
portrait of Garry Winogrand *181*

G
Gambarini, Federico: portrait of Andreas Gursky *297*
Gandhi, Mohandas ('Mahatma') 123, 135, *148* (Janah), 149
Garbo, Greta *30* (Steichen)
Giacomelli, Mario 7, **176–9**
Godeau, Abigail Solomon 9
Goerhardt, Frank: portrait of Sebastião Salgado *257*
Goldberg, Whoopi 277, *278* (Leibovitz)
Goldin, Nan **288–91**
*The Hug 291*
*Jimmy Paulette and Taboo! in the Bathroom 288*
*Sisters 290*
*Swan-like Embrace 290*
Grosz, George 41
Gursky, Andreas 25, 189, **296–9**
*99 Cent II Diptychon 298–9*
*Rhein II 297*

H
Hampton Institute, Virginia 17, *18–19*, 285
*Harper's Bazaar* 99, 171, 175
Hasegawa, Akira 225
Hausmann, Raoul **40–3**, 45
*ABCD 41, 43*
*The Art Critic 42*
*Tatlin at Home 40*, 41
Heartfield, John 41, **56–9**
cover of Sinclair's *So Macht Man Dollars* 57, *59*
*The Meaning of Geneva* 57, *58*
*The Meaning of the Hitler Salute 56*, 57
Hijikata, Tatsumi 197
Hine, Lewis 6, 7, **20–3**, 55
*Self-portrait with Newspaper Boy 20*
Hitler, Adolf *56*, 57, 125
Höch, Hannah 41, **44–7**
*Cut with the Kitchen Knife* 45, *46*
'Ethnographic Museum' series 45, *47*
*Tamer 44*, 45
Horst, Horst P.: portrait of George Hoyningen-Huene *97*
Hosoe, Eikoh **196–9**
*Kamaitachi #31* 197, *198*
*Man and Woman 199*
*Yukio Mishima, Ordeal by Roses 196*, 197
*House and Garden* (magazine) 65
Hoyningen-Huene, George **96–9**
*Colette Salomon 98*
*Divers 96*
*Mrs Hubbell 99*
*Lee Miller Wearing Yraide Sailcloth Overalls 99*
Hubbell, Mrs *99* (Hoyningen-Huene)
Hughes, Langston: *The Sweet Flypaper...* (with DeCarava) 161, 273
Hujar, Peter 101

Hurston, Zora Neale: *Their Eyes Were Watching God* 285

I
Iturbide, Graciela **244–7**
*Magnolia 244*
*Mujer Angel (Angel Woman) 246*
*Nuesta Señora de las Iguanas 247*
*Procesión 247*
Ivens, Joris 83
*Rain* 81

J
Jacobs, Karen Folger 237
Janah, Sunil **148–51**, 249
Johns, Jasper 217
Johnston, Frances Benjamin **16–9**, 285
Joshi, J. C. 149

K
Kennedy, John F. 181, *182* (Winogrand)
Kertész, André **64–7**
*Circus* 67
*Meudon* 65, *66*
*Mondrian's Glasses and Pipe 67*
*Wandering Violinist* 65
*Washington Square with Arch 64*
Kinski, Nastassja 169
Kloss, Karlie *279* (Leibovitz)
Koudelka, Josef **220–3**
Krull, Germaine **80–3**
*Métal 80*, 81, *82*

L
Lange, Dorothea **72–5**, 105
*Migrant Mother* 72, *73*
*White Angel Breadline 74*
Lederer, William, and Burdick, Eugene: *The Ugly American* 173
Leibovitz, Annie **276–9**
Lelyveld, Joseph 249
Lennon, John *276*, 277 (Leibovitz)
Levitt, Helen 113, **140–3**, 229
Lhote, André 135
Libarry, Irene 'Bobby' 33, *35* (Cunningham)
*Life* magazine 65, 121, 137, 153, 237
Little Galleries of the PhotoSecession, New York 13
Liu Zheng **304–7**
*Convicts Fetching Water 307*
*Three Country Strippers 306*
*Three Women at a Country Funeral 307*
*Two Miners 304*
Loeb, Janice 142
López, Nacho **164–7**
*Pachuco* or *Gigolo 166*
Lorant, Stefan 153
Lorentz, Pare: *The Plow that Broke the Plains* 55

M
Maar, Dora 45
McCullin, Don **208–11**
McMillan, Jerry: portrait of Ed Ruscha *217*
Magnum photographic agency 133, 147, 155, 223, 239, 259
Magubane, Peter **192–5**
Mandela, Nelson *192* (Magubane), 193
Mark, Mary Ellen **236–9**
*Homeless Damm Family 236*
*Marie Frances in the Bathtub 239*
*'Rat' and Mike with a Gun 238*
*Marlon Brando fascinated by a dragonfly... 239*
Marshall, Brigadier General S. L. A. 157
Masters, Edgar Lee 177
Matisse, Henri 13
Mayakovsky, Vladimir: 'Pro Eto' 61, *62*
Metropolitan Museum of Art, New York 35, 65, 142, 271
Meyer, Pedro **204–7**
*Destroyed Somoza 206–7*
*The Temptation of the Angel 204*
Michener, James 157
Miller, Henry 93
Miller, Lee *48* (Man Ray) *99* (Hoyningen-Huene), **124–7**
*Charred Bones, Buchenwald 124*, 125
*Mary Chess cosmetics shot 126*
*Portrait of Space 127*
*Untitled, man and tar 126*
Minimalism 189
*Minotaure* (magazine) 93
Mishima, Yukio 197
*Ordeal by Roses* (with Hosoe) 197, *1989*, 199
*Spring Snow 264*, 265
Model, Lisette **100–3**
*Belmont Park Race Track, Arms 102*
*Wall Street 103*
*Westminster Kennel Club, Royal Poodle 103*
*Woman with Veil, San Francisco 100*
Modernism/Modernists 37, 113, 121, 125
Modotti, Tina 111
Mofokeng, Santu **300–3**
*Afoor Fmily Bedroom 302*
*Democracy is Forever 302*
*Ishmael: Eyes Wide Shut 300*
Moholy, Lucia: portrait of László Moholy-Nagy 77
Moholy-Nagy, László **767–9**
*The Eccentric II* 77
*Fotogramm* 77, *78*
*Love Your Neighbour; Murder on the Railway 76*
MoMA *see* Museum of Modern Art
Moore, Marcel (Suzanne Malherbe) 69, *70* (Cahun)
Moriyama, Daidō *197*, **224–7**
*Lips 224*
*Shinjuku Station 227*
*Stray Dog* 225, *226*
*Münchner Illustrierte* (magazine) 65
Murphy, Tom *128* (White)
Museum of Modern Art (MoMA), New York 55, 87, 91, 107, 133, 135, 223, 229, 230, 271
'The Family of Man' (1955) 27, 29, 111, 127, 141, 182
'Looking at Photographs' (1963) 179
'Meta-Monumental Garage Sale' (2012) 253
'The Photographer's Eye' (1964) 182, 203
'Photographs of Children by Helen Levitt' 141
'Photography 18391937' (1937) 35, 141
retrospectives 39 (Weston), 47 (Höch), 59 (Heartfield), 111 (Bravo), 267 (Wall), 299 (Gursky)
Mydans, Carl: *W. Eugene Smith 153*

N
Nagasaki, bombing of 185
Naipaul, V. S. 249
Narayan, R. K. 249
Nast, Condé 31, 99, 125
National Child Labor Committee, USA 21
National Gallery of Art, Washington, DC 155, 182
National Portrait Gallery, Washington, DC 279
'New Bauhaus', Chicago 78
'New Topographics' movement 213, 261, 263, 269
'New Woman', the 77, 81
New York *140*, 141, *142*, *143* (Levitt)
An American Place 15, 107
Armory Show (1913) 15, 51
*The Flatiron* (Steichen) *28*
Little Galleries of the PhotoSecession (291) 13
Metropolitan Museum of Art 35, 65, 142, 271
Shomburg Center for Research in Black Culture 273
*see also* Eastman House; Museum of Modern Art
*New Yorker* magazine 171
Newby, Eric 249
Newhall, Beaumont 131
Nixon, Richard 181

O
Obama, President Barack 273
Obama, Michelle 273, 279
O'Keeffe, Georgia 13
Ono, Yoko *276*, 277 (Leibovitz)
Orozco, José Clemente 109

P
Paris *8*, 9, *1011* (Atget), 65, 97
Parks, Rosa 193
Parks, Gordon **136–9**
*Evening Wraps 138*
*People's War* (newspaper) 149
Philadelphia Museum of Art, Pennsylvania 55
photocollages 61, 69
photograms 77
photomontage 41, 45, 57, 77
Photorealists 289
Photo-Secession/Photo-Secessionists 13, 29
Picasso, Pablo 13, 45, 93, *945* (Brassaï)
Pictorialism 37, 65
Pittsburgh, Pennsylvania 153
Pittsburgh Survey, the 21
Postmodernism/Postmodernists 9, 237, 265, 293

R
Ray, Man 67, 9, 11, **48–51**, 85, 97, 117, 125, 281
rayographs 49, *51*
*Le Violon d'Ingres* 49, *50*
Ray, Satyajit 149, 249
Riesman, David: *The Lonely Crowd* 173
Rivera, Diego 39, 105, 109
Robertson, Struan: *Ernest Cole 233*
Rodchenko, Alexander **60–3**
*Pro Eto* 61, *62*
*White Sea Canal* 61, *62–3*
*Rolling Stone* magazine *276*, 277
Roosevelt, Alice *16*, 17 (Johnston)
Rosenberg, Harold 169
Rosler, Martha **252–5**
'Body Beautiful' panels *252*, 253
*Saddam's Palace 254–5*
Roussow, Marguerite: *Roger Ballen 281*
Rubinstein, Eva 101
Ruscha, Ed **216–9**

S
Salgado, Sebastião **256–9**
Salomon, Colette *98* (HoyningenHuene)
San Francisco Museum of Modern Art 142, 182, 227
Sander, August **24–7**, 55, 189
Schiaparelli, Elsa 137
Schönberg, Arnold 101
Schweitzer, Albert 153
Seliger, Mark: portrait of Cindy Sherman *293*
*Shaft* (film) 137
Sharpeville massacre (1960) 195
Sheeler, Charles: *Manhatta* 55
Shelley, Percy Bysshe 6
Sherman, Cindy **292–5**, 297
*Untitled #74 295*
*Untitled #96 293*
*Untitled #193 292*
*Untitled #224 294*
Shields, Brooke 169
Shomburg Center for Research in Black Culture, New York 273
Shore, Stephen 213, 229, **268–71**
Sims, Lowery 273
Sinclair, Upton: *So Macht Man Dollars* (cover, Heartfield) 57, *59*
Singh, Raghubir **248–51**
*Barber and Goddess Kali 250–1*
*Below the Howra Bridge a Marwari bride and groom... 248*
*Member of a middle-class family of North Calcutta... 251*
*The Pilgrim and Ambassador Car 250–1*

Smith, W. Eugene **152–5**, 257
*Industrial Waste from the Chisso Chemical Company 152*
solarization 49, 125
Sontag, Susan 279
*Regarding the Pain of Others* 267
Spanish Civil War 145
Steichen, Edward **28–31**, 53, 125, 271
Stein, Gertrude 65
Stieglitz, Alfred 7, **12–5**, 29, 37, 53, 105, 129, 131, 297
*Apples and Gable 15*
'Equivalents' 13, *15*
*The Steerage 12*, 13
*Sun's Rays – Paula* 14
Sting 277
stopaction effect 65
Strand, Paul **52–5**, 101, 111, 135, 141
*The Court* 52
*Double Akeley* 54
*Pears and Bowls* 55
*Wire Wheel* 54
Stuttgart, Germany: 'Film und Foto' exhibition (1929) 35, 39, 67, 99
Surrealism/Surrealists 9, 45, 49, 65, 69, 81, 93, 97, 109, 117, 125, 133
Szarkowski, John 203, 229

T
Taylor, Paul S. 73
*Dorothea Lange in Texas on the Plains 73*
Thomas, Hank Willis 273
Tōmatsu, Shōmei **183–7**
*Bottle Melted and Deformd... 184*, 185
*Coca-Cola 186*
*Eros, Tokyo 186*
Trotsky, Leon *147* (Capa)

U
Uemura, Tomoko 153
Ulmer, Alan: *William Eggleston 229*
Universal Exposition, Paris (1900) 17

V
*Vanity Fair* (magazine) 29, 49, 99
Varèse, Edgard 93
Veruschka (von Lehndorff) *170* (Avedon)
Vietnam War 157, 169, 209, *210–11*, 253
*Vogue* (magazine) 29, 97, 125, 137, 171
*Vu* (magazine) 65

W
Wade, Dwyane *279* (Leibovitz)
Wall, Jeff **264–7**, 293
*The Destroyed Room 266*
*In Front of a Nightclub 266–7*
*'Invisible Man' by Ralph Ellison 267*
*After 'Spring Snow' by Yukio Mishima... 264*, 265
Warhol, Andy 89, *168* (Avedon), 217, 269
Washington, DC
Corcoran Gallery of Art 139, 279
National Gallery of Art 155, 182
National Portrait Gallery 279
Western High School *19*
Watson, Ella 137
Weber, Bruce 101
Weegee **88–91**, 289
*At Sammy's on the Bowery 88*
*Tenement Fire 90–1*
*Their First Murder 90*
Weems, Carrie Mae **284–7**
*Descending the Throne... 286*
*You Became Mammie... 286*
Weston, Edward **36–9**, 73, 111, 129, 141
*Dunes, Oceano 38*
*Epilogue 36*
*Excusado 37, 39*
*Nude 38*
*Pepper #30 39*
White, Minor 13, **128–31,** *131* (Cunningham)
*Three-Thirds 130*
*Tom Murphy, San Francisco 128*
*Windowsill Daydreaming 131*
Willis, Deborah 137, **27–25**, 285
*Firehouse Memorial 274–5*
*To Catch a Lover 272*
Wilson, Sloan: *The Man in the Grey Flannel Suit* 173
Winogrand, Garry **180–3**, *181* (Friedlander), 201
World War II 25, 29, 121, 125, 145, 149, 153

Y
Yosemite National Park, California *104*, 105, 213

Z
Ziff-Davis (publishers) 153

## Picture Credits



## Acknowledgements

Books are collaborative efforts and I have had the good fortune to work with editors Kara Hattersley-Smith and Sophie Wise, picture researcher Peter Kent and designer Jon Allan. I am grateful to the photographers and scholars who have shared their knowledge with me and to Michael Marien, my live-in editor and spouse.

## The Author

Mary Warner Marien is Professor Emerita in the Department of Fine Arts at Syracuse University, New York. She lectures in the US and Europe and in 2008 won an Andy Warhol Foundation Arts Writer award. She is the author of *Photography: A Cultural History* and *100 Ideas that Changed Photography* as well as numerous articles on photography.